Protecting Children in the Digital Era

International Studies in Human Rights

Volume 105

Protecting Children in the Digital Era

The Use of Alternative Regulatory Instruments

By

Eva Lievens

MARTINUS
NIJHOFF
PUBLISHERS

LEIDEN • BOSTON
2010

This book is printed on acid-free paper.

Library of Congress Cataloging-in-Publication Data

Lievens, Eva, 1979–
Protecting children in the digital era : the use of alternative regulatory instruments / by Eva Lievens.
p. cm. — (International studies in human rights ; v. 105)
Includes bibliographical references and index.
ISBN 978-90-04-18477-0 (hardback : alk. paper)
1. Internet—Law and legislation—European Union countries. 2. Digital media—Law and legislation—European Union countries. 3. Children—Legal status, laws, etc.—European Union countries. 4. Computers and children—European Union countries. 5. Mass media and children—European Union countries. 6. Internet and children—European Union countries. I. Title.
KJE959.5.C65L54 2010
343.2409'944—dc22

2010018077

ISSN 0924-4751
ISBN 978 90 04 18477 0

PRINTED BY DRUKKERIJ WILCO B.V. - AMERSFOORT, THE NETHERLANDS

Contents

Preface xiii
Acknowledgements xv
Abbreviations xvii

Introduction 1
1. Background 1
2. Delineation 3
3. Structure 4

PART I

Chapter 1. Setting: Notions, Issues & Policy History 9
1.1. Clarification of the constitutive elements 9
1.1.1. Digital media content 9
A. Introduction 9
B. Recent developments in the media environment 12
B.1. The emergence of new technologies 12
B.2. Digitisation 14
B.3. Convergence 17
B.4. Control revolution, social networking and user-generated content 20
C. Conclusion: digital media content 25
1.1.2. Minor 27
1.1.3. Harmful content 30
A. Social science: history and theories of media content and media effects 30
A.1. Social science and harmful media content 30
A.2. Media effects research 32
B. Why regulate harmful content?: the precautionary principle 38
C. Exploration of the concept 'harmful content' 44
C.1. Definitions of harmful content 44
C.2. Harmful content versus illegal content 47

C.3. Social science inspired concepts of harmful content 50
C.4. Varieties of risks and varieties of harmful content 52
D. Legal aspects and implications of harmful content 57
D.1. Lack of legal definitions 57
D.2. Harmful content and freedom of expression 59
E. Concluding remarks 60
1.2. Protecting minors against harmful digital media content: identifying the regulatory challenges 61
1.2.1. Introduction 61
A. Old versus new media 61
B. Statistics 63
C. Implications for policy and regulation? 66
1.2.2. Characteristics of the new information and communication networks 69
1.2.3. Obstacles to the use of traditional (content) regulation in the digital media environment 73
1.2.4. The United States legislative approach to protect minors on the Internet 78
1.2.5. The need for a broader regulatory framework 87
1.2.6. EU policy history: the protection of minors against harmful digital media content 88
A. Communication Illegal and Harmful Content on the Internet 89
B. Green Paper on the protection of minors and human dignity in audiovisual and information services 93
C. Council Resolution on illegal and harmful content on the Internet 97
D. Green Paper on the protection of minors and human dignity: Follow-up & Consultation 98
E. Recommendations on the protection of minors and human dignity 101
F. Successive Safer Internet programmes 122
G. Council of Europe: a variety of policy documents 135
H. Concluding remarks 139
1.3. Conclusion 140

Chapter 2. Alternative Regulatory Instruments ... 143
2.1. "Regulation" ... 143
2.1.1. Regulation: conceptual elements ... 144
2.1.2. Centred or 'command-and-control' regulation ... 147
A. Notion ... 147
B. Drawbacks ... 148
2.1.3. Away from pure command-and-control regulation ... 150
2.1.4. Interim conclusion ... 153
2.2. "Alternative regulation" in policy documents ... 154
2.2.1. General policy documents ... 154
A. International: OECD ... 154
A.1. Recommendation on improving the quality of government regulation ... 154
A.2. Report on regulatory reform ... 155
B. European Union ... 157
B.1. White Paper on European Governance ... 158
B.2. The Final Report of the Mandelkern Group on Better Regulation ... 162
B.3. Better Legislation Action Plan ... 164
B.4. Interinstitutional Agreement on Better Lawmaking ... 166
B.5. Other EU policy documents ... 170
B.6. Interim conclusion ... 173
2.2.2. Media policy documents ... 173
A. European Union ... 174
B. Council of Europe ... 186
C. Interim conclusion ... 188
2.3. Overview and analysis of different alternative regulatory instruments ... 188
2.3.1. Alternative regulatory instruments (ARIs) ... 188
2.3.2. Self-regulation ... 189
A. Concept ... 191
B. Self-regulation in the media sector: studies ... 195
C. Illustration: codes of conduct ... 200
D. Assets and drawbacks ... 203
E. Interim conclusion ... 207
2.3.3. Co-regulation ... 208
A. Concept ... 208
B. Co-regulation in the media sector: the HBI and EMR study ... 214
C. Illustrations ... 217

C.1. Netherlands 217
C.2. Germany 220
C.3. Australia 222
D. Assets and drawbacks 225
E. Interim conclusion 227
2.3.4. Self- and co-regulation: Interim conclusion 228
2.3.5. Regulatory tools: Technology 230
A. Technology: alternative regulatory instrument or regulatory tool? 230
B. Technology and the protection of minors 236
C. Illustrations 238
C.1. Filtering 238
C.2. Rating and labelling 243
C.3. Parental monitoring and notification software 247
C.4. Identification mechanisms 248
C.5. Domain names 251
D. Interim conclusion 252
2.3.6. Regulatory tools: Supporting mechanisms 253
2.4. Conclusion 259

PART II

Chapter 1. Legal Framework (‘*de lege lata*’) 263
1.1. Introduction 263
1.2. Human Rights – Children’s rights 264
1.2.1. International 266
A. United Nations Convention on the Rights of the Child 266
B. International Covenant on Civil and Political Rights and International Covenant on Economic, Social and Cultural Rights 280
1.2.2. Council of Europe 283
A. European Convention on the protection of Human Rights and Fundamental Freedoms 284
B. European Social Charter 286
C. Documents related to human rights and the information society 287
D. Documents related specifically to children’s rights 289

1.2.3. European Union 293
A. EU Treaties 293
B. Charter of Fundamental Rights of the European Union 295
C. EU strategy on the rights of the child 297
1.2.4. Concluding remark 302
1.3. Human Rights: freedom of expression, privacy and procedural guarantees 303
1.3.1. Freedom of expression 303
A. Article 10 ECHR 303
B. Freedom of expression and the information society 310
C. Freedom of expression and children 312
D. Concluding remarks 315
1.3.2. Privacy 315
A. Privacy and children 315
B. Article 8 ECHR and the EU Privacy Directives 316
C. The right to anonymity 319
D. Concluding remark 323
1.3.3. Procedural guarantees 323
A. Article 6 ECHR 323
B. Article 13 ECHR 327
1.4. Content regulation 330
1.4.1. Introduction 330
1.4.2. Regulation of audiovisual content 334
A. Television without Frontiers Directive 334
B. Revision process: from Television without Frontiers to Audiovisual Media Services 338
C. Audiovisual Media Services Directive 341
D. Council of Europe Convention on Transfrontier Television 351
1.4.3. Regulation of information society services: e-Commerce Directive 354
1.4.4. Indirect content regulation: liability of intermediaries 356
A. Introduction 356
B. e-Commerce liability regime 357
C. Issues of concern 362
1.5. Internal market and competition 366
1.5.1. Internal market principles 366
1.5.2. Competition rules 368
1.6. General EU legislative principles and requirements 369

1.6.1. Proportionality 369
1.6.2. Subsidiarity 372
1.6.3. Article 288 para. 3 TFEU [ex 249 EC Treaty] 375
1.7. Conclusion 377

Chapter 2. Using ARIs to Protect Minors from Harmful Content: Compliance with the Legal Framework 379
2.1. Introduction 379
2.2. Evaluation of different alternative regulatory instruments: compliance with the legal framework 381
2.2.1. Human rights 381
A. Freedom of expression 383
A.1. General principle 383
A.2. Infringement by 'public authorities' 384
A.3. Freedom of expression and horizontal effect 385
A.4. Restrictions on freedom of expression and their justification 388
A.5. Freedom of expression and self-regulation 392
A.6. Freedom of expression and technology 396
A.7. Concluding remarks 400
B. Privacy 402
B.1. General principle 402
B.2. Privacy and alternative regulatory instruments 403
B.3. Privacy and technology 405
B.4. Concluding remarks 410
C. Right to a fair trial 411
C.1. General principle and delineation 411
C.2. Scope of application 411
C.3. The notion 'tribunal established by law' 413
C.4. Procedural guarantees 415
C.5. Concluding remark 417
D. Right to an effective remedy 418
D.1. General principle 418
D.2. Article 13 ECHR and alternative regulatory instruments 419
D.3. Horizontal effect of article 13 ECHR 421
D.4. Article 6 and article 13 ECHR 422
D.5. Concluding remarks 423
E. Interim conclusion: ARIs and fundamental rights 424

2.2.2. Internal market legislation 427
A. Free movement of goods 428
A.1. General principles 428
A.2. Conceptual elements 429
A.3. Member States, individuals and responsibility 435
A.4. Application of theory in practice: Dynamic Medien v. Avides Media 440
B. Free movement of services 443
B.1. General principles 443
B.2. Scope 443
B.3. Applicability to actions of private parties 449
B.4. Free movement of services and the media sector 451
C. Interim conclusion 454
2.2.3. Competition rules 456
A. Article 101 TFEU [ex 81 EC Treaty] 458
A.1. General principle 458
A.2. Undertaking 458
A.3. Agreements 461
A.4. Inapplicability of article 101 para. 1 TFEU [ex 81 EC Treaty] 467
A.5. Delegation to private bodies 470
B. Article 102 TFEU [ex 82 EC Treaty] 472
C. Article 106 TFEU [ex 86 EC Treaty] 475
D. Interim conclusion 478
2.2.4. Article 288 para. 3 TFEU [ex 249 EC Treaty] 480
A. General principle 480
B. Requirements 481
B.1. Content 483
B.2. Nature 485
B.3. Application and enforcement 488
B.4. Liability in case of inadequate implementation 490
C. Article 288 TFEU [ex 249 EC Treaty] and ARIs 492
D. Interim conclusion 495
2.3. Conclusion: ARIs and their compatibility with the European legal framework 496

Concluding Remarks and Recommendations for the Future 499
1. Retrospective of the research undertaken 499
2. Conclusions 518
3. Recommendations and indications for future research 520
   A. Recommendations 520
   B. Indications for future research 523

Bibliography 525

Index 583

Preface

When asked what was the best and the worst of things, Aesop famously replied in both cases "the tongue": it is both the basis of any social life but also of all disputes and conflicts. Today, the answer would probably be "the Internet". Indeed, as a mirror of human society, Internet encompasses an infinite amount of information about all possible subjects, an inexhaustible source of knowledge, but also the most offensive and criminal content. Illegal activities such as promotion of terrorism or child pornography are prohibited on the Internet as in real life. However a whole range of content, while not illegal, can have disturbing effects on children, and should nevertheless be available to responsible adults. Minors have a fundamental right to be protected, but this protection must respect other fundamental rights and in particular the freedom of expression and information.

Eva Lievens' book presents an original reflection on ways to respond to this challenge. It provides a well-documented overview of policy evolutions and challenges at EU level in the field of the protection of minors in digital media as well as the use of self- and co-regulation. It further provides an in-depth analysis of the compatibility of the use of self-regulation, co-regulation as well as technology in the field of the protection of minors with other policy objectives: protection of fundamental rights, free-provision of services and promotion of competition.

Legislation can have many drawbacks, in particular in areas where technical, commercial and social evolution is very fast. Because of the heavy procedures needed to amend law, the situation is frozen at a given moment which may have negative social effects when it is no longer adapted. Experience also demonstrates that disproportionate restrictions are imposed by law, and substantial time will elapse before this is corrected. Co- and self-regulation represent a useful alternative in cases where the free-functioning of the market could interfere with objectives of general interest while legislation would not be appropriate. For these reasons, the use of alternative regulatory instruments (ARIs), such as self-regulation, co-regulation, technology and supporting mechanisms are high on the policy agendas of both the European Commission and many national governments. Eva Lievens' book provides useful guidance not only regarding the establishment of these initiatives but also with respect to their subsequent interpretation by the addressees (e.g. media companies, regulatory bodies), as well as by academia.

The research is innovative as it provides a comprehensive analysis of relevant EU and Council of Europe law. Beyond an in-depth examination of the notions of "digital media content", "minor" and "harmful content", we are presented with interesting developments on co- and self-regulation. Contrary to other authors, Eva Lievens considers that strict categorisations of self- and co-regulation are irrelevant and she proposes to adopt a general concept of 'alternative regulatory instruments', which can be situated along a regulatory continuum, some ARIs leaning towards 'self-regulation', where there is no, or a very limited, level of government involvement while others incline towards 'co-regulation', where there is a higher degree of government involvement.

Eva Lievens convincingly concludes that there are no legal obstacles which exclude ARIs to protect minors against harmful digital content, provided the necessary conditions are met. She rightly stresses that one of the major challenges in this area is the balance between various fundamental rights; she also underlines the need carefully to structure ARIs with respect to procedural guarantees and the provision of effective remedies. An important reminder is the fact that protection of minors is a shared responsibility, with parents and educators having a primary role to play next to the State and industry. Relying only on State intervention would create great dangers in terms of freedom of expression and information.

A remarkable feature of this book is the modesty with which it concludes that it should not be seen as a terminus, but rather as one stop on a long, and possibly never-ending journey. The indications for future research are therefore of particular interest. This is the case regarding notably the use of regulatory impact assessment in this area: it is indeed a major challenge to balance economic and non-economic costs and benefits. While economic costs can be quite easily quantified, the cost of inadequate protection of minors, or the cost of a disproportionate protection of minors which would hinder freedom of expression, are very difficult to assess. An in-depth study of the use of ARIs in respect of conduct- and contact-related risks such as cyberbullying or issues linked to social networking websites, could also yield very interesting results. I hope that these ideas for future research will inspire authors with the same talent as Eva Lievens.

Jean-Eric de Cockborne
15 January 2010

Head of Unit "Audiovisual and Media Policies"
Directorate General "Information Society and Media" of the
European Commission

Acknowledgements

In December 2003, I embarked on a fascinating journey at the Interdisciplinary Centre for Law & ICT (ICRI) at the Faculty of Law of the K.U. Leuven. Over the past six years I have had the privilege of conducting research into the legal and regulatory challenges that arise from the emergence and evolution of new communication technologies, particularly in the field of the protection of minors from harmful content.

I would like to extend my gratitude to Prof. dr. Jos Dumortier, for giving me the opportunity to conduct this research, which intrigued me from the start. His level of expertise and his progressive thinking about law and technology have been an inspiration throughout this journey. Being a researcher at the centre he built with such determination, is an honour.

I will never be able to thank Prof. dr. Peggy Valcke enough. I have had the pleasure of working with her since my first day at ICRI. She introduced me to the world of media law research and has been a role model throughout the past six years. Her incredible expertise is stimulating and her ceaseless enthusiasm is infectious. I hope there are many more years of cooperation to come.

I would also like to thank Prof. dr. Stephan Parmentier, Prof. dr. Dirk Voorhoof and Prof. dr. Wolfgang Schulz, for inspiring me and providing me with valuable comments. A special word of thanks goes to Prof. Voorhoof, whose media law course I took in the final year of my law studies. Without his passion for media law, I would not be working in this field.

I would also like to thank everyone at ICRI, especially Nicole, David, Katleen, Eleni, Evi, Katrien, and Aleksandra. Although research is often perceived as a lonely activity, my fellow ICRI-ots have been excellent company, both in good and more difficult times.

I would also like to express my gratitude to Martinus Nijhoff Publishers, an imprint of Brill, and to Lindy Melman, Birgitta Poelmans and Bea Timmer in particular.

A heartfelt thank you goes to my parents, my brother and sister, my parents-in-law, my brothers and sisters-in-law, and my friends for their love, support and encouragement.

This book is dedicated to Fred, Lou and Stella.

Eva Lievens
15 January 2010

Abbreviations

AVMSD	Audiovisual Media Services Directive
ARI	Alternative Regulatory Instrument
CFI	Court of First Instance
CoE	Council of Europe
ECCT	European Convention on Transfrontier Television
ECHR	European Convention on Human Rights
ECJ	European Court of Justice
EU	European Union
ICCPR	International Covenant on Civil and Political Rights
ICESCR	International Covenant on Economic, Social and Cultural Rights
TEU	Treaty on European Union
TFEU	Treaty on the Functioning of the European Union
TVWFD	Television Without Frontiers Directive
UNCRC	United Nations Convention on the Rights of the Child

Introduction

1. Background

Children and new media – Children are curious beings. From a very young age they are on a mission to discover the world, in all its facets. One environment in which this exploratory expedition occurs is the media environment. Over the past decades, children have been faced with an increasing array of different media, from toddlerhood into their late teens. Television – analogue or digital –, DVDs, the Internet, video games and mobile phones, for instance, are part of many children's and young people's (daily) media menu. Whereas this provides them with unprecedented opportunities to learn, communicate and explore the world, it also means that, unavoidably, they will be faced with content which could be potentially harmful to them or even outright illegal. Such content has always been a concern with respect to any new medium which surfaced, be it books, comics or movies. However, the new types of media, such as the Internet, have a much lower access threshold as well as an exponentially higher content offer. As a consequence, this long-standing concern now needs to cope with new challenges.

Instruments for protection – Just as every parent teaches his or her child to look left and right before crossing the road or not to talk to strangers, children also need to be guided and protected – at least to a certain extent – with respect to their media use. Traditionally, this aim of protecting minors against harmful content has been aspired to by means of legislation. However, from the mid-1990s onwards, doubts were expressed with respect to the use of this traditional legal instrument to regulate certain aspects of the continually changing media environment. As a result, the use of other instruments, such as self-regulation, co-regulation and technology, was pushed to the fore. Policy documents, especially at the EU level, started to pick up and promote these instruments, and initiatives to set up such mechanisms were undertaken in several EU Member States.

Research purpose – This background is the context for my research, which intended to deepen the understanding of the use of 'alternative regulatory instruments' (ARIs) to protect minors against harmful content. Hence, its purpose was fourfold. First, the issue of protecting minors against harmful content is described and analysed. Second, the use of alternative regulatory instruments is explored. Third, the legal framework which surrounds both the protection of minors against harmful content as well as the use of alternative regulatory instruments is mapped. Fourth, the compliance of the use of such instruments to protect minors against harmful content with the broader legal framework is assessed.

Research topic – The research topic of this book sprouts from the research tradition of the Interdisciplinary Centre for Law & ICT (ICRI) and builds on research that has been carried out at this centre, in particular on the PhD theses of Caroline Uyttendaele and Peggy Valcke. Both these theses dealt with challenges posed to our traditional understanding of legislation and normative goals, by the many developments to which the media environment was subject from the early 1990s onwards. This study looks at this broader topic from a specific angle. Using the traditional public interest goal of protecting minors against harmful content as a case study, I first examined the hypothesis that traditional legislation is not adapted to the converged or networked digital media environment and, moreover, that the use of alternative regulatory instruments is better suited to achieve this public interest goal in an efficient manner. In a second phase, I then based my approach to this issue on the thesis that the use of such alternative regulatory instruments to protect minors against harmful content inevitably occurs within a broader legal framework, which needs to be respected; a fact that is often – conveniently – overlooked.

Research question – Hence, in essence, the legal research question was the following: "are there legal obstacles to the use of alternative regulatory instruments, such as self- and co-regulation, to protect minors against digital harmful content"? En route to answering this key question, of course, other questions, related to the research topic, were examined. Examples are, for instance, "what is harmful content?", "what is the policy history in the field of protecting minors against harmful content in the digital media environment?", "what are alternative regulatory instruments?" and "which legal provisions influence both the issues of protecting minors against harmful content and the use of alternative regulatory instruments to achieve this goal?".

2. Delineation

Research scope – Whereas this study attempts to provide an as complete picture as possible of the research issue at hand – the use of alternative regulatory instruments to protect minors against harmful digital media content –, due to its vastness, it has been necessary to carefully delineate the precise scope of research. My choice of research topic, made in 2004, was based on a preliminary literature review, which not only uncovered the many intricacies related to protecting minors against harmful digital content, but also revealed the importance and urgency of the debate that was pursued at the European level not only with respect to this delicate policy goal, but also with respect to the use of alternative regulatory instruments in an attempt to simplify and improve regulation.

European level – In this context, I have opted to carry out this research with respect to the European level; this includes the European Union (EU) level as well as the Council of Europe (CoE) level. In the course of the preliminary research, I found that, instead of concentrating on specific countries and national legal systems, focusing on the EU and CoE policy and legislative frameworks would provide an added value. Not only do these frameworks contain crucial 'umbrella' provisions with respect to the use of alternative regulatory instruments to protect minors against harmful digital media content, but the analysis of the relevant EU and CoE provisions also lead to research results which can be applied not only throughout the EU and CoE but also to other regulatory areas. However, occasionally, references are made to specific country systems by means of illustration.

Digital media – Furthermore, with respect to the different 'media' within in the digital media environment, the reader will notice that the most prominent medium in this study is the Internet (as in the 'the World Wide Web', hence excluding e-mail and other communication applications such as instant messaging). The reasons for the predominance of the Internet are simple; not only were concerns regarding minors and media since the mid-1990s mainly directed at the Internet, but the Internet also was the first medium with certain characteristics which significantly differed from traditional media, such as television broadcasting. This does not mean, however, that other media, such as audiovisual media (e.g., digital television or video-on-demand platforms), mobile telephony and videogames, are excluded from the scope of this study. References to these media and communication technologies, however, occur on a more occasional basis.

Harmful content versus illegal content – Moreover, I have made the conscious decision to focus on harmful content and to exclude illegal content from the scope of this study. Although these notions are often mentioned in the same breath, in fact – as will be clarified in the first chapter of the first part of this book – they require a totally different approach and are faced with other difficulties.

Content versus conduct – In addition, concerns with respect to minors and media are not restricted to harmful content; harmful conduct by adults as well as minors, such as grooming, happy-slapping and cyberbullying, is at least as problematic (cf. *infra*, Part 1, Chapter 1). Since the issues of harmful conduct are relatively new and could be the subject of several other theses, I have opted to leave them outside of the scope of this study. I would like to point out, however, that these issues urgently require further research.

Alternative regulatory instruments – The concept of 'alternative regulatory instruments', including self- and co-regulation, will be clarified and analysed in detail in the second chapter of the first part of this study. At this point, however, I would like to emphasise that this study deals with regulation at sector level. This means that I looked at regulatory systems which aim to regulate the behaviour of a group of actors (for instance, the content industry), and that, consequently, I did not address regulation between individual actors, for instance, by means of contracts (although contracts are sometimes also put under the heading 'self-regulation').

Research at the crossroads of law and social science – Finally, the issue of protecting minors against harmful content is closely connected to social science studies. As will be clarified in the first chapter of the first part of this work, the exact scope and impact of 'harmfulness' of content is a – controversial – subject, addressed by many social scientists. A brief excursion into social theories regarding harmful content was thus necessary to reach thorough understanding of this kind of content.

3. Structure

This study is composed of two main parts, which both contain two chapters, and which are followed by a conclusion.

Setting – The first chapter aims to gain a clearer understanding of the research issues. A first logical step in this direction implies a clarification of the notions 'digital media content', 'minor' and 'harmful content'. To this end, first, recent evolutions in the media environment, such as the emergence of new technologies, digitisation, convergence, the control revolution, and the uprise of user-generated content and social networking sites, are described. Second, the concept 'minor' is explored not only on the basis of international, European Union, Council of Europe and United States legislative or policy documents, but also from a social science angle. Third, the concept of 'harmful content' is pursued in greater depth. Following a brief exploration into social science theories on media content and media effects, the question why harmful content should be regulated is looked into more closely, based on the precautionary principle theory. Next, which content can actually be considered harmful is examined in greater detail, again, by examining social science literature, but also by considering the juxtaposition between harmful content and illegal content. Finally, harmful content is looked at from a legal angle, identifying a number of legal aspects and implications.

The second part of the first chapter then intends to identify the regulatory challenges linked to the protection of minors against harmful digital media content. Starting from the assumption that this traditional goal of public interest remains valid in the new media environment, the concrete repercussions of particular characteristics of these new media on the use of traditional (content) regulation are examined. To illustrate the potential difficulties of using such traditional forms of regulation, a brief comparison is made with US legislation which aims (or aimed) to protect minors against harmful content. Finally, to conclude the chapter, an analysis of the EU policy history concerning the protection of minors against harmful digital media content, which suggests that using alternative regulatory instruments, such as self- and co-regulation, can achieve this goal in a more efficient way, is presented.

Alternative regulatory instruments – The second chapter of the first part focuses on framing the use of alternative regulatory instruments and gaining a better understanding of how these instruments are conceptualised. First, by means of introduction, 'regulation' as a broad concept is looked into. The distinction between command-and-control regulation and decentred regulation in particular is explored, as a prelude to the subsequent analysis of what is understood by the notion 'alternative regulatory instruments'. This analysis starts with an in-depth investigation of policy documents – international as well as EU documents, and general as well as specific media policy documents – which refer to such instruments. Next, the actual instruments, i.e., self- and co-regulation, possibly accompanied by the use of regulatory tools (such as technology or supporting mechanisms), are analysed on the basis of regulatory theory, studies and illustrations, and assets and drawbacks of using such instruments are identified.

Legal framework – The first chapter of the second part of this study concentrates on the legal framework and requirements which are relevant to the use of alternative regulatory instruments to protect minors against harmful digital media content. Legal provisions which surround both elements of our research subject are described and explained. More specifically, five sets of regulation are concentrated upon. First, the development and different sources of children's fundamental rights are outlined. Second, specific and crucial fundamental rights, i.e., the right to freedom of expression, the right to privacy and the right to a fair trial and to an effective remedy, are discussed in greater detail. Third, different aspects of the (direct and indirect) regulation of content are examined; this includes a closer investigation of the new Audiovisual Media Services Directive, and certain elements of the e-Commerce Directive. Fourth, EU legislation with respect to the internal market and competition is briefly introduced. Finally, several general legislative principles and requirements, such as proportionality, subsidiarity and formal requirements regarding the implementation of EU Directives are clarified.

Compliance of the use of ARIs with the legal framework – The second chapter of this part then seeks to respond to the central research question which aims to discover whether there are legal obstacles to the use of alternative regulatory instruments to protect minors against digital harmful content – given that the use of such instruments does not occur in a legal vacuum. To this end, the relevant provisions are selected from the legal framework presented in the previous chapter and analysed with respect to the requirements they impose on the use of such instruments, based on an interpretation of the normative texts in question, as well as jurisprudence.

Conclusion – Finally, the conclusion compiles the research results, presents a number of recommendations for the future and indicates issues for further research.

* * *

Note to the reader: References to articles of the Treaty on European Union [TEU] and the Treaty on the Functioning of the European Union [TFEU], as amended by the Treaty of Lisbon[1] are – for the sake of clarity – accompanied by their old numbering. In (indented) quotations the numbering prior to the adoption of the Treaty of Lisbon has been maintained, and this has been noted after the quotation.

---

[1] The Treaty of Lisbon entered into force on 1 December 2009.

Part I

Chapter 1

Setting: Notions, Issues & Policy History

Introduction – In this chapter, first, the three essential components of the research topic – the digital media environment, minors and harmful content – are explored as a necessary prelude to the analytical research. In a second phase, these components are combined, with a discussion of recent policy history, to illustrate the issue of protecting minors against harmful media content and, in particular, the regulatory challenges accompanying this issue.

1.1. Clarification of the constitutive elements

1.1.1. *Digital media content*

A. *Introduction*

Changing media environment – Over the past decade the media and communications environment has changed beyond recognition. In addition to the very important technological revolution, social and cultural evolutions have also shaped the current media setting.[1] The technical aspects of these changes have already been described and analysed in great detail over the past few years. Consequently, in this chapter the focus will be on the

[1] Wetenschappelijke Raad voor het Regeringsbeleid, Focus op functies – Uitdagingen voor een toekomstbestendig mediabeleid [*Focus on functions – Challenges for a future proof media policy*], Amsterdam, Amsterdam University Press, 2005, retrieved from http://www.wrr.nl/dsc?c=getobject&s=obj&!sessionid=1o7p!cnhb9o!M9xXGwuyBPekM35UuYCWRZ1zyOvsfxauyo3h50uVxzYXp1K38HdW&objectid=2799&!dsname=default&isapidir=/gvisapi/ (on 27.07.2007), 11 [in Dutch].

impact these different developments have had on (media) content, which is an essential element of culture and modern society.[2]

MEDIA CONTENT – The relative simplicity of the 'old' media environment, which was focused on newspapers, film and television broadcasting, has truly been abandoned.[3] Today, an enormous amount of content is available on an increased number of content platforms, such as, for instance, the PC broadband platform, the digital television platform and the mobile platform.[4] The 'content' industry encompasses a wide range of activities. In addition to the so-called 'core content industries', i.e., the media and related creative industries – such as printing and publishing, television and radio broadcasters, music, video and cinema players, and the online content market –

> *content is also produced and/or distributed by all those who produce art, i.e. painters, architects, actors, musicians and photographers, as well as by cultural institutions such as theatres, concert halls and museums, by players in the market whose function is to deliver certain types of information (such as stock exchange prices), by governmental institutions that provide information important to the public (for instance in the fields of culture, education and health), and, last but not least, by the consumers themselves, e.g. by participating in Internet fora or by providing content via weblogs which are publicly accessible.*[5]

In this study, the notion 'content' primarily refers to 'media' content, and occasionally to user-generated content (*infra*).

THE EUROPEAN UNION AND THE CONTENT INDUSTRY – Over the past decade, the European Union (EU) has touched upon the importance of the con-

---

[2] HOLOUBEK, Michael (ed.), *Regulating content – European regulatory framework for the media and related creative sectors*, Alphen a/d Rijn, Kluwer Law International, 2007, 3.

[3] WETENSCHAPPELIJKE RAAD VOOR HET REGERINGSBELEID, Focus op functies – Uitdagingen voor een toekomstbestendig mediabeleid [*Focus on functions – Challenges for a future proof media policy*], Amsterdam, Amsterdam University Press, 2005, retrieved from http://www.wrr.nl/dsc?c=getobject&s=obj&!sessionid=1o7p!cnhb9o!M9xXGwuyBPekM35UuYCWRZ1zyOvsfxauyo3h50uVxzYXp1K38HdW&objectid=2799&!dsname=default&isapidir=/gvisapi/ (on 27.07.2007), 23 [in Dutch].

[4] HOLOUBEK, Michael (ed.), *Regulating content – European regulatory framework for the media and related creative sectors*, Alphen a/d Rijn, Kluwer Law International, 2007, 15.

[5] HOLOUBEK, Michael (ed.), *Regulating content – European regulatory framework for the media and related creative sectors*, Alphen a/d Rijn, Kluwer Law International, 2007, 15.

tent industry in different policy documents. The Lisbon strategy[6],[7] as well as the i2010 policy[8] have provided an impetus for the development of this industry.[9] The i2010 strategy in particular provided a number of guidelines for the dissemination and the safe use of information and communication technologies.[10] Its aim is threefold: first, to create a Single European Information Space, which promotes an open and competitive internal market for the information society and media services, second, to strengthen investment in innovation in research and ICT, and third, to foster social inclusion, better public services and improved quality of life through the use of ICT.[11] The 2008 Commission Communication on Creative Content Online in the Single Market is another important document in this area and also has a threefold aim: to ensure "*that European content achieves its full potential in contributing to European competitiveness and in fostering the availability and circulation of the great diversity of European content creation and of Europe's cultural and linguistic heritage*"; to update and clarify "*possible legal provisions that unnecessarily hinder online distribution of creative content in the EU, while acknowledging the importance of copyright for creation*"; and, finally, to

---

[6] Commission of the European Communities, The Lisbon European Council – An agenda of economic and social renewal for Europe (Contribution of the European Commission to the special European Council in Lisbon), 23-24.03.2000, retrieved from http://ec.europa.eu/growthandjobs/pdf/lisbon_en.pdf (on 27.07.2007). The Lisbon Strategy's aim is to transform the European Union into a competitive knowledge economy, in which the information society – and hence also the content industry – plays an important role.

[7] Commission of the European Communities, Communication to the Spring European Council Working together for growth and jobs: a new start for the Lisbon Strategy, COM (2005) 24, 02.02.2005, retrieved from http://ec.europa.eu/growthandjobs/pdf/COM2005_024_en.pdf (on 27.07.2007).

[8] Commission of the European Communities, Communication from the Commission to the Council, the European Parliament, the European Economic and Social Committee and the Committee of the Regions: "i2010 – A European Information Society for growth and employment", COM (2005) 229 final, 01.06.2005. For more details on the i2010 policy, cf. Harcourt, Alison, "Institutionalising soft governance in the European Information Society", in: Ward, David (ed.), *The European Union and the culture industries: regulation and the public interest*, Aldershot, Ashgate, 2008, 22–25.

[9] Holoubek, Michael (ed.), *Regulating content – European regulatory framework for the media and related creative sectors*, Alphen a/d Rijn, Kluwer Law International, 2007, 45.

[10] Holoubek, Michael (ed.), *Regulating content – European regulatory framework for the media and related creative sectors*, Alphen a/d Rijn, Kluwer Law International, 2007, 46.

[11] European Commission, What is i2010?, retrieved from http://ec.europa.eu/information_society/eeurope/i2010/what_is_i2010/index_en.htm (on 27.07.2007).

foster "*users' active role in content selection, distribution and creation*".[12, 13] In order to be able to deal in a timely manner with the challenges posed by the increased availability and accessibility of content, the EU Commission set up a 'Content Online Platform'[14] as a framework for discussion on relevant issues.[15] It is thus clear that the Commission attaches great value to the recent technological and social evolutions with respect to content.

B. *Recent developments in the media environment*

TRENDS – A number of trends have contributed to the recent media developments. The emergence of new technologies, digitisation, convergence, and the phenomena of social networking and the control revolution are the four trends that are the most relevant to the subject at hand. These trends will be briefly commented upon to clarify the research subject. It is important to note, however, that it is not the intention here to sketch a comprehensive overview of all these recent developments.

B.1. *The emergence of new technologies*

NEW TECHNOLOGIES – Changes in the media sector have always been driven by technological developments and the emergence of new technologies. Each new medium – from the printing press, to movies, television, VCRs, videogames and the Internet – has brought about fundamental transformations in the way people consume media content. Some transitions between different media were smooth, others more revolutionary.

---

[12] COMMISSION OF THE EUROPEAN COMMUNITIES, Communication from the Commission to the European Parliament, the Council, the European Economic and Social Committee and the Committee of the Regions on Creative Content Online in the Single Market, COM (2007) 836 final, 03.01.2008. The Commission identifies "*content and services such as audiovisual media online (film, television, music and radio), games online, online publishing, educational content as well as user-generated content*" as 'creative content online' (p. 3).

[13] Cf. also REDING, Viviane, Towards next generation media for the digital age?, Speech at the Conference organised by the IMPRESA Group and RADIO RENASCENCA on the Future of the Media, Lisbon, 17.07.2007, retrieved from http://ec.europa.eu/commission_barroso/reding/docs/speeches/lisbon_20070717.pdf (on 27.07.2007).

[14] Several meetings of this Platform took place in 2008 and 2009: cf. EUROPEAN COMMISSION, Final report on the Content Online Platform, May 2009, retrieved from http://ec.europa.eu/avpolicy/docs/other_actions/col_platform_report.pdf (on 24.05.2009).

[15] COMMISSION OF THE EUROPEAN COMMUNITIES, Communication from the Commission to the European Parliament, the Council, the European Economic and Social Committee and the Committee of the Regions on Creative Content Online in the Single Market, COM (2007) 836 final, 03.01.2008, 8–9.

Table 1: Common set of attributes

Interactivity	The extent to which a person is actually able to interact with the technology in a meaningful way
Structure	The extent to which a medium is linear or non-linear
Control	Amount of control provided to the user (extent to which the user can easily alter the pace of presentation, the order of presentation and the amount of content presented)
Channel	Presentation of information: visually, acoustically or via both channels at once
Textuality	Amount of information in a medium that is communicated in text form
Content	Actual information conveyed by a medium (e.g. violence, sex, persuasive messages or information)

Inspired by Sparks, Glenn G., *Media effects research: a basic overview*, London, Thomson, 2006, 220 and Eveland, William. P. Jr., "A mix of attributes approach to the study of media effects and new communication technologies", *Journal of Communication* 2003, Volume 53, Issue 3, 395–410.

Thinking about new technologies – Although it is tempting to magnify the differences between these technologies and their corresponding media, they, of course, share a considerable number of characteristics. An interesting approach in this context is advocated by the sociologist William Eveland, who characterises media according to a 'common set of attributes', such as interactivity, structure, control, channel, textuality and content.[16, 17]

Each medium possesses each of these characteristics to a different degree. The value of this approach primarily lies in demonstrating not only the differences and parallels between the various media, but also the evolution of a medium over time along the continuum of each attribute. Sparks, for instance, points to the increased degree of textuality of certain television channels through the inclusion of text banners at the bottom of the screen on which news headlines are continuously published. Another example is the branching out of newspapers into the online world, which often also complement their textual articles with news video clips. In our view, this approach

[16] Sparks, Glenn G., *Media effects research: a basic overview*, London, Thomson, 2006, 220–221.

[17] Eveland, William. P. Jr., "A mix of attributes approach to the study of media effects and new communication technologies", *Journal of Communication* 2003, Vol. 53, No. 3, 395–410. Eveland stresses that his list of attributes is not exhaustive and that other attributes exist (p. 398).

provides a nuanced method of thinking about 'old' and 'new' media that transcends blunt and impulsive statements about developments within and between media.

CHANGES – It can, however, not been denied that the rise of digital technologies brought about significant changes with respect to the availability, accessibility and volume of content. The Internet, for instance, is a medium that is easily accessible – all you need is a computer, a modem and an Internet connection – and makes available an unprecedented amount of information.[18] This would not have been possible without a technical process called digitisation.

B.2. *Digitisation*

> *At its simplest, digital content means the forms of content that we understand in the analogue media world turned into bits and bytes so they can be manipulated, processed and transmitted by computer systems.*
>
> Tony FELDMAN[19]

DIGITAL CONTENT – Harry NEWTON defines 'digital' in the context of telecommunications, recording or computing as "*the use of a binary code to represent information*".[20] Hence, digitisation implies the conversion of analogue information into bits.[21] This process then "*enables computer controlled*

[18] For a 'definition' of the Internet, cf. for instance, NEWTON, Harry, *Newton's Telecom Dictionary*, San Francisco, CMP Books, 2003, 419: "*The Internet is both a transport network – moving every form of data around the world (voice, video, data and images) – and a network of computers which allow you to access, retrieve, process and store all manner of information. Increasingly, the most important part of the Internet for all of us normal people is something called the World Wide Web, as characterized by all those web sites starting with www. […] The Internet is basically a packet switched network based on a family of protocols called TCP/IP, which stands for Transmission Control Protocol/Internet Protocol, a family of networking protocols providing communication across interconnected networks, between computers with diverse hardware architectures and between various computer operating systems*". For more information on the Internet, cf. OFCOM, Ofcom's submission to the Byron Review: Annex 1: How does the Internet work?, 30.11.2007, retrieved from http://www.ofcom.org.uk/research/telecoms/reports/byron/annex1.pdf (on 02.07.2008). For statistics on Internet usage, cf. EUROSTAT, Use of the Internet among individuals and enterprises, 2006, retrieved from http://epp.eurostat.ec.europa.eu/cache/ITY_OFFPUB/KS-NP-06-012/EN/KS-NP-06-012-EN.PDF (on 02.08.2007).

[19] FELDMAN, Tony, *An introduction to digital media*, London, Routledge, 1997, 154.

[20] NEWTON, Harry, *Newton's Telecom Dictionary*, San Francisco, CMP Books, 2003, 241.

[21] SVANTESSON, Dan Jerker B., "The characteristics making Internet communication challenge traditional models of regulation – What every international jurist should know about

storage, manipulation and display of this information and its transmission in an integrated bit stream on a common channel".[22]

Characteristics – According to Feldman, digital content has five characteristics which analogue information lacks: digital information is manipulable, networkable, dense, compressible and impartial.[23] First, digitalised information is easily and infinitely manipulable. Changing analogue information, such as, for instance, a book, is a difficult process compared to modifying, taking apart, dividing or assembling digital information, which can be done quickly, easily and an unlimited number of times. Second, digital information is networkable. This means that the information can "*be shared and exchanged by large numbers of users simultaneously*" on a large geographical scale. Furthermore, digital information is dense and compressible. While digital information is already much more compact than analogue information (depending on the storage technology used), it can also be compressed even more. Digital compression technologies play a crucial role in switching from analogue to digital technology, and have particularly led to a multiplication of the amount of information that can be distributed. Finally, digital information is said to be impartial. As a result of the use of binary code, computer systems function independently from the sort of information that needs to be digitally transmitted. As long as the code is comprehensible to the machine, the information will be sent through. Hence, it does not matter if the code constitutes text, photos, video or music.

Consequences of digitisation – Due to the characteristics mentioned above, digital technologies have the advantage of being more efficient, flexible and cost-effective than analogue media,[24] and have consequently influenced different elements of the media value chain.[25] The digitisation of media infrastructure is leading – due to its more efficient storage and transmission, and the reduced volume of information – to the reduction of technological

---

the Internet", *International Journal of Law and Information Technology* 2005, Vol. 13, No. 1, 60.

[22] Garnham, Nicholas, "What is multimedia", 1999, retrieved from http://europa.eu.int/ISPO/legal/en/lab/lisbon/garnham.html (on 30.07.2007, no longer available).

[23] Feldman, Tony, *An introduction to digital media*, London-New York, Routledge, 1997, 4–8.

[24] Commission of the European Communities, Green Paper on the convergence of the telecommunications, media and information technology sectors, and the implications for regulation, COM (1997) 623 final, 03.12.1997, 2.

[25] Goldberg, David, Prosser, Tony and Verhulst, Stefaan (eds), *Regulating the changing media: a comparative study*, Oxford, Oxford University Press, 1998, 1.

scarcity (such as spectrum scarcity),[26] and the increase of media capacity.[27] Whereas analogue cable television networks, for instance, can carry around forty channels, cable networks using digital technology can offer hundreds of television channels as well as telephony, Internet access and interactive services.[28] Furthermore, digitisation of the production, distribution and consumption of media services is leading to a more diversified, and again amplified, offering of these services to the consumer.[29] The breakdown of the barriers between different media sectors, distribution channels, services and interfaces,[30] prompted by the digitisation trend, has led to a very important phenomenon that is referred to as 'convergence'.[31]

---

[26] Wetenschappelijke Raad voor het Regeringsbeleid, Focus op functies – Uitdagingen voor een toekomstbestendig mediabeleid [*Focus on functions – Challenges for a future proof media policy*], Amsterdam, Amsterdam University Press, 2005, retrieved from http://www.wrr.nl/dsc?c=getobject&s=obj&!sessionid=1o7p!cnhb9o!M9xXGwuyBPekM35UuYCWRZ1zyOvsfxauyo3h50uVxzYXp1K38HdW&objectid=2799&!dsname=default&isapidir=/gvisapi/ (on 27.07.2007), 23 [in Dutch].

[27] Goldberg, David, Prosser, Tony and Verhulst, Stefaan (eds), *Regulating the changing media: a comparative study*, Oxford, Oxford University Press, 1998, 11; Council of Europe (Media Division, Directorate General of Human Rights), Public service media in the information society – Report prepared for the Council of Europe's Group of Specialists on Public Service Broadcasting in the Information Society by Christian S. Nissen, February 2006, retrieved from http://www.coe.int/t/dghl/standardsetting/media/Doc/H-Inf(2006)003_en.pdf (on 30.05.2006), 8.

[28] Commission of the European Communities, Communication from the Commission to the Council, the European Parliament, the Economic and Social Committee and the Committee of the Regions, Principles and guidelines for the Community's audiovisual policy in the digital age, COM (1999) 657 final, 14.12.1999, 5.

[29] Wetenschappelijke Raad voor het Regeringsbeleid, Focus op functies – Uitdagingen voor een toekomstbestendig mediabeleid [*Focus on functions – Challenges for a future proof media policy*], Amsterdam, Amsterdam University Press, 2005, retrieved from http://www.wrr.nl/dsc?c=getobject&s=obj&!sessionid=1o7p!cnhb9o!M9xXGwuyBPekM35UuYCWRZ1zyOvsfxauyo3h50uVxzYXp1K38HdW&objectid=2799&!dsname=default&isapidir=/gvisapi/ (on 27.07.2007), 23 [in Dutch].

[30] Garnham, Nicholas, "What is multimedia", 1999, retrieved from http://europa.eu.int/ISPO/legal/en/lab/lisbon/garnham.html (on 30.07.2007, no longer available).

[31] Valcke, Peggy, *Digitale diversiteit – Convergentie van media-, telecommunicatie en mededingingsrecht* [*Digital diversity – Convergence of media, telecommunication and competition law*], Brussel, Larcier, 2004, 24 [in Dutch]; Goldberg, David, Prosser, Tony and Verhulst, Stefaan (eds), *Regulating the changing media: a comparative study*, Oxford, Oxford University Press, 1998, 1; Verhulst, Stefaan G., "The regulation of digital content", in: Lievrouw, Leah A. and Livingstone, Sonia, *Handbook of new media – Social shaping and social consequences of ICTs*, London, Sage Publications, 2006, 332.

B.3. *Convergence*

What is convergence? – Convergence has been one of the buzzwords in the media environment for the past decade. Literally 'convergence' means "*to tend or move toward one point or one another*", "*come together*" or "*to come together and unite in a common interest or focus*".[32] A more specific definition, which can be applied to the media environment, is "*the merging of distinct technologies, industries, or devices into a unified whole*".[33] The EU Green Paper on the convergence of the telecommunications, media and information technology sectors and the implications for regulation describes the phenomenon as "*the ability of different network platforms to carry essentially similar kinds of services, or the coming together of consumer devices such as the telephone, television and personal computer*".[34]

Different kinds of convergence – Within the media environment, different types of convergence have been distinguished.[35] Technological convergence refers to the blurring of boundaries between the different communication technologies, which implies that media services can now be offered over various networks[36] (unlike before, when services were much more medium-dependent). This kind of convergence is directly based on the "*common application of digital technologies to systems and networks associated with the delivery of services*".[37] A second type of convergence is economic convergence, which relates to the economic entwining of different sectors. This leads to mergers between media companies, the diversification

---

32 Merriam's-Webster's Online Dictionary, Converge, retrieved from http://www.webster.com/dictionary/converge (on 31.07.2007).

33 Merriam's-Webster's Online Dictionary, Convergence, retrieved from http://www.webster.com/dictionary/convergence (on 31.07.2007).

34 Commission of the European Communities, Green Paper on the convergence of the telecommunications, media and information technology sectors, and the implications for regulation, COM (1997) 623 final, 03.12.1997, 1.

35 Uyttendaele, Caroline, *Openbare informatie – Het juridisch statuut in een convergerende mediaomgeving* [*Public information – The legal status in a converging media environment*], Antwerpen, Maklu, 2002, 25–26 [in Dutch]; Valcke, Peggy, *Digitale diversiteit – Convergentie van media-, telecommunicatie en mededingingsrecht* [*Digital diversity – Convergence of media, telecommunication and competition law*], Brussel, Larcier, 2004, 74 [in Dutch].

36 Commission of the European Communities, Green Paper on the convergence of the telecommunications, media and information technology sectors, and the implications for regulation, COM (1997) 623 final, 03.12.1997, ii.

37 Commission of the European Communities, Green Paper on the convergence of the telecommunications, media and information technology sectors, and the implications for regulation, COM (1997) 623 final, 03.12.1997, 2.

of services that are offered by media companies and the expansion of activities of media companies, traditionally active in one market segment, into other market segments.[38] The final category of convergence then is legal or policy convergence, which denotes a unified model of law for the different elements of a converged media environment. It is necessary to bear in mind, however, that technological convergence does not automatically lead to legal convergence.[39]

Levels and impact of convergence – Whereas the convergence phenomenon has been at the forefront of almost all discussions related to the media landscape over the past decade,[40] it has only recently been declared as being an "*everyday reality*".[41] Convergence has occurred – and still is occur-

---

[38] Uyttendaele, Caroline, *Openbare informatie – Het juridisch statuut in een convergerende mediaomgeving* [*Public information – The legal status in a converging media environment*], Antwerpen, Maklu, 2002, 26 [in Dutch]. See also: Commission of the European Communities, Green Paper on the convergence of the telecommunications, media and information technology sectors, and the implications for regulation, COM (1997) 623 final, 03.12.1997, 6 *et seq.*

[39] Different challenges in this domain were identified by the EC's Green Paper on convergence: Commission of the European Communities, Green Paper on the convergence of the telecommunications, media and information technology sectors, and the implications for regulation, COM (1997) 623 final, 03.12.1997, 26 *et seq.*

[40] The European Commission Green Paper on convergence (Commission of the European Communities, Green Paper on the convergence of the telecommunications, media and information technology sectors, and the implications for regulation, COM (1997) 623 final, 03.12.1997), for instance, dates from 1997.

[41] Commission of the European Communities, Communication from the Commission to the Council, the European Parliament, the European Economic and Social Committee and the Committee of the Regions: "i2010 – A European Information Society for growth and employment", COM (2005) 229 final, 01.06.2005: "*The digital convergence of information society and media services, networks and devices is finally becoming an everyday reality*". See also: Arino, Monica and Llorens, Carles, "Back to the future: new media, same principles? Convergence regulation re-visited", in: Ward, David (ed.), *The European Union and the culture industries: regulation and the public interest*, Aldershot, Ashgate, 2008, 141. Jakubowicz lists the characteristics of 'fully developed convergent digital communication': "*Multimedia communication; non-linear, on-demand delivery of content; interactivity; asynchronous communication; individualisation/personalisation (customisation); portability of receivers and mobile reception; disintermediation (elimination of intermediaries, e.g. media organisations, as anyone can offer information and other content to be directly accessed by users and receivers); and "neo-intermediation" (emergence of new intermediaries, especially on the Internet, capable of offering new services or aggregating and packaging content in new ways)*": Jakubowicz, Karl, "A new notion of media?", Background text, 1st Council of Europe Conference of Ministers responsible for media and new communications services: A new notion of media?, Reykjavik, 28-29.05.2009, retrieved from http://www.ministerialconference.is/media/images/a_new_notion_of_media_web_version.df (on 27.05.2009).

ring – at different levels of the media sector; the three most important being the infrastructure level, the device or terminal level, and the services level.[42] At the infrastructure level, convergence has led to the de-specialisation of networks. On the one hand, different networks can be used to transmit the same type of media services, and, on the other hand, one type of network can now also carry different types of media content.[43] Whereas cable operators, for example, only used to carry television signals over their networks, they are now also able to offer telephony and Internet access. In this context, the notion 'networked media' was introduced by the European Commission in 2007. This concept implies that "*all kinds of media including text, image, 3D graphics, audio and video are produced, distributed, shared, managed and consumed through various networks like the Internet, WiFi, GPRS, 3G and so on, in a converged manner*".[44] At the same time, devices or terminals can now be used to consult many different types of media services. A mobile phone, for instance, now has the potential to provide voice telephony, Internet access and transmission of audiovisual images, such as television broadcasting or movies, whereas before one would have needed three different devices, i.e., a telephone, a computer and a television, to access these services.[45] As regards services, convergence has produced hybrid multimedia services.[46] Audiovisual images, text and music can be combined in an infinite number of ways and then be distributed in different formats on a variety of networks. Newspapers, for instance, can thus be enhanced with pictures, film or audio fragments, and then be distributed electronically. The slogan "anywhere-anytime-anything" is, as a result, often used to describe this

[42] Commission of the European Communities, Green Paper on the protection of minors and human dignity in audiovisual and information services, COM (1996) 483 final, 10.

[43] Verhulst, Stefaan G., "The regulation of digital content", in: Lievrouw, Leah A. and Livingstone, Sonia, *Handbook of new media – Social shaping and social consequences of ICTs*, London, Sage Publications, 2006, 332.

[44] European Commission, Networked Media of the Future, October 2007, retrieved from ftp://ftp.cordis.europa.eu/pub/fp7/ict/docs/netmedia/networked-media-of-the-future_en.pdf (on 28.01.2008), 6.

[45] Economist.com, Your television is ringing, 12.10.2006, retrieved from http://www.economist.com/research/articlesBySubject/displayStory.cfm?subjectid=349005&story_id=7995312 (on 16.10.2006).

[46] Commission of the European Communities, Green Paper on the convergence of the telecommunications, media and information technology sectors, and the implications for regulation, COM (1997) 623 final, 03.12.1997, 9.

evolution.[47] Hence, convergence in general creates a wealth of opportunities and is a powerful driver for innovation.[48]

B.4. *Control revolution, social networking and user-generated content*

Control revolution and individualisation – In comparison to the traditional media environment where content providers, such as broadcasters, were in control of what content viewers would see at what time, users are now gradually exercising more and more control over their media consumption patterns.[49] This phenomenon has been called the 'control revolution'.[50] Because of the opportunities provided by the two former trends – digitisation and convergence – the kinds of media services that are now offered have changed considerably. As such, the offering of services has shifted from being supply-driven to being much more demand-driven.[51] On-demand services, such as on-demand movies distributed over digital platforms, have become increasingly more available in the current landscape. This evolution goes hand in hand with the rise of digital personal video recorders, which allow a greater freedom to watch content whenever it is convenient. Furthermore, the Internet is, by its nature, an on-demand medium: content can be consulted where and when the user wishes to do so. By the same token, mobile phones increasingly provide the opportunity to consult content on the move

[47] O'Connell, Rachel and Bryce, Jo, Children and young people in on-line and related off-line environments: Promoting well-being and minimising risk of harm, Study commissioned by the Council of Europe, not published, 18.

[48] Reding, Viviane, Digital convergence: a whole new way of life, Speech at the Digital Lifestyle Exhibition, Brussels, 30.05.2006, retrieved from http://ec.europa.eu/commission_barroso/reding/docs/speeches/dle_20060530.pdf (on 31.07.2007), 2.

[49] Reding, Viviane, Digital convergence: a whole new way of life, Speech at the Digital Life style Exhibition, Brussels, 30.05.2006, retrieved from http://ec.europa.eu/commission_barroso/reding/docs/speeches/dle_20060530.pdf (on 31.07.2007), 2.

[50] Van Eijck, Nico, Asscher, Lodewijk, Helberger, Natali and Kabel, Jan, De regulering van media in internationaal perspectief [*The regulation of media in an international perspective*], Den Haag, February 2005, retrieved from http://www.ivir.nl/publicaties/overig/Media/regulering%20van%20media%20in%20internationaal%20perspect.pdf (on 01.08.2007), 62 [in Dutch].

[51] Wetenschappelijke Raad voor het Regeringsbeleid, Focus op functies – Uitdagingen voor een toekomstbestendig mediabeleid [*Focus on functions – Challenges for a future proof media policy*], Amsterdam, Amsterdam University Press, 2005, retrieved from http://www.wrr.nl/dsc?c=getobject&s=obj&!sessionid=1o7p!cnhb9o!M9xXGwuyBPekM35UuYCWRZ1zyOvsfxauyo3h50uVxzYXp1K38HdW&objectid=2799&!dsname=default&isapidir=/gvisapi/ (on 27.07.2007) 37 [in Dutch]; Commission of the European Communities, Green Paper on the convergence of the telecommunications, media and information technology sectors, and the implications for regulation, COM (1997) 623 final, 03.12.1997, 21.

and at the moment of the user's choosing. Hence, media consumption is becoming much more individualised.[52] At the same time, the new media services also have the potential to provide a higher level of interactivity.[53] Voting mechanisms, for instance, are regularly used in television broadcasting. It is important to be aware of the importance of this control revolution from a regulatory perspective. Regulation of traditional media services has for a large part been based on the rationale that the media content provider, such as the broadcaster, had total control over what content the user or viewer would be confronted with. Therefore, it was considered necessary to impose a number of rules on these content providers. Of course, when users gain more and more control over their media use, this rationale loses strength (cf. *infra*).

SOCIAL NETWORKING – Another expression of interactivity, but between users instead of between the media content provider and the user, can be found in the rapidly growing social networking trend.[54] The trend is found especially on the Internet: social networking websites such as MySpace, Facebook or Bebo, are immensely successful. For example, a 2007 US study found that 55 percent of all of online American 12–17 year-olds are active

---

[52] COUNCIL OF EUROPE (MEDIA DIVISION, DIRECTORATE GENERAL OF HUMAN RIGHTS), Public service media in the information society – Report prepared for the Council of Europe's Group of Specialists on Public Service Broadcasting in the Information Society by Christian S. NISSEN, February 2006, retrieved from http://www.coe.int/t/dghl/standard setting/media/Doc/H-Inf(2006)003_en.pdf (on 30.05.2006), 13.

[53] REDING, Viviane, Digital convergence: a whole new way of life, Speech at the Digital Life style Exhibition, Brussels, 30.05.2006, retrieved from http://ec.europa.eu/commission_bar roso/reding/docs/speeches/dle_20060530.pdf (on 31.07.2007); COMMISSION OF THE EUROPEAN COMMUNITIES, Green Paper on the protection of minors and human dignity in audiovisual and information services, COM (1996) 483 final, 16.10.1996, 9.

[54] The European Commission describes 'social networking' as follows: "*Social networking sites makes [sic] it possible to create and design a personal website, blog, journal or diary using graphics, colour, music and images to represent a unique style and identity. On these sites, children and young people share thoughts and information about areas of interest and themselves, they publish and share their own music, they receive comments from friends or guests, they publish images and videos, also of themselves and their family and friends and they link to other friends' websites. On many sites they can also interact with friends in real-time through instant messaging, chat rooms or message boards and they can meet new friends, play online games, join communities where they can discuss their interests with others and take part in competitions and quizzes*": EUROPEAN COMMISSION, What is social networking?, retrieved from http://ec.europa.eu/information_society/activities/sip/safety_tips/index_en.htm#1.1_what_is_social_networking (on 17.03.2008). See also: EUROPEAN COMMISSION, Public consultation on online social networking – Summary report, November 2008, retrieved from http://ec.europa.eu/information_society/activities/sip/docs/pub_consult_age_rating_sns/summaryreport.pdf (on 19.11.2008).

on online social networking sites.[55] Predominantly used by young people,[56, 57] such sites provide them with the opportunity to connect to friends, talk, blog, create personal profiles with information about them, exchange pictures or movies and make new friends based, for instance, on common interests.[58, 59] Although these networking sites have an enormous potential in terms of creativity, communication and friendship, they have also been confronted with abuses, such as adults posing as children in order to contact children, and cyberbullying.[60]

---

55 Lenhart, Amanda and Madden, Mary, Social networking websites and teens: an overview, Pew Internet and American Life Project, 2007, retrieved from www.pewinternet.org/PPF/r/198/report_display.asp (on 17.03.2008).

56 European Commission, What is social networking?, retrieved from http://ec.europa.eu/information_society/activities/sip/safety_tips/index_en.htm#1.1_what_is_social_networking (on 17.03.2008); O'Connell, Rachel and Bryce, Jo, Children and young people in on-line and related off-line environments: Promoting well-being and minimising risk of harm, Study commissioned by the Council of Europe, not published, 111.

57 Although not exclusively: LinkedIn, for instance, is a professional networking site which allows professionals to create personal profiles and connect with other professionals (www.linkedin.com).

58 OECD, Participative web: user-created content, DSTI/ICCP/IE(2006)7/FINAL, 12.04.2007, retrieved from http://www.oecd.org/dataoecd/57/14/38393115.pdf (on 02.08.2007), 19.

59 A 2007 US study claims that 9–17 year-olds spend almost as much time (nine hours per week) using social networking services and Web sites as they spend watching television: National School Boards Association, Creating and connecting – Research and guidelines on online social – and educational – networking, July 2007, retrieved from http://www.nsba.org/SecondaryMenu/TLN/CreatingandConnecting.aspx (on 11.01.2007), ii.

60 BBC News, Warnings over social site 'abuse', 14.09.2006, retrieved from http://news.bbc.co.uk/2/hi/technology/5344722.stm (on 18.09.2006). Other studies report that the dangers of social networking are often overestimated: National School Boards Association, Creating and connecting – Research and guidelines on online social – and educational – networking, July 2007, retrieved from http://www.nsba.org/SecondaryMenu/TLN/CreatingandConnecting.aspx (on 11.01.2007), 1: "*[...] parents and students report few problem behaviours online*" and also "*Students and parents report fewer recent and current problems, such as cyberstalking, cyberbullying and unwelcome personal encounters than school fears and policies seem to imply. Only a minority of students has had any kind of negative experience with social networking in the last three months; even fewer parents report that their children have had a negative experience over a longer, six-month period*" (p. 5). See also: European Commission, Public consultation: Safer Internet and online technologies for children, 2007, retrieved from http://ec.europa.eu/information_society/activities/sip/docs/public_consultation_prog/pc_2007_info_en.pdf (on 02.04.2008), 3. Other qualitative (as well as quantitative) research on social networking was published by Ofcom: Ofcom, Social networking: A quantitative and qualitative research report into attitudes, behaviours and use, April 2008, retrieved from http://www.ofcom.org.uk/advice/media_literacy/medlitpub/medlitpubrss/socialnetworking/ (on 01.07.2008).

User-generated content – Another important trend in the current media landscape is the vastly lowered threshold for content production. Whereas before, a limited number of media content providers had control over which content was distributed, now each user has the possibility to supply and distribute content.[61] This phenomenon mainly arises on the Internet – fixed and mobile – which has been dubbed the 'participative web'.[62] This concept is based on

> *an Internet increasingly influenced by intelligent web services that empower the user to contribute to developing, rating, collaborating on and distributing Internet content and customising Internet applications.*[63]

These web services such as (we)blogs,[64] and video and photo portals (e.g. YouTube and Flickr) are very user-friendly and provide an instrument to easily distribute content (such as text, video fragments or pictures) on a worldwide scale.[65] No significant costs or technical skills are required to become a content provider. The content created in this way has been labelled 'user-created' or 'user-generated' content; i.e., "*i) content made publicly available over the Internet, ii) which reflects a certain amount of creative effort, and iii)*

---

[61] Commission of the European Communities, Green Paper on the protection of minors and human dignity in audiovisual and information services, COM (1996) 483 final, 8. Also: Jakubowicz, Karl, "A new notion of media?", Background text, 1st Council of Europe Conference of Ministers responsible for media and new communications services: A new notion of media?; Reykjavik, 28-29.05.2009, retrieved from http://www.ministerialconference.is/media/images/a_new_notion_of_media_web_version.df (on 27.05.2009), 15 *et seq.*

[62] Another popular term is 'Web 2.0'. Definitions of 'Web 2.0' exist in great numbers. The European Commission distinguishes the following differences between 'Web 1.0' and 'Web 2.0': downloading versus uploading, consuming versus creating, corporate versus personal, separate media versus converging media, and static versus interactive: European Commission, Safer Internet and online technologies for children: Summary of the results of the online public consultation and 20–21 June 2007 Safer Internet Forum Report, January 2008, retrieved from http://ec.europa.eu/information_society/activities/sip/docs/public_consultation_prog/summary_report.pdf (on 09.01.2008), 4.

[63] OECD, Participative web: user-created content, DSTI/ICCP/IE(2006)7/FINAL, 12.04.2007, retrieved from http://www.oecd.org/dataoecd/57/14/38393115.pdf (on 02.08.2007), 4.

[64] A blog can be defined as "*a webpage that serves as a publicly accessible personal journal for an individual, i.e., a collection of text and multimedia postings*": O'Connell, Rachel and Bryce, Jo, Children and young people in on-line and related off-line environments: Promoting well-being and minimising risk of harm, Study commissioned by the Council of Europe, not published, 111.

[65] Cf. European Commission, Networked Media of the Future, October 2007, retrieved from ftp://ftp.cordis.europa.eu/pub/fp7/ict/docs/netmedia/networked-media-of-the-future_en.pdf (on 28.01.2008), 12.

which is created outside of professional routines and practices".[66] It has been argued that the rise of these forms of content leads towards democratisation of media production, increased user autonomy, increased participation, and increased diversity.[67] Thus, user-generated content can play a role in the exercise of the right to freedom of expression (*infra*) and the promotion of the free flow of information.[68] Without a shadow of a doubt, user-generated content can be very valuable. Young people, who are especially active in this context and have access to an enormous amount of information from all over the world, can express their own creativity in the production of content and can interact through the enormously popular social networking sites such as MySpace or Facebook. By so acting, they become "*integrated members of a knowledge-based society*".[69] At the same time, however, when content is created and distributed, inevitably, content that is potentially harmful to children or young persons will circulate as well. Another challenge connected with the growth of user-generated content concerns the accuracy and quality of content.[70] The amount of content and the number of content providers make it very difficult, if not impossible, to control both the accuracy and quality of content, which are usually associated more with the output of traditional media content providers, such as, for instance, newspapers. To somewhat counter this problem, systems such as peer review, ratings and recommendations have been put in place by the users themselves.[71] Other issues which can be a cause for concern are infringements of privacy, identity theft and copyright matters. As the user-generated content trend is still in its

[66] OECD, Participative web: user-created content, DSTI/ICCP/IE(2006)7/FINAL, 12.04.2007, retrieved from http://www.oecd.org/dataoecd/57/14/38393115.pdf (on 02.08.2007), 4.

[67] OECD, Participative web: user-created content, DSTI/ICCP/IE(2006)7/FINAL, 12.04.2007, retrieved from http://www.oecd.org/dataoecd/57/14/38393115.pdf (on 02.08.2007), 5.

[68] OECD, Participative web: user-created content, DSTI/ICCP/IE(2006)7/FINAL, 12.04.2007, retrieved from http://www.oecd.org/dataoecd/57/14/38393115.pdf (on 02.08.2007), 6.

[69] O'Connell, Rachel and Bryce, Jo, Children and young people in on-line and related off-line environments: Promoting well-being and minimising risk of harm, Study commissioned by the Council of Europe, not published, 26.

[70] Cf. O'Connell, Rachel and Bryce, Jo, Children and young people in on-line and related off-line environments: Promoting well-being and minimising risk of harm, Study commissioned by the Council of Europe, not published, 47 *et seq.* on source criticism. O'Connell and Bryce point to the importance of including information literacy in school curricula and educating children on interpreting and evaluating the content of newsblogs and user generated blogs.

[71] OECD, Participative web: user-created content, DSTI/ICCP/IE(2006)7/FINAL, 12.04.2007, retrieved from http://www.oecd.org/dataoecd/57/14/38393115.pdf (on 02.08.2007), 54.

infancy, it will be important to address these challenges without losing sight of the many opportunities[72] this evolution offers.[73]

C. *Conclusion: digital media content*

Focus – In this book, the focus lies primarily on 'online' content, particularly text and audiovisual content, made available on digital platforms (such as the Internet, digital television or mobile platforms). Comparisons with the offline content context are made where relevant. Only 'public media' content are taken into consideration; private content, such as e-mails, are remain outside the scope of this analysis. Video and online games also fall within the scope of the concept of digital media content, but are only treated on the margin, since they are a quite specific form of content to which a whole new study could be devoted.[74]

Digital media content and children – Children nowadays grow up in a digital media environment. Digital media content, with all its specific characteristics, is a part of their daily reality.[75] Studies reveal that children

---

[72] European Commission, Safer Internet and Online Technologies for children: Summary of the results of the online public consultation and 20–21 June 2007 Safer Internet Forum Report, January 2008, retrieved from http://ec.europa.eu/information_society/activities/sip/docs/public_consultation_prog/summary_report.pdf (on 09.01.2008), 3: "*Many respondents expressed a need to keep in mind the overwhelmingly positive potential of the internet, to inform, educate, entertain and – as far as industry is concerned – to drive business success*". See also: Byron, Tanya, Safer children in a digital world: the report of the Byron review, 27.03.2008, retrieved from http://www.dfes.gov.uk/byronreview/ (on 04.07.2008), 27 and 60–62; Ofcom, Ofcom's response to the Byron Review – Statement, 27.03.2008, retrieved from http://www.ofcom.org.uk/research/telecoms/reports/byron/byron_review.pdf (on 04.07.2008), 15–19.

[73] For an overview concerning legal challenges related to user-generated content, cf. Carlisle, George and Scerri, Jackie, "Web 2.0 and user-generated content: legal challenges in the new frontier", *Journal of Information, Law and Technology* 2007, No. 2, retrieved from http://www2.warwick.ac.uk/fac/soc/law/elj/jilt/2007_2/george_scerri (on 21.01.2008).

[74] For more information on video and online games, cf. Byron, Tanya, Safer children in a digital world: the report of the Byron review, 27.03.2008, retrieved from http://www.dfes.gov.uk/byronreview/ (on 04.07.2008), Chapter 6–8; Council of Europe, Human rights guidelines for online games providers – Developed by the Council of Europe in co-operation with the Interactive Software Federation of Europe, July 2008, retrieved from http://www.coe.int/t/dghl/standardsetting/media/Doc/H-Inf(2008)008_en.pdf (on 17.12.2008).

[75] Even very young children, under the age of twelve, are already very active media consumers. Cf. Etsi, Human Factors (HF); Specification and guidelines for service providers on the provision of information services to young children under twelve years of age, ETSI DTS/HF 102 745, 2008, retrieved from http://portal.etsi.org/stfs/STF_HomePages/STF323/DTS%20102745v6b.doc (on 07.04.2008).

and adolescents spend a large – and continually increasing – amount of time watching television, surfing the Internet, blogging, chatting and playing games.[76] Furthermore, due to the changes in technology, the nature of the media experience has also modified: images and sounds are increasingly realistic, the boundaries between the real and virtual worlds are increasingly blurred and the media are much more interactive than before.[77] The diversification of content types, services and delivery channels potentially increases the possibilities for children to have access to and engage with 'harmful content'.[78] Whereas adults can compare the former media landscape with the profoundly changed one, children and young people only know the current media landscape. Growing up in this media context also leads to children often having better technical skills than their parents or teachers (also referred to as the 'generational gap').[79] However, this does not automati-

---

[76] Kaiser Family Foundation Study, Generation M: media in the lives of 8–18 year-olds, March 2005, retrieved from http://www.kff.org/entmedia/upload/Generation-M-Media-in-the-Lives-of-8-18-Year-olds-Report.pdf (on 25.02.2008); IPPR, A generation of youth are being raised 'online', 24.03.2008, retrieved from http://www.ippr.org.uk/pressreleases/?id=3059 (on 27.03.2008); Livingstone, Sonia and Haddon, Leslie, *EU Kids Online: Final report*, 2009, retrieved from http://www.lse.ac.uk/collections/EUKidsOnline/Reports/EUKidsOnlineFinalReport.pdf (on 21.01.2010).

[77] Strasburger, Victor C. and Wilson, Barbara J., *Children, adolescents & the media*, Thousand Oaks, Sage Publications, 2002, 6.

[78] O'Connell, Rachel and Bryce, Jo, Children and young people in on-line and related off-line environments: Promoting well-being and minimising risk of harm, Study commissioned by the Council of Europe, not published, 67.

[79] Commission of the European Communities, Proposal for a Decision of the European Parliament and of the Council establishing a multiannual Community programme on protecting children using the Internet and other communication technologies, COM (2008) 106 final, 27.02.2008, 7; European Commission, Public consultation: Safer Internet and online technologies for children, 2007, retrieved from http://ec.europa.eu/information_society/activities/sip/docs/public_consultation_prog/pc_2007_info_en.pdf (on 02.04.2008), 3; Carlsson, Ulla, "Violence and pornography in the media – Public views on the influence media violence and pornography exert on young people", in: Carlsson, Ulla (ed.), *Regulation, awareness, empowerment: Young people and harmful media content in the digital age*, Göteborg, Nordicom, 2006, 145; Buckingham, David, "Children and new media", in: Lievrouw, Leah A. and Livingstone, Sonia, *Handbook of new media – Social shaping and social consequences of ICTs*, 2006, London, Sage Publications, 76 and 87; Buckingham, David, "Is there a digital generation?", 1–13, in: Buckingham, David and Willett, Rebekah, *Digital generations: children, young people and new media*, Mahwah NJ and London, Lawrence Erlbaum Associates, 2006, 337 p.; Etsi, Human Factors (HF); Specification and guidelines for service providers on the provision of information services to young children under twelve years of age, ETSI DTS/HF 102 745, 2008, retrieved from http://portal.etsi.org/stfs/STF_HomePages/STF323/DTS%20102745v6b.doc (on 07.04.2008); Byron, Tanya, Safer children in a digital world: the report of the Byron review, 27.03.2008, retrieved from http://www.dfes.gov.uk/byronreview/ (on 04.07.2008), 22–24. Peter Hinssen

cally mean that they are also equipped to deal with the enormous amount of content they are confronted with in a responsible, cautious manner.[80] It is important to keep this in mind when studying the potential pitfalls of the new media environment vis-à-vis children and young people. At the same time, however, it is also necessary to remind ourselves that, aside from any potential bad influences media may have on the development of children,[81] media provide children with vast opportunities to learn and develop their personality and knowledge.[82]

1.1.2. *Minor*

CHILDREN, MINORS AND YOUNG PERSONS – When researching a topic that relates to 'minors', one finds very quickly that different notions are used to indicate which persons are targeted. 'Minors', 'children', 'adolescents', 'youth' and 'young persons' are only a few of the terms that are frequently used. The United Nations Convention on the Rights of the Child opts to use the notion 'child', which it defines as "*every human being below the age of eighteen years of age unless under the law applicable to the child, majority is attained earlier*".[83] The Council of Europe Cybercrime Convention talks

---

(http://www.peterhinssen.com) argues that people below the age of 20 (in 2008) are 'digital natives' and people above the age of 20 are 'digital immigrants' (HINSSEN, Peter, Speech at the IBBT researchers' day, We-BBT, 19.03.2008, not published); cf. also PRENSKY, Marc, "Digital natives, digital immigrants", 2001, retrieved from http://www.marcprensky.com/writing/Prensky%20-%20Digital%20Natives,%20Digital%20Immigrants%20-%20Part1.pdf (on 07.04.2008).

[80] COMMISSION OF THE EUROPEAN COMMUNITIES, Proposal for a Decision of the European Parliament and of the Council establishing a multiannual Community programme on protecting children using the Internet and other communication technologies, COM (2008) 106 final, 27.02.2008, 2.

[81] SPARKS lists a number of motivations for children's media use: learning, companionship, habit, arousal, relaxation, escape or passing time: SPARKS, Glenn G., *Media effects research: a basic overview*, London, Thomson, 2006, 65–68.

[82] RUXTON, Sandy, *What about us? Children's rights in the European Union? Next Steps*, Brussels, The European Children's Network, 2005, 105; STRASBURGER, Victor C. and WILSON, Barbara J., *Children, adolescents & the media*, Thousand Oaks, Sage Publications, 2002, 305; BYRON, Tanya, Safer children in a digital world: the report of the Byron review, 27.03.2008, retrieved from http://www.dfes.gov.uk/byronreview/ (on 04.07.2008), 60–62; OFCOM, Ofcom's response to the Byron Review – Statement, 27.03.2008, retrieved from http://www.ofcom.org.uk/research/telecoms/reports/byron/byron_review.pdf (on 04.07.2008), 15–19; BBC NEWS, Online time 'is good for teens', 21.11.2008, retrieved from http://news.bbc.co.uk/2/hi/technology/7740895.stm (on 21.11.2008).

[83] Article 1 UNITED NATIONS, Convention of the Rights of the Child, 20.11.1989, retrieved from http://www.unhchr.ch/html/menu3/b/k2crc.htm (on 12.09.2006).

about 'minors', by which is meant "*all persons under 18 years of age*" (unless a Party requires a lower age limit not less than 16 years of age).[84] In other policy documents, such as the 2006 Recommendation on the protection of minors and human dignity in audiovisual and online information services (*infra*),[85] the words child[86] and minor[87] are used alternately, without any clarification or definition. Some scholars advance their own interpretation of the different concepts.[88] ETZIONI, for instance, clarifies the distinction between children, teenagers and minors as follows:

> *Children refers to those twelve and under, and teenagers refers to those between the ages of thirteen and eighteen. Minors is used to refer to both groups together.*[89]

Taking a closer look at the two most frequently used notions, 'child' and 'minor', one could argue that whereas child is a more general term, used in different contexts, the notion 'minor' is linked to the age of majority, and more often used in a 'legal' context.

DISTINCTION ACCORDING TO AGE – Even though different notions are used, it is clear that the decisive criterion for labelling a person a 'child' or a 'minor' is age.[90] Most policy documents set eighteen years as the 'age of majority'. This age of majority is laid down in most countries' national legislation. In addition, countries also set age limits for the acquisition of other rights, such

---

[84] Article 9, para. 3 COUNCIL OF EUROPE, Convention on Cybercrime, ETS No. 185, 23.11.2001, Budapest, retrieved from http://conventions.coe.int/Treaty/EN/Treaties/Html/185.htm (on 13.03.2007).

[85] EUROPEAN PARLIAMENT AND COUNCIL Recommendation 2006/952/EC of 20 December 2006 on the protection of minors and human dignity and on the right of reply in relation to the competitiveness of the European audiovisual and on-line information services industry, *OJ* 27.12.2007, *L* 378, 72: cf. *infra*.

[86] Defined as "*a young person especially between infancy and youth*" in MERRIAM WEBSTER'S ONLINE DICTIONARY, Child, retrieved from http://www.m-w.com/dictionary/child (on 03.08.2007).

[87] Defined as "*a person who has not attained majority*" in MERRIAM WEBSTER'S ONLINE DICTIONARY, Minor, retrieved from http://www.m-w.com/dictionary/minor (on 03.08.2007).

[88] Another scholar argues that any definition of childhood is inevitably artificial, and that the notion 'minor' is somewhat discriminatory, since it is "*imbued with the notion that children are lesser or incomplete beings because they are not always able to determine and in their own best interests, something arguably which they share with many adults*". Cf. VAN BUEREN, Geraldine, *The international law on the rights of the child*, Dordrecht, Martinus Nijhoff Publishers, 1995, 32.

[89] ETZIONI, Amitai, "On protecting children from speech (Symposium Do children have the same First Amendment rights as adults?)", *Chicago-Kent Law Review* 2004, Vol. 79, No. 1, 43.

[90] On interpretations of the beginning and ending of childhood, cf. BAINHAM, Andrew, *Children – the modern law*, Bristol, Family Law, 2005, 86 *et seq.*

as the age of sexual consent, or the age required to marry.[91] HODGKIN and NOWELL note that "*setting an age for the acquisition of certain rights or for the loss of certain protections is a complex matter*", which "*balances the concept of the child as a subject of rights whose evolving capacities must be respected with the concept of the State's obligation to provide special protection*".[92]

SOCIAL SCIENCE RESEARCH – 'Childhood' is also a subject of interest in social science research. However, the interpretation of this concept is far from straightforward and varies across cultures.[93] Yet, agreement exists amongst social scientists on the fact that age is an important factor in evaluating the effect certain media content has on children (*infra*). Research has shown that younger children "*attend to and interpret information in different ways than do their older counterparts*".[94] Categories that are often used and are linked to stages of cognitive development are, for instance, 3–7 years, 8–12 years and 13–16/18 years of age.[95] However, it has also been emphasised that, capacities and skills of children of the same age can vary widely, for instance due to personality differences or gender characteristics.[96]

USE OF NOTIONS – In this book, the notions 'child' and 'minor', as well as 'young people', are used interchangeably. Where the age is of particular importance to the topic that is discussed this is emphasised and explained.

---

[91] HODGKIN, Rachel and NEWELL, Peter, *Implementation handbook for the Convention on the Rights of the Child*, New York, Unicef, 2002, 5.

[92] HODGKIN, Rachel and NEWELL, Peter, *Implementation handbook for the Convention on the Rights of the Child*, New York, Unicef, 2002, 1.

[93] HUTCHBY, Ian and MORAN-ELLIS, Jo, "Introduction: relating children, technology and culture" in: HUTCHBY, Ian and MORAN-ELLIS, Jo (eds), *Children, technology and culture: The impacts of technologies in children's everyday lives*, Oxford, Routledge, 2001, 1: "*Thus across different cultures, children are looked after in periods of dependency in a variety of social arrangements, are cultural participants in varying degrees of inter- and intragenerational segregation and integration, and occupy the status of 'child' for varying lengths of time*". For an overview of the approach of childhood throughout history cf.: VERHELLEN, Eugeen, *Convention on the Rights of the Child: background, motivation, strategies, main themes*, Antwerpen, Garant, 2006, 11 *et seq.*; BAINHAM, Andrew, *Children – the modern law*, Bristol, Family Law, 2005, 85.

[94] STRASBURGER, Victor C. and WILSON, Barbara J., *Children, adolescents & the media*, Thousand Oaks, Sage Publications, 2002, 12.

[95] STRASBURGER, Victor C. and WILSON, Barbara J., *Children, adolescents & the media*, Thousand Oaks, Sage Publications, 2002, 12–14.

[96] STRASBURGER, Victor C. and WILSON, Barbara J., *Children, adolescents & the media*, Thousand Oaks, Sage Publications, 2002, 13.

1.1.3. *Harmful content*

PREVIEW – Harmful content stands at the centre of this book. Which content may be considered harmful to the development of minors is a delicate and controversial issue, and one that is addressed extensively in social science literature. Hence, a brief excursion into the social theories concerning (potential) harmful media content is essential to gain a good understanding of the issue. However, as was mentioned in the introduction of this book, it is not and cannot be the goal of this book to express a value judgment about the accuracy of these theories. After this excursion, the question why harmful content should be regulated will be looked into, the concept of harmful content will be explored further, and a number of legal aspects and implications will be identified.

A. *Social science: history and theories of media content and media effects*

A.1. *Social science and harmful media content*

HISTORY OF HARMFUL MEDIA CONTENT – Concerns about the "*evil influence*"[97] or potential damaging effect of media content on children are intrinsically linked with the rise of each (mass) medium.[98] Social science research findings suggest that, from 1770 onwards, measures have been taken to protect children from certain 'inappropriate' material.[99] These measures have included, for instance, the adaptation of fairytales such as Little Red Riding Hood (the deletion of sexual elements), or the censoring of certain Bible passages.[100] VALKENBURG argues that censoring media with a view to protecting children finds its origin in the ideas of the Enlightenment philosophers, and more specifically in the writings of Jean-Jacques Rousseau, who put forward the argument that children "*should be raised in freedom in a protected envi-*

[97] KIRSH, Steven J., *Children, adolescents and media violence: A critical look at the research*, Thousand Oaks CA, Sage Publications, 2006, 5.

[98] PAIK, Haejung, "The history of children's use of electronic media", in: SINGER, Dorothy G. and SINGER, Jerome, L., *Handbook of children and the media*, Thousand Oaks, Sage Publications, 2001, 7; VALKENBURG, Patti M., *Children's responses to the screen: a media psychological approach*, Mahwah NJ, Erlbaum, 2004, 1. Sparks also refers to the explosive popularity of movies in the 1920s as a catalyst for media effects research: SPARKS, Glenn G., *Media effects research: a basic overview*, London, Thomson, 2006, 45.

[99] VALKENBURG, Patti M., *Children's responses to the screen: a media psychological approach*, Mahwah NJ, Erlbaum, 2004, 2.

[100] VALKENBURG, Patti M., *Children's responses to the screen: a media psychological approach*, Mahwah NJ, Erlbaum, 2004, 2.

ronment separate from the distorting influences of the adult world".[101] Opinions on the level of protection that children need, fluctuated in the following centuries but the appearance of (electronic) mass media, such as television, certainly revived the debate concerning the potential harmful influence of certain media content. Sexual[102] and violent[103] images have especially been regarded as problematic, be they in print, movies, television programmes, video games[104] or on the Internet.[105]

Vulnerable versus empowered child – Different views on the level of protection a child needs from potentially damaging material exist in the social sciences. The two main theories, which are on the opposite sides of the spectrum are that of the 'vulnerable' child on the one hand and that of the 'empowered' child on the other.[106] Whereas the first theory posits that children are susceptible and helpless beings who are greatly influenced by media content, the second school of thought focuses on children as autonomous, intelligent individuals who are difficult to deceive.[107] Another view is that the reality is probably somewhere in between these two extremes and

---

[101] Valkenburg, Patti M., *Children's responses to the screen: a media psychological approach*, Mahwah NJ, Erlbaum, 2004, 2.

[102] Cf. Sparks, Glenn G., *Media effects research: a basic overview*, London, Thomson, 2006, 106–126.

[103] Weaver, C. Kay and Carter, Cynthia, *Critical Readings: Violence and the media*, Maidenhead, Open University Press, 2006, 379 p.; Hamilton, James T., *Television violence and public policy*, Ann Arbor, The University of Michigan Press, 1998, 394 p. Valkenburg, for instance, concludes that "*all meta-analyses conducted so far on media effects studies have shown that media violence leads to aggression in children. Yet, it is common to read in newspapers and magazines that the effect of media violence has never been demonstrated. This chapter has shown that such claims are based on misinterpretations of empirical research [...]*": Valkenburg, Patti M., *Children's responses to the screen: a media psychological approach*, Mahwah NJ, Erlbaum, 2004, 39–57 (Chapter 3: Media violence and aggression). Along the same lines: Liebert, Robert M. and Sprafkin, Joyce, *The early window: effects of television on children and youth*, Oxford, Pergamon, 1988, 59–161. See also: Anderson, Craig A., Gentile, Douglas A. and Buckley, Katherine E., *Violent video game effects on children en adolescents: theory, research and public policy*, Oxford, Oxford University Press, 2007, 190 p.

[104] Kirsh, Steven J., *Children, adolescents and media violence: A critical look at the research*, Thousand Oaks CA, Sage Publications, 2006, 409 p.

[105] Critcher, Cras, *Critical Readings: Moral panics and the media*, Maidenhead, Open University Press, 2006, 329 p.

[106] Ribak, Rivka, "Children & new media: some reflections on the ampersand", *Journal for Children and Media* 2007, Vol. 1, No. 1, 71; Valkenburg, Patti M., *Children's responses to the screen: a media psychological approach*, Mahwah (N.J.), Erlbaum, 2004, 7.

[107] Buckingham, David, "Children and new media", in: Lievrouw, Leah A. and Livingstone, Sonia, *Handbook of new media – Social shaping and social consequences of ICTs*,

that as children get older, they amass more knowledge that can help them to make sense of media messages.[108]

A.2. *Media effects research*

> *[...] for some children, under some conditions, some television is harmful. For some children under other conditions, it may be beneficial. For most children, under most conditions, most television is probably neither harmful nor particularly beneficial.*
>
> Wilbur Schramm, Jack Lyle and Edwin Parker[109]

Origin media effects research – Studying the influence of media on children falls within the extensive body of social science research on media effects.[110] This research stream arose during the Interbellum and has since undergone an enormous evolution. Whereas in the first half of the twentieth century a large and powerful effect was ascribed to media,[111] from 1950 onwards research increasingly focused on a limited effects model.[112] This model also applies to children and assumes that they are not passive receivers, but "*active and motivated users of media, who critically evaluate what they are shown*".[113] Currently, however, most media scholars assume that the

London, Sage Publications, 2006, 77 and 79; Valkenburg, Patti M., *Children's responses to the screen: a media psychological approach*, Mahwah NJ, Erlbaum, 2004, 7.

108 Strasburger, Victor C. and Wilson, Barbara J., *Children, adolescents & the media*, Thousand Oaks, Sage Publications, 2002, 10.

109 Schramm, Wilbur, Lyle, Jack, and Parker, Edwin B., *Television in the Lives of Our Children*, Stanford, Stanford University Press, 1961, 11. As cited in Livingstone, Sonia and Millwood Hargrave, Andrea, "Harmful to children? Drawing conclusions from empirical research on media effects", in: Carlsson, Ulla (ed.), *Regulation, awareness, empowerment. Young people and harmful media content in the digital age*, Göteborg, The International Clearinghouse on Children, Youth and Media, 2006, 32.

110 For a extensive overview of media effects research, cf. Sparks, Glenn G., *Media effects research: a basic overview*, London, Thomson, 2006, 250 p. See also: Eveland, William P. Jr., "A mix of attributes approach to the study of media effects and new communication technologies", *Journal of Communication* 2003, Vol. 53, No. 3, 395–410.

111 Sparks, Glenn G., *Media effects research: a basic overview*, London, Thomson, 2006, 51–52: this line of thought was dubbed the 'magic bullet' – model or the 'hypodermic needle' – model: "*According to this view, the communication of a message in a mass medium can be compared to shooting a gun that contains a magic bullet or to injecting someone with a hypodermic needle. Once the message reaches the audience, it will exert powerful, relatively uniform effects on everyone who processes it*".

112 Valkenburg, Patti M., *Children's responses to the screen: a media psychological approach*, Mahwah NJ, Erlbaum, 2004, 7–8.

113 Valkenburg, Patti M., *Children's responses to the screen: a media psychological approach*, Mahwah NJ, Erlbaum, 2004, 8.

issue is much more complex and that the effects of media largely depend on the message, the medium, the audience and the type of effect focused on.[114, 115]

Specific research – Throughout the years, innumerable studies have been conducted with the aim of discovering what effect, if there is one at all, particular media have on their users. Following the rise in popularity of movies in the 1920s in the United States, the Payne Fund sponsored a study into the real impact of movies on children and adolescents, which found that a bad influence could be distinguished.[116] This 1930s research has been followed by an enormous array of studies, ranging from an analysis of the "*evil of comic books*" (by Frederic Wertham),[117] over inquiries into copycat crimes inspired by television programmes,[118] to the currently omnipresent studies on the effects of violent videogames.[119] As might be expected, studies on the effect of new media, such as the Internet, are not yet great in number.[120] However, it has been pointed out that the new media, which are much

---

114 Sparks, Glenn G., *Media effects research: a basic overview*, London, Thomson, 2006, 58.

115 With respect to children, it is also argued that the effects of media on children depend "*on the manner in which the child deals with the media content they are exposed to*": Valkenburg, Patti M., *Children's responses to the screen: a media psychological approach*, Mahwah NJ, Erlbaum, 2004, 8.

116 Kirsh, Steven J., *Children, adolescents and media violence: A critical look at the research*, Thousand Oaks CA, Sage Publications, 2006, 9; Sparks, Glenn G., *Media effects research: a basic overview*, London, Thomson, 2006, 49.

117 Kirsh, Steven J., *Children, adolescents and media violence: A critical look at the research*, Thousand Oaks CA, Sage Publications, 2006, 301: "*Wertham claimed that the murder and mayhem illustrated in crime comics and the grisly depictions of death in horror comics were sure to promote deceit and increase antisocial behavior in children*"; Sparks, Glenn G., *Media effects research: a basic overview*, London, Thomson, 2006, 57. Wertham's research was widely criticised and found to be exaggerated and unfounded.

118 Sparks, Glenn G., *Media effects research: a basic overview*, London, Thomson, 2006, 82.

119 Anderson, Craig A., Gentile, Douglas A. and Buckley, Katherine E., *Violent video game effects on children en adolescents: theory, research and public policy*, Oxford, Oxford University Press, 2007, 190 p.; Kirsh, Steven J., *Children, adolescents and media violence: A critical look at the research*, Thousand Oaks CA, Sage Publications, 2006, 409 p; BBC News, Violent games 'affect behaviour'; 09.01.2006, retrieved from http://news.bbc.co.uk/1/hi/health/4594376.stm (on 29.02.2008).

120 Strasburger, Victor C. and Wilson, Barbara J., *Children, adolescents & the media*, Thousand Oaks, Sage Publications, 2002, 303; Millwood Hargrave, Andrea and Livingstone, Sonia, *Harm and offence in media content: a review of the evidence*, Bristol, Intellect, 2006, 141. For a report on media effects related to the Internet (and video games): cf. Buckingham, David, The impact of the media on children and young people with a particular focus on computer games and the internet – prepared for the Byron Review on children and new technology, December 2007, retrieved from http://www

more individualised, decentralised and interactive, put the traditional mass communication model under pressure (*infra*). These changes in the media environment need to be reflected in research into the effects of these new media. Importantly, it has been stressed that it is not possible to straightforwardly apply research on the effects of traditional media to new media, since "*people's response to media content is strongly shaped by the particularities of each medium*".[121] This finding raises potential questions as to the current trend towards technological neutrality as the basis for media regulation.[122]

New media effects – An important element with respect to the issue of harmful content in new media to which attention has already been drawn is that of 'context'. Whereas linear media, such as television or film, offer content within a context "*that tells a story or establishes a framework of expectations that is recognised by and makes sense to the consumer*", non-linear technologies permit content to be seen out of context (as seen, e.g., with short clips on YouTube, and images received via mobile phone).[123] Millwood Hargrave and Livingstone observe that, from research on children's accidental confrontation with pornographic images on the Internet, it can be deduced that "*unexpected and decontextualised content can be particularly upsetting*". Other significant differences, which may have an impact on the effect of new media, are the facilitated access to (more extreme forms of) content, the growing element of 'choice' and the lowered threshold for content production (making it possible, for instance, to take pictures and disseminate them across the whole world by uploading them to the Internet).[124] In this context, Valkenburg identifies six trends that will potentially increase children's exposure to harmful content:

.dfes.gov.uk/byronreview/pdfs/Buckingham%20Impact%20of%20Media%20Literature%20Review%20for%20the%20Byron%20Review.pdf (on 04.07.2008).

121 Millwood Hargrave, Andrea and Livingstone, Sonia, *Harm and offence in media content: a review of the evidence*, Bristol, Intellect, 2006, 203 and 205.

122 Livingstone, Sonia, "Do the media harm children? Reflections on new approaches to an old problem", *Journal of Children and Media* 2007, Vol. 1, No. 1, 10. Cf. also: Arino, Monica, "Content regulation and new media: a casestudy of online video portals", *Communications and Strategies* 2007, No. 66, 128 and Arino, Monica and Llorens, Carles, "Back to the future: new media, same principles? Convergence regulation re-visited", in: Ward, David (ed.), *The European Union and the culture industries: regulation and the public interest*, Aldershot, Ashgate, 2008, 139–140.

123 Millwood Hargrave, Andrea and Livingstone, Sonia, *Harm and offence in media content: a review of the evidence*, Bristol, Intellect, 2006, 205.

124 Millwood Hargrave, Andrea and Livingstone, Sonia, *Harm and offence in media content: a review of the evidence*, Bristol, Intellect, 2006, 206.

- the commercialisation of media content: which leads to an increase in commercial – often sexual or violent – content;
- the potential of new media for social interaction: which can lead to online or offline harassment;
- influence of interactive media on children's identities: availability of personal profile pages can attract negative comments, insults, bullying or even threats;
- the level of privacy even young children acquire: children's media use occurs increasingly outside parents' field of vision, which can lead to increased exposure to harmful content or people with bad intentions;
- the blurring of the boundaries between reality and virtuality: an enormous amount of information is put online (also by non-professionals) without a clear context; exposure to content like that, which children cannot easily place within a context of reality or virtuality, can be potentially more harmful; and
- media-multitasking: using different media simultaneously can lead to a decreased ability to place certain content within a story line or genre; since children's attention is divided, the chance increases that they encounter certain content unprepared.[125]

Furthermore, O'Connell and Bryce emphasise the important transition of children from passive (mostly television) consumers to (inter)active participants in the new media environment.[126] Within this new media environment they play different roles (for instance, by producing content or interacting on social networks), which influence the potentially 'harmful' experiences they have.

However, very little actual qualitative research on these developments is available at the moment. Keeping the changing media environment in mind, Livingstone thus calls for changes in media effects research. She argues that "*the focus on simple and direct causal effects of the media is no longer appropriate*".[127] Instead, she suggests concentrating on the more complex question: "*in what way and to what extent do the media contribute, if at all,*

---

[125] Valkenburg, Patti, "Expert opinion Schadelijke media en weerbare jeugd: een beleidsvisie 2005–2010" ["*Expert opinion Harmful media and youth: a policy vision 2005–2010*"], retrieved from http://www.ivir.nl/publicaties/vaneijk/Wijzerkijken.pdf (on 03.03.2008), 34–36 [in Dutch].

[126] O'Connell, Rachel and Bryce, Jo, Children and young people in on-line and related off-line environments: Promoting well-being and minimising risk of harm, Study commissioned by the Council of Europe, not published, 16.

[127] Livingstone, Sonia, "Do the media harm children? Reflections on new approaches to an old problem", *Journal of Children and Media* 2007, Vol. 1, No. 1, 8.

as one among several identifiable factors that, in combination, account for the social phenomenon under consideration (violence, racism, etc.)"?[128]

CONCLUDING REMARKS REGARDING MEDIA EFFECTS – There seems to be an overall consensus that confrontation with particular types of content at an early age may have negative consequences on a child's development.[129] Within media effects research, the most studied topic clearly is the effect of violence on viewers and media users.[130] There seems to be an agreement amongst the majority of media scholars that violent content has the tendency to contribute to aggressive behaviour and desensitisation.[131] SPARKS argues, however, that this effect is rather small, although it is definitely not unimportant.[132] Another recurring observation is that media violence is only one of many other factors which together may lead to an increase in aggression.[133] Research into the effect of sexual content is less abundant, especially with respect to children, due to ethical restrictions concerning experiments.[134] Furthermore, there also is a higher degree of disagreement as to the potential effects of sexual imagery.[135] However, keeping in mind the results of research

---

128 LIVINGSTONE, Sonia, "Do the media harm children? Reflections on new approaches to an old problem", *Journal of Children and Media* 2007, Vol. 1, No. 1, 9.

129 O'CONNELL, Rachel and BRYCE, Jo, Children and young people in on-line and related off-line environments: Promoting well-being and minimising risk of harm, Study commissioned by the Council of Europe, not published, 5.

130 SPARKS, Glenn G., *Media effects research: a basic overview*, London, Thomson, 2006, 57.

131 KIRSH, Steven J., *Children, adolescents and media violence: A critical look at the research*, Thousand Oaks CA, Sage Publications, 2006, 9 and 18; SPARKS, Glenn G., *Media effects research: a basic overview*, London, Thomson, 2006, 93 and 102; STRASBURGER, Victor C. and WILSON, Barbara J., *Children, adolescents & the media*, Thousand Oaks, Sage Publications, 2002, 83 and 113; BUSHMAN, Brad J. and ROWELL HUESMANN, L., "Effects of televised violence on aggression", in: SINGER, Dorothy G. and SINGER, Jerome, L., *Handbook of children and the media*, Thousand Oaks, Sage Publications, 2001, 248.

132 SPARKS, Glenn G., *Media effects research: a basic overview*, London, Thomson, 2006, 103.

133 CARLSSON, Ulla, "Violence and pornography in the media – Public views on the influence media violence and pornography exert on young people", in: CARLSSON, Ulla (ed.), *Regulation, awareness, empowerment: Young people and harmful media content in the digital age*, Göteborg, Nordicom, 2006, 139; STRASBURGER, Victor C. and WILSON, Barbara J., *Children, adolescents & the media*, Thousand Oaks, Sage Publications, 2002, 113.

134 MILLWOOD HARGRAVE, Andrea and LIVINGSTONE, Sonia, *Harm and offence in media content: a review of the evidence*, Bristol, Intellect, 2006, 78 and 121–122; SPARKS, Glenn G., *Media effects research: a basic overview*, London, Thomson, 2006, 112 and 121–122; ETZIONI, Amitai, On protecting children from speech (Symposium Do children have the same First Amendment rights as adults?), *Chicago-Kent Law Review* 2004, Vol. 79, No. 1, 38.

135 HELSPER, Ellen, "R18 material: its potential impact on people under 18: An overview of the available literature", research conducted for Ofcom, May 2005, retrieved from http://www.ofcom.org.uk/research/radio/reports/bcr/r18.pdf (on 27.02.2008), 20: "*there is no*

into other areas of media impact, concerns related to exposing children (as opposed to adults) to sexual content might be justified.[136] Anyhow, it is necessary to be aware of the very complex nature of media effects research, and the resulting divergent conclusions that have been drawn. In this light, it is neither possible nor desirable in the framework of this legal study to adopt a conclusive stance on harmful media effects. Therefore, we limit ourselves to noting that at least a number of social science researchers assert that certain content can potentially have a negative impact on children's development.[137] In the next section, the question whether this finding in itself can be

---

conclusive empirical evidence for a causal relationship between exposure to R18 material and impairment of the mental, physical or moral development of minors"; MILLWOOD HARGRAVE, Andrea and LIVINGSTONE, Sonia, *Harm and offence in media content: a review of the evidence*, Bristol, Intellect, 2006, 131: "*The evidence that viewing pornography harms children remains scarce, given ethical restrictions on the research, though many experts believe it to be harmful*", and 199: "*[...] despite widespread public concern over the exposure of children to adult or pornographic images, there remains little evidence that such exposure has harmful effects, with the notable exception of material that combines sexual and violent content. This lack of evidence partly reflects the methodological limitations of the evidence [...] But it may also suggest that, at least in our present largely regulated content environment, the images available to children are not harmful, though they may be offensive or even briefly disturbing*". There are of course also experts who believe pornography is very damaging: WIRED NEWS (Ryan SINGEL), Internet porn: worse than crack?, 19.11.2004, retrieved from http://www.wired.com/news/technology/0,1282,65772,00.html?tw=wn_tophead_4 (on 29.02.2008).

136 STRASBURGER, Victor C. and WILSON, Barbara J., *Children, adolescents & the media*, Thousand Oaks, Sage Publications, 2002, 186; SPARKS, Glenn G., *Media effects research: a basic overview*, London, Thomson, 2006, 122; MALAMUTH, Neil M. and IMPETT, Emily A., "Research on sex in the media: what do we know about effects on children and adolescents?", in: SINGER, Dorothy G. and SINGER, Jerome, L., *Handbook of children and the media*, Thousand Oaks, Sage Publications, 2001, 282: "*Under some conditions, exposure to sexual content in the media is likely to affect some young people's judgments and attitudes regarding sexual behaviors (e.g., premarital and extramarital sex) and possibly influence their sexual behaviors*"; DONNERSTEIN, Ed and SMITH, Stacy, "Sex in the media: theory, influences and solutions", in: SINGER, Dorothy G. and SINGER, Jerome, L., *Handbook of children and the media*, Thousand Oaks, Sage Publications, 2001, 289: "*[...] teenagers' attitudes toward coital behavior are influenced by exposure to sexual content on television. Viewing scenes of pre- or extra-marital sex may be having a negative effect on young viewers' attitudes and beliefs about early initiation of intercourse. [...] [E]xposure to the mixture of sex and violence may be desensitizing young viewers*".

137 BYRON emphasised that this is also linked to current knowledge about children's brain and functional development, which implies that children have certain under-developed abilities, i.e., critical evaluation, lack of inhibition, ability to judge sources of information and make socially appropriate decisions (all of which are crucial in dealing with media in a responsible way). Cf. BYRON, Tanya, Safer children in a digital world: the report of

considered as a sufficient trigger for policy and regulation in this area, will be looked into.[138]

B. *Why regulate harmful content?: the precautionary principle*

> *It is better to be roughly right in due time, bearing in mind the consequences of being very wrong, than to be precisely right too late.*
>
> NORWEGIAN RESEARCH COUNCIL FOR SCIENCE AND THE HUMANITIES[139]

NO CONCLUSIVE EVIDENCE – One could wonder why regulation is at all necessary if there is no conclusive scientific evidence that children's development can be harmed by certain media content. Regulation imposes restrictions on certain behaviours or actors and, hence, there should be a compelling reason to regulate. However, with respect to delicate issues, such as the protection of children, it could be argued that one should always defer to the 'precautionary principle'. Simply put, this concept, which finds its origins in environmental policy, embraces the 'better safe than sorry' approach.[140] The precautionary principle compels society to act cautiously if there are certain – but not necessarily absolute – scientific indications of a potential danger and if not acting upon these indications could inflict harm.[141] The *Wingspread statement on the precautionary principle*, adopted by experts at an environmental conference, described the principle as follows:

---

the Byron review, 27.03.2008, retrieved from http://www.dfes.gov.uk/byronreview/ (on 04.07.2008), 38–40 and 59.

[138] See also: KIRSH, Steven J., *Children, adolescents and media violence: A critical look at the research*, Thousand Oaks CA, Sage Publications, 2006, 297–298: "*As a risk factor for aggression, violent media can be viewed as a health threat, and when viewed as a health threat, violent entertainment becomes a legitimate target of policy makers*", and "*If the goal of public policy is to protect the welfare of children and adolescents, then there can be no doubt that public policy related to media violence is necessary even if the effects are small*".

[139] As cited in: JORDAN, Andrew and O'RIORDAN, Timothy, "The precautionary principle: a legal and policy history", in: WORLD HEALTH ORGANISATION (edited by Marco MARTUZZI and Joel A. TICKNER), Background document for the Fourth Ministerial Conference on Environment and Health "The precautionary principle: Public Health, the protection of children and sustainability", 07.06.2004, retrieved from http://www.euro.who.int/document/EEHC/ebakdoc09.pdf (on 11.03.2008), 31.

[140] HARREMOËS, Poul *et al.* (eds), *The precautionary principle in the 20th century: late lessons from early warnings, London*, Earthscan, 2002, 4.

[141] Furthermore, "*in such circumstances, the burden of proof is said to lie with those who downplay the risk of disaster, rather than with those who argue that the risks are real, even if they might be quite small*": RUNCIMAN, David, "The precautionary principle – David Runciman writes about Tony Blair and the language of risk", *London Review of books*, 01.04.2008, retrieved from http://www.lrb.co.uk/v26/n07/runc01_.html (on 11.03.2008).

Where an activity raises threats of harm to the environment or human health, precautionary measures should be taken even if some cause and effect relationships are not fully established scientifically.[142]

HISTORY – Contrary to popular belief, the precautionary principle has been, although not always under this exact term, present in regulatory policy for a couple of decades.[143] Its origins are often traced back to the '*Vorsorgeprinzip*' concept used in 1970s West German environmental policy,[144] as well as the thoughts of the German philosopher Hans JONAS.[145] Gradually, the precautionary principle was introduced in international law and policy

[142] ASHFORD, Nicholas et al., Wingspread statement on the precautionary principle, January 1998, retrieved from http://www.gdrc.org/u-gov/precaution-3.html (on 04.03.2008).

[143] Of course, 'precaution' in general is inherent to human existence. Mankind has always tried to limit or rule out risks. Cf. LIERMAN, Steven, "Het voorzorgsbeginsel en gezondheidsbescherming, oude wijn in nieuwe zakken?" [*The precautionary principle and health protection: old wine in new barrels?*], in: VAN CALSTER, Geert and VOS, Ellen, *Risico en voorzorg in de rechtsmaatschappij* [*Risk, precaution and the rule of law*], Antwerpen, Intersentia, 2004, 47 [in Dutch]. HARREMOËS *et al.* refer to the use of the precautionary principle in the late 19th century: HARREMOËS, Poul *et al.* (eds), *The precautionary principle in the 20th century: late lessons from early warnings*, London, Earthscan, 2002, 5–8.

[144] FISHER, Elizabeth, "Opening Pandora's Box: contextualising the precautionary principle in the European Union", University of Oxford Faculty of Law Legal Studies Research Paper Series, Working Paper No 2/2007, retrieved from http://papers.ssrn.com/sol3/papers.cfm?abstract_id=956952 (on 11.03.2008), 3; WORLD HEALTH ORGANISATION (edited by Marco MARTUZZI and Joel A. TICKNER), Background document for the Fourth Ministerial Conference on Environment and Health "The precautionary principle: public health, the protection of children and sustainability", 07.06.2004, retrieved from http://www.euro.who.int/document/EEHC/ebakdoc09.pdf (on 11.03.2008), 20; JORDAN, Andrew and O'RIORDAN, Timothy, "The precautionary principle: a legal and policy history", in: WORLD HEALTH ORGANISATION (edited by Marco MARTUZZI and Joel A. TICKNER), Background document for the Fourth Ministerial Conference on Environment and Health "The precautionary principle: Public Health, the protection of children and sustainability", 07.06.2004, retrieved from http://www.euro.who.int/document/EEHC/ebakdoc09.pdf (on 11.03.2008), 31 *et seq.*

[145] WHITESIDE, Kerry H., *Precautionary politics: Principle and practice in confronting environmental risk*, Cambridge MA, The MIT Press, 2006, 74 *et seq.* The precautionary principle can also be linked to the concept of the 'risk society' advanced by Ulrich Beck, cf. VAN CALSTER, Geert and VOS, Ellen, *Risico en voorzorg in de rechtsmaatschappij* [*Risk, precaution and the rule of law*], Antwerpen, Intersentia, 2004, 255 p. [in Dutch].

documents,[146] national legislation,[147] EU case law[148] and EU legislative documents.[149]

---

146 Examples are, for instance, the 1987 Ministerial Declaration of the Second International Conference on the North Sea, London, 24-25.11.1987, retrieved from http://www.seas-at-risk.org/1mages/1987%20London%20Declaration.pdf (on 11.03.2008); and the 1992 Rio Declaration on environment and development which stated in its principle 15: "*In order to protect the environment, the precautionary approach shall be widely applied by States according to their capabilities. Where there are threats of serious or irreversible damage, lack of full scientific certainty shall not be used as a reason for postponing cost-effective measures to prevent environmental degradation*": United Nations, Report of the United Nations conference on environment and development (Rio de Janeiro, 3-14.06.1992), A/CONF.151/26 (Vol. I), 12.08.1992, retrieved from http://www.un.org/documents/ga/conf151/aconf15126–1annex1.htm (on 10.03.2008).

147 The principle was, for instance, incorporated into the French constitution (*Constitution* [*French constitution*], 04.10.1958, retrieved from http://www.conseil-constitutionnel.fr/conseil-constitutionnel/francais/la-constitution/la-constitution-du-4–octobre-1958/texte-integral-de-la-constitution-de-1958.5074.html (on 11.03.2008) [in French]), through the reference to the *Charte de l'environnement* (*Charte de l'environnement* [*Charter of the environment*], 2004, retrieved from http://www.conseil-constitutionnel.fr/conseil-constitutionnel/francais/la-constitution/la-constitution-du-4–octobre-1958/charte-de-l-environnement-de-2004.5078.html (on 11.03.2008) [in French]), which states in its article 5: "*Lorsque la réalisation d'un dommage, bien qu'incertaine en l'état des connaissances scientifiques, pourrait affecter de manière grave et irréversible l'environnement, les autorités publiques veillent, par application du principe de précaution et dans leurs domaines d'attributions, à la mise en oeuvre de procédures d'évaluation des risques et à l'adoption de mesures provisoires et proportionnées afin de parer à la réalisation du dommage*". In Belgian legislation, references are made to the precautionary principle in: Wet van 20 januari 1999 ter bescherming van het mariene milieu in de zeegebieden onder de rechtsbevoegdheid van België [*Law of 20 January 1999 on the protection of the marine environment in the seas under the legal competence of Belgium*], *BS* 12.03.1999 [in Dutch], and the Decreet van 5 april 1999 houdende algemene bepalingen inzake milieubeleid [*Decree of 5 April 1999 holding general provisions regarding environmental policy*], *BS* 03.06.1995 (amended repeatedly) [in Dutch]. See: Lierman, Steven, "Het voorzorgsbeginsel en gezondheidsbescherming, oude wijn in nieuwe zakken?" ["*The precautionary principle and health protection: old wine in new barrels?*"], in: Van Calster, Geert and Vos, Ellen, *Risico en voorzorg in de rechtsmaatschappij* [*Risk, precaution and the rule of law*], Antwerpen, Intersentia, 2004, 47 [in Dutch].

148 For an overview, cf. Alemanno, Alberto, "The shaping of the precautionary principle by European Courts: from scientific uncertainty to legal certainty", in: Cuocolo, Lorenzo and Lupária, Luca (eds), *Valori costituzionali e nuove politiche del diritto: scritti raccolti del decennale della rivisat "Cahiers Européens"*, Matelica, Halley Editrice, 2007, 232 p., retrieved from http://papers.ssrn.com/sol3/papers.cfm?abstract_id=1007404 (on 01.07.2008).

149 For instance: Council Resolution on Community consumer policy 1999–2001, 28.06.1999, *OJ* 21.07.1999, *C* 206, 1; European Parliament and Council Regulation (EC) No 178/2002 of 28 January 2002 laying down the general principles and requirements of food

The precautionary principle in the European Union – The precautionary principle was officially introduced into EU legislation by the Treaty of Maastricht. Since 1992, article 191 TFEU [ex 174 of EC Treaty] refers to the precautionary principle in the title on environmental policy.[150] The Treaty itself provides no definition of the principle, but the European Commission issued a Communication on the principle which clarifies a number of aspects.[151] First and foremost, the Commission emphasises that, although the precautionary principle is mentioned in the context of environmental policy, the principle has a much wider scope, i.e.,

> *where preliminary objective scientific evaluation indicates that there are reasonable grounds for concern that the potentially dangerous effects on the environment, human, animal or plant health may be inconsistent with the high level of protection chosen for the Community.*[152]

This has also been explicitly confirmed by the Court of First Instance, who stated that the precautionary principle, which it labeled a general principle of Community law, is "*intended to be applied in order to ensure a high level of protection of health, consumer safety and the environment in all the Community's spheres of activity*".[153] The application of the precautionary principle should occur where scientific information is lacking or inconclusive, and where there are potential dangers for the environment or human, animal or

---

law, establishing the European Food Safety Authority and laying down procedures in matters of food safety, *OJ* 01.02.2002, *L* 31, 1, recitals 20–21, article 6, para. 3 and article 7.

150 Article 191 para. 2 TFEU [ex 174 EC Treaty] states: "*Union policy on the environment shall aim at a high level of protection taking into account the diversity of situations in the various regions of the Union. It shall be based on the precautionary principle and on the principles that preventive action should be taken, that environmental damage should as a priority be rectified at source and that the polluter should pay [...]*".

151 The Commission Communication was an answer to an appeal from the Council to "*be in the future even more determined to be guided by the precautionary principle in preparing proposals for legislation and in its other consumer-related activities and develop as a priority clear and effective guidelines for the application of this principle*": Council Resolution on Community consumer policy 1999–2001, 28.06.1999, *OJ* 21.07.1999, *C* 206, 1.

152 Commission of the European Communities, Communication from the Commission on the precautionary principle, COM (2000) 1 final, 02.02.2000, 3.

153 CFI, Artegodan GmbH v. Commission, Joined Cases T-74/00, 76/00, 83/00, 84/00, 85/00, 132/00, 137/00 and 141/00, 26.11.2002. For a detailed overview of various EU court cases concerning the precautionary principle: cf. Alemanno, Alberto, "The shaping of the precautionary principle by European Courts: from scientific uncertainty to legal certainty", in: Cuocolo, Lorenzo and Lupária, Luca (eds), *Valori costituzionali e nuove politiche del diritto: scritti raccolti del decennale della rivisat "Cahiers Européens"*, Matelica, Halley Editrice, 2007, 232 p. and Heyvaert, Veerle, "Facing the consequences of the precautionary principle in European Community Law", *European Law Review* 2006, Vol. 31, Issue 2, 185–206.

plant health.[154] The Commission Communication also puts forward a number of conditions that need to be adhered to when applying the precautionary principle. Thus, measures taken on the basis of the principle need to be proportional, non-discriminatory, consistent with similar measures already taken, based on an examination of the potential benefits and costs of action or lack of action, subject to review in the light of new scientific data, and capable of assigning responsibility for producing the scientific evidence necessary for a more comprehensive risk assessment.[155]

Controversial issue – The application of the precautionary principle, and certainly the increased scope, has been the cause of much debate.[156] Sceptics of the principle have put forward a wide range of criticisms. Some argue that the (rigorous) application of the principle hampers innovation,[157] while others declare the principle to be self-contradictory,[158] or an open door to arbitrary decision making.[159] As Heyvaert succinctly summarises, the precautionary principle is:

> *[...] a principle that has received strong official endorsement, that is considered by some as a powerful tool to better the relations between administration and the citizens, by others as a potentially dangerous licence for arbitrary decisionmaking and protectionism, or as an irresponsible brake on innovation, and by still others as a tempest in a teacup.*[160]

---

154 Commission of the European Communities, Communication from the Commission on the precautionary principle, COM (2000) 1 final, 02.02.2000, 8.

155 Commission of the European Communities, Communication from the Commission on the precautionary principle, COM (2000) 1 final, 02.02.2000, 4.

156 Commission of the European Communities, Communication from the Commission on the precautionary principle, COM (2000) 1 final, 02.02.2000, 3.

157 Guldberg, Helene, "Challenging the precautionary principle", 01.07.2003, retrieved from http://www.spiked-online.com/Articles/00000006DE2F.htm (on 04.03.2008); Heyvaert, Veerle, "Facing the consequences of the precautionary principle in European Community Law", *European Law Review* 2006, Vol. 31, Issue 2, 187.

158 Runciman, David, "The precautionary principle – David Runciman writes about Tony Blair and the language of risk", *London Review of books*, 01.04.2008, retrieved from http://www.lrb.co.uk/v26/n07/runc01_.html (on 11.03.2008).

159 Fisher, Elizabeth, "Opening Pandora's Box: contextualising the precautionary principle in the European Union", University of Oxford Faculty of Law Legal Studies Research Paper Series, Working Paper No 2/2007, retrieved from http://papers.ssrn.com/sol3/papers.cfm?abstract_id=956952 (on 11.03.2008), 7.

160 Heyvaert, Veerle, "Facing the consequences of the precautionary principle in European Community Law", *European Law Review* 2006, Vol. 31, Issue 2, 189.

It has also been claimed that enthusiasm for the precautionary principle has been by far greater in Europe than in the United States.[161] Others maintain, however, that although the concept is interpreted differently on the two sides of the Atlantic, these supposed diametrical attitudes are a fallacy, and much more complex in reality.[162]

THE PRECAUTIONARY PRINCIPLE AND HARMFUL MEDIA CONTENT – In the past decade, the application of the precautionary principle has evolved from the rather narrow field of environmental law to an increasing number of other areas of life.[163] Recently, some scholars have also referred to the precautionary principle with respect to harmful media content.[164] It is true that if one reads the many theoretical descriptions concerning the precautionary principle, it seems possible and even logical to apply this principle to the protection of minors against harmful new media content, precisely because the scientific evidence in this field can be considered inconclusive (*supra*). However, it needs to be noted that, to our knowledge, policymakers have never[165] explicitly referred to this principle to justify the creation of regulatory measures in this field. This might be because the protection of minors

---

[161] WHITESIDE, Kerry H., Precautionary politics: Principle and practice in confronting environmental risk, Cambridge MA, The MIT Press, 2006, 69 *et seq.*

[162] VAN DER HAEGEN, Tony, EU view of precautionary principle in food safety, 23.10.2003, New York, retrieved from http://www.eurunion.org/news/speeches/2003/031023tvdh.htm (on 11.03.2008); HARREMOËS, Poul *et al.* (eds), *The precautionary principle in the 20th century: late lessons from early warnings, London*, Earthscan, 2002, 2–3.

[163] GULDBERG, Helene, Challenging the precautionary principle, 01.07.2003, retrieved from http://www.spiked-online.com/Articles/00000006DE2F.htm (on 04.03.2008). The precautionary principle has, for instance, also been applied to the decision to go to war in Iraq: cf. RUNCIMAN, David, "The precautionary principle – David Runciman writes about Tony Blair and the language of risk", *London Review of books*, 01.04.2008, retrieved from http://www.lrb.co.uk/v26/n07/runc01_.html (on 11.03.2008).

[164] MILLWOOD HARGRAVE, Andrea and LIVINGSTONE, Sonia, *Harm and offence in media content: A review of the evidence*, Bristol, UK, Portland, OR, USA, Intellect Press, 2006, 179; LIVINGSTONE, Sonia, "Do the media harm children? Reflections on new approaches to an old problem", *Journal of Children and Media* 2007, Vol. 1, No. 1, 9; FÜG, Oliver C., "Save the children: the protection of minors in the Information Society and the Audiovisual Media Services Directive", *Journal of Consumer Policy* 2008, Issue 31, No. 1, 47.

[165] One reference can be found in: EUROPEAN COMMISSION, Summary of the results of the public consultation 'Child safety and mobile phone services', 2006, retrieved from http://ec.europa.eu/information_society/activities/sip/docs/public_consultation_mobile/public_consultation_rsults_en.pdf (on 11.03.2008). This reference, however, is most likely inspired by the contribution of Andrea MILLWOOD HARGRAVE and Sonia LIVINGSTONE to the consultation (retrieved from http://ec.europa.eu/information_society/activities/sip/docs/public_consultation_mobile/results/millwoodhargrave_livingstone_a337711.pdf (on 11.03.2008)); cf. previous footnote.

against harmful media content benefits from its 'acquired status' as a goal of public interest which it had had since mass media first appeared.[166] The decision to pursue this goal of public interest is of a political nature and one that has usually been favourably received, even when one is unable to fall back on sound, unanimously agreed upon scientific evidence. It has traditionally been accepted that is justified to err on the side of caution when it comes to the protection of vulnerable beings against potential harm. So, in fact, one could argue that this decision has always been made with a sort of precautionary principle in mind.

C. *Exploration of the concept 'harmful content'*

> *"harmful: something that is harmful has a bad effect on something else, especially a person's health"*[167]
>
> *"harmful: causing or likely to cause harm" – "harm: physical injury, especially that which is deliberately inflicted, material damage, actual or potential ill effect"*[168]

C.1. *Definitions of harmful content*

Definition harmful content – Although many policy documents and other writings talk about the issue of 'harmful content', few actually provide a definition of the concept. In addition, when the concept is discussed, a number of different terms are used to describe it, such as, for instance, 'unwanted content', 'inappropriate' or age-inappropriate content', 'unsuitable content', or 'offensive content'. When focused on sexual content, often-heard notions are 'indecent content' or 'obscene content'. Differences or variations between the panoply of notions are often subtle, as is demonstrated in the following overview of a number of definitions found mostly in EU policy documents:

---

166 Commission of the European Communities, Communication from the Commission to the Council, the European Parliament, the Economic and Social Committee and the Committee of the Regions, Principles and guidelines for the Community's audiovisual policy in the digital age, COM (1999) 657 final, 14.12.1999, 2; Carlsson, Ulla, "Introduction: Media Governance – Harm and Offence in Media Content", in: Carlsson, Ulla (ed.), *Regulation, awareness, empowerment. Young people and harmful media content in the digital age*, Göteborg, The International Clearinghouse on Children, Youth and Media, 2006, 12.

167 Collins Cobuild, English Dictionary for Advanced Learners, Glasgow, HarperCollins Publishers, 2001, 715.

168 Pearshall, Judy (ed.), The Concise Oxford Dictionary, Oxford, Oxford University Press, 1999, 649.

- *Harmful information covers both content which is legal but the distribution of which is restricted (adults only, for example), and content which could give offence to certain users.*[169]
- *Harmful content is either authorized content with restricted distribution (e.g. reserved for adults) or content which may offend certain users, but whose publication is not restricted because of the principle of freedom of expression. Under no circumstances does the legality of such content detract from the fact that it is harmful to minors and to their physical, mental or moral development.*[170]
- *Harmful content is content that potentially can be harmful or dangerous for children, and includes content which parents and carers do not want their child to have access to.*[171]
- *Harmful content is content which parents, teachers or other adults responsible for children consider harmful to them. Definitions vary from one culture – and one person – to the next.*[172]

Time and place dependence – The interpretation of what is considered harmful content differs from place to place, from culture to culture and

[169] European Economic and social committee, Opinion of the Economic and Social Committee on the 'Proposal for a Council Decision adopting a Multiannual Community Action Plan on promoting safe use of the Internet', 98/C 214/08, 29.04.1998, *OJ* 10.07.1998, C 214, 29.

[170] European Parliament, Report on the proposal for a recommendation of the European Parliament and of the Council on the protection of minors and human dignity and the right of reply in relation to the competitiveness of the European audiovisual and information services industry, A6-0244/2005, 19.07.2006, retrieved from http://www.europarl.europa.eu/sides/getDoc.do?pubRef=-//EP//NONSGML+REPORT+A6-2005-0244+0+DOC+PDF+V0//EN&language=EN (on 05.07.2007), 29.

[171] European Commission, European Commission, Public consultation: Safer Internet and online technologies for children, 2007, retrieved from http://ec.europa.eu/information_society/activities/sip/docs/public_consultation_prog/pc_2007_info_en.pdf (on 02.04.2008), 9; idem: European Commission, Safer Internet and Online Technologies for children: Summary of the results of the online public consultation and 20–21 June 2007 Safer Internet Forum Report, January 2008, retrieved from http://ec.europa.eu/information_society/activities/sip/docs/public_consultation_prog/summary_report.pdf (on 09.01.2008), 20.

[172] European Commission, Factsheet n° 18 – Making the Internet a safer place, retrieved from http://ec.europa.eu/information_society/doc/factsheets/018–saferinternetplus-en.pdf (on 27.02.2008); along the same lines: Commission of the European Communities, Proposal for a Decision of the European Parliament and of the Council establishing a multiannual Community programme on protecting children using the Internet and other communication technologies, COM (2008) 106 final, 27.02.2008.

from time to time.[173] This has often been stressed in policy documents[174] and was confirmed by the European Court of Human Rights, for instance in the *Handyside* case.[175] This case concerned the sanctioning of the publisher of *The Little Red Schoolbook* on the basis of the *UK Obscene Publications Acts*. The Court noted that this issue concerned "*the protection of morals within a democratic society*", of which there is no uniform European conception, and which varies from time to time and from place to place.[176]

Age dependence – Furthermore, the degree of harm that can be caused to children also varies according to their age. It seems logical to assume that the younger the child, the more damage certain content can cause. Hence, what might be considered harmful for a six-year-old is probably less harmful for a fifteen-year-old.[177] This assumption is supported by social science and media effects research. Today's media scholars thus make important theoretical distinctions between younger and older children.[178]

---

173 Ukrow, Jörg, "Protection of minors and public order", in: Castendyk, Oliver, Dommering, Egbert J. and Scheuer, Alexander (eds), *European media law*, Alphen a/d Rijn, Kluwer Law International, 2008, 703 and 706; Mifsud Bonnici, Jeanne P. and De Vey Mestdagh, Cees N.J., "Right vision, wrong expectations: the European Union and self-regulation of harmful Internet content", *Information & Communications Technology Law* 2005, Vol. 14, No. 2, 136; European Commission, Public consultation: Safer Internet and online technologies for children, 2007, retrieved from http://ec.europa.eu/information_society/activities/sip/docs/public_consultation_prog/pc_2007_info_en.pdf (on 02.04.2008), 10; Akdeniz, Yaman, "Who watches the watchmen? The role of filtering software in Internet content regulation", in: Möller, Christian and Amouroux, Arnaud (eds), *The media freedom Internet cookbook*, Vienna, OSCE, 2004, retrieved from http://www.osce.org/publications/rfm/2004/12/12239_89_en.pdf (on 29.02.2008), 105.

174 Commission of the European Communities, Communication to the European Parliament, the Council, the Economic and Social Committee and the Committee of the Regions, Illegal and harmful content on the Internet, COM (1996) 487, 16.10.1996; Commission of the European Communities, Proposal for a Decision of the European Parliament and of the Council on establishing a multiannual Community programme on promoting safer use of the Internet and new online technologies, COM (2004) 91 final, 12.03.2004, 4.

175 European Court of Human Rights, Handyside v. the United Kingdom, 493/72, 07.12.1976. Cf. also *infra*.

176 European Court of Human Rights, Handyside v. the United Kingdom, 493/72, 07.12.1976, 46 and 48.

177 European Internet Co-regulation Network, Protecting minors from exposure to harmful content on mobile phones, July 2005, retrieved from http://www.foruminternet.org/specialistes/international/multi-fr-rapports-et-guides-en-reports-and-guides-multi/IMG/pdf/reco-mobile-20050728.pdf (on 03.03.2008), 5.

178 Sparks, Glenn G., *Media effects research: a basic overview*, London, Thomson, 2006, 47. For more details on age-related impacts on behaviour and anxiety, cf. Byron, Tanya, Safer

No uniform interpretation – Hence, there is no uniform, clear-cut interpretation of the concept of harmful content, but rather a multitude of different factors that play a role in its delineation. It is, however, possible to gain a more detailed understanding of the issue by juxtaposing it with other concepts or by referring to social theory.

C.2. *Harmful content versus illegal content*

Reference to illegal content – A recurring element in definitions or descriptions of harmful content is the reference to 'illegal content'. Contrary to content which is illegal, such as child pornography,[179] harmful content is content which is legal.[180] In other words, a distinction is made between content which is banned for everyone (because it violates human dignity and has therefore been branded illegal and has been criminalised), and content which may harm vulnerable persons, such as children, but is legal for adults to consume.[181] As Akdeniz puts it:

> *The difference between illegal and harmful content is that the former is criminalized by national laws, while the latter is considered offensive, objectionable, unwanted, or disgusting by some people but is generally not criminalized by national laws.*[182]

---

children in a digital world: the report of the Byron review, 27.03.2008, retrieved from http://www.dfes.gov.uk/byronreview/ (on 04.07.2008), 43–46.

179 For a detailed analysis of the legal implications of child pornography, see for instance: Forum des droits sur l'Internet, Recommandation Les enfants du Net – II: Pédo-pornographie et pédophilie sur Internet [*Recommendation Children of the Net – II: Childpornography and paedophila on Internet*], 25.01.2005, retrieved from http://www.foruminternet.org/telechargement/documents/reco-enfance2–20050125.pdf (on 03.03.2008) [in French].

180 Of course, illegal content is always considered harmful. This was, for instance, illustrated in European Parliament, Resolution on the Commission Communication on illegal and harmful content on the Internet, A4-0098/97, 24.07.1997, retrieved from http://europa.eu.int/ISPO/legal/en/internet/98–97en.html (on 17.05.2006, no longer available), where in the context of child pornography the adjective 'harmful' was used. In our view, however, it is important to make unambiguous distinctions and for the sake of clarity the ambiguous use of the different notions should thus be avoided, especially in policy documents.

181 Commission of the European Communities, Green Paper on the protection of minors and human dignity in audiovisual and information services, COM (1996) 483 final, 16.10.1996. Akdeniz, Yaman, "Who watches the watchmen? The role of filtering software in Internet content regulation", in: Möller, Christian and Amouroux, Arnaud (eds), *The media freedom Internet cookbook*, Vienna, OSCE, 2004, retrieved from http://www.osce.org/publications/rfm/2004/12/12239_89_en.pdf (on 29.02.2008), 104.

182 Akdeniz, Yaman, "Who watches the watchmen? The role of filtering software in Internet content regulation", in: Möller, Christian and Amouroux, Arnaud (eds), *The media*

Obscene versus non-obscene content in the United States – In the United States, the distinction between illegal and harmful content is, at least in the sexual content sphere, echoed by the distinction between obscene and non-obscene content.[183] Thus, in the case *Miller v. California*,[184] the US Supreme Court established three conditions for content to be found obscene:

> *(a) whether 'the average person, applying contemporary community standards' would find that the work, taken as whole, appeals to the prurient interest; (b) whether the work depicts or describes, in a patently offensive way, sexual conduct specifically defined by the applicable state law; and (c) whether the work, taken as a whole, lacks serious literary, artistic, political, or scientific value.*[185]

Obscene content falls outside of the protection of the First Amendment of the US Constitution and, hence, cannot be accessed by anyone, adults included.[186] Conversely, "*if sexually-themed expression falls outside of Miller's definition of obscene speech, adults enjoy a constitutional right to access it, which the government cannot (constitutionally) restrict or substantially burden*".[187] Because the three cumulative criteria are strictly interpreted, not many attempts at declaring media content obscene have succeeded.[188] However, content can also be found to be 'obscene for minors'. US case law[189] has repeatedly found that legislators may constitutionally confine minors' access

freedom Internet cookbook, Vienna, OSCE, 2004, retrieved from http://www.osce.org/publications/rfm/2004/12/12239_89_en.pdf (on 29.02.2008), 104.

183 Birnhack, Michael and Rowbottom, Jacob, Shielding children: the European way, *Chicago-Kent Law Review* 2004, Issue 79, 183.

184 Miller v. California, 413 U.S. 15 (1973).

185 Birnhack, Michael and Rowbottom, Jacob, Shielding children: the European way, *Chicago-Kent Law Review* 2004, Issue 79, 183.

186 Interestingly, in the United States, images of violence are protected by the First Amendment (although more evidence on the harmful nature of violence exists; *supra*). Cf. Etzioni, Amitai, On protecting children from speech (Symposium Do children have the same First Amendment rights as adults?), *Chicago-Kent Law Review*, Vol. 79, No. 1, 2004, 35. In a number of European countries the same higher tolerance level for violent images, as opposed to obscene images, is noticeable. In Belgium, article 383 of the Criminal Code criminalises offences against public decency. In the EU, it has only been since the creation of the Television without Frontiers Directive (*infra*) that violent content has explicitly been brought under the umbrella of harmful media content (article 22).

187 Nunziato, Dawn C., Technology and pornography, The George Washington University Law School Public Law and Legal Theory Working Paper No. 324, retrieved from http://papers.ssrn.com/sol3/papers.cfm?abstract_id=1003394 (on 11.01.2007), 6.

188 Sparks, Glenn G., *Media effects research: a basic overview*, London, Thomson, 2006, 57.

189 For instance: Ginsberg v. New York, 390 U.S. 629 (1968).

to sexually-themed content that is permitted for adults, provided that they are cautious not to limit adults' rights by such legislation.[190]

Different approaches – Both categories of content – illegal and harmful – require a different approach and a different solution.[191] With respect to illegal content, the approach is rather straightforward.[192] Most countries have included outright prohibitions on specific types of material, because of their danger to individuals as well as society in general.[193] Examples are child pornography, violent pornography and incitement to racial hatred.[194] Such material is banned (and activities associated with such material, punishable by fines or imprisonment) for everyone, irrespective of medium or the addressee's age.[195] Herein lies an important difference with harmful content, which can be restricted for minors, but should be allowed for adults. In this vein, Mifsud Bonnici and De Vey Mestdagh distinguish the two approaches particularly eloquently:

---

190 Nunziato, Dawn C., Technology and pornography, The George Washington University Law School Public Law and Legal Theory Working Paper No. 324, retrieved from http://papers.ssrn.com/sol3/papers.cfm?abstract_id=1003394 (on 11.01.2007), 11. See also *infra*.

191 Recital 17 Council Recommendation 98/560/EC of 24 September 1998 on the development of the competitiveness of the European audiovisual and information services industry by promoting national frameworks aimed at achieving a comparable and effective level of protection of minors and human dignity, *OJ* 07.10.1998, *L* 270, 48; Commission of the European Communities, Green Paper on the protection of minors and human dignity in audiovisual and information services, COM (1996) 483 final, 16.10.1996; Commission of the European Communities, Communication to the European Parliament, the Council, the Economic and Social Committee and the Committee of the Regions, Illegal and harmful content on the Internet, COM (1996) 487, 16.10.1996, retrieved from http://ec.europa.eu/archives/ISPO/legal/en/internet/communic.html (on 25.03.2008).

192 In a nutshell, with respect to illegal content, the adage "*what is illegal offline, is illegal online*" is always repeated. Although a number of serious problems can be distinguished with respect to dealing with this kind of content in the new media environment, for instance relating to enforcement, this book focuses on regulatory issues surrounding harmful content, particularly because of the tension with the right to freedom of expression (*infra*).

193 Commission of the European Communities, Green Paper on the protection of minors and human dignity in audiovisual and information services, COM (1996) 483 final, 16.10.1996.

194 One could wonder if there are types of racist speech which would not be categorised as 'illegal', for instance, because there is no actual incitement to hatred. In our opinion, however, such types of content could nevertheless be considered harmful.

195 Commission of the European Communities, Green Paper on the protection of minors and human dignity in audiovisual and information services, COM (1996) 483 final, 16.10.1996. In Belgium, for instance, article 383bis of the Criminal Code criminalises the production, distribution and even possession of child pornography.

> *In regulating illegal content, the role of the regulator is both to determine what content should be considered illegal and in what way should the publication and the distribution of the so defined illegal content be suppressed. In the regulation of harmful content, the decision on the content lies with the individual and not with the state. The role of regulation is to create conditions where the citizen can exercise his or her right to decide what content is accessed and received and to ensure that the citizen is not importuned by content he or she considers harmful.*[196]

As was mentioned in the introduction to this book, illegal content falls outside the scope of this study, and will thus not be further examined.

C.3. *Social science inspired concepts of harmful content*

SOCIAL SCIENCE RESEARCH – To gain a clearer understanding of the concept of harmful content, it is useful to briefly examine some relevant social science research.

HARM VERSUS OFFENCE – In the definitions listed *supra*, 'offence' is a recurring definitional element. MILLWOOD HARGRAVE and LIVINGSTONE, who have conducted much research on the topic, also distinguish between 'harm' and 'offence'. According to these researchers, harm can be conceived in objective terms, i.e., as observable by others, and hence measurable in a reliable fashion.[197] Offence, on the other hand, is regarded in subjective terms, i.e., as experienced and reported by the individual.[198] Thus, whereas harm may have consequences for the media user or society in general, offence is much more individual in its effect.[199] Another important distinction, especially relevant with respect to children, is the fact that, contrary to offence, harm is related to vulnerability.[200] Hence, harm, to which the focus of this book is limited, is thought to be greater for children (and vulnerable adults). Without entering at length into the complexity of the concept of harm, however, it is important to acknowledge MILLWOOD HARGRAVE and LIVINGSTONE's finding that it is a notion which depends on a wide range of complex factors.

---

196 MIFSUD BONNICI, Jeanne P. and DE VEY MESTDAGH, Cees N.J., "Right vision, wrong expectations: the European Union and self-regulation of harmful Internet content", *Information & Communications Technology Law* 2005, Vol. 14, No. 2, 134.

197 MILLWOOD HARGRAVE, Andrea and LIVINGSTONE, Sonia, Harm and offence in media content: a review of the evidence, Bristol, Intellect, 2006, 194.

198 MILLWOOD HARGRAVE, Andrea and LIVINGSTONE, Sonia, Harm and offence in media content: a review of the evidence, Bristol, Intellect, 2006, 15 and 194.

199 MILLWOOD HARGRAVE, Andrea and LIVINGSTONE, Sonia, Harm and offence in media content: a review of the evidence, Bristol, Intellect, 2006, 194.

200 MILLWOOD HARGRAVE, Andrea and LIVINGSTONE, Sonia, Harm and offence in media content: a review of the evidence, Bristol, Intellect, 2006, 195.

TAXONOMY OF HARM – A study commissioned by the Council of Europe and carried out by researchers Rachel O' CONNELL and Jo BRYCE concluded that, in the context of the protection of children and young people in digital media, an examination of harmful content alone does not deal with the "*nature, scope, scale or extent of the risk of harm that may be associated with children and young people's use of the Internet and new communications services*" in a satisfactory way.[201] Instead, they advance the concept "*Risk of Harm from Online and Related Offline Activities*" (RHOOA) which puts forward a taxonomy of activities in five areas that may create a risk of harm to the physical, psychological and social well-being of children and young people. These five areas are

- Commerce and information (for instance misuse of personal data and information);
- Social networking (for instance blogging, cyberbullying and happy slapping);
- Sexual health (for instance legal and illegal pornography);
- Sharing perspectives (for instance on race, religion and violence); and
- Mind, body and spirit (for instance, pro-suicide, pro-anorexia and pro-bulimia, and pro-self-harm material; game and gambling addiction).[202]

Within each of these five areas, different activities can be categorised as (1) having a *positive* effect on children, (2) posing a '*risk of harm*' (potentially harmful but not illegal), or (3) outright *illegal* (and hence prohibited).[203] Thus, for example, within the 'sexual health' area, one can distinguish, first, websites which supply useful information on sexual health issues, second, types of adult pornography (which are not illegal), and third, illegal types of pornography or grooming activities. The second category relating to 'risk

---

[201] COUNCIL OF EUROPE (GROUP OF SPECIALISTS ON HUMAN RIGHTS IN THE INFORMATION SOCIETY), Young people, well-being and risk on-line (abridged), Study by Rachel O'CONNELL and Jo BRYCE, 25.04.2006, retrieved from http://www.coe.int/t/dghl/standardsetting/media/doc/H-Inf(2006)005_en.pdf (on 30.05.2006), 4.

[202] COUNCIL OF EUROPE (GROUP OF SPECIALISTS ON HUMAN RIGHTS IN THE INFORMATION SOCIETY), Young people, well-being and risk on-line (abridged), Study by Rachel O'CONNELL and Jo BRYCE, 25.04.2006, retrieved from http://www.coe.int/t/dghl/standardsetting/media/doc/H-Inf(2006)005_en.pdf (on 30.05.2006), 4.

[203] O'CONNELL, Rachel and BRYCE, Jo, Children and young people in on-line and related off-line environments: Promoting well-being and minimising risk of harm, Study commissioned by the Council of Europe, not published, 4; for examples also cf. WESTHEAD, Bill, "Cyberwellness and harm reduction strategies: forging a new approach", Teen works 2005: Young people and the Internet, Swansea, 15.11.2005, retrieved from http://www.wisekids.org.uk/postconference/pdfs/UCLAN.pdf (on 06.03.2008).

of harm' is the one that can be compared to the more traditional concept of harmful content.[204]

With this taxonomy-based risk identification methodology, which is based on the recognition that there are varying levels of content – positive, harmful, illegal – associated with particular behaviours that are dependent on an array of multifaceted factors, the authors hope to create a better understanding of, and to be better able to respond, to various potentially risky activities.[205] They also stress that censorship is certainly not their suggested tool to deal with 'risk of harm' activities; rather, they promote educational activities and the supply of the necessary skills for safe and responsible use of the Internet.[206] In our view, the methodology developed by O'Connell and Bryce could prove to be a useful tool to assess certain risks in the digital media environment. This is not only because it is constructive to refer to the positive effect certain activities can have, but also because the five areas of activities, coupled with the three categories of possible effects, also provide a detailed and comprehensive overview that, in the future, could be used by policymakers to identify regulatory gaps.

C.4. *Varieties of risks and varieties of harmful content*

Wide range of risks – As can be deduced from the previous section, there is a whole spectrum of material that can be considered potentially harmful. Aside from the 'usual suspects', i.e., sexual content and violence, informa-

---

[204] The scope of this category, however, is not limited to violent or sexual content but also covers "*abusive communications including; bullying, abusive cybersex, or solicitation and exposure to or engagement in fora dedicated to e.g., self, harm, suicide or eating disorders, which occur in interactive online and related offline environments*": O'Connell, Rachel and Bryce, Jo, Children and young people in on-line and related off-line environments: Promoting well-being and minimising risk of harm, Study commissioned by the Council of Europe, not published, 64.

[205] O'Connell, Rachel and Bryce, Jo, Children and young people in on-line and related off-line environments: Promoting well-being and minimising risk of harm, Study commissioned by the Council of Europe, not published, 5–6.

[206] O'Connell, Rachel and Bryce, Jo, Children and young people in on-line and related off-line environments: Promoting well-being and minimising risk of harm, Study commissioned by the Council of Europe, not published, 6.

tion promoting anorexia,[207, 208] drugs and suicide,[209] advertising[210] and gambling can fall within the scope of the concept as well. These different kinds of harmful material fit into a larger framework of 'risks' to which children are exposed in digital media, and especially the Internet. These 'risks' can be divided into three categories: content-related risks, commerce-related risks and contact-related risks.[211, 212]

- CONTENT-RELATED RISKS: A first category of risks relates to actual content, such as, for instance, photographs, moving images or text.
  - SEXUAL CONTENT: There are different kinds of sexual content with which children can be confronted. One distinction that is made is between embedded sexual content versus sexually explicit content.[213]

---

207 A whole array of 'pro-ana' websites can be found on the Internet.

208 STRASBURGER, Victor C. and WILSON, Barbara J., *Children, adolescents & the media*, Thousand Oaks, Sage Publications, 2002, 238 *et seq.*

209 EUROPEAN COMMISSION, Public consultation: Safer Internet and online technologies for children, 2007, retrieved from http://ec.europa.eu/information_society/activities/sip/docs/public_consultation_prog/pc_2007_info_en.pdf (on 02.04.2008), 10.

210 COMMISSION OF THE EUROPEAN COMMUNITIES, Commission Staff working document accompanying the Communication from the Commission Towards an EU Strategy on the Rights of the Child, Preliminary inventory of EU actions affecting children's rights, COM (2006) 367 final, SEC (2006) 889, 04.07.2006, retrieved from http://register.consilium.europa.eu/pdf/en/06/st12/st12107-ad02.en06.pdf (on 29.08.2006).

211 After: WALRAVE, Michel (ed.), "Cyberteens@risk: Opportunities and risks of teens' ICT use analysed", TIRO (Teens and ICT: risks and opportunities) research project, February 2008, retrieved from http://www.e-privacy.be/TIRO-summary.pdf (on 29.02.2008).

212 Of course, a myriad of classifications of the different risks children are exposed to exists. Another classification, put forward by a group of Belgian social scientists, for instance, is: "*1. The nature of the Internet and the age level of the Internet users make it difficult to evaluate the information being presented, 2. The danger associated with giving out personal derails or setting up personal meetings with individuals they met via the Internet, 3. The negative impact of exposure to unsolicited pornography, 4. The occurrence and subsequent impact of sexual solicitation, 5. The impact of anti-racist sites, hate sites and threatening or harassing materials*": VALCKE, Martin, SCHELLENS, Tamara, VAN KEER, Hilde and GERARTS, Marjan, "Primary school children's safe and unsafe use of the Internet at home and at school: An exploratory study", *Computers in Human Behaviour* 2007, Vol. 23, Issue 6, 2839. A group of UK researchers have used the classification 'content-contact-conduct': HASEBRINK, Uwe, LIVINGSTONE, Sonia, HADDON, Leslie, KIRWIL, Lucyna and PONTE, Christina (eds), Comparing children's online activities and risks across Europe, June 2007, retrieved from http://www.eukidsonline.net/ (on 04.07.2008), 12.

213 MALAMUTH, Neil M. and IMPETT, Emily A., "Research on sex in the media: what do we know about effects on children and adolescents?", in: SINGER, Dorothy G. and SINGER, Jerome, L., *Handbook of children and the media*, Thousand Oaks, Sage Publications, 2001, 270.

The first category of sexual content is embedded within a larger context that includes considerable non-sexual content, whereas the latter category encompasses material that mainly depicts nudity and (simulated or actual) sexual acts which are not interwoven with larger amounts of non-sexual content.[214] Another differentiation is that between pornography and erotic media. SPARKS, for instance, attributes the notion pornography to

> *material that features explicit sexual behavior and nudity in a context frequently characterized by depictions of one character exerting physical or psychological dominance over another, often this type of material contains explicit violence that is shown at the same time as explicit sexuality.*[215]

According to him, the term erotic media "*seems to be associated more with material that features explicit sexual content in the absence of violence and without the overt power dynamics that appear in pornography*".[216] MILLWOOD HARGRAVE and LIVINGSTONE, on the other hand, discern different levels of pornography, from images of consensual activity to violent or non-consensual (even criminal) activity.[217] They also stress that whereas sexual content has always been available and often restricted in a quite informal way ("*from age-restricted access to the sex shop to the embarrassment of buying a top shelf magazine*"), the enormously increased access and anonymity with which this content can be accessed, for instance on the Internet, are new – and challenging – elements.[218] Furthermore, they note that there is an emergent body of research on children's distress following accidental confrontations with online pornography (*supra*).[219]

- VIOLENCE: Violent content is another category of content which has caused a lot of concern over the years. Violence is not only often found in television programmes or movies, but is also a popular element of

---

[214] MALAMUTH, Neil M. and IMPETT, Emily A., "Research on sex in the media: what do we know about effects on children and adolescents?", in: SINGER, Dorothy G. and SINGER, Jerome, L., *Handbook of children and the media*, Thousand Oaks, Sage Publications, 2001, 270.

[215] SPARKS, Glenn G., *Media effects research: a basic overview*, London, Thomson, 2006, 108.

[216] SPARKS, Glenn G., *Media effects research: a basic overview*, London, Thomson, 2006, 108.

[217] MILLWOOD HARGRAVE, Andrea and LIVINGSTONE, Sonia, Harm and offence in media content: a review of the evidence, Bristol, Intellect, 2006, 141.

[218] MILLWOOD HARGRAVE, Andrea and LIVINGSTONE, Sonia, Harm and offence in media content: a review of the evidence, Bristol, Intellect, 2006, 154–155.

[219] MILLWOOD HARGRAVE, Andrea and LIVINGSTONE, Sonia, Harm and offence in media content: a review of the evidence, Bristol, Intellect, 2006, 155.

certain types of music and video and Internet games.[220] As has been noted above, exposure to violent content is generally thought to be potentially harmful for children (*supra*).

- Other categories of content: Aside from sexual and violent content, scholars have recently drawn attention to an increasing number of other categories of content that might be problematic:[221]
  - Swearing and offensive language (although, arguably, this type of content could be catalogued under 'offence' instead of 'harm');
  - Racism and discrimination (race, disability) (however, it can be noted that sometimes racist content can also be qualified as illegal content);[222]
  - Substance abuse (alcohol, drugs or cigarettes);
  - Body image issue (for instance, anorexia or bulimia); and
  - Suicide[223] and self-harm.

- Commerce-related risks: Another category of potentially damaging content is commerce-related.
  - Advertising: Over the past decades, much research into the adverse effects of advertising on children has been undertaken by media scholars.[224] One claim that has been made is that (especially very young) children do not always have the skills to distinguish advertising from other media content. This concern is also valid with respect to new media advertising, because children may lack the literacy to discern advertising messages from other content, particularly when advertising is more and more embedded in virtual worlds, television programmes or interactive games.[225] Furthermore, advertising could also provide misleading information or promote false values.[226] It is important to point out

---

[220] Millwood Hargrave, Andrea and Livingstone, Sonia, Harm and offence in media content: a review of the evidence, Bristol, Intellect, 2006, 133–140.

[221] Cf. also 'Taxonomy of harm' (*supra*).

[222] Akdeniz, Yaman, "Stocktaking on efforts to combat racism on the Internet", Background Paper for the High Level Seminar on Racism and the Internet, Intergovernmental Working Group on the Effective Implementation of the Durban Declaration and Programme of Action, Fourth session, Geneva, 16-27.01.2006, E/CN.4/2006/WG.21/BP.1, retrieved from http://www.cyber-rights.org/reports/ya_un_paper_int_06.pdf (on 23.04.2007).

[223] BBC News, Call to ban pro-suicide websites, 09.09.2006, retrieved from http://news.bbc.co.uk/2/hi/health/5327354.stm (on 18.09.2006).

[224] Strasburger, Victor C. and Wilson, Barbara J., *Children, adolescents & the media*, Thousand Oaks, Sage Publications, 2002, 34 *et seq.*

[225] Millwood Hargrave, Andrea and Livingstone, Sonia, Harm and offence in media content: a review of the evidence, Bristol, Intellect, 2006, 173.

[226] Ruxton, Sandy, *What about us? Children's rights in the European Union? Next Steps*, Brussels, The European Children's Network, 2005, 106 *et seq.*

that (audiovisual) advertising is regulated on the national as well as the European Union level, especially with respect to children.[227]

- GAMBLING: Another commerce-related category of content is gambling. The anonymity of the Internet has made it possible for children and young people to gamble on offshore gambling websites. All that is needed to do so are their parents' credit card data. It should also be noted that, in some instances, online gambling is illegal.
- SPAM: A final type of commerce-related content (although arguably not so much a kind of content but a manner of delivering content) is spam (i.e., unwanted e-mail messages).[228] Not only can it be confusing for children to receive unwanted advertising messages (for instance, after they entered their e-mail address on a website in order to win a prize), but spam often also is a vehicle to lead people to sexually explicit websites.[229]

- CONTACT-RELATED RISKS: A third category of risks that children are exposed to, especially on the Internet, is not content-related, but rather contact- or conduct-related.[230] Different problems can be classified under this heading. The most worrying issue is that of (sexual) 'grooming', i.e., contact between paedophiles and potential victims that can occur, for instance, in chatrooms or via social networking websites that assemble personal profile pages and which can lead to the sexual abuse of these victims in real life.[231] A 2007 Council of Europe Convention addressed this issue. Article 23 of the Convention states that

[227] Cf. articles 3e–3g and 10–20 AVMS Directive (*infra,* Part 2, Chapter 1): for instance, article 3e (e) "*audiovisual commercial communications for alcoholic beverages shall not be aimed specifically at minors and shall not encourage immoderate consumption of such beverages*"; and article 3e (g) "*audiovisual commercial communications shall not cause physical or moral detriment to minors*".

[228] For more on this issue, cf. O'CONNELL, Rachel and BRYCE, Jo, Children and young people in on-line and related off-line environments: Promoting well-being and minimising risk of harm, Study commissioned by the Council of Europe, not published, 107–110.

[229] OUT-LAW.COM, Michigan prosecutes spammers to protect kids, 15.08.2006, retrieved from http://www.out-law.com/page-7196 (on 29.02.2008).

[230] THIERER describes the difference between these categories as 'bad people' versus 'bad pictures': THE PROGRESS & FREEDOM FOUNDATION BLOG (Adam THIERER), A response to Sen. Lieberman's Online Child Protection Manifesto, 12.10.2006, retrieved from http://blog.pff.org/archives/2006/10/a_response_to_s.html#more (on 16.10.2006).

[231] COUNCIL OF EUROPE, Explanatory report to the Convention on the Protection of Children against Sexual Exploitation and Sexual Abuse, retrieved from http://conventions.coe.int/Treaty/EN/Reports/Html/201.htm (on 29.02.2008), 155–156.

> *[e]ach Party shall take the necessary legislative or other measures to criminalise the intentional proposal, through information and communication technologies, of an adult to meet a child who has not reached the age set in application of Article 18, paragraph 2, for the purpose of committing any of the offences established in accordance with Article 18, paragraph 1.a, or Article 20, paragraph 1.a, against him or her, where this proposal has been followed by material acts leading to such a meeting.*[232]

Another recent problem in this area is cyberbullying, i.e., bullying which occurs via the Internet in chatrooms or on social networking sites, by e-mail or by mobile phone.[233] Cyberbullying is a very serious issue that is hard to tackle in an efficient way, due to the use of tools such as mobile phone cameras or webcams, which facilitate the uploading of photos of cyberbully victims, and the lowered threshold to anonymously distribute content – images, movie clips or text – on a worldwide scale.[234]

Subject delineation – The scope of this book is limited to content-related risks,[235] and within this category neither offence, nor illegal content (for instance, illegal pornography), will be taken into consideration. Hence, with respect to content, the focus lies on categories of content that may be, from an objective point of view, harmful to children and young people, but legal for adults to view and consume.

D. *Legal aspects and implications of harmful content*

D.1. *Lack of legal definitions*

Legal definition of harmful content – EU legal texts and documents often refrain from including a detailed definition of harmful content. This can

---

232 Council of Europe, Convention on the Protection of Children against Sexual Exploitation and Sexual Abuse, CETS No. 201, 25.10.2007, Lanzarote, retrieved from http://conventions.coe.int/Treaty/EN/treaties/Html/201.htm (on 29.02.2008).

233 EU policy documents on the protection of minors in digital media have recently started to include this phenomenon: for instance, Commission of the European Communities, Proposal for a Decision of the European Parliament and of the Council establishing a multiannual Community programme on protecting children using the Internet and other communication technologies, COM (2008) 106 final, 27.02.2008, 2.

234 BBC News, Warning over 'bullying by mobile', 07.06.2005, retrieved from http://news.bbc.co.uk/1/hi/education/4614515.stm (on 29.02.2008); cf. also O'Connell, Rachel and Bryce, Jo, Children and young people in on-line and related off-line environments: Promoting well-being and minimising risk of harm, Study commissioned by the Council of Europe, not published, 119–120.

235 Hence issues related to advertising, for instance, fall outside of the scope of this book.

of course be explained by the argument that harmful content varies across cultures and, hence, Member States. The exact description and implementation of the concept is thus left to the Member States, and the interpretation is ultimately in the hands of the national courts. The European Court of Human Rights as well as the European Court of Justice have confirmed that the protection of children against content injurious to their well-being is a legitimate interest on the basis of which national measures can be taken.[236]

ECHR – In this context, it is also useful to note that judgments of the European Court of Human Rights have clarified that the freedom of expression[237] also covers information that shocks, offends or disturbs.[238] Hence, whereas this kind of information can be particularly harmful to children, it can thus nevertheless count on a certain level of protection (cf. *infra*, Part 2, Chapter 1).

TWF & AVMS Directives – The Television without Frontiers Directive and its successor the Audiovisual Media Services Directive – two very important EU instruments with respect to the protection of minors against harmful content which will be discussed in the second part of this book – also refrain from defining harmful content. However, an indication of what can be considered harmful is provided, since both these directives refer to pornography and gratuitous violence as examples of programmes which might *seriously* impair the physical, mental or moral development of minors.[239] The establishment of measures regarding pornographic and violent images is a mini-

236 ECJ, Dynamic Medien v. Avides Media AG, C-244/06, 14.02.2008, 42 and 47; ECHR, Handyside v. the United Kingdom, 7.12.1976, *Publ. Eur. Court H.R.*, Series, A, Vol. 24, 52. Also: Voorhoof, Dirk, "Media(recht) en kinder(recht)en" [*"Media(law) and children('s rights"*], Deel 1, 1.9., update 1995, in: Verhellen, Eugeen (ed.), *Kinderrechtengids (KIDS): Commentaren, regelgeving, rechtspraak en nuttige informatie over de maatschappelijke en juridische positie van het kind* [*Guide to children's rights: Comments, regulation, case law and useful information about the social and legal status of the child*], Gent, Mys en Breesch, 1994, 22 [in Dutch].

237 A more detailed analysis of the right to freedom of expression is provided *infra*, Part 2, chapter 1.

238 European Court of Human Rights, Handyside v. the United Kingdom, 7.12.1976, para. 49; see also European Court of Human Rights, Perna v. Italy, 06.05.2003, *Reports* 2003, § 39.

239 Article 22 para. 1 Council Directive 89/552/EEC of 3 October 1989 on the coordination of certain provisions laid down by law, regulation or administrative action in Member States concerning the pursuit of television broadcasting activities, *OJ L* 298, 17.10.1989, 23, amended by European Parliament and Council Directive 97/36/EC of 30 June 1997, *OJ L* 202, 30.07.1997, 60; article 22 para. 1 European Parliament and Council Directive 2007/65/EC of 11 December 2007 amending Council Directive 89/552/EEC on the coordination of certain provisions laid down by law, regulation or administrative action in

mum requirement included in both directives, which means that Member States can extend their concept of seriously harmful content to include other categories of harmful content.[240] With respect to content which is *likely* to harm minors, however, no examples are provided in the directives.[241]

Implicit understanding – So, although there is no formal (legal) definition of harmful content, there still seems to be an implicit understanding of the concept at the EU level.[242] However, from the examples given above, in our view, it is important that – keeping the recent above-mentioned social science theories in mind – this understanding is adapted to current interpretations of the notion 'harmful content', which is no longer limited to sexual and violent content, but covers a wide array of material and images.

D.2. *Harmful content and freedom of expression*

Legal relevance – One could wonder why a legal study undertakes research into aspects and consequences of harmful content, which is not illegal. Our analysis has been motivated by the legal relevance of the interaction of harmful content with the fundamental right to freedom of expression.

Safeguarding adults' rights – In a democratic society, any regulation of communication needs to be balanced with the fundamental right to freedom of expression.[243] The content which is the focal point of this book, i.e., harmful content, is legal for adults to access; hence, when restricting access to this kind of content to protect children, the freedom of expression of adults needs to be adequately protected.[244] As the Council of Europe puts it:

> *The development of new communication technologies and the evolution of the Internet have led to a vacuum in appropriate measures to protect children against*

Member States concerning the pursuit of television broadcasting activities, *OJ* 18.12.2007, *L* 332, 27.

240 Füg, Oliver C., "Save the children: the protection of minors in the Information Society and the Audiovisual Media Services Directive", *Journal of Consumer Policy* 2008, Issue 31, No. 1, 47.

241 Article 22 para. 2 TWFD and article 22 para. 2 AVMSD.

242 Livingstone, Sonia, "Do the media harm children? Reflections on new approaches to an old problem", *Journal of Children and Media* 2007, Vol. 1, No. 1, 6.

243 Holznagel, Bernd, "Responsibility for harmful and illegal content as well as free speech on the Internet in the United States of America and Germany", 2002, retrieved from http://www.coll.mpg.de/pdf_dat/holznag.pdf (on 12.03.2008), 11.

244 Birnhack, Michael and Rowbottom, Jacob, Shielding children: the European way, *Chicago-Kent Law Review* 2004, Issue 79, 188.

> *content carrying a risk of harm. While the protection against content in the offline world is, in most cases, much easier to guarantee, it has become significantly more difficult to do so in the online world, especially considering that every action to restrict access to content is potentially in conflict with the right to freedom of expression and information as enshrined in Article 10 of the European Convention on Human Rights (ETS No. 5). It should be recalled that this fundamental right and freedom is a primary objective of the Council of Europe and its member states; at the same time states also have a legitimate right, and even an obligation, to protect children from content which is unsuitable or inappropriate.*[245]

Consequently, creating measures to protect children against harmful content is a very delicate exercise of which the aim should be to minimise 'spillover' restrictions to adults.[246, 247] The compliance of such measures with the relevant fundamental rights provisions (as well as other legal provisions) thus always needs to be carefully checked. This challenging issue will be thoroughly examined and clarified in the second part of this book.

E. *Concluding remarks*

Exploration of 'harmful content' – This section explored the concept of harmful content. First, social science theories related to media content and its impact were briefly looked into. We found that although media effects research has shown that certain types of content (for instance, violent imagery) might have a negative influence on children's development, there is no overall consensus on the exact degree of harmfulness of different types of content. We then examined whether such indications are sufficient to trigger regulation, and, based on the precautionary principle, found that this is indeed the case. Next, we delved deeper into the concept of harmful content and looked at definitions, the link with illegal content, and a number of recently constructed social science concepts (for instance, the "*Risk of Harm*

---

245 Council of Europe (Committee of Ministers), Recommendation CM/REC(2009)5 on measures to protect children against harmful content and behaviour and to promote their active participation in the new information and communications environment, 08.07.2009, retrieved from https://wcd.coe.int/ViewDoc.jsp?id=1470045&Site=CM (on 20.01.2010).

246 Etzioni, Amitai, On protecting children from speech (Symposium Do children have the same First Amendment rights as adults?), *Chicago-Kent Law Review*, Vol. 79, No. 1, 2004, 29.

247 'Spillover' is a concept used by Eugene Volokh in the framework of US First Amendment law. Volokh, Eugene, "Speech and spillover", 19.07.1996, retrieved from http://www.slate.com/id/2371 (on 12.03.2008). With respect to the regulation of harmful content to protect children he states: "*The law can allow public display of this material, protecting adults' access but also making it available to children; or the law can prohibit public display, insulating children but also restricting adults. Either way there's spillover. Either the restriction spills over onto speech that should be free, or the freedom spills over onto speech that, in the judgment of most legislators, voters, and judges, should be restricted*".

from Online and Related Offline Activities" model advanced by O'Connell and Bryce). We further pointed out the variety of risks and the wide array of types of content that are potentially harmful. Today it is accepted that sexual and violent content are no longer the only types of harmful content. Content related to eating disorders, suicide or substance abuse, for instance, also fall within this category. Next, we established that although there is no actual legal definition of 'harmful content', it seems that there is an implicit understanding of the concept. Finally, we clarified that our choice to study harmful content was motivated by its relationship with the fundamental right to freedom of expression, which always needs to be taken into account when content is restricted in one way or another.

Harmful content and regulation – Although we have tried to provide a detailed and balanced analysis of 'harmful content', it cannot be denied that the concept is not clear-cut. This is not only because the concept is very much culture-dependent and evolves in time, but also because, as our foray into social science literature demonstrated, it is very hard to obtain objective results on the precise impact of certain content on children. The fact that this concept is not clear-cut entails that regulation of harmful content to protect minors is challenging. The next section will explore the regulatory challenges in this area, particularly with respect to digital media.

1.2. Protecting minors against harmful digital media content: identifying the regulatory challenges

1.2.1. *Introduction*

A. *Old versus new media*

> *An increasing number of children use the Internet for various purposes: finding information for school work, read [sic] news, searching for information about hobbies/interests, playing games, participating in competitions and quizzes, downloading, listening and watching music and films, communicating with friends and getting new friends through own home pages, social networking sites, chats, instant messaging services, e-mail and mobile phones. However, when doing so children are also exposed to a wide range of risks.*
>
> European Commission[248]

[248] European Commission, Public consultation: Safer Internet and online technologies for children, 2007, retrieved from http://ec.europa.eu/information_society/activities/sip/docs/public_consultation_prog/pc_2007_info_en.pdf (on 02.04.2008), 3.

Continuing concern – The previous section touched upon the fact that the protection of minors against harmful content has been a concern for centuries. With each new medium that appears, these concerns have modified and often also intensified.[249] The rise of digital media, such as the Internet and 3G mobile telephony, has inspired such concerns as well; at certain points during the past decade, it was even possible to discern a certain 'moral panic' concerning harmful content on the Internet.[250]

New elements? – Without a doubt, the media environment in which children are active nowadays is much more complex than a decade ago.[251] Whereas the risks children run on the new digital media are certainly not exclusively present in the online world, there are, however, elements that, arguably, have a great impact on children's use of this medium (*supra*).[252] Hence, in light of the exponentially growing popularity of digital media, concerns regarding the exposure to harmful content have increased accordingly.

---

[249] Etsi identified the three main differences between old and new media as 'increased accessibility', 'increased opportunity' and 'increased vulnerability': Etsi, Human Factors (HF); Specification and guidelines for service providers on the provision of information services to young children under twelve years of age, ETSI DTS/HF 102 745, 2008, retrieved from http://portal.etsi.org/stfs/STF_HomePages/STF323/DTS%20102745v6b.doc (on 07.04.2008), 12–13.

[250] Critcher, Cras, *Critical Readings: Moral panics and the media*, Maidenhead, Open University Press, 2006, 207 p.; Tufte, Brigitte and Tufte, Thomas, "Parental control of broadcasting, film, audiovisual and online", *Nordicom Review* 1999, Issue 2, retrieved from http://www.nordicom.gu.se/common/publ_pdf/37_tufte&tufte.pdf (on 13.03.2008), 54. Another example of moral panic was directed towards violent video games following the Columbine High School shootings (Buckingham, David, "Children and new media", in: Lievrouw, Leah A. and Livingstone, Sonia, *Handbook of new media – Social shaping and social consequences of ICTs*, London, Sage Publications, 76).

[251] Füg, Oliver Carsten, "Content ratings harmonization and the protection of minors in the European Information Society", in: Ward, David (ed.), *The European Union and the culture industries: regulation and the public interest*, Aldershot, Ashgate, 2008, 180: "*The increase in the amount of content available and the detachment of delivery from particular devices and geo-spatial situations of consumption have on the one hand challenged traditional regulatory logic and at the same time increased the need for guidance and information on behalf of viewers. Under these circumstances, the protection of minors from unsuitable content has developed into a far more complex endeavour spanning multiple regulatory venues, with a varying number of content originators and varying technical means of intervention and control that legislators can dispose of*".

[252] European Commission, Public consultation: Safer Internet and online technologies for children, 2007, retrieved from http://ec.europa.eu/information_society/activities/sip/docs/public_consultation_prog/pc_2007_info_en.pdf (on 02.04.2008), 3.

B. *Statistics*

Research – In recent years research into children's and young people's Internet use has greatly increased.[253] Several of these studies have also investigated accidental (and sometimes deliberate) exposure to upsetting content. The table below provides a brief overview of a few statistics related to such harmful content exposure.[254]

Table 2: Youth and exposure to harmful online content

Study	Country	Key findings
UK Children Go Online, Final report of key project findings, 2005,[255] 3	UK	– 57 per cent of 9–19 year old daily and weekly users have come into contact with online pornography. – Most online pornography is viewed unintentionally: 38 per cent of such users have seen a pornographic pop-up advert while doing something else, 36 per cent have accidentally found themselves on a pornographic site when looking for something else, and 25 per cent have received pornographic junk mail. – 22 per cent of 9–19 year old daily and weekly users have accidentally ended up on a site with violent or gruesome pictures and nine per cent on a site that is hostile or hateful to a group of people.

[253] For more general statistics on children's Internet use: cf. Ofcom, Media literacy audit: Report on media literacy among children, 02.05.2006, retrieved from www.ofcom.org.uk/advice/media_literacy/medlitpub/medlitpubrss/children/ (on 14.03.2008); European Commission, Eurobarometer Safer Internet, May 2006, retrieved from http://ec.europa.eu/information_society/activities/sip/docs/eurobarometer/eurobarometer_2005_25_ms.pdf (on 14.03.2008); European Commission, Eurobarometer Safer Internet for Children: Qualitative study in 29 European studies, May 2007, retrieved from http://ec.europa.eu/information_society/activities/sip/docs/eurobarometer/qualitative_study_2007/summary_report_en.pdf (on 14.03.2008); Pew Internet, Parent and teen Internet use, 24.10.2007, retrieved from http://www.pewinternet.org/PPF/r/225/report_display.asp (on 14.01.2008); OIVO, Jongeren en nieuwe technologieën [*Youth and new technologies*], May 2006, retrieved from http://www.oivo-crioc.org/teksten/pdf/1769nl.pdf (on 19.10.2006) [in Dutch]; Ofcom, Ofcom's submission to the Byron review – Annex 5: The evidence base – the views of children, young people and parents, 30.11.2007, retrieved from http://www.ofcom.org.uk/research/telecoms/reports/byron/annex3.pdf (on 04.07.2008).

[254] The aim is certainly not to provide a comprehensive overview, nor to pronounce a judgment on the validity of the research that is cited, but rather to give an idea of existing research and some of its outcomes.

[255] Retrieved from http://personal.lse.ac.uk/bober/UKCGOfinalReport.pdf (on 14.03.2008).

Table 2 (*cont.*)

Study	Country	Key findings
Kidsonline@home: Internet Use in Australian homes, 2005, 44[256]	AUS	Almost one in five children (19 per cent) said that they had accidentally found websites their parents would prefer them not to see 'a few times'. Children who had accidentally come across websites that their parents would prefer them not to see were asked what types of sites they had seen. Almost half of the sites (45 per cent) contained nudity / pornography and a further one in five (22 per cent) were 'rude' / adult sites. Other online content mentioned by fewer than five per cent of these children included obscene language, violence and gambling.
Ofcom, Media literacy audit, Report on media literacy among children, 2006[257]	UK	Across all children who use the Internet, one in six (16 per cent) has come across anything of concern to them, with this being more common for 12–15 than 8–11 year olds.
Valcke, Martin, Schellens, Tamara, Van Keer, Hilde and Gerarts, Marjan, "Primary school children's safe and unsafe use of the Internet at home and at school: An exploratory study", *Computers in Human Behaviour* 2007, Vol. 23, Issue 6, 2845	BE	When surfing on the Internet, 40,7 per cent of pupils surveyed have been shocked by inappropriate content (violence, sexual content, racial content) and 16,7 per cent of the pupils felt threatened while being online.
smit vub, cita & crid fundp and osc Universiteit Antwerpen, Teens and ICT: Risks and opportunities, Summary, 2008, 2[258]	BE	Six out of ten (61,2 per cent) adolescents declared that they already by accident came across web sites that showed nude images, and half (52,6 per cent) of the interviewed group already arrived at porn sites. Six out of ten adolescents (60,7 per cent) were also already confronted with images that they considered to be horrible or disgusting or with pictures / films of violent actions. One out of four (26,3 per cent) young Internet users was already confronted with racism on the net.

256 Retrieved from http://www.acma.gov.au/webwr/aba/about/recruitment/kidsonline.pdf (on 14.03.2008).

257 Retrieved from www.ofcom.org.uk/advice/media_literacy/medlitpub/medlitpubrss/children/ (on 14.03.2008).

258 Retrieved from http://www.e-privacy.be/TIRO-summary.pdf (on 14.03.2008).

Table 2 (*cont.*)

Study	Country	Key findings
Livingstone, Sonia and Haddon, Leslie, EU Kids Online: Final report, 2009, retrieved from http://www.lse.ac.uk/collections/EUKidsOnline/Reports/KidsOnlineFinalReport.pdf (on 21.01.2010), 16	EU	– Giving out personal information is the most common risky behaviour at around half of online teenagers. Note that, as anonymity removes conventional constraints on communication, there are risks associated both with disclosing and not disclosing personal details. – Seeing pornography online is the second most common risk at around 4 in 10 teenagers across Europe. This risk is widely regarded with ambivalence by both adults and children, with considerable disagreement over the potential harm involved. – Seeing violent or hateful content is the third most common risk, experienced by approximately one third of teenagers. As with pornography, the nature or level of violent content encountered is little researched, partly for ethical reasons. – Being bullied (i.e., 'cyber-bullied) comes fourth, affecting some 1 in 5 or 6 teenagers online, along with receiving unwanted sexual comments – experienced by between 1 in 10 teenagers (Germany, Ireland, Portugal) and as many as 1 in 3 or 4 teenagers in Iceland, Norway, UK and Sweden, even rising to 1 in 2 in Poland. – Last, meeting an online contact offline appears the least common though arguably the most dangerous risk. There is a fair degree of consistency in the findings across Europe: around 9 per cent (1 in 11) of online teenagers go to such meetings, rising to 1 in 5 in Poland, Sweden and the Czech Republic. Often these meetings are with teenagers of a similar age. – In several countries, there is evidence that around 15 per cent – 20 per cent of online teenagers report a degree of distress or of feeling uncomfortable or threatened online. This provides some indication, arguably, of the proportion of teenagers for whom risk poses a degree of harm.

Without passing judgment on the consistency or correctness of the studies above – an endeavour reserved for social scientists – the figures indicate that exposure to harmful content occurs, and hence, concerns may be justified.

C. *Implications for policy and regulation?*

Valid policy goal – Protecting children is a legitimate interest.[259] Protecting children against harmful media content has always been and continues to be a concern for policy- and law-makers at the international, regional and national levels.[260] In almost every country, this concern has been a central driver of regulation,[261] resulting, for instance, in legislation with respect to film classification and the broadcasting of television programmes. Hence, it is not surprising that, as the Internet grew increasingly popular, questions were asked about the validity of this policy goal in the new media environment. However, there has been surprisingly little doubt as to the continuing legitimacy of protecting children against harmful media content.[262] As the European Commission put it back in 1999

> *Regulatory policy in the sector is aimed at safeguarding certain public interests, such as cultural and linguistic diversity, the protection of minors and consumer protection. These are not called into question by technological development.*[263]

---

259 ECJ, Dynamic Medien v. Avides Media AG, C-244/06, 14.02.2008, 42.

260 United Nations General Assembly, Resolution A world fit for children, A/RES/S-27/2, 11.10.2002, retrieved from http://www.unicef.org/specialsession/docs_new/documents/A-RES-S27-2E.pdf (on 27.09.2006), 16; Commission of the European Communities, Proposal for a Decision of the European Parliament and of the Council establishing a multiannual Community programme on protecting children using the Internet and other communication technologies, COM (2008) 106 final, 27.02.2008, 2; Goldberg, David, Prosser, Tony and Verhulst, Stefaan (eds), *Regulating the changing media: A comparative study*, Oxford, Oxford University Press, 1998, 303.

261 Tambini, Damien and Forgan, Liz, "Content", Communications White Paper, retrieved from http://www.communicationswhitepaper.gov.uk/cwp_consultation/contentregulation.pdf (18.12.2003, no longer available); O'Connell, Rachel and Bryce, Jo, Children and young people in on-line and related off-line environments: Promoting well-being and minimising risk of harm, Study commissioned by the Council of Europe, not published, 27.

262 Uyttendaele, Caroline, *Openbare informatie – Het juridisch statuut in een convergerende mediaomgeving* [*Public information – The legal status in the converging media environment*], Antwerpen, Maklu, 2002, 225 [in Dutch]; Palzer, Carmen, "Horizontal rating of audiovisual content in Europe – An alternative to multi-level classification?", *Iris Plus* 2003, No. 10, 2–8.

263 Commission of the European Communities, Communication from the Commission to the Council, the European Parliament, the Economic and Social Committee and the Committee of the Regions, Principles and guidelines for the Community's audiovisual policy in the digital age, COM (1999) 657 final, 14.12.1999, 2.

Shared responsibility – The achievement of this public policy goal has traditionally been a joint effort between government and parents.[264] The government has been argued to have a duty of care to provide an environment in which children's exposure to harmful content is minimised,[265] and parents need to exercise some form of supervision within this environment.[266, 267] If one of the actors does not take up this responsibility, however, no effective protection can be guaranteed. For instance, if governments create 'watershed' provisions, but parents allow children to have a television in their

[264] Reding, Viviane, Minors and media: towards a more effective protection – Workshop of scientists in the field of protection of minors on media violence, self-regulation and media literacy, 10.09.2003, retrieved from http://europa.eu.int/rapid/pressReleasesAction.do?reference=SPEECH/03/400&format=HTML&aged=0&language=EN&guiLanguage=en (on 14.03.2008): "*It should be borne in mind that the responsibility to protect minors from harmful effects of the media is a shared one. Regulators, the audiovisual industry and parents all have to play their part to achieve the goal*". On domestic (or parental) regulation of children's access to Internet content, see also: Livingstone, Sonia and Bober, Magdalena, "Regulating the Internet at home: contrasting the perspectives of children and parents", 93–113, in: Buckingham, David and Willett, Rebekah, *Digital generations: children, young people and new media*, Mahwah NJ and London, Lawrence Erlbaum Associates, 2006, 337 p.

[265] van der Stoel, Anne Lize, van Eijk, Nico, Hoogland, Duco, van Noorduyn, Els and Wermuth, Mir, Wijzer Kijken – Schadelijkheid, geschiktheid en kennisbevordering bij het gebruik van audiovisuele producten door jeugdigen [*Watching wiser – Harmfulness, appropriateness and advancement of knowledge*], November 2005, retrieved from http://www.ivir.nl/publicaties/vaneijk/Wijzerkijken.pdf (on 14.03.2008) [in Dutch]. Cf. also article 17 UNCRC: *infra*, Part 2, Chapter 1.

[266] However, research indicates that, in reality, parents are not always taking up this responsibility: Ruxton, Sandy, *What about us? Children's rights in the European Union? Next Steps*, Brussels, The European Children's Network, 2005, 108: "*Results from a recent Eurobarometer survey 29 of parental attitudes in the 25 Member States also indicate that a significant proportion of children face no parental limitations on their use of television, the internet, mobile phones, or game consoles. This is the case for 22 % of 7–11 year olds, 27 % of 12–15 year olds, and 40 % of 15–16 year olds*". Valcke et al. found that "*Of 1626 pupils who responded to this question 52% reported that they did not or hardly ever experience being controlled when using the Internet at home*" (Valcke, Martin, Schellens, Tamara, Van Keer, Hilde and Gerarts, Marjan, "Primary school children's safe and unsafe use of the Internet at home and at school: An exploratory study", *Computers in Human Behaviour* 2007, Vol. 23, Issue 6, 2846).

[267] Cf. also: Ofcom, Initial assessments of when to adopt self- or co-regulation – Consultation, 27.03.2008, retrieved from http://www.ofcom.org.uk/consult/condocs/coregulation/condoc.pdf (on 01.07.2008), 7: "*In addition Ofcom believes that it is important that a model of shared responsibility is developed that gives people the tools they need to take personal responsibility and which supports effective means of different type [o]f regulation whether it is self-, co- or statutory regulation*".

bedroom on which they can easily watch television after the watershed time, the chance that they will be confronted with harmful content increases. Another example, related to film classification, is if there is legislation which classifies films according to age, but parents still allow their fourteen year olds to go to films that are classified 'sixteen plus', again, the protection fails. The reverse is also true:[268] if no regulation were to exist, it would be much more difficult for parents to take up their responsibility. The new media and communications environment, however, does not facilitate this assumption of parental responsibility.[269] Media use is increasingly individual and private and occurs on many different devices. In such a context it is very difficult to keep track of the content children and young people are confronted with across different digital media. Furthermore, government and parents are not the only actors involved in the protection of minors using digital media, the number of which has increased spectacularly over the past decade.[270] Private actors, such as access and content providers, for instance, play an increasingly

[268] In *Ginsberg v. New York*, 390 U.S. 629 (1968), the US Supreme Court argued that "*parents and others, teachers for example who have this primary responsibility for children's wellbeing are entitled to the support of laws designed to aid discharge of that responsibility*". Nunziato, Dawn, "Toward a constitutional regulation of minors' access to harmful internet speech", *Chicago-Kent Law Review* 2004, Issue 79, 129.

[269] Livingstone, Sonia and Bober, Magdalena, "Regulating the Internet at home: contrasting the perspectives of children and parents", in: Buckingham, David and Willett, Rebekah, *Digital generations: children, young people and new media*, Mahwah NJ and London, Lawrence Erlbaum Associates, 2006, 98 and 104 *et seq.* Livingstone and Bober identified two main difficulties of domestic regulation: "*The first is that although parents are responsible for their children's safety, they must also manage their children's growing independence and rights to privacy – something that children feel strongly about. The second is that, as parents and children agree, children are more often expert on the internet than their parents*". They even concluded that "*relying on parents to implement consistent, effective regulation within the home is problematic – not necessarily because parents are unwilling or incompetent, but rather because for both practical and theoretical reasons, this is a difficult and, in some ways, inappropriate burden to rest on parents' shoulders*" (p. 110).

[270] The European Commission has identified the following actors: "*content providers, Internet service providers and mobile network operators, regulators, standards bodies, industry self-regulatory bodies, national, regional and local authorities responsible for industry, education, consumer protection, families, children's rights and child welfare and non-governmental organisations active in consumer protection, families, children's rights and child welfare*": Commission of the European Communities, Proposal for a Decision of the European Parliament and of the Council on establishing a multiannual Community programme on promoting safer use of the Internet and new online technologies, COM (2004) 91 final, 12.03.2004, 7.

important role. Taking into account this myriad of actors involved in the protection of minors from harmful content, it has been argued that the promotion of a 'shared responsibility' strategy is the only way forward.[271]

Implications for regulation – The characteristics of the new media and communications technologies do not only pose a problem with respect to parental supervision. Regulation to achieve an optimal protection for young people from unsuitable content also faces a number of difficulties as a consequence of the nature of these technologies. This is a key element of this book and will be explored in the following section.

Overview – In this section, first, a number of the characteristics of the new information and communication networks are outlined. These characteristics are then considered in light of a few typical features of the use of legislation, to determine what difficulties need to be overcome when trying to apply traditional laws to new, digital media. Third, the legislative approach to protecting minors against harmful content in the United States is analysed. This analysis leads to an interim conclusion concerning the need for a broader regulatory framework. Finally, illustrating the move towards the use of an alternative regulatory framework, the policy history of the protection of minors against harmful online content in the European Union is described and analysed.

1.2.2. *Characteristics of the new information and communication networks*

Problem definition – In a digital world, the traditional regulatory goal of protecting minors against harmful content runs into a number of obstacles caused by the characteristics and nature of the new information and

[271] Cf. Byron, Tanya, Safer children in a digital world: the report of the Byron review, 27.03.2008, retrieved from http://www.dfes.gov.uk/byronreview/ (on 04.07.2008), 2. See also: Ofcom, Ofcom's response to the Byron Review – Statement, 27.03.2008, retrieved from http://www.ofcom.org.uk/research/telecoms/reports/byron/byron_review.pdf (on 04.07.2008), 8.

communication networks. This is because these characteristics,[272] and particularly those of the Internet,[273] affect the use of traditional regulation.[274]

Decentralisation and Borderlessness – The digital media environment is global. The architecture of the Internet is decentralised,[275] and information flows are not hampered by physical borders.[276] Information can be consulted from anywhere in the world regardless of where the information is

---

272 These networks of course possess many other features. In this book however, the discussion is limited to those characteristics that are of importance to the use of traditional state regulation. For a detailed overview of the (technical) nature of digital information and communications networks, see: Svantesson, Dan Jerker B., "The characteristics making Internet communication challenge traditional models of regulation – What every international jurist should know about the Internet", *International Journal of Law and Information Technology* 2005, Vol. 13, No. 1, 39–69.

273 As was mentioned above, when using the notion 'Internet', reference is made to what is also called the World Wide Web. Private communications such as e-mail are excluded from the scope of this book.

274 Cf. Commission of the European Communities, Communication to the European Parliament, the Council, the Economic and Social Committee and the Committee of the Regions, Illegal and harmful content on the Internet, COM (1996) 487, 16.10.1996, retrieved from http://ec.europa.eu/archives/ISPO/legal/en/internet/communic.html (on 25.03.2008): "*It is widely recognised that the international nature of the Internet and its unique characteristics (extremely decentralised structure, resistance to tampering, high degree of automation, global reach, wide usage) clearly pose novel, and specific problems*". See also: Verhulst, Stefaan G., "The regulation of digital content", in: Lievrouw, Leah A. and Livingstone, Sonia, *Handbook of new media – Social shaping and social consequences of ICTs*, London, Sage Publications, 2006, 329.

275 Thornburgh, Dick and Lin, Herbert S. (eds), *Youth, Pornography and the Internet*, Washington, D.C., National Academies Press, 2002, retrieved from http://books.nap.edu/html/youth_internet/ (on 22.02.2007); Baird, Zoë and Verhulst, Stefaan, "A new model for Global Internet Governance", 2004, retrieved from http://www.markle.org/downloadable_assets/ahs_global_internet_gov.pdf (on 23.04.2007), 4; Akdeniz, Yaman, "Stocktaking on efforts to combat racism on the Internet", Background Paper for the High Level Seminar on Racism and the Internet, Intergovernmental Working Group on the Effective Implementation of the Durban Declaration and Programme of Action, Fourth session, Geneva, 16-27.01.2006, E/CN.4/2006/WG.21/BP.1, retrieved from http://www.cyber-rights.org/reports/ya_un_paper_int_06.pdf (on 23.04.2007), 9.

276 Commission of the European Communities, Green Paper on the protection of minors and human dignity in audiovisual and information services, COM (1996) 483 final, 16.10.1996, 3: "*In geographical terms, distribution networks are less national and increasingly global in nature, Internet being a world-wide network of networks*".

stored, and can be transmitted worldwide with very little effort or cost.[277, 278] The impact of this obsolescence of geographical frontiers cannot be underestimated in a world where traditionally legislation is confined to national territories.

Multiplicity of players and user-generated content – Broadcasting information via television or radio is an expensive and technically complicated endeavour reserved for a limited number of media organisations.[279] The Internet, however, offers anyone who disposes of an Internet connection the possibility to distribute information. Hence, the threshold for content production has been significantly lowered, which has lead to an explosion of 'user-generated content'.[280] This does not mean that there is an absolute 'level playing field'; large companies still have more means to attract a significant number of visitors. However, a single user can now communicate information to anyone anywhere at any time. With respect to the regulation of content, this development results in a multiplication of actors that potentially need to be controlled.

---

277 Svantesson, Dan Jerker B., "The characteristics making Internet communication challenge traditional models of regulation – What every international jurist should know about the Internet", *International Journal of Law and Information Technology* 2005, Vol. 13, No. 1, 46.

278 Related to the borderlessness of the Internet is the so-called 'cyberreach' phenomenon, which is the "*Internet's ability to extend the impact of one's words beyond typical real space limits*": Newman, Abraham and Bach, David, "Self-regulatory trajectories in the shadow of public power: Resolving digital dilemmas in Europe and the United States", *Governance* 2004, Vol. 17, No. 3, 399.

279 Svantesson, Dan Jerker B., "The characteristics making Internet communication challenge traditional models of regulation –What every international jurist should know about the Internet", *International Journal of Law and Information Technology* 2005, Vol. 13, No. 1, 50.

280 Commission of the European Communities, Communication to the European Parliament, the Council, the Economic and Social Committee and the Committee of the Regions, Illegal and harmful content on the Internet, COM (1996) 487, 16.10.1996, retrieved from http://ec.europa.eu/archives/ISPO/legal/en/internet/communic.html (on 25.03.2008): "*Unlike other traditional networks such as broadcasting, the Internet is essentially user-driven, with users themselves, rather than established publishers, generating a substantial part of the 'content'. A unique characteristic of the Internet is that it functions simultaneously as a medium for publishing and for communication. [...] This constant shift from 'publishing mode' to 'private communication' mode – two modes governed traditionally by very different legal regimes – constitutes one of the main challenges of Internet regulation*". See also: Commission of the European Communities, Green Paper on the protection of minors and human dignity in audiovisual and information services, COM (1996) 483 final, 16.10.1996, 8: "*[E]ach user becomes a potential supplier of material*".

Individualisation and choice – Furthermore, one of the long-established rationales for regulating traditional broadcasting, which is a one-way mass communication medium,[281] is the potential large impact on its audience.[282] If viewers across a country watch the same programme at the same time, the effect on public opinion is judged to be significant and hence regulation is considered justified. Digital media, however, are highly individualised. The Internet, which can be seen as a collection of many one-to-many and many-to-many communications,[283] or digital television platforms, offer the user or viewer a much greater individual choice[284] and hence also more control over what he or she wishes to see.[285] It has been argued that such 'on-demand' services have significantly less impact on the persons that use them.[286] This could lead to a diminished need for top-down state regulation. Also related to the highly individualised character of digital media is the possibility to communicate anonymously.[287] Although this can be seen as an element of the right to privacy,[288] it could lead to difficulties regarding enforcement of regulation.

Multiplicity and portability of devices – Over the past decade, the number of devices that can be used to consult information has multiplied. The same content, for instance, a television programme, can now be watched

---

[281] Cf. Commission of the European Communities, Green Paper on the protection of minors and human dignity in audiovisual and information services, COM (1996) 483 final, 16.10.1996, 1.

[282] Helberger, Natali, "From eyeball to creator – Toying with audience empowerment in the Audiovisual Media Service Directive", *Entertainment Law Review* 2008, No. 6, 128–137; Grünwald, Andreas, Report on possible options for the review of the European Convention on Transfrontier Television, 24.04.2003, retrieved from http://www.coe.int/t/dghl/standardsetting/media/T-TT/T-TT(2003)002_en.pdf (on 19.05.2008).

[283] Peer-to-peer networks, for instance, are increasingly being used.

[284] Commission of the European Communities, Green Paper on the protection of minors and human dignity in audiovisual and information services, COM (1996) 483 final, 16.10.1996, 3.

[285] Cf. *supra*.

[286] Recital 42 European Parliament and Council Directive 2007/65/EC of 11 December 2007 amending Council Directive 89/552/EEC on the coordination of certain provisions laid down by law, regulation or administrative action in Member States concerning the pursuit of television broadcasting activities, *OJ* 18.12.2007, *L* 332, 27.

[287] Thornburgh, Dick and Lin, Herbert S. (eds), *Youth, Pornography and the Internet*, Washington, D.C., National Academies Press, 2002, retrieved from http://books.nap.edu/html/youth_internet/ (on 22.02.2007).

[288] Cf. *infra*, Part 2, Chapter 1.

on a television, a computer screen, a handheld PDA, a game console or a mobile phone. This requires a technology-neutral[289] and medium-independent regulatory approach.

1.2.3. *Obstacles to the use of traditional (content) regulation in the digital media environment*

DISCORDANCE – Different characteristics of the new information and communication networks, whether separately or combined, are at odds with a number of basic elements of traditional state regulation.[290]

GLOBALISATION, TERRITORIALITY OF THE LAW AND ENFORCEMENT ISSUES – One of the major problems traditional state regulation faces with respect to new information and communication networks is the discordance between the global, border-crossing nature of these networks and the territoriality of traditional legislation.[291] States are usually only able to enforce legislation within their borders. Confronted with a global network on which information circulates regardless of geographical restrictions, governments have

289 VAN EIJCK, Nico, ASSCHER, Lodewijk, HELBERGER, Natali and KABEL, Jan, De regulering van media in internationaal perspectief [*The regulation of media in an international perspective*], Den Haag, February 2005, retrieved from http://www.ivir.nl/publicaties/overig/Media/regulering%20van%20media%20in%20internationaal%20perspect..pdf (on 01.08.2007), 7 [in Dutch].

290 REDING, Viviane, Commission study points the way forward for better regulation of new media and the digital economy (press release on Safer Internet Day 2007), IP/07/138, Brussels, 06.02.2007, retrieved from http://www.europa.eu/rapid/pressReleasesAction.do?reference=IP/07/138&format=HTML&aged=0&language=EN&guiLanguage=fr (on 07.02.2007): "*Particularly in the digital economy, driven by rapid technological change and enhanced user control, traditional regulations are finding it difficult to keep up with the speed of technological, economical and social changes, and the problem of decentralised information. Traditional regulatory approaches also may suffer from enforcement problems*".

291 BAIRD, Zoë and VERHULST, Stefaan, "A new model for Global Internet Governance", 2004, retrieved from http://www.markle.org/downloadable_assets/ahs_global_internet_gov.pdf (on 23.04.2007), 4; GOLDBERG, David, PROSSER, Tony and VERHULST, Stefaan (eds), *Regulating the changing media: a comparative study*, Oxford, Oxford University Press, 1998, 3; UYTTENDAELE, Caroline, *Openbare informatie – Het juridisch statuut in een convergerende mediaomgeving* [*Public information – The legal status in a converging media environment*], Antwerpen, Maklu, 2002, 332 [in Dutch].

found that effective enforcement is extremely difficult.[292, 293, 294] Furthermore, since state enforcement is at odds with the international nature of the Internet, citizens or companies increasingly take conscious decisions with respect

[292] RAPID, Commission study points the way forward for better regulation of new media and the digital economy (press release on Safer Internet Day 2007), IP/07/138, 06.02.2007, retrieved from http://www.europa.eu/rapid/pressReleasesAction.do?reference=IP/07/138&format=HTML&aged=0&language=EN&guiLanguage=fr (on 07.02.2007); KLEINSTEUBER, Hans, "State – Regulation – Media", OSCE Conference "Guaranteeing Media Freedom on the Internet", Amsterdam, 27–28.08.2004, retrieved from http://www.osce.org/documents/rfm/2004/08/3430_en.pdf (on 23.04.2007), 7; UYTTENDAELE, Caroline, *Openbare informatie – Het juridisch statuut in een convergerende mediaomgeving* [*Public information – The legal status in a converging mediaenvironment*], Antwerpen, Maklu, 2002, 335 [in Dutch]; REIDENBERG, Joel R., "States and Internet Enforcement", *University of Ottawa Law & Technology Journal* 2004, Vol. 1, No. 1–2, 213–230; REIDENBERG, Joel R., "Technology and Internet Jurisdiction", *University of Pennsylvania Law Review* 2005, Vol. 153, 2005, 1951–1974.

[293] An important example of a practical case where enforcement issues arose was the famous Yahoo!- case. The US-based company Yahoo! was ordered by a French court to make certain images of Nazi objects unavailable for French Internet users as such images are illegal in France (whereas they are protected by the United States Constitution). Yahoo! claimed in vain that the French court did not have jurisdiction and that French law could not be applied given that the images were stored on a server in the United States. For detailed information on this case, cf.: CENTER FOR DEMOCRACY AND TECHNOLOGY, "Jurisdiction", retrieved from http://www.cdt.org/jurisdiction/ (on 23.04.2007); GEIST, Michael, "New Yahoo decisions raises old questions", 22.01.2006, retrieved from http://michaelgeist.ca/index.php?option=com_content&task=view&id=1083&Itemid=113 (on 23.04.2007); FRYDMAN, Benoît and RORIVE, Isabelle, "Fighting Nazi and anti-Semitic material on the internet: The Yahoo! case and its global implications", Conference: "Hate and Terrorist Speech on the Internet: The Global Implications of the Yahoo! Ruling in France", Cardozo School of Law, 11.02.2002, retrieved from http://pcmlp.socleg.ox.ac.uk/YahooConference/ (on 23.04.2007); REIDENBERG, Joel R., "Technology and Internet Jurisdiction", *University of Pennsylvania Law Review* 2005, Vol. 153, 2005, 1951–1974.

[294] However, this does not alter the fact that some countries do exercise some sort of border control. The most famous example is China. The Chinese government censors Chinese as well as foreign Internet content on a massive scale. The filtering system used has been dubbed the 'Great Wall 2.0', or the 'Golden Shield'. Moreover, international companies, such as Microsoft and Google, surrendered to the Chinese government's pressure and agreed to create censored versions of their products (a censored Google search engine, for instance, since their regular search engine had been blocked). Cf. SVANTESSON, Dan Jerker B., "The characteristics making Internet communication challenge traditional models of regulation – What every international jurist should know about the Internet", *International Journal of Law and Information Technology* 2005, Vol. 13, No. 1, 45; SLATE (Tim WU), "The filtered future: China's bid to divide the Internet", 11.07.2005, retrieved from http://www.slate.com/id/2122270/ (on 30.06.2008); SPIEGEL ONLINE (Hilmar SCHMUNDT and Wieland WAGNER), "Great Wall 2.0: how China leads the world in web censorship", 02.05.2008, retrieved from http://www.spiegel.de/international/world/0,1518,551110,00

to the jurisdiction to which they want to be subjected. In this respect, forum shopping increasingly occurs,[295] since differences between legislative regimes push people with intentions that are illegal in one jurisdiction to establish their activities in another which offers a legal safe haven.[296] It could seem logical to resort to international legislation, such as conventions or treaties, to deal with this issue. Today, however, a consensus exists on the fact that drafting international legislation which would be applicable to the 'global Internet' is a utopian idea.[297]

Slowness linked to a knowledge gap – Given the fact that technology evolves at a very fast pace, it is not surprising that governments, who function within a strict administrative structure, struggle to keep up with these developments.[298] As the Children's Charities Coalition for Internet Safety has put it:

.html (on 30.06.2008); Deibert, Ron, Written statement for the Congress, Bipartisan US-China Economic and Security Review Commission Hearing on 'Access to Information and Media Control in the People's Republic of China', 18.06.2008, retrieved from http://deibert.citizenlab.org/deibertcongresstestimony.pdf (on 30.06.2008). For more details, cf. the research results of the OpenNet Initiative (a project which aims to document patterns of Internet censorship and surveillance across the globe): http://cyber.law.harvard.edu/research/opennet (on 30.06.2008). See also: Deibert, Ronald, Palfrey, John, Rohozinski, Rafal and Zittrain, Jonathan, *Access denied: the practice and policy of Internet filtering*, Cambridge MA, The MIT Press, 2008, 320 p.

295 Hans-Bredow-Institut and EMR, Study on co-regulation measures in the media sector: Final report, Study commissioned by the European Commission, June 2006, retrieved from http://ec.europa.eu/avpolicy/docs/library/studies/coregul/final_rep_en.pdf (on 28.07.2006), 13; Uyttendaele, Caroline, *Openbare informatie – Het juridisch statuut in een convergerende mediaomgeving* [*Public information – The legal status in a converging media environment*], Antwerpen, Maklu, 2002, 336 [in Dutch].

296 Reidenberg, Joel R., "Technology and Internet Jurisdiction", *University of Pennsylvania Law Review* 2005, Vol. 153, 2005, 1958; see also: Froomkin, Michael, T*he Internet as a Source of Regulatory Arbitrage,* in: Kahin, Brian and Nesson, Charles (eds.), *Borders in Cyberspace – Information policy and the global information infrastructure*, Cambridge MA, MIT Press, 1997, 142.

297 Rorive, Isabelle, "Réguler l'Internet" ["*Regulating the Internet*"], Intervention présentée au Palais de l'Europe le 31 mai 2003 dans le cadre d'une journée consacrée à La convention du Conseil de l'Europe sur l'information et la coopération juridique concernant les 'Services de la société de l'information', retrieved from http://www.coe.int/t/e/legal_affairs/legal_co%2Doperation/information_society_services/Riguler%20l%27Internet%20–%20CoE%20–%2021%20%20Mai%202003%20_version%20icrite_.pdf (on 03.04.2008) [in French].

298 Reding, Viviane, Commission study points the way forward for better regulation of new media and the digital economy (press release on Safer Internet Day 2007), IP/07/138, Brussels, 06.02.2007, retrieved from http://www.europa.eu/rapid/pressReleasesAction.do?reference=

> *No sooner has a technologically-based problem been identified and a response formulated than it has moved or changed. No one wants to legislate in haste and repent at leisure. In this area, the government definitely does need, and generally can only benefit from, the active collaboration and involvement of the Internet industry.*[299]

Private actors who operate in this rapidly changing environment often have a far superior and more detailed expertise. Hence, it has been argued that governments should take advantage of this knowledge, and should cooperate with these actors.[300, 301]

UNIDIRECTIONAL MODEL OF REGULATION VERSUS A MULTIPLICITY OF ACTORS – Traditional regulation- or legislation-making has the tendency to be unidirectional: the state or government takes the initiative, drafts the law or regulation, and operates the enforcement mechanisms[302] as well. Most often, little or no consultation with involved parties is organised. Linked with the knowledge gap issue, as mentioned above, this can be deemed problematic in an increasingly complex environment in which information, knowledge and understanding of the often specialised issues are key to successful regu-

IP/07/138&format=HTML&aged=0&language=EN&guiLanguage=fr (on 07.02.2007); HOLOUBEK, Michael (ed.), *Regulating content – European regulatory framework for the media and related creative sectors*, Alphen a/d Rijn, Kluwer Law International, 2007, 134; SINCLAIR, Darren, "Self-regulation versus command and control? Beyond false dichotomies", *Law & Policy* 1997, Vol. 19, No. 4, 542.

299 CHILDREN'S CHARITIES COALITION FOR INTERNET SAFETY, "Child safety online – A digital manifesto", 2004, retrieved from http://www.nch.org.uk/uploads/documents/Digital_Manifesto_web.pdf (on 23.02.2007), 6.

300 HANS-BREDOW-INSTITUT AND EMR, Study on co-regulation measures in the media sector: Final report, Study commissioned by the European Commission, June 2006, retrieved from http://ec.europa.eu/avpolicy/docs/library/studies/coregul/final_rep_en.pdf (on 28.07.2006), 12, KLEINSTEUBER, Hans, "State – Regulation – Media", OSCE Conference "Guaranteeing Media Freedom on the Internet", Amsterdam, 27–28.08.2004, retrieved from http://www.osce.org/documents/rfm/2004/08/3430_en.pdf (on 23.04.2007), 8.

301 However, it has been argued that "*[e]qually there is something fundamentally unhealthy in a democracy for the government to be so heavily reliant on technical advice that is provided by the very industry they are meant to be overseeing on behalf of the wider public interest*": CHILDREN'S CHARITIES COALITION FOR INTERNET SAFETY, "Child safety online – A digital manifesto", 2004, retrieved from http://www.nch.org.uk/uploads/documents/Digital_Manifesto_web.pdf (on 23.02.2007), 6.

302 Of course, the actual enforcement is often delegated to regulators and courts. However, notwithstanding the theory of separation of powers, in the context of this book such actors, although independent, are considered to belong to the (broadly interpreted concept of) 'government'.

lation.[303] Furthermore, the fact that traditional regulation does not take into account the interests of the subjects it regulates can lead to resistance vis-à-vis the regulation, rather than cooperation.[304] In addition (and especially in the sphere of content regulation), although a limited number of players, such as broadcasters or traditional publishers, can be controlled with relative ease in a top-down regulatory system, control over the current multitude of content producers is much more difficult. This is because the volume and global character of content reduces the possibility of central control.[305]

WEAKENING OF TRADITIONAL RATIONALES FOR CONTENT REGULATION? – Different traditional justifications for content – especially broadcasting – regulation lose much of their strength in the digital era. Spectrum scarcity, for instance, is one of the traditional grounds upon which regulation has been based.[306] Digital media, however, are characterised by abundance rather than scarcity.[307] Another fading rationale is the special impact on the formation of opinion, the spread effect and the simultaneity of impact of mass media such as broadcasting (*supra*).[308] VERHULST clarifies this further by attributing four features to broadcasting that were the grounds for regulating this medium:

---

303 HANS-BREDOW-INSTITUT AND EMR, Study on co-regulation measures in the media sector: Final report, Study commissioned by the European Commission, June 2006, retrieved from http://ec.europa.eu/avpolicy/docs/library/studies/coregul/final_rep_en.pdf (on 28.07.2006), 12–13.

304 HANS-BREDOW-INSTITUT AND EMR, Study on co-regulation measures in the media sector: Final report, Study commissioned by the European Commission, June 2006, retrieved from http://ec.europa.eu/avpolicy/docs/library/studies/coregul/final_rep_en.pdf (on 28.07.2006), 12.

305 KELLER, Daphne and VERHULST, Stefaan, Parental control in a converged communications environment. Self-regulation, technical devices and meta-information (Final report for the DVB regulatory group), October 2000, retrieved from http://ec.europa.eu/avpolicy/docs/reg/minors/dvbgroup.pdf (on 23.04.2007), 4.

306 VALCKE, Peggy and STEVENS, David, "Graduated regulation of 'regulatable' content and the European Audiovisual Media Services Directive: one small step for the industry and one giant leap for the legislator?", *Telematics & Informatics* 2007, Vol. 24, Issue 4, 288; NOORLANDER, Peter, "Freedom of expression and Internet regulation", in: HARDY, Christiane and MÖLLER, Christian (eds), *Spreading the Word on the Internet: 16 Answers to 4 Questions (Reflections on Freedom of the Media and the Internet Amsterdam Conference, June 2003)*, Vienna, OSCE, 2003, retrieved from http://www.osce.org/publications/rfm/2003/06/12245_103_en.pdf (on 23.04.2007),108.

307 VERHULST, Stefaan G., "The regulation of digital content", in: LIEVROUW, Leah A. and LIVINGSTONE, Sonia, *Handbook of new media – Social shaping and social consequences of ICTs*, London, Sage Publications, 2006, 332–333.

308 VALCKE, Peggy and STEVENS, David, "Graduated regulation of 'regulatable' cntent and the European Audiovisual Media Services Directive: one small step for the industry and one giant leap for the legislator?", *Telematics & Informatics* 2007, Vol. 24, Issue 4, 288.

i.e., pervasiveness, invasiveness, publicness and influence.[309] First, a limited number of channels and programming (due, for instance, to spectrum scarcity) implies that each programme is perceived to be pervasive, and hence, pluralist safeguards and public service obligations have been put in place. Second, content is considered to be more invasive if the broadcaster decides upon what is viewed when and the user can not actively choose which content he or she wants to receive. Again, this justifies content controls. Third, broadcast media constitute a forum for public thinking and confrontation with common values. There are certain taboos that are not a part of such a public discussion and that are regulated. Finally, broadcast programmes can exert a large influence (cf. *supra*), and certainly so, if there are only a limited number of information sources. Therefore, regulatory measures ensuring that content is not harmful nor undemocratic have been considered warranted. These features of traditional broadcasting are not transposed to digital media, which embody a multitude of information sources and channels, individualised patterns of media consumption and a high degree of choice and control. However, although it is true that, at first sight, one could conclude that the traditional content regulation rationales are consequently obsolete, the reality is more complex.[310] Especially with respect to the motivation for regulation that is central to this study, the protection of minors, the question is not so much 'is regulation still necessary in the digital era?' – yes! – but rather 'how should this regulation be constructed in order to be efficient and reconcilable with the characteristics of the media in question?'.

1.2.4. *The United States legislative approach to protect minors on the Internet*

Issues with respect to freedom of expression – Notwithstanding the regulatory issues concerning the specific characteristics of the new media technologies and platforms, it is important not to lose sight of another fundamental regulatory challenge associated with the protection of minors against harmful content. As was mentioned *supra*, regulatory measures aiming to protect minors against such content inevitably have an impact on the right to freedom of expression. Hence, and this will be analysed in-depth in part 2 of this book, any regulatory measure with such an impact needs to

---

309 Verhulst, Stefaan G., "The regulation of digital content", in: Lievrouw, Leah A. and Livingstone, Sonia, *Handbook of new media – Social shaping and social consequences of ICTs*, London, Sage Publications, 2006, 332–333.

310 Verhulst, Stefaan G., "The regulation of digital content", in Lievrouw, Leah A. and Livingstone, Sonia, *Handbook of new media – Social shaping and social consequences of ICTs*, London, Sage Publications, 2006, 336–337.

be constructed in a way which respects the fundamental right to freedom of expression or free speech.

United States: illustration – In this context, it is useful to take a brief look at the situation in the United States, where there has been a tendency to fall back on (traditional) legislation to achieve the policy goal of shielding children from harmful online content.[311, 312, 313] At least two of these legislative initiatives have, been constitutionally challenged, which reveals certain flaws of this *modus operandi*.[314]

[311] It is important to note that US Courts have repeatedly stressed that there is a compelling interest to protect children from harmful material that should still remain freely accessible to adults. Cf. *Reno v. American Civil Liberties Union*, 521 U.S. 844 (1997), 846; *American Civil Liberties Union v. Gonzales*, 478 F.Supp.2d 775 (E.D.Pa. 2007), 776. Also: Etzioni, Amitai, On protecting children from speech (Symposium Do children have the same First Amendment rights as adults?), *Chicago-Kent Law Review* 2004, Vol. 79, No. 1, 33.

[312] For more information on which kinds of speech are exactly considered as 'harmful to minors' under First Amendment doctrine in the United States, cf. Lessig, Lawrence and Resnick, Paul, "Zoning speech on the Internet: a legal and technical model", *Michigan Law Review* 1999, Vol. 98, Issue 2, 395–431; Nunziato, Dawn, "Toward a constitutional regulation of minors' access to harmful internet speech", *Chicago-Kent Law Review* 2004, Issue 79, 124 *et seq.*; Nunziato, Dawn C., "Technology and pornography", *Brigham Young University Law Review* 2007, Issue 6, 1535–1584. In some acts, the notion 'harmful to minors' is defined. For instance, in the *Children's Internet Protection Act* (*infra*): "*The term 'harmful to minors' means any picture, image, graphic image file, or other visual depiction that (A) taken as a whole and with respect to minors, appeals to a prurient interest in nudity, sex or excretion; (B) depicts, describes, or represents, in a patently offensive way with respect to what is suitable for minors, an actual or simulated sexual act or sexual contact, actual or simulated normal or perverted sexual acts, or a lewd exhibition of the genitals; and (C) taken as a whole, lacks serious literary, artistic, political, or scientific value as to minors*" (SEC 1703).

[313] Regulating Internet content can be seen as part of a broader current trend in the United States towards regulating material that can be harmful to minors in other media, such as 'indecent' broadcasting and violent video games. Cf. *Broadcast Decency Enforcement Act*, Pub. L. No. 109–235, 120 Stat. 491; Washington Post (Adam Thierer), New worlds to censor, 07.06.2005, retrieved fromhttp://www.washingtonpost.com/wp-dyn/content/article/2005/06/06/AR2005060601506_pf.html (on 04.05.2007); Gamasutra (David Jenkins), Tenessee violent game bill withdrawn, 23.05.2006, retrieved from http://www.gamasutra.com/php-bin/news_index.php?story=9416 (on 29.05.2006); Ars Technica (Nate Anderson), With Katrina behind it, Louisiana tackles next big problem: video games, 19.05.2006, retrieved from http://arstechnica.com/news.ars/post/20060519-6874.html (on 29.05.2006); Ars Technica (Eric Bangeman), ESA backs Maryland video game sales restrictions, 24.05.2006, retrieved from http://arstechnica.com/news.ars/post/20060524-6907.html (on 29.05.2006).

[314] Etzioni, Amitai, On protecting children from speech (Symposium Do children have the same First Amendment rights as adults?), *Chicago-Kent Law Review* 2004, Vol. 79, No. 1, 6.

COMMUNICATIONS DECENCY ACT – The *Communications Decency Act* of 1996 (CDA) set the tone of this intervention.[315] As a result of the CDA, "*knowingly*" transmitting "*indecent*", "*obscene*" or "*patently offensive*" online content to recipients under eighteen years of age could result in a fine or imprisonment.[316, 317] However, the Supreme Court judged that these provisions abridged the freedom of speech principles protected by the First Amendment, and overturned them.[318] The Court considered these aspects of the CDA too vague, given the inconsistent and undefined terms 'indecent' and 'patently offensive',[319] and deemed this vagueness problematic for two reasons: first, because the CDA is a content-based regulation of speech, and second, because of the severity of the criminal sanctions. Both of these factors, linked to the use of vague notions, raised serious First Amendment concerns because they could lead to a chilling effect on free speech. The serious penalties, for instance, may have caused "*speakers to remain silent rather than communicate even arguably unlawful words, ideas and images*".[320] The Court summarised as follows:

> *[a]lthough the Government has an interest in protecting children from potentially harmful materials [. . .] the CDA pursues that interest by suppressing a large*

---

[315] *Communications Decency Act*, Pub. L. No. 104–104, 110 Stat. 133.

[316] *Communications Decency Act*, SEC 502.

[317] In two circumstances one can defend oneself against prosecution: if one "*(A) has taken, in good faith, reasonable, effective, and appropriate actions under the circumstances to restrict or prevent access by minors to a communication specified in such subsections, which may involve any appropriate measures to restrict minors from such communications, including any method which is feasible under available technology; or (B) has restricted access to such communication, by requiring use of a verified credit card, debit account, adult access code, or adult personal identification number*" (*Communications Decency Act*, SEC. 502).

[318] *Reno v. American Civil Liberties Union*, 521 U.S. 844 (1997), 844. For an analysis of the Court's decision, cf. SOSNAY, Jacob A., "Regulating minors' access to pornography via the Internet: what options do Congress have left?", *The John Marshall Journal of Computer & Information Law* 2005, Vol. 23, No. 2, 461–465.

[319] The Court argued: "*Given the absence of definition of either term, this difference in language will provoke uncertainty among speakers about how the two standards relate to each other and just what they mean. [. . .] This uncertainty undermines the likelihood that the CDA has been carefully tailored enough to the congressional goal of protecting minors from potentially harmful materials*". Furthermore, the Court observed that "*[t]he general, undefined terms 'indecent' and 'patently offensive' cover large amounts of non-pornographic material with serious educational or other value*". Cf. *Reno v. American Civil Liberties Union*, 521 U.S. 844 (1997), 846 and 877.

[320] *Reno v. American Civil Liberties Union*, 521 U.S. 844 (1997), 872.

amount of speech that adults have a constitutional right to send and receive […]".[321, 322]

Moreover, the Court reasoned that this heavy burden on (adult) speech was "*unacceptable if less restrictive alternatives would be at least as effective in achieving the legitimate purpose that the statute was enacted to serve*".[323] Given the breadth of the CDA, the Court argued that it would be difficult for the government to clarify why there were no less restrictive alternatives available,[324] and decided that the government indeed had failed to do so. Overall, the Supreme Court carefully balanced the governmental interest in protecting children from harmful materials against the freedom of speech of adults and concluded that the latter was disproportionately restricted.[325]

Child Online Protection Act – The *Child Online Protection Act of 1998* (COPA), although slightly more narrowly tailored,[326] roughly met with the same fate.[327] Assuming that "*a prohibition on the distribution of material harmful to minors, combined with legitimate defenses, currently is the most effective and least restrictive means by which to satisfy the compelling*

---

[321] *Reno v. American Civil Liberties Union*, 521 U.S. 844 (1997), 846.

[322] Along the same lines, the Court noted: "*Given the vague contours of the coverage of the statute, it unquestionably silences some speakers whose messages would be entitled to constitutional protection*", *Reno v. American Civil Liberties Union*, 521 U.S. 844 (1997), 874.

[323] *Reno v. American Civil Liberties Union*, 521 U.S. 844 (1997), 874.

[324] A less restrictive alternative could for instance be user-based filtering software: Nunziato, Dawn, "Toward a constitutional regulation of minors' access to harmful internet speech", *Chicago-Kent Law Review* 2004, Issue 79, 132.

[325] Judge Stevens' opinion also referred to earlier Supreme Court cases (such as *Denver Area Ed. Telecommunications Consortium, Inc. v. FCC*, 518 U.S. 727 (1996); and *Sable Communications v. FCC*, 492 U.S. 115 (1989)) which stated that "*the Government may not reduce adult population to only what is fit for children*". Along the same lines in *Bolger v. Young Drugs Products Corp.*, 463 U.S. 60 (1983), the Court argued that "*[t]he level of discourse reaching a mailbox simply cannot be limited to that which would be suitable for a sandbox*" (pp. 74–75).

[326] Lessig, Lawrence and Resnick, Paul, "Zoning speech on the Internet: a legal and technical model", *Michigan Law Review* 1999, Vol. 98, Issue 2, 398; Sosnay, Jacob A., "Regulating minors' access to pornography via the Internet: what options do Congress have left?", *The John Marshall Journal of Computer & Information Law* 2005, Vol. 23, No. 2, 455 and 465: "*Specifically, in response to the Court's concerns with the CDA's over-breadth, Congress limited COPA in three ways. First, unlike the CDA, which applied to the Internet as a whole, COPA only applied to content displayed on the World Wide Web. Second, COPA only applied to communications made for 'commercial purposes'. Finally, unlike the CDA, which sought to prohibit indecent and patently offensive communications, COPA only restricted that material which is 'harmful to minors'*".

[327] *Child Online Protection Act*, Pub. L. No. 105–227, 112 Stat. 2681–736.

government interest",[328] this Act criminalised the communication of content 'harmful to minors'[329] for commercial purposes, except when access by minors had been restricted through verification of the Internet user's identity (e.g., by requiring a credit card number, digital age certificate, or any other reasonable measures feasible under available technology).[330] Again, severe penalties were established. After being reviewed a number of times in different courts,[331] the Supreme Court decided in June 2004 to enjoin the enforcement of COPA because of its probable violation of the First Amendment, given the fact that the government failed to meet its burden to prove that the alternatives proposed by the plaintiffs (for instance blocking and filtering software) would not be as effective as COPA.[332] The Supreme Court pointed out that filters, although not a perfect solution,[333] "*impose selective restric-*

[328] *Child Online Protection Act*, SEC. 1402 (Congressional findings).

[329] Defined as: "*any communication, picture, image, graphic image file, article, recording, writing, or other matter of any kind that is obscene or that – (A) the average person, applying contemporary community standards, would find, taking the material as a whole and with respect to minors, is designed to appeal to, or is designed to pander to, the prurient interest; (B) depicts, describes, or represents, in a manner patently offensive with respect to minors, an actual or simulated sexual act or sexual contact, an actual or simulated normal or perverted sexual act, or a lewd exhibition of the genitals or post-pubescent female breast; and (C) taken as a whole, lacks serious literary, artistic, political, or scientific value for minors*" (*Child Online Protection Act*, SEC. 1403).

[330] *Child Online Protection Act*, SEC. 1403: "*It is an affirmative defense to prosecution under this section that the defendant, in good faith, has restricted access by minors to material that is harmful to minors – (A) by requiring use of a credit card, debit account, adult access code, or adult personal identification number; (B) by accepting a digital certificate that verifies age; or (C) by any other reasonable measures that are feasible under available technology*".

[331] For instance, the District Court: *ACLU v. Reno*, 31 F. Supp. 2d 473 (E.D. Pa.1999), 476; the Third Circuit Court: *ACLU v. Reno*, 217 F.3d 162 (3d. Cir. 2000), 173–174; the Supreme Court: *Ashcroft v. ACLU*, 535 U.S. 564 (2002) and the Third Circuit Court on remand: *ACLU v. Ashcroft*, 322 F.3d 240 (C.A.3 (Pa.) 2003), 265–67. For a thorough analysis of these decisions: cf. Nunziato, Dawn, "Toward a constitutional regulation of minors' access to harmful internet speech", *Chicago-Kent Law Review* 2004, Issue 79, 133–140; Corn-Revere, Robert, "Ashcroft v. ACLU II: the beat goes on", *Cato Supreme Court Review* 2003–2004, 299–326.

[332] *Ashcroft v. American Civil Liberties Union*, 542 U.S. 656 (2004), 658.

[333] More specifically, filters may "*block some materials that are not harmful to minors and fail to catch some that are*": *Ashcroft v. American Civil Liberties Union*, 542 U.S. 656 (2004), 657–658. For strong criticism on the use of filters, see Judge Breyers's dissenting opinion: *Ashcroft v. American Civil Liberties Union*, 542 U.S. 656 (2004), 676–691. Interestingly, with respect to the argument that filtering is not an available alternative because Congress may not require it to be used and hence its success depends on the actual application of the software by parents, the Court stated that "*the need for parental cooperation does not automatically disqualify a proposed less restrictive alternative*" (*Ashcroft v. American Civil Liberties Union*, 542 U.S. 656 (2004), 669) and, furthermore, "*Congress undoubtedly may*

tions on speech at the receiving end, not universal restrictions at the source", and thus may well have been more effective than COPA.[334] Reverting to the *Playboy* case,[335] the Court recalled the line of reasoning that "*absent a showing that a less restrictive technological alternative already available to parents would not be as effective as a blanket speech restriction, the more restrictive option preferred by Congress could not survive strict scrutiny*".[336] In the end, the case was thus remanded to the E.D. Pennsylvania District Court with the order to undertake an investigation into recent technological developments to protect minors that would inflict fewer restrictions on freedom of expression and to examine whether the District Court's original decision that the use of filtering was better than COPA still prevailed.[337] Judge Reed of the District Court issued his (remanded) judgment in March 2007,[338] upholding the decision that COPA facially violates the First (and Fifth) Amendment. Arguments supporting the decision are that COPA was not narrowly tailored to Congress's compelling interest; the defendant (the US government) failed to meet its burden of showing that COPA is the least restrictive, most effective alternative in achieving the compelling interest; and COPA was impermissibly vague and overbroad.[339] The District Court's decision contains an analysis of the amount of sexually explicit material available on the Internet, and of the effectiveness of filtering technology and age and data verification technologies.[340] Based on this evidence, Judge Reed was of the opinion

---

act to encourage the use of filters" (*Ashcroft v. American Civil Liberties Union,* 542 U.S. 656 (2004), 669). Cf. also Corn-Revere, Robert, "Ashcroft v. ACLU II: the beat goes on", *Cato Supreme Court Review* 2003–2004, 312.

334 "*Promoting filter use does not condemn as criminal any category of speech, and so the potential chilling effect is eliminated, or at least much diminished. Filters, moreover, may well be more effective than COPA*": *American Civil Liberties Union,* 542 U.S. 656 (2004), 667.

335 *United States v. Playboy Entertainment Group, Inc.*, 529 U.S. 803 (2000).

336 *American Civil Liberties Union*, 542 U.S. 656 (2004), 670.

337 The Court reasoned that "*[i]t [was] reasonable to assume that technological developments important to the First Amendment analysis [had] occurred since the District Court made its factfindings*": *Ashcroft v. American Civil Liberties Union,* 542 U.S. 656 (2004), 658.

338 *American Civil Liberties Union v. Gonzales*, 478 F.Supp.2d 775 (E.D.Pa. 2007).

339 *American Civil Liberties Union v. Gonzales*, 478 F.Supp.2d 775 (E.D.Pa. 2007), final adjudication.

340 The latter services are mentioned in the affirmative defenses included in COPA, cf. *supra* footnote 330. The use of these technologies cause privacy concerns, cf. *American Civil Liberties Union v. Gonzales*, 478 F.Supp.2d 775 (E.D.Pa. 2007), 805 *et seq*. The Court found that credit cards, debit accounts, adult access codes and adult personal identification numbers do not actually verify age. Furthermore, these measures also give rise to significant First Amendment concerns: the chilling effect on free speech, the impermissible burden on Web site operators to demonstrate that their speech is lawful, the substantial economic burdens on the exercise of protected speech because the technologies involve significant

that COPA is both over and under-inclusive and that again, the government failed to show that it was the least restrictive alternative:

> *Although filters are not perfect and are prone to some over and under blocking, the evidence shows that they are at least as effective, and in fact, are more effective than COPA in furthering Congress' stated goal for a variety of reasons.*[341]

Together with the finding that COPA is unconstitutionally vague and overbroad, this led the Judge to enter a permanent injunction against the enforcement of COPA.[342] This judgment was confirmed by the 3rd U.S. Circuit Court of Appeals in July 2008.[343]

Children's Internet Protection Act – In contrast to the two previous Acts, the 2000 *Children's Internet Protection Act* (CIPA),[344] aimed at children's use of the Internet in schools and libraries, was found to be constitutional by the Supreme Court.[345] CIPA links the funding for schools and libraries to the use of filtering technology on computer terminals that provide access to the Internet. Computers that are used by minors need to be equipped with 'a technology protection measure' that protects against access to visual depictions that are obscene, involve child pornography, or are harmful to minors, and, additionally, the operation of this protection measure needs to be enforced during any use of such computers by minors.[346] Computers that are not used by minors need to be able to filter out obscene and child pornography content.[347] This Act was challenged as well. However, this time – after being found "*facially invalid*" by the District Court for the Eastern District of Pennsylvania –[348] the Supreme Court decided that the Act complies with the Constitution.[349] According to the Supreme Court, the use of Internet filtering software by libraries does not violate their patrons' First Amendment

cost and the loss of visitors, especially to operators who provide their content for free: cf. *American Civil Liberties Union v. Gonzales*, 478 F.Supp.2d 775 (E.D.Pa. 2007), 811 *et seq.*

341 *American Civil Liberties Union v. Gonzales*, 478 F.Supp.2d 775 (E.D.Pa. 2007), 814 *et seq.*

342 *American Civil Liberties Union v. Gonzales*, 478 F.Supp.2d 775 (E.D.Pa. 2007), 820. Interestingly, Judge Reed noted that he personally regretted "*having to set aside yet another attempt to protect our children from harmful material*" (p. 820).

343 *American Civil Liberties Union v. Mukasey*, 534 F.3d 181 (C.A.3 (Pa.) 2008).

344 *Children's Internet Protection Act*, Pub. L. No. 106–554, 114 Stat. 2763, 2763A-336.

345 *United States et al. v. American Library Association Inc. et al.*, 539 U.S. 194 (2003).

346 *Children's Internet Protection Act*, SEC. 1711 and SEC. 1712.

347 *Children's Internet Protection Act*, SEC. 1711 and SEC. 1712.

348 *United States et al. v. American Library Association Inc. et al.*, 539 U.S. 194 (2003), 194.

349 *United States et al. v. American Library Association Inc. et al.*, 539 U.S. 194 (2003), 194.

rights.[350] The Court justified its position by referring to the societal role of libraries as a main argument:

> *Internet terminals are not acquired by a library in order to create a public forum for Web publishers to express themselves. Rather a library provides such access for the same reasons it offers other library resources: to facilitate research, learning, and recreational pursuits by furnishing materials of requisite and appropriate quality.*[351]

To fulfil these tasks, it is considered necessary that libraries can decide what material to provide to their patrons.[352] It is, for instance, possible for libraries to decide to ban pornography from their print collections. Hence, according to the Court, it would be irrational to approach libraries' judgments to block online pornography in a different manner.[353] The argument that filtering software 'overblocks' useful content is countered by the Court by referring to the ease with which patrons may ask for filtering software to be disabled.[354] Consequently, the Supreme Court reversed the decision of the District Court and found that CIPA does not induce libraries to violate the Constitution, since public libraries' use of Internet filtering software does not violate their patrons' First Amendment rights.[355] Although this legislative initiative was held up in court, it is important to recall that CIPA's scope was much more limited than the CDA and COPA.[356]

Constitutional test – So far, the use of legislation to protect minors against harmful online content has in the majority of cases not stood the constitutional

---

[350] *United States et al. v. American Library Association Inc. et al.*, 539 U.S. 194 (2003), 194.

[351] *United States et al. v. American Library Association Inc. et al.*, 539 U.S. 194 (2003), 194.

[352] *United States et al. v. American Library Association Inc. et al.*, 539 U.S. 194 (2003), 204.

[353] *United States et al. v. American Library Association Inc. et al.*, 539 U.S. 194 (2003), 195.

[354] *United States et al. v. American Library Association Inc. et al.*, 539 U.S. 194 (2003), 195–196. CIPA states (SEC. 1711) that "*an administrator, supervisor or other person authorized by the certifying authority under subparagraph (A)(1) may disable the technology protection measures concerned, during use by an adult, to enable access for bona fide research or other lawful purpose*". The District Court had argued that this possibility was inadequate because some patrons may be too embarrassed to request the disabling (*American Library Association Inc. et al. v. United States et al.*, 201 F.Supp.2d 401 (E.D. Pa. 2002, 411). The Supreme Court, however, argued that "*the Constitution does not guarantee the right to acquire information at a public library without any risk of embarrassment*" (*United States et al. v. American Library Association Inc. et al.*, 539 U.S. 194 (2003), 209).

[355] *United States et al. v. American Library Association Inc. et al.*, 539 U.S. 194 (2003), 214.

[356] However, it has been argued that this approach is also not optimal: Etzioni, Amitai, On protecting children from speech (Symposium Do children have the same First Amendment rights as adults?), *Chicago-Kent Law Review* 2004, Vol. 79, No. 1, 9.

test in the United States.[357] Achieving the right balance between the fundamental right of freedom of expression and the protection of vulnerable Internet users is an intricate task, which is even more complicated due to the inherent characteristics of legislative instruments, such as rigidity, the fact that the initiative and implementation are solely left to the government, and the propensity for 'censorship' – i.e., infringing the First Amendment – when regulating content issues. Hence, it could be deduced from the CDA and COPA decisions that initiatives in which the private sector plays a greater role, or schemes aimed at the empowering and educating of children would probably meet with greater approval from the courts.[358, 359] A recent proposal in this context, which might be accepted by the courts is the *Safeguarding America's Families by Enhancing and Reorganizing New and Efficient Technologies Act of 2007* (the *SAFER NET Act*), which aims to improve public

[357] Apart from CDA, COPA and CIPA, several other legislative proposals aimed at the online protection of minors have been submitted over the past years. Almost all of these proposals, however, have been the target of fierce criticism. Cf. Center for Democracy and Technology, "Child safety and free speech issues in the 110th Congress", 15.02.2007, retrieved from http://www.cdt.org/speech/20070215freespeechincongress.pdf (on 27.04.2007).

[358] In the *ACLU v. Gonzales* case, Judge Reed emphasised that "*in conjunction with the private use of filters, the government may promote and support their use by, for example, providing further education and training programs to caregivers, giving incentives or mandates to ISP's to provide filters to their subscribers, directing the developers of computer operating systems to provide filters and parental controls as a part of their products [...], subsidizing the purchase of filters for those who cannot afford them, and by performing further studies and recommendations regarding filters*": *American Civil Liberties Union v. Gonzales*, 478 F.Supp.2d 775 (E.D.Pa. 2007), 814. Cf. also: Center for Democracy & Technology, Policy Post 13.4: Federal Court rejects censorship, endorses user empowerment, 23.03.2007, retrieved from http://www.cdt.org/publications/policyposts/2007/4 (on 07.05.2007).

[359] The Progress & Freedom Foundation Blog (Adam Thierer), Summary of latest ICRA Summit on Internet free expression and child protection, 15.09.2006, retrieved from http://blog.pff.org/archives/2006/09/summary_of_late.html#more (on 20.09.2006). However, Thierer also points to the danger that "*[i]f the government somehow convinced the courts that filters were not an effective tool of private content control, then we could be on the verge of a major legislative / regulatory push for more government content regulation in the name of 'protecting the children'*". According to him, "*[t]hat's why it is important for industry to coordinate and redouble their efforts now to head-off this threat. If the courts see industry stepping-up and doing more, it could help tip the balance in important cases currently pending or coming soon before them for consideration*". Furthermore, it can be noted that the United States already have a tradition of trying to empower parents by means of a technological tool, i.e., the V-chip used in broadcasting (cf. http://www.fcc.gov/vchip/ – used in broadcasting). However, not everyone has deemed the use of the V-chip an overwhelming success: Etzioni, Amitai, On protecting children from speech (Symposium Do children have the same First Amendment rights as adults?), *Chicago-Kent Law Review* 2004, Vol. 79, No. 1, 24–27.

awareness in the United States of the safe use of the Internet through the establishment of an Office of Internet Safety and Public Awareness within the Federal Trade Commission.[360] Awareness, education and promotion of Internet safety are the key elements of the bill. It has been stressed by various commentators that such an approach would fall within the boundaries of the First Amendment.[361]

1.2.5. *The need for a broader regulatory framework*

Thinking out of the 'legislation box' – A number of factors have led to the realisation that (traditional) legislation might not be the panacea to efficiently regulate the digital media environment.

General factors: clashing characteristics – The complexity of the new media landscape is irreconcilable with a legislative model that is built around detailed regulation and central control.[362] As described above, various characteristics of the new information and communication networks clash with a number of features typical of legislation.

Specific factors: protection minors against harmful content – Protecting minors against harmful content is an extremely delicate issue with regard to which competing interests must be appropriately balanced. As can be deduced from the situation in the United States, it is very hard to delineate the scope of the legislation in a sufficiently careful manner.

---

[360] H.R. 1008, 110th Congress, retrieved from http://thomas.loc.gov/cgi-bin/query/D?c110:1:./temp/~c110Pufhnj:: (on 19.12.2008).

[361] Cf. Thierer, Adam, "Rep. Bean's 'SAFER NET Act': an education-based approach to online child safety", Progress on Point 14.3, February 2007, retrieved from http://www.pff.org/issues-pubs/pops/pop14.3beanbillinternetsafety.pdf (on 27.04.2007); Center for Democracy and Technology, "Child safety and free speech issues in the 110th Congress", 15.02.2007, retrieved from http://www.cdt.org/speech/20070215freespeechincongress.pdf (on 27.04.2007), 9; The Progress & Freedom Foundation, Cyber Safety in a Web 2.0 World: what parents and policymakers need to know, 25.12.2007, retrieved from http://www.pff.org/issues-pubs/pops/pop14.25cybersafetyweb.pdf (on 16.01.2008).

[362] Wetenschappelijke Raad voor het Regeringsbeleid, Focus op functies – Uitdagingen voor een toekomstbestendig mediabeleid [*Focus on functions – Challenges for a future proof media policy*], Amsterdam, Amsterdam University Press, 2005, retrieved from http://www.wrr.nl/dsc?c=getobject&s=obj&!sessionid=1o7p!cnhb9o!M9xXGwuyBPekM35UuYCWRZ1zyOvsfxauyo3h50uVxzYXp1K38HdW&objectid=2799&!dsname=default&isapidir=/gvisapi/ (on 27.07.2007) [in Dutch].

Alternative approaches – At the EU level, from very early on, it was stressed that legislation might not be the most suitable means to achieve the policy goal of protecting minors in the digital media environment.[363] The next section will thus examine the history of such policies at the EU level, from which a preference for the use of alternative regulatory mechanisms will become apparent. In this respect, the issue of responsibility is essential (cf. *supra*). Different actors play a role in keeping minors from harmful material: public authorities, industry, parents, teachers and other caregivers[364] all therefore need to assume some responsibility to achieve this goal in an effective manner. The concept of 'alternative regulatory instruments' – often suggested as the solution to the deficit of legislation in this area – will then be described and analysed in the next chapter.

1.2.6. *EU policy history: the protection of minors against harmful digital media content*

Policy goal still valid – As discussed above, there has never been any doubt that the policy goal of protecting children and young people against harmful media content remains valid in the new media environment.[365] Thus, early on, the European Commission emphasised that "*the protection*

[363] Commission of the European Communities, Green Paper on the protection of minors and human dignity in audiovisual and information services, COM (1996) 483 final, 16.10.1996 (cf. *infra*); Commission of the European Communities, Communication to the European Parliament, the Council, the Economic and Social Committee and the Committee of the Regions, Illegal and harmful content on the Internet, COM (1996) 487, 16.10.1996, retrieved from http://ec.europa.eu/archives/ISPO/legal/en/internet/communic.html (on 25.03.2008) (cf. *infra*); Commission of the European Communities, Communication from the Commission to the Council, the European Parliament, the Economic and Social Committee and the Committee of the Regions on the follow-up to the Green Paper on the protection of minors and human dignity in audiovisual and information services, including a Proposal for a Council Recommendation concerning the protection of minors and human dignity in audiovisual and information services, COM (97) 570 final, 18.11.1997, 1 (cf. *infra*): "*In the field of television, a coherent and tested regulatory framework is in place at national and Community level, but the use of digital technology makes it necessary to look at new methods of protecting minors. There have been real difficulties in applying laws and general principles to the online services sector: the first national initiatives to adapt to the new services have taken the form of self-regulation as a supplement to existing legislation, in the form of voluntary action by the parties concerned*".

[364] Commission of the European Communities, Green Paper on the protection of minors and human dignity in audiovisual and information services, COM (1996) 483 final, 16.10.1996.

[365] Commission of the European Communities, Green Paper on the protection of minors and human dignity in audiovisual and information services, COM (1996) 483 final,

of minors and human dignity is an essential prerequisite to establishing the climate of trust needed for the development of the audiovisual and information services industry".[366]

Overview and analysis – In this section, we take a closer look at the most important policy documents concerning the protection of minors against harmful digital media content, from the mid-1990s onwards.

A. *Communication Illegal and Harmful Content on the Internet*

Communication – The specific issue of 'illegal and harmful Internet content' was first addressed by the European Commission in 1996.[367] A first official Commission document, the Communication on 'Illegal and harmful content on the Internet',[368] was adopted in October of that year. While it assumed that although the majority of Internet content has a legitimate purpose, the Commission pointed to the fact that – as is the case with any communication technology – certain online information is potentially harmful or illegal. In this respect, national security, protection of minors, protection of human dignity, economic security, information security, protection of privacy, protection of reputation and intellectual property were (and still are) considered to be areas of concern. With regard to these possibly threatened values, the Commission attached major importance to "*the need to strike the*

16.10.1996, 38: "*The protection of minors against material which might harm their physical or mental development is an almost universal objective*".

[366] Commission of the European Communities, Communication from the Commission to the Council, the European Parliament, the Economic and Social Committee and the Committee of the Regions on the follow-up to the Green Paper on the protection of minors and human dignity in audiovisual and information services, including a Proposal for a Council Recommendation concerning the protection of minors and human dignity in audiovisual and information services, COM (97) 570 final, 18.11.1997.

[367] In April, at an informal Council meeting of the Ministers of Telecommunications and Culture, the issue of illegal and harmful content on the Internet was identified as an urgent priority for analysis and action: Commission of the European Communities, Working party on illegal and harmful content on the Internet – Report, presented to the Council on 28.11.1996, retrieved from http://europa.eu.int/ISPO/legal/en/internet/wpen.html (on 18.05.2006). Cf. *infra*.

[368] Commission of the European Communities, Communication to the European Parliament, the Council, the Economic and Social Committee and the Committee of the Regions, Illegal and harmful content on the Internet, COM (1996) 487, 16.10.1996, retrieved from http://ec.europa.eu/archives/ISPO/legal/en/internet/communic.html (on 25.03.2008).

right balance between ensuring the free flow of information and guaranteeing protection of the public interest".[369]

The Communication did not specifically address the protection of minors and human dignity,[370] but concentrated instead on the opportunities offered by the Internet (social, cultural, educational and economic),[371] the description of the technical environment of the Internet, the identification of variations of illegal and harmful content, and policy options for immediate action to counter such content on the Internet. The two latter topics are of interest to our research subject. It was stressed that the Internet does not exist in a legal vacuum, and, furthermore, that it is thus crucial to distinguish between illegal[372] and harmful content. In the words of the Commission:

> *[t]hese different categories of content pose radically different issues of principle, and call for very different legal and technological responses. It would be dangerous to amalgamate separate issues such as children accessing pornographic content for adults, and adults accessing pornography about children.*[373]

With respect to regulation of content, the availability of practical means to limit access by vulnerable persons to harmful material was considered key. First, however, the importance of respecting the freedom of expression, as well as the principles governing the internal market (more specifically, the free provision of services, *infra*)[374] and competition rules, was reiterated.

---

[369] Commission of the European Communities, Communication to the European Parliament, the Council, the Economic and Social Committee and the Committee of the Regions, Illegal and harmful content on the Internet, COM (1996) 487, 16.10.1996, retrieved from http://ec.europa.eu/archives/ISPO/legal/en/internet/communic.html (on 25.03.2008), 4.

[370] Cf. *infra*: Green Paper on the protection of minors and human dignity in audiovisual and information services, COM (1996) 483 final, 16.10.1996.

[371] "*The framework for the Internet should, therefore,* foster economic development, *while taking account of* justified social and societal concerns" [original italics]: Commission of the European Communities, Communication to the European Parliament, the Council, the Economic and Social Committee and the Committee of the Regions, Illegal and harmful content on the Internet, COM (1996) 487, 16.10.1996, retrieved from http://ec.europa.eu/archives/ISPO/legal/en/internet/communic.html (on 25.03.2008), 7.

[372] With respect to illegal content it was made clear that the maxim "*what is illegal offline, remains illegal online*" is fully applicable. Moreover, Member States carry the responsibility of enforcing their existing legislation. There is, however, a Community aspect which needs to be taken into account as adopting new Internet services regulations could lead to distortions of competition and the re-fragmentation of the internal market.

[373] Commission of the European Communities, Communication to the European Parliament, the Council, the Economic and Social Committee and the Committee of the Regions, Illegal and harmful content on the Internet, COM (1996) 487, 16.10.1996, retrieved from http://ec.europa.eu/archives/ISPO/legal/en/internet/communic.html (on 25.03.2008), 10.

[374] The freedom to provide services may only be limited when the principle of proportionality is adhered to, i.e., "*the measure must be appropriate to achieve the pursued objective and may not exceed what is necessary to achieve this aim*" (*infra*).

With these principles in mind, the Commission proposed to turn to practical instruments, such as parental control software, filtering technology, European rating systems and education to deal with harmful content. Significantly, the Commission argued that contrary to 'upstream censorship' by official agencies (i.e., prevention of illegal content from being published at all), filtering provides for 'downstream control' by parents (i.e., prevention of harmful content from reaching minors). The filtering model, which can – according to the Commission – be used in three different manners, i.e., blacklisting,[375] whitelisting[376] or neutral labelling,[377] was considered a pragmatic, instead of a legal, approach to the availability of harmful online content, although legal implications could not be ruled out (for instance, by exonerating access providers from liability). The Commission was, at that moment in time, inclined towards an overall positive evaluation of filtering systems. Furthermore, to ensure a comprehensive approach, the development of European rating mechanisms, filtering software, reporting mechanisms (i.e., hotlines), and awareness activities was encouraged. To conclude, the Commission proposed a number of measures for immediate action. Regarding harmful content, the main point of action was labelled "*Community action to support use of filtering software and rating systems*".[378]

---

375 Access to listed sites is blocked.

376 Access is only possible to listed sites.

377 Sites are labelled or rated (for example, using the PICS standard), but the user decides how to use the label or rating. PICS (Platform for Internet Selection) is a global standard developed and launched by the World Wide Web Consortium which 'tags' sites with 'value-neutral labels': Commission of the European Communities, Communication to the European Parliament, the Council, the Economic and Social Committee and the Committee of the Regions, Illegal and harmful content on the Internet, COM (1996) 487, 16.10.1996, retrieved from http://ec.europa.eu/archives/ISPO/legal/en/internet/communic.html (on 25.03.2008), 5.d. PICS: a global industry standard). The Commission claimed in the Communication that "*PICS-compatible applications [...] provide an effective technology for the indexing and screening of content – and a flexible and inexpensive solution to the differences of sensibilities between various families and cultures*" (p. 22). Cf. *infra*.

378 More specifically: "*(1) A Council recommendation could be envisaged setting out a clear political message encouraging the use of filtering software such as PICS, and for one or more European rating systems. The Commission has already called upon the industry to form a common platform enabling the use of filtering systems Community-wide; (2) European content producers should be encouraged to co-operate in this system by adopting their own Code of Conduct for content published on the Internet; including systematic self-rating of content; and (3) A Commission initiative will support national awareness actions for parents and teachers*": Commission of the European Communities, Communication to the European Parliament, the Council, the Economic and Social Committee and the Committee of the Regions, Illegal and harmful content on the Internet, COM (1996) 487, 16.10.1996, retrieved from http://ec.europa.eu/archives/ISPO/legal/en/internet/communic.html (on 25.03.2008), 6.2. In comparison, the measures to be taken in the field of illegal

Parliament resolution – In April 1997, the European Parliament issued a Resolution on the Communication[379] in which fundamental rights, such as privacy and the free communication of ideas and opinions, and public interest goals, such as the protection of children, were put forward as being primordial. It should be noted, however, that although the Parliament stresses the distinction between illegal and harmful content as being fundamental, the notion 'illegal' and 'harmful' are used in an inconsistent and confusing way throughout the text of the Resolution.[380]

Specifically, with respect to harmful content, the Parliament insisted on the "*primacy of individual responsibility, especially within the family*".[381] Public action, however, could also play a complementary role. Furthermore, in line with the European Commission, self-regulation and the use of technology seemed to be the tools favoured by the European Parliament: the establishment of a common European rating system, parental control systems using filtering techniques[382] and reporting mechanisms such as hotlines were

---

content were: cooperation between Member States, liability of access providers and host service providers, and encouragement of self-regulation.

[379] European Parliament, Resolution on the Commission Communication on illegal and harmful content on the Internet, A4-0098/97, 24.07.1997, retrieved from http://ec.europa.eu/archives/ISPO/legal/en/internet/98–97en.html (on 17.05.2006, no longer available).

[380] For instance: "*17. Underlines that the Internet can be used as a tool for the distribution of harmful sex-related material when and if the persons depicted are sexually exploited and their personal integrity and dignity degraded; finds the misuse of children for these purposes particularly harmful and despicable; is convinced that national legislation is insufficient to reduce the harmful effects of this truly global industry*". Although this recital concerns child pornography the notion 'harmful' is used twice. Although there can be no question that this kind of content is harmful, it is foremost illegal. It would be helpful if such adjectives be used in a consistent and coherent manner.

[381] European Parliament, Resolution on the Commission Communication on illegal and harmful content on the Internet, A4-0098/97, 24.07.1997, retrieved from http://ec.europa.eu/archives/ISPO/legal/en/internet/98–97en.html (on 17.05.2006, no longer available), 33. See also para. O: "*whereas telematic networks can easily bring into the home material denying human dignity and can encourage certain forms of criminal behaviour; whereas therefore it is above all essential for the individual and the family to take a responsible and critical approach when using telematic equipment*"; and para. 9: "*urges Member States to introduce suitable forms of instruction in their education systems to enable children to develop a capacity for critical analysis of visual messages on the electronic media in parallel with the written word; underlines parents' role in this respect*".

[382] On the other hand, the Parliament notes that "*the problem of harmful content on the Internet resembles the problem that also arises with conventional means of communication, so that the introduction of filtering software (PICS) will not solve the problem until questions of classification and coding have been sufficiently clarified*": European Parliament, Resolution on the Commission Communication on illegal and harmful content on the

encouraged.[383] The Parliament also suggested creating a cross-border quality rating system for Internet service providers,[384] to guarantee that service providers do not work together with persons who disseminate illegal and harmful content and, hence, service providers would be prompted to scrutinise and maintain the quality of the information content of their systems.

B. *Green Paper on the protection of minors and human dignity in audiovisual and information services*[385]

Green Paper – In 1996, the protection of minors was identified as a legal priority in the annual report of the Information Society Forum.[386] The

Internet, A4-0098/97, 24.07.1997, retrieved from http://ec.europa.eu/archives/ISPO/legal/en/internet/98–97en.html (on 17.05.2006, no longer available), 12.

383 Also, a rather bizarre and vaguely formulated suggestion was made to establish "*measures at the European level that [would] impose unique sender-recognition codes for all providers of data over the Internet and commit access and service providers to the following minimum standards: in respect of data made available by themselves, to accept full responsibility, including full criminal-law responsibility; in respect of any criminally unlawful content of third-party services provided by them, to accept responsibility if they are expressly aware of the specific contents and if it is technically possible and reasonable for them to prevent their use; in the case of non-criminal content, access and service providers must establish effective self-regulation mechanisms*": European Parliament, Resolution on the Commission Communication on illegal and harmful content on the Internet, A4-0098/97, 24.07.1997, retrieved from http://ec.europa.eu/archives/ISPO/legal/en/internet/98–97en.html (on 17.05.2006, no longer available), 35. Cf. under para. Q: "*whereas regulation requires that each level of responsibility be defined, with a clear distinction drawn between the access or service provider and the user*"; and under para. 22: "*underlines that access and service providers' liability should be regulated at the international level*". It is important to note that these statements concerning liability precede the e-Commerce Directive, in which a liability regime for Internet service providers was established (cf. *infra*, Part 2, Chapter 1).

384 European Parliament, Resolution on the Commission Communication on illegal and harmful content on the Internet, A4-0098/97, 24.07.1997, retrieved from http://ec.europa.eu/archives/ISPO/legal/en/internet/98–97en.html (on 17.05.2006, no longer available), 7.

385 "*Green papers are discussion papers published by the Commission on a specific policy area. Primarily they are documents addressed to interested parties – organisations and individuals – who are invited to participate in a process of consultation and debate. In some cases they provide an impetus for subsequent legislation*": http://europa.eu.int/documents/comm/index_en.htm.

386 Information Society Forum, Networks for people and their communities – Making the most of the information society in the European Union, First Annual Report to the European Commission from the Information Society Forum, June 1996, retrieved from http://europa.eu.int/ISPO/policy/isf/documents/rep-96/ISF-REPORT-96.html#ch4 (on 30.05.2006, no longer available). The Information Society Forum was set up in 1995 by the European Commission as an independent advisory body.

adoption by the Commission of the Green Paper on the protection of minors and human dignity in audiovisual and information services,[387] on the same day as the Communication on Illegal and harmful content on the Internet, was thus not surprising.[388]

Balance – The Green Paper again pointed to the importance of "*striking the right balance between freedom of speech and public interest considerations, between policies designed to foster the emergence of new services and the need to ensure that the opportunities they create are not abused by the few at the expense of the many*" in the new information environment. It was stressed that if no effective steps to protect the public interest were taken, it could be feared that the new information and communication services would not reach their full economic, social and cultural potential.[389]

Changing media environment – The first chapter of the Green Paper also addressed the need to distinguish between illegal and harmful content on the one hand, and the changing audiovisual and information services context on the other hand. Thus, the Commission emphasised that whereas it is doubtful that new information and communication services carry more contentious material than the traditional media, these new services do make this material more visible and relatively more accessible.[390]

Legal framework – In the second chapter of the Green Paper the existing legal and constitutional arrangements at the EU and national levels were analysed (mostly with respect to harmful content). Freedom of expression and respect for privacy were put forward as fundamental EU principles. Furthermore, a number of patterns and specific problems emerged from an

---

[387] Commission of the European Communities, Green Paper on the protection of minors and human dignity in audiovisual and information services, COM (1996) 483 final, 16.10.1996.

[388] The Commission considers the two documents to be fully complementary regarding both their timing and scope: whereas the Communication proposes a number of short-term action items, the Green Paper is a consultative and more specific document with a longer term view. See: Commission of the European Communities, Green Paper on the protection of minors and human dignity in audiovisual and information services, COM (1996) 483 final, 16.10.1996, 1.

[389] Commission of the European Communities, Green Paper on the protection of minors and human dignity in audiovisual and information services, COM (1996) 483 final, 16.10.1996, 3.

[390] Commission of the European Communities, Green Paper on the protection of minors and human dignity in audiovisual and information services, COM (1996) 483 final, 16.10.1996, 11.

analysis of national regulations and other measures relating to the protection of minors and human dignity.

Illegal content – As mentioned above, a distinction was made between content that violates human dignity ('illegal content') and content that is harmful to children. According to the Green Paper, the protection of human dignity aims at "*prohibiting certain kinds of material considered as intolerable both for the individual and for the community at large and as going to the very roots of society, and, in particular human dignity*".[391] Examples of this kind of material are child pornography, violent pornography and material that incites to racial hatred or violence. With respect to this category of material, a coherent approach at the EU level, which would facilitate the application of national law while avoiding disproportionate obstacles to the trans-frontier development of services, was advocated.

Harmful content: controlling access – On the subject of harmful content, the Commission highlighted the need to ensure that children do not normally have access to material which could damage their physical or mental development, while at the same time allowing adults access to such material.[392] In this context, attention was brought to two topics: controlling access by minors to questionable material and labelling of material. Regarding the first topic, four systems of controlling access by minors to online content were proposed:

- "*Restrictions on computer use*", which "*enable parents to limit access by children to times when they are present*";
- "*Memory storage of navigation on the networks (sites accessed, messages exchanged, etc.)*", which "*enables parents to monitor the use their children actually make of services*";
- "*Systematic filtering of material*" which "*allows controversial material to be intercepted automatically [...]*"; and
- "*Blocking sites on a selective basis on the basis of a labelling system allowing material to be filtered by suitable software*".[393]

---

[391] Commission of the European Communities, Green Paper on the protection of minors and human dignity in audiovisual and information services, COM (1996) 483 final, 16.10.1996, 13.

[392] Commission of the European Communities, Green Paper on the protection of minors and human dignity in audiovisual and information services, COM (1996) 483 final, 16.10.1996, 15.

[393] Commission of the European Communities, Green Paper on the protection of minors and human dignity in audiovisual and information services, COM (1996) 483 final, 16.10.1996, 18.

At the time the document was issued these parental control systems were not functioning optimally, and therefore exploration of the potential in this field offered by digital technology was earmarked as a priority.[394] Furthermore, the question was asked whether the approach taken in the area of parental control should be based on legislation or self-regulation. It can be noted that, at that time, a number of self-regulatory or voluntary mechanisms had already been developed by the industry.

Harmful content: labelling and rating – In order for filtering and blocking systems[395] to function, information needs to be labelled. Hence, the Commission considered encouraging suppliers of content and third parties to label material made available as a priority for the harmonious development of control of material in general, and parental control in particular.[396] The chapter concluded with some comments on the topic of media education, stressing that parents and children must learn to use the new communication tools.[397]

Conclusion – The Green Paper concluded by emphasising the fundamental role the European Union had to play in the field of protecting minors against harmful new media content and by clarifying that the aim of the paper and the questions that were put forward were to help create the conditions for the establishment of a coherent framework for the protection of minors and human dignity in audiovisual and information services in the European Union.

[394] Annex IV of the Green Paper provides a description of technical and other non-regulatory protection measures, 47 *et seq*.

[395] Such possible systems involve blacklisting, whitelisting and neutral labelling: "*[1] black list filtering aims to block access to sites identified as problematic in view of the material they distribute (nudity, violence, sex, etc.) […]; [2] white list filtering authorizes access only to pre-determined sites; access to material is heavily limited; and [3] filtering based on neutral labelling gives users access to information on material loaded by suppliers or third parties on the basis of their own selection criteria*": Commission of the European Communities, Green Paper on the protection of minors and human dignity in audiovisual and information services, COM (1996) 483 final, 16.10.1996, 19.

[396] Commission of the European Communities, Green Paper on the protection of minors and human dignity in audiovisual and information services, COM (1996) 483 final, 16.10.1996, 20.

[397] Commission of the European Communities, Green Paper on the protection of minors and human dignity in audiovisual and information services, COM (1996) 483 final, 16.10.1996, 20.

C. *Council Resolution on illegal and harmful content on the Internet*

Working party – Another – parallel – series of policy documents concerning illegal and harmful content on the Internet were issued at EU Council level. In April 1996, at an informal Council meeting of the Ministers of Telecommunications and Culture, the issue of illegal and harmful content on the Internet was identified as "*an urgent priority for analysis and action*".[398] One of the results of the meeting was the establishment of a Working Party entrusted with analysing problems relating to illegal and harmful content.[399] The Telecommunications Council Meeting of 27 September 1996 extended the Working Party to including representatives of the Ministers of Telecommunication, access and service providers, content industries and users.[400] The Working Party was asked to create concrete proposals for possible measures to combat the illegal use of the Internet and similar networks.

Reports – At the November meeting of the Telecommunications Council, the first report of the Working Party on illegal and harmful content on the Internet was presented. A few months later, the Interim report on initiatives in EU Member States with respect to combating illegal and harmful content on the Internet, drafted by the Working Party, was published.[401] This report contained a detailed analysis of initiatives at the national and international levels and presented a number of proposals for further action relating to self-regulation, liability, technical measures, international cooperation and support measures (e.g., awareness and parental education).

---

398 Commission of the European Communities, Working party on illegal and harmful content on the Internet – Report, presented to the Council on 28.11.1996, retrieved from http://europa.eu.int/ISPO/legal/en/internet/wpen.html (last consulted on 18.05.2006, no longer available).

399 Commission of the European Communities, Working party on illegal and harmful content on the Internet – Report, presented to the Council on 28.11.1996, retrieved from http://europa.eu.int/ISPO/legal/en/internet/wpen.html (last consulted on 18.05.2006, no longer available).

400 Council of the European Communities, Press release Telecommunications Council 1949, Brussels, 27.09.1996, No. 10259/96, Press No. 247, retrieved from http://www.consilium.europa.eu/ueDocs/cms_Data/docs/pressdata/en/trans/019a0005.htm (on 18.05.2006).

401 Commission of the European Communities, Interim report on initiatives in EU Member States with respect to combating illegal and harmful content on the Internet, 04.06.1997, retrieved from http://ec.europa.eu/archives/ISPO/legal/en/internet/wp2en.html (on 17.05.2006).

Council Resolution – Following the Commission Communication on illegal and harmful content, and the activities of the Working Party, the Council issued a Resolution on illegal and harmful content on the Internet, in which the initiatives and activities of the Working Party were welcomed.[402] In addition, the Council invited the Member States to start undertaking concrete action (for instance, encouraging and facilitating self-regulatory systems and encouraging the use of filtering systems and the setting up of rating systems). Furthermore, the Council requested the Commission to ensure that these efforts were coherent and followed up, to foster coordination of self-regulatory and representative bodies, to promote and facilitate the exchange of information on best practices, to foster research into technical issues and, finally, to further reflect on the issue of legal liability for Internet content.[403]

D. *Green Paper on the protection of minors and human dignity: Follow-up & Consultation*

Working document – In June 1997 the Commission published the results of a consultation on the Green Paper in a working document.[404] Points of consensus and divergence between the consulted actors were clarified and a number of provisional conclusions were presented.

Consensus – Consulted parties, for instance, agreed on the principle that respect for the protection of minors and human dignity is a *sine qua non* for the development of new services. Furthermore, the importance of the fundamental rights of freedom of expression and respect for privacy was emphasised. Another point of agreement was the need to distinguish between illegal and harmful content, given that both kinds of content require different approaches and dissimilar solutions. A last – general – point of consensus was the need for the European Union to play a role in this field.

With respect to the legal framework, the Commission clarified that there was a broad agreement that there is no legal vacuum with regard to the protection of minors and human dignity, these principles being clearly enshrined

---

402 Council of the European Communities, Resolution of the Council and the Representatives of the Governments of the Member States, meeting within the Council of 17 February 1997 on illegal and harmful content on the Internet, *OJ* 06.03.1997, *C* 70, 1–2.

403 Council of the European Communities, Resolution of the Council and the Representatives of the Governments of the Member States, meeting within the Council of 17 February 1997 on illegal and harmful content on the Internet, *OJ* 06.03.1997, *C* 70, 1–2.

404 Commission of the European Communities, Commission working document Protection of minors and human dignity in audiovisual and information services: Consultations on the Green Paper, SEC (97) 1203, 13.06.1997.

in international and national law. At the same time, there also was a consensus that it is the *application* of these laws that pose problems, especially with respect to online services.

Specifically regarding the protection of minors and the use of parental control systems the consultations underlined a number of elements to keep in mind. First, it was agreed that parental control systems must not lead to a shift in responsibility from broadcasters to parents, and must complement rather than replace other existing systems. Second, emphasis was put on the need to introduce these mechanisms on a voluntary basis. Finally, it was considered essential to experiment with and evaluate different parental control systems. On that note, and particularly with regard to online services, attention was brought to the idea that although parental control systems, such as filter software, are indispensable, they are not in themselves sufficient. The adoption of good practices for the identification and presentation of offending material, promoted by self-regulation and possibly backed up by government measures, was considered primordial in this context. A related concern, i.e., the need to develop, with regard to the efficiency of parental control devices, a consistent system for labelling content, was also touched upon. In this context, a consensus emerged for the promotion of the PICS protocol.[405] Finally, information, education, awareness-raising, and positive measures promoting the access of children to the new services in public places and encouraging high-quality material aimed at minors were stated as additional essential elements of a strategy to protect children against harmful content.

Divergence – The most important quoted points of divergence between the different actors were the varying levels of maturity of the protection of minors debate itself across the European Union, the different degrees to which the involved parties had organised representative structures (for instance, related to self-regulation) and the priority objectives or approaches adopted in response to the problem. The different situations of Member States notwithstanding, there was a consensus on the need to share information and experiences at the EU level.

Proposals – Hence, the Commission working document concluded by suggesting two areas for development at the EU level: the coordination of national responses and community objectives[406] and closer cooperation and

[405] Cf. footnote 377.

[406] These objectives were described as follows: "*(1) to promote, in partnership with the public authorities and the different parties concerned, a framework of self-regulation of online services for the protection of minors and human dignity, (2) to encourage experimentation*

the pooling of experience at European and international level (especially in the field of justice and home affairs).[407] Regarding the former suggestion – the coordination of national responses – the Commission proposed to develop a framework of *self-regulation* of online services for the protection of minors and human dignity. To this end, all parties concerned were encouraged to participate in defining the rules of self-regulation, contribute to the supervision of their application, and play a part in the evaluation of the implemented system. The framework was supposed to supplement the existing regulatory systems and fully respect the powers of legal bodies, by adopting minimum rules.[408] Other points of action put forward were the clarification and adaptation of existing national legislation on the protection of minors and human dignity, the encouragement of broadcasters to experiment with new methods of protecting minors and informing consumers,[409] and the evaluation of the effectiveness of new arrangements. The Commission pointed out that the implementation of these actions would necessitate the fostering of cooperation within the Community by networking between the national self-regulation and control bodies, the provision of the appropriate framework to pool experiences and increase cooperation (in order to strengthen the coherence of national action by researching common methodologies and concepts), and the continuous tackling of questions that are crucial for the development of new audiovisual and information services.

---

with new methods of protecting minors and informing consumers in the world of television, (3) to promote the access of minors to the new services in educational institutions and public places, (4) to promote high-quality content and services aimed at young people, (5) to assess the appropriateness and effectiveness of the measures being used to protect minors and human dignity": Commission of the European Communities, Commission working document Protection of minors and human dignity in audiovisual and information services: Consultations on the Green Paper, SEC (97) 1203, 13.06.1997, 9.

407 Topics addressed in this part related to judicial and police cooperation (regarding illegal content), the development of relations between children and the media, international cooperation and evaluation and monitoring.

408 The following minimum rules were stressed: special presentation for content that is likely to harm minors (good practices as regards warning pages and age checks); the labelling of content (which may be done by third parties) and the promotion of filtering systems based on the PICS protocol; procedures, principles and practical measures to be applied to relations between operators and users, and the police and courts in order to prevent the dissemination of illegal content, and, in particular, to make it easier to identify and prosecute offenders; a centralised system for handling users' complaints and identifying illegal content; information and awareness-raising measures for users to encourage responsible use of the new services; and procedures and penalties to be applied when self-regulations are breached.

409 Such as the use of special symbols, technical systems to help parental control, awareness-raising programmes, etc.

COMMUNICATION – The Consultation working document was followed by a Commission Communication in November of the same year,[410] which contained a proposal for a Recommendation on the protection of minors and human dignity in audiovisual and information services.

E. *Recommendations on the protection of minors and human dignity*

FOLLOW-UP GREEN PAPER – The 1997 Commission Communication on the follow-up to the Green Paper started from the finding – i.e., the conclusion from the Consultation – that the European Union should

1) *coordinate the development of national self-regulation by promoting common codes of practice and principles to be applied by the Member States, industries and interested parties and the European Union*; and
2) *reinforce cooperation, including that between businesses, and pool know-how at European and international level.*

with a view to improve the effectiveness of relevant national measures.[411] To achieve this goal, the Commission developed a proposal for a Council Recommendation on the protection of minors and human dignity in audiovisual and information services.[412] A recommendation represented, at that moment, according to the Commission, an "*appropriate instrument strictly proportionate to the objectives defined at 1) above and identifies the*

[410] COMMISSION OF THE EUROPEAN COMMUNITIES, Communication from the Commission to the Council, the European Parliament, the Economic and Social Committee and the Committee of the Regions on the follow-up to the Green Paper on the protection of minors and human dignity in audiovisual and information services, including a Proposal for a Council Recommendation concerning the protection of minors and human dignity in audiovisual and information services, COM (97) 570 final, 18.11.1997.

[411] COMMISSION OF THE EUROPEAN COMMUNITIES, Communication from the Commission to the Council, the European Parliament, the Economic and Social Committee and the Committee of the Regions on the follow-up to the Green Paper on the protection of minors and human dignity in audiovisual and information services, including a Proposal for a Council Recommendation concerning the protection of minors and human dignity in audiovisual and information services, COM (97) 570 final, 18.11.1997, 2.

[412] COMMISSION OF THE EUROPEAN COMMUNITIES, Communication from the Commission to the Council, the European Parliament, the Economic and Social Committee and the Committee of the Regions on the follow-up to the Green Paper on the protection of minors and human dignity in audiovisual and information services, including a Proposal for a Council Recommendation concerning the protection of minors and human dignity in audiovisual and information services, COM (97) 570 final, 18.11.1997.

Community instruments and frameworks already available for strengthening the cooperation referred to at 2) above".[413]

Proposal for a Recommendation – The scope of application of the proposed Recommendation was defined in a broad, technologically-neutral manner: the common reference framework was directed at all audiovisual and information services, regardless of the medium.[414] Three different strategic elements could be distinguished in the proposal. First of all, a specific methodology for tackling the issue of the protection of minors and human dignity was adopted. Second, common guidelines for the implementation of a self-regulation framework at national level were devised. The Commission considered these common guidelines as a major component of the Community "*added value*" in the Recommendation. Finally, attention was paid to initiatives aimed at giving the public greater access to new services in educational and/or public places, promoting quality content for minors, fighting against content offensive to human dignity, and developing means of parental control.[415]

The Commission stressed the importance of coherence with existing instruments (such as the Safer Internet Action Plan,[416] the Television without Frontiers directive,[417] the Action Plan for a European education initiative[418]

---

413 On the legal force of a recommendation, see article I-33 Constitution of the European Union: "*Recommendations and opinions shall have no binding force*"; also I-35: "*3. The Council shall adopt recommendations. It shall act on a proposal from the Commission in all cases where the Constitution provides that it shall adopt acts on a proposal from the Commission. It shall act unanimously in those areas in which unanimity is required for the adoption of a Union act. The Commission, and the European Central Bank in the specific cases provided for in the Constitution, shall adopt recommendations*". Cf. also article 288 TFEU [ex 249 EC Treaty]: "*Recommendations and opinions shall have no binding force*".

414 Such as broadcasting / television, proprietary online services or services on the Internet.

415 Commission of the European Communities, Communication from the Commission to the Council, the European Parliament, the Economic and Social Committee and the Committee of the Regions on the follow-up to the Green Paper on the protection of minors and human dignity in audiovisual and information services, including a Proposal for a Council Recommendation concerning the protection of minors and human dignity in audiovisual and information services, COM (97) 570 final, 18.11.1997, 4.

416 Cf. *infra*.

417 Cf. *infra*.

418 Commission of the European Communities, Learning in the information society – Action plan for a European education initiative (1996–1998), COM (1996) 471 final, 02.10.1996, retrieved from http://aei.pitt.edu/1200/01/education_gp_follow_COM_96_471.pdf (on 05.01.2009).

and article K of the Treaty on the European Union),[419] and concluded that the proposed Recommendation would allow the EU to launch a coherent cooperation framework and hence participate in the debate on the protection of fundamental rights in the information society, as well as produce common instruments for the protection of minors and human dignity in the new media environment.[420]

Recommendation – The following year, in 1998, the Council Recommendation on the development of the competitiveness of the European audiovisual and information services industry by promoting national frameworks aimed at achieving a comparable and effective level of protection of minors and human dignity was adopted.[421] With the exception of some differences in phrasing, the Recommendation does not significantly differ from the Proposal.[422] The legal basis of the Recommendation is article 173 TFEU [ex 157 EC Treaty], which provides that "*the Community and the Member States shall ensure that the conditions necessary for the competitiveness of the Community's industry exist*".[423]

Scope of application – The Recommendation is considered to be the most comprehensive legal instrument establishing a framework for the protection of minors in new media services,[424] and was the first legal instrument at the

[419] Article K of the Treaty on the European Union deals with co-operation in the fields of justice and home affairs. Provisions regarding this matter are currently included in Title V of the TFEU ("*Area of freedom, security and justice*").

[420] Commission of the European Communities, Communication from the Commission to the Council, the European Parliament, the Economic and Social Committee and the Committee of the Regions on the follow-up to the Green Paper on the protection of minors and human dignity in audiovisual and information services, including a Proposal for a Council Recommendation concerning the protection of minors and human dignity in audiovisual and information services, COM (97) 570 final, 18.11.1997, 4–5.

[421] Council Recommendation 98/560/EC of 24 September 1998 on the development of the competitiveness of the European audiovisual and information services industry by promoting national frameworks aimed at achieving a comparable and effective level of protection of minors and human dignity, *OJ* 07.10.1998, *L* 270, 48.

[422] The European Parliament put forward certain amendments, most of which were not retained in the final version of the Recommendation: European Parliament, Legislative resolution embodying Parliament's opinion on the proposal for a Council Recommendation concerning the protection of minors and human dignity in audiovisual and information services, *OJ* 01.06.1998, *C* 167, 128.

[423] Cf. http://eur-lex.europa.eu/LexUriServ/LexUriServ.do?uri=CELEX:11992E130:EN:HTML (retrieved on 03.01.2007).

[424] Although a recommendation is a non-binding instrument, it sets out the policy at the European Union level and is therefore considered to be of significant authority. Given that

EU level concerning the content of all electronic audiovisual and information services ("*whatever the means of conveyance*").[425] However, the guidelines for implementation of national self-regulation frameworks included in the Annex to the Recommendation are only applicable to services provided at a distance by electronic means. Hence broadcasting services covered by the Television without Frontiers directive (*infra*) are excluded from the Annex. Furthermore, it is noteworthy that the Recommendation is aimed at harmful as well as illegal content. Again, it was accentuated that the distinction between both types of content is important and that a different approach and solution are necessary.[426]

RATIONALE – The Recommendation was based on the idea that the development of a competitive audiovisual and information services industry depends on the creation of a climate of confidence, and hence on the protection of certain important general interests, such as the protection of minors and human dignity.[427] Furthermore, the development of a common indicative framework at the EU level was considered necessary given the global character of the communication networks.[428] However, since the protection of

the harmonisation of laws of the Member States is excluded from industrial and cultural policies, a recommendation was the logical choice; cf. article 167 TFEU [ex 151 EC Treaty] and article 294 TFEU [ex 251 EC Treaty]. For more information on the concept of division of competences between the European Union and the Member States in cultural affairs, cf.: HOLOUBEK, Michael (ed.), *Regulating content – European regulatory framework for the media and related creative sectors*, Alphen a/d Rijn, Kluwer Law International, 2007, 41 *et seq.*

425 Recital 5 COUNCIL Recommendation 98/560/EC of 24 September 1998 on the development of the competitiveness of the European audiovisual and information services industry by promoting national frameworks aimed at achieving a comparable and effective level of protection of minors and human dignity, *OJ* 07.10.1998, *L* 270, 48.

426 Recital 17 COUNCIL Recommendation 98/560/EC of 24 September 1998 on the development of the competitiveness of the European audiovisual and information services industry by promoting national frameworks aimed at achieving a comparable and effective level of protection of minors and human dignity, *OJ* 07.10.1998, *L* 270, 48.

427 Recital 10 and 11, I COUNCIL Recommendation 98/560/EC of 24 September 1998 on the development of the competitiveness of the European audiovisual and information services industry by promoting national frameworks aimed at achieving a comparable and effective level of protection of minors and human dignity, *OJ* 07.10.1998, *L* 270, 48.

428 Recital 16 COUNCIL Recommendation 98/560/EC of 24 September 1998 on the development of the competitiveness of the European audiovisual and information services industry by promoting national frameworks aimed at achieving a comparable and effective level of protection of minors and human dignity, *OJ* 07.10.1998, *L* 270, 48.

minors is a culture-dependent issue (*supra*), the importance of the subsidiarity principle[429] was highlighted.[430]

Focus on Self-regulation – The Recommendation is highly oriented towards self-regulation, and creates guidelines for the development of national self-regulation frameworks to protect minors (as a supplement to the regulatory framework).[431] The choice for self-regulation, according to the Commission, is justified because

> *[w]hereas, as a supplementary measure, and with full respect for the relevant regulatory frameworks at national and Community level, greater self-regulation by operators should contribute to the rapid implementation of concrete solutions to the problems of the protection of minors and human dignity, while maintaining the flexibility needed to take account of the rapid development of audiovisual and information services.*[432]

Two comments can be made with respect to this statement. First, it is interesting that the Commission explicitly referred to self-regulation as a supplementary measure,[433] and not as an alternative to regulation.[434] Second, the Commission put forward two advantages of the use of self-regulatory instruments: swift implementation[435] and flexibility.[436]

Key elements and addressees – Key building blocks of the recommendation are codes of conduct, parental control tools, hotlines, awareness actions,

---

[429] Cf. *infra*, Part 2, Chapter 1.

[430] Recital 18 Council Recommendation 98/560/EC of 24 September 1998 on the development of the competitiveness of the European audiovisual and information services industry by promoting national frameworks aimed at achieving a comparable and effective level of protection of minors and human dignity, *OJ* 07.10.1998, *L* 270, 48.

[431] Recitals 9, 13, 20; I (1), II; and Annex Council Recommendation 98/560/EC of 24 September 1998 on the development of the competitiveness of the European audiovisual and information services industry by promoting national frameworks aimed at achieving a comparable and effective level of protection of minors and human dignity, *OJ* 07.10.1998, *L* 270, 48.

[432] Recital 20 Council Recommendation 98/560/EC of 24 September 1998 on the development of the competitiveness of the European audiovisual and information services industry by promoting national frameworks aimed at achieving a comparable and effective level of protection of minors and human dignity, *OJ* 07.10.1998, *L* 270, 48.

[433] See also: I (1) Council Recommendation 98/560/EC of 24 September 1998 on the development of the competitiveness of the European audiovisual and information services industry by promoting national frameworks aimed at achieving a comparable and effective level of protection of minors and human dignity, *OJ* 07.10.1998, *L* 270, 48.

[434] Cf. *infra*, Part 1, Chapter 2.

[435] The ability of self-regulation to be quickly adapted is also mentioned in recital 13.

[436] Cf. *infra*, Part 1, Chapter 2.

multi-stakeholder involvement and cooperation across borders. On the one hand, the Recommendation is addressed to the *Member States*. They are encouraged to (1) promote the establishment of voluntary national frameworks (according to the guidelines in the Annex), (2) encourage broadcasters to undertake research on new means to protect minors, (3) set up hotlines and cooperation between complaints-handling structures to fight illegal content and (4) promote awareness on responsible use of information services and identification of and access to quality content. On the other hand, the *industries and 'parties concerned'* should (1) set up structures to improve coordination at the EU and international levels, (2) draw up codes of conduct, (3) develop and experiment with new means of protecting minors and informing viewers, (4) develop positive measures for the benefit of minors, and (5) collaborate in regular follow-ups and evaluations of initiatives in the framework of the Recommendation. Additionally, the *Commission* is allotted the task of facilitating the networking between the different actors, encouraging cooperation – and the sharing of experiences and good practices – between Member States and between self-regulatory and complaints-handling structures, promoting international cooperation and developing an evaluation methodology.[437]

Annex: guidelines for self-regulation frameworks – The Annex to the Recommendation proposes "*Indicative guidelines for the implementation, at national level, of a self-regulation framework for the protection of minors and human dignity in on-line audiovisual and information services*". These guidelines are built around four key elements: consultation with and representativeness of the parties concerned, codes of conduct, national bodies facilitating cooperation at the EU level and national evaluation of self-regulation frameworks. First of all, it is stressed that *all parties* concerned, i.e., public authorities, users, consumers and businesses, need to *participate* fully in the creation of the self-regulatory frameworks, since the acceptance and effectiveness of such a framework largely depends on the degree of participation of the various actors.[438] More details on how this could be put into practice, however, were not given. Secondly, *codes of conduct* must be adopted and implemented voluntarily by businesses. Guidelines referring to the content of these codes of conduct are reasonably detailed. With respect

[437] III (1)–(4) Council Recommendation 98/560/EC of 24 September 1998 on the development of the competitiveness of the European audiovisual and information services industry by promoting national frameworks aimed at achieving a comparable and effective level of protection of minors and human dignity, *OJ* 07.10.1998, *L* 270, 48.

[438] Of course, and this will be discussed in the next chapter, it can be argued that 'pure' self-regulation does not require the involvement of public authorities or users / consumers.

to the protection of minors ('harmful' content), the provision of information to users on the risks of online content as well as the available means of protection, the presentation of legal contents that may harm minors (utilising, for example, labelling or age verification systems), the supply of parental control tools (e.g., filtering software), and the management of complaints about content which does not abide by the rules for the protection of minors are the topics that need to be included in the codes. As regards the protection of human dignity ('illegal' content), three content requirements are put forward: informing users regarding the risks inherent in the use of online services, handling of complaints about illegal content through hotlines and cooperation of operators with judicial and police authorities. Furthermore, and this is a general requirement, the inclusion of sanctions in the case of code violations, is deemed essential for the credibility of the code. Thirdly, the Annex highlights the need for *cooperation* between national bodies at the Community level. On the one hand, a representative national body should be set up to facilitate the sharing of experiences and good practices at the EU and international levels, while on the other hand, cooperation procedures between national contact points set up by the complaints-handling structures also need to be developed. Finally, the Annex insists that national *evaluation* mechanisms be set up, in order to measure the effectiveness of the framework and to adapt it when necessary.

First evaluation – In February 2001, the Commission published the first evaluation report on the application of the 1998 Recommendation.[439, 440] The evaluation was carried out by means of a questionnaire. The questions were focused on themes such as self-regulation, codes of conduct, technical and educational measures, the required degree of coherence between the activities to protect minors across different media, and the potential of a common approach to ratings that cover all audiovisual media.[441] After analysing the responses to the questionnaire, the Commission concluded that, on the whole,

---

[439] Commission of the European Communities, Evaluation report from the Commission to the Council and the European Parliament on the application of Council Recommendation of 24 September 1998 concerning the protection of minors and human dignity, COM (2001) 106 final, 27.02.2001, retrieved from http://ec.europa.eu/comm/avpolicy/docs/reg/minors/ermin_en.pdf (on 04.01.2006).

[440] Point III (4) of the Recommendation required the Commission to publish an evaluation report two years after the adoption of the Recommendation.

[441] Commission of the European Communities, Evaluation report from the Commission to the Council and the European Parliament on the application of Council Recommendation of 24 September 1998 concerning the protection of minors and human dignity, COM (2001) 106 final, 27.02.2001, retrieved from http://ec.europa.eu/comm/avpolicy/docs/reg/minors/ermin_en.pdf (on 04.01.2006), 5.

the effect of the Recommendation's application was encouraging. One minus that was quoted, however, was the fact that the involvement of interested parties – specifically consumers – in the development of the codes of conduct was not satisfactory. Furthermore, the Recommendation seemed to have been applied quite heterogeneously and with unequal degrees of enthusiasm across the different Member States. Possible explanations were, according to the Commission, cultural heterogeneity, varied Internet development between States, and the relatively short time frame of application. On the other hand, the Commission found the industry development of reliable filter and rating systems for the Internet (in particular through the ICRA system) encouraging.[442] Finally, according to the report, the most significant contribution of the Commission to the promotion of EU and international cooperation was the implementation of the Safer Internet Action Plan (*infra*). To conclude its report, the Commission noted a few points of interest. First of all, it was observed that the protection of minors and human dignity should be strived for across all media. Hence, a coherent approach should be aspired to. Second, the involvement of users and consumers should be promoted. Finally, attention was drawn to the potential of self- and co-regulation for the further implementation of the Recommendation.[443] It should be noted that this was the very first time that 'co-regulation'[444] was mentioned in documents relating to the Recommendation. The conclusions of the evaluation were adopted by the Council on the 21 June 2001.[445]

Parliament resolution – Almost a year later, the European Parliament issued a Resolution on the evaluation report,[446] in which a few surprising

[442] Commission of the European Communities, Evaluation report from the Commission to the Council and the European Parliament on the application of Council Recommendation of 24 September 1998 concerning the protection of minors and human dignity, COM (2001) 106 final, 27.02.2001, retrieved from http://ec.europa.eu/comm/avpolicy/docs/reg/minors/ermin_en.pdf (on 04.01.2006), 14.

[443] Commission of the European Communities, Evaluation report from the Commission to the Council and the European Parliament on the application of Council Recommendation of 24 September 1998 concerning the protection of minors and human dignity, COM (2001) 106 final, 27.02.2001, retrieved from http://ec.europa.eu/comm/avpolicy/docs/reg/minors/ermin_en.pdf (on 04.01.2006), 15.

[444] No definition or further clarification of the concept was, however, given.

[445] European Council, 2361st meeting of the Council (Culture), held in Luxembourg on 21.06.2001, 10308/01, retrieved from http://register.consilium.europa.eu/pdf/en/01/st10/10308en1.pdf (on 29.01.2007).

[446] European Parliament, Resolution on the evaluation report from the Commission to the Council and the European Parliament on the application of the Council Recommendation of 24 September 1998 concerning the protection of minors and human dignity,

comments were made. First of all, the Parliament twice stressed the primary responsibility of legal guardians for the protection of minors against harmful content, without, however, absolving content providers or the legislators.[447] Furthermore, the Parliament was of the opinion that self-regulation is an effective additional, but insufficient, means to protect minors against harmful content.[448] A last – peculiar – comment related to the fact that "*technical measures cannot be a substitute for the liability of service providers for the content for which they are responsible, and that consequently a legal duty for service providers to comply with certain provisions, with a view to protecting minors from harmful content is unavoidable*".[449] The comments were rather short, not clarified and not put into context, which makes it quite difficult to assess their value.

Second evaluation – The second evaluation report, requested by the Parliament in its Resolution,[450] was published in 2003.[451] Again the evaluation was based on a questionnaire. Aside from the traditional subjects (self-regulation frameworks, codes of conduct, etc.), a number of 'new' topics were discussed,

---

COM(2001) 106 – C5-0191/2001 – 2001/2087(COS), 11.04.2002, *OJ* 29.05.2003, *C* 127 E, 671.

[447] European Parliament, Resolution on the evaluation report from the Commission to the Council and the European Parliament on the application of the Council Recommendation of 24 September 1998 concerning the protection of minors and human dignity, COM(2001) 106 – C5-0191/2001 – 2001/2087(COS), 11.04.2002, *OJ* 29.05.2003, *C* 127 E, 671, A and 5.

[448] European Parliament, Resolution on the evaluation report from the Commission to the Council and the European Parliament on the application of the Council Recommendation of 24 September 1998 concerning the protection of minors and human dignity, COM(2001) 106 – C5-0191/2001 – 2001/2087(COS), 11.04.2002, *OJ* 29.05.2003, *C* 127 E, 671, C.

[449] European Parliament, Resolution on the evaluation report from the Commission to the Council and the European Parliament on the application of the Council Recommendation of 24 September 1998 concerning the protection of minors and human dignity, COM(2001) 106 – C5-0191/2001 – 2001/2087(COS), 11.04.2002, *OJ* 29.05.2003, *C* 127 E, 671, 10.

[450] European Parliament, Resolution on the evaluation report from the Commission to the Council and the European Parliament on the application of the Council Recommendation of 24 September 1998 concerning the protection of minors and human dignity, COM(2001) 106 – C5-0191/2001 – 2001/2087(COS), 11.04.2002, *OJ* 29.05.2003, *C* 127 E, 671, 20.

[451] Commission of the European Communities, Second evaluation report from the Commission to the Council and the European Parliament on the application of Council Recommendation of 24 September 1998 concerning the protection of minors, COM (2003) 776 final, 12.12.2003, retrieved from http://eur-lex.europa.eu/LexUriServ/site/en/com/2003/com2003_0776en01.pdf (on 25.07.2006).

such as UMTS, chatrooms, media literacy, right of reply, video games and discrimination. The report found that the protection of minors remained a concern and an increasingly challenging issue.[452] Positive developments mentioned were the growing number of hotlines and codes of conduct and the launch of campaigns to encourage safer use of the Internet.[453] Negative points, according to the Commission, however, were the lack of measures in place in the accession countries, and the still lacking involvement of consumer associations and other parties in the establishment of codes of conduct and other self-regulatory initiatives.[454] Large parts of the report focused on the importance of rating and classification of audiovisual content.[455] Initiatives in this area, such as the PEGI system (cf. *infra*), were discussed. The Commission reiterated that rating and classification of audiovisual content plays an essential role in the protection of minors.[456] Although this remained a largely national activity, the Commission suggested there could be a

---

452 Commission of the European Communities, Second evaluation report from the Commission to the Council and the European Parliament on the application of Council Recommendation of 24 September 1998 concerning the protection of minors, COM (2003) 776 final, 12.12.2003, retrieved from http://eur-lex.europa.eu/LexUriServ/site/en/com/2003/com2003_0776en01.pdf (on 25.07.2006), 17.

453 Commission of the European Communities, Second evaluation report from the Commission to the Council and the European Parliament on the application of Council Recommendation of 24 September 1998 concerning the protection of minors, COM (2003) 776 final, 12.12.2003, retrieved from http://eur-lex.europa.eu/LexUriServ/site/en/com/2003/com2003_0776en01.pdf (on 25.07.2006), 17.

454 Commission of the European Communities, Second evaluation report from the Commission to the Council and the European Parliament on the application of Council Recommendation of 24 September 1998 concerning the protection of minors, COM (2003) 776 final, 12.12.2003, retrieved from http://eur-lex.europa.eu/LexUriServ/site/en/com/2003/com2003_0776en01.pdf (on 25.07.2006), 17.

455 The European Commission commissioned a study on the different rating regimes across Europe: Olsberg / SPI et al., Empirical study on the practice of the rating of films distributed in cinemas, television, DVD and videocassettes in the EU and EEA Member States: Final report, Study commissioned by the European Commission, May 2003, retrieved from http://ec.europa.eu/avpolicy/docs/library/studies/finalised/studpdf/rating_finalrep2.pdf, (on 22.12.2008). The results of the study were presented in the evaluation report (pp. 4–5).

456 Commission of the European Communities, Second evaluation report from the Commission to the Council and the European Parliament on the application of Council Recommendation of 24 September 1998 concerning the protection of minors, COM (2003) 776 final, 12.12.2003, retrieved from http://eur-lex.europa.eu/LexUriServ/site/en/com/2003/com2003_0776en01.pdf (on 25.07.2006), 18.

> *'bottom-up' harmonisation through collaboration between self-regulatory and co-regulatory bodies in the Member States, and through the exchange of best practices concerning such issues as a system of common, descriptive symbols which would help viewers assess the content of programmes.*[457]

Of note here is the increased attention that was drawn to 'co-regulation'. In the introduction to the report it was stressed that a co-regulatory approach might be "*more flexible, adaptable and effective than straightforward regulation and legislation*". Furthermore, "*with regard to the protection of minors, where many sensibilities have to be taken into account, co-regulation can often better achieve the given aims*". The only further clarification that was given on this matter was that co-regulation implies an "*appropriate level of involvement by the public authorities*", and should "*consist of cooperation between the public authorities, industry and the other interested parties, such as consumers*". Remarkably, the Commission stated that that was "*the approach laid out in the Recommendation*". Hence, one can wonder if the Commission had always meant to promote 'co-regulatory' measures (as a concept) in the Recommendation, but used the notion 'self-regulation' for lack of a better term at that time. Nevertheless, it is unfortunate that the Commission did not clarify its view on these different regulatory instruments more consistently.

Updating the 1998 Recommendation – In the second evaluation report, the Commission gave the initial impetus to update the Recommendation. In 2004, the first steps towards this update were taken,[458] and over the next two years, different proposals were reviewed by the European Parliament, the Commission and the Council.[459] The proposal put forward by the Commission in 2004 changed considerably over the following two years. Initially, it was endorsed by the Council in November 2004. The Parliament, however, then adopted a significant number of amendments in 2005, in reply to which the

---

457 Commission of the European Communities, Second evaluation report from the Commission to the Council and the European Parliament on the application of Council Recommendation of 24 September 1998 concerning the protection of minors, COM (2003) 776 final, 12.12.2003, retrieved from http://eur-lex.europa.eu/LexUriServ/site/en/com/2003/com2003_0776en01.pdf (on 25.07.2006), 18.

458 Commission of the European Communities, Proposal for a recommendation of the European Parliament and of the Council on the protection of minors and human dignity and the right of reply in relation to the competitiveness of the European audiovisual and information services industry, COM (2004) 341 final, 30.04.2004.

459 One aspect of the revision was the inclusion of a right of reply in relation to online media. This aspect falls outside the scope of this book and will thus not be addressed.

Commission presented an adapted proposal in 2006.[460] The Council reached a political agreement on this modified version in May 2006.[461] The Culture Committee of the Parliament endorsed this common position, without any amendments.[462] The vote in plenary on 12 December 2006 also resulted in a full endorsement.[463] The Council and the Parliament then, finally, officially adopted the Recommendation on 20 December 2006.[464]

Recommendation – The Commission again justified the choice of a 'recommendation' in its proposal by referring to the exclusion of the harmonisation of laws from cultural policies.[465] The Parliamentary Committee on Civil Liberties, Justice and Home Affairs strongly criticised this choice since the "*mandatory content [of a recommendation] legally enforceable before the*

---

460 Commission of the European Communities, Amended proposal for a Recommendation of the European Parliament and of the Council on the protection of minors and human dignity and the right of reply in relation to the competitiveness of the European audiovisual and information services industry, COM (2006) 31 final, 20.01.2006 [hereinafter: Amended proposal Recommendation].

461 Council of the European Union, Proposal for a Recommendation of the European Parliament and of the Council on the protection of minors and human dignity and on the right of reply in relation to the competitiveness of the European audiovisual and online information services industry – Political agreement, No. 8956/06, Interinstitutional file 2004/0117 (COD), Brussels, 11.05.2006, retrieved from http://register.consilium.europa.eu/pdf/en/06/st08/st08956.en06.pdf (on 30.05.2006). However, the Dutch, UK and Slovak delegations revealed their plans to abstain from voting when the act was adopted: Council of the European Union, Press release 2729th Council Meeting, Education, Youth and Culture, Brussels, 18-19.05.2006, retrieved from http://www.consilium.europa.eu/ueDocs/cms_Data/docs/pressData/en/educ/89661.pdf (on 29.05.2006), 16.

462 European Parliament, Draft Recommendation for second reading on the Council common position for adopting a recommendation of the European Parliament and of the Council on protection of minors and human dignity and the right of reply in relation to the competitiveness of the European audiovisual and online information services industry, 2004/0117(COD), 06.11.2006, retrieved from http://www.europarl.europa.eu/meetdocs/2004_2009/documents/pr/637/637009/637009en.pdf (on 28.11.2006).

463 Cf. *infra*, also http://ec.europa.eu/prelex/detail_dossier_real.cfm?CL=en&DosId=190796 (retrieved on 19.11.2008).

464 European Parliament and Council Recommendation 2006/952/EC of 20 December 2006 on the protection of minors and human dignity and on the right of reply in relation to the competitiveness of the European audiovisual and on-line information services industry, *OJ* 27.12.2007, *L* 378, 72.

465 Commission of the European Communities, Proposal for a recommendation of the European Parliament and of the Council on the protection of minors and human dignity and the right of reply in relation to the competitiveness of the European audiovisual and information services industry, COM (2004) 341 final, 30.04.2004, 3; cf. *supra* footnote 424.

courts is practically zero".[466] The European Economic and Social Committee also expressed its displeasure with the fact that laws cannot be harmonised in the audiovisual sector.[467] Furthermore, the Commission emphasised in its proposal that a Recommendation from the Parliament and Council (contrary to the 1998 Recommendation which was a 'Council only' initiative) was preferable to one of the Commission. This was because, first, according to the Commission, the goal of the Recommendation, i.e., the development of the competitiveness of the European audiovisual and information services industry through the promotion of national frameworks aimed at achieving a comparable and effective level of protection of minors and human dignity, could be better achieved if the Recommendation was discussed and adopted by the Council. Second, the Commission was of the opinion that involving the Parliament would result in a more public debate and a bigger impact of the Recommendation.

Scope and legal basis – The scope, i.e., "*content of audiovisual and information services covering all forms of delivery, from broadcasting to the Internet*",[468] as well as the legal basis,[469] i.e., article 173 TFEU [ex 157 EC Treaty] on

---

[466] Cf. European Parliament, Opinion of the Committee on Civil Liberties, Justice and Home Affairs, for the Committee on Culture and Education on the 'Proposal for a recommendation of the European Parliament and of the Council on the protection of minors and human dignity and the right of reply in relation to the competitiveness of the European audiovisual and information services industry', 15.04.2005, retrieved from http://www.europarl.europa.eu/registre/commissions/libe/avis/2005/353374/LIBE_AD(2005)353374_EN.pdf (on 02.01.2006), 4.

[467] Cf. European Economic and Social Committee, Opinion of the European Economic and Social Committee on the 'Proposal for a European Parliament and Council recommendation on the protection of minors and human dignity and the right of reply in relation to the competitiveness of the European audiovisual and information services industry', COM(2004) 341 final – 2004/0117 (COD), 09.02.2005, *OJ* 08.09.2005, *C* 221, 87.

[468] European Communities, Proposal for a recommendation of the European Parliament and of the Council on the protection of minors and human dignity and the right of reply in relation to the competitiveness of the European audiovisual and information services industry, COM (2004) 341 final, 30.04.2004, 3. Recital 19 of the Recommendation clarifies that the scope of the Recommendation includes "*audiovisual and on-line information services made available to the public via fixed or mobile electronic networks*": European Parliament and Council Recommendation 2006/952/EC of 20 December 2006 on the protection of minors and human dignity and on the right of reply in relation to the competitiveness of the European audiovisual and on-line information services industry, *OJ* 27.12.2007, *L* 378, 72.

[469] Commission of the European Communities, Proposal for a recommendation of the European Parliament and of the Council on the protection of minors and human dignity and the right of reply in relation to the competitiveness of the European audiovisual and information services industry, COM (2004) 341 final, 30.04.2004, 4: "*The audiovisual and*

guaranteeing the competitiveness of the industry, of the new Recommendation are identical to that of the 1998 Recommendation. The choice of article 173 TFEU [ex 157 EC Treaty] as the legal basis for the Recommendation could not count on the approval of the Parliamentary Committee on Civil Liberties, Justice and Home affairs, which was of the opinion that article 169 TFEU [ex 153 EC Treaty], which aims at protecting the interests of consumers, would be more appropriate.[470] The European Economic and Social Committee had already voiced a similar concern. The Committee was of the opinion that it is

> *illogical that, in order to protection minors and human dignity, [...] it should be necessary to invoke as a key factor not rights relating to the personality as such, but 'the development of the competitiveness of the European audiovisual and information services industry'. Protecting this core of fundamental citizen's rights must not be seen as a merely incidental aspect of achieving the aim of developing the audiovisual market.*

However, the Committee agreed that the Recommendation as proposed by the Commission, including its legal basis, was the best way forward.[471]

Proposal – The original Commission proposal, inspired by the second evaluation report, was rather short and to-the-point. Member States, on the one hand, were encouraged to promote awareness of the potential of new services and of the means whereby they may be made safe for minors, media literacy and education, and action to facilitate the identification of and access to quality content and services for minors.[472] Industries and parties concerned,

---

information industry in Europe has great potential for creating employment and contributing to economic growth. The conditions for the competitiveness of these industrial activities need to be improved, especially as regards better use of technological developments, such as digitisation".

[470] Cf. European Parliament, Opinion of the Committee on Civil Liberties, Justice and Home Affairs, for the Committee on Culture and Education on the 'Proposal for a recommendation of the European Parliament and of the Council on the protection of minors and human dignity and the right of reply in relation to the competitiveness of the European audiovisual and information services industry', 15.04.2005, retrieved from http://www.europarl.europa.eu/registre/commissions/libe/avis/2005/353374/LIBE_AD(2005)353374_EN.pdf (on 02.01.2006), 4.

[471] Cf. European Economic and Social Committee, Opinion of the European Economic and Social Committee on the 'Proposal for a European Parliament and Council recommendation on the protection of minors and human dignity and the right of reply in relation to the competitiveness of the European audiovisual and information services industry', COM(2004) 341 final – 2004/0117 (COD), 09.02.2005, *OJ* 08.09.2005, *C* 221, 87.

[472] Commission of the European Communities, Proposal for a recommendation of the European Parliament and of the Council on the protection of minors and human dignity

on the other hand, were urged to initiate positive measures for the benefit of children,

> *including a bottom-up harmonisation through cooperation between self-regulatory and co-regulatory bodies in the Member States, and through the exchange of best practices concerning such issues as a system of common, descriptive symbols that would help viewers assess program content.*

First reading parliament – The Parliament heavily amended the Commission's proposal. This version of the text, based on a report by rapporteur Marielle De Sarnez, was much lengthier and more detailed.[473] A number of general amendments related to the usefulness of different regulatory approaches. The Parliament assumed that prevention and improved parental control would always be the best method of protection against the hazards of the Internet.[474] Self-regulation, on the other hand, was not considered

---

and the right of reply in relation to the competitiveness of the European audiovisual and information services industry, COM (2004) 341 final, 30.04.2004, I.

473 European Parliament, Report on the proposal for a recommendation of the European Parliament and of the Council on the protection of minors and human dignity and the right of reply in relation to the competitiveness of the European audiovisual and information services industry, A6-0244/2005, 19.07.2006, retrieved from http://www.europarl.europa.eu/sides/getDoc.do?pubRef=-//EP//NONSGML+REPORT+A6-2005-0244+0+DOC+PDF+V0//EN&language=EN (on 05.07.2007). In March 2005, a draft report had been presented by rapporteur De Sarnez (European Parliament, Draft Report on the proposal for a recommendation on the protection of minors and human dignity and the right of reply in relation to the competitiveness of the European audiovisual and information services industry, 2004/0117 (COD), 14.03.2004, retrieved from http://www.europarl.europa.eu/meetdocs/2004_2009/documents/pr/547/547671/547671en.pdf (on 05.02.2007)). This draft report was heavily amended before its approval on 7 September 2005 (cf. for instance: European Parliament, Draft report Marielle De Sarnez, Amendments 24–53, PE 355.734v01-00, 01.04.2005, retrieved from http://www.europarl.europa.eu/meetdocs/2004_2009/documents/am/561/561514/561514en.pdf (on 08.02.2007)). A number of the amendments were inspired by the Opinion of the Committee on Civil Liberties, Justice and Home Affairs: European Parliament, Opinion of the Committee on Civil Liberties, Justice and Home Affairs, for the Committee on Culture and Education on the 'Proposal for a recommendation of the European Parliament and of the Council on the protection of minors and human dignity and the right of reply in relation to the competitiveness of the European audiovisual and information services industry', 15.04.2005, retrieved from http://www.europarl.europa.eu/registre/commissions/libe/avis/2005/353374/LIBE_AD(2005)353374_EN.pdf (on 02.01.2006).

474 European Parliament, Report on the proposal for a recommendation of the European Parliament and of the Council on the protection of minors and human dignity and the right of reply in relation to the competitiveness of the European audiovisual and information services industry, A6-0244/2005, 19.07.2006, retrieved from http://www

sufficient to protect minors from messages with harmful content.[475] Moreover, "*the development of a European audiovisual area based on freedom of expression and respect for citizen's rights should be based on an ongoing dialogue between national and European law makers, regulatory authorities, industries, associations, consumers and civil society actors*".[476] Along the same lines, the explanatory memorandum stressed the need for all actors to take responsibility for what happens on the Internet: politicians (at the national as well as the EU level) should provide education programmes and information campaigns, access providers must provide parental software and access services aimed at children with automatic filtering at the source, content producers ought to classify their content, and parents, educators and teachers should be trained to provide guidance.[477] Further amendments to the body of the text, aimed at making sure that these different actors involved would really fulfil their responsibilities, put forward specific lists of action points. Although concrete proposals make the issue more tangible, some of the propositions could be considered unfeasible or impractical: the imposed classification of content by all content providers seemed especially difficult to enforce.[478] Other

.europarl.europa.eu/sides/getDoc.do?pubRef=-//EP//NONSGML+REPORT+A6-2005-0244+0+DOC+PDF+V0//EN&language=EN (on 05.07.2007), amendment 11, 10.

[475] European Parliament, Report on the proposal for a recommendation of the European Parliament and of the Council on the protection of minors and human dignity and the right of reply in relation to the competitiveness of the European audiovisual and information services industry, A6-0244/2005, 19.07.2006, retrieved from http://www.europarl.europa.eu/sides/getDoc.do?pubRef=-//EP//NONSGML+REPORT+A6-2005-0244+0+DOC+PDF+V0//EN&language=EN (on 05.07.2007), amendment 12, 11.

[476] European Parliament, Report on the proposal for a recommendation of the European Parliament and of the Council on the protection of minors and human dignity and the right of reply in relation to the competitiveness of the European audiovisual and information services industry, A6-0244/2005, 19.07.2006, retrieved from http://www.europarl.europa.eu/sides/getDoc.do?pubRef=-//EP//NONSGML+REPORT+A6-2005-0244+0+DOC+PDF+V0//EN&language=EN (on 05.07.2007), justification amendment 12, 11.

[477] European Parliament, Report on the proposal for a recommendation of the European Parliament and of the Council on the protection of minors and human dignity and the right of reply in relation to the competitiveness of the European audiovisual and information services industry, A6-0244/2005, 19.07.2006, retrieved from http://www.europarl.europa.eu/sides/getDoc.do?pubRef=-//EP//NONSGML+REPORT+A6-2005-0244+0+DOC+PDF+V0//EN&language=EN (on 05.07.2007), Explanatory memorandum, IV. 1, 29–30.

[478] The European Economic and Social Committee had, already in 1998, deemed the classification of all information on the Internet to be impracticable: European Economic and social committee, Opinion of the Economic and Social Committee on the 'Proposal for a Council Decision adopting a Multiannual Community Action Plan on promoting safe use of the Internet', 98/C 214/08, 29.04.1998, *OJ* 10.07.1998, *C* 214, 32.

proposals were: to put banners, warning of possible dangers, on the homepage of every search engine; to establish a free telephone number which provides information on filtering tools; and to create a top level domain name '.kid'. The latter suggestion is, particularly controversial, since it has been argued that such a domain attracts adults with questionable intentions. Moreover, a similar domain was established in the United States, but proved unsuccessful.[479]

The report of DE SARNEZ and a draft legislative Resolution were approved by the Committee on Culture and Education in July 2005 and adopted in plenary on 7 September 2005.[480]

AMENDED PROPOSAL – The Commission considered the Parliament's amendments and published a modified version of the proposal in January 2006.[481] Although quite a number of the amendments were adopted, it was clear that the Commission tried to water down the Parliament's sometimes radical suggestions. Wordings such as "*adopting a directive*" or "*binding legislation at national level*", for instance, were not taken up in the revised Commission proposal. Furthermore, the Commission moved the lists of specific action points to the Annexes ("*Annex II: Examples of possible actions concerning media literacy* and *Annex III: Examples of possible actions by the industries and the parties concerned for the benefit of minors*"), which again reduced the body of the text.

The modified version of the proposal rested on four main pillars: first, awareness, education and information campaigns (mainly aimed at the Member States); second, filtering systems linked with content labelling (primarily aimed at industry and other parties involved); third, codes of conduct by professionals and regulatory authorities linked with quality labelling (aimed at industry and Member States); and last, a number of separate proposals to be initiated by the Commission (e.g., a free telephone number informing

---

479 REUTERS (Andy SULLIVAN), PluggedIn: Not much to do in kids' online domain, 03.06.2005, retrieved from http://massis.lcs.mit.edu/telecom-archives/TELECOM_Digest_Online2005-1/4801.html (on 20.12.2008).

480 EUROPEAN PARLIAMENT, Legislative resolution on the proposal for a recommendation of the European Parliament and of the Council on the protection of minors and human dignity and the right of reply in relation to the competitiveness of the European audiovisual and information services industry, COM(2004)0341 – C6-0029/2004 – 2004/0117(COD), 07.09.2005, *OJ* 17.8.2006, *C* 193E, 217.

481 COMMISSION OF THE EUROPEAN COMMUNITIES, Amended proposal for a Recommendation of the European Parliament and of the Council on the protection of minors and human dignity and the right of reply in relation to the competitiveness of the European audiovisual and information services industry, COM (2006) 31 final, 20.01.2006.

users about complaint mechanisms and the effectiveness of filtering software, and a second level domain name '.kid.eu').

Council common position – The Council reached a political agreement on the draft Recommendation in May 2006,[482] and published their common position in September 2006.[483, 484] The majority of the differences between the Commission's amended proposal and the Council's common position boiled down to rephrasing or the reversal of the order of the recitals or recommendations. A number of modifications to the content were made,[485] but the core and the spirit of the Recommendation remained the same.

[482] Council of the European Union, Proposal for a Recommendation of the European Parliament and of the Council on the protection of minors and human dignity and on the right of reply in relation to the competitiveness of the European audiovisual and online information services industry – Political agreement, No. 8956/06, Interinstitutional file 2004/0117 (COD), Brussels, 11.05.2006, retrieved from http://register.consilium.europa.eu/pdf/en/06/st08/st08956.en06.pdf (on 30.05.2006). However, the delegations from the United Kingdom and Slovakia expressed their intention to abstain when the act was to be adopted. The delegation from the Netherlands announced that it would agree to the Recommendation, but that it would make a statement in the minutes. Cf. Council of the European Union, Press release 2729th Council Meeting, Education, Youth and Culture, Brussels, 18–19.05.2006, retrieved from http://www.consilium.europa.eu/ueDocs/cms_Data/docs/pressData/en/educ/89661.pdf (on 29.05.2006); European Council, Draft minutes 2729th meeting of the Council of the European Union (Education, Youth and Culture), held in Brussels on 18–19 May 2006, 9547/06, retrieved from http://register.consilium.europa.eu/pdf/en/06/st09/st09547.en06.pdf (on 08.02.2007). The objection of the three countries related to the inclusion of online media, such as newspapers and magazine services, within the scope of the Recommendation. Cf. Council of the European Union, Proposal for a Recommendation of the European Parliament and of the Council on the protection of minors and human dignity and on the right of reply in relation to the competitiveness of the European audiovisual and online information services industry – Political agreement, No. 8956/06, Interinstitutional file 2004/0117 (COD), Brussels, 11.05.2006, retrieved from http://register.consilium.europa.eu/pdf/en/06/st08/st08956.en06.pdf (on 30.05.2006).

[483] Council of the European Union, Common Position (EC) No 24/2006 of 18 September 2006 adopted by the Council, acting in accordance with the procedure referred to in Article 251 of the Treaty establishing the European Community, with a view to adopting a Recommendation of the European Parliament and of the Council on the protection of minors and human dignity and on the right of reply in relation to the competitiveness of the European audiovisual and on-line information services industry, *OJ* 05.12.2006, *C* 295E, 48.

[484] Comparing both documents (footnotes 482 and 483), small differences in wording can be observed.

[485] Two noteworthy alterations regarding the use of regulatory instruments are the omission of the references to the adoption of a directive and the setting up of a legal framework.

The European Commission reacted to this common position,[486] and observed that the Council implemented several changes, which it considered, acceptable "*because they will help ensure that the Recommendation's aims are ultimately achieved*".[487] Hence, the Council's common position was supported and a prompt adoption encouraged.[488]

Parliament's Second Reading – The European Parliament found, after its second reading, that the Council's common position was satisfactory since it acknowledged the principal concerns of the political groups (better information and guidance, a more responsible approach, right of reply in the online media and monitoring by the Commission).[489] Hence, the Council's common position was approved without amendments in plenary during the mid-December 2006 meeting.[490]

---

[486] Commission of the European Communities, Communication from the Commission to the European Parliament pursuant to the second subparagraph of Article 251 (2) of the EC Treaty concerning the common position of the Council on the adoption of a Recommendation on the protection of minors and human dignity and on the right of reply in relation to the competitiveness of the European audiovisual and on-line information services industry, COM (2006) 546 final, 21.09.2006.

[487] Commission of the European Communities, Communication from the Commission to the European Parliament pursuant to the second subparagraph of Article 251 (2) of the EC Treaty concerning the common position of the Council on the adoption of a Recommendation on the protection of minors and human dignity and on the right of reply in relation to the competitiveness of the European audiovisual and on-line information services industry, COM (2006) 546 final, 21.09.2006, 2.

[488] Commission of the European Communities, Communication from the Commission to the European Parliament pursuant to the second subparagraph of Article 251 (2) of the EC Treaty concerning the common position of the Council on the adoption of a Recommendation on the protection of minors and human dignity and on the right of reply in relation to the competitiveness of the European audiovisual and on-line information services industry, COM (2006) 546 final, 21.09.2006, 4.

[489] European Parliament, Recommendation for second reading on the Council common position for adopting a recommendation of the European Parliament and of the Council on protection of minors and human dignity and the right of reply in relation to the competitiveness of the European audiovisual and online information services industry, A6-0433/2006, 29.11.2006, retrieved from http://www.europarl.europa.eu/sides/getDoc.do?pubRef=-//EP//NONSGML+REPORT+A6-2006-0433+0+DOC+PDF+V0//EN&language=EN (on 02.01.2006); based on European Parliament, Draft Recommendation for second reading on the Council common position for adopting a recommendation of the European Parliament and of the Council on protection of minors and human dignity and the right of reply in relation to the competitiveness of the European audiovisual and online information services industry, 2004/0117(COD), 06.11.2006, retrieved from http://www.europarl.europa.eu/meetdocs/2004_2009/documents/pr/637/637009/637009en.pdf (on 28.11.2006).

[490] European Parliament, Legislative resolution on the Council common position for adopting a recommendation of the European Parliament and of the Council on the protection

Adoption of new recommendation – The Recommendation of the European Parliament and of the Council on the protection of minors and human dignity and on the right of reply in relation to the competitiveness of the European audiovisual and on-line information services industry was adopted on 20 December 2006, and published in the Official Journal on 27 December 2006.[491]

Different regulatory approaches – In the 2006 Recommendation there are references to the use of legislation, self-regulation and co-regulation, whereas the 1998 Recommendation was solely focused on self-regulation. Without a clear explanation,[492] the European Parliament inserted recital 3 into the 2006 Recommendation, which stated that

> *[l]egislative measures need to be enacted at Union level on the protection of the physical, mental and moral development of minors in relation to the content of all audiovisual and information services and the protection of minors from access to inappropriate adult programmes or services.*

As this is the only mention of the use of 'legislation' in the text of the Recommendation, it could be assumed that what was meant is the Recommendation itself. It is, however, debatable whether recommendations are 'legislative measures', since they do not have binding force. Hence, if *in casu* the Recommendation was what was being referred to (rather than an actual desire by the European Union to adopt legislation to protect minors against harmful audiovisual or on-line content), then the wording 'legislative measures' can be considered rather ill-chosen. However, it is more likely that the recital

---

of minors and human dignity and on the right of reply in relation to the competitiveness of the European audiovisual and online information services industry, 9577/1/2006-C6-0313/2006-2004/0117(COD), 12.12.2006, retrieved from http://www.europarl.europa.eu/sides/getDoc.do?Type=TA&Reference=P6–TA-2006–0537&language=EN (on 26.03.2008).

491 European Parliament and Council Recommendation 2006/952/EC of 20 December 2006 on the protection of minors and human dignity and on the right of reply in relation to the competitiveness of the European audiovisual and on-line information services industry, *OJ* 27.12.2007, *L* 378, 72.

492 European Parliament, Report on the proposal for a recommendation of the European Parliament and of the Council on the protection of minors and human dignity and the right of reply in relation to the competitiveness of the European audiovisual and information services industry, A6-0244/2005, 19.07.2006, retrieved from http://www.europarl.europa.eu/sides/getDoc.do?pubRef=-//EP//NONSGML+REPORT+A6-2005-0244+0+DOC+PDF+V0//EN&language=EN (on 05.07.2007), amendment 6: "*The audiovisual and information media have brought information of all kinds within the reach of minors, and the content of and access to this information must be in keeping with their physical, mental and moral development*".

is the result of a compromise, for the benefit of the European Parliament who desired more binding measures in this field.[493] The adoption of the 'Audiovisual Media Services Directive' (*infra*) could be seen as a step in this direction.

Other suggested regulatory instruments in the 2006 Recommendation are self-regulation and co-regulation. As was mentioned above, the concept 'co-regulation' first appeared, in the context of the Recommendation, in the second evaluation report of the 1998 Recommendation. From then on, self- and co-regulation have been mentioned together, but have never been clearly distinguished. Hence, one can wonder whether the 'sudden' inclusion of co-regulation from 2003 onwards was purely a matter of using another notion, instead of the introduction of a different concept. Looking at the text of the 1998 Recommendation[494] and the second evaluation report[495] one could argue that the regulatory concept that was strived for always had characteristics of co-regulation (for instance, cooperation and dialogue between the different actors, cf. *infra*).

Another interesting observation relates to the apparent determination of the Parliament to toughen their approach. The original Commission proposal was concisely formulated in rather moderate terms.[496] Amendments by the Parliament, on the other hand, were extensive and very detailed, and suggested an inclination for further-reaching action, promoting, for instance,

---

[493] Cf. a number of the amendments the Parliament proposed regarding binding legislation and directives: footnote 497.

[494] E.g. II (1), which: "*Recommends that the industries and parties involved cooperate, in accordance with national traditions and practices, with the relevant authorities in setting up structures representing all the parties concerned at national level [...]*"; or Annex 1, which states that: "*The objective is to ensure that the definition, implementation and evaluation of national self-regulation framework benefits from the full participation of the parties concerned, such as the public authorities, the users, consumers and the businesses which are directly or indirectly involved in the audiovisual and on-line information services industry. The respective responsibilities and functions of the parties concerned, both public and private, should be set out clearly*".

[495] Commission of the European Communities, Second evaluation report from the Commission to the Council and the European Parliament on the application of Council Recommendation of 24 September 1998 concerning the protection of minors, COM (2003) 776 final, 12.12.2003, retrieved from http://eur-lex.europa.eu/LexUriServ/site/en/com/2003/com2003_0776en01.pdf (on 25.07.2006), 5.

[496] Commission of the European Communities, Proposal for a recommendation of the European Parliament and of the Council on the protection of minors and human dignity and the right of reply in relation to the competitiveness of the European audiovisual and information services industry, COM (2004) 341 final, 30.04.2004.

the use of legislative measures and a directive.[497] The Commission, however, succeeded in moderating the tendency towards the use of legislation in its amended proposal.

F. *Successive Safer Internet programmes*

Safer Internet Action Plan – The Safer Internet Action Plan was established in 1999 with the objective of promoting safer use of the Internet and encouraging, at a European level, an environment favourable to the development of the Internet industry.[498, 499] The Action Plan originally ran from 1 January 1999 to 31 December 2002,[500] but was extended by the Parliament and the Council until the end of 2004.[501] It was explicitly stressed that the

---

[497] European Parliament, Legislative resolution on the proposal for a recommendation of the European Parliament and of the Council on the protection of minors and human dignity and the right of reply in relation to the competitiveness of the European audiovisual and information services industry, COM(2004)0341-C6–0029/2004-2004/0117(COD), 07.09.2005, *OJ* 17.8.2006, *C* 193E, 217. For instance: "*Legislative measures need to be enacted at European Union level for the protection of the physical, mental and moral development of minors in relation to the content of all audiovisual and information services, the adoption of measures preventing the circulation of illegal content and the protection of minors from access to adult programmes or services*", recital 4; and "*The inevitable development of new information and communication technologies makes it urgent for the European Community to ensure full and adequate protection for consumers' interests in this field, by adopting a directive which will, throughout its territory, one the one hand guarantee the free delivery and free provision of information services and on the other ensure that their content is legal, respects the principle of human dignity and does not impair the overall development of minors*", recital 5 [own emphasis].

[498] Parliament and Council of the European Communities, Decision No 276/1999/EC of the European Parliament and Council adopting a multiannual Community action plan on promoting safer use of the Internet by combating illegal and harmful content on the global networks, 25.01.1999, *OJ* 06.02.1999, *L* 33, 1, article 2.

[499] The legal basis for the Action Plan was article 153, par. 2 EC Treaty [currently article 12 TFEU]: "*Consumer protection requirements shall be taken into account in defining and implementing other Community policies and activities*": Commission of the European Communities, Proposal for a Decision of the European Parliament and of the Council on establishing a multiannual Community programme on promoting safer use of the Internet and new online technologies, COM (2004) 91 final, 12.03.2004, 9.

[500] Parliament and Council of the European Communities, Decision No 276/1999/EC of the European Parliament and Council adopting a multiannual Community action plan on promoting safer use of the Internet by combating illegal and harmful content on the global networks, 25.01.1999, *OJ* 06.02.1999, *L* 33, article 1 para. 2.

[501] Parliament and Council of the European Communities, Decision No 1151/2003/EC of the European Parliament and of the Council, amending Decision No 276/1999/EC adopting a Multiannual Community Action Plan on promoting safer use of the Internet by combating illegal and harmful content on global networks, 16.06.2003,

Action Plan needed to be put into practice in close coordination with the 1998 Recommendation on the protection of minors and human dignity (cf. *supra*).[502]

Lines of action – Greatly inspired by self-regulatory principles, the Action Plan was implemented through three main lines of action: creating a safer environment (through the creation of a European network of hotlines, and the encouragement of self-regulation and codes of conduct),[503] developing filtering and rating systems,[504] and increasing public awareness.[505, 506] The Annex to the Action Plan clarified the objectives of these lines: to incite

OJ 01.07.2003, *L* 162, 1. It was deemed that more time was needed for the implementation of actions, to attain the Action Plan's goals and to take new online technologies into account (recital 6).

502 Parliament and Council of the European Communities, Decision No 276/1999/EC of the European Parliament and Council adopting a multiannual Community action plan on promoting safer use of the Internet by combating illegal and harmful content on the global networks, 25.01.1999, *OJ* 06.02.1999, *L* 33, recital 11 and Annex I.

503 This line of action, particularly the suggested implementation of the network of hotlines, seems to be directed primarily at restricting circulation of illegal material.

504 It is interesting to note that the Economic and Social Committee was not persuaded that the Commission's technological approach was the most effective way of dealing with a social problem: Economic and Social Committee, Opinion of the Economic and Social Committee on the 'Proposal for a Council Decision adopting a Multiannual Community Action Plan on promoting safer use of the Internet', *OJ* 10.07.1998, *C* 214, 30. Indeed, the Committee started by saying that, in general, it is "*very favourably disposed towards the Commission's action plan*", since the Action Plan "*actually attempts to address the problem*". However, in its conclusions, the Committee deemed the Action Plan to be over-ambitious, unrealistic and impracticable (p. 32, 4.1 *et seq.*).

505 Parliament and Council of the European Communities, Decision No 276/1999/EC of the European Parliament and Council adopting a multiannual Community action plan on promoting safer use of the Internet by combating illegal and harmful content on the global networks, 25.01.1999, *OJ* 06.02.1999, *L* 33, article 3 and Annex I; Commission of the European Communities, Communication from the Commission to the Council, the European Parliament, the European Economic and Social Committee and the Committee of the Regions, concerning the evaluation of the Multiannual Community Action Plan on promoting safer use of the Internet and new online technologies by combating illegal and harmful content primarily in the area of the protection of children and minors, COM (2003) 653 final, 03.11.2006.

506 Apart from the three main lines of action, a number of supporting actions were identified in Annex I of the Action Plan: assessment of legal implications, coordination with similar international initiatives and the evaluation of the impact of Community measures: Parliament and Council of the European Communities, Decision No 276/1999/EC of the European Parliament and Council adopting a multiannual Community action plan on promoting safer use of the Internet by combating illegal and harmful content on the global networks, 25.01.1999, *OJ* 06.02.1999, *L* 33, 9–10.

the relevant actors – i.e., industry and users – to develop and implement adequate systems of self-regulation; to pump-prime developments by supporting demonstrations and stimulating application of technical solutions; to alert and inform parents and teachers; to foster cooperation and exchange of experiences and best practices at the EU and international levels; to promote coordination throughout the European Union and between actors concerned; and to ensure compatibility between the approach taken in the European Union and elsewhere.[507] The Action Plan essentially functioned by co-financing projects that attempted to contribute to one of these aims.[508] In this first phase, 37 projects were approved.

Extension of the Action Plan – During its second stage (2003–2004),[509] the programme's scope was extended to new online technologies such as mobile and broadband content, online games, peer-to-peer file transfer, and all forms of real-time communications such as chat rooms and instant messaging.[510] Other innovations were the establishment of a Safer Internet

507 Parliament and Council of the European Communities, Decision No 276/1999/EC of the European Parliament and Council adopting a multiannual Community action plan on promoting safer use of the Internet by combating illegal and harmful content on the global networks, 25.01.1999, *OJ* 06.02.1999, *L* 33, Annex I.

508 Cf. Parliament and Council of the European Communities, Decision No 276/1999/EC of the European Parliament and Council adopting a multiannual Community action plan on promoting safer use of the Internet by combating illegal and harmful content on the global networks, 25.01.1999, *OJ* 06.02.1999, *L* 33, Annex II (The means for implementing the Action Plan).

509 Parliament and Council of the European Communities, Decision No 1151/2003/EC of the European Parliament and of the Council, amending Decision No 276/1999/EC adopting a Multiannual Community Action Plan on promoting safer use of the Internet by combating illegal and harmful content on global networks, 16.06.2003, *OJ* 01.07.2003, *L* 162, 1.

510 Parliament and Council of the European Communities, Decision No 1151/2003/EC of the European Parliament and of the Council, amending Decision No 276/1999/EC adopting a Multiannual Community Action Plan on promoting safer use of the Internet by combating illegal and harmful content on global networks, 16.06.2003, *OJ* 01.07.2003, *L* 162, 1: Annex I, 2, (i). See also: Commission of the European Communities, Communication from the Commission to the European Parliament, the Council, the European Economic and Social Committee and the Committee of the Regions, Communication, Final evaluation of the implementation of the multiannual Community action plan on promoting safer use of the Internet by combating illegal and harmful content on global networks, COM (2006) 663 final, 06.11.2006, 2. See also: Parliament and Council of the European Communities, Decision No 1151/2003/EC of the European Parliament and of the Council, amending Decision No 276/1999/EC adopting a Multiannual Community Action Plan on promoting safer use of the Internet by combating illegal and harmful content on global networks, 16.06.2003, *OJ* 01.07.2003, *L* 162, 1, recital 4: "*New online*

Forum,[511] aimed at enhanced networking, and a greater emphasis on fostering cooperation and exchange of experiences and best practices at the European and international levels.[512]

Assessment – An intermediary evaluation, carried out in 2001, found that the Action Plan was being successfully implemented and that problems encountered until then were relatively minor.[513] In November 2003, the Action Plan again received fairly positive evaluations.[514] The Commission observed that the positive impact of the Action Plan was primarily achieved through the fostering of networking and the provision of an enormous amount of information on issues of safer use of the Internet and their solutions.[515] A final

---

technologies, new users and new usage patterns create new dangers and exacerbate existing dangers at the same time as opening a wealth of opportunities".

511 Commission of the European Communities, Communication from the Commission to the Council, the European Parliament, the European Economic and Social Committee and the Committee of the Regions, concerning the evaluation of the Multiannual Community Action Plan on promoting safer use of the Internet and new online technologies by combating illegal and harmful content primarily in the area of the protection of children and minors, COM (2003) 653 final, 03.11.2006. The Safer Internet Forum has been described as "*a unique discussion forum including representatives of industry, child welfare organizations and policymakers*" and "*a platform for national co- and self-regulatory bodies to exchange experience*": Commission of the European Communities, Proposal for a Decision of the European Parliament and of the Council on establishing a multiannual Community programme on promoting safer use of the Internet and new online technologies, COM (2004) 91 final, 12.03.2004, 8.

512 Commission of the European Communities, Communication from the Commission to the European Parliament, the Council, the European Economic and Social Committee and the Committee of the Regions, Communication, Final evaluation of the implementation of the multiannual Community action plan on promoting safer use of the Internet by combating illegal and harmful content on global networks, COM (2006) 663 final, 06.11.2006, 3.

513 Commission of the European Communities, Communication from the Commission to the Council, the European Parliament, the Economic and Social Committee and the Committee of the Regions, Intermediate evaluation of the implementation of the multiannual Community action plan on promoting safer use of the Internet by combating illegal and harmful content on global networks, COM (2001) 690 final, 23.11.2001, 3–4.

514 Commission of the European Communities, Communication from the Commission to the Council, the European Parliament, the European Economic and Social Committee and the Committee of the Regions, concerning the evaluation of the Multiannual Community Action Plan on promoting safer use of the Internet and new online technologies by combating illegal and harmful content primarily in the area of the protection of children and minors, COM (2003) 653 final, 03.11.2003, 3.

515 Commission of the European Communities, Communication from the Commission to the Council, the European Parliament, the European Economic and Social Committee and the Committee of the Regions, concerning the evaluation of the Multiannual Community Action Plan on promoting safer use of the Internet and new online technologies by

evaluation of the Action Plan, published in November 2006, deemed the implementation successful, and the attribution of grants and the management in general transparent, efficient and satisfactory.[516] The main achievements of the Action Plan were identified as being the launching of national hotlines and the development of awareness nodes.[517] The evaluation also found that filtering tools are essential and of growing importance, and that their availability had increased. The progress made in the area of rating and labelling, however, was considered unsatisfactory.[518] Furthermore, it was pointed out that the harmonisation of national legislation was an important issue, and that new difficulties were emerging such as social networking, Internet blogging and file sharing.[519] As a result of the final evaluation, seven recommendations were issued: (1) increase the visibility of hotlines, (2) improve the cooperation between hotlines and other stakeholders (in particular, the police and ISPs), (3) awareness-raising should focus on specific target groups and improve outreach, (4) involve children and young people in identifying problems and designing solutions, (5) increase end user awareness of the options available for filtering harmful content, (6) encourage industry

---

combating illegal and harmful content primarily in the area of the protection of children and minors, COM (2003) 653 final, 03.11.2003, 3.

516 Parliament and Council of the European Communities, Decision No 1151/2003/EC of the European Parliament and of the Council, amending Decision No 276/1999/EC adopting a Multiannual Community Action Plan on promoting safer use of the Internet by combating illegal and harmful content on global networks, 16.06.2003, *OJ* 01.07.2003, *L* 162, 4.

517 Parliament and Council of the European Communities, Decision No 1151/2003/EC of the European Parliament and of the Council, amending Decision No 276/1999/EC adopting a Multiannual Community Action Plan on promoting safer use of the Internet by combating illegal and harmful content on global networks, 16.06.2003, *OJ* 01.07.2003, *L* 162, 4. In the period 2003–2004, these two areas received the majority of the funding. Filtering, labelling, rating, self-regulation and codes of conduct were left to the industry according to the independent evaluation report: Idate (Philippe Mathonnet and Philippe Baudouin), Final evaluation of the Safer Internet Action Plan – Final report of the expert panel, May 2006, retrieved from http://ec.europa.eu/information_society/activities/sip/docs/prog_evaluation/final_evaluation_en_siap_06112006.pdf (on 14.11.2006), 4.

518 Parliament and Council of the European Communities, Decision No 1151/2003/EC of the European Parliament and of the Council, amending Decision No 276/1999/EC adopting a Multiannual Community Action Plan on promoting safer use of the Internet by combating illegal and harmful content on global networks, 16.06.2003, *OJ* 01.07.2003, *L* 162, 4.

519 Parliament and Council of the European Communities, Decision No 1151/2003/EC of the European Parliament and of the Council, amending Decision No 276/1999/EC adopting a Multiannual Community Action Plan on promoting safer use of the Internet by combating illegal and harmful content on global networks, 16.06.2003, *OJ* 01.07.2003, *L* 162, 4.

self-regulatory solutions at the EU level, and (7) map possibilities for future technological developments and user options.[520] Overall, however, the Action Plan was judged, by a three member Expert Panel, to be relevant and effective, and thus needing to be continued.[521]

Proposal Safer Internet Plus – As the end date of the Action Plan approached, it was felt that the complexity of the issues dealt with by the Action Plan and the multiplicity of the actors with which it was concerned, meant that a follow-up was necessary.[522] As a result, in March 2004, the Commission adopted a proposal for the Safer Internet Plus Programme, which the EU Telecommunications Council approved on 9 December 2004. Prior to the adoption of this proposal, wide public consultations had been undertaken and an ex ante evaluation had been carried out.[523] Both these efforts led to the conclusion that safer use of the Internet continued to be a real concern.[524] Moreover, new technologies and new ways of using these technologies only appeared to make the challenge of protecting children greater, both in a quantitative and qualitative way.[525]

---

520 Idate (Philippe Mathonnet and Philippe Baudouin), Final evaluation of the Safer Internet Action Plan – Final report of the expert panel, May 2006, retrieved from http://ec.europa.eu/information_society/activities/sip/docs/prog_evaluation/final_evaluation_en_siap_06112006.pdf (on 14.11.2006), 43–44.

521 Idate (Philippe Mathonnet and Philippe Baudouin), Final evaluation of the Safer Internet Action Plan – Final report of the expert panel, May 2006, retrieved from http://ec.europa.eu/information_society/activities/sip/docs/prog_evaluation/final_evaluation_en_siap_06112006.pdf (on 14.11.2006), 4.

522 Commission of the European Communities, Proposal for a Decision of the European Parliament and of the Council on establishing a multiannual Community programme on promoting safer use of the Internet and new online technologies, COM (2004) 91 final, 12.03.2004, 2.

523 Commission of the European Communities, Commission Staff working paper Ex ante evaluation of Safer Internet Plus (2005–2008), SEC (2004) 148, retrieved from http://eur-lex.europa.eu/LexUriServ/LexUriServ.do?uri=CELEX:52004PC0091:EN:HTML (on 23.11.2006).

524 Commission of the European Communities, Proposal for a Decision of the European Parliament and of the Council on establishing a multiannual Community programme on promoting safer use of the Internet and new online technologies, COM (2004) 91 final, 12.03.2004, 2 and 5.

525 Commission of the European Communities, Proposal for a Decision of the European Parliament and of the Council on establishing a multiannual Community programme on promoting safer use of the Internet and new online technologies, COM (2004) 91 final, 12.03.2004, 2 and 5.

Instruments – Interestingly, the proposal pointed out that a variety of means (e.g., enforcement of legal provisions, self-regulation, technical means such as filtering, and awareness raising) must be combined in order to deal with unwanted and harmful content efficiently.[526] This statement could be understood to indicate that self-regulation was no longer regarded as the only regulatory instrument that could be used in the struggle for more safety on the Internet. The proposal also asserted that self-regulation does not exclude the need for a legal underpinning, clarifying that "*a more pro-active approach may be required in order to stimulate agreement on an appropriate set of rules and their implementation*".[527] During the preparatory phase, other EU institutions expressed their preference for legislative measures.[528] This legislative approach, however, was not the one opted for in the end, as self-regulation still remained an important element of the scheme.[529]

---

[526] Commission of the European Communities, Proposal for a Decision of the European Parliament and of the Council on establishing a multiannual Community programme on promoting safer use of the Internet and new online technologies, COM (2004) 91 final, 12.03.2004, 4. In: Commission of the European Communities, Commission Staff working paper Ex ante evaluation of Safer Internet Plus (2005–2008), SEC (2004) 148, retrieved from http://eur-lex.europa.eu/LexUriServ/LexUriServ.do?uri=CELEX:52004PC0091:EN:HTML (on 23.11.2006), it is argued that "*according to the Safer Internet 1999–2002 programme evaluation, there was a consensus among those consulted that relying on the regulatory framework alone was not enough to deal with the global nature of the problem*".

[527] Commission of the European Communities, Proposal for a Decision of the European Parliament and of the Council on establishing a multiannual Community programme on promoting safer use of the Internet and new online technologies, COM (2004) 91 final, 12.03.2004, 8. With respect to the use of legally binding rules, the proposal states: "*Reaching international agreement on legally binding rules is desirable but will [be] a challenge to achieve and, even then, will not be achieved rapidly. Even if such agreement is reached, it will not be enough in itself to ensure implementation of the rules or to ensure protection of those at risk*" (p. 6). See also: Parliament and Council of the European Communities, Decision No 854/2005/EC of the European Parliament and of the Council establishing a multiannual Community programme on promoting safer use of the Internet and new online technologies, 11.05.2005, *OJ* 11.06.2005, *L* 149, recital 5.

[528] The opinion of the Economic and Social Committee on the proposal, for instance, was clearly in favour of adopting legislative measures. A number of the suggestions made, such as requiring a general obligation for all operators to protect children and users in general, were formulated in a vague manner and can be deemed rather ill-considered: European Economic and Social Committee, Opinion of the European Economic and Social Committee on the 'Proposal for a Decision of the European Parliament and of the Council on establishing a multiannual Community programme on promoting safer use of the internet and new online technologies', COM(2004) 91 final – 2004/0023 (COD), 16.12.2004, *OJ* 28/06/2005, *C* 157, 136.

[529] "*A fully functioning system of self-regulation is an essential element in limiting the flow of unwanted, harmful and illegal content. Self-regulation involves a number of components: consultation and appropriate representation of the parties concerned; codes of conduct;*

Safer Internet Plus Concept – The main aim of the Safer Internet Plus Programme,[530] adopted on 11 May 2005, was to promote safer use of the Internet and new technologies, and to protect the end-users, particularly children, from unwanted content.[531] Four key actions to undertake were distinguished: (1) fighting against illegal content (with a focus on hotlines), (2) tackling unwanted and harmful content (with a focus on filtering and rating),[532] (3) promoting a safer online environment (with a focus on self-regulation), and (4) awareness-raising.[533] Co-financing projects that attempt to achieve one or more of these aims remained the conceptual basis of the programme. Half of the available budget was earmarked for the awareness action line.[534] Principles of continuity – taking account of lessons learnt and

---

national bodies facilitating cooperation at Community level; and national evaluation of self-regulation frameworks. There is a continuing need for Community work in this area to encourage the European Internet and new online technologies industries to implement codes of conduct": Parliament and Council of the European Communities, Decision No 854/2005/EC of the European Parliament and of the Council establishing a multiannual Community programme on promoting safer use of the Internet and new online technologies, 11.05.2005, *OJ* 11.06.2005, *L* 149, Annex I.3.

530 Parliament and Council of the European Communities, Decision No 854/2005/EC of the European Parliament and of the Council establishing a multiannual Community programme on promoting safer use of the Internet and new online technologies, 11.05.2005, *OJ* 11.06.2005, *L* 149, 1.

531 Parliament and Council of the European Communities, Decision No 854/2005/EC of the European Parliament and of the Council establishing a multiannual Community Programme on promoting safer use of the Internet and new online technologies, 11.05.2005, *OJ* 11.06.2005, *L* 149, recital 1.

532 With respect to this line of action, the report of the European Parliament stressed that additional investment in the *development* of filtering software and rating systems should not be the priority; the priority should rather be research into the performance and transparency of filtering software: European Parliament, Report on the proposal for a decision of the European Parliament and of the Council on establishing a multiannual Community programme on promoting safer use of the Internet and new online technologies, A6–0033/2004, 18.11.2004, retrieved from http://www.europarl.europa.eu/omk/sipade3?PUBREF=-//EP//NONSGML+REPORT+A6–2004–0033+0+DOC+PDF+V0//EN&L=EN&LEVEL=2&NAV=S&LSTDOC=Y on (15.11.2006). This was changed accordingly in the adopted version of the Decision: Parliament and Council of the European Communities, Decision No 854/2005/EC of the European Parliament and of the Council establishing a multiannual Community programme on promoting safer use of the Internet and new online technologies, 11.05.2005, *OJ* 11.06.2005, *L* 149, recital 7.

533 Parliament and Council of the European Communities, Decision No 854/2005/EC of the European Parliament and of the Council establishing a multiannual Community programme on promoting safer use of the Internet and new online technologies, 11.05.2005, *OJ* 11.06.2005, *L* 149, article 1, para. 2.

534 Parliament and Council of the European Communities, Decision No 854/2005/EC of the European Parliament and of the Council establishing a multiannual

building on achievements of the previous Action Plan's initiatives – and enhancement – meeting new threats and ensuring European added-value – were the main inspiration behind the programme.[535]

Scope – The scope of the Programme, as far as technologies are concerned, was similar to the second phase of the Safer Internet Action Plan.[536] Regarding types of content, however, the range was extended to violence.[537] The focus of the programme clearly was the end-user,[538] and user-empowerment, i.e., enabling users to make their own decisions on how to deal with unwanted and harmful content, for instance with the help of technical tools, was one of the projected aims.[539]

Safer Internet Forum – The Safer Internet Forum concept, an element of the third line of action promoting a safer environment, was clarified in the Annex to the Decision.[540] The Forum functions as a discussion forum for

Community programme on promoting safer use of the Internet and new online technologies, 11.05.2005, *OJ* 11.06.2005, *L* 149, Annex II.

535 Commission of the European Communities, Proposal for a Decision of the European Parliament and of the Council on establishing a multiannual Community programme on promoting safer use of the Internet and new online technologies, COM (2004) 91 final, 12.03.2004, 6. See also: Parliament and Council of the European Communities, Decision No 854/2005/EC of the European Parliament and of the Council establishing a multiannual Community programme on promoting safer use of the Internet and new online technologies, 11.05.2005, *OJ* 11.06.2005, *L* 149, recital 6.

536 Cf. *supra*.

537 Commission of the European Communities, Communication from the Commission to the European Parliament, the Council, the European Economic and Social Committee and the Committee of the Regions, Communication, on the implementation of the multiannual Community programme on promoting safer use of the Internet and new online technologies (Safer Internet plus), COM (2006) 661 final, 06.11.2006, 3.

538 Parliament and Council of the European Communities, Decision No 854/2005/EC of the European Parliament and of the Council establishing a multiannual Community programme on promoting safer use of the Internet and new online technologies, 11.05.2005, *OJ* 11.06.2005, *L* 149, recital 1 and article 1.1; Commission of the European Communities, Proposal for a Decision of the European Parliament and of the Council on establishing a multiannual Community programme on promoting safer use of the Internet and new online technologies, COM (2004) 91 final, 12.03.2004, 6.

539 Parliament and Council of the European Communities, Decision No 854/2005/EC of the European Parliament and of the Council establishing a multiannual Community programme on promoting safer use of the Internet and new online technologies, 11.05.2005, *OJ* 11.06.2005, *L* 149, Annex I.2.

540 Parliament and Council of the European Communities, Decision No 854/2005/EC of the European Parliament and of the Council establishing a multiannual Com-

all actors involved, as a platform for the exchange of experiences, views and information, and as a platform to drive consensus.[541]

Evaluation – According to the reporting requirement embedded in article 5(3) of the Decision adopting the Programme,[542] a first implementation report was published by the Commission in November 2006.[543] The Programme sponsored thirty-seven projects in 2005–2006.[544]

Achievements – The Safer Internet Forum was convened each year since its inception: in 2005, it discussed the topic of 'Child safety and mobile

---

munity programme on promoting safer use of the Internet and new online technologies, 11.05.2005, *OJ* 11.06.2005, *L* 149, Annex I.3.

541 The specific objectives of the Forum are formulated as follows: "*(1) stimulating networking of the appropriate structures within Member States and developing links with self-regulatory bodies outside Europe, (2) stimulating consensus and self-regulation on issues such as quality rating of websites, cross-media content rating, rating and filtering techniques, extending them to new forms of content such as online games and new forms of access such as mobile phones, (3) encouraging service providers to draw up codes of conduct on issues such as handling notice and take down procedures in a transparent and conscientious manner and informing users about safer use of Internet and the existence of hotlines reporting illegal content, and (4) promoting research into the effectiveness of rating projects and filtering technologies – user organisations and scientific research institutes can be valuable partners in this effort*": Parliament and Council of the European Communities, Decision No 854/2005/EC of the European Parliament and of the Council establishing a multiannual Community programme on promoting safer use of the Internet and new online technologies, 11.05.2005, *OJ* 11.06.2005, *L* 149, Annex I.3.

542 Parliament and Council of the European Communities, Decision No 854/2005/EC of the European Parliament and of the Council establishing a multiannual Community programme on promoting safer use of the Internet and new online technologies, 11.05.2005, *OJ* 11.06.2005, *L* 149.

543 Commission of the European Communities, Communication from the Commission to the European Parliament, the Council, the European Economic and Social Committee and the Committee of the Regions, Communication, on the implementation of the multiannual Community programme on promoting safer use of the Internet and new online technologies (Safer Internet plus), COM (2006) 661 final, 06.11.2006.

544 Hotlines: 1 network coordinator and 16 hotlines; awareness nodes and helplines: 1 network coordinator and 16 awareness nodes; user empowerment: 1 thematic network; self-regulation: 1 thematic network; and media: 1 thematic network: Commission of the European Communities, Communication from the Commission to the European Parliament, the Council, the European Economic and Social Committee and the Committee of the Regions, Communication, on the implementation of the multiannual Community programme on promoting safer use of the Internet and new online technologies (Safer Internet plus), COM (2006) 661 final, 06.11.2006.

phones';[545] in 2006, 'Children's use of new media and blocking access to child sexual abuse images';[546] in 2007, 'Online-related sexual abuse of children, with a special focus on the process of grooming and the consequences for children', 'Awareness-raising' and 'The impact and consequences of convergence of online technologies';[547] in 2008 'Social networking' and in 2009 'Promoting online safety in schools'.[548] In the context of the Safer Internet Plus Programme, the Commission also presented the results of the Eurobarometer surveys on Internet safety.[549] Furthermore, in February 2005, 2006, 2007, 2008 and 2009, Safer Internet Days were organised, as part of the awareness-raising goal.[550]

FUTURE – The 2006 evaluation also announced the future enhancement of the impact of the Safer Internet Plus Programme activities by consolidating and extending the geographical coverage of the hotlines and awareness-raising networks, fostering close cooperation between all stakeholders in Safer Internet activities, helping EU citizens to find practical information about how they can use the Internet more safely, and increasing the visibility of the Safer Internet Plus Programme among EU citizens, both adults and children.[551]

---

[545] More information on: http://europa.eu.int/information_society/activities/sip/si_forum/mobile_2005/index_en.htm (retrieved on 20.11.2006).

[546] More information on: http://europa.eu.int/information_society/activities/sip/si_forum/forum_june_2006/agenda/index_en.htm (retrieved on 20.11.2006).

[547] More information on http://ec.europa.eu/information_society/activities/sip/si_forum/forum_june_2007/index_en.htm (retrieved on 26.03.2008).

[548] More information on http://ec.europa.eu/information_society/activities/sip/si_forum/index_en.htm (retrieved on 26.11.2008).

[549] EUROPEAN COMMISSION, Eurobarometer Safer Internet, May 2006, retrieved from http://europa.eu.int/information_society/activities/sip/docs/eurobarometer/eurobarometer_2005_25_ms.pdf (on 20.11.2006) and EUROPEAN COMMISSION, Eurobarometer Safer Internet for Children: Qualitative study in 29 European studies, May 2007, retrieved from http://ec.europa.eu/information_society/activities/sip/docs/eurobarometer/qualitative_study_2007/summary_report_en.pdf (on 14.03.2008).

[550] More information on: http://ec.europa.eu/information_society/activities/sip/si_day/index_en.htm (retrieved on 26.11.2008). This initiative has been considered a "*valuable opportunity to improve communication among stakeholders and to reach out to the broader public*": COMMISSION OF THE EUROPEAN COMMUNITIES, Communication from the Commission to the European Parliament, the Council, the European Economic and Social Committee and the Committee of the Regions, Communication, on the implementation of the multiannual Community programme on promoting safer use of the Internet and new online technologies (Safer Internet plus), COM (2006) 661 final, 06.11.2006, 7.

[551] COMMISSION OF THE EUROPEAN COMMUNITIES, Communication from the Commission to the European Parliament, the Council, the European Economic and Social Committee and the Committee of the Regions, Communication, on the implementation of the multiannual

Impact assessment and new proposal – A second impact assessment procedure was launched in April 2007,[552] and was aimed at creating a basis for deciding whether or not to put forward a follow-up programme starting 2009 onwards or not. The consultation revealed that the actions carried out under the previous programme were effective, but that they must be adapted to new needs resulting from the emergence of new technologies and services.[553] Consequently, a follow-up Programme appeared justified and a proposal for the extension of the Programme from 2009 until 2013 was put forward by the Commission.[554] The proposal aimed to provide practical help for the end-user (children, parents, carers and educators), and sought to involve and bring together the different stakeholders whose cooperation is essential.[555] The scope of the Programme would be extended so as to focus on grooming and cyberbullying and to provide more knowledge on the ways children use new technologies.[556] Four lines of action were again put forward: (1) reducing illegal content and tackling harmful conduct online, (2) promoting a safer online environment, (3) ensuring public awareness, and (4) establishing a knowledge base of all issues related to the achievement of a safer Internet (such as, for instance, the (evolving) ways children use online technologies, associated risks and the possible harmful effects the use of online technologies can have on them, including technical, psychological and sociological issues).[557] Again, it was stressed that to achieve the aim of the Programme it

---

Community Programme on promoting safer use of the Internet and new online technologies (Safer Internet plus), COM (2006) 661 final, 06.11.2006, 6.

552 European Commission, Public consultation: Safer Internet and online technologies for children, 2007, retrieved from http://ec.europa.eu/information_society/activities/sip/docs/public_consultation_prog/pc_2007_info_en.pdf (on 02.04.2008).

553 Commission of the European Communities, Proposal for a Decision of the European Parliament and of the Council establishing a multiannual Community programme on protecting children using the Internet and other communication technologies, COM (2008) 106 final, 27.02.2008, 3.

554 Commission of the European Communities, Proposal for a Decision of the European Parliament and of the Council establishing a multiannual Community programme on protecting children using the Internet and other communication technologies, COM (2008) 106 final, 27.02.2008.

555 Commission of the European Communities, Proposal for a Decision of the European Parliament and of the Council establishing a multiannual Community programme on protecting children using the Internet and other communication technologies, COM (2008) 106 final, 27.02.2008, 7.

556 Commission of the European Communities, Proposal for a Decision of the European Parliament and of the Council establishing a multiannual Community programme on protecting children using the Internet and other communication technologies, COM (2008) 106 final, 27.02.2008, 7.

557 Commission of the European Communities, Proposal for a Decision of the European Parliament and of the Council establishing a multiannual Community programme on

would be necessary to combine several measures and actions (such as supporting technologies and codes of conduct).[558] The proposal for the new Safer Internet Programme was adopted by the Parliament on 23 October 2008,[559] and by the Council of Ministers on 9 December 2008.[560]

SUPPORT FOR 'SELF-REGULATION' – Within the framework of the Safer Internet Programmes two initiatives merit a special mention. Both initiatives have been labelled self-regulation, but were developed in close cooperation with the European Commission. The first initiative is the 'European Framework for safer mobile use by younger teenagers and children', adopted by a number of mobile operators and content providers in 2007.[561] This framework was "*brokered by the European Commission*"[562] and concerns the implementation of principles and measures regarding access controls, awareness raising campaigns, classification of content and the fight against illegal content on mobile phones. A second evaluation report has been published by GSM-Europe in April 2009.[563] Although the framework has been widely adopted

protecting children using the Internet and other communication technologies, COM (2008) 106 final, 27.02.2008, 8–9.

558 COMMISSION OF THE EUROPEAN COMMUNITIES, Proposal for a Decision of the European Parliament and of the Council establishing a multiannual Community programme on protecting children using the Internet and other communication technologies, COM (2008) 106 final, 27.02.2008, 13.

559 RAPID, Commission welcomes European Parliament's strong support for a new Safer Internet Programme, IP/08/1571, 22.10.2008, retrieved from http://europa.eu/rapid/pressReleasesAction.do?reference=IP/08/1571&format=HTML&aged=0&language=EN&guiLanguage=fr (on 26.11.2008).

560 RAPID, EU adopts new Safer Internet Programme: € 55 million to make the Internet a safer place for children, IP/08/1899, 09.12.2008, retrieved from http://europa.eu/rapid/pressReleasesAction.do?reference=IP/08/1899&format=HTML&aged=0&language=EN&guiLanguage=en (on 20.12.2008). Cf. PARLIAMENT AND COUNCIL OF THE EUROPEAN UNION, Decision No 1351/2008/EC of the European Parliament and of the Council establishing a multiannual Community programme on protecting children using the Internet and other communication technologies, 16.12.2008, *OJ* 24.12.2008, *L* 348, 118.

561 X, European framework for safer mobile use by younger teenagers and children, February 2007, retrieved from http://ec.europa.eu/information_society/activities/sip/docs/mobile_2005/europeanframework.pdf (on 28.05.2009).

562 RAPID, Commission calls on mobile operators to continue to improve child safety policies, IP/09/596, 20.04.2009, retrieved from http://europa.eu/rapid/pressReleasesAction.do?reference=IP/09/596&format=HTML&aged=0&language=EN&guiLanguage=en (on 28.05.2009).

563 GSMEUROPE, European framework for safer mobile use by younger teenagers and children: Implementation report, 16.04.2009, retrieved from http://www.gsmeurope.org/documents/PwC_Implementation_Report.pdf (on 28.05.2009). A first report was published in March 2008: GSMEUROPE, European framework for safer mobile use by younger teenagers

(in 22 Member States, by 81 mobile operators through national codes of conduct), the requirements of the framework are not fully complied with, according to the report. In a reaction to this, the European Commission has called on mobile operators to keep improving child safety policies.[564] The second initiative introduced the 'Safer social networking principles for the EU', which aim to "*provide good practice recommendations for the providers of social networking and other user interactive sites, to enhance the safety of children and young people using their services*".[565] These principles have been adopted – voluntarily – by 18 social networks and were created with the help of researchers, child welfare organisations and the European Commission, who brought all these actors together. The European Commission will evaluate this scheme after twelve months.

G. *Council of Europe: a variety of policy documents*

Recurring theme – The protection of minors in digital media has also been a recurring theme in a number of policy documents issued by the Council of Europe. The issue is most often raised in relation to the protection of human rights in the digital environment,[566] in particular the protection of the freedom of expression.[567] In this context, the importance of

---

and children: one year after – Implementation report, 06.03.2008, retrieved from http://www.gsmeurope.org/documents/gsma_implementation_report.pdf (on 28.05.2009).

564 Rapid, Commission calls on mobile operators to continue to improve child safety policies, IP/09/596, 20.04.2009, retrieved from http://europa.eu/rapid/pressReleasesAction.do?reference=IP/09/596&format=HTML&aged=0&language=EN&guiLanguage=en (on 28.05.2009).

565 X, Safer social networking principles for the EU, 10.02.2009, retrieved from http://ec.europa.eu/information_society/activities/social_networking/docs/sn_principles.pdf (on 25.05.2009), 1. Also: Reding, Viviane, How can we empower youngsters to stay safe online? Innovative solutions in Europe, Speech at the World Childhood Foundation Seminar, Stockholm, 17 September 2009, retrieved from http://ec.europa.eu/commission_barroso/reding/docs/speeches/2009/stockholm-170909.pdf (on 21.01.2010).

566 Cf. *infra*, Part 2, Chapter 1.

567 Council of Europe (Committee of Ministers), Declaration on a European policy for new information technologies, 07.05.1999, retrieved from https://wcd.coe.int/ViewDoc.jsp?id=448133&Site=CM&BackColorInternet=9999CC&BackColorIntranet=FFBB55&BackColorLogged=FFAC75 (on 24.04.2007), (v); Council of Europe (Committee of Ministers), Recommendation Rec(2001)8 on self-regulation concerning cyber content (self-regulation and user protection against illegal or harmful content on new communications and information services), 05.09.2001, retrieved from https://wcd.coe.int/ViewDoc.jsp?id=220387&Site=COE&BackColorInternet=DBDCF2&BackColorIntranet=FDC864&BackColorLogged=FDC864 (on 24.04.2007), § 7; Council of Europe (Committee of Ministers), Recommendation CM/Rec(2007)11 on promoting freedom of expression and information in the new information and communications environment, 26.09.2007,

protecting minors against harmful content (without infringing on the freedom of expression of adults) has been stressed repeatedly.[568] Mostly, the approach favoured throughout the Council of Europe documents is in line with the strategies advocated at the EU level. Thus, whereas in the earlier documents emphasis was put on self- (and co-) regulation, the development of codes of conduct and the use of technical measures,[569] gradually

retrieved from https://wcd.coe.int/ViewDoc.jsp?id=1188541&Site=COE&BackColorInternet=DBDCF2&BackColorIntranet=FDC864&BackColorLogged=FDC864 (on 26.03.2008).

568 Council of Europe (Committee of Ministers), Declaration on human rights and the rule of law in the Information Society, 13.05.2005, retrieved from https://wcd.coe.int/ViewDoc.jsp?Ref=CM(2005)56&Sector=secCM&Language=lanEnglish&Ver=final&BackColorInternet=9999CC&BackColorIntranet=FFBB55&BackColorLogged=FFAC75 (on 19.05.2008), II.4 § 3; Council of Europe, Pan-European forum on "Human rights in the Information Society: responsible behaviour by key actors", Strasbourg, 12-13.09.2005, retrieved from http://www.coe.int/t/dghl/standardsetting/media/doc/forumstbgsept2005_EN.asp (on 25.04.2007): "*The need for balance between competing rights and freedoms is ever more necessary within a rapidly evolving technological and economic context at both the Member State and European/international level*"; Council of Europe (Committee of Ministers), Recommendation CM/REC(2009)5 on measures to protect children against harmful content and behaviour and to promote their active participation in the new information and communications environment, 08.07.2009, retrieved from https://wcd.coe.int/ViewDoc.jsp?id=1470045&Site=CM (on 20.01.2010): "*Protecting freedom of expression and human dignity in the information and communications environment by ensuring a coherent level of protection for minors against harmful content and behaviour and developing children's media literacy skills is a priority for the Council of Europe*"; Council of Europe (Parliamentary Assembly), Recommendation 1882 (2009) The promotion of Internet and online media services appropriate for minors, 28 September 2009, retrieved from http://assembly.coe.int/Mainf.asp?link=/Documents/AdoptedText/ta09/EREC1882.htm (on 20 January 2010).

569 Council of Europe (Committee of Ministers), Recommendation Rec(2001)8 on self-regulation concerning cyber content (self-regulation and user protection against illegal or harmful content on new communications and information services), 05.09.2001, retrieved from https://wcd.coe.int/ViewDoc.jsp?id=220387&Site=COE&BackColorInternet=DBDCF2&BackColorIntranet=FDC864&BackColorLogged=FDC864 (on 24.04.2007), § 10–12; Council of Europe, Democracy, human rights and the rule of law in the Information Society, Contribution by the Council of Europe to the 2nd Preparatory Committee for the World Summit on the Information Society, 07.12.2002, retrieved from http://www.coe.int/t/e/integrated_projects/democracy/02_activities/04_w.s.i.s/90IP1(2002)27.asp (on 24.04.2007), I § 5; Council of Europe (Committee of Ministers), Declaration on freedom of communications on the Internet, 28.05.2003, retrieved from https://wcd.coe.int/rsi/common/renderers/rend_standard.jsp?DocId=37031&SecMode=1&SiteName=cm&Lang=en (on 24.04.2007), principle 2–3; Council of Europe (Committee of Ministers), Declaration on human rights and the rule of law in the Information Society, 13.05.2005, retrieved from https://wcd.coe.int/ViewDoc.jsp?Ref=CM(2005)56&Sector=secCM&Language=lanEnglish&Ver=final&BackColorInternet=9999CC&BackColorIntranet=FFBB55&BackColorLogged=FFAC75 (on 19.05.2008), II.1 § 3.

more and more attention was paid to media literacy, education, awareness and empowerment.[570]

EMPOWERING CHILDREN – Especially in recent years, the Council of Europe intensified its efforts with respect to the protection of children and young people in new media. In 2005, the Council of Europe commitment to this goal was expressed in the Warsaw Summit Action Plan:

> *The Council of Europe shall also continue its work on children in the information society, in particular as regards developing their media literacy skills and ensuring their protection against harmful content.*[571]

The Council of Europe also commissioned a study entitled 'Young people, well-being and risk on-line',[572] in which the concept of 'harm' was extensively studied.[573] Furthermore, since 2004, almost every year a Pan-European Forum was organised, which dealt with this theme.[574]

RECOMMENDATION ON EMPOWERMENT OF CHILDREN – In preparation of the Pan-European Forum on 'Human Rights in the Information Society: Empowering children and young people', held in Yerevan on 5 and 6 October 2006,

---

570 COUNCIL OF EUROPE, Pan-European forum on "Human rights in the Information Society: responsible behaviour by key actors", Strasbourg, 12-13.09.2005, retrieved from http://www.coe.int/t/dghl/standardsetting/media/doc/forumstbgsept2005_EN.asp (on 25.04.2007); COUNCIL OF EUROPE, Pan-European forum on "Human rights in the Information Society: empowering children and young people", Yerevan, 5-6.10.2006, retrieved from http://www.coe.int/t/e/human_rights/media/links/events/1GalREPORT_Yerevan_FrauMeigs_en.pdf (on 25.04.2007, no longer available).

571 COUNCIL OF EUROPE (MINISTERS' DEPUTIES), Warsaw Summit Action Plan, CM(2005)80 final, Warsaw, 17.05.2005, retrieved from http://www.coe.int/t/dcr/summit/20050517_plan_action_en.asp (on 30.05.2006), II.5 § 3.

572 COUNCIL OF EUROPE (GROUP OF SPECIALISTS ON HUMAN RIGHTS IN THE INFORMATION SOCIETY), Young people, well-being and risk on-line (abridged), Study by Rachel O'CONNELL and Jo BRYCE, 25.04.2006, retrieved from http://www.coe.int/t/dghl/standardsetting/media/doc/H-Inf(2006)005_en.pdf (on 30.05.2006).

573 Cf. *supra*.

574 COUNCIL OF EUROPE AND EUROPEAN UNION, European Forum: Internet with a human face – a common responsibility, Warsaw, 26–27.03.2004, http://www.coe.int/t/dghl/standarsetting/media/Doc/MM-S-OD(2004)003_en.asp#TopOfPage (on 25.04.2007); COUNCIL OF EUROPE, Pan-European forum on "Human rights in the Information Society: responsible behaviour by key actors", Strasbourg, 12-13.09.2005, retrieved from http://www.coe.int/t/dghl/standardsetting/media/doc/forumstbgsept2005_EN.asp (on 25.04.2007); COUNCIL OF EUROPE, Pan-European forum on "Human rights in the Information Society: empowering children and young people", Yerevan, 5-6.10.2006, retrieved from http://www.coe.int/t/e/human_rights/media/links/events/1GalREPORT_Yerevan_FrauMeigs_en.pdf (on 25.04.2007, no longer available).

the Committee of Ministers adopted a Recommendation on empowering children in the new information and communications environment.[575] The Recommendation opens with the reaffirmation of the Member States' commitment to the fundamental right of freedom of expression, incorporated in article 10 ECHR (*infra*).[576] Interestingly, having emphasised that information and communication technologies can positively, as well as negatively, impact on the enjoyment of fundamental rights, the Recommendation pursues the notion of harm in greater depth. Examples of content and behaviour that are not necessarily illegal, but that may "*adversely [affect] the physical, emotional and psychological well-being of children*" are, for instance, online pornography, the portrayal and glorification of violence and self-harm, demeaning, discriminatory or racist expressions or apologia for such conduct, solicitation (grooming), bullying, and stalking and other forms of harassment. Such content and behaviour may, according to the Recommendation, be tackled through

> *the development and provision of information literacy, defined as the competent use of tools providing access to information, the development of critical analysis of content and the appropriation of communications skills to foster citizenship and creativity, and training initiatives for children and their educators in order for them to use information and communication technologies and services in a positive and responsible manner.*[577]

Empowerment, education and media literacy are put forward as key elements of a strategy for the protection of children against harmful content. Furthermore, the Recommendation stresses the importance of a multi-stakeholder approach involving governmental organisations, the private sector and civil society actors. This need for a multi-stakeholder approach had also been highlighted at the Pan-European Forum in 2005 and 2006.[578] Of particular

---

575 Council of Europe (Committee of Ministers), Recommendation Rec(2006)12 on empowering children in the new information and communications environment, 27.09.2006, retrieved from https://wcd.coe.int/ViewDoc.jsp?Ref=Rec(2006)12&Sector=secCM&Language=lanEnglish&Ver=original&BackColorInternet=9999CC&BackColorIntranet=FFBB55&BackColorLogged=FFAC75 (on 16.10.2006).

576 The right to privacy, as guaranteed by article 8 EHCR, is highlighted as well.

577 Council of Europe (Committee of Ministers), Recommendation Rec(2006)12 on empowering children in the new information and communications environment, 27.09.2006, retrieved from https://wcd.coe.int/ViewDoc.jsp?Ref=Rec(2006)12&Sector=secCM&Language=lanEnglish&Ver=original&BackColorInternet=9999CC&BackColorIntranet=FFBB55&BackColorLogged=FFAC75 (on 16.10.2006), recital 9.

578 Council of Europe, Pan-European Forum on "Human rights in the Information Society: responsible behaviour by key actors", Strasbourg, 12-13.09.2005, retrieved from http://www.coe.int/t/dghl/standardsetting/media/doc/forumstbgsept2005_EN.asp (on 25.04.2007) and Council of Europe, Pan-European forum on "Human Rights in the

importance here is the fact that there was a high level of consensus that the state should remain the primary guarantor of human rights. However, collaboration with industry and non-governmental organisations within civil society, international governmental organisations and young people was considered essential.

Recommendation on protection against harmful content and behaviour – In July 2009, the Committee of Ministers adopted a Recommendation on measures to protect children against harmful content and behaviour and to promote their active participation in the new information and communications environment.[579] The Recommendation identifies the "*need to provide children with the knowledge, skills, understanding, attitudes, human rights values and behaviour necessary to participate actively in social and public life, and to act responsibly while respecting the rights of others*". Member States are encouraged to develop coherent strategies to protect children against content and behaviour carrying a risk of harm. These strategies should focus on providing safe and secure spaces for children on the Internet, encouraging the development of a pan-European trustmark and labelling systems, and promoting Internet skills and literacy for children, parents and educators.

H. *Concluding remarks*

Consistent approach – From the overview of the EU and Council of Europe documents, we can conclude that the approach opted for, since concerns related to the protection of minors in the digital media environment first appeared, has been rather consistent. Early policy documents were infected with enthusiasm for technological solutions and self-regulation. This can be linked with the liberal and technology-oriented atmosphere which characterised the early years of the Internet boom. Gradually, however, co-regulation sneaked its way into the documents, and more and more attention was paid to cooperation, dialogue, literacy and awareness. In the past few years, policy documents even increasingly pointed to the fact that only a combination of tools and instruments would succeed in effectively protecting

Information Society: empowering children and young people", Yerevan, 5-6.10.2006, retrieved from http://www.coe.int/t/e/human_rights/media/links/events/1GalREPORT_Yerevan_FrauMeigs_en.pdf (on 25.04.2007, no longer available).

579 Council of Europe (Committee of Ministers), Recommendation CM/REC(2009)5 on measures to protect children against harmful content and behaviour and to promote their active participation in the new information and communications environment, 08.07.2009, retrieved from https://wcd.coe.int/ViewDoc.jsp?id=1470045&Site=CM (on 20.01.2010).

minors against harmful content. It is, however, essential to have a clear understanding of the separate mechanisms before being able to grasp how an optimal combination would function.

Vague notions – Yet, most policy documents refrain from defining or describing the different proposed regulatory instruments, such as self- and co-regulation, in a clear and unambiguous manner. The next chapter attempts to provide an overview and an analysis of these different instruments.

1.3. Conclusion

Constitutive elements – In this chapter, the central elements of this study were delineated and analysed. First, the essential building blocks, i.e., 'digital media', 'minor' and 'harmful content' were explored. We found that there are indications that certain content may harm the development of children. Hence, given the fact that media regulation is traditionally founded on an evaluation of the "*detriment caused to society or individuals by the availability of certain content*" and should "*aim to be a proportionate response to that risk*",[580] the protection of children against such content, whether in traditional media or new, digital media, is a justified normative goal.

Regulatory challenges – Second, the fundamental problem, i.e., the need for a broader regulatory framework to achieve this policy goal of protecting minors against harmful content, was presented. In this section we addressed the fact that although this policy goal is still valid, the instruments with which to reach this goal – traditionally national legislation – display a number of flaws when applied to the changed information and communications environment. Certain inherent characteristics of this new media environment, such as its global and decentralised nature, the multiplicity of involved actors, its rapidly evolving character and its complexity, clash with features of traditional legislation, such as its national nature, its lack of involvement of stakeholders and the slowness of adaptation. Furthermore, in areas where freedom of expression is at stake, the use of legislation is very delicate and needs to be carefully balanced. We examined the situation in the United

[580] Millwood Hargrave, Andrea and Livingstone, Sonia, Harm and offence in media content: a review of the evidence (abbreviated version of the book), retrieved from http://www.lse.ac.uk/collections/media@lse/pdf/Harm%20and%20Offence,%20summary.pdf (on 11.03.2008), 13.

States where this appeared to be quite problematic. Hence, we came to the conclusion that it is increasingly necessary to think out of the 'legislation box'. Next, we took a look at the past decade's European Union and Council of Europe policy documents in the area of the protection of minors against harmful content, and found that these documents confirmed our conclusion. The use of alternative regulatory instruments such as self- and co-regulation, as well as technological tools, was promoted from the outset, both at the EU and Council of Europe levels. However, we also found that definitions or descriptions of these alternative regulatory instruments were lacking in the different policy documents. Hence, in the next chapter these instruments and their use will be described and analysed in greater detail.

Chapter 2

Alternative Regulatory Instruments

Structure – The aim of this chapter is to elucidate the nature and use of the 'alternative regulatory instruments' which increasingly appeared in policy documents regarding the protection of minors against digital harmful content (*supra*). Recent regulatory trends are examined and general, as well as media policy documents are analysed. Furthermore, an overview of existing alternative regulatory instruments is provided, the concepts of self-regulation and co-regulation are clarified and illustrated, and the use of regulatory tools such as technology and supporting mechanisms are discussed.

2.1. 'Regulation'

Regulation: a rule or directive made and maintained by an authority.[1]

Pragmatic approach – Regulation is at the same time a seemingly obvious and a difficult to grasp concept. It is a concept which varies across centuries, cultures and countries. Much academic writing has been devoted to different theories of regulation.[2] However, whereas general conceptual analysis is undoubtedly of great importance, in this study we have instead opted for an approach that focuses on a specific element of 'regulation', i.e., the involvement of different actors in the regulatory process. Therefore in this section we will not reiterate the rich body of legal theory concerning regulation, but

---

1 Pearshall, Judy (ed.), *The concise Oxford dictionary*, Oxford, Oxford University Press, 1999, 1207.

2 Examples of recent academic works are: Baldwin, Robert, Scott, Colin and Hood, Christopher (eds), *A reader on regulation*, Oxford, Oxford University Press, 1998, 522 p.; Black, Julia, *Rules and regulators*, Oxford, Clarendon Press Oxford, 1997, 285 p.; Ayres, Ian and Braithwaite, John, *Responsive regulation: transcending the deregulation debate*, Oxford, Oxford University Press, 1992, 205 p.; Braithwaite, John, *Restorative justice and responsive regulation*, Oxford, Oxford University Press, 2002, 314 p.

rather select a number of conceptual elements that are crucial to our research subject and provide some thoughts on these elements.

From command-and-control to decentred regulation – The second and third part of this section aim to clarify the concepts of command-and-control regulation and decentred regulation as a prelude to the subsequent analysis of different alternative regulatory instruments.

2.1.1. *Regulation: conceptual elements*

> *Public authorities regulate in the public interest to achieve a variety of goals – to ensure a fair and competitive market place, to protect health, to provide safety, to stimulate innovation, to preserve the natural environment. Regulation is a tool for delivering policies and meeting citizen's expectations.*
>
> European Commission[3]

Public policy objective – Regulation is an essential and accepted aspect of a contemporary society.[4] The goal of every democratic government should be to advance the economic and social wellbeing of its citizens,[5] and regulation is a tool to achieve the different public policy goals that aim to attain this greater democratic ideal.[6] This is a very broad approach of regulation which encompasses a great number of regulatory instruments. No uniform, universally agreed-upon concept of regulation, however, exists.[7] Instead, a whole array of definitions has been conceived by scholars, ranging from the very narrow to the very broad (*infra*).[8]

---

[3] European Commission, Better regulation: simply explained, 2006, retrieved from http://ec.europa.eu/governance/better_regulation/documents/brochure/br_brochure_en.pdf (on 14.05.2008), 3.

[4] European Commission, Better regulation: simply explained, 2006, retrieved from http://ec.europa.eu/governance/better_regulation/documents/brochure/br_brochure_en.pdf (on 14.05.2008), 3.

[5] OECD, The OECD Report on Regulatory Reform, 1997, retrieved from http://www.oecd.org/dataoecd/17/25/2391768.pdf (on 09.04.2008), 5.

[6] Mandelkern group on better regulation, Final Report, 13.11.2001, retrieved from http://ec.europa.eu/governance/impact/docs/key_docs/mandelkern_report_en.pdf (on 13.05.2008), i; OECD, The OECD Report on Regulatory Reform, 1997, retrieved from http://www.oecd.org/dataoecd/17/25/2391768.pdf (on 09.04.2008), 5.

[7] Baldwin, Robert, Scott, Colin and Hood, Christopher (eds), *A reader on regulation*, Oxford, Oxford University Press, 1998, 2.

[8] Majone, for instance, argued that "*European scholars tend to identify regulation with the whole realm of legislation, governance and social control*": Majone, Giandomenico, "The rise of the regulatory state in Europe", in: Baldwin, Robert, Scott, Colin and Hood, Christopher (eds), *A reader on regulation*, Oxford, Oxford University Press, 1998, 193.

Terminological confusion – The use of the notion 'regulation' is by no means uniform or consistent.[9] Regulation, legislation and governance are only a few of the words that are often used to express the same or a similar concept. Furthermore, 'regulation' is often used in combination with other words, such as 'command-and-control', 'self', 'co' or 'soft', that attach a qualification to the sort of regulation that is being discussed.

Avoiding overly narrow definitions – For the purpose of this book, overly narrow definitions of 'regulation' are avoided, so as to adopt an open-minded approach to instruments that are used to regulate digital media content. This is consistent with recent trends that stress that social activity is as much a matter of regulatory interest[10] as economic activity, which, according to a certain tradition in regulatory theory, is usually emphasised as the object of regulation.[11] Furthermore, 'regulation' is often taken to be the prerogative of 'agencies'.[12] With this approach, 'regulation' is seen to be the product of the decision making of regulators. This is an interpretation that we do not pursue in this book, as it, in our opinion, would lead to a too narrow a scope of enquiry.

Categories of definitions – Julia Black, who is one of the scholars who in recent years addressed many of the issues concerning regulation that are relevant to our research subject, argued that there are three main definitions of regulation:

> *In the first, regulation is the promulgation of rules by government accompanied by mechanisms for monitoring and enforcement, usually assumed to be performed through a specialist public agency. In the second, it is any form of direct state intervention in the economy, whatever form that intervention might take. In*

---

[9] Black, Julia, "Critical reflections on regulation", Discussion paper, January 2002, retrieved from http://www.lse.ac.uk/collections/CARR/pdf/DPs/Disspaper4.pdf (on 08.04.2008), 8.

[10] Black, Julia, "Critical reflections on regulation", Discussion paper, January 2002, retrieved from http://www.lse.ac.uk/collections/CARR/pdf/DPs/Disspaper4.pdf (on 08.04.2008), 11; OECD, The OECD Report on Regulatory Reform, 1997, retrieved from http://www.oecd.org/dataoecd/17/25/2391768.pdf (on 09.04.2008), 6: The OECD classifies 'regulations' into three categories: economic regulations, social regulations and administrative regulations. Social regulations "*protect public interests such as health, safety, the environment and social cohesion*".

[11] On the rationales for economic regulation, cf. Breyer, Stephen, "Typical justifications for regulation", 59–92, in: Baldwin, Robert, Scott, Colin and Hood, Christopher (eds), *A reader on regulation*, Oxford, Oxford University Press, 1998, 522 p.

[12] Cf. Majone, Giandomenico, "The rise of the regulatory state in Europe", 192–215, in: Baldwin, Robert, Scott, Colin and Hood, Christopher (eds), *A reader on regulation*, Oxford, Oxford University Press, 1998, 522 p.

> *the third, regulation is all mechanisms of social control or influence affecting all aspects of behaviour from whatever source, whether they are intentional or not.*[13]

She concluded that the first two definitions have an essential link with the 'government' or 'state', and are hence 'centred' definitions.[14] An example of a (rather narrow) centred definition is one advocated by the OECD. This definition describes regulation as "*the full range of legal instruments by which governing institutions, at all levels of government, impose obligations or constraints on private sector behaviour*", including "*[c]onstitutions, parliamentary laws, subordinate legislation, decrees, orders, norms, licenses, plans, codes and even some forms of administrative guidance*".[15] Baldwin, Scott and Hood, who used the same categories of definitions as Black, clarified that the second definition – direct state intervention in the economy – allows for the use of a variety of tools and is hence not limited to the use of command-and-control regulation (*infra*).[16] The third category of definition is the broadest one, and allows a large number of actors to play a role. Black, however, criticised this last definition for not providing any limits and thus having little analytical value.[17] She instead developed a definition herself, which described 'regulation' as:

> *the sustained and focused attempt to alter the behaviour of others according to defined standards or purposes with the intention of producing a broadly identi-*

[13] Black, Julia, "Critical reflections on regulation", Discussion paper, January 2002, retrieved from http://www.lse.ac.uk/collections/CARR/pdf/DPs/Disspaper4.pdf (on 08.04.2008), 8.

[14] Black, Julia, "Critical reflections on regulation", Discussion paper, January 2002, retrieved from http://www.lse.ac.uk/collections/CARR/pdf/DPs/Disspaper4.pdf (on 08.04.2008), 8. An example of such a definition was put forward by Baldwin, Robert, Scott, Colin and Hood, Christopher, *A reader on regulation*, Oxford, Oxford University Press, 1998, 3: "*At its simplest, regulation refers to the promulgation of an authoritative set of rules, accompanied by some mechanism, typically a public agency, for monitoring and promoting compliance with these rules*".

[15] Organisation for Economic Co-operation and Development, Recommendation of the Council of the OECD on improving the quality of government regulation, OCDE/GD(95)95, 09.03.1995, retrieved from http://www.olis.oecd.org/olis/1995doc.nsf/LinkTo/NT000009E6/$FILE/PME5205.PDF (on 16.05.2008), 20. In another document, the OECD defined regulation as "*the diverse set of instruments by which governments set requirements on enterprises and citizens*", including "*laws, formal and informal orders and subordinate rules issued by all levels of government, and rules issues by non-governmental or self-regulatory bodies to whom governments have delegated regulatory powers*": Organisation for Economic Co-operation and Development, The OECD Report on Regulatory Reform, 1997, retrieved from http://www.oecd.org/dataoecd/17/25/2391768.pdf (on 09.04.2008), 6.

[16] Baldwin, Robert, Scott, Colin and Hood, Christopher, *A reader on regulation*, Oxford, Oxford University Press, 1998, 2 *et seq.*

[17] Black, Julia, "Critical reflections on regulation", Discussion paper, January 2002, retrieved from http://www.lse.ac.uk/collections/CARR/pdf/DPs/Disspaper4.pdf (on 08.04.2008), 8.

> *fied outcome or outcomes, which may involve mechanisms of standard-setting, information-gathering and behaviour-modification.*[18]

Black stressed that this definition entails that regulation is not the prerogative of the state, and, moreover, it enables "*the identification, creation and analysis of regulatory arrangements that involve complex interactions between state and non-state actors*". This aspect of regulation – the involvement of different actors – is crucial to the subject of this study and, hence, will be the focus of this chapter.

From centred to decentred regulation – In the next two sections, we will focus on the evolution from centred or traditional 'command-and-control' regulation to more decentred forms of regulation. This evolution has seen a gradual move from regulation in which the state is the only regulatory actor, to the inclusion of other actors who are considered to add value to the regulatory process.

2.1.2. *Centred or 'command-and-control' regulation*

A. *Notion*

Concept – Centred or 'command-and-control regulation', again, has been referred to using a myriad of notions. 'Legislation', 'statutory regulation' or 'direct public ordering',[19] for instance, are often used as interchangeable expressions. Black described command-and-control regulation as "*regulation by the state through the use of legal rules backed by (often) criminal sanctions*".[20] Prosser found that a characterisation of regulation as command-and-control regulation assumes that "*a public authority gaining its legitimacy from the political process issues orders to companies or individuals requiring them to meet public policy goals; the implication is that these orders are obeyed*".[21] Schulz and Held followed a similar reasoning for their characterisation: "*[t]he state lays down a set of rules to be followed by the subjects of regulation, as well as prohibitions that they must adhere to, thus ensuring*

---

[18] Black, Julia, "Critical reflections on regulation", Discussion paper, January 2002, retrieved from http://www.lse.ac.uk/collections/CARR/pdf/DPs/Disspaper4.pdf (on 08.04.2008), 20.

[19] Birnhack, Michael and Rowbottom, Jacob, "Shielding children: the European way", *Chicago-Kent Law Review* 2004, Issue 79, 177.

[20] Black, Julia, "Critical reflections on regulation", Discussion paper, January 2002, retrieved from http://www.lse.ac.uk/collections/CARR/pdf/DPs/Disspaper4.pdf (on 08.04.2008), 2.

[21] Prosser, Tony, "Self-regulation, co-regulation and the Audio-Visual Media Services Directive", *Journal of Consumer Policy* 2008, Vol. 31, No. 1, 100.

that the objectives of regulation are fulfilled".[22] In the field of environmental policy, SINCLAIR depicted it as when a "*government literally* commands *industry to meet specific environmental standards, either directly through legislation or indirectly through delegated authority, and* controls *its behaviour through the threat of negative sanctions*".[23] What all these definitions have in common is what interests us the most within the framework of our research, namely, that the state performs all regulatory tasks: creation, implementation and monitoring, and enforcement.[24] In other words, command-and-control regulation is a 'centred' type of regulation. As BLACK puts it:

> *It is 'centred' in that it assumes the state to have the capacity to command and control, to be the only commander and controller, and to be potentially effective in commanding and controlling. It is assumed to be unilateral in its approach (governments telling, others doing), to be based on simple cause-effect relations and to envisage a linear progression from policy information through to implementation.*[25]

B. *Drawbacks*

FAILURE OF COMMAND-AND-CONTROL REGULATION – Command-and-control regulation, however, has lost some of its lustre over the past decade,[26] as it has gradually become clear that this type of regulation, in which the state

[22] SCHULZ, Wolfgang and HELD, Thorsten, Regulated Self-Regulation as a Form of Modern Government, Study commissioned by the German Federal Commissioner for Cultural and Media Affairs, 2001, retrieved from http://www.humanrights.coe.int/Media/documents/interim-report-self-regulation.pdf (on 02.06.2008), 6.

[23] SINCLAIR, Darren, "Self-regulation versus command and control? Beyond false dichotomies", *Law & Policy* 1997, Vol. 19, No. 4, 534 [original emphasis].

[24] PROSSER, however, warns against a too restricted view of the government being the only actor in the regulatory process: "*Thus even where regulation ostensibly takes the form of command and control, the reality has been shown to involve extensive negotiation between regulators and those they regulate, either through consultation when rules are made or even more importantly through selective enforcement in which rules are enforced not as binding orders but as the basis for negotiation to achieve reasonable results*": PROSSER, Tony, "Self-regulation, co-regulation and the Audio-Visual Media Services Directive", *Journal of Consumer Policy* 2008, Vol. 31, No. 1, 101.

[25] BLACK, Julia, "Critical reflections on regulation", Discussion paper, January 2002, retrieved from http://www.lse.ac.uk/collections/CARR/pdf/DPs/Disspaper4.pdf (on 08.04.2008), 2.

[26] Before that, "*[u]ntil the seventies and eighties regulators in Britain and North America appeared to be highly respected as expert officials who acted in the public interest in controlling the behaviour of the private sector*": BALDWIN, Robert, "Is regulation right?", Carr Launch paper, 2000, retrieved from http://www.lse.ac.uk/collections/CARR/pdf/IsRegulationRight.pdf (on 16.04.2008), 1.

is the sole regulatory actor, suffers from a number of drawbacks.[27] BLACK identified these shortcomings as instrument failure, information and knowledge failure, implementation failure, motivation failure and capture theory.[28] The first problem, instrument failure, implies that the instruments that are used, i.e., laws, are "*inappropriate and unsophisticated*". Secondly, the state often does not enough have knowledge or expertise to be capable of identifying the causes of problems, designing adequate solutions and detecting non-compliance. A third issue with command-and-control regulation is its often ineffective implementation. And, finally, it has been found that command-and-control regulation often does not provide enough incentives for regulatees to comply (motivation failure), and, moreover, that regulators often do not act in the public's interest, but rather in favour of the regulated industry or themselves (capture theory).[29] Other criticisms directed at command-and-control regulation are, for instance, that it is slow,[30] costly and stifles innovation.[31] On the other hand, having listed these weaknesses of command-and-control regulation, it would be easy to totally lose sight of its benefits. As PROSSER argued, command-and-control regulation is at least "*based on some form of democratic mandate*", and the government is in any case "*subject to some form of democratic scrutiny*".[32] However, due to the significant pathologies that have been especially strongly felt in complex

[27] BALDWIN, Robert, "Is regulation right?", Carr Launch paper, 2000, retrieved from http://www.lse.ac.uk/collections/CARR/pdf/IsRegulationRight.pdf (on 16.04.2008), 1. Cf. also *supra*, Part 1, Chapter 1.

[28] BLACK, Julia, "Critical reflections on regulation", Discussion paper, January 2002, retrieved from http://www.lse.ac.uk/collections/CARR/pdf/DPs/Disspaper4.pdf (on 08.04.2008), 2.

[29] BALDWIN, Robert, "Is regulation right?", Carr Launch paper, 2000, retrieved from http://www.lse.ac.uk/collections/CARR/pdf/IsRegulationRight.pdf (on 16.04.2008), 1. See also: MAKKAI, Toni and BRAITHWAITE, John, "In and out of the revolving door: making sense of regulatory capture", 173–191, in: BALDWIN, Robert, SCOTT, Colin and HOOD, Christopher, *A reader on regulation*, Oxford, Oxford University Press, 1998, 522 p.

[30] RAND EUROPE (Chris MARSDEN, Stephen SIMMONS, Jonathan CAVE, Eddy NASON, Neil ROBINSON), Options for and effectiveness of Internet self- and co-regulation, Phase 1 Report: Mapping existing co- and self-regulatory institutions on the Internet, Study commissioned by the European Commission, June 2007, retrieved from http://ec.europa.eu/dgs/information_society/evaluation/data/pdf/studies/s2006_05/phase1.pdf (on 02.06.2008), 11.

[31] SINCLAIR, Darren, "Self-regulation versus command and control? Beyond false dichotomies", *Law & Policy* 1997, Vol. 19, No. 4, 530.

[32] PROSSER, Tony, "Self-regulation, co-regulation and the Audio-Visual Media Services Directive", *Journal of Consumer Policy* 2008, Vol. 31, No. 103.

sectors such as the digital media environment,[33] a shift from command-and-control regulation to 'decentred' forms of regulation has occurred in the past decades.

2.1.3. *Away from pure command-and-control regulation*

From welfare state to regulatory state to post-regulatory state – Regulation, and its interpretation and application across time and space, are by no means static. Different trends and developments have been distinguished and have become the subject of scholarly thought and writing. Near the end of the last century, a shift was noted from the welfare state[34] to the regulatory state. During this transformation, the regulatory debate was dominated by the notion of 'deregulation', a reaction of public policy makers to the "*pathologies of command*" (cf. *supra*).[35] Harcourt and Weatherill simply stated that deregulation "*refers to the removal of state controls on a particular activity*".[36] Majone clarified, however, that deregulation is not a synonym for 'no regulation' but rather implies less restrictive or rigid regulation: "*a search for ways of achieving the relevant regulatory objectives by less burdensome methods of government intervention, as when command-and-control methods are replaced by economic incentives*".[37] Where the welfare state relied upon public ownership, planning, centralised administration, direct state provision of benefits and services, and the integration of policy making and operational functions,[38] the regulatory state was observed to

[33] Cf. also *supra*, Part 1, Chapter 1. See also: Murray, Andrew and Scott, Colin, "Controlling the new media: hybrid responses to new forms of power", *The Modern Law Review* 2002, Vol. 65, No. 4, 491.

[34] Or 'dirigist' state, according to Majone: Majone, Giandomenico, "The rise of the regulatory state in Europe", 192–215, in Baldwin, Robert, Scott, Colin and Hood, Christopher (eds), *A reader on regulation*, Oxford, Oxford University Press, 1998, 522 p.

[35] Moran, Michael, "Understanding the regulatory state", *British Journal of Political Science* 2002, Vol. 2, No. 2, 397; Majone, Giandomenico, "The rise of the regulatory state in Europe", in: Baldwin, Robert, Scott, Colin and Hood, Christopher (eds), *A reader on regulation*, Oxford, Oxford University Press, 1998, 212.

[36] Harcourt, Alison and Weatherill, Stephen, "The Consumer, the European Union, and Media Law", *Journal of Consumer Policy* 2008, Vol. 31, No. 1, 1.

[37] Majone, Giandomenico, "The rise of the regulatory state in Europe", in: Baldwin, Robert, Scott, Colin and Hood, Christopher (eds), *A reader on regulation*, Oxford, Oxford University Press, 1998, 195.

[38] Scott, Colin, "Regulation in the age of governance: the rise of the post-regulatory state", National Europe Center Paper No. 100, Australian National University, 2003, retrieved from http://dspace.anu.edu.au/bitstream/1885/41716/2/scott1.pdf (on 29.11.2008), 4; Majone, Giandomenico, "The rise of the regulatory state in Europe", in: Baldwin, Robert,

instead place its trust in 'regulation'.[39] According to SCOTT, this transformation was characterised by

> *a complex set of changes in public management involving the separation of operational from regulatory activities in some policy areas (sometimes linked to privatization), a trend towards separating purchasers and providers of public services (through policies of contracting out and market testing) and towards separation of operational from policy tasks within government departments and the creation of executive agencies.*[40]

Generally, he argued that this boils down to a shift of "*emphasis of control, to a greater or lesser degree, from traditional bureaucratic mechanisms towards instruments of regulation*".[41] SCOTT did go one step further and discerned an evolution from the regulatory state to the post-regulatory state. He earmarked the relaxation of the "*distinction between states and markets and between the public and the private*" as a central characteristic of this latest concept.[42] This evolution has also been described by BLACK, who used the notion 'de-centring'.[43]

OPENING UP REGULATION – Different regulatory theories have influenced the conceptualisation of this 'decentred' form of regulation. TEUBNER's autopoietic law theory,[44] AYRES AND BRAITHWAITE's responsive regulation

---

SCOTT, Colin and HOOD, Christopher (eds), *A reader on regulation*, Oxford, Oxford University Press, 1998, 193.

39 The 'regulatory state' originated in the United States. MORAN argues that "*Americans virtually invented the modern regulatory state, in the sense that the United States was the great pioneer of the administrative technology of controlling business through law-backed specialized agencies rather than through the technique of public ownership*": MORAN, Michael, "Understanding the regulatory state", *British Journal of Political Science* 2002, Vol. 2, No. 2, 392.

40 SCOTT, Colin, "Regulation in the age of governance: the rise of the post-regulatory state", National Europe Center Paper No. 100, Australian National University, 2003, retrieved from http://dspace.anu.edu.au/bitstream/1885/41716/2/scott1.pdf (on 29.11.2008), 4.

41 SCOTT, Colin, "Regulation in the age of governance: the rise of the post-regulatory state", National Europe Center Paper No. 100, Australian National University, 2003, retrieved from http://dspace.anu.edu.au/bitstream/1885/41716/2/scott1.pdf (on 29.11.2008), 4.

42 SCOTT, Colin, "Regulation in the age of governance: the rise of the post-regulatory state", National Europe Center Paper No. 100, Australian National University, 2003, retrieved from http://dspace.anu.edu.au/bitstream/1885/41716/2/scott1.pdf (on 29.11.2008), 3.

43 BLACK, Julia, "Critical reflections on regulation", Discussion paper, January 2002, retrieved from http://www.lse.ac.uk/collections/CARR/pdf/DPs/Disspaper4.pdf (on 08.04.2008), 2.

44 TEUBNER built on Niklas LUHMANN's theory of *autopoiesis*. For detailed information on this concept, cf. TEUBNER, Gunther (ed.), *Autopoietic law: a new approach to law and society*, Berlin, Walter de Gruyter, 1988, 380 p.; TEUBNER, Gunther, *Law as an autopoietic system*, Oxford, Blackwell, 1993, 203 p.; TEUBNER, Gunther, NOBLES, Richard and SCHIFF,

model,[45] and recent 'governance' paradigms[46] all have contributed to the opening up of the traditional understanding of regulation.[47] These types of theories stress the importance of the involvement of different actors or

---

David, "The autonomy of law: an introduction to legal autopoiesis", chapter 18, in: PENNER, James, SCHIFF, David and NOBLES, Richard (eds), *Introduction to jurisprudence and legal theory*, Oxford, Oxford University Press, 2005, 1194 p., retrieved from http://www.jura.uni-frankfurt.de/ifawz1/teubner/dokumente/autonomy_of_law.pdf (on 23.06.2008). See also: LOUGHLIN, Martin, *Public law and political theory*, Oxford, Oxford University Press, 1992, 250–264; SCOTT, Colin, "Regulation in the age of governance: the rise of the post-regulatory state", National Europe Center Paper No. 100, Australian National University, 2003, retrieved from http://dspace.anu.edu.au/bitstream/1885/41716/2/scott1.pdf (on 29.11.2008), 7–10; BLACK, Julia, "Constitutionalising self-regulation", *Modern Law Review* 1996, Vol. 59, Issue 1, 44 *et seq.*

45 AYRES, Ian and BRAITHWAITE, John, *Responsive regulation: transcending the deregulation debate*, Oxford, Oxford University Press, 1995, 205 p. BRAITHWAITE clarified the notion of 'responsive regulation' as follows: "*The basic idea of responsive regulation is that governments should be responsive to the conduct of those they seek to regulate in deciding whether a more or less interventionist response is needed [...]. In particular, law enforcers should be responsive to how efficiently citizens or corporations are regulating themselves before deciding whether to escalate intervention*": BRAITHWAITE, John, *Restorative justice and responsive regulation*, Oxford, Oxford University Press, 2002, 29. On the concept of responsive law, cf. also NONET, Philippe and SELZNICK, Philip, *Law and society in transition: toward responsive law*, New York, Harper Colophon Books, 1978, 122 p.

46 For descriptions of governance, cf.: UNESCO, Media education – A kit for teachers, students, parents and professionals (ed. Divina Frau-Meigs), Paris, L'exprimeur, 2006, retrieved from http://unesdoc.unesco.org/images/0014/001492/149278E.pdf (on 09.01.2007), 88: "*Governance is a form of government that aims at re-founding the democratic basis for the exercise of power, by proceeding with directives and recommendations rather than laws and sanctions. It implies a multiplicity of actors, at all levels, local, national, regional and even international. It encourages participation and responsible behaviour from citizens in the face of today's complexity, to which the media environment contributes massively*"; BAIRD, Zoë and VERHULST, Stefaan, "A new model for Global Internet Governance", 2004, retrieved from http://www.markle.org/downloadable_assets/ahs_global_internet_gov.pdf (on 23.04.2007); JAKUBOWICZ, Karol, "Co-regulation as an instrument of media policy: how effective?", Presentation at the Expert Conference on European Media Policy "More trust in content – The potential of co- and self-regulation in digital media", Leipzig, 9–11.05.2007, not published, 2. Also on 'soft governance' (i.e., "*non-binding agreements made between participating actors established outside the Community method*"): HARCOURT, Alison, "Institutionalising soft governance in the European Information Society", 7–31, in WARD, David (ed.), *The European Union and the culture industries: regulation and the public interest*, Aldershot, Ashgate, 2008, 264 p.

47 SCOTT, Colin, "Regulation in the age of governance: the rise of the post-regulatory state", National Europe Center Paper No. 100, Australian National University, 2003, retrieved from http://dspace.anu.edu.au/bitstream/1885/41716/2/scott1.pdf (on 29.11.2008), 7–15. SCOTT calls these theories 'theories of the post-regulatory state'.

'sub-systems' in the regulatory process, and consequently, have provided fertile ground for the development of self- and co-regulatory mechanisms.[48]

2.1.4. *Interim conclusion*

TRADITIONAL REGULATION VERSUS ALTERNATIVE REGULATION – We propose to use two concepts of regulation in this study. One the hand, we discern 'traditional regulation' (or 'command-and-control' regulation, *supra*), a centred concept in which the government or state is the only player and performs all regulatory tasks (creation, implementation, enforcement).[49, 50] On the other hand, we discern what we will call 'alternative regulation' (as it is an alternative for the use of traditional regulation), which is a decentred concept (*supra*), and implies that different actors play a role in the regulatory process.

For the remainder of this chapter, our focal point will be 'alternative regulation' or 'alternative regulatory instruments' (ARIs).[51] First, the occurrence of such instruments in policy documents (general as well as specific media policy documents) will be studied. Second, different alternative regulatory instruments (self-regulation and co-regulation) will be analysed and illustrated.

---

[48] RAND EUROPE (Chris MARSDEN, Stephen SIMMONS and Jonathan CAVE), Options for effectiveness of Internet self- and co-regulation – Inception report, Study commissioned by the European Commission, 30.04.2007, retrieved from http://ec.europa.eu/dgs/information_society/evaluation/data/pdf/studies/s2006_05/inception_final.pdf (on 08.01.2008), 36; SCOTT, Colin, "Regulation in the age of governance: the rise of the post-regulatory state", National Europe Center Paper No. 100, Australian National University, 2003, retrieved from http://dspace.anu.edu.au/bitstream/1885/41716/2/scott1.pdf (on 29.11.2008), 15 *et seq*.

[49] JAKUBOWICZ, Karl, "A new notion of media?", Background text, 1st Council of Europe Conference of Ministers responsible for media and new communications services : A new notion of media?; Reykjavik, 28–29.05.2009, retrieved from http://www.ministerialconference.is/media/images/a_new_notion_of_media_web_version.df (on 27.05.2009), 31.

[50] Cf. *supra*, footnote 302 (Chapter 1).

[51] This notion finds its origin in environmental law where the use of self-regulation in particular has been advocated for a long time (cf. *infra*). We have found this notion ('alternative regulatory instruments') to be the most useful notion in terms of our research, as it not only adequately describes the fact that such instruments provide an alternative, *in casu* to command-and-control regulation, but also because it is an 'umbrella' term, which covers an array of instruments in which the involvement of different actors can vary widely. This suits our argument that different alternative regulatory instruments can be situated along a regulatory continuum (*infra*).

2.2. 'Alternative regulation' in policy documents

Increasing references in policy documents – The use of alternative regulatory instruments has gained importance over the past decade, and has been increasingly referred to in policy documents issued by organisations at different levels, most importantly the European Union. These references usually occur in the framework of a 'Better Regulation' discourse. Improving the creation and implementation of legislation and regulation is a topic that started to concern policymakers since a couple of decades. The involvement of different stakeholders and the use of alternative regulatory instruments have often been put forward as tools to achieve this goal.

Overview – In this section, an overview is given of the different policy documents at the international, EU and CoE levels that refer to the use of alternative regulatory instruments. First, a number of general policy documents are analysed and second, specific media policy documents are studied. The aim of this overview is to provide a comprehensive picture of the increasing attention that has been paid to the use of these alternative methods of regulation.

2.2.1. *General policy documents*

A. *International: OECD*

A.1. *Recommendation on improving the quality of government regulation*

Recommendation on improving the quality of government regulation – In 1995, the Organisation for Economic Co-operation and Development (OECD) issued its Recommendation on improving the quality of government regulation, including a 'Reference checklist for regulatory decision-making'.[52] The Recommendation, which claimed to be the first international standard on regulatory quality, resulted from the finding that "*regulatory quality is crucial for economic performance and government effectiveness in improving the quality of life of citizens*".[53] One of the objectives of

[52] Organisation for Economic Co-operation and Development, Recommendation of the Council of the OECD on improving the quality of government regulation, OCDE/GD(95)95, 09.03.1995, retrieved from http://www.olis.oecd.org/olis/1995doc.nsf/LinkTo/NT000009E6/$FILE/PME5205.PDF (on 16.05.2008).

[53] Organisation for Economic Co-operation and Development, Recommendation of the Council of the OECD on improving the quality of government regulation, OCDE/

the Recommendation, especially relevant to the subject of this book, was the promotion of the use of alternative instruments by providing further insight into how public policy goals could be achieved through a combination of regulatory and non-regulatory methods.[54]

Checklist and alternative instruments – The reference checklist, the annex to the Recommendation, which was based on ten questions in which principles on good regulatory decision-making were embedded, contained the question whether regulation is the best form of government action. The OECD argued that, in practice, regulators most often favoured command-and-control regulation (because of a "*preference for standardised solutions, ease of enforcement, clarity for regulated groups and certainty of intent*"), notwithstanding a number of clear shortcomings of this form of regulation (for instance, "*its rigidity, tendency to be over-detailed, inability to adapt to changing conditions, high costs, adversarial nature, and ineffectiveness in many situations*)".[55] In order to minimise these disadvantages and to better achieve certain policy goals, the OECD promoted using a mix of state regulation and other instruments amongst which voluntary agreements and self-regulation were mentioned.[56]

A.2. *Report on regulatory reform*

Report on regulatory reform – Following the Recommendation, the OECD issued The OECD Report on Regulatory Reform in 1997.[57] The starting point of the OECD's reasoning was the risk that, in a time of quickly

GD(95)95, 09.03.1995, retrieved from http://www.olis.oecd.org/olis/1995doc.nsf/LinkTo/NT000009E6/$FILE/PME5205.PDF (on 16.05.2008), 3.

54 Organisation for Economic Co-operation and Development, Recommendation of the Council of the OECD on improving the quality of government regulation, OCDE/GD(95)95, 09.03.1995, retrieved from http://www.olis.oecd.org/olis/1995doc.nsf/LinkTo/NT000009E6/$FILE/PME5205.PDF (on 16.05.2008), 3.

55 Organisation for Economic Co-operation and Development, Recommendation of the Council of the OECD on improving the quality of government regulation, OCDE/GD(95)95, 09.03.1995, retrieved from http://www.olis.oecd.org/olis/1995doc.nsf/LinkTo/NT000009E6/$FILE/PME5205.PDF (on 16.05.2008), 15. See also: *supra*.

56 Organisation for Economic Co-operation and Development, Recommendation of the Council of the OECD on improving the quality of government regulation, OCDE/GD(95)95, 09.03.1995, retrieved from http://www.olis.oecd.org/olis/1995doc.nsf/LinkTo/NT000009E6/$FILE/PME5205.PDF (on 16.05.2008), 15.

57 Organisation for Economic Co-operation and Development, The OECD report on regulatory reform, 1997, retrieved from http://www.oecd.org/dataoecd/17/25/2391768.pdf (on 09.04.2008).

changing economic and social conditions, "*regulations can become an obstacle to achieving the very economic and social well-being for which they are intended*".[58] Furthermore,

> *[r]egulations which impede innovation or create unnecessary barriers to trade, investment, and economic efficiency; duplication between regulatory authorities and different layers of government, and even among governments of different countries; the influence of vested interests seeking protection from competition; and regulations that are outdated or poorly designed to achieve their intended policy goals are all part of the problem.*[59]

The Report attempted to remedy these problems, and intended to assist governments in assessing and improving the quality of their regulatory systems. One of the key goals of regulatory reform was deemed by the OECD to be the improvement of government credibility and effectiveness in attaining significant public policy goals. A way of accomplishing this was considered to be the use of alternative policy tools,[60] based on the idea that "*incentives are better than commands*".[61]

Voluntary and co-operative approaches – In this context, the OECD pointed out that 'voluntary and co-operative approaches' (which could, in our opinion, possibly be labelled self- and co-regulation) "*can exceed regulatory results because solutions are better fitted to practical realities and the speed of response and updating can be faster*".[62] On the other hand, the OECD also warned of potential disadvantages of such regulatory approaches, such as issues regarding competition, free riding regulatory capture, transparency and accountability. Another allusion was made to self-regulation, stating that (although governments still play a significant role in regulating safety, health

[58] Organisation for Economic Co-operation and Development, The OECD report on regulatory reform, 1997, retrieved from http://www.oecd.org/dataoecd/17/25/2391768.pdf (on 09.04.2008), 5.

[59] Organisation for Economic Co-operation and Development, The OECD report on regulatory reform, 1997, retrieved from http://www.oecd.org/dataoecd/17/25/2391768.pdf (on 09.04.2008), 5.

[60] Organisation for Economic Co-operation and Development, The OECD report on regulatory reform, 1997, retrieved from http://www.oecd.org/dataoecd/17/25/2391768.pdf (on 09.04.2008), 7.

[61] Organisation for Economic Co-operation and Development, The OECD report on regulatory reform, 1997, retrieved from http://www.oecd.org/dataoecd/17/25/2391768.pdf (on 09.04.2008), 28.

[62] Organisation for Economic Co-operation and Development, The OECD report on regulatory reform, 1997, retrieved from http://www.oecd.org/dataoecd/17/25/2391768.pdf (on 09.04.2008), 18.

and consumer protection), voluntary codes of conduct to protect consumers may in certain circumstances be effective, especially in innovative markets.[63]

B. *European Union*

Better regulation – At the EU level, a trend towards 'Better Regulation' or 'Better Lawmaking' has been noticeable for a couple of decades.[64] Particularly since the beginning of the 21st century, the simplification and improvement of the regulatory environment has been an essential item on the EU agenda,[65] as the conclusions of the Lisbon European Council revealed.[66] In

---

[63] Organisation for Economic Co-operation and Development, The OECD report on regulatory reform, 1997, retrieved from http://www.oecd.org/dataoecd/17/25/2391768.pdf (on 09.04.2008), 23.

[64] Cf., for instance: European Council, Presidency conclusions, 11–12.12.1992, Edinburgh, retrieved from http://www.europarl.europa.eu/summits/edinburgh/a0_en.pdf (on 14.05.2008); Commission of the European Communities, Commission report to the European Council: Better lawmaking 1998 A shared responsibility, COM (1998) 715 final, 01.12.1998, retrieved from http://aei.pitt.edu/926/01/subsidiarity_COM_98_715.pdf (on 14.05.2008); Commission of the European Communities, Commission report to the European Council: Better lawmaking 1999, COM (1999) 562 final, 03.11.1999, retrieved from http://aei.pitt.edu/3541/01/000689_1.pdf (on 14.05.2008). See also: Senden, Linda, "Soft law, self-regulation and co-regulation in European law: where do they meet?", *Electronic Journal of Comparative Law* 2005, Vol. 9, No. 1, retrieved from http://www.ejcl.org/91/abs91-3.html (on 30.05.2008).

[65] Cf. European Commission, Better regulation: simply explained, 2006, retrieved from http://ec.europa.eu/governance/better_regulation/documents/brochure/br_brochure_en.pdf (on 14.05.2008).

[66] It is worth noting that almost all documents relating to 'Better Regulation' refer to the general EU law principles of proportionality and subsidiarity (*infra*). For instance: European Parliament, Council, and Commission, Interinstitutional agreement on better law-making, 2003/C 321/01, *OJ* 31.12.2003, *C* 321, 1; Commission of the European Communities, Communication from the Commission Action Plan "Simplifying and improving the regulatory environment", COM (2002) 278 final, 05.06.2002; Commission of the European Communities, Communication from the Commission to the Council and the European Parliament – Better regulation for growth and jobs in the European Union, COM (2005) 97 final, 16.03.2005; Commission of the European Communities, Communication from the Commission to the European Parliament, the Council, the European Economic and Social Committee and the Committee of the Regions – Implementing the Community Lisbon programme: A strategy for the simplification of the regulatory environment, COM (2005) 535 final, 25.10.2005. The latter document stressed that "*[f]ollowing these principles, the EU should only regulate if a proposed action can be better achieved at EU level. Any such action should not go beyond what is necessary to achieve the policy objectives pursued. It needs to be cost efficient and take the lightest form of regulation called for. In this respect simplification intends to make legislation at both Community and national level less burdensome easier to apply and thereby more effective in achieving their goals*" (p. 2).

these conclusions, the Council urged the Commission, the Council and the Member States "*to set out by 2001 a strategy for further coordinated action to simplify the regulatory environment*".[67] Below, the most important EU policy documents in this area are explored, with a clear emphasis on the use of alternative regulatory instruments.

B.1. *White Paper on European Governance*

Good governance – The White Paper on European Governance[68] was adopted as an answer to the increasing loss of confidence of European citizens in the European Union (the so-called democratic deficit)[69] and dealt with the manner in which this supranational organisation uses the power granted by its citizens.[70, 71] The starting point of the White Paper was the idea that "*a better use of those powers should connect the EU more closely to its citizens and lead to more effective policies*".[72] To that aim, five principles

[67] European Council, Presidency conclusions, 23–24.03.2000, Lisbon, retrieved from http://www.europarl.europa.eu/summits/lis1_en.htm (on 13.05.2008).

[68] Commission of the European Communities, European Governance – A White Paper, COM (2001) 428 final, 25.07.2001.

[69] Cf. Europa, Glossary, retrieved from http://europa.eu/scadplus/glossary/democratic_deficit_en.htm (on 30.04.2008). See also: Commission of the European Communities, Communication from the Commission 'Simplifying and improving the regulatory environment', COM (2001) 726 final, 05.12.2001, 2: "*The need to strengthen the democratic legitimacy of the European project means that the EU has to work towards legislation which is better, simpler, more responsive to the real problems, and more accessible. This is a sine qua non if EU action is to be better understood, better applied and more readily accepted by the people of Europe*".

[70] Commission of the European Communities, European Governance – A White Paper, COM (2001) 428 final, 25.07.2001, 3.

[71] The White Paper on European Governance was preceded by an interim report (Commission of the European Communities, Interim report from the Commission to the Stockholm European Council: Improving and simplifying the regulatory environment, COM (2001) 130 final, 07.03.2001, retrieved from http://ec.europa.eu/fisheries/publications/factsheets/legal_texts/com_03_130_en.pdf (on 14.05.2008)) in which the plans for the adoption of the White Paper were laid out. In this interim report, already considerable attention was paid to the use of alternative and complementary approaches. Self- and co-regulation were put forward as potential options. Self-regulation was described as being voluntary, and based on cooperation between all interested parties (p. 7); and co-regulation as combining the advantages of legislation – more especially its predictable and binding nature – with the more flexible approach under self-regulation (p. 7).

[72] Commission of the European Communities, European Governance – A White Paper, COM (2001) 428 final, 25.07.2001, 8.

of 'good' (or more democratic) governance[73] were established: openness,[74] participation, accountability, effectiveness, and coherence; the application of which underpin the general EU principles of proportionality and subsidiarity (cf. *infra*).[75] It was stated that these five principles should be adhered to at all times and also form the basis for four proposed changes: better involvement; better policies, regulation and delivery; contribution to global governance; and refocused policies and institutions.

Better regulation – Most relevant to our subject are the changes related to 'Better Regulation'.[76] Problematic issues concerning regulation mentioned were, for instance, the level of detail in EU legislation which made adaptation to market or technical changes "*complex and time-consuming*",[77] and the lack of use of expertise in decision-making.[78] Hence, the Commission stressed the importance of "*improving the quality, effectiveness and simplicity of regulatory acts*",[79] and proposed "*following a less top-down approach and complementing its policy tools more effectively with non-legislative*

---

[73] 'Governance' is defined by the White Paper as: "*rules, processes and behaviour that affect the way in which powers are exercised at European level, particularly as regards openness, participation, accountability, effectiveness and coherence*".

[74] The Commission proposed "*opening up the policy-making process to get more people and organisations involved in shaping and delivering EU policy*": Commission of the European Communities, European Governance – A White Paper, COM (2001) 428 final, 25.07.2001, 3.

[75] Commission of the European Communities, European Governance – A White Paper, COM (2001) 428 final, 25.07.2001, 10.

[76] It has been stressed time and again that better regulation or simplification of regulation is not a synonym for 'deregulation': Mandelkern group on better regulation, Final Report, 13.11.2001, retrieved from http://ec.europa.eu/governance/impact/docs/key_docs/mandelkern_report_en.pdf (on 13.05.2008), 4; Commission of the European Communities, Communication from the Commission to the European Parliament, the Council, the European Economic and Social Committee and the Committee of the Regions – Implementing the Community Lisbon programme: A strategy for the simplification of the regulatory environment, COM (2005) 535 final, 25.10.2005, 3; Commission of the European Communities, Communication from the Commission to the European Parliament, the Council, the European Economic and Social Committee and the Committee of the Regions – Second strategic review of Better Regulation in the European Union, COM (2008) 32 final, 30.01.2008, 2; etc.

[77] Commission of the European Communities, European Governance – A White Paper, COM (2001) 428 final, 25.07.2001, 18.

[78] Commission of the European Communities, European Governance – A White Paper, COM (2001) 428 final, 25.07.2001, 19.

[79] Commission of the European Communities, European Governance – A White Paper, COM (2001) 428 final, 25.07.2001, 20.

instruments".[80] It was suggested that a three-step approach would improve the quality of the EU policies. Thus, first, it must be assessed whether action is needed, and second, if action is needed at the EU level. If the answer to both questions is affirmative, only then the combination of different policy tools should be considered.[81]

Co-regulation – One of the policy instruments put forward to help implement these principles was 'co-regulation'. According to the White Paper, co-regulation "*combines binding legislative and regulatory action with actions taken by the actors most concerned, drawing on their practical expertise*".[82] A set of conditions for the establishment of co-regulatory regimes was provided. First, a co-regulatory regime necessitates that "*a framework of overall objectives, basic rights, enforcement and appeal mechanisms, and conditions for monitoring compliance is set in the legislation*".[83] Furthermore, such a regime must only be opted for where it clearly provides added value, serves the general interest, and where fundamental rights or major political choices are not called into question. Regimes should not be created for situations where rules need to apply in a uniform way in every Member State. The participating organisations must also adhere to conditions of representation, accountability and openness. Moreover, European competition rules must be complied with and the established rules must be adequately visible so that people are conscious of the rules and rights. In case of failure of co-regulatory measures, public authorities need to be able to intervene by creating the necessary rules.[84]

Analysis – The concept of co-regulation as constructed in the White Paper could be deemed quite strict, depending on the breadth of interpretation.[85] For instance, a large number of measures which, at first sight, might be classified as co-regulation, may fall short of meeting the above-mentioned definition of co-regulation, assuming that a great level of detail is manda-

[80] Commission of the European Communities, European Governance – A White Paper, COM (2001) 428 final, 25.07.2001, 4.
[81] Commission of the European Communities, European Governance – A White Paper, COM (2001) 428 final, 25.07.2001, 5.
[82] Commission of the European Communities, European Governance – A White Paper, COM (2001) 428 final, 25.07.2001, 5.
[83] Commission of the European Communities, European Governance – A White Paper, COM (2001) 428 final, 25.07.2001, 21.
[84] Commission of the European Communities, European Governance – A White Paper, COM (2001) 428 final, 25.07.2001, 21.
[85] Cf. also Prosser, Tony, "Self-regulation, co-regulation and the Audio-Visual Media Services Directive", *Journal of Consumer Policy* 2008, Vol. 31, No. 1, 106.

tory with regard to the description of enforcement and appeals mechanisms in the legislation. On the other hand, a much broader interpretation could be applied in which general guidelines on the part of the government are considered sufficient. Moreover, it is important to reflect on the specification in the White Paper that co-regulation should not be used in situations where rules need to apply in a uniform way in every Member State. With this thought in mind, the media sector appears to be a sector in which co-regulation could function well. Media regulation is still, and will probably remain, very much culture and country-specific, and certainly so regarding the protection of minors. On the other hand, the description of co-regulation included in the White Paper also states that co-regulation can only be used in cases where fundamental rights or major political choices are not called into question. Yet, in matters related to the protection of minors against harmful content the fundamental right to freedom of expression might be restricted to a certain degree (*infra*). Poullet, however, claimed that the White Paper (and other documents on the same subject) does not preclude co-regulatory intervention in this field; instead, he suggested that such an intervention should have a more limited, although certainly not insignificant, scope than it does in other fields.[86] Furthermore, Prosser argued that this condition seems to indicate that "*co-regulation may be part of the cocktail with other protections for basic rights alongside them*".[87]

Criticism by the European Parliament – In its Resolution on the Commission White Paper on European Governance, the European Parliament clearly showed its disgruntlement with a number of aspects of the White Paper.[88] It was especially displeased with the fact that it had not been consulted by the Commission beforehand; much emphasis was thus placed on the importance of democratic legitimacy and parliamentary deliberation.[89]

---

[86] Poullet, Yves, "Technologies de l'information et de la communication et 'co-régulation': une nouvelle approche?" ["*Information and communication technologies and 'co-regulation': a new approach?*"], *Droit et Nouvelles Technologies*, 27.05.2004, retrieved from http://www.droit-technologie.org/upload/dossier/doc/120-1.pdf (on 29.11.2008), 11 [in French].

[87] Prosser, Tony, "Self-regulation, co-regulation and the Audio-Visual Media Services Directive", *Journal of Consumer Policy* 2008, Vol. 31, No. 1, 106.

[88] European Parliament, Resolution on the Commission White Paper on European Governance, A5-0399/2001, 29.11.2001, *OJ* 27.06.2002, *C* 153 E, 314.

[89] For instance: "*democratic legitimacy presupposes that the political will underpinning decisions is arrived at through parliamentary deliberation; this is a substantive and not merely formal requirement; there is also an urgent need for democratic legitimacy and scrutiny when implementing rules are adopted by the executive*": European Parliament, Resolution on the Commission White Paper on European Governance, A5-0399/2001, 29.11.2001, *OJ* 27.06.2002, *C* 153 E, 318.

Concerning the use of co-regulation, the Parliament also expressed its doubts by noting that it:

> *[c]onsiders that there are currently no interinstitutional agreements on co-regulation which guarantee Parliament effective exercise of its political role and responsibility, either with regard to the appropriate choice of legal instrument (while respecting the Commission's right of initiative), or with regard to the form and implementation of a proposed co-regulation.*[90]

B.2. *The Final Report of the Mandelkern Group on Better Regulation*

Better regulation – In November 2000, the Mandelkern Group on Better Regulation, chaired by Dieudonné Mandelkern, was established by the Ministers for Public Administration to develop a coherent strategy to improve the European regulatory environment.[91] In November 2001, the group delivered its final report, which clarified what was meant by the term 'Better Regulation':

> *Regulation is essential to achieve the aims of public policy in many areas, and better regulation is not about unthinking removal of such regulation. Rather, it is about ensuring that regulation is only used when appropriate, and about ensuring that the regulation that is used is high quality. Improving the quality of regulation is a public good in itself, enhancing the credibility of the governance process and contributing to the welfare of citizens, business and other stakeholders alike. High quality regulation prevents the imposition of the unnecessary burdens on businesses, citizens and public administrations that cost them time and money. It helps avoid the damage to firms' competitiveness that comes from increased costs and market distortions (particularly for small firms). [...] High quality regulation assists in the restoration of confidence in government and is better able to accomplish its desired purpose. Implementation of such regulation is also less problematic for public administrations and compliance is easier for citizens. For all these reasons it is strongly in the public interest to improve the quality of regulation at both national and EU levels.*[92]

[90] European Parliament, Resolution on the Commission White Paper on European Governance, A5-0399/2001, 29.11.2001, *OJ* 27.06.2002, *C* 153 E, 321. In 2003, such an Interinstitutional Agreement was created (*infra*).

[91] The establishment of the Group was inspired by conclusions of the Lisbon European Council (European Council, Presidency conclusions, 23–24.03.2000, Lisbon, retrieved from http://www.europarl.europa.eu/summits/lis1_en.htm (on 13.05.2008), which urged "*to set out by 2001 a strategy for further coordinated action to simplify the regulatory environment*" (*supra*).

[92] Mandelkern group on better regulation, Final Report, 13.11.2001, retrieved from http://ec.europa.eu/governance/impact/docs/key_docs/mandelkern_report_en.pdf (on 13.05.2008).

The Final Report proposed an Action Plan, which contained a comprehensive overall approach to Better Regulation based on a set of seven core principles: necessity, proportionality, subsidiarity, transparency, accountability, accessibility and simplicity.[93] Several recommendations were made, one of these relating to 'policy implementation options'. In this area, a case was made for the use of alternative regulatory instruments where appropriate. Motivations for the use of such alternative instruments could be found in the potential disadvantages of the use of 'traditional' regulation, identified as excessively lengthy regulatory processes, the disproportionate cost of drafting and implementing, taking responsibility away from the relevant parties, and the loss of credibility of regulatory processes (also *supra*).[94]

Co-regulation – The report stressed that "*solutions that better combine public authority objectives and the responsibility of users or groups of users*", such as co-regulation, could be one of the most appropriate ways of implementing public policies efficiently.[95] The report found that no single definition of co-regulation exists,[96] and that different combinations of legislative and regulatory rules and alternatives to regulation are possible. Amongst all these different combinations, the report distinguished two main approaches: (1) a *top-down* approach, in which the regulatory authority sets objectives and delegates implementation details, and (2) a *bottom-up* approach, in which rules stemming from self-regulation are validated by the regulatory authority.[97] In the top-down approach, regulation enacts the global objectives, main implementation mechanisms and methods for monitoring the application of a public policy, and private players are asked to define a comprehensive set of

---

93 Mandelkern group on better regulation, Final Report, 13.11.2001, retrieved from http://ec.europa.eu/governance/impact/docs/key_docs/mandelkern_report_en.pdf (on 13.05.2008), i.

94 Mandelkern group on better regulation, Final Report, 13.11.2001, retrieved from http://ec.europa.eu/governance/impact/docs/key_docs/mandelkern_report_en.pdf (on 13.05.2008), 14.

95 Mandelkern group on better regulation, Final Report, 13.11.2001, retrieved from http://ec.europa.eu/governance/impact/docs/key_docs/mandelkern_report_en.pdf (on 13.05.2008), 17.

96 In the glossary in Annex D of the Report, co-regulation was defined as "*control of activities by a combination of action from private parties and public authorities*": Mandelkern group on better regulation, Final Report, 13.11.2001, retrieved from http://ec.europa.eu/governance/impact/docs/key_docs/mandelkern_report_en.pdf (on 13.05.2008), 81.

97 Mandelkern group on better regulation, Final Report, 13.11.2001, retrieved from http://ec.europa.eu/governance/impact/docs/key_docs/mandelkern_report_en.pdf (on 13.05.2008), 17.

rules.[98] The bottom-up approach, on the other hand, involves the conversion of a non-compulsory rule established by private partners into a mandatory rule established by the public authority.[99] In other words, in this scenario, a public authority executes a self-regulatory mechanism, with or without some modifications by that authority.[100, 101] The Mandelkern report also established two conditions for co-regulation.[102] First of all, the report stressed that the primacy of the public authority must remain intact.[103] Second, certain guarantees were deemed necessary:[104] co-regulatory activities should be appropriate and proportionate, and participating organisations should be credible, representative and supervised by the regulatory authority.[105]

B.3. *Better Legislation Action Plan*

BETTER LEGISLATION ACTION PLAN – The recommendations made by the Mandelkern group were included in a Commission Communication titled

98 MANDELKERN GROUP ON BETTER REGULATION, Final Report, 13.11.2001, retrieved from http://ec.europa.eu/governance/impact/docs/key_docs/mandelkern_report_en.pdf (on 13.05.2008), 17.

99 MANDELKERN GROUP ON BETTER REGULATION, Final Report, 13.11.2001, retrieved from http://ec.europa.eu/governance/impact/docs/key_docs/mandelkern_report_en.pdf (on 13.05.2008), 17.

100 POULLET, Yves, "Technologies de l'information et de la communication et 'co-régulation': une nouvelle approche?" ["*Information and communication technologies and 'co-regulation': a new approach?*"], *Droit et Nouvelles Technologies*, 27.05.2004, retrieved from http://www.droit-technologie.org/upload/dossier/doc/120–1.pdf (on 29.11.2008), 13 [in French].

101 One could argue (and deduce from certain policy documents, such as the White Paper on European Governance) that the European Commission has shown a light inclination towards the top-down approach. Cf. also: POULLET, Yves, "Technologies de l'information et de la communication et 'co-régulation': une nouvelle approche?" ["*Information and communication technologies and 'co-regulation': a new approach?*"], *Droit et Nouvelles Technologies*, 27.05.2004, retrieved from http://www.droit-technologie.org/upload/dossier/doc/120–1.pdf (on 29.11.2008), 12 [in French].

102 MANDELKERN GROUP ON BETTER REGULATION, Final Report, 13.11.2001, retrieved from http://ec.europa.eu/governance/impact/docs/key_docs/mandelkern_report_en.pdf (on 13.05.2008), 17.

103 MANDELKERN GROUP ON BETTER REGULATION, Final Report, 13.11.2001, retrieved from http://ec.europa.eu/governance/impact/docs/key_docs/mandelkern_report_en.pdf (on 13.05.2008), 17.

104 MANDELKERN GROUP ON BETTER REGULATION, Final Report, 13.11.2001, retrieved from http://ec.europa.eu/governance/impact/docs/key_docs/mandelkern_report_en.pdf (on 13.05.2008), 17.

105 MANDELKERN GROUP ON BETTER REGULATION, Final Report, 13.11.2001, retrieved from http://ec.europa.eu/governance/impact/docs/key_docs/mandelkern_report_en.pdf (on 13.05.2008), 17.

Action plan Simplifying and improving the regulatory environment.[106] With this 'Better Legislation Action Plan' the Commission's aim was to introduce "*a strategy for further coordinated action to simplify the regulatory environment*".[107] Simplifying and improving EU regulation should ensure that Community legislation is better adapted to the problems posed by opaque legislation, to EU enlargement and technical and local conditions, and should ultimately guarantee a high level of legal certainty throughout the European Union.[108]

Self- and co-regulation – Making more appropriate use of legislative instruments was one of the action points reserved for the European Parliament and the Council.[109] The Action Plan described co-regulation and self-regulation[110] as "*tools which in specific circumstances can be used to achieve the objectives of the Treaty of the European Union while simplifying lawmaking activities and legislation itself*".[111] Co-regulation, in particular, was judged to facilitate the implementation of the objectives identified by the legislator in the context of measures carried out by actors in the field concerned. Moreover, the Commission suggested that co-regulation could prove useful "*when it comes to adjusting legislation to the problems and sectors concerned,*

---

106 Commission of the European Communities, Communication from the Commission Action Plan "Simplifying and improving the regulatory environment", COM (2002) 278 final, 05.06.2002. The Action Plan was accompanied by another Communication from the Commission, in which the most important elements of the Better Regulation strategy were clarified: Commission of the European Communities, Communication from the Commission – European Governance: better lawmaking, COM (2002) 275 final, 05.06.2002.

107 Commission of the European Communities, Communication from the Commission Action Plan "Simplifying and improving the regulatory environment", COM (2002) 278 final, 05.06.2002, 3.

108 Commission of the European Communities, Communication from the Commission Action Plan "Simplifying and improving the regulatory environment", COM (2002) 278 final, 05.06.2002, 3.

109 Commission of the European Communities, Communication from the Commission Action Plan "Simplifying and improving the regulatory environment", COM (2002) 278 final, 05.06.2002, 11.

110 Defined in the Action Plan as "*a large number of practices, common rules, codes of conduct and voluntary agreements which economic actors, social players, NGOs and organised groups establish themselves on a voluntary basis in order to regulate and organise their activities*". It was stressed that "*[u]nlike co-regulation, self-regulation does not involve a legislative act*": Commission of the European Communities, Communication from the Commission Action Plan "Simplifying and improving the regulatory environment", COM (2002) 278 final, 05.06.2002, 11.

111 Commission of the European Communities, Communication from the Commission Action Plan "Simplifying and improving the regulatory environment", COM (2002) 278 final, 05.06.2002, 11.

reducing the burden of legislative work by focusing on the essential aspects of legislation, and drawing on the experience of interested parties, particularly operators and social partners".[112] Furthermore, the Better Legislation Action Plan put forward 'A framework for co-regulation' and set out a number of co-regulatory criteria. In summary, these criteria are:

- *Co-regulation [should] be used on the basis of a legislative act.*
- *The co-regulation mechanism, within the framework of a legislative act, must be in the interests of the general public.*
- *The legislator [should establish] the essential aspects of the legislation: the objectives to achieve; the deadlines and mechanisms relating to its implementation; methods of monitoring the application of the legislation and any sanctions which are necessary to guarantee the legal certainty of the legislation.*[113]
- *The legislator determines to what extent defining and implementing the measures can be left to the parties concerned because of [their] experience.*
- *The principle of the transparency of legislation applies to the co-regulation mechanism.*
- *The parties concerned must be considered to be representative, organised and responsible by the Commission, Council and European Parliament.*[114]

While these criteria were particularly oriented to the EU legislative and regulatory process, they could also prove quite useful for building co-regulatory concepts in other settings as well, although the criteria are rather strict.

B.4. *Interinstitutional Agreement on Better Lawmaking*

Agreement – In December 2003, the European Parliament, Council, and Commission drafted the Interinstitutional Agreement on Better Lawmaking,[115, 116]

---

[112] Commission of the European Communities, Communication from the Commission Action Plan "Simplifying and improving the regulatory environment", COM (2002) 278 final, 05.06.2002, 12.

[113] Again, the narrowness or broadness with which this criterion is interpreted is of crucial importance and can have significant consequences regarding whether or not measures could be classified as co-regulation.

[114] Commission of the European Communities, Communication from the Commission Action Plan "Simplifying and improving the regulatory environment", COM (2002) 278 final, 05.06.2002, 13.

[115] European Parliament, Council, and Commission, Interinstitutional agreement on better law-making, 2003/C 321/01, *OJ* 31.12.2003, *C* 321, 1.

[116] The importance of the involvement of the different EU institutions in the Better Regulation initiatives was already emphasised in Commission of the European Communities, Communication from the Commission Simplifying and improving the regulatory envi-

the goal of which was to improve the quality of law-making. To achieve this aim, the three institutions all agreed "*to observe general principles such as democratic legitimacy, subsidiarity and proportionality, and legal certainty*", as well as "*to promote simplicity, clarity and consistency in the drafting of laws and the utmost transparency of the legislative process*".[117] Again, one of the strategies to improve EU regulation was considered to be the use of alternative methods of regulation. The Interinstitutional Agreement can be considered the first general legal framework for the use of self- and co-regulation at the EU level, as it created general rules and conditions with which alternative regulatory methods need to comply.

CO-REGULATION – The Interinstitutional Agreement defined co-regulation as "*the mechanism whereby a Community legislative act entrusts the attainment of the objectives defined by the legislative authority to parties which are recognised in the field (such as economic operators, the social partners, non-governmental organisations, or associations)*".[118] The legislative act on which the co-regulatory mechanism is based should respect the principle of proportionality,[119] and should specify the level of authority that the recognised parties possess and the relevant measures to be taken in the event of non-compliance by one or more parties or of failure of agreements.[120] These agreements can be established voluntarily by different parties to set up practical arrangements.[121] According to the Interinstitutional Agreement, opting

ronment, COM (2001) 726 final, 05.12.2001, 4. In this Communication, the Commission revealed its intention to consult with the other institutions.

[117] EUROPEAN PARLIAMENT, COUNCIL, AND COMMISSION, Interinstitutional agreement on better law-making, 2003/C 321/01, *OJ* 31.12.2003, *C* 321, recital 2.

[118] EUROPEAN PARLIAMENT, COUNCIL, AND COMMISSION, Interinstitutional agreement on better law-making, 2003/C 321/01, *OJ* 31.12.2003, *C* 321, recital 18.

[119] EUROPEAN PARLIAMENT, COUNCIL, AND COMMISSION, Interinstitutional agreement on better law-making, 2003/C 321/01, *OJ* 31.12.2003, *C* 321, recital 18.

[120] EUROPEAN PARLIAMENT, COUNCIL, AND COMMISSION, Interinstitutional agreement on better law-making, 2003/C 321/01, *OJ* 31.12.2003, *C* 321, recital 21.

[121] EUROPEAN PARLIAMENT, COUNCIL, AND COMMISSION, Interinstitutional agreement on better law-making, 2003/C 321/01, *OJ* 31.12.2003, *C* 321, recital 20. The Agreement specified that any draft agreement would be "*forwarded by the Commission to the legislative authority*", and that the Commission would "*verify whether or not those draft agreements comply with Community law (and, in particular, with the basic legislative act*" (recital 20, para. 2). Furthermore, it was stipulated that "*[a]t the request of inter alia the European Parliament or of the Council, on a case-by-case basis and depending on the subject, the basic legislative act may include a provision for a two-month period of grace following notification of a draft agreement to the European Parliament and the Council. During that period, each Institution may either suggest amendments, if it is considered that the draft agreement does not meet the objectives laid down by the legislative authority, or object to the entry into force*

for such a mechanism would enable legislation to be adapted to the problems and sectors concerned, help reduce the legislative burden by concentrating on essential aspects of the matter that needs to be regulated, and allow the parties concerned to draw on their experience.[122]

SELF-REGULATION – Self-regulation, on the other hand, was described as "*the possibility for economic operators, social partners, non-governmental organisations or associations to adopt amongst themselves and for themselves guidelines at European level (particularly codes of practice or sectoral agreements)*".[123]

GENERAL CONDITIONS – The Agreement specified that the use of alternative instruments (self- and co-regulation) should always conform to Community law and respect the values of transparency and representativeness of the parties involved.[124] Furthermore, opting for alternative methods should add value to the general interest. On the other hand, such methods should not be opted for where fundamental rights or important political options are at stake or in situations where full harmonisation across Member States is strived for. Finally, the Agreement stipulated that alternative regulatory

of that agreement and, possibly, ask the Commission to submit a proposal for a legislative act" (recital 20 para. 3). These provisions relate to co-regulatory mechanisms at the EU level, but of course inspiration can be drawn from them for mechanisms at other levels.

122 EUROPEAN PARLIAMENT, COUNCIL, AND COMMISSION, Interinstitutional agreement on better law-making, 2003/C 321/01, *OJ* 31.12.2003, *C* 321, recital 18.

123 EUROPEAN PARLIAMENT, COUNCIL, AND COMMISSION, Interinstitutional agreement on better law-making, 2003/C 321/01, *OJ* 31.12.2003, *C* 321, recital 22. Again, certain specifications were included that specifically relate to the Community institutions and their responsibilities in the creation, implementation and oversight of self-regulatory mechanisms. The Commission, for instance, was ordered to scrutinise the self-regulation mechanisms in order to verify that they comply with the provisions of the EC Treaty (recital 22 para. 2). Moreover, "*[t]he Commission will notify the European Parliament and the Council of the self-regulation practices which it regards, on the one hand, as contributing to the attainment of the EC Treaty objectives and as being compatible with its provisions and, on the other, as being satisfactory in terms of the representativeness of the parties concerned, sectoral and geographical cover and the added value of the commitments given. It will, nonetheless, consider the possibility of putting forward a proposal for a legislative act, in particular at the request of the competent legislative authority or in the event of a failure to observe the above practices*" (recital 23). It is worth noting that this is a stipulation (particularly the last sentence) which is inclined more towards co- than self-regulation.

124 EUROPEAN PARLIAMENT, COUNCIL, AND COMMISSION, Interinstitutional agreement on better law-making, 2003/C 321/01, *OJ* 31.12.2003, *C* 321, recital 17.

methods should guarantee swift and flexible regulation that does not affect the principles of competition or unity of the market.[125]

ANALYSIS – It has been argued that these definitions and conditions are highly restrictive, and in stark contrast to the existing mechanisms throughout the European Union.[126] PROSSER, for instance, pointed out that the co-regulation concept in the Agreement is "*very much a 'top-down' view with minimal discretion for the co-regulatory body, and appears not to cover the 'bottom-up' development of private regulation with state back-up powers, or the contracting out of regulatory functions to such bodies*".[127] SENDEN agreed that the EU approach to co-regulation seems to be rather top-down, and argued that co-regulation seems to be considered as an implementation mechanism and a complement to legislation, rather than as an alternative.[128] According to her, self-regulation, on the other hand, takes a bottom-up approach, and is thus rather an alternative to legislation.[129] Finally, one can also wonder whether the elaborate conditions included in the Agreement do not pre-empt flexibility and adaptability, two characteristics for which alternative regulatory instruments are usually renowned.

[125] EUROPEAN PARLIAMENT, COUNCIL, AND COMMISSION, Interinstitutional agreement on better law-making, 2003/C 321/01, *OJ* 31.12.2003, *C* 321, recital 17.

[126] PROSSER, Tony, "Self-regulation, co-regulation and the Audio-Visual Media Services Directive", *Journal of Consumer Policy* 2008, Vol. 31, No. 1, 107 and 108.

[127] PROSSER, Tony, "Self-regulation, co-regulation and the Audio-Visual Media Services Directive", *Journal of Consumer Policy* 2008, Vol. 31, No. 1, 107.

[128] SENDEN, Linda, "Soft law, self-regulation and co-regulation in European law: where do they meet?", *Electronic Journal of Comparative Law* 2005, Vol. 9, No. 1, retrieved from http://www.ejcl.org/91/abs91-3.html (on 30.05.2008), 27: "*European co-regulation presupposes the prior establishment of a general legislative framework by the European legislature and thus also takes place within the scope of the Union's competence. It merely leaves the further execution and implementation of this framework to the various private actors in the field concerned. Hence, co-regulation primarily aims at complementing legislation*".

[129] SENDEN, Linda, "Soft law, self-regulation and co-regulation in European law: where do they meet?", *Electronic Journal of Comparative Law* 2005, Vol. 9, No. 1, retrieved from http://www.ejcl.org/91/abs91-3.html (on 30.05.2008), 27: "*European self-regulation occurs outside such a legislative framework, where there is deemed to be no need (yet) for legislation or where a European legal basis for legislation may be lacking. As such it may be perceived as an alternative to legislation*".

B.5. *Other EU policy documents*

Better Regulation for Growth and Jobs in the European Union – In 2005,[130] the Commission issued its Communication Better regulation for growth and jobs in the European Union.[131] This Communication re-emphasised the importance of improving the regulatory environment and observed that, although the European Union had achieved a lot in a relatively short space of time, much still needed to be done.[132] Concerning the 'Better Regulation' policy at the EU level, the Commission proposed three main focus points: improving and extending the use of impact assessment for new proposals, screening pending legislative proposals, and the introduction of a new method of simplifying existing legislation.[133] With respect to the use of self- and co-regulation, references were made to definitions and criteria included in the Interinstitutional Agreement, and the Commission stressed that the use of such instruments would reinforce the effective application of the principles of proportionality and subsidiarity.[134]

---

[130] In January 2005, the Commission reiterated the importance of the Better Regulation policy, stating that "*[l]egislation should aim at the highest level of quality, coherence and effectiveness. Better Regulation means that legislation should be well-prepared and as simple as possible. Impact assessment, including on competitiveness, before initiatives are launched and throughout the legislative process must become second nature. Reviews of legislation in force should systematically be done. Subsidiarity and proportionality must be applied in full. Better regulation should be a priority also at the Member States' level*": Commission of the European Communities, Strategic objectives 2005–2009, Europe 2010: a partnership for European renewal, prosperity, solidarity and security, COM (2005) 12 final, 26.01.2005, 5.

[131] Commission of the European Communities, Communication from the Commission to the Council and the European Parliament – Better regulation for growth and jobs in the European Union, COM (2005) 97 final, 16.03.2005.

[132] Commission of the European Communities, Communication from the Commission to the Council and the European Parliament – Better regulation for growth and jobs in the European Union, COM (2005) 97 final, 16.03.2005, 4.

[133] Commission of the European Communities, Communication from the Commission to the European Parliament, the Council, the European Economic and Social Committee and the Committee of the Regions – Implementing the Community Lisbon programme: a strategy for the simplification of the regulatory environment, COM (2005) 535 final, 25.10.2005, 3. Another proposal was the creation of a high-level group of national regulatory experts, who would advise the Commission on better regulation issues in general (p. 10). This group was set up in February 2006: Commission of the European Communities, Commission Decision of 28 February 2006 setting up a group of high-level regulatory experts, 2006/210/EC, *OJ* 15.03.2006, *L* 76, 3.

[134] Commission of the European Communities, Communication from the Commission to the Council and the European Parliament – Better regulation for growth and jobs in the European Union, COM (2005) 97 final, 16.03.2005, 4.

Strategy for the simplification of the regulatory environment – In October 2005, another communication by the Commission was issued, this time titled Implementing the Community Lisbon programme: a strategy for the simplification of the regulatory environment.[135] This Communication focused on the third action point put forward in the Better regulation for growth and jobs in the European Union Communication (*supra*), i.e., the introduction of a new method for simplification of legislation. One element of this new method was the modification to the regulatory approach, which involved – among other suggestions – using co-regulation as "*a more efficient and expedient method for addressing certain policy objectives than the classical legislative tools*".[136] Standardisation of independent bodies and technical harmonisation with respect to CE marking[137] were given as examples of co-regulatory measures.[138]

Strategic reviews of better regulation – In 2006 and 2008, the Commission published A strategic review of better regulation in the European Union, and A second strategic review of better regulation in the European Union,[139] both of which scrutinised the progress achieved with respect to previous Better Regulation documents and identified remaining challenges

---

[135] Commission of the European Communities, Communication from the Commission to the European Parliament, the Council, the European Economic and Social Committee and the Committee of the Regions – Implementing the Community Lisbon programme: a strategy for the simplification of the regulatory environment, COM (2005) 535 final, 25.10.2005.

[136] Commission of the European Communities, Communication from the Commission to the European Parliament, the Council, the European Economic and Social Committee and the Committee of the Regions – Implementing the Community Lisbon programme: a strategy for the simplification of the regulatory environment, COM (2005) 535 final, 25.10.2005, 7.

[137] For more information on CE marking, cf. http://ec.europa.eu/enterprise/newapproach/legislation/guide/document/chap07.pdf (retrieved on 29.11.2008).

[138] Commission of the European Communities, Communication from the Commission to the European Parliament, the Council, the European Economic and Social Committee and the Committee of the Regions – Implementing the Community Lisbon programme: a strategy for the simplification of the regulatory environment, COM (2005) 535 final, 25.10.2005, 7–8.

[139] Commission of the European Communities, Communication from the Commission to the European Parliament, the Council, the European Economic and Social Committee and the Committee of the Regions – A strategic review of Better Regulation in the European Union, COM (2006) 689 final, 14.11.2006; Commission of the European Communities, Communication from the Commission to the European Parliament, the Council, the European Economic and Social Committee and the Committee of the Regions – Second strategic review of better regulation in the European Union, COM (2008) 32 final, 30.01.2008.

with respect to the Better Regulation policy. In these reviews, only fleeting references were made to the use of self- and co-regulation, in the framework of using impact assessments to decide upon the kind of legislative or regulatory instrument needed to achieve a certain goal.[140]

BETTER REGULATION EXPLAINED SIMPLY – The Commission also issued a 'vulgarised' document in which they attempted to explain the Better Regulation policy in a simple way.[141] Alternatives to regulation were discussed as one of the elements of the policy. In the document, the Commission defined co-regulation as "*entrusting the achievement of the goals set out in law, for example to social partners or to non-governmental organisations*", and self-regulation as "*voluntary agreements between private bodies to solve problems by taking commitments between themselves*".[142] Such instruments were judged to be more cost efficient and effective ways to deal with certain policy objectives than the traditional legislative instruments.[143] Again, the standardisation of technical requirements by independent bodies (with respect to the CE marking) was cited as a classic co-regulation example.[144]

DOCUMENTS PROMOTING MULTI-STAKEHOLDER INVOLVEMENT – There are also a number of documents which do not fit in directly with the EU Better Regulation policy, but which are nonetheless interesting to the subject of this study since they promote the involvement of many stakeholders in policy,

---

140 COMMISSION OF THE EUROPEAN COMMUNITIES, Communication from the Commission to the European Parliament, the Council, the European Economic and Social Committee and the Committee of the Regions – A strategic review of Better Regulation in the European Union, COM (2006) 689 final, 14.11.20068; COMMISSION OF THE EUROPEAN COMMUNITIES, Communication from the Commission to the European Parliament, the Council, the European Economic and Social Committee and the Committee of the Regions – Second strategic review of better regulation in the European Union, COM (2008) 32 final, 30.01.2008, 5.

141 COMMISSION, Better regulation: simply explained, 2006, retrieved from http://ec.europa.eu/governance/better_regulation/documents/brochure/br_brochure_en.pdf (on 14.05.2008).

142 COMMISSION, Better regulation: simply explained, 2006, retrieved from http://ec.europa.eu/governance/better_regulation/documents/brochure/br_brochure_en.pdf (on 14.05.2008), 13.

143 COMMISSION, Better regulation: simply explained, 2006, retrieved from http://ec.europa.eu/governance/better_regulation/documents/brochure/br_brochure_en.pdf (on 14.05.2008), 13.

144 COMMISSION, Better regulation: simply explained, 2006, retrieved from http://ec.europa.eu/governance/better_regulation/documents/brochure/br_brochure_en.pdf (on 14.05.2008), 13: "*For many industrial and consumer products, the 'CE' marking attests that a product has been certified and can be marketed in the EU. EU legislation only sets certification requirements and mandates private bodies*".

regulation or decision-making.[145] A Communication from the Commission following the World Summit on the Information Society, for instance, stressed that involvement of the private sector and civil society organisations was of prime importance to achieve the Summit goals.[146]

B.6. *Interim conclusion*

TREND – It is obvious from the overview of these general policy documents that the 'Better Regulation' paradigm has been studied, documented and debated thoroughly. Yet, this does not mean that the approach to alternative regulatory instruments, such as self- and co-regulation, has been consistent throughout the different policy documents. Whereas the gist of these concepts remained rather similar, different nuances are noticeable in the various definitions and descriptions.

FROM GENERAL TO SECTOR-SPECIFIC – The general 'Better Regulation' discourse is not, however, restricted to the abstract EU level. On the contrary, certain sectors, such as the media sector, preceded the trend at this general level, having referred to the use of alternative regulatory instruments a few years before the first general documents were issued.

2.2.2. *Media policy documents*

REFERENCES TO SELF- AND CO-REGULATION – From the mid-1990s onwards, media policy documents, particularly EU and CoE documents, started to refer to the use of self- (and later co-) regulation to achieve certain policy goals in the digital media environment.[147] As mentioned in the previous part, the new

---

[145] Multi-stakeholder involvement is also promoted at the international level. Cf., for instance: UNITED NATIONS GENERAL ASSEMBLY, United Nations Millennium Declaration, 55th session, 18.09.2000, retrieved from http://www.un.org/millennium/declaration/ares552e.htm (on 29.08.2006): "*To give greater opportunities to the private sector, non-governmental organizations and civil society, in general, to contribute to the realization of the Organization's goals and programmes*".

[146] COMMISSION OF THE EUROPEAN COMMUNITIES, Communication from the Commission to the Council, the European Parliament, the European Economic and Social Committee and the Committee of the Regions, Towards a global partnership in the Information Society: Follow-up to the Tunis Phase of the World Summit on the Information Society (WSIS), COM (2006) 181 final, 27.04.2006, 8 and 9.

[147] It has been suggested in the United States as well, also from the mid-1990s onwards, that self-regulation would be an appropriate tool to regulate cyberspace: cf. THE WHITE HOUSE, A framework for global electronic commerce, 01.07.1997, retrieved from http://

information and communication technologies possess certain characteristics which clash with the use of traditional legislation. The overview of the policy documents with respect to the protection of minors against harmful content, provided in the previous chapter, already showed the inclination towards the use of alternative regulatory instruments to remedy this problem.[148] In the following section, the references to the use of self- and co-regulation in these, and other media policy documents, will be studied in greater detail.

A. *European Union*

Table – The table below presents an analysis of the most important EU media policy documents (related to the protection of minors against harmful content).[149] The analysis focuses on which regulatory instruments were mentioned in these policy documents, how often they were mentioned, and how these regulatory methods were presented or interpreted.

---

www.technology.gov/digeconomy/framewrk.htm (on 26.05.2008, no longer available): "*governments should encourage industry self-regulation wherever appropriate and support the efforts of private sector organizations to develop mechanisms to facilitate the successful operation of the Internet*".

[148] For instance: Reding, Viviane, Commission study points the way forward for better regulation of new media and the digital economy (press release on Safer Internet Day 2007), IP/07/138, Brussels, 06.02.2007, retrieved from http://www.europa.eu/rapid/pressReleasesAction.do?reference=IP/07/138&format=HTML&aged=0&language=EN&guiLanguage=fr (on 07.02.2007): "*Self regulation, where industry regulates itself, and co-regulation, the combination of state and non-state regulation, will help cope with the increasing risk of failure of traditional approaches, and will hand back responsibility to society and interested parties where appropriate*".

[149] The policy documents chosen are documents that have been issued by the EU in the field of media policy with the aim (as a sole goal or as one goal amongst other goals) of protecting minors against harmful content. There are, of course, other EU documents that relate to self- and/or co-regulation. For instance: Council, Conclusions of 27 September 1999 on the role of self-regulation on the light of the development of new media services, 1999/C 283/02, *OJ* 06.10.1999, *C* 283, 3; European Parliament, Resolution on the Commission communication 'Study on Parental Control of Television Broadcasting', COM(1999) 371 – C5-0324/1999 – 1999/2210(COS), 05.10.2000, retrieved from http://www.europarl.europa.eu/omk/omnsapir.so/pv2?PRG=DOCPV&APP=PV2&LANGUE=EN&SDOCTA=7&TXTLST=1&POS=1&Type_Doc=RESOL&TPV=PROV&DATE=051000&PrgPrev=TYPEF@A5|PRG@QUERY|APP@PV2|FILE@BIBLIO00|NUMERO@258|YEAR@00|PLAGE@1&TYPEF=A5&NUMB=1&DATEF=001005 (on 26.05.2008): The Parliament "*[b]elieves that, as a matter of urgency, all television operators in the EU should agree a code of self-regulation in respect of the protection of minors*".

Table 3: Self- and co-regulation in media policy documents

Year	Document	Which alternative regulatory instruments? (number of mentions)	Presentation / Interpretation
1996	Green paper on the protection of minors and human dignity	Self-regulation (25)	Codes of conduct Parental control systems Frameworks of self-regulation
		Co-regulation?	Not mentioned, but mention of "*self-regulation, possibly supervised / possibly backed up by legislation*"
1996	Communication on Illegal and harmful content on the Internet	Self-regulation (10)	Network of Associations of ISPs
1998	Recommendation on the protection of minors and human dignity	Self-regulation (20)	National self-regulation frameworks Cooperation between enterprises/operators Codes of conduct
1999	Safer Internet Action Plan	Self-regulation (19)	Industry self-regulation Codes of conduct Self-regulatory bodies
2001	First evaluation report Recommendation	Self-regulation (25)	Codes of conduct Self-regulatory networks of operators Rating
		Co-regulation (2)	NICAM and UK Communications White Paper
2003	Second evaluation report Recommendation	Self-regulation (35)	Codes of conduct Self-regulatory networks of operators NICAM Rating
		Co-regulation (9)	Rating (complaints systems)
2004	Proposal new Recommendation	Self-regulation (2) Co-regulation (1)	Rating Self- and co-regulatory bodies
2005	Safer Internet Programme Plus	Self-regulation (16)	Rating and labelling Codes of conduct Self-regulatory bodies
		Co-regulation (1)	Co-regulatory bodies
2005	Proposal AVMS	Self-regulation (6) Co-regulation (10)	Not specified Not specified

Table 3 (*cont.*)

Year	Document	Which alternative regulatory instruments? (number of mentions)	Presentation / Interpretation
2006	Recommendation on the protection of minors and human dignity	Self-regulation (6)	Rating Self-regulatory bodies Codes of conduct Rating
		Co-regulation (3)	Co-regulatory bodies
2008	AVMSD	Self-regulation (10) Co-regulation (5)	Definition (*infra*) Definition (*infra*)
2008	Safer Internet Programme	Self-regulation (13)	Rating Industry bodies
		Co-regulation (2)	Not specified
2008	Communication on video games[150]	Self-regulation (13) Co-regulation (3)	Rating (PEGI) Not specified

Conclusions drawn from table – A first deduction that can be made from the table is that, in the earliest documents, only self-regulation was alluded to: it is only since the beginning of the 21st century that co-regulation started to appear. It is quite obvious, however, that self-regulation is still mentioned more often, notwithstanding the recently increased enthusiasm for the use of co-regulation. As to what exactly is meant by the notions 'self-regulation' and 'co-regulation', the relevant policymakers can certainly not be accused of being abundantly clear. In the first documents, codes of conduct and self-regulation frameworks were most often referred to. Additionally, rating was also mentioned regularly in relation to self- (and later also co-) regulation. Finally, references to co-regulation in the later documents were usually not very specific. Nevertheless, there are a limited number of clues regarding both concepts that can be extracted from certain policy documents.

Clues in the 1998 Recommendation – An early document in which certain specifications on self-regulation were given was the 1998 Recommendation on the protection of minors. The recitals to the Recommendation clarified that the use of self-regulation could allow businesses to adapt themselves quickly

[150] Commission of the European Communities, Communication from the Commission to the European Parliament, the Council, the European Economic and Social Committee and the Committee of the Regions on the protection of consumers, in particular minors, in respect of the use of video games, COM (2008) 207 final, 22.04.2008.

to technical progress and market globalisation.[151] Furthermore, it could play a part in a fast implementation of solutions for protecting minors, while benefiting from the high degree of flexibility necessary to keep up with the above-mentioned fast technological developments.[152] The Annex to the Recommendation provided some indications for the establishment of national self-regulation frameworks. The importance of the full participation of the relevant actors, such as public authorities, users, consumers and businesses that are directly or indirectly involved in the media sector was stressed, as well as the significance of a clear division of responsibilities and functions of these different actors.[153] As will become clearer later on, we can wonder if the emphasis on the involvement of public authorities does not rather point in the direction of co-regulation instead of self-regulation.[154] The Annex also suggested that because self-regulation is, usually, voluntary, the acceptance and effectiveness of such a framework will be dependent on the degree of participation and cooperation of the relevant actors in the establishment, implementation and evaluation of the self-regulation framework.[155]

---

151 Recital 13 Council Recommendation 98/560/EC of 24 September 1998 on the development of the competitiveness of the European audiovisual and information services industry by promoting national frameworks aimed at achieving a comparable and effective level of protection of minors and human dignity, *OJ* 07.10.1998, *L* 270, 48.

152 Recital 20 Council Recommendation 98/560/EC of 24 September 1998 on the development of the competitiveness of the European audiovisual and information services industry by promoting national frameworks aimed at achieving a comparable and effective level of protection of minors and human dignity, *OJ* 07.10.1998, *L* 270, 48.

153 Annex Council Recommendation 98/560/EC of 24 September 1998 on the development of the competitiveness of the European audiovisual and information services industry by promoting national frameworks aimed at achieving a comparable and effective level of protection of minors and human dignity, *OJ* 07.10.1998, *L* 270, 48.

154 Commissioner Reding also seemed to believe that the 1998 Recommendation supported co-regulation: "*The necessary mix of self- and co-regulation, of technical measures and of media literacy initiative is reflected as well in the 1998 Recommendation on Protection of minors in the online environment, which offers guidelines for the development of national self-regulation regarding the protection of minors and human dignity*": Reding, Viviane, Freedom of the media, effective co-regulation and media literacy: cornerstones for an efficient protection of minors in the European Union, Speech at the ICRA Roundtable Brussels 'Mission Impossible', Brussels, 14.06.2006, retrieved from http://europa.eu.int/rapid/pressReleasesAction.do?reference=SPEECH/06/374&type=HTML&aged=0&language=EN&guiLanguage=en (on 15.06.2006).

155 Annex Council of the European Communities, Council Recommendation on the development of the competitiveness of the European audiovisual and information services industry by promoting national frameworks aimed at achieving a comparable and effective level of protection of minors and human dignity, 98/560/EC, *OJ* 07.10.1998, *L* 270, 48. Cf. also Reding, Viviane, Freedom of the media, effective co-regulation and media literacy: cornerstones for an efficient protection of minors in the European Union, Speech

Clues in the second evaluation report of the 1998 Recommendation – The second evaluation report of the 1998 Recommendation was a very significant document with respect to co-regulation. The document sung the praises of this instrument – especially for the protection of minors – for the very first time, and provided some indications as to the interpretation of the concept as well. More specifically, it was argued that a "*coregulatory approach may be more flexible, adaptable and effective than straightforward regulation and legislation*".[156] Particularly with regard to the protection of minors, "*where many sensibilities have to be taken into account*", it was suggested that co-regulation could better attain this goal.[157] The Commission also clarified that co-regulation should entail an appropriate level of involvement by the public authorities and should involve cooperation between public authorities, industry and other interested parties, such as consumers.[158] In this context, one can of course wonder what an appropriate level of public authority involvement is.

Clues in Safer Internet Programmes – The Safer Internet Plus Programme (2005–2008) decision clarified which elements constitute a self-regulatory mechanism: "*consultation and appropriate representation of the parties concerned; codes of conduct; national bodies facilitating cooperation*

at the ICRA Roundtable Brussels 'Mission Impossible', Brussels, 14.06.2006, retrieved from http://europa.eu.int/rapid/pressReleasesAction.do?reference=SPEECH/06/374&type=HTML&aged=0&language=EN&guiLanguage=en (on 15.06.2006): "*Self-regulation is based on three key elements: first, the involvement of all the interested parties (Government, industry, service and access providers, user associations) in the production of codes of conduct; secondly, the implementation of codes of conduct by the industry; thirdly, the evaluation of measures taken*". Again, the reference to the involvement of the government leans more toward the concept of co-regulation (*infra*).

[156] Commission of the European Communities, Second evaluation report from the Commission to the Council and the European Parliament on the application of Council Recommendation of 24 September 1998 concerning the protection of minors, COM (2003) 776 final, 12.12.2003, retrieved from http://eur-lex.europa.eu/LexUriServ/site/en/com/2003/com2003_0776en01.pdf (on 25.07.2006), 5.

[157] Commission of the European Communities, Second evaluation report from the Commission to the Council and the European Parliament on the application of Council Recommendation of 24 September 1998 concerning the protection of minors, COM (2003) 776 final, 12.12.2003, retrieved from http://eur-lex.europa.eu/LexUriServ/site/en/com/2003/com2003_0776en01.pdf (on 25.07.2006), 5.

[158] Commission of the European Communities, Second evaluation report from the Commission to the Council and the European Parliament on the application of Council Recommendation of 24 September 1998 concerning the protection of minors, COM (2003) 776 final, 12.12.2003, retrieved from http://eur-lex.europa.eu/LexUriServ/site/en/com/2003/com2003_0776en01.pdf (on 25.07.2006), 5.

at Community level; and national evaluation of selfregulation frameworks".[159] Even in the proposal for this Decision the Commission had already stressed the fact that it supported the use of self-regulation due to its "*flexibility and understanding of the needs of the media in an area combining high technology, rapid change and cross-border activity*".[160] Interestingly, this proposal also pointed out that self-regulation does not exclude the need for some type of legal underpinning, for instance, to achieve agreement on an appropriate set of rules and their implementation.[161] The most recent Safer Internet Programme proposal decision (2009–2013) stressed that in order to achieve a high degree of effectiveness in dealing with harmful content, a number of methods, such as enforcement of legal provisions, self-regulation, parental control tools, awareness-raising and education need to be combined.[162] We can also recall the 'European Framework for safer mobile use by younger teenagers and children' and the 'Safer social networking principles for the EU', two initiatives taken within the framework of the Safer Internet Programmes (*supra*, Chapter 1). It can be noted that, whereas these initiatives are assigned the label 'self-regulation', the European Commission played an important role in gathering the stakeholders and facilitating the creation of the principles, and will continue to participate in the process by monitoring the progress of the initiatives.[163]

---

[159] Parliament and Council of the European Communities, Decision No 854/2005/EC of the European Parliament and of the Council establishing a multiannual Community programme on promoting safer use of the Internet and new online technologies, 11.05.2005, *OJ* 11.06.2005, *L* 149, 7.

[160] Commission of the European Communities, Proposal for a Decision of the European Parliament and of the Council on establishing a multiannual Community programme on promoting safer use of the Internet and new online technologies, COM (2004) 91 final, 12.03.2004, 8.

[161] Commission of the European Communities, Proposal for a Decision of the European Parliament and of the Council on establishing a multiannual Community programme on promoting safer use of the Internet and new online technologies, COM (2004) 91 final, 12.03.2004, 8.

[162] Commission of the European Communities, Proposal for a Decision of the European Parliament and of the Council establishing a multiannual Community programme on protecting children using the Internet and other communication technologies, COM (2008) 106 final, 27.02.2008, 5. Similar statements had already been included in other policy documents as well, cf. for instance: Commission of the European Communities, Proposal for a Decision of the European Parliament and of the Council on establishing a multiannual Community programme on promoting safer use of the Internet and new online technologies, COM (2004) 91 final, 12.03.2004, 4.

[163] Jakubowicz, Karl, "A new notion of media?", Background text, 1st Council of Europe Conference of Ministers responsible for media and new communications services : A new

Clues in the AVMS Directive – The documents relating to the Audiovisual Media Services Directive[164] (AVMSD, *infra*, Part 2, Chapter 1) probably provide the clearest indications of the Commission's interpretation of the use of self- and co-regulation.[165] The first text – the 2005 Commission proposal – could, however, be considered somewhat doubtful or contradictory with respect to the instruments it proposes given that, while self-regulation was mentioned in the introduction and the recitals,[166] only co-regulation was referred to in the text of the Directive itself, in article 3 para. 3 ("*Member States shall encourage co-regulatory regimes in the fields coordinated by this Directive*"). Prosser argued that the reason for this ambiguity can be found in the reference in the proposal to the definitions included in the Interinstitutional Agreement on Better Lawmaking,[167] which, as mentioned above, were highly restrictive.[168] According to him, the Commission's lawyers worried that the definition of self-regulation in the Interinstitutional agreement was not suitable and, furthermore, that self-regulation, given its undeveloped state in certain Member States, could not be stipulated for all of them.[169] Fur-

notion of media?; Reykjavik, 28–29.05.2009, retrieved from http://www.ministerialconference.is/media/images/a_new_notion_of_media_web_version.df (on 27.05.2009), 32.

164 European Parliament and Council Directive 2007/65/EC of 11 December 2007 amending Council Directive 89/552/EEC on the coordination of certain provisions laid down by law, regulation or administrative action in Member States concerning the pursuit of television broadcasting activities, *OJ* 18.12.2007, *L* 332, 27.

165 The usefulness of alternative regulatory instruments in the areas covered by the Directive was already stressed in documents preceding the actual review process of the Television without Frontiers Directive, for instance: Commission of the European Communities, Communication from the Commission to the Council, the European Parliament, the European Economic and Social Committee and the Committee of the Regions, The future of European regulatory audiovisual policy, COM (2003) 784 final, 15.12.2003, 23; and Commission of the European Communities, Commission interpretative communication on certain aspects of the provisions on televised advertising in the 'Television without Frontiers' Directive, 2004/C 102/02, *OJ* 28.04.2004, *C* 102, 2: "*73. Finally, the Commission wishes to stress the potentially important role which codes of conduct and co-regulation may play in the practical implementation of the principles and rules of the Directive*".

166 It was stated, for instance, that the proposed instruments were "*directive, co-regulation, self-regulation*": Commission of the European Communities, Proposal for a Directive of the European Parliament and of the Council amending Council Directive 89/552/EEC on the coordination of certain provisions laid down by law, regulation or administrative action in Member States concerning the pursuit of television broadcasting activities, COM (2005) 646 final, 13.12.2005, 9. Cf. also recital 25.

167 Recital 25 AVMS Directive.

168 Prosser, Tony, "Self-regulation, co-regulation and the Audio-Visual Media Services Directive", *Journal of Consumer Policy* 2008, Vol. 31, No. 1, 108.

169 Prosser, Tony, "Self-regulation, co-regulation and the Audio-Visual Media Services Directive", *Journal of Consumer Policy* 2008, Vol. 31, No. 1, 108.

thermore, it has been suggested that referring to the Interinstitutional Agreement with regard to the definitions and criteria (recital 25 of the proposal) would have led to a high degree of inflexibility,[170] which is precisely the problem for which a remedy was sought by suggesting to use alternative regulatory instruments.[171] Moreover, the already existing self- and co-regulatory measures that had already been established in different Member States would probably not satisfy all the requirements of the Interinstitutional Agreement.[172] Suffice to say that the proposal was rather problematic with respect to the description and requirements for the use of alternative regulatory mechanisms. Finally, article 3 para. 3 of the AVMSD proposal added two criteria: co-regulatory regimes should be broadly accepted by the main stakeholders, and they should provide for effective enforcement. DOMMERING, SCHEUER and ADER noted that the notions 'broadly accepted' and 'main stakeholders' are not clear and will give rise to interpretation problems.[173]

The original proposal was commented upon and amended by the Council, the Parliament and then again the Commission. In the April 2007 Consolidated Draft,[174] all references to the Interinstitutional Agreement had disappeared and article 3 para. 7 included co- as well as self-regulation. The new recital 25 also offered much less restrictive descriptions of self- and co-regulation.[175] This more relaxed approach found its way into the final – adopted – version of the Directive. Recital 36 states:

> *In its Communication to the European Parliament and the Council on Better Regulation for Growth and Jobs in the European Union, the Commission stressed*

---

170 PROSSER, Tony, "Self-regulation, co-regulation and the Audio-Visual Media Services Directive", *Journal of Consumer Policy* 2008, Vol. 31, No. 1, 108.

171 PROSSER also suggested that there could also be a problem regarding article 288 TFEU [ex 249 EC Treaty]: PROSSER, Tony, "Self-regulation, co-regulation and the Audio-Visual Media Services Directive", *Journal of Consumer Policy* 2008, Vol. 31, No. 1, 108. This issue will be dealt with in detail in the next part.

172 For example: cf. PROSSER, Tony, "Self-regulation, co-regulation and the Audio-Visual Media Services Directive", *Journal of Consumer Policy* 2008, Vol. 31, No. 1, 109.

173 DOMMERING, Egbert, SCHEUER, Alexander and ADER, Thorsten, "Article 3 AVMSD", in: CASTENDYK, Oliver, DOMMERING, Egbert J. and SCHEUER, Alexander (eds), *European Media Law*, Alphen a/d Rijn, Kluwer Law International, 2008, 850–851.

174 EUROPEAN COMMISSION, Audiovisual Media Services Directive: Draft consolidated amended version 2007, March 2007, retrieved from http://ec.europa.eu/information_society/newsroom/cf/itemlongdetail.cfm?item_id=2343 (on 26.03.2007).

175 PROSSER noted that this relaxation probably was influenced to a certain extent by the results of the Hans Bredow Study on Co-regulatory Measures in the Media Sector, which was published in June 2006: PROSSER, Tony, "Self-regulation, co-regulation and the Audio-Visual Media Services Directive", *Journal of Consumer Policy* 2008, Vol. 31, No. 1, 109. This study will be analysed in greater detail in the next section.

> *that a careful analysis of the appropriate regulatory approach is necessary, in particular, in order to establish whether legislation is preferable for the relevant sector and problem, or whether alternatives such as co-regulation or self-regulation should be considered. Furthermore, experience has shown that both co- and self-regulation instruments, implemented in accordance with the different legal traditions of the Member States, can play an important role in delivering a high level of consumer protection. Measures aimed at achieving public interest objectives in the emerging audiovisual media services sector are more effective if they are taken with the active support of the service providers themselves.*
>
> *Thus self-regulation constitutes a type of voluntary initiative which enables economic operators, social partners, non-governmental organisations or associations to adopt common guidelines amongst themselves and for themselves. Member States should, in accordance with their different legal traditions, recognise the role which effective self-regulation can play as a complement to the legislative and judicial and/or administrative mechanisms in place and its useful contribution to the achievement of the objectives of this Directive. However, while self-regulation might be a complementary method of implementing certain provisions of this Directive, it should not constitute a substitute for the obligations of the national legislator.*
>
> *Co-regulation gives, in its minimal form, a legal link between self-regulation and the national legislator in accordance with the legal traditions of the Member States. Co-regulation should allow for the possibility of State intervention in the event of its objectives not being met. Without prejudice to Member States' formal obligations regarding transposition, this Directive encourages the use of co-regulation and self-regulation. This should neither oblige Member States to set up co- and/or self-regulatory regimes nor disrupt or jeopardise current co- or self-regulatory initiatives which are already in place within Member States and which are working effectively.*

The final article 3 para. 7 AVMSD stipulates that "*Member States shall encourage co- and/or self-regulatory regimes at national level in the field coordinated by this Directive to the extent permitted by their legal systems*". The two normative criteria, broad acceptance by the main stakeholders and effective enforcement, remained unchanged.[176] A few remarks can be made regarding this adopted text. A first noteworthy element in recital 36 is the clarification of the rationale for choosing self- and co-regulation. Not only it is mentioned that experience has demonstrated that these instruments have the potential to provide a high degree of consumer protection, but it is also emphasised that the active participation of the relevant actors ('service providers') is crucial for effectively reaching certain policy goals.

A second remark relates to the description of self-regulation. Although the definition is broad, it is highlighted that self-regulation can only be a

[176] Although it can be noted that, in the final text, the wording was slightly different: "*These regimes shall be such that they are broadly accepted by the main stakeholders <u>in the Member States concerned</u> and provide for effective enforcement*" (added emphasis).

complementary method, and "*should not constitute a substitute for the obligations of the national legislator*". This is an awkward specification, from which it could possibly be deduced that self-regulation is not considered a real alternative to legislation (although the first paragraph of the recital clearly considers both self- and co-regulation alternatives to legislation), and that at least a minimal level of government involvement is required for the implementation of the obligations included in the Directive. Given that the same recital describes co-regulation as entailing "*in its minimal form, a legal link between self-regulation and the national legislator in accordance with the legal traditions of the Member States*", which allows for government intervention in the case of failure of the self-regulatory mechanism, one can wonder if co-regulation is preferred above self-regulation to implement the Directive. Of course, following this interpretation, the inclusion of 'self-regulation' in article 3 para. 7 AVMSD seems somewhat contradictory. The choice, however, to refer to self-regulation probably was foremost a political one, urged on by Member States who dearly hold on to their own national traditions of self-regulation.

A final observation is linked to the final sentence of recital 36, which accentuates that Member States should not feel obliged to set up such mechanisms, nor should existing – effective – mechanisms be put at risk. This provision shows the respect for the discretion of the Member States[177] and existing self- and co-regulatory mechanisms. However, in our opinion, Member States should at least consider the take-up of such instruments,[178] especially to protect minors against harmful content, and not use this stipulation as an excuse to completely disregard article 3 para. 7.

STATEMENTS BY THE COMMISSION – Over the past few years, Commissioner Viviane REDING (responsible for Information Society and Media) has frequently referred to the use of self- and co-regulation to achieve certain media policy goals.[179] Already at the time of her appointment as Commissioner,

---

[177] This also relates to article 288 TFEU [ex 249 EC Treaty] (cf. *infra*).

[178] DOMMERING, SCHEUER and ADER argue that Member States are obliged "*to thoroughly assess whether co- or self-regulation is an option*": DOMMERING, Egbert, SCHEUER, Alexander and ADER, Thorsten, "Article 3 AVMSD", in: CASTENDYK, Oliver, DOMMERING, Egbert J. and SCHEUER, Alexander (eds), *European Media Law*, Alphen a/d Rijn, Kluwer Law International, 2008, 850.

[179] REDING, Viviane, The new Television without Frontiers Directive: the Commission proposal to boost Europe's audiovisual sector, Speech at the High level conference on the future of the television sector of the Association for Commercial Television (ACT), Brussels, 27.04.2006, retrieved from http://europa.eu/rapid/pressReleasesAction.do?reference=SPEECH/06/268&format=HTML&aged=0&language=EN&guiLanguage=en (on 21.05.2008); REDING, Viviane, Audiovisual media services directive: the right instrument

Reding emphasised that self- and co-regulation would be the Commission's preferred instrument.[180] On Safer Internet Day 2007, the Commissioner expressed the Commission's desire, with respect to the media and Internet sector, to strive for a regulatory framework that finds a balance "*between firmness and fairness*", while at the same time offering the private sector to swiftly react to change.[181] To achieve this, she expressed a firm belief in the use of self- and co-regulation as alternatives to traditional legislative approaches.[182] In June 2006, Commissioner Reding stated that in relation to the protection

---

to provide legal certainty for Europe's media businesses in the next decade, Speech at the Seminar "Regulating the new media landscape", Brussels, 07.06.2006, retrieved from http://europa.eu.int/rapid/pressReleasesAction.do?reference=SPEECH/06/352&format=HTML&aged=0&language=EN&guiLanguage=en (on 12.07.2006); Reding, Viviane, Freedom of the media, effective co-regulation and media literacy: cornerstones for an efficient protection of minors in the European Union, Speech at the ICRA Roundtable Brussels 'Mission Impossible', Brussels, 14.06.2006, retrieved from http://europa.eu.int/rapid/pressReleasesAction.do?reference=SPEECH/06/374&type=HTML&aged=0&language=EN&guiLanguage=en (on 15.06.2006); Reding, Viviane, Commission study points the way forward for better regulation of new media and the digital economy (press release on Safer Internet Day 2007), IP/07/138, Brussels, 06.02.2007, retrieved from http://www.europa.eu/rapid/pressReleasesAction.do?reference=IP/07/138&format=HTML&aged=0&language=EN&guiLanguage=fr (on 07.02.2007); Reding, Viviane, Self regulation applied to interactive games: success and challenges, speech at the ISFE Expert Conference, Brussels, 26.06.2007, retrieved from http://europa.eu/rapid/pressReleasesAction.do?reference=SPEECH/07/429&type=HTML&aged=0&language=EN&guiLanguage=en (on 22.05.2008); Reding, Viviane, Le nouveau contexte des médias audiovisuels – Tendances et enjeux publics [*The new context of audiovisual media – Trends and public challenges*], Speech at the Colloque international pour les 10 ans du Conseil supérieur de l'audiovisuel de la Communauté française de Belgique, Brussels, 21.09.2007, retrieved from http://europa.eu/rapid/pressReleasesAction.do?reference=SPEECH/07/560 (on 14.01.2008) [in French]; Reding, Viviane, Video games: let's go for PEGI Plus, Speech at the Annual Conference Interactive Software Federation of Europe, Brussels, 07.05.2008, retrieved from http://ec.europa.eu/commission_barroso/reding/docs/speeches/2008/brussels-20080507.pdf (on 21.05.2008).

180 Euractiv, New Commission pledges 'improved cooperation' with media industry, 19.11.2004, retrieved from http://www.euractiv.com/en/pa/new-commission-pledges-improved-operation-media-industry/article-132296 (on 23.05.2008).

181 Reding, Viviane, Commission study points the way forward for better regulation of new media and the digital economy (press release on Safer Internet Day 2007), IP/07/138, Brussels, 06.02.2007, retrieved from http://www.europa.eu/rapid/pressReleasesAction.do?reference=IP/07/138&format=HTML&aged=0&language=EN&guiLanguage=fr (on 07.02.2007).

182 Reding, Viviane, Commission study points the way forward for better regulation of new media and the digital economy (press release on Safer Internet Day 2007), IP/07/138, Brussels, 06.02.2007, retrieved from http://www.europa.eu/rapid/pressReleasesAction.do?reference=IP/07/138&format=HTML&aged=0&language=EN&guiLanguage=fr (on 07.02.2007).

of minors, self-regulation functions optimally when it is underpinned by a legal framework.[183] In fact, she thus seemed to show, at least with respect to this policy goal, a preference for co-regulation, which she defined as a system "*where public authorities accept that the protection of societal values can be left to self-regulatory mechanisms and codes of conduct, but where they reserve the right to step in in case that self-regulation should prove to be inefficient*".[184] Recently, most of her comments regarding self- and co-regulation have related to the creation and implementation of the AVMSD. She has, for instance, expressed her pride in having succeeded in including self- and co-regulation in the AVMSD and stressed it was the first time that the use of co-regulation was included in Community legislation.[185] As to the concrete implementation of the AVMSD, she clarified that Member States would not have an obligation to create such instruments,[186] but only an obligation to examine whether co-regulation would be an appropriate implementation tool, and that, if self-regulatory organisations would be involved in implementing the Directive, an intervention mechanism must be clearly defined in case of failure of the self-regulatory mechanism.[187] Reding also emphasised

[183] Reding, Viviane, Freedom of the media, effective co-regulation and media literacy: cornerstones for an efficient protection of minors in the European Union, Speech at the ICRA Roundtable Brussels 'Mission Impossible', Brussels, 14.06.2006, retrieved from http://europa.eu.int/rapid/pressReleasesAction.do?reference=SPEECH/06/374&type=HTML&aged=0&language=EN&guiLanguage=en (on 15.06.2006).

[184] Reding, Viviane, Freedom of the media, effective co-regulation and media literacy: cornerstones for an efficient protection of minors in the European Union, Speech at the ICRA Roundtable Brussels 'Mission Impossible', Brussels, 14.06.2006, retrieved from http://europa.eu.int/rapid/pressReleasesAction.do?reference=SPEECH/06/374&type=HTML&aged=0&language=EN&guiLanguage=en (on 15.06.2006).

[185] Reding, Viviane, Le nouveau contexte des médias audiovisuels – Tendances et enjeux publics [*The new context of audiovisual media – Trends and public challenges*], Speech at the Colloque international pour les 10 ans du Conseil supérieur de l'audiovisuel de la Communauté française de Belgique, Brussels, 21.09.2007, retrieved from http://europa.eu/rapid/pressReleasesAction.do?reference=SPEECH/07/560 (on 14.01.2008) [in French]; and Reding, Viviane, Audiovisual media services directive: the right instrument to provide legal certainty for Europe's media businesses in the next decade, Speech at the Seminar "Regulating the new media landscape", Brussels, 07.06.2006, retrieved from http://europa.eu.int/rapid/pressReleasesAction.do?reference=SPEECH/06/352&format=HTML&aged=0&language=EN&guiLanguage=en (on 12.07.2006).

[186] Due to article 288 para. 3 TFEU [ex 249 EC Treaty], cf. *infra*, Part 2, Chapters 1 and 2.

[187] Reding, Viviane, Audiovisual media services directive: the right instrument to provide legal certainty for Europe's media businesses in the next decade, Speech at the Seminar "Regulating the new media landscape", Brussels, 07.06.2006, retrieved from http://europa.eu.int/rapid/pressReleasesAction.do?reference=SPEECH/06/352&format=HTML&aged=0&language=EN&guiLanguage=en (on 12.07.2006).

that the effectiveness of a self- or co-regulatory mechanisms greatly depends on the awareness of the public of the existence of such mechanisms.[188]

B. *Council of Europe*

ARIs and CoE Recommendations and Declarations – The Council of Europe has also frequently referred to the use of self- and co-regulatory measures in various policy documents. The 2001 Council of Europe Recommendation on self-regulation concerning cyber content (self-regulation and user protection against illegal and harmful content on new communications and information services)[189] encouraged the establishment of organisations whose members represent a variety of Internet actors (e.g., Internet Service Providers, content providers, and users). Furthermore, the 2003 Declaration of freedom of communication on the Internet[190] declared that Member States should encourage self- or co-regulation of content disseminated on the Internet. This opinion was repeated in the 2005 Declaration on human rights and the rule of law in the Information Society, which stressed the importance of promoting self- and co-regulation by private sector actors to reduce the availability of illegal and of harmful content and to enable users to protect themselves from both.[191] Over the past decade, the Council of Europe has thus clearly supported the take-up of alternative regulatory instruments in the information society.

---

188 Reding, Viviane, Self regulation applied to interactive games: success and challenges, speech at the ISFE Expert Conference, Brussels, 26.06.2007, retrieved from http://europa.eu/rapid/pressReleasesAction.do?reference=SPEECH/07/429&type=HTML&aged=0&language=EN&guiLanguage=en (on 22.05.2008). Cf. also *infra*: Regulatory tools: supporting mechanisms.

189 Council of Europe (Committee of Ministers), Recommendation Rec(2001)8 on self-regulation concerning cyber content (self-regulation and user protection against illegal or harmful content on new communications and information services), 05.09.2001, retrieved from https://wcd.coe.int/ViewDoc.jsp?id=220387&Site=COE&BackColorInternet=DBDCF2&BackColorIntranet=FDC864&BackColorLogged=FDC864 (on 19.05.2008).

190 Council of Europe, Declaration of freedom of communication on the Internet, 28.03.2003, retrieved from https://wcd.coe.int/rsi/common/renderers/rend_standard.jsp?DocId=37031&SecMode=1&SiteName=cm&Lang=en (on 19.05.2008).

191 Council of Europe (Committee of Ministers), Declaration on human rights and the rule of law in the Information Society, 13.05.2005, retrieved from https://wcd.coe.int/ViewDoc.jsp?Ref=CM(2005)56&Sector=secCM&Language=lanEnglish&Ver=final&BackColorInternet=9999CC&BackColorIntranet=FFBB55&BackColorLogged=FFAC75 (on 19.05.2008).

Other documents – Other documents issued by the Council of Europe also mentioned the use of self- and co-regulation in the media sector. The report by Andreas Grunwäld, for instance, which provided certain recommendations for the review of the European Convention on Transfrontier Television (cf. *infra*), suggested using self- and co-regulation, rather than mandatory regulation, to achieve certain policy goals, such as the protection of minors.[192] This was confirmed by the Parliamentary Assembly in its Recommendation on The regulation of audio-visual media services, in which it was stated that policy guidelines need to be developed "*for new means of content control, including through media self- and co-regulation*".[193] Another document, not related to the protection of minors but rather to the complaints handling of media organisations, was the Report on self-regulation within the media in the handling of complaints.[194] This report was drawn up as part of a study which aimed to develop a catalogue of indicators for an appropriate legal and policy framework for well-functioning, democratic media. Within the report, the motivations for and effectiveness of journalists' codes of conduct were assessed. The rapporteur concluded that whereas

> *[j]ournalists' associations seem keen on self-regulatory measures in keeping their independence from both the elected authorities and powerful corporations, [t]here is however increased awareness concerning the failure of self-regulation in the present media landscape as they are urgently calling for legislative initiatives to address the gaps in the protection.*[195]

In any case, self- and co-regulation are regulatory instruments that also have received a substantial degree of attention in Council of Europe documents related to media.

---

[192] Grünwald, Andreas, Report on possible options for the review of the European Convention on Transfrontier Television, 24.04.2003, retrieved from http://www.coe.int/t/dghl/standardsetting/media/T-TT/T-TT(2003)002_en.pdf (on 19.05.2008).

[193] Council of Europe (Parliamentary Assembly), Recommendation 1855 (2009) The regulation of audio-visual media services, 27.01.2009, retrieved from http://assembly.coe.int/Main.asp?link=/Documents/AdoptedText/ta09/EREC1855.htm#1 (on 28.05.2009), 12.4.

[194] Council of Europe (Venice Commission), Report on self-regulation within the media in the handling of complaints, CDL(2008)039, 07.04.2008, retrieved from http://www.venice.coe.int/docs/2008/CDL(2008)039-e.asp (on 19.05.2008).

[195] Council of Europe (Venice Commission), Report on self-regulation within the media in the handling of complaints, CDL(2008)039, 07.04.2008, retrieved from http://www.venice.coe.int/docs/2008/CDL(2008)039-e.asp (on 19.05.2008).

C. *Interim conclusion*

Important, but not coherent – From the description and analysis of the general and media policy documents, we can conclude that, whereas alternative regulatory instruments have been at the top of the policy agenda for the past decade, and particularly with respect to the protection of minors, it cannot be said that the concepts of self- and co-regulation have been clearly delineated. Neither concept has been approached in a coherent and consistent manner. Therefore, to obtain a clearer conceptual view, in the next section, self- and co-regulation will be analysed thoroughly, on the basis of doctrine and research results.

2.3. Overview and analysis of different alternative regulatory instruments

2.3.1. *Alternative regulatory instruments (ARIs)*

What are ARIs? – As concluded in the previous part, policy documents have not always provided much clarity on what is really meant when references are made to self- and/or co-regulation. In general, we assume that these regulatory mechanisms are an alternative (or, as is sometimes argued, a supplement) to traditional forms of regulation, such as legislation, in which the government is the major – and often the only – player.[196] Their key characteristic is the involvement of non-governmental players, such as the industry and/or users in the regulatory process.[197] The required degree of involvement of these different actors is the issue that most often causes controversy or confusion in the ARIs debate. Whereas self-regulation is sometimes conceived very strictly, rejecting any kind of interference from the outside, others interpret this concept less rigorously, allowing the involvement of dif-

[196] Notions such as 'soft law' or 'governance' have also been used to indicate forms of regulation in which the government is not the chief player. Cf. Marsden, Christopher T., "Beyond Europe: the Internet, regulation and multistakeholder governance – Representing the consumer interest?", *Journal of Consumer Policy* 2008, Vol. 31, No. 1, 116–117.

[197] Latzer, Michael, "Trust in the industry – Trust in the users: self-regulation and self-help in the context of digital media content in the EU", Report for working group 3 of the Expert Conference on European media policy "More trust in content – The potential of co- and self-regulation in digital media", Leipzig, 9–11.05.2007, retrieved from http://www.leipzig-eu2007.de/en/downloads/dokumente.asp (on 21.05.2008), 36.

ferent actors.[198] Who exactly can participate in forms of co-regulation and to what extent, is usually no more clear-cut. This section aims to elucidate both concepts, by analysing existing definitions, studies and practical examples. Following this analysis, an attempt is made to distinguish a number of positive and negative aspects of each instrument.

Regulatory tools – Alternative regulatory instruments often make use of various – what we call – 'regulatory tools'. Technology is one of these regulatory tools. Filtering instruments, age verification measures and parental notification software, for instance, are mechanisms that are often suggested as being helpful in protecting minors against harmful content. Another increasingly important regulatory tool in this context is the use of 'supporting mechanisms', such as education, media literacy and awareness. In the third and fourth part of this section both these types of regulatory tools are examined.

2.3.2. *Self-regulation*

History – Self-regulation is by no means a novel phenomenon.[199] A PhD thesis defended at KULeuven in 2007 by Anne-Lies Verdoodt analysed the history of the concept and its place in the field of sociology of law, and found that the origins of self-regulation go back to the theories of Max Weber, Emile Durkheim, Niklas Luhmann, Gunter Teubner and John Griffiths (also *supra*).[200] Over the years, self-regulation as a regulatory mechanism

---

198 Verdoodt, Anne-Lies, Zelfregulering in de journalistiek: de formulering en de handhaving van deontologische standaarden in en door het journalistieke beroep [*Self-regulation in journalism: the formulation and enforcement of deontological standards in and by the journalistic profession*], PhD Thesis (promotor: Prof. dr. Stephan Parmentier), 2007, iii [in Dutch].

199 Sinclair, Darren, "Self-regulation versus command and control? Beyond false dichotomies", *Law & Policy* 1997, Vol. 19, No. 4, 530.

200 Verdoodt, Anne-Lies, Zelfregulering in de journalistiek: de formulering en de handhaving van deontologische standaarden in en door het journalistieke beroep [*Self-regulation in journalism: the formulation and enforcement of deontological standards in and by the journalistic profession*], PhD Thesis (promotor: Prof. dr. Stephan Parmentier), 2007 [in Dutch]. Verdoodt presented a detailed theoretical analysis of the concept of self-regulation. We have opted to present a briefer overview since self-regulation is not sole focus of our work, but would like to refer the reader to her outstanding work for more details.

has been used in different sectors, such as financial services, environmental protection,[201] insurance, sports and, of course, the media sector.[202]

SELF-REGULATION AND THE MEDIA – Self-regulation is an instrument that has a history within the field of media regulation,[203] especially with respect to press and journalist associations,[204] and in the field of advertising.[205] On the other side of the Atlantic as well, the protection of minors against harmful content has sometimes been addressed with the help of self-regulatory instruments. As early as the 1950s, for instance, the Comics Magazine Association of America created a self-regulatory code of conduct and a self-regulatory body, the Comics Code Authority, to protect children from harmful content in comic books.[206] Self-regulation also played a role in the establishment of the voluntary warning labels 'Parental advisory: explicit content' by the Recording Industry Association of America.[207]

---

[201] SINCLAIR, Darren, "Self-regulation versus command and control? Beyond false dichotomies", *Law & Policy* 1997, Vol. 19, No. 4, 529–559. See also: COMMISSION OF THE EUROPEAN COMMUNITIES, Communication from the Commission to the Council and to the European Parliament on environmental agreements, COM (1996) 561 final, 27.11.1996 and COMMISSION OF THE EUROPEAN COMMUNITIES, Communication from the Commission to the European Parliament, the Council, the Economic and Social Committee and the Committee of the Regions of 17 July 2002 on environmental agreements at Community Level within the framework of the Action Plan on the 'Simplification and improvement of the regulatory environment', COM (2002) 412 final, 17.07.2002 (also *infra*, Part 2, Chapter 2).

[202] OGUS, Anthony, "Rethinking self-regulation", *Oxford Journal of Legal Studies* 1995, Vol. 15, No. 1, 97; MIFSUD BONNICI, Jeanne, *Self-regulation in cyberspace*, Malta, 2007, 10.

[203] LATZER, Michael, "Trust in the industry – Trust in the users: self-regulation and self-help in the context of digital media content in the EU", Report for working group 3 of the Expert Conference on European media policy "More trust in content – The potential of co- and self-regulation in digital media", Leipzig, 9–11.05.2007, retrieved from http://www.leipzig-eu2007.de/en/downloads/dokumente.asp (on 21.05.2008), 42.

[204] VERDOODT, Anne-Lies, Zelfregulering in de journalistiek: de formulering en de handhaving van deontologische standaarden in en door het journalistieke beroep [*Self-regulation in journalism: the formulation and enforcement of deontological standards in and by the journalistic profession*], PhD Thesis (promotor: Prof. dr. Stephan Parmentier), 2007 [in Dutch].

[205] BODDEWYN, Jean, *Advertising self-regulation and outside participation: a multinational comparison*, New York, Quorum Books, 1988, 384 p.

[206] KIRSCH, Steven J., *Children, adolescents and media violence: a critical look at the research*, Thousand Oaks CA, Sage Publications, 2006, 301.

[207] KIRSCH, Steven J., *Children, adolescents and media violence: A critical look at the research*, Thousand Oaks CA, Sage Publications, 2006, 304–305.

SELF-REGULATION AND DIGITAL MEDIA – The rise of the Internet – or 'cyberspace' – which was, at the time, considered by many a 'free' social space in which involvement or interference from governments was unwanted and unnecessary,[208] sparked an intensified interest in the use of 'self-regulation'.[209] As we have seen in the previous section, in policy documents, 'self-regulation' was often presented as the panacea to 'regulate' the Internet. At different levels – international,[210] supranational as well as national – the enthusiasm for the use of this ARI was substantial. This does not mean, however, that there was a uniform, unambiguous understanding of what was meant by 'self-regulation'.

A. *Concept*

WHAT IS SELF-REGULATION? – According to The Oxford Dictionary, 'self-regulating' means "*regulating itself without intervention from external bodies*".[211] In its most basic form, self-regulation could thus be interpreted as regulation by a group of actors without intervention from others that do not belong to this group; in reality this latter specification is mostly interpreted as 'without

---

208 The most well-known expression of this idea was the 'Declaration of the Independence of Cyberspace', written by John Perry BARLOW (BARLOW, John Perry, Declaration of the Independence of Cyberspace, 08.02.1996, retrieved from http://homes.eff.org/~barlow/Declaration-Final.html (on 09.12.2008)): "*Governments of the Industrial World, you weary giants of flesh and steel, I come from Cyberspace, the new home of Mind. On behalf of the future, I ask you of the past to leave us alone. You are not welcome among us. You have no sovereignty where we gather*". Cf. also LESSIG, Lawrence, *Code and other laws of cyberspace*, New York, Basic Books, 1999, 4–5.

209 JOHNSON, David, "Let's let the Net self-regulate – The case for allowing decentralized, emergent self-ordering to solve the public policy problems created by the Internet", 1998, retrieved from http://web.archive.org/web/19990210085611/www.cli.org/selford/essay.htm (on 26.05.2008).

210 For instance: ORGANISATION FOR ECONOMIC CO-OPERATION AND DEVELOPMENT, Summary record of the BIAC/OECD Forum on Internet Content Self-regulation, 25.03.1998, retrieved from http://www.oecd.org/document/31/0,3343,fr_2649_34255_1893343_1_1_1_1,00.html (on 26.05.2008); UNITED NATIONS, Durban Declaration and Programme for Action at the World Conference against Racism, Racial Discrimination, Xenophobia and Related Intolerance, 2001, retrieved from http://www.un.org/WCAR/durban.pdf (on 30.05.2008); as referred to by AKDENIZ, Yaman, "Stocktaking on efforts to combat racism on the Internet", Background Paper for the High Level Seminar on Racism and the Internet, Intergovernmental Working Group on the Effective Implementation of the Durban Declaration and Programme of Action, Fourth session, Geneva, 16–27.01.2006, E/CN.4/2006/WG.21/BP.1, retrieved from http://www.cyber-rights.org/reports/ya_un_paper_int_06.pdf (on 23.04.2007).

211 PEARSHALL, Judy (ed.), *The concise Oxford dictionary*, Oxford, Oxford University Press, 1999, 1301.

intervention from government'. As was mentioned in the introduction, the self-regulation concept that is studied in this book concerns regulation of a group of actors. Hence, regulation between individual actors, for instance, by means of contracts, falls outside the scope of our self-regulation concept.

Definitions – An endless array of definitions of self-regulation – also referred to as 'private ordering' –[212] exists. Marais defined self-regulation as "*l'élaboration et le respect, par les acteurs eux-mêmes, de règles qu'ils ont formulées (sous la forme par exemple, de codes de bonne conduite ou de bonnes pratiques) et dont ils assurent eux-mêmes l'application)*".[213] Gunningham and Rees described (industry) self-regulation as the "*regulatory process whereby an industry-level (as opposed to a governmental or firm-level) organization sets rules and standards (codes of practice) relating to the conduct of firms in the industry*".[214] Palzer characterised self-regulation as a system in which "*non-state groups (producers, providers, etc.) draw up their own regulations in order to achieve their objectives and take full responsibility for monitoring compliance with those regulations*".[215] Ofcom qualified a system as self-regulation "*when industry administers and enforces its own solution to address a particular issue without formal oversight or participation of the regulator or government; in particular there is no ex ante legal backstop in a self-regulatory scheme to act as the ultimate guarantor of enforcement*".[216] Rand Europe described 'self-regulatory organisations' as "*institutions which by rule or the formation of norms exercise a function which shapes or controls the behaviour*

---

[212] Birnhack, Michael and Rowbottom, Jacob, "Shielding children: the European way", *Chicago-Kent Law Review* 2004, Issue 79, 211–213; Mifsud Bonnici, Jeanne, *Self-regulation in cyberspace*, Malta, 2007, 20. For more on self-regulation in the United States, cf. Newman, Abraham and Bach, David, "Self-regulatory trajectories in the shadow of public power: resolving digital dilemmas in Europe and the United States", *Governance* 2004, Vol. 17, Iss. 3, 387–413.

[213] du Marais, Bertrand, "Auto regulation, regulation et co-régulation des réseaux" [*Auto regulation, regulation and co-regulation of networks*], Colloque "Droit de l'Internet: approches européennes et internationales, 2001, retrieved from http://droit-internet-2001.univ-paris1.fr/pdf/vf/Marais.pdf (on 26.05.2008), 3 [in French].

[214] Gunningham, Neil and Rees, Joseph, "Industry self-regulation: an institutional perspective", *Law & Policy* 1997, Vol. 19, No. 4, 364.

[215] Palzer, Carmen, "Self-monitoring v. self-regulation v. co-regulation", in: Nikoltchev, Susanne (ed.), *Co-regulation of the media in Europe*, IRIS Special, Strasbourg, European Audiovisual Observatory, 2003, 29.

[216] Ofcom, Initial assessments of when to adopt self- or co-regulation – Consultation, 27.03.2008, retrieved from http://www.ofcom.org.uk/consult/condocs/coregulation/condoc.pdf (on 04.04.2008), 3.

of actors in that environment".[217] Finally, we can remind ourselves of the definition used in the EU Interinstitutional Agreement on Better Lawmaking, where self-regulation was defined as "*the possibility for economic operators, social partners, non-governmental organisations or associations to adopt amongst themselves and for themselves guidelines at European level (particularly codes of practice or sectoral agreements)*".[218]

Analysis – What this brief and randomly selected overview of definitions, which vary from the narrow (the Interinstitutional Agreement definition) to the very broad (as per Marais),[219] teaches us is that whereas all definitions contain more or less similar elements, there are still slight variations between them. One agreed-upon definition certainly does not exist, but it has been argued that this is not necessary, since self-regulation varies across sectors and states anyway.[220] However, we would like to take two elements from the different definitions: first, a group of actors create, implement and enforce rules; and second, there is a minimal involvement of government. The rationale for this last specification can be found in the often repeated argument that 'pure' self-regulation,[221] i.e., without any kind of government involvement, hardly exists in reality;[222] even the threat of government

---

217 Rand Europe (Chris Marsden, Stephen Simmons and Jonathan Cave), Options for effectiveness of Internet self- and co-regulation – Inception report, Study commissioned by the European Commission, 30.04.2007, retrieved from http://ec.europa.eu/dgs/information_society/evaluation/data/pdf/studies/s2006_05/inception_final.pdf (on 08.01.2008), 4.

218 European Parliament, Council, and Commission, Interinstitutional agreement on better law-making, 2003/C 321/01, *OJ* 31.12.2003, *C* 321, recital 22.

219 For a detailed overview of different classifications of definitions: cf. Latzer, Michael, "Trust in the industry – Trust in the users: self-regulation and self-help in the context of digital media content in the EU", Report for working group 3 of the Expert Conference on European media policy "More trust in content – The potential of co- and self-regulation in digital media", Leipzig, 9–11.05.2007, retrieved from http://www.leipzig-eu2007.de/en/downloads/dokumente.asp (on 21.05.2008), 38–41.

220 Price, Monroe and Verhulst, Stefaan, "In search of the self: charting the course of self-regulation on the Internet in a global environment", in: Marsden, Christopher, *Regulating the global information society*, London, Routledge, 2000, 58.

221 Also referred to by PCMLP as 'enlightened self-interest', defined as when a "*industry sets standards and polices them merely to increase product trust with consumers*": PCMLP, Self-regulation of digital media converging on the Internet: industry codes of conduct in sectoral analysis, Study commissioned by the European Commission, 30.04.2004, retrieved from http://pcmlp.socleg.ox.ac.uk/selfregulation/iapcoda/0405-iapcode-final.pdf (on 29.05.2008), 11.

222 Prosser, Tony, "Self-regulation, co-regulation and the Audio-Visual Media Services Directive", *Journal of Consumer Policy* 2008, Vol. 31, No. 1, 99 and 102; Gunningham, Neil and Rees, Joseph, "Industry self-regulation: an institutional perspective", *Law & Policy* 1997, Vol. 19, No. 4, 365; Price, Monroe and Verhulst, Stefaan, "In search of

regulation as motivation for the creation of a self-regulatory mechanism is by some seen as 'government involvement' (and hence precludes the label 'pure' self-regulation).[223] Other forms of relatively limited or 'soft' government involvement could, for instance, be the encouragement of self-regulation, symbolic support or low-key cooperation with government agencies.[224] Of course, what exactly can be considered as a 'minimal' level of government involvement is open to interpretation. This might become clearer in the next section, where the level of government involvement required with respect to co-regulation will be discussed. For now, we assume that self-regulation entails the creation, implementation and enforcement of rules by a group of actors with no – or at least minimal – involvement of actors that do not belong to this group.

Economic versus social self-regulation – For the subject of this study, it is important to draw attention to the distinction that is sometimes made between economic and social self-regulation. Economic self-regulation is aimed at controlling markets or other facets of economic life; social self-regulation attempts to "*protect people or the environment from the damaging consequences of industrialization*".[225] Price and Verhulst clarified this latter form of self-regulation further:

---

the self: charting the course of self-regulation on the Internet in a global environment", in: Marsden, Christopher, *Regulating the global information society*, London, Routledge, 2000, 58; Latzer, Michael, "Trust in the industry – Trust in the users: self-regulation and self-help in the context of digital media content in the EU", Report for working group 3 of the Expert Conference on European media policy "More trust in content – The potential of co- and self-regulation in digital media", Leipzig, 9–11.05.2007, retrieved from http://www.leipzig-eu2007.de/en/downloads/dokumente.asp (on 21.05.2008), 38.

223 Latzer, Michael, "Trust in the industry – Trust in the users: self-regulation and self-help in the context of digital media content in the EU", Report for working group 3 of the Expert Conference on European media policy "More trust in content – The potential of co- and self-regulation in digital media", Leipzig, 9–11.05.2007, retrieved from http://www.leipzig-eu2007.de/en/downloads/dokumente.asp (on 21.05.2008), 46; Price, Monroe and Verhulst, Stefaan, "In search of the self: charting the course of self-regulation on the Internet in a global environment", in: Marsden, Christopher, *Regulating the global information society*, London, Routledge, 2000, 66 and 68.

224 Latzer, Michael, "Trust in the industry – Trust in the users: self-regulation and self-help in the context of digital media content in the EU", Report for working group 3 of the Expert Conference on European media policy "More trust in content – The potential of co- and self-regulation in digital media", Leipzig, 9–11.05.2007, retrieved from http://www.leipzig-eu2007.de/en/downloads/dokumente.asp (on 21.05.2008), 46.

225 Gunningham, Neil and Rees, Joseph, "Industry self-regulation: an institutional perspective", *Law & Policy* 1997, Vol. 19, No. 4, 365; and Price, Monroe and Verhulst, Stefaan, "In search of the self: charting the course of self-regulation on the Internet in a global

> *Social self-regulation is thus usually taken to include mechanisms whereby firms or their associations, in their undertaking of business activities, seek to assure that their actions avoid unacceptable consequences to the environment, the workforce, or consumers and clients.*[226]

In the light of our case study, the protection of minors against harmful content, our focus is clearly on social self-regulation.

'Self' in self-regulation – Who exactly personifies the 'self' in self-regulation differs from mechanism to mechanism and from sector to sector. Mifsud Bonnici presented the 'self' as a group who consists of members ("*natural and/or artificial persons who share a number of similar or common interests and goals and accept regulation by the group they participate in*") who regulate their own behaviour (to some extent).[227] It has been argued that when discussing the actors who embody the 'self' in self-regulation, emphasis is too often placed on industry or business.[228] Although industry is often an important player,[229] in some instances, the involvement of other actors, such as NGOs or users, can provide added value.[230]

B. *Self-regulation in the media sector: studies*

Studies commissioned by the European Commission – The European Commission commissioned a number of studies aimed at shedding light on the concepts of self- and co-regulation. Two studies on self-regulation and one study on co-regulation (*infra*) were carried out by various consultants over the past decade. Before looking at the self-regulation studies in greater

---

environment", in: Marsden, Christopher, *Regulating the global information society*, London, Routledge, 61, referring to Hawkins, Keith and Hutter, Bridget, "The response of business to social regulation in England and Wales: an enforcement perspective", *Law & Policy* 1993, Vol. 15, No. 3, 199 and Hawkins, Keith, "Rule and discretion in comparative perspective: the case of social regulation", *The Ohio State Law Journal* 1989, Vol. 50, No. 3, 663.

226 Price, Monroe and Verhulst, Stefaan, "In search of the self: charting the course of self-regulation on the Internet in a global environment", in: Marsden, Christopher, *Regulating the global information society*, London, Routledge, 2000, 61.

227 Mifsud Bonnici, Jeanne, *Self-regulation in cyberspace*, Malta, 2007, 27.

228 Price, Monroe and Verhulst, Stefaan, "In search of the self: charting the course of self-regulation on the Internet in a global environment", in: Marsden, Christopher, *Regulating the global information society*, London, Routledge, 2000, 69.

229 For instance, Internet Service Providers Associations in self-regulatory mechanisms in the Internet sector.

230 Price, Monroe and Verhulst, Stefaan, "In search of the self: charting the course of self-regulation on the Internet in a global environment", in: Marsden, Christopher, *Regulating the global information society*, London, Routledge, 2000, 75.

detail, however, it needs to be said that the concept of self-regulation has not been clearly delineated in either study. Often, the notions self- and co-regulation seemed to be used in an inconsistent manner, and without much explanation as to why sometimes the notion self-regulation, and sometimes the concept co-regulation, was preferred.

IAPCODE STUDY – The IAPCODE study (Self-regulation of digital media converging on the Internet: Industry codes of conduct in sectoral analysis), carried out by the Oxford University Centre for Socio-Legal Studies / Programme in Comparative Media Law & Policy and published in 2004, examined the regulation of harmful content and self-regulation of content by the media industry.[231] The focus of the study was the analysis of media[232] self-regulatory codes of conduct, according to a comparative analysis framework dubbed the 5C approach ('Constitution, Coverage, Content, Communication and Compliance').[233] The study concluded that self-regulation can respond faster and more efficiently than traditional state regulation to technical change.[234] No single generally acceptable formula for self-regulation, however, was found;[235] variations across sectors and circumstances were numerous.[236] One deduction the authors could make was that legacy and

[231] PCMLP, Self-regulation of digital media converging on the Internet: Industry codes of conduct in sectoral analysis, Study commissioned by the European Commission, 30.04.2004, retrieved from http://pcmlp.socleg.ox.ac.uk/selfregulation/iapcoda/0405–iapcode-final.pdf (on 29.05.2008). The research results were also published: cf. TAMBINI, Damien, LEONARDI, Danilo and MARSDEN, Chris, *Codifying cyberspace: communications self-regulation in the age of Internet convergence*, London, Routledge, 2008, 323 p.

[232] Across different media sectors: press, broadcasting, film, games, Internet and mobile services.

[233] PCMLP, Self-regulation of digital media converging on the Internet: Industry codes of conduct in sectoral analysis, Study commissioned by the European Commission, 30.04.2004, retrieved from http://pcmlp.socleg.ox.ac.uk/selfregulation/iapcoda/0405–iapcode-final.pdf (on 29.05.2008), 17–18.

[234] PCMLP, Self-regulation of digital media converging on the Internet: Industry codes of conduct in sectoral analysis, Study commissioned by the European Commission, 30.04.2004, retrieved from http://pcmlp.socleg.ox.ac.uk/selfregulation/iapcoda/0405–iapcode-final.pdf (on 29.05.2008), 70.

[235] PCMLP, Self-regulation of digital media converging on the Internet: Industry codes of conduct in sectoral analysis, Study commissioned by the European Commission, 30.04.2004, retrieved from http://pcmlp.socleg.ox.ac.uk/selfregulation/iapcoda/0405–iapcode-final.pdf (on 29.05.2008), 70.

[236] PCMLP, Self-regulation of digital media converging on the Internet: Industry codes of conduct in sectoral analysis, Study commissioned by the European Commission, 30.04.2004, retrieved from http://pcmlp.socleg.ox.ac.uk/selfregulation/iapcoda/0405–iapcode-final.pdf (on 29.05.2008), 84: "*While we cannot conclude with certainty under which institutional conditions self-regulation develops, we found evidence that in order to fully understand the*

history are important in the adoption or transformation of self-regulation.[237] Causes for concern related primarily to safeguards with respect to freedom of expression. Whereas self-regulation may provide a positive alternative to government involvement – a delicate issue since this may lead to censorship – the authors found that avenues of redress might be problematic, since sanctions and compensation might be lacking.[238] Therefore, they suggested building in a number of safeguards, such as, for instance, an audit procedure for the establishment of self-regulatory codes and institutions, including an assessment of market structure and interest in self-regulation, and a fundamental rights impact assessment.[239] They also called for the European Commission and the Council of Europe to develop and publish benchmarks for acceptable levels of transparency, accountability, due process and appeal.[240] It is important to note that throughout the study references were made to co-regulation, often without a clear explanation why this notion was used instead of self-regulation.[241] However, the final conclusion seemed to reveal a preference for the use of co-regulation:

> *An imperfect self-regulatory solution may be better than no solution at all, and we must not raise our standards so high that self-regulation is never attempted.*

---

pattern of media self-regulation development in Europe we must take into account national factors such as economic foundations, political culture, civil society and regulatory trends".

237 PCMLP, Self-regulation of digital media converging on the Internet: Industry codes of conduct in sectoral analysis, Study commissioned by the European Commission, 30.04.2004, retrieved from http://pcmlp.socleg.ox.ac.uk/selfregulation/iapcoda/0405–iapcode-final.pdf (on 29.05.2008), 71. For instance, in the press sector there was a long-standing self-regulatory tradition contrary to the broadcasting sector.

238 PCMLP, Self-regulation of digital media converging on the Internet: Industry codes of conduct in sectoral analysis, Study commissioned by the European Commission, 30.04.2004, retrieved from http://pcmlp.socleg.ox.ac.uk/selfregulation/iapcoda/0405–iapcode-final.pdf (on 29.05.2008), 73.

239 PCMLP, Self-regulation of digital media converging on the Internet: Industry codes of conduct in sectoral analysis, Study commissioned by the European Commission, 30.04.2004, retrieved from http://pcmlp.socleg.ox.ac.uk/selfregulation/iapcoda/0405–iapcode-final.pdf (on 29.05.2008), 72 and 93.

240 PCMLP, Self-regulation of digital media converging on the Internet: Industry codes of conduct in sectoral analysis, Study commissioned by the European Commission, 30.04.2004, retrieved from http://pcmlp.socleg.ox.ac.uk/selfregulation/iapcoda/0405–iapcode-final.pdf (on 29.05.2008), 73.

241 We also note that in a book chapter presenting the results of the study, the emphasis was put mostly on co-regulation. Cf. Marsden, Christopher, "Co- and self-regulation in European media and Internet sectors: the results of Oxford University's study www.self-regulation.info", in: Möller, Christian and Amouroux, Arnaud (eds), *The media freedom Internet cookbook*, 76–100, Vienna, OSCE Representative on Freedom of the Media, 2004, retrieved from http://www.osce.org/item/13570.html (on 30.05.2008), 274 p.

> *But there are limits to how much imperfection can be tolerated, and for how long. If self-regulatory codes and institutions are insufficiently transparent and accountable, and if they do not observe accepted standards of due diligence, they will lose the trust of the public and fail. There is a danger that some aspects of internet self-regulation fail to conform to accepted standards. We recommend co-regulatory audit as the best balance of fundamental rights and responsive regulation.*[242]

Rand Study – The most recent study related to Internet self- (but also co-) regulation was carried out by Rand Europe in 2007.[243] The objective of this study was to assist the European Commission in developing a coherent and effective approach to future self- and co-regulation initiatives in the Information Society.[244] Rand Europe produced three reports: an inception report which mapped existing co- and self-regulatory institutions on the Internet; an informative case study report in which 21 self- and co-regulatory institutions (dubbed 'XROs') were thoroughly analysed; and a final report. Along the same lines of the PCMLP research results, one of the key conclusions of the study was that there is no 'magic bullet' in Internet regulation. Although the study focused for a large part on regulatory impact assessment, a subject which falls outside the scope of this study, it also produced an interesting classification of the XROs according to the degree of government involvement (their 'Beaufort scale of self-regulation').[245]

---

[242] PCMLP, Self-regulation of digital media converging on the Internet: Industry codes of conduct in sectoral analysis, Study commissioned by the European Commission, 30.04.2004, retrieved from http://pcmlp.socleg.ox.ac.uk/selfregulation/iapcoda/0405–iapcode-final.pdf (on 29.05.2008), 94.

[243] Rand Europe (Jonathan Cave, Chris Marsden and Stephen Simmons), Options for effectiveness of Internet self- and co-regulation – Phase 3 (Final) Report, Study commissioned by the European Commission, 2008, retrieved from http://ec.europa.eu/dgs/information_society/evaluation/data/pdf/studies/s2006_05/final_report.pdf (on 30.05.2008).

[244] Rand Europe (Jonathan Cave, Chris Marsden and Stephen Simmons), Options for effectiveness of Internet self- and co-regulation – Phase 3 (Final) Report, Study commissioned by the European Commission, 2008, retrieved from http://ec.europa.eu/dgs/information_society/evaluation/data/pdf/studies/s2006_05/final_report.pdf (on 30.05.2008), ii.

[245] Rand Europe (Jonathan Cave, Chris Marsden and Stephen Simmons), Options for effectiveness of Internet self- and co-regulation – Phase 3 (Final) Report, Study commissioned by the European Commission, 2008, retrieved from http://ec.europa.eu/dgs/information_society/evaluation/data/pdf/studies/s2006_05/final_report.pdf (on 30.05.2008), 27.

Table 4: A 'Beaufort Scale' of self-regulation

Scale	Regulatory scheme	Example	Government involvement
0	'Pure' unenforced self-regulation	CC / SecondLife	Informal interchange only – evolving partial industry forum building on players' own terms
1	Acknowledged self-regulation	ATVOD	Discussion but no formal recognition / approval
2	Post-facto standardised self-regulation	W3C	Later approval of standards
3	Standardised self-regulation	IETF	Formal approval of standards
4	Discussed self-regulation	IMCB	Prior principled informal discussion – but no sanction/ approval/process audit
5	Recognised self-regulation	ISPA	Recognition of body – informal policy role
6	Co-founded self-regulation	FOSI	Prior negotiation of body; no outcome role
7	Sanctioned self-regulation	PEGI / Euro Mobile	Recognition of body – formal policy role (contact committee / process)
8	Approved self-regulation	Hotline	Prior principled less formal discussion with government – with recognition / approval
9	Approved compulsory co-regulation	KJM / ICANN	Prior principled discussion with government – with sanction / approval / process audit
10	Scrutinised co-regulation	NICAM	As 9, with annual budget / process approval
11	Independent body (with stakeholder forum)	ICSTIS	Government imposed and co-regulated with taxation / compulsory levy

Source: Rand Europe (Jonathan Cave, Chris Marsden and Stephen Simmons), Options for effectiveness of Internet self- and co-regulation – Phase 3 Final Report, retrieved from http://ec.europa.eu/dgs/information_society/evaluation/data/pdf/studies/s2006_05/final_report.pdf (on 30.05.2008), 27.

In the table, the level of government involvement intensifies from 0 to 11. 0 represents 'pure' self-regulation (which, however, in reality is extremely rare).[246] Only the three last classifications 9, 10 and 11 are considered to be 'co-regulation' (*infra*). That leaves eight possible forms of self-regulation, in which the degree of government involvement is hence limited (according to Rand, too limited to qualify as co-regulation), ranging from acknowledgment to actual approval by government. Whereas this scale is an interesting theoretical exercise, which does show that many different levels of government occur with respect to ARIs, one can wonder whether this detailed classification is relevant in practice. We will refer back to this classification in the section with respect to co-regulation.

C. *Illustration: codes of conduct*

PART OF SELF-REGULATORY STRATEGY – Codes of conduct are often part of a self-regulatory strategy to protect minors against harmful content.[247] Such codes of conduct (or codes of practice) exist in all shapes and sizes. They range from being merely declarations of principles to agreements which incorporate mutual obligations by different actors.[248] European policy documents have strongly promoted such codes since the advent of the Internet

[246] RAND EUROPE (Jonathan CAVE, Chris MARSDEN and Stephen SIMMONS), Options for effectiveness of Internet self- and co-regulation – Phase 3 (Final) Report, Study commissioned by the European Commission, 2008, retrieved from http://ec.europa.eu/dgs/information_society/evaluation/data/pdf/studies/s2006_05/final_report.pdf (on 30.05.2008), 28.

[247] Cf. PCMLP, Self-regulation of digital media converging on the Internet: Industry codes of conduct in sectoral analysis, Study commissioned by the European Commission, 30.04.2004, retrieved from http://pcmlp.socleg.ox.ac.uk/selfregulation/iapcoda/0405-iapcode-final.pdf (on 29.05.2008). See also: POULLET, Yves, "How to regulate Internet: new paradigms for Internet governance self-regulation: value and limits", in MONVILLE, Claire (ed.), *Variations sur le droit de la société de l'information*, Cahiers du Crid, n° 20, Brussels, Bruylant, 81; HUYSE, Luc and PARMENTIER, Stephan, "Decoding codes: the dialogue between consumers and suppliers through codes of conduct in the European Community", *Journal of Consumer Policy* 1990, Vol. 13, No. 3, 253–272; GRABOSKY, Peter and BRAITHWAITE, John, Of manners gentle: enforcement strategies of Australian business regulatory agencies, Melbourne, Oxford University Press, 1986, 183: "*[Self-regulation] can occur by negotiating agreements with industry associations for the writing of voluntary codes or guidelines*".

[248] PRICE, Monroe and VERHULST, Stefaan, "In search of the self: charting the course of self-regulation on the Internet in a global environment", in: MARSDEN, Christopher, *Regulating the global information society*, London, Routledge, 2000, 62.

and 3G mobile technology (*supra*). One example of such a code is the UK code of conduct related to mobile content.

UK Mobile Operators Code of Conduct – The UK mobile operators (O2, Orange, T-Mobile, Virgin Mobile, Vodafone and Hutchison 3G) initiated the creation of a self-regulatory code of conduct in 2004.[249] The intention of the operators was to provide parents with information and to empower them to decide what content their children cannot have access to via their mobile phone. The code covers visual content, online gambling, mobile gaming, chat rooms and Internet access. An independent classification body (the Independent Mobile Classification Body), appointed and funded by the mobile operators, was charged with the task of providing a framework for classifying (commercial) content inappropriate for children (under the age of 18).[250] A first edition of the classification framework set up by the IMCB was published in February 2005.[251] The commercial content providers for their part are required to self-classify their content according to this framework. Content not classified as '18' is freely accessible, whereas content classified as '18' needs to be restricted with access controls[252] operated by the mobile operators. '18' content is then only available to persons who have been verified as being indeed 18 or over.[253] The classification framework

---

249 O2, Orange, T-Mobile, Virgin Mobile, Vodafone, Hutchison 3G, UK Code of Practice for the self-regulation of new forms of content on mobiles, 2004, retrieved from http://www.imcb.org.uk/assets/documents/10000127Codeofpractice.pdf (on 23.06.2008).

250 O2, Orange, T-Mobile, Virgin Mobile, Vodafone, Hutchison 3G, UK Code of Practice for the self-regulation of new forms of content on mobiles, 2004, retrieved from http://www.imcb.org.uk/assets/documents/10000127Codeofpractice.pdf (on 23.06.2008). For more information, cf. http://www.imcb.org.uk/.

251 Independent Mobile Classification Body, IMCB guide and classification framework for UK mobile operator commercial content services, 2005, retrieved from http://www.imcb.org.uk/assets/documents/ClassificationFramework.pdf (on 23.06.2008).

252 Defined in the code as "*methods of preventing unrestricted access to content, including barring, PIN controlled access and subscription only services*": O2, Orange, T-Mobile, Virgin Mobile, Vodafone, Hutchison 3G, UK Code of Practice for the self-regulation of new forms of content on mobiles, 2004, retrieved from http://www.imcb.org.uk/assets/documents/10000127Codeofpractice.pdf (on 23.06.2008), 5.

253 According to the Code, 'age verification' can entail the following: "*a) at point of mobile device sale for new customers: inspection of document containing customer's date of birth (e.g. Driving licence, Citizen Card etc.); visual check (is the customer clearly over 18?); b) "customer not present": a valid credit card transaction for the customer; age confirmation using 3rd party agencies (e.g. Experian or Dun & Bradstreet etc.); c) documents and/or process used for contract mobile phone customers, combined with a process by which customers can manage access controls*": O2, Orange, T-Mobile, Virgin Mobile, Vodafone,

itself is strongly linked to the classification of other media (for instance films – BBFC,[254] and video games – PEGI)[255] to achieve rating consistency across the media spectrum. As a result, mobile content providers need to ensure that content rated '18' by the BBFC, for example, is also rated '18' within the IMCB classification framework.[256] Language, sex, nudity, violence, drugs, horror and imitable techniques are criteria on which – in specific circumstances – potential '18' classification can be based.[257] The IMCB carries the responsibility to deal with complaints about possible misclassification. So far, however, merely one ruling has been given by the IMCB.[258] The code of conduct also stipulates that mobile operators should offer the possibility to apply a filter to the mobile operator's Internet access service – set at a level that is intended to filter out content approximately equivalent to commercial content classified as '18'.

Adoption and evaluation – The creation of the code exemplifies the swift reaction of industry to growing social concerns, more than likely prompted by the desire to deter rigid government legislation. The early adoption has been considered exceptional and illustrative of industry players' awareness both of possible harms and of the potential value of self-regulation.[259] However, for some time it was not clear how successful the implementation of the code was. In January 2008, reports surfaced that Ofcom was ordered by the Home Office to review the voluntary code after children's charities expressed their

---

Hutchison 3G, UK Code of Practice for the self-regulation of new forms of content on mobiles, 2004, retrieved from http://www.imcb.org.uk/assets/documents/10000127Codeofpractice.pdf (on 23.06.2008), 5.

[254] British Board of Film Classification, more info at www.bbfc.co.uk.

[255] Pan European Game Information, more info at www.pegi.info.

[256] Independent Mobile Classification Body, IMCB guide and classification framework for UK mobile operator commercial content services, 2005, retrieved from http://www.imcb.org.uk/assets/documents/ClassificationFramework.pdf (on 23.06.2008), 6–7.

[257] For instance: 'real or simulated sexual intercourse'. However, it should be pointed out that strong emphasis is put on the fact that "*material which genuinely seeks to inform and educate such as in matters of sexuality, safe sex and health and where explicit images are the minimum necessary to illustrate and educate in a responsible manner may be permissible*": Independent Mobile Classification Body, IMCB guide and classification framework for UK mobile operator commercial content services, 2005, retrieved from http://www.imcb.org.uk/assets/documents/ClassificationFramework.pdf (on 23.06.2008), 7.

[258] Or at least only one ruling is made available on the IMCB website. See http://www.imcb.org.uk/latestrulings/.

[259] European Internet Coregulation Network, "Coregulation of Internet content accessed on mobile phones – Summary report and recommendations", 2005, retrieved from http://network.foruminternet.org/article.php3?id_article=24 (on 23.06.2008), 6.

concern about the efficiency of the system.[260] Ofcom published its review in August 2008 and concluded that, overall, the code is effective in restricting young people's access to inappropriate mobile content.[261] It also proclaimed the code a good example of industry self-regulation, argued that the code is understood and readily adopted by all concerned, and stressed that that the mobile industry had made significant investment in the development and implementation of content controls and put much effort in enforcing compliance.[262] Points of critique included poor information provided to consumers in retail outlets and the lack of availability of data on complaints by consumers.[263]

D. *Assets and drawbacks*

Pros and cons – The identification of assets and drawbacks of self-regulation is a subject that has been written about extensively in academic circles over the past decade. It can be noted that most of these advantages and disadvantages counter, in some way or another, the known disadvantages and advantages of government regulation.

Assets – Often cited assets of self-regulation are its flexibility,[264] its capacity to adapt quickly to fast developing technologies and increasingly global

---

[260] The Times (Elizabeth Judge), Mobile firms face tough rules on internet access for children, 21.01.2008, retrieved from http://business.timesonline.co.uk/tol/business/industry_sectors/telecoms/article3221526.ece (on 23.06.2008); Moconews.net (Dianne See Morrison), Ofcom to review code of conduct for mobile content, 21.08.2008, retrieved from http://www.moconews.net/entry/419–ofcom-to-review-code-of-conduct-for-mobile-content/ (on 23.06.2008). See also: Ofcom, Ofcom's response to the Byron Review – Annex 2: Current tools and approaches to protecting children from harmful content online, 30.11.2007, retrieved from http://www.ofcom.org.uk/research/telecoms/reports/byron/annex2.pdf (on 04.07.2008), 36.

[261] Ofcom, UK Code of Practice for the self-regulation of new forms of content on mobiles: Review, 11.08.2008, retrieved from http://www.ofcom.org.uk/advice/media_literacy/medlitpub/ukcode/ukcode.pdf (on 18.08.2008).

[262] Ofcom, UK Code of Practice for the self-regulation of new forms of content on mobiles: Review, 11.08.2008, retrieved from http://www.ofcom.org.uk/advice/media_literacy/medlitpub/ukcode/ukcode.pdf (on 18.08.2008), 1.

[263] Ofcom, UK Code of Practice for the self-regulation of new forms of content on mobiles: Review, 11.08.2008, retrieved from http://www.ofcom.org.uk/advice/media_literacy/medlitpub/ukcode/ukcode.pdf (on 18.08.2008), 3.

[264] Ofcom, Initial assessments of when to adopt self- or co-regulation – Consultation, 27.03.2008, retrieved from http://www.ofcom.org.uk/consult/condocs/coregulation/condoc.pdf (on 04.04.2008), 9; Mifsud Bonnici, Jeanne, *Self-regulation in cyberspace*, Malta, 2007, 14; Gunningham, Neil and Rees, Joseph, "Industry self-regulation: an institutional

issues,[265] its higher degree of incorporated expertise,[266] and its lower cost.[267] As a result of the high degree of incorporated expertise, it has been suggested that the rules created offer a more suitable solution tailored to the needs identified by the group.[268] It has also been claimed that incentives for commitment and compliance are higher[269] because the actors themselves are closely involved in the creation of the rules and because of the exercise of peer pressure.[270]

---

perspective", *Law & Policy* 1997, Vol. 19, No. 4, 366; RAND EUROPE (Jonathan CAVE, Chris MARSDEN and Stephen SIMMONS), Options for effectiveness of Internet self- and co-regulation – Phase 3 (Final) Report, Study commissioned by the European Commission, 2008, retrieved from http://ec.europa.eu/dgs/information_society/evaluation/data/pdf/studies/s2006_05/final_report.pdf (on 30.05.2008), 48: "*It is generally believed that self-regulation offers enhanced flexibility, responsiveness and speed of implementation and modification*".

265 PRICE, Monroe and VERHULST, Stefaan, "In search of the self: charting the course of self-regulation on the Internet in a global environment", in: MARSDEN, Christopher, *Regulating the global information society*, London, Routledge, 2000, 75; GUNNINGHAM, Neil and REES, Joseph, "Industry self-regulation: an institutional perspective", *Law & Policy* 1997, Vol. 19, No. 4, 366.

266 OGUS, Anthony, "Rethinking self-regulation", *Oxford Journal of Legal Studies* 1995, Vol. 15, No. 1, 97; MIFSUD BONNICI, Jeanne, *Self-regulation in cyberspace*, Malta, 2007, 14.

267 GUNNINGHAM, Neil and REES, Joseph, "Industry self-regulation: an institutional perspective", *Law & Policy* 1997, Vol. 19, No. 4, 366; OGUS, Anthony, "Rethinking self-regulation", *Oxford Journal of Legal Studies* 1995, Vol. 15, No. 1, 98; MIFSUD BONNICI, Jeanne, *Self-regulation in cyberspace*, Malta, 2007, 14; PRICE, Monroe and VERHULST, Stefaan, "In search of the self: charting the course of self-regulation on the Internet in a global environment", in: MARSDEN, Christopher, *Regulating the global information society*, London, Routledge, 2000, 75; LATZER, Michael, "Trust in the industry – Trust in the users: self-regulation and self-help in the context of digital media content in the EU", Report for working group 3 of the Expert Conference on European media policy "More trust in content – The potential of co- and self-regulation in digital media", Leipzig, 9–11.05.2007, retrieved from http://www.leipzig-eu2007.de/en/downloads/dokumente.asp (on 21.05.2008), 54.

268 MIFSUD BONNICI, Jeanne, *Self-regulation in cyberspace*, Malta, 2007, 14; GUNNINGHAM, Neil and REES, Joseph, "Industry self-regulation: an institutional perspective", *Law & Policy* 1997, Vol. 19, No. 4, 366.

269 PRICE, Monroe and VERHULST, Stefaan, "In search of the self: charting the course of self-regulation on the Internet in a global environment", in: MARSDEN, Christopher, *Regulating the global information society*, London, Routledge, 2000, 75.

270 LATZER, Michael, "Trust in the industry – Trust in the users: self-regulation and self-help in the context of digital media content in the EU", Report for working group 3 of the Expert Conference on European media policy "More trust in content – The potential of co- and self-regulation in digital media", Leipzig, 9–11.05.2007, retrieved from http://www.leipzig-eu2007.de/en/downloads/dokumente.asp (on 21.05.2008), 54; GUNNINGHAM, Neil and REES, Joseph, "Industry self-regulation: an institutional perspective", *Law & Policy* 1997, Vol. 19, No. 4, 366.

Drawbacks – The drawbacks of self-regulation are, however, at least as numerous as the assets. One of the most frequent criticisms is that self-regulatory mechanisms often lack effective enforcement.[271] Sanctions may be mild,[272] and reluctantly imposed.[273] Self-regulatory processes also have been known to suffer from a low level of transparency. [274] Compliance with other standard principles of good regulation (accountability, proportionality, consistency, etc.) has been judged problematic as well.[275] Moreover, it has been argued that self-regulation has the potential to establish cartel-like agreements that close markets, thereby infringing competition law principles (*infra*).[276] Another crucial objection, especially within the framework of this study, is the fact that self-regulation does not protect the fundamental rights

[271] Ogus, Anthony, "Rethinking self-regulation", *Oxford Journal of Legal Studies* 1995, Vol. 15, No. 1, 99; Prosser, Tony, "Self-regulation, co-regulation and the Audio-Visual Media Services Directive, *Journal of Consumer Policy* 2008, Vol. 31, No. 1, 104–105; Gunningham, Neil and Rees, Joseph, "Industry self-regulation: an institutional perspective", *Law & Policy* 1997, Vol. 19, No. 4, 370.

[272] Gunningham, Neil and Rees, Joseph, "Industry self-regulation: an institutional perspective", *Law & Policy* 1997, Vol. 19, No. 4, 370.

[273] Rand Europe (Jonathan Cave, Chris Marsden and Stephen Simmons), Options for effectiveness of Internet self- and co-regulation – Phase 3 (Final) Report, Study commissioned by the European Commission, 2008, retrieved from http://ec.europa.eu/dgs/information_society/evaluation/data/pdf/studies/s2006_05/final_report.pdf (on 30.05.2008), 49.

[274] Latzer, Michael, "Trust in the industry – Trust in the users: self-regulation and self-help in the context of digital media content in the EU", Report for working group 3 of the Expert Conference on European media policy "More trust in content – The potential of co- and self-regulation in digital media", Leipzig, 9–11.05.2007, retrieved from http://www.leipzig-eu2007.de/en/downloads/dokumente.asp (on 21.05.2008), 57; Rand Europe (Jonathan Cave, Chris Marsden and Stephen Simmons), Options for effectiveness of Internet self- and co-regulation – Phase 3 (Final) Report, Study commissioned by the European Commission, 2008, retrieved from http://ec.europa.eu/dgs/information_society/evaluation/data/pdf/studies/s2006_05/final_report.pdf (on 30.05.2008), 47.

[275] Rand Europe (Jonathan Cave, Chris Marsden and Stephen Simmons), Options for effectiveness of Internet self- and co-regulation – Phase 3 (Final) Report, Study commissioned by the European Commission, 2008, retrieved from http://ec.europa.eu/dgs/information_society/evaluation/data/pdf/studies/s2006_05/final_report.pdf (on 30.05.2008), 50.

[276] Prosser, Tony, "Self-regulation, co-regulation and the Audio-Visual Media Services Directive", *Journal of Consumer Policy* 2008, Vol. 31, No. 1, 103; Latzer, Michael, "Trust in the industry – Trust in the users: self-regulation and self-help in the context of digital media content in the EU", Report for working group 3 of the Expert Conference on European media policy "More trust in content – The potential of co- and self-regulation in digital media", Leipzig, 9–11.05.2007, retrieved from http://www.leipzig-eu2007.de/en/downloads/dokumente.asp (on 21.05.2008), 57; Newman, Abraham and Bach, David, "Self-Regulatory trajectories in the shadow of public power: resolving digital dilemmas in Europe and the United States", *Governance* 2004, Vol. 17, Iss. 3, 390–391.

of users or citizens in an adequate manner, or otherwise put, as adequately as traditional government legislation.[277] In addition, self-regulatory mechanisms have been accused of putting the private interest (of the group) before the public interest.[278] GUNNINGHAM and REES formulated this as follows:

> *Indeed, self-regulation has an extremely tarnished image, and is often reviled by conservationists, consumer organizations and other public interest groups for being a charade – a cynical attempt by self-interested parties to give the appearance of regulation (thereby warding off more direct and effective government intervention) while serving private interests at the expense of the public).*[279]

Related to this issue is the 'legitimacy' or 'democratic deficit' argument,[280] which implies that, whereas traditional legislation is created by democratically elected people and is subject to some form of democratic scrutiny, self-regulatory mechanisms are created by private actors who are not accountable to the public.[281] PRICE and VERHULST argue that for this reason self-regulation can never totally replace government regulation in the media sector, since the state ultimately carries the responsibility to safeguard fundamental rights and the public interest.[282]

SUCCESS FACTORS – GUNNINGHAM and REES argue that two factors are essential for the success of a self-regulatory mechanism: first, "*a strong natural coincidence between the public and private interest in establishing self-regulation*", and second, "*the existence of one or more external pressures sufficient to create such a coincidence of interest*".[283] An example of the latter success

---

277 MIFSUD BONNICI, Jeanne, *Self-regulation in cyberspace*, Malta, 2007, 14.

278 GUNNINGHAM, Neil and REES, Joseph, "Industry self-regulation: an institutional perspective", *Law & Policy* 1997, Vol. 19, No. 4, 366; MIFSUD BONNICI, Jeanne, *Self-regulation in cyberspace*, Malta, 2007, 14.

279 GUNNINGHAM, Neil and REES, Joseph, "Industry self-regulation: an institutional perspective", *Law & Policy* 1997, Vol. 19, No. 4, 370.

280 SCHULZ, Wolfgang, "Regulating search engines? On the use of self- and co-regulation in the field of Internet search", 79–86, in: NIKOLTCHEV, Susanne (ed.), *Searching for audiovisual content*, IRIS Special, Strasbourg, European Audiovisual Observatory, 2008, 83.

281 PROSSER, Tony, "Self-regulation, co-regulation and the Audio-Visual Media Services Directive", *Journal of Consumer Policy* 2008, Vol. 31, No. 1, 103; OGUS, Anthony, "Rethinking self-regulation", *Oxford Journal of Legal Studies* 1995, Vol. 15, No. 1, 98.

282 PRICE, Monroe and VERHULST, Stefaan, "In search of the self: charting the course of self-regulation on the Internet in a global environment", in: MARSDEN, Christopher, *Regulating the global information society*, London, Routledge, 2000, 65.

283 GUNNINGHAM, Neil and REES, Joseph, "Industry self-regulation: an institutional perspective", *Law & Policy* 1997, Vol. 19, No. 4, 390.

factor may be the mere threat of government intervention.[284] With respect to the first factor, it could be argued that the achievement of a delicate public policy goal such as the protection of minors against harmful content could lead to an overlap of private and public interest, as industry would want to be seen to care about this issue of societal importance. LATZER identified further success factors: operational objectives and clearly defined responsibilities, transparent regulatory processes and measurable results, defined fall-back scenarios in case of malfunction, adequate sanction powers, periodical reviews and external control by the general public and the state, and participation possibilities for interested stakeholders.[285]

E. *Interim conclusion*

FROM SELF- TO CO-REGULATION – As a result of the often repeated list of drawbacks of self-regulation, and certainly with respect to fields in which fundamental rights are crucial – such as the media sector and, more specifically, the protection of children against harmful content – calls for another, 'improved' regulatory instrument steadily grew louder. Such an instrument could unify the advantages of both self-regulation and command-and-control regulation, while eliminating their drawbacks. This middle way between the two extremes, often cited as an optimal regulatory solution,[286] is 'co-regulation'.[287]

---

[284] GUNNINGHAM, Neil and REES, Joseph, "Industry self-regulation: an institutional perspective", *Law & Policy* 1997, Vol. 19, No. 4, 391.

[285] LATZER, Michael, "Trust in the industry – Trust in the users: self-regulation and self-help in the context of digital media content in the EU", Report for working group 3 of the Expert Conference on European media policy "More trust in content – The potential of co- and self-regulation in digital media", Leipzig, 9–11.05.2007, retrieved from http://www.leipzig-eu2007.de/en/downloads/dokumente.asp (on 21.05.2008), 56.

[286] SINCLAIR, Darren, "Self-regulation versus command and control? Beyond false dichotomies", *Law & Policy* 1997, Vol. 19, No. 4, 533; GUNNINGHAM, Neil and REES, Joseph, "Industry self-regulation: an institutional perspective", *Law & Policy* 1997, Vol. 19, No. 4, 404.

[287] COMMISSION OF THE EUROPEAN COMMUNITIES, Interim report from the Commission to the Stockholm European Council: Improving and simplifying the regulatory environment, COM (2001) 130 final, 07.03.2001, retrieved from http://eur-lex.europa.eu/LexUriServ/LexUriServ.do?uri=COM:2001:0130:FIN:EN:PDF (on 14.05.2008), 7: "*[co-regulation] combines the advantages of legislation – more especially its predictable and binding nature – with the more flexible approach under self-regulation*".

2.3.3. *Co-regulation*

Government steers and industry rows.
Adam THIERER[288]

A. *Concept*

WHAT IS CO-REGULATION? – Simply put, co-regulation is a regulatory strategy which consists of elements of state regulation and elements of self-regulation.[289] Different stakeholders are thus involved in the co-regulatory process: on the one hand, the state, and on the other, a number of industry actors, and possibly users, consumers or NGOs as well. This description, however, is deceivingly simple. It took a lot of time and many academic writings before the concept of co-regulation was somewhat elucidated.[290]

EARLY DEFINITIONS – It might seem, also from the overview of the European policy documents (discussed *supra* in this chapter), that 'co-regulation' is a phenomenon of the 21st century. However, Australian scholars GRABOSKY and BRAITHWAITE already used the concept in 1986. They considered voluntary industry codes containing provisions for monitoring of compliance by the government to be co-regulation.[291] Almost a decade later, AYRES and BRAITHWAITE distinguished between *enforced self-regulation* and co-regulation.[292] Whereas 'co-regulation' was defined as "*industry-association self-regulation with some oversight and/or ratification by government*",

[288] THE PROGRESS & FREEDOM FOUNDATION BLOG (Adam THIERER), Reflections on Brussels Summit on Future of free expression and child protection, 16.06.2006, retrieved from http://blog.pff.org/archives/2006/06/reflections_on_3.html#more (on 06.07.2006).

[289] RAND EUROPE (Chris MARSDEN, Stephen SIMMONS and Jonathan CAVE), Options for effectiveness of Internet self- and co-regulation – Inception report, Study commissioned by the European Commission, 30.04.2007, retrieved from http://ec.europa.eu/dgs/information_society/evaluation/data/pdf/studies/s2006_05/inception_final.pdf (on 08.01.2008), 39: "*The term co-regulation encompasses a range of different regulatory phenomena, which basically have in common the fact that the regulatory regime is made up of a complex interaction of general legislation and a self-regulatory body*".

[290] Parts of the overview of notions and definitions can also be found in: LIEVENS, Eva, DUMORTIER, Jos and RYAN, Patrick S., "The co-protection of minors in new media: a European approach to co-regulation", *UC Davis Journal of Juvenile Law & Policy* 2006, Vol. 10, 97–151.

[291] GRABOSKY, Peter and BRAITHWAITE, John, *Of manners gentle: enforcement strategies of Australian business regulatory agencies*, Melbourne, Oxford University Press, 1986, 183.

[292] AYRES, Ian and BRAITHWAITE, John, *Responsive regulation: Transcending the deregulation debate*, Oxford, Oxford University Press, 1995, 102. The same distinction and similar definitions were referred to by GOLDBERG, David, PROSSER, Tony and VERHULST, Stefaan

enforced 'self-regulation' – "*an extension and individualization of 'co-regulation' theory*" – was described as follows:

> *The enforced self-regulation model presented in this chapter is about negotiation occurring between the state and individual firms to establish regulations that are particularized to each firm. Each firm in an industry is required to propose its own regulatory standards if it is to avoid harsher (and less tailored) standards imposed by the state. This individual-firm, as opposed to industry association, self-regulation is 'enforced' in two senses. First, the firm is required by the state to do the self-regulation. Second, the privately written rules can be publicly enforced.*[293]

Other notions and definitions – Over the years, an array of notions and descriptions of regulatory strategies that could be interpreted as 'co-regulation' circulated.[294] Price and Verhulst used the term *two-tiered regulation* when referring to a combination of self-regulation and formal legal systems,[295] and argued that such a combination is the optimal choice for addressing public concerns or market or policy failures, both management- and efficiency-wise. In addition, they pointed out that two-tiered regulation is especially relevant in complex and transnational industries and areas, such

---

(eds), *Regulating the changing media: A comparative study*, Oxford, Oxford University Press, 1998, 313.

293 Ayres, Ian and Braithwaite, John, *Responsive regulation: Transcending the deregulation debate*, Oxford, Oxford University Press, 1995, 101.

294 In the United States, the term *audited self-regulation* is used, which has been legally defined as "*congressional or agency delegation of power to a private self-regulatory organization to implement and enforce laws or agency regulations with respect to the regulated entities, with powers of independent action and review retained by the agency*": Administrative Conference of the United States, The use of audited self-regulation as a regulatory technique, Recommendation 94–1, 30.08.1994, retrieved from http://www.law.fsu.edu/library/admin/acus/305941.html (on 02.06.2008). Also cf. Marsden, Christopher, "Co- and self-regulation in European media and Internet sectors: the results of Oxford University's study www.selfregulation.info", in Möller, Christian and Amouroux, Arnaud (eds), *The media freedom Internet cookbook*, Vienna, OSCE, 2004, 86. Other notions used, mainly in Europe, are, for instance, mandated full self-regulation, mandated partial self-regulation, subcontracting, concerted action and incorporation. These notions all incorporate different nuances, mostly related to the actual level of government involvement. Cf. Gunningham, Neil and Rees, Joseph, "Industry self-regulation: an institutional perspective", Law & Policy 1997, Vol. 19, No. 4, 365 and Huyse, Luc and Parmentier, Stephan, "Decoding codes: the dialogue between consumers and suppliers through codes of conduct in the European Community", *Journal of Consumer Policy* 1990, Vol. 13, No. 3, 259–260.

295 Price, Monroe and Verhulst, Stefaan, "In search of the self: charting the course of self-regulation on the Internet in a global environment", in: Marsden, Christopher, *Regulating the global information society*, London, Routledge, 2000, 59.

as content regulation.[296] PAUL built on this idea and described *co-regulation* as a technique by which a consensus between different actors in the regulation process (such as legislators, judges, enterprises, civil associations, and regulatory authorities) can be reached.[297] Together, these actors coordinate, exchange information, and establish a body entrusted with supervision, provision of information, consultation, and advice.[298, 299] In other words, in this description, co-regulation appears to be a 'pre-normative' process that occurs in the preliminary phases that precede the passage of a regulation. Such a process could reinforce the legitimacy and efficacy of the ensuing regulation, especially when the state or another regulatory authority takes into account the interests of all actors concerned and obtains their agreement that they will respect the consensus reached.[300] In an important article, writ-

[296] PRICE, Monroe and VERHULST, Stefaan, "In search of the self: charting the course of self-regulation on the Internet in a global environment", in: MARSDEN, Christopher, *Regulating the global information society*, London, Routledge, 2000, 59.

[297] PAUL, Christian, Du Droits et des Libertés sur l'Internet – La Corégulation, Contribution Française pour une Réglementation Mondiale [*On rights and freedoms on the Internet – Co-regulation, a French contribution to universal regulation*], Rapport au Premier Ministre, May 2000, retrieved from http://lesrapports.ladocumentationfrancaise.fr/BRP/004001056/0000.pdf (on 02.06.2008), as described in POULLET, Yves, "Technologies de l'information et de la communication et 'co-régulation': une nouvelle approche?" ["*Information and communication technologies and 'co-regulation': a new approach?*"], *Droit et Nouvelles Technologies*, 27.05.2004, retrieved from http://www.droit-technologie.org/upload/dossier/doc/120–1.pdf (on 29.11.2008), 5–6 [in French].

[298] PAUL, Christian, Du Droits et des Libertés sur l'Internet – La Corégulation, Contribution Française pour une Réglementation Mondiale [*On rights and freedoms on the Internet – Co-regulation, a French contribution to universal regulation*], Rapport au Premier Ministre, May 2000, retrieved from http://lesrapports.ladocumentationfrancaise.fr/BRP/004001056/0000.pdf (on 02.06.2008), as described in POULLET, Yves, "Technologies de l'information et de la communication et 'co-régulation': une nouvelle approche?" ["*Information and communication technologies and 'co-regulation': a new approach?*"], *Droit et Nouvelles Technologies*, 27.05.2004, retrieved from http://www.droit-technologie.org/upload/dossier/doc/120–1.pdf (on 29.11.2008), 5–6 [in French].

[299] Along the same lines, DU MARAIS defined co-regulation as "*un lieu d'échange, de négociation entre les 'parties prenantes' et les titulaires de la contrainte légitime et où se comparent les bonnes pratiques, afin de les ériger en recommandations, ce lieu peut également servir d'instance de médiation*": DU MARAIS, Bertrand, "Auto regulation, regulation et co-régulation des réseaux" [*Auto regulation, regulation and co-regulation of networks*], Colloque "Droit de l'Internet: approches européennes et internationales, 2001, retrieved from http://droit-internet-2001.univ-paris1.fr/pdf/vf/Marais.pdf (on 26.05.2008), 3 [in French].

[300] PAUL, Christian, Du Droits et des Libertés sur l'Internet – La Corégulation, Contribution Française pour une Réglementation Mondiale [*On rights and freedoms on the Internet – Co-regulation, a French contribution to universal regulation*], Rapport au Premier Ministre, May 2000, retrieved from http://lesrapports.ladocumentationfrancaise.fr/BRP/004001056/0000.pdf (on 02.06.2008), as described in POULLET, Yves, "Technologies de l'information et de la communication et 'co-régulation': une nouvelle approche?"

ten in 2001, SCHULZ and HELD preferred the term *regulated self-regulation*, defined as "*self-regulation that fits in with a legal framework or has a basis laid down in law*".[301, 302] SCHULZ and HELD wondered at that time if co-regulation could perhaps be the 'middle road' that regulators in the information society might follow.[303] HOFFMANN-RIEM, from whom they borrowed the term *regulated self-regulation*, saw this concept as "*a kind of self-regulation with a state safety net*".[304] Along the same lines, LATZER ET AL. identified co-regulation as "*self-regulation with public oversight or ratified by the state; in other words, it is self-regulation with a legal basis*".[305] Examples of this kind of strong state involvement include supervision of regulatory activities by the state and state-dictated instructions regarding structure, transparency, or goals.[306, 307] In PALZER's opinion, 'co-regulation' is an ambiguous

["*Information and communication technologies and 'co-regulation': a new approach?*"], *Droit et Nouvelles Technologies*, 27.05.2004, retrieved from http://www.droit-technologie.org/upload/dossier/doc/120–1.pdf (on 29.11.2008), 5–6 [in French].

301 SCHULZ, Wolfgang and HELD, Thorsten, Regulated Self-Regulation as a Form of Modern Government, Study commissioned by the German Federal Commissioner for Cultural and Media Affairs, 2001, retrieved from http://www.humanrights.coe.int/Media/documents/interim-report-self-regulation.pdf (on 02.06.2008), 7.

302 KLEINSTEUBER distinguished co-regulation and regulated self-regulation as follows: "*If the State and the private regulators co-operate in joint institutions, this is called 'co-regulation'. If this type of self-regulation is structured by the State but the State is not involved the appropriate term is 'regulated selfregulation'*": KLEINSTEUBER, Hans, "State – regulation – media", OSCE Conference "Guaranteeing media freedom on the Internet, Amsterdam, 27–28.08.2004, retrieved from http://www.osce.org/documents/rfm/2004/08/3430_en.pdf (on 06.06.2008), 2–3.

303 SCHULZ, Wolfgang and HELD, Thorsten, Regulated Self-Regulation as a Form of Modern Government, Study commissioned by the German Federal Commissioner for Cultural and Media Affairs, 2001, retrieved from http://www.humanrights.coe.int/Media/documents/interim-report-self-regulation.pdf (on 02.06.2008), 5.

304 HOFFMANN-RIEM, Wolfgang, *Regulating Media: The licensing and supervision of broadcasting in six countries*, New York, The Guilford Press, 1996, 326.

305 LATZER, Michael, JUST, Natascha, SAURWEIN, Florian and SLOMINSKI, Peter, "Regulation remixed: Institutional change through self- and co-regulation in the mediamatics sector", *Communications & Strategies* 2003, 135.

306 LATZER, Michael, JUST, Natascha, SAURWEIN, Florian and SLOMINSKI, Peter, "Regulation remixed: Institutional change through self- and co-regulation in the mediamatics sector", *Communications & Strategies* 2003, 135.

307 Interestingly, LATZER ET AL. distinguished two rationales for applying alternative regulatory mechanisms: as a 'makeshift solution' for when the failure of traditional regulation forces the state to choose an appropriate regulatory mechanism, and as an 'ideal solution' specifically chosen because of the advantages it offers over traditional state regulation: LATZER, Michael, JUST, Natascha, SAURWEIN, Florian and SLOMINSKI, Peter, "Regulation remixed: Institutional change through self- and co-regulation in the mediamatics sector", *Communications & Strategies* 2003, 142. For an overview of the advantages of alternative regulatory mechanisms, cf. *infra*.

and generic term commonly applied to cooperative forms of regulation that (1) are designed to achieve public authority objectives and that (2) contain elements of both self-regulation and traditional public authority regulation.[308] As she put it,

> *The co-regulation model is based on a self-regulation framework (in its broadest sense), which is anchored in public authority regulations in one of two ways: the public authority either lays down a legal basis for the self-regulation framework so that it can begin to function, or integrates an existing self-regulation system into a public authority framework.*[309]

Indeed, many different forms of co-regulation can be placed under this umbrella definition, depending on the combination of public (authority) and private (sector) elements. Palzer used a common distinction between a top-down approach (where the public authority prescribes a legal basis for co-regulation) and a bottom-up approach (where the public authority integrates an existing self-regulatory system).[310] The UK's Communications White Paper, issued by the former UK telecommunications regulator Oftel, described co-regulation as a regulatory approach that "*implies a more active involvement of government or regulator in seeking a solution to an emerging concern or perceived need for regulation*".[311] As the White Paper also noted, this involvement may manifest itself in "*setting objectives which are to be achieved, or providing support for the sanctions available, while still leaving space for self-regulatory initiatives by industry, taking due account of the interests and views of other stakeholders, to meet the objectives in the most efficient way*".[312] If the industry response would prove ineffective or not forthcoming in a sufficiently timely manner, the regulator would have the authority to impose more formal regulations. In a more recent document published by Ofcom, the current UK communications authority, co-regulation was described as "*an extension of self-regulation that involves both*

[308] Palzer, Carmen, "European provisions for the establishment of co-regulation frameworks", in: Nikoltchev, Susanne (ed.), *Co-regulation of the media in Europe*, IRIS Special, Strasbourg, European Audiovisual Observatory, 2003, 4.

[309] Palzer, Carmen, "European provisions for the establishment of co-regulation frameworks", in: Nikoltchev, Susanne (ed.), *Co-regulation of the media in Europe*, IRIS Special, Strasbourg, European Audiovisual Observatory, 2003, 4.

[310] Palzer, Carmen, "Co-regulation of the media in Europe: European provisions for the establishment of co-regulation frameworks", *Iris Plus* 2002, No. 6, 4. This distinction was also proposed in the Mandelkern report (*supra*).

[311] Oftel, Communications White Paper, retrieved from http://www.communicationswhitepaper.gov.uk/pdf/ch8.pdf (on 05.05.2005, no longer available), 83.

[312] Oftel, Communications White Paper, retrieved from http://www.communicationswhitepaper.gov.uk/pdf/ch8.pdf (on 05.05.2005, no longer available), 83.

industry and the government (or regulator) administering and enforcing a solution in a variety of combinations; thus the aim is to harness the benefits of self-regulation in circumstances where some oversight by Ofcom may still be required".[313] A final definition was pronounced by Commissioner Reding in a 2006 speech: "*[a] co-regulatory system is one where public authorities accept that the protection of societal values can be left to self-regulatory mechanisms and codes of conduct, but where they reserve the right to step in in case that self-regulation should prove to be inefficient*".[314]

ANALYSIS – From this overview of definitions it appears that again no consensus on the exact scope of the concept of co-regulation exists. It is often not clear where self-regulation ends and co-regulation starts. However, what we can deduce from the overview is that there are certain characteristics that can distinguish co-regulation from either state regulation or self-regulation, most importantly the degree of involvement and participation of the different actors and the roles these actors play.[315] It is important to point out that there are authors who consider co-regulation as a form of self-regulation.[316] This, however, is a position that we do not endorse, despite the fact that, if self-regulation is interpreted very broadly, it could be understood where this view is coming from, especially since it was most often expressed before thorough studies of co-regulation were carried out. Nonetheless, we prefer to distinguish between the two forms depending on the degree of government involvement.

---

313 OFCOM, Initial assessments of when to adopt self- or co-regulation – Consultation, 27.03.2008, retrieved from http://www.ofcom.org.uk/consult/condocs/coregulation/condoc.pdf (on 04.04.2008), 5–6.

314 REDING, Viviane, Freedom of the media, effective co-regulation and media literacy: cornerstones for an efficient protection of minors in the European Union, Speech at the ICRA Roundtable Brussels 'Mission Impossible', Brussels, 14.06.2006, retrieved from http://europa.eu.int/rapid/pressReleasesAction.do?reference=SPEECH/06/374&type=HTML&aged=0&language=EN&guiLanguage=en (on 15.06.2006).

315 See, for instance, the analytical approach used by LATZER ET AL. regarding regulatory institutions and state involvement, operational scope and regulatory objectives, international involvement and stakeholder participation, and regulatory processes and instruments: LATZER, Michael, JUST, Natascha, SAURWEIN, Florian and SLOMINSKI, Peter, "Regulation remixed: Institutional change through self- and co-regulation in the mediamatics sector", *Communications & Strategies* 2003, 137.

316 MIFSUD BONNICI, Jeanne, *Self-regulation in cyberspace*, Malta, 2007, 16; SINCLAIR, Darren, "Self-regulation versus command and control? Beyond false dichotomies", *Law & Policy* 1997, Vol. 19, No. 4, 532; PRICE, Monroe and VERHULST, Stefaan, "In search of the self: charting the course of self-regulation on the Internet in a global environment", in: MARSDEN, Christopher, *Regulating the global information society*, London, Routledge, 59.

Quest for clarity – The fact that many different opinions, definitions and classifications regarding co-regulation circulated did not escape the European Commission's attention. In a quest for clarity vis-à-vis this regulatory concept, especially in the media sector, it commissioned a study in 2005.

B. *Co-regulation in the media sector: the HBI and EMR study*

Aim of the study – The 'Study on co-regulation measures in the media sector' was carried out by the Hans-Bredow-Institut and the Institut für Europäisches Medienrecht (EMR).[317] The study's aim was to clarify the concept of co-regulation, to identify co-regulatory systems and to critically appraise these systems. The authors of the study developed a definition and a number of classification criteria which enable a more reasoned approach to existing, as well as future, co-regulatory mechanisms.

Definition and classification criteria – In the study, co-regulation was defined as "*a specific combination of state and non-state regulation*".[318] More specifically, the authors took co-regulation to mean "*combining non-state regulation and state regulation in such a way that a non-state regulatory system links up with state regulation*".[319] The non-state component included in the definition was considered carefully, and the authors proposed that at least three conditions should be fulfilled. First, specific organisations, rules or processes (such as, for instance, codes of conduct or self-regulatory bod-

[317] Hans-Bredow-Institut and EMR, Study on co-regulation measures in the media sector: Final report, Study commissioned by the European Commission, June 2006, retrieved from http://ec.europa.eu/avpolicy/docs/library/studies/coregul/final_rep_en.pdf (on 28.07.2006). Cf. also: Kleist, Thomas and Palzer, Carmen, "Co-regulation as an instrument of modern regulation", Report for working group 4 of the Expert Conference on European media policy "More trust in content – The potential of co- and self-regulation in digital media", Leipzig, 9–11.05.2007, retrieved from http://www.leipzig-eu2007.de/en/downloads/dokumente.asp (on 21.05.2008); Schulz, Wolfgang and Held, Thorsten, "Together they are strong? Co-regulatory approaches for the protection of minors in the European Union", 49–65, in: Carlsson, Ulla (ed.), *Regulation, awareness, empowerment. Young people and harmful media content in the digital age*, Göteborg, The International Clearinghouse on Children, Youth and Media, 2006, 286 p.

[318] Hans-Bredow-Institut and EMR, Study on co-regulation measures in the media sector: Final report, Study commissioned by the European Commission, June 2006, retrieved from http://ec.europa.eu/avpolicy/docs/library/studies/coregul/final_rep_en.pdf (on 28.07.2006), 35.

[319] Hans-Bredow-Institut and EMR, Study on co-regulation measures in the media sector: Final report, Study commissioned by the European Commission, June 2006, retrieved from http://ec.europa.eu/avpolicy/docs/library/studies/coregul/final_rep_en.pdf (on 28.07.2006), 35.

ies) should be created. Second, these organisations, rules or processes should be aimed at influencing decisions by persons or by or within organisations. Hence, the non-state system should participate in the creation, implementation or enforcement of rules; pure consultation cannot be considered adequate. Finally, all of this should – at least partly – be done by or within the organisations or parts of society to whose members the (non-state) regulation is addressed.[320] Furthermore, four criteria were developed to which the link between the state and the non-state component needs to adhere in order to be qualified as 'co-regulation':

1. The system is established to achieve public policy goals targeted at social processes (such as, for instance, the protection of minors). Systems that merely advance the private sector's individual interest do not qualify.
2. There is a legal connection between the non-state regulatory system and the state regulation. As a clarification, it was added that the use of non-state regulation need not necessarily be mentioned in Acts of Parliament; regulator's guidelines or contracts can suffice. However, informal agreements or a mention in a minister's speech fall outside the scope of the criterion.
3. The state leaves discretionary power to a non-state regulatory system (at the level of making, implementing, and/or enforcing the regulations). The authors clarified that there needs to be a real division of labour.
4. The state uses regulatory resources, such as money or power, to influence the outcome of the regulatory process to guarantee the fulfilment of the regulatory goals.[321]

Case-studies and results – The study then proceeded with an analysis of 19 regulatory systems in Europe and four abroad (Australia, Canada, Malaysia and South Africa).[322] These case-studies resulted in the formulation of a number of requirements and factors that characterise well-functioning co-regulatory systems. Two prerequisites for a successful system were put forward by the authors: sufficient incentives for the industry to participate, on the one hand, and proportional deterrents to enforce regulation on the

---

[320] Hans-Bredow-Institut and EMR, Study on co-regulation measures in the media sector: Final report, Study commissioned by the European Commission, June 2006, retrieved from http://ec.europa.eu/avpolicy/docs/library/studies/coregul/final_rep_en.pdf (on 28.07.2006), 35.

[321] Hans-Bredow-Institut and EMR, Study on co-regulation measures in the media sector: Final report, Study commissioned by the European Commission, June 2006, retrieved from http://ec.europa.eu/avpolicy/docs/library/studies/coregul/final_rep_en.pdf (on 28.07.2006), 35 *et seq.*

[322] Cf. *infra*, illustrations of co-regulatory systems: Netherlands, Germany and Australia.

other.[323] The first is of crucial importance since it would be illusory to assume that the private sector would undertake regulatory efforts for completely altruistic reasons. Pending regulatory intervention might already provide a sufficient incentive, but other possibilities, such as the requirement to follow non-state regulation in order to receive state aid, exist as well.[324] The latter essential success factor involves the establishment of effective sanctions and backstop powers, which are necessary to provide the systems with some 'teeth'. Regulatory culture and countries' openness to innovative regulatory concepts, the availability of state resources to assure satisfactory protection levels, unambiguous legal bases and clear divisions of work, and respecting key process objectives – such as proportionality, openness, transparency and clarity – were also considered fundamental for a thriving co-regulatory system.[325] Furthermore, the authors of the study concluded that co-regulation could be a particularly suitable regulatory option to protect minors across all media.[326, 327]

Analysis – Undoubtedly, the development of the working definition and the classification criteria could be considered an important step forward in the co-regulation debate. The study presents the first detailed reflection on and analysis of the concept, and provides some useful clues, particularly as to the requirements one could place on the level of government involvement in order to qualify a system as co-regulation. In our opinion, the study developed a balanced concept, without resorting to criteria that would be either

[323] Hans-Bredow-Institut and EMR, Study on co-regulation measures in the media sector: Final report, Study commissioned by the European Commission, June 2006, retrieved from http://ec.europa.eu/avpolicy/docs/library/studies/coregul/final_rep_en.pdf (on 28.07.2006), 179.

[324] Hans-Bredow-Institut and EMR, Study on co-regulation measures in the media sector: Final report, Study commissioned by the European Commission, June 2006, retrieved from http://ec.europa.eu/avpolicy/docs/library/studies/coregul/final_rep_en.pdf (on 28.07.2006), 119 and 179.

[325] Hans-Bredow-Institut and EMR, Study on co-regulation measures in the media sector: Final report, Study commissioned by the European Commission, June 2006, retrieved from http://ec.europa.eu/avpolicy/docs/library/studies/coregul/final_rep_en.pdf (on 28.07.2006), 119–120.

[326] Hans-Bredow-Institut and EMR, Study on co-regulation measures in the media sector: Final report, Study commissioned by the European Commission, June 2006, retrieved from http://ec.europa.eu/avpolicy/docs/library/studies/coregul/final_rep_en.pdf (on 28.07.2006), 178.

[327] The study also analysed the legal framework surrounding the use of co-regulatory systems (Hans-Bredow-Institut and EMR, Study on co-regulation measures in the media sector: Final report, Study commissioned by the European Commission, June 2006, retrieved from http://ec.europa.eu/avpolicy/docs/library/studies/coregul/final_rep_en.pdf (on 28.07.2006), 147–176). This part of the study will be dealt with *infra* (Part 2, Chapter 2).

too strict or too lenient. If we now take a look back at the 'Beaufort scale' developed by the Rand study (*supra*), which identified three types of co-regulation ('approved compulsory co-regulation', 'scrutinised co-regulation' and 'independent body with stakeholder forum') we doubt whether this classification actually provides an added value to the concept developed by HBI/EMR study.

C. *Illustrations*

SUCCESSFUL CO-REGULATORY SYSTEMS – Although many co-regulatory systems are still in their infancy, there are a few systems that have already been repeatedly judged to function in an efficient way: the '*Kijkwijzer*' system in the Netherlands, the German co-regulatory framework to protect minors in media, and the Australian codes of practice system underpinned by a governmental safety net.

C.1. *Netherlands*

KIJKWIJZER – The Dutch cross-media content classification scheme, *Kijkwijzer* [*Watch Smarter*], is one of Europe's most often praised co-regulatory systems aiming to protect minors against harmful content. It consists of a 'self-regulatory' organisation, NICAM, which functions on the basis of a legal act and within a governmental supervisory framework. The legal basis for the scheme can be found in the Dutch Media Act [recently amended]. Article 4.1. Media Act [ex 52d Media Act] stipulates that programmes can only contain content which is potentially harmful for minors if the broadcaster has joined an organisation certified by the government. According to article 4.2 Media Act [ex 53 Media Act], this organisation has the task to create classification criteria, and to decide when potentially harmful content can be broadcast and to develop symbols which indicate that such content is being broadcast.[328] In 1999, the *Nederlands Instituut voor de Classificatie van Audiovisuele Media* (NICAM) [*the Dutch Institute for Classification of Audiovisual Media*] was established. An independent institution broadly supported by more than 2200 institutions and companies in the audiovisual industry,[329] NICAM was created in close collaboration with the Ministry of Education, Culture and Science, the Ministry of Health, Welfare and Sport, and the

[328] Article 4.2 *et seq.* Media Act also contains other stipulations regarding the organisation.

[329] RAND EUROPE (Chris MARSDEN et al.), Options for and effectiveness of Internet self- and co-regulation – Phase 2: Case study report, Study commissioned by the European Commission, 15.01.2008, retrieved from http://ec.europa.eu/dgs/information_society/evaluation/data/pdf/studies/s2006_05/phase2.pdf (on 06.06.2008), 159.

Ministry of Justice.[330] NICAM coordinates the *Kijkwijzer* system, which is made up of a single content classification system for television, videos, film, games, and – since April 2005 – mobile content. *Kijkwijzer* is structured as follows: (1) content providers classify their own content by responding to a list of standardised questions, to which (2) NICAM subsequently applies a formula and then assigns an age recommendation and pictograms indicating which aspects of the content have led to the recommended age restrictions (for instance, violence, sex, fear, swearing, etc.). The government, aside from co-funding the system, closely monitors the proceedings. The *Commissariaat voor de media* [*the Dutch Media Authority*] is charged with the meta-supervision of the scheme. NICAM needs to report to the Media Authority on its functioning and the Media Authority regulates companies that have not joined NICAM. This latter stipulation provides a significant incentive for industry to participate.[331] Although *Kijkwijzer* was often cited as being self-regulatory in the early days of the system, recent studies have now clearly pronounced it to be co-regulatory.[332] This is sup-

[330] Rand Europe (Chris Marsden et al.), Options for and effectiveness of Internet self- and co-regulation – Phase 2: Case study report, Study commissioned by the European Commission, 15.01.2008, retrieved from http://ec.europa.eu/dgs/information_society/evaluation/data/pdf/studies/s2006_05/phase2.pdf (on 06.06.2008), 160.

[331] Rand Europe (Chris Marsden et al.), Options for and effectiveness of Internet self- and co-regulation – Phase 2: Case study report, Study commissioned by the European Commission, 15.01.2008, retrieved from http://ec.europa.eu/dgs/information_society/evaluation/data/pdf/studies/s2006_05/phase2.pdf (on 06.06.2008), 162.

[332] Hans-Bredow-Institut and EMR, Study on co-regulation measures in the media sector: Final report, Study commissioned by the European Commission, June 2006, retrieved from http://ec.europa.eu/avpolicy/docs/library/studies/coregul/final_rep_en.pdf (on 28.07.2006), 75 *et seq.*; Rand Europe (Chris Marsden et al.), Options for and effectiveness of Internet self- and co-regulation – Phase 2: Case study report, Study commissioned by the European Commission, 15.01.2008, retrieved from http://ec.europa.eu/dgs/information_society/evaluation/data/pdf/studies/s2006_05/phase2.pdf (on 06.06.2008), 159–160. Rand Europe classified the system as being 'scrutinised co-regulatory' (cf. *supra*: Beaufort Scale: Rand Europe (Jonathan Cave, Chris Marsden and Stephen Simmons), Options for effectiveness of Internet self- and co-regulation – Phase 3 (Final) Report, Study commissioned by the European Commission, 2008, retrieved from http://ec.europa.eu/dgs/information_society/evaluation/data/pdf/studies/s2006_05/final_report.pdf (on 30.05.2008), 27). See also: Reding, Viviane, Minors and media: Towards a more effective protection, Speech at the Workshop of scientists in the field of the protection of minors on media violence, self-regulation and media literacy, Brussels, 10.09.2003, retrieved from http://europa.eu.int/rapid/pressReleasesAction.do?reference=SPEECH/03/400&format=HTML&aged=0&language=EN&guiLanguage=en (on 06.06.2008); McGonagle, Tarlach, "The potential for practice of an intangible idea", in: Nikoltchev, Susanne (ed.), *Co-regulation of the media in Europe*, IRIS Special, Strasbourg, European Audiovisual Observatory, 2003, 6.

ported by the fact that it ticks many of the boxes put forward by the HBI/EMR study.

Evaluation – An assessment conducted by Palzer at the end of 2002 concluded that NICAM functioned well, met its objectives, and that both the industry and consumers were satisfied with the system.[333] Both the HBI/EMR study and the Rand study found the Dutch system to be a particularly well-functioning system.[334] The former study even dubbed the system "*a role model worth considering*".[335] In 2005, an expert report, commissioned by the Dutch Commission 'Youth, violence and media', which reviewed the system, was issued.[336] The experts concluded that, although there was room for improvement in some areas,[337] experiences with NICAM and the

---

333 Palzer, Carmen, "Horizontal rating of audiovisual content in Europe – An alternative to multi-level classification?", *Iris Plus* 2003, No. 10, 4.

334 Hans-Bredow-Institut and EMR, Study on co-regulation measures in the media sector: Final report, Study commissioned by the European Commission, June 2006, retrieved from http://ec.europa.eu/avpolicy/docs/library/studies/coregul/final_rep_en.pdf (on 28.07.2006), 180; Rand Europe (Chris Marsden et al.), Options for and effectiveness of Internet self- and co-regulation – Phase 2: Case study report, Study commissioned by the European Commission, 15.01.2008, retrieved from http://ec.europa.eu/dgs/information_society/evaluation/data/pdf/studies/s2006_05/phase2.pdf (on 06.06.2008), 159 and 170. This system was also praised by other organisations and academics, for instance: Ofcom, Initial assessments of when to adopt self- or co-regulation – Consultation, 27.03.2008, retrieved from http://www.ofcom.org.uk/consult/condocs/coregulation/condoc.pdf (on 04.04.2008), 6 and Prosser, Tony, "Self-regulation, co-regulation and the Audio-Visual Media Services Directive", *Journal of Consumer Policy* 2008, Vol. 31, No. 1, 108.

335 Hans-Bredow-Institut and EMR, Study on co-regulation measures in the media sector: Final report, Study commissioned by the European Commission, June 2006, retrieved from http://ec.europa.eu/avpolicy/docs/library/studies/coregul/final_rep_en.pdf (on 28.07.2006), 180.

336 van der Stoel, Anne Lize, van Eijk, Nico, Hoogland, Duco, van Noorduyn, Els and Wermuth, Mir, Wijzer Kijken – Schadelijkheid, geschiktheid en kennisbevordering bij het gebruik van audiovisuele producten door jeugdigen [*Watch smarter – Harmfulness, appropriateness and advancement of knowledge related to the use of audiovisual products by young persons*], November 2005, retrieved from http://www.ivir.nl/publicaties/vaneijk/Wijzerkijken.pdf (on 06.06.2008).

337 Recommendations related, for instance, to increasing industry participation, strengthening enforcement, the inclusion of independent members on the board, and improving quality control. Cf. van der Stoel, Anne Lize, van Eijk, Nico, Hoogland, Duco, van Noorduyn, Els and Wermuth, Mir, Wijzer Kijken – Schadelijkheid, geschiktheid en kennisbevordering bij het gebruik van audiovisuele producten door jeugdigen [*Watch smarter – Harmfulness, appropriateness and advancement of knowledge related to the use of audiovisual products by young persons*], November 2005, retrieved from http://www.ivir.nl/publicaties/vaneijk/Wijzerkijken.pdf (on 06.06.2008), 5–6.

Kijkwijzer system were predominantly positive and that the system provided an excellent basis for further regulation.

C.2. *Germany*

Co-regulatory framework – In 2003, the *Jugendmedienschutz-Staatsvertrag* [*Interstate Treaty for the Protection of Minors in Media*][338] entered into force in Germany. This co-regulatory (or regulated self-regulatory, as is the most common term in Germany) framework attributed the responsibility of protecting minors[339] to non-state actors, which need to be certified by the state on the basis of certain conditions laid down in the Treaty.[340, 341] For Internet services, for instance, the *Freiwillige Selbstkontrolle Multimedia-Diensteabieter* [FSM: *Association for the Voluntary Self-Monitoring of Multimedia Service Providers*] obtained such a certification.[342] The FSM set up a code[343] and can take action if certain content breaches the law. The voluntary associations are supervised by a central regulatory body called the *Commission for the protection of minors in the media* [*Kommission für Jugendmedienschutz*, or KJM],[344] composed of twelve experts nominated from amongst

338 *Jugendmedienschutz-Staatsvertrag* [*Interstate Treaty on the protection of minors*], vom 10. bis 27.9.2002 (GBl. S. 93), zuletzt geändert durch Artikel 4 des Zehnten Staatsvertrages zur Änderung rundfunkrechtlicher Staatsverträge vom 19.12.2007 (GBI. S. 249), retrieved from http://www.kjm-online.de/public/kjm/downloads/2051_(2008)_2_jmstv_080901.pdf (on 05.01.2009) [in German]. English translation retrieved from http://www.kjm-online.de/public/kjm/downloads/JMStV2007–englisch.pdf (on 06.06.2008).

339 The co-regulatory system is aimed at the protection against 'content not suitable for certain age groups'. 'Harmful content' is rated by an official administrative authority, the *Bundesprüfstelle für jugendgefährdende Medien* [the Federal Department for Media Harmful to Young Persons]: Schulz, Wolfgang, Held, Thorsten, Dreyer, Stephan (in cooperation with Thilo Wind), "Regulation of broadcasting and Internet services in Germany: A brief overview", Arbeitspapiere des Hans-Bredow-Instituts No. 13, March 2008, retrieved from http://www.hans-bredow-institut.de/english/publications/ap/13–2Mediaregulation.pdf (on 06.06.2008), 14.

340 Article 19 para. 3 *Jugendmedienschutz-Staatsvertrag.*

341 Hans-Bredow-Institut and EMR, Study on co-regulation measures in the media sector: Final report, Study commissioned by the European Commission, June 2006, retrieved from http://ec.europa.eu/avpolicy/docs/library/studies/coregul/final_rep_en.pdf (on 28.07.2006), 49.

342 Other bodies were recognised for other media: for instance, the *Freiwillige Selbstkontrolle Fernsehen* for the broadcasting sector (http://www.fsf.de), and the *Freiwillige Selbstkontrolle der Filmwirtschaft* (http://www.fsk.de) for the film industry.

343 Retrieved from: http://www.fsm.de/de/Verhaltenskodex.

344 Kommission für Jugendmedienschutz, Website, retrieved from http://www.kjm-online.de/ (on 26.07.2006) and Freiwillige Selbstkontrolle Multimedia-Diensteabieter, Website, retrieved from http://www.fsm.de/ (on 26.07.2006).

the highest state and federal authorities.[345] The task of the KJM is to ensure compliance with norms defining the protection of minors, to recognise and license the voluntary self-regulation organisations and to approve technical measures.[346] If the licensed body acts outside the scope of its discretionary power, the KJM can step in and revoke the license.[347] Only in this case, where the voluntary organisation acts outside the scope of its competences, may the KJM impose sanctions on providers that breach the law.[348] According to the criteria put forward by the HBI/EMR study, the system can be labelled co-regulatory. The Rand Europe study classified the system as being 'approved compulsory co-regulatory' (*supra*).[349]

Evaluation – An assessment by the KJM six months into the application of the new regulatory framework claimed that the new system worked satisfactorily,[350] not only because it balances the needs of content providers, consumers, and the state, but also because it fosters a paradigm of consistency throughout different media sectors. The HBI/EMR study also found that – although the system is still in its infancy – the system is more effective than the former one based solely on state regulation.[351] So, whereas there is still room for improvement, for instance regarding transparency[352] or the low

[345] Article 14, para. 3 *Jugendmedienschutz-Staatsvertrag.*

[346] Article 16, *Jugendmedienschutz-Staatsvertrag.*

[347] Hans-Bredow-Institut and EMR, Study on co-regulation measures in the media sector: Final report, Study commissioned by the European Commission, June 2006, retrieved from http://ec.europa.eu/avpolicy/docs/library/studies/coregul/final_rep_en.pdf (on 28.07.2006), 53.

[348] Article 20, para. 5 *Jugendmedienschutz-Staatsvertrag.* See also: Hans-Bredow-Institut and EMR, Study on co-regulation measures in the media sector: Final report, Study commissioned by the European Commission, June 2006, retrieved from http://ec.europa.eu/avpolicy/docs/library/studies/coregul/final_rep_en.pdf (on 28.07.2006), 53.

[349] Rand Europe (Jonathan Cave, Chris Marsden and Stephen Simmons), Options for effectiveness of Internet self- and co-regulation – Phase 3 (Final) Report, Study commissioned by the European Commission, 2008, retrieved from http://ec.europa.eu/dgs/information_society/evaluation/data/pdf/studies/s2006_05/final_report.pdf (on 30.05.2008), 27.

[350] KJM, The new German regulation for the protection of minors and digital media – The first six months, retrieved from http://ec.europa.eu/comm/avpolicy/docs/reg/minors/workshop_ring.pdf (on 26.06.2007), 4.

[351] Hans-Bredow-Institut and EMR, Study on co-regulation measures in the media sector: Final report, Study commissioned by the European Commission, June 2006, retrieved from http://ec.europa.eu/avpolicy/docs/library/studies/coregul/final_rep_en.pdf (on 28.07.2006), 134–135.

[352] Hans-Bredow-Institut and EMR, Study on co-regulation measures in the media sector: Final report, Study commissioned by the European Commission, June 2006, retrieved from http://ec.europa.eu/avpolicy/docs/library/studies/coregul/final_rep_en.pdf (on 28.07.2006), 180.

membership of the FSM,[353] on the whole, the scheme has received a rather positive rating.

C.3. *Australia*

Co-regulatory codes of practice – Another illustration of co-regulation, adopted early and often proclaimed a leading example, is the Australian Internet content regulation scheme. This scheme took effect on 1 January 2000. Inspiration was drawn from the co-operative regulatory system established with respect to broadcasting by the federal *Broadcasting Services Act 1992*.[354] This system grants broadcasters the primary responsibility for managing content by means of codes of practice which describe which content may be broadcast. This responsibility, however, is exercised within a framework of rules and 'reserve' regulatory powers, entailing that the regulator in charge – formerly the Australian Broadcasting Authority (ABA), now the Australian Communications and Media Authority (ACMA)[355] – approves and monitors compliance with the codes.[356] The *Broadcasting Services Amendment (Online Services) Act 1999* introduced the current Internet content co-regulatory scheme.[357] The scheme is based on an optimal fusion of public and industry interest, and hence enables "*public interest considerations to be addressed in a way that does not impose unnecessary financial and administrative burdens on Internet content hosts and Internet service providers*".[358]

---

353 Rand Europe (Chris Marsden et al.), Options for and effectiveness of Internet self- and co-regulation – Phase 2: Case study report, Study commissioned by the European Commission, 15.01.2008, retrieved from http://ec.europa.eu/dgs/information_society/evaluation/data/pdf/studies/s2006_05/phase2.pdf (on 06.06.2008), 123.

354 Hans-Bredow-Institut and EMR, Study on co-regulation measures in the media sector: Final report, Study commissioned by the European Commission, June 2006, retrieved from http://ec.europa.eu/avpolicy/docs/library/studies/coregul/final_rep_en.pdf (on 28.07.2006), 92.

355 The ACMA is the result of the merger of the former Australian Broadcasting Authority and the Australian Communications Authority.

356 Wright, Andree, "Coregulation of fixed and mobile Internet content, Safety and security in a networked world: balancing cyber-rights and responsibilities", Oxford Internet Institute, 8–10.09.2005, retrieved from http://www.oii.ox.ac.uk/research/cybersafety/extensions/pdfs/papers/andree_wright.pdf (on 06.06.2008), 1.

357 This Act can be found at http://www.aph.gov.au/parlinfo/billsnet/99077.pdf.

358 *Broadcasting Services Amendment (Online Services) Act*, No. 90, 1999, retrieved from http://www.comlaw.gov.au/comlaw/Legislation/Act1.nsf/0/6e2d62f72aacb92bca256f710082447e?OpenDocument&VIEWCAT=amending&COUNT=999&START=1 (on 05.01.2009), 4 (3).

Key concepts and players – The two key concepts of the scheme are the industry codes of practice and the legislative framework which encircles the codes of practice and which functions as a safety net.[359] Hence, the two key actors in the scheme are the industry and the government. On the one hand, the Internet Industry Association (IIA) develops the codes, while, on the other, the government, and more specifically ACMA, is able to intervene in two ways: firstly, it can order a non-compliant Internet Service Provider (ISP) or Internet Content Host to comply with a code, and secondly, it can establish a compulsory standard if no satisfactory code is developed by industry, or if it can be demonstrated that a registered code does not provide adequate community safeguards in relation to the matters it covers.[360] The fact that the government 'lurks' in the background is an incentive for the ISPs to act in accordance with the codes. A further incentive for compliance is the 'Family Friendly ISP' seal programme which has been created by the IIA.[361] ISPs that abide by the codes of practice are entitled to display the IIA-endorsed 'ladybird' logo on their website.[362] This seal demonstrates the engagement of the ISP with parental concerns.[363]

---

359 Wright, Andree, "Coregulation of fixed and mobile Internet content, Safety and security in a networked world: balancing cyber-rights and responsibilities", Oxford Internet Institute, 8–10.09.2005, retrieved from http://www.oii.ox.ac.uk/research/cybersafety/extensions/pdfs/papers/andree_wright.pdf (on 06.06.2008), 5.

360 Wright, Andree, "Coregulation of fixed and mobile Internet content, Safety and security in a networked world: balancing cyber-rights and responsibilities", Oxford Internet Institute, 8–10.09.2005, retrieved from http://www.oii.ox.ac.uk/research/cybersafety/extensions/pdfs/papers/andree_wright.pdf (on 06.06.2008), 7.

361 See, for instance, Part A, 5. "IIA Family Friendly Program" in: Australian Internet Industry Association, Internet Industry Codes of Practice – Codes for industry co-regulation in areas of mobile content (pursuant to the requirements of the Broadcasting Services Act 1992) as registered by the Australian Broadcasting Authority, May 2005, retrieved from http://www.iia.net.au/ContentCodes10_4.pdf (on 01.09.2005, no longer available).

362 Wright, Andree, "Coregulation of fixed and mobile Internet content, Safety and security in a networked world: balancing cyber-rights and responsibilities", Oxford Internet Institute, 8–10.09.2005, retrieved from http://www.oii.ox.ac.uk/research/cybersafety/extensions/pdfs/papers/andree_wright.pdf (on 06.06.2008), 8.

363 Coroneos, Peter, "Industry facilitated end user empowerment within a co-regulatory environment: the history and practice of online content regulation in Australia", Safety and security in a networked world: balancing cyber-rights and responsibilities, Oxford Internet Institute, 8–10.09.2005, not published, 7.

Evaluation – Evaluations of the scheme are generally positive, from the industry perspective[364] as well as the government's viewpoint.[365, 366] One of the most often cited drawbacks of pure self-regulation (especially by means of codes of practice), i.e., inefficient enforcement, seems to be effectively countered by the government safety net. In May 2004, a large-scale review of the Australian online content co-regulatory scheme was carried out. The majority of review submissions clearly supported the scheme, suggesting that it effectively meets its objectives and is in line with community views on this

---

364 The industry perspective has been voiced by Peter Coroneos, chief executive of the IIA: "*Overall, the IIA believes that the co-regulatory policy model is well suited to the rapidly evolving internet environment because it combines two key strengths: firstly, the flexibility of the rules which can adapt more easily than legislation to the changes in technology, and secondly, the backing of government which ensures the adequacy of end user protections and the uniformity of application and compliance across industry sectors to which the codes apply*": Coroneos, Peter, "Industry facilitated end user empowerment within a co-regulatory environment: the history and practice of online content regulation in Australia", Safety and security in a networked world: balancing cyber-rights and responsibilities, Oxford Internet Institute, 8–10.09.2005, not published, 9.

365 The government perspective has been expressed by Andree Wright, ACMA: "*A legislative framework administered by a competent regulatory body helps to ensure that safeguards are enforceable, and that the scheme is transparent and accountable. Reliance on industry codes of practice allows industry to meet regulatory objectives in a way that is technically and commercially feasible, and provides flexibility to address emerging concerns. An emphasis on community education, informed by research, has provided users with tools and information with which they can manage access to the internet for themselves and their children*": Wright, Andree, "Coregulation of fixed and mobile Internet content, Safety and security in a networked world: balancing cyber-rights and responsibilities", Oxford Internet Institute, 8–10.09.2005, retrieved from http://www.oii.ox.ac.uk/research/cybersafety/extensions/pdfs/papers/andree_wright.pdf (on 06.06.2008), 15.

366 See, for instance: Council of Europe, Pan-European Forum on "Human Rights in the Information Society: responsible behaviour by key actors", Palais de l'Europe, Strasbourg, France, 12–13.09.2005, retrieved from http://www.coe.int/t/dghl/standardsetting/media/doc/ForumStbgSept2005Report_en.asp#TopOfPage (on 26.07.2006), 4, which described it as a "*noteworthy example of a responsible and successful collaboration between the state and the Information Society Industry in regulating harmful content*", and that "*[o]verall, it would appear that this is a model which shows successful and effectively working co-regulation between different stakeholders*". Also Andree Wright: "*[...a] coregulatory strategic approach to managing problematic content on the 'fixed' Internet and mobile devices has delivered favourable outcomes for industry and the community, and has positioned Australia well to deal with emerging regulatory issues posed by convergence, such as those associated with new forms of mobile content*". See also: Wright, Andree, "Coregulation of fixed and mobile Internet content, Safety and security in a networked world: balancing cyber-rights and responsibilities", Oxford Internet Institute, 8–10.09.2005, retrieved from http://www.oii.ox.ac.uk/research/cybersafety/extensions/pdfs/papers/andree_wright.pdf (on 06.06.2008), 1.

issue.[367] A new code of practice for online and mobile content services was adopted in July 2008.[368]

D. *Assets and drawbacks*

Assets – The asset of a co-regulatory system mainly lies in the combination of the advantages of self-regulation – flexibility, fast adaptation, expertise and engagement of the industry – with the advantages of command-and-control regulation – most importantly legal certainty, democratic guarantees and more efficient enforcement (cf. table).[369] Especially with respect to important public policy goals, such as the protection of minors against harmful content, it is important to be able to fall back on a governmental backbone if private interests threaten to undermine them.[370] Gunningham and Rees stated that "*there is reason to believe that self-regulatory mechanisms underpinned by some form of state intervention are more resilient and effective than self-regulation in isolation*".[371] The HBI/EMR study also identified a number of advantages related to the cooperation of state and non-state regulation. According to the authors, co-regulatory systems have a chance of higher industry accountability, can benefit from the faster pace of decision-making and demonstrate a greater sustainability.[372]

---

367 Australian government, Review of the Operation of Schedule 5 to the Broadcasting Services Act 1992 – Report, 13.05.2004, retrieved from http://www.dcita.gov.au/__data/assets/pdf_file/10920/118872.pdf (on 28.07.2006, no longer available), 14.

368 Australian Internet Industry Association, Internet Industry Code of Practice – Content services code for industry co-regulation in the area of content services (pursuant to the requirements of Schedule 7 of the Broadcasting Services Act 1992 as amended), 10.07.2008, retrieved from http://www.iia.net.au/images/content_services_code_registration_version_1.0.pdf (on 24.07.2008).

369 Also, for instance: Commission of the European Communities, Communication from the Commission Simplifying and improving the regulatory environment, COM (2001) 726 final, 05.12.2001, 8: "*Co-regulation is a way of achieving flexibility and greater effectiveness*".

370 In the field of environmental policy, this asset has been recognised as well. Cf. Commission of the European Communities, Communication from the Commission to the European Parliament, the Council, the Economic and Social Committee and the Committee of the Regions of 17 July 2002 on environmental agreements at Community Level within the framework of the Action Plan on the 'Simplification and improvement of the regulatory environment', COM (2002) 412 final, 17.07.2002, 8: "*Coregulation can therefore offer the advantages of environmental agreements with the legal guarantees provided through a legislative approach*".

371 Gunningham, Neil and Rees, Joseph, "Industry self-regulation: an institutional perspective", *Law & Policy* 1997, Vol. 19, No. 4, 366.

372 Hans-Bredow-Institut and EMR, Study on co-regulation measures in the media sector: Final report, Study commissioned by the European Commission, June 2006, retrieved from http://ec.europa.eu/avpolicy/docs/library/studies/coregul/final_rep_en.pdf (on 28.07.2006), 119.

Table 5: Assets and drawbacks of legislation, self-regulation and co-regulation

Regulatory Instrument	Advantages	Disadvantages
Legislation	▪ Legal certainty (if, and only if, notions used are defined in a precise way!) ▪ Democratic guarantee ▪ Public interest is main objective	▪ Rigidity ▪ Initiative and implementation by government (thus, very limited involvement of other players) ▪ Propensity to 'censorship' when regulating content issues (for instance vis-à-vis adults) / chilling effect due to severe penalties ▪ National borders (impede effective enforcement in a borderless information society) ▪ Large regulatory cost
Self-regulation	▪ Swift reaction to public concerns ▪ Flexible tool ▪ Expertise of industry players ▪ Higher commitment if sector creates rules ▪ No / limited cost to taxpayer	▪ Credibility? Accountability? ▪ Enforceability? Compliance? ▪ Independence? (will 'independent' self-regulatory bodies dare to bite the hand that feeds them?) ▪ Private censorship? (private – commercial – organisations should not decide what content can be considered harmful) ▪ Private sector puts its own interest before the public interest ▪ Decrease in democratic quality
Co-regulation	▪ Multi-player involvement (e.g. technical expertise from industry) ▪ Higher compliance and commitment ▪ Flexibility (self-regulatory mechanisms, such as codes, can be adapted more easily than legislation) ▪ Safety net / backing of government leads to a more effective enforcement ▪ Greater democratic guarantee (attention for public interest) ▪ Higher level of transparency (when legal basis and division of tasks are clear), accountability, legitimacy	▪ Confusion / uncertainty when structure and procedures are not carefully laid out from the start, or when normative requirements are not respected

Drawbacks – However, it would not be correct to present co-regulation as a panacea without any drawbacks whatsoever. Prosser has pointed out that, in certain circumstances, co-regulatory systems do not offer the best of both worlds but the worst, "*in which neither [private or public interests are] respected and any values are subjected to unprincipled bargaining between the state and private interests*".[373] It is important to stress that co-regulatory systems need to be carefully drawn up. Normative requirements or 'process values',[374] such as transparency, adequate participation, and independence, need to be respected and the division of tasks between the different actors needs to be clearly established. Accountability and credibility are crucial requirements for the non-state components of regulation. In this context, we can remind ourselves of the success factors noted by the HBI/EMR study (*supra*). Furthermore, the exact combination of state and non-state elements will need to be structured carefully, so as not to lose the advantages of both self-regulation and traditional state regulation.[375]

E. *Interim conclusion*

Concept – In our opinion, the analysis of co-regulation proposed by the HBI/EMR study is useful, especially for conceptual purposes. It provides a number of balanced and carefully considered criteria, which are neither too strict, nor too lenient. In our opinion this framework might prove especially valuable for policymakers who contemplate using co-regulation in a certain field. They could consult this study to gain a better understanding of the concept, and to find inspiration and acquire knowledge about how a co-regulation mechanism can and should be structured in order to reach a high level of efficiency.

Added value co-regulation – Although it falls outside the scope of this legal study to provide a detailed impact assessment of co-regulation, we have attempted to provide some indications as to the potential assets and drawbacks of this regulatory instrument. We have assumed that co-regulation provides an opportunity to unite the strong points of both self- and

[373] Prosser, Tony, "Self-regulation, co-regulation and the Audio-Visual Media Services Directive", *Journal of Consumer Policy* 2008, Vol. 31, No. 1, 103.

[374] Prosser, Tony, "Self-regulation, co-regulation and the Audio-Visual Media Services Directive", *Journal of Consumer Policy* 2008, Vol. 31, No. 1, 103.

[375] Marsden, Christopher, "Co- and self-regulation in European media and Internet sectors: the results of Oxford University's study www.selfregulation.info", in: Möller, Christian and Amouroux, Arnaud (eds), *The media freedom Internet cookbook*, Vienna, OSCE, 2004, 80.

command-and-control regulation, which, in our view, is especially relevant with respect to the protection of minors against harmful media content. Of course, though, the actual success of such mechanisms will need to be evaluated on a case-by-case basis.

Co- and self-regulation – Latzer stated that "*[s]elf-regulation starts where co-regulation ends*".[376] The obvious difference between the two ARIs undoubtedly lies in the intensity of the level of government involvement in a given system. Where exactly the line can be drawn, however, is extremely complex and highly dependent on concrete circumstances. In the final chapter of this study, which will verify the compliance of the use of ARIs to protect minors against harmful content with the broader legal framework, part of the focus will be on the different levels of government involvement in self- and co-regulation, and their subsequent legal impact.

2.3.4. *Self- and co-regulation: Interim conclusion*

Regulatory continuum – We started this chapter with a brief conceptualisation of 'regulation', and proceeded with a clarification of the concepts 'command-and-control'-regulation, 'self-regulation' and 'co-regulation'. It might thus seem unexpected to state that it does not really matter which label is attached to a given regulatory instrument. This is, however, a position that is increasingly being adopted. Several scholars have argued that the different regulatory instruments can be situated along a 'regulatory continuum'.[377]

---

[376] Latzer, Michael, "Trust in the industry – Trust in the users: self-regulation and self-help in the context of digital media content in the EU", Report for working group 3 of the Expert Conference on European media policy "More trust in content – The potential of co- and self-regulation in digital media", Leipzig, 9–11.05.2007, retrieved from http://www.leipzig-eu2007.de/en/downloads/dokumente.asp (on 21.05.2008), 38.

[377] Prosser, Tony, "Self-regulation, co-regulation and the Audio-Visual Media Services Directive", *Journal of Consumer Policy* 2008, Vol. 31, No. 1, 101; Sinclair, Darren, "Self-regulation versus command and control? Beyond false dichotomies", *Law & Policy* 1997, Vol. 19, No. 4, 532; Gunningham, Neil and Rees, Joseph, "Industry self-regulation: an institutional perspective", *Law & Policy* 1997, Vol. 19, No. 4, 366; Ofcom, Initial assessments of when to adopt self- or co-regulation – Consultation, 27.03.2008, retrieved from http://www.ofcom.org.uk/consult/condocs/coregulation/condoc.pdf (on 04.04.2008), 2; Ofcom, Identifying appropriate regulatory solutions: principles for analysing self- and co-regulation: Statement, 10.12.2008, retrieved from http://www.ofcom.org.uk/consult/condocs/coregulation/statement/statement.pdf (on 30.12.2008).

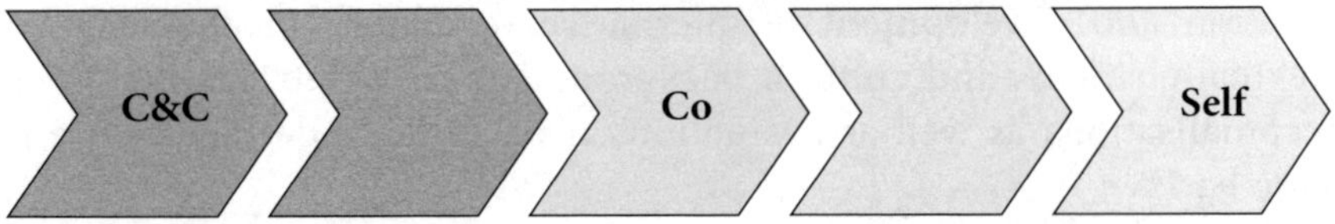

Along this continuum, different types of regulation can be positioned according to the varying levels of involvement of different players.[378] The proponents of such an approach argue that compartmentalising is artificial[379] and does not conform to reality, since perfect or idealised forms of 'pure' self-regulation or 'pure' command-and-control regulation are hardly ever found in practice.[380] We agree with the fact that restrictive definitions of regulatory concepts are 'unhelpful'[381] and, more importantly, endorse PROSSER's position that rather than categorising the different regulatory instruments, it is "*much more important to assess them through the application of normative principles*".[382] Criteria such as legitimacy, openness, participation and accountability are essential in this respect. In the next part of this study, we will go a step further and assess the compliance of self- and co-regulatory instruments with the broader legal framework.

NO MAGIC BULLET – A conclusion that has frequently been drawn with respect to conceptualisations of self- and co-regulation is that a 'magic bullet' does not exist.[383] It is not possible to devise the perfect recipe for the

---

378 PROSSER states: "*There is a continuum between different regulatory regimes with varying degrees of public and private input; what is apparent in practice is a cocktail of different techniques dependent on context*": PROSSER, Tony, "Self-regulation, co-regulation and the Audio-Visual Media Services Directive", *Journal of Consumer Policy* 2008, Vol. 31, No. 1, 101.

379 Recent examples of alternative regulatory instruments which are difficult to label are the 'European Framework for safer mobile use by younger teenagers and children' and the 'Safer social networking principles for the EU' (*supra*). These initiatives are labelled 'self-regulation' by the European Commission, but since the Commission played an active role in the establishment of the instruments and closely monitors their functioning it could also be argued that these instruments are co-regulatory.

380 GUNNINGHAM, Neil and REES, Joseph, "Industry self-regulation: an institutional perspective", *Law & Policy* 1997, Vol. 19, No. 4, 366; PROSSER, Tony, "Self-regulation, co-regulation and the Audio-Visual Media Services Directive", *Journal of Consumer Policy* 2008, Vol. 31, No. 1, 99 and 111.

381 PROSSER, Tony, "Self-regulation, co-regulation and the Audio-Visual Media Services Directive", *Journal of Consumer Policy* 2008, Vol. 31, No. 1, 111.

382 PROSSER, Tony, "Self-regulation, co-regulation and the Audio-Visual Media Services Directive", *Journal of Consumer Policy* 2008, Vol. 31, No. 1, 99.

383 MARSDEN, Christopher, "Co- and self-regulation in European media and Internet sectors: the results of Oxford University's study www.selfregulation.info", in: MÖLLER, Christian and AMOUROUX, Arnaud (eds), *The media freedom Internet cookbook*, Vienna, OSCE,

conception and development of alternative regulatory mechanisms, since contextual elements and cultural backgrounds play a critical role.[384] Hence, conceptualisations as well as evaluations need to be undertaken on a case-by-case basis.

ARIs and the protection of minors against harmful content – Protecting minors against harmful media content is one of the fields in which especially co-regulatory mechanisms have mushroomed. Furthermore, these systems have often proved successful. The overview of assets and drawbacks offered above provided some – theoretical – indications as to the reasons for this success. There remains, however, one aspect of the use of alternative regulatory instruments to protect minors that we have so far not elaborated on. From our literature review (and some of the illustrations provided above), it emerged that alternative regulatory instruments often fall back on or make use of what we call 'regulatory tools', i.e., technology and supporting mechanisms, such as media literacy, education and awareness. The next section aims to delve deeper into the use of these 'regulatory tools'.

2.3.5. *Regulatory tools: Technology*

A. *Technology: alternative regulatory instrument or regulatory tool?*

The answer to the machine is in the machine.
Charles Clark[385]

Technology and public policy goals – Since the rise of the Internet, and especially during the early years of its rapidly growing popularity, it has often been suggested that technology be used to deal with emerging problematic issues, such as the protection of minors against harmful content. It was claimed that if the problem originated in the technology, then the

---

2004, 86; Hans-Bredow-Institut and EMR, Study on co-regulation measures in the media sector: Final report, Study commissioned by the European Commission, June 2006, retrieved from http://ec.europa.eu/avpolicy/docs/library/studies/coregul/final_rep_en.pdf (on 28.07.2006), 177.

384 Marsden, Christopher, "Co- and self-regulation in European media and Internet sectors: the results of Oxford University's study www.selfregulation.info", in: Möller, Christian and Amouroux, Arnaud (eds), *The media freedom Internet cookbook*, Vienna, OSCE, 2004, 86.

385 Clark, Charles, "The answer to the machine is in the machine", in: Hugenholtz, P. Bernt (ed.), *The future of copyright in a digital environment*, The Hague, Kluwer Law International, 139.

answer was also to be found in the technology.[386] Of course, this was not a totally new phenomenon uniquely related to the Internet. In the United States and Canada, for instance, the 'V-chip' was implemented to protect minors against harmful broadcasting content. This system entailed that a technical device – the so-called 'viewer'-chip or 'violence'-chip – was built into the television set or into a decoder to enable blocking of inappropriate content according to its classification.[387]

Regulation or regulatory tool? – It has been argued that technology is a form of regulation, similar to law (cf. 'Code is law', *infra*). Others, on the other hand, see it as "*tools that those regulating might use*".[388] This was an issue that Black touched upon in her discussion of the different definitions of 'regulation': although she did not offer a final opinion on whether technology by itself constitutes regulation, she referred to both possibilities. In our opinion, however, the use of technology to regulate, or to implement a policy goal, seldom stands alone. More often, it is part of a regulatory strategy, frequently an alternative regulatory strategy.[389] It is important to

---

[386] Cf. Clark, Charles, "The answer to the machine is in the machine", in: Hugenholtz, P. Bernt (ed.), *The future of copyright in a digital environment*, The Hague, Kluwer Law International, 139.

[387] For more information on the v-chip, cf. Price, Monroe (ed.), *The V-chip debate: content filtering from television to the internet*, Mahwah, Lawrence Erlbaum Associates, 1998, 363 p.; Spitzer, Matthew, "A first glance at the constitutionality of the V-chip ratings system", 335–384, in Hamilton, James T. (ed.), *Television violence and public policy*, Ann Arbor, The University of Michigan Press, 1998, 394 p.; Kirsch, Steven J., *Children, adolescents and media violence: A critical look at the research*, Thousand Oaks CA, Sage Publications, 2006, 311; Etzioni, Amitai, "On protecting children from speech", *Chicago-Kent Law Review* 2004, Issue 79, 24 *et seq.* Cf. also http://www.fcc.gov/vchip/ and http://www.cbsc.ca/english/agvot/index.php; Federal Communications Commission, Report in the matter of Implementation of the Child Safe Viewing Act; Examination of parental control technologies for video or audio programming, 31.08.2009, retrieved from http://hraunfoss.fcc.gov/edocs_public/attachmatch/FCC-09-69A1.pdf (on 20.01.2010).

[388] Black, Julia, "Critical reflections on regulation", Discussion paper, January 2002, retrieved from http://www.lse.ac.uk/collections/CARR/pdf/DPs/Disspaper4.pdf (on 08.04.2008), 14 and 16. Brownsword and Yeung also use the notion 'technology as a regulatory tool': Brownsword, Roger and Yeung, Karen (eds), *Regulating technologies: legal futures, regulatory frames and technological fixes*, Oxford, Hart Publishing, 2008, 7.

[389] Cf. also Latzer, Michael, "Trust in the industry – Trust in the users: self-regulation and self-help in the context of digital media content in the EU", Report for working group 3 of the Expert Conference on European media policy "More trust in content – The potential of co- and self-regulation in digital media", Leipzig, 9–11.05.2007, retrieved from http://www.leipzig-eu2007.de/en/downloads/dokumente.asp (on 21.05.2008), 61: "*Forms of self-help can be used in various combinations with self-, co- and governmental regulation (e.g. in filter and rating systems) […]*".

note, however, that this does not mean that we disagree totally with the proponents of the other view. It is possible that for other policy goals than the one we are working with, this theory is perfectly applicable. However, with respect to the protection of minors against harmful digital content, we have observed that the use of technology is almost always part of a larger (often alternative) regulatory strategy (*infra*).

Code is law – Although we do not fully agree with the "*Code is law*"-theorem,[390] the ideas behind it are of great value to any writing regarding regulation and technology.[391] In 1999 – still early days in Internet history – Lessig advanced the idea that cyberspace could be regulated, not, however, by statutes, but instead primarily through 'code'.[392, 393] He stated that there are

---

390 Another notion that is used is "*Code as Code*", the second 'Code' meaning Civil Code or Penal Code. Cf. Koops, Bert-Jaap and Lips, Miriam, "Wie reguleert het internet? Horizontalisering en rechtsmacht bij de technische regulering van het internet" ["*Who regulates the internet? Horizontalisation and jurisdiction with regard to technical regulation of the internet*"], in: Franken, Hans et al., *Zeven essays over informatietechnologie en recht* [*Seven essays on information technology and law*], Den Haag, SDU, 262 [in Dutch]. Lessig also distinguishes between 'East Coast Code' (code as in statutes; East Coast since the issuing of federal statutes in the United States is a Washington D.C. or 'East Coast' activity) and 'West Coast Code' (code as in code that writers create, i.e., the instructions embedded in software and hardware; West Coast since in the United States this is primarily a Silicon Valley or 'West Coast' activity). Cf. Lessig, Lawrence, *Code and other laws of cyberspace*, New York, Basic Books, 1999, 53.

391 Lessig, Lawrence, *Code and other laws of cyberspace*, New York, Basic Books, 1999, 297 p. An update of this book is also available: Lessig, Lawrence, *Code version 2.0*, New York, Basic Books, 2006, retrieved from http://pdf.codev2.cc/Lessig-Codev2.pdf (on 09.06.2008). Cf. also Lessig, Lawrence, "The Code is the law", The Industry Standard, 09.04.199, retrieved from http://www.lessig.org/content/standard/0,1902,4165,00.html (on 09.06.2008). Lessig also discusses his theory elsewhere: Lessig, Lawrence, "What things regulate speech: CDA 2.0 vs. filtering", *Jurimetrics* 1998, Vol. 38, No. 4, 629–670.

392 Lessig, Lawrence, *Code and other laws of cyberspace*, New York, Basic Books, 1999, 20.

393 Lessig's theory has provoked substantial criticism: Kleve, Pieter and De Mulder, Richard, "Code is Murphy's law", *International Review of Law, Computers and Technology* 2005, Vol. 19, No. 3, 317–327; Post, David, "What Larry doesn't get: code, law, and liberty in Cyberspace", *Stanford Law Review* 2000, Vol. 52, 1439–1459; Dommering, Egbert, "Regulating technology: code is not law", 1–16, in Dommering, Egbert and Asscher, Lodewijk (eds), *Coding regulation: essays on the normative role of information technology*, The Hague, TMC Asser Press, 301 p.; Wu, Tim, "When Code isn't law", *Virginia Law Review* 2003, Vol. 89, 101–170.

four different constraints on human behaviour: the law, social norms,[394] the market and architecture[395] (i.e., 'technology').[396] LESSIG clarified:

> *The constraints are distinct, yet they are plainly interdependent. Each can support or oppose the others. Technologies can undermine norms and laws; they can also support them. Some constraints make others possible; others make some impossible. Constraints work together, though they function differently and the effect of each is distinct. Norms constrain through the stigma that a community imposes; markets constrain through the price that they exact; architectures constrain through the physical burdens they impose; and law constrains through the punishment it threatens.*[397]

LESSIG argued that, in cyberspace, these four types of constraints – law (e.g. copyright law), norms (e.g., so-called 'netiquette'), market (e.g., pricing) and technology or 'code' (e.g., hardware or software) – are active.[398] He observed that code can set certain features, embed certain values or make certain values impossible.[399] Hence, in his view, code too is regulation.[400] However, further on, LESSIG noted that "*the code of cyberspace is becoming just another tool of state regulation*".[401] What we can deduce from these statements is that, in all probability, it does not matter that much whether we perceive technology to

---

394 I.e., "*the many slight and sometimes forceful sanctions that members of a community impose on each other*", "*a norm governs socially salient behaviour, deviation from which makes you socially abnormal*": LESSIG, Lawrence, *Code and other laws of cyberspace*, New York, Basic Books, 1999, 234.

395 MURRAY and SCOTT pointed out that the importance of architecture as a basis for regulation was not new. They referred to Jeremy BENTHAM's design of the 'Panopticon prison' as an illustration of the potential for controls to be built into architecture. Cf. MURRAY, Andrew and SCOTT, Colin, "Controlling the new media: hybrid responses to new forms of power", *The Modern Law Review* 2002, Vol. 65, No. 4, 500. Cf. also LAMBERS, Rik, "Code and speech. Speech control through network architecture", in: DOMMERING, Egbert and ASSCHER, Lodewijk (eds), *Coding regulation: essays on the normative role of information technology*, The Hague, TMC Asser Press, 91.

396 LESSIG, Lawrence, *Code and other laws of cyberspace*, New York, Basic Books, 1999, 87. For more on these different constraints, cf. the Appendix, 235 *et seq*.

397 LESSIG, Lawrence, *Code and other laws of cyberspace*, New York, Basic Books, 1999, 88.

398 These four modalities of regulation were reconceived by Andrew MURRAY and Colin SCOTT as 'hierarchy', 'community', 'competition' and 'design'. Cf. MURRAY, Andrew and SCOTT, Colin, "Controlling the new media: hybrid responses to new forms of power", *The Modern Law Review* 2002, Vol. 65, No. 4, 491–516.

399 LESSIG, Lawrence, *Code and other laws of cyberspace*, New York, Basic Books, 1999, 89.

400 LESSIG, Lawrence, *Code and other laws of cyberspace*, New York, Basic Books, 1999, 89.

401 LESSIG, Lawrence, *Code and other laws of cyberspace*, New York, Basic Books, 1999, 99.

be 'regulation' or a 'regulatory tool'. The fact that technology can be used to further a public interest goal is the conclusion that matters most.[402]

DARK CLOUDS ON THE TECHNO-REGULATORY SKY? – It is of the utmost importance, however, to point out that using technology as a regulatory tool has not been presented as a uniquely positive response to the clash of current information and communication networks and the use of traditional regulation. This is because, although in certain instances, resorting to technology or 'code' can have a positive influence on rights and freedoms, 'code' can also, at the same time, be used to limit freedoms. AHLERT, for instance, has argued that it should be carefully assessed who asserts control over code.[403] Private parties, for example, could quite easily use code to censor certain kinds of speech, without being held accountable. He warned:

> *Technical systems incorporate 'political properties' and the code and standards design and implementation processes for the Internet are 'regulative mechanisms' which have to be examined in detail in order to understand their various and subtle impacts on the way we are able to communicate online.*[404]

Furthermore, it is not always clear when code has been altered to achieve certain goals – and these goals are not necessarily in the valid public interest. In this context, LESSIG emphasised the importance of transparency when building regulatory objectives into code. He argued that *"[w]hat a code regu-*

---

[402] Other scholars have also contributed to the development of theories regarding technology and regulation. Cf., for instance: REIDENBERG, Joel, "Lex informatica: the formulation of information policy rules through technology", *Texas Law Review* 1998, Vol. 76, No. 3, 553–584; AHLERT, Christian, "Technologies of control: how code controls communication", 199–136, in: HARDY, Christiane and MÖLLER, Christian (eds), *Spreading the word on the Internet: 16 answers to 4 questions (Reflections on Freedom of the Media and the Internet Amsterdam Conference, June 2003)*, Vienna, OSCE, 2003, 224 p., retrieved from http://www.osce.org/publications/rfm/2003/06/12245_103_en.pdf (on 23.04.2007); BROWNSWORD, Roger, "Code, control, and choice: why East is East and West is West", *Legal Studies* 2005, Vol. 25, No. 1, 1–21; DOMMERING, Egbert and ASSCHER, Lodewijk (eds), *Coding regulation: essays on the normative role of information technology*, The Hague, TMC Asser Press, 301 p.; KESAN, Jay and SHAH, Rajiv, "Deconstructing code", *Yale Journal of Law & Technology* 2003, Vol. 64, 277–389; SHAH, Rajiv C. and KESAN, Jay P., "Manipulating the Governance Characteristics of Code", *Info* 2003, Vol. 5, No. 4, 3–9.

[403] AHLERT, Christian, "Technologies of control: how code controls communication", in: HARDY, Christiane and MÖLLER, Christian (eds), *Spreading the word on the Internet: 16 answers to 4 questions (Reflections on Freedom of the Media and the Internet Amsterdam Conference, June 2003)*, Vienna, OSCE, 2003, 129.

[404] AHLERT, Christian, "Technologies of control: how code controls communication", in: HARDY, Christiane and MÖLLER, Christian (eds), *Spreading the word on the Internet: 16 answers to 4 questions (Reflections on Freedom of the Media and the Internet Amsterdam Conference, June 2003)*, Vienna, OSCE, 2003, 134.

lation does should be at least as apparent as what a legal regulation does".[405] In his approach to 'techno-regulation', BROWNSWORD detected concerns related to accountability, transparency, responsibility, respect and human dignity.[406] On the one hand, he argued that democratic and efficient governance entails that regulatees should be informed of regulatory objectives and formal regulatory positions.[407] BROWNSWORD warned that these values are put at risk if regulatory objectives are attained through unclear and indirect 'techno-regulation'.[408] He identified two problems:

> *One threat arises from regulators, who, favouring indirect over direct approaches, and insouciant to the values of transparency and accountability, deviate from the canons of good governance. The other arises from the embedded nature of West Coast Solutions; even where regulators act with meticulous concern for transparency and accountability, designed solutions may become so embedded in everyday life that it is only outsiders and historians who can trace the invisible hand of regulation.*[409]

On the other hand, BROWNSWORD also expressed his worries about the lack of choice for regulatees when the technological design of products or spaces only offers one 'appropriate' way of acting (of which the regulatees might, moreover, not even be aware). In his opinion,

> *Ultimately, then, the question boils down to this: if we are regulated so that we can only do the right thing, does it matter that we lose the opportunity to do the wrong thing? To which, I am inclined to respond: if techno-regulators know how to stop us from being bad, but only by, at the same time stopping us from being good, maybe the East Code, for all its imperfections, has something going for it.*[410]

TECHNOLOGY IN COMPLIANCE WITH THE LEGAL FRAMEWORK? – Within the scope of this legal study, our main concern is that the use of technology to achieve certain policy goals, often functioning as a tool to implement alternative regulatory strategies, is in compliance with the broader legal framework. This issue will be addressed in the next part.

---

405 LESSIG, Lawrence, *Code and other laws of cyberspace*, New York, Basic Books, 1999, 224.

406 BROWNSWORD, Roger, "Code, control, and choice: why East is East and West is West", *Legal Studies* 2005, Vol. 25, No. 1, 14–20.

407 BROWNSWORD, Roger, "Code, control, and choice: why East is East and West is West", *Legal Studies* 2005, Vol. 25, No. 1, 14.

408 BROWNSWORD, Roger, "Code, control, and choice: why East is East and West is West", *Legal Studies* 2005, Vol. 25, No. 1, 15.

409 BROWNSWORD, Roger, "Code, control, and choice: why East is East and West is West", *Legal Studies* 2005, Vol. 25, No. 1, 17.

410 BROWNSWORD, Roger, "Code, control, and choice: why East is East and West is West", *Legal Studies* 2005, Vol. 25, No. 1, 20.

B. *Technology and the protection of minors*

Policy documents: is technology the panacea? – In the early policy documents related to Internet content,[411] emphasis was already often put on technology to deal with the growing concerns regarding minors and harmful content.[412] Filtering tools, for instance, for online and mobile content, and 'child lock' systems applicable to digital television content, were promoted from the outset of the digital era,[413] and have frequently been hailed as the

---

[411] Such as Commission of the European Communities, Green Paper on the protection of minors and human dignity in audiovisual and information services, COM (1996) 483 final, 16.10.1996, Annex IV Technical and other non-regulatory protection measures, 2. Parental control devices applied to on-line services; Commission of the European Communities, Communication to the European Parliament, the Council, the Economic and Social Committee and the Committee of the Regions, Illegal and harmful content on the Internet, COM (1996) 487 final, 16.10.1996; recital 12 Council Recommendation 98/560/EC of 24 September 1998 on the development of the competitiveness of the European audiovisual and information services industry by promoting national frameworks aimed at achieving a comparable and effective level of protection of minors and human dignity, *OJ* 07.10.1998, *L* 270, 48. For a detailed overview cf. also: Füg, Oliver Carsten, "Content ratings harmonization and the protection of minors in the European Information Society", 165–186, in: Ward, David (ed.), *The European Union and the culture industries: regulation and the public interest*, Aldershot, Ashgate, 2008, 264 p.

[412] As mentioned above, technology had already been proposed as a regulatory tool for broadcasting. Cf. Commission of the European Communities, Green Paper on the protection of minors and human dignity in audiovisual and information services, COM (1996) 483 final, 16.10.1996, Annex IV Technical and other non-regulatory protection measures, 1. Parental control devices applied to television broadcasting. See also: PCMLP, Study on parental control of television broadcasting, 1999, retrieved from http://ec.europa.eu/comm/avpolicy/info_centre/library/studies/index_en.htm (on 11.06.2008); Commission of the European Communities, Communication from the Commission to the Council, the European Parliament, and the Economic and Social Committee – Study on parental control of television broadcasting, COM (99) 371 final, 19.07.1999; PCMLP, Parental control in a converged communications environment: self-regulation, technical devices and meta-information (Final report for the DVB Regulatory Group), October 2000, retrieved from http://ec.europa.eu/comm/avpolicy/docs/reg/minors/dvbgroup.pdf (on 11.06.2008).

[413] Commission of the European Communities, Green Paper on the protection of minors and human dignity in audiovisual and information services, COM (1996) 483 final, 16.10.1996; Commission of the European Communities, Communication to the European Parliament, the Council, the Economic and Social Committee and the Committee of the Regions, Illegal and harmful content on the Internet, COM (1996) 487 final, 16.10.1996, retrieved from http://ec.europa.eu/archives/ISPO/legal/en/internet/communic.html (on 27.07.2006). The proposal for the 2006 Recommendation also promoted the use of filtering systems: Commission of the European Communities, Amended proposal for a Recommendation of the European Parliament and of the Council on the protection of minors and human dignity and the right of reply in relation to the competitiveness

answer to all concerns regarding children and potentially damaging images and information. However, at the same time, the use of technical solutions has often been the object of harsh criticism. The ease with which these tools can be circumvented, even by people with rather limited technical skills, has been one of the most often cited drawbacks. In an era where children and teenagers often have a far greater knowledge of new technologies than their parents or teachers, this is not an unrealistic worry.

User empowerment – On the other hand, technical tools embody the promising trend towards user empowerment.[414] Mifsud Bonnicci and De Vey Mestdagh have argued that this concept of 'user empowerment' can be seen as the mirror image of the right to free speech: "*one has the right to publish harmful content (since it is not illegal to do so), while the recipient has the right to determine what content to receive and not to receive*".[415] Furthermore, they claimed that the "*role of regulation of harmful content is to create the necessary conditions within which the user can freely exercise his or her right to decide what content to receive and block*".[416] Technology can be a tool to implement this decision. Latzer calls this 'self-help by users' or 'technology-based self-restriction'.[417] Hence, control over which content is thought appropriate to watch is shifted from governments – who need to be very careful when restricting the distribution of content and, therefore, the freedom of expression of its citizens, children included (*infra*) – to parents and teachers, who can then decide for themselves which content

of the European audiovisual and information services industry, COM (2006) 31 final, 20.01.2006, II.1.

414 Commission of the European Communities, Proposal for a Decision of the European Parliament and of the Council on establishing a multiannual Community programme on promoting safer use of the Internet and new online technologies, COM (2004) 91 final, 12.03.2004, 17; Helberger, Natali, "From eyeball to creator – Toying with audience empowerment in the Audiovisual Media Service Directive", *Entertainment Law Review* 2008, No. 6, 128–137.

415 Mifsud Bonnici, Jeanne P. and De Vey Mestdagh, Cees N.J., "Right vision, wrong expectations: the European Union and self-regulation of harmful Internet content", *Information & Communications Technology Law* 2005, Vol. 14, No. 2, 144.

416 Mifsud Bonnici, Jeanne and De Vey Mestdagh, Cees, "Right vision, wrong expectations: the European Union and self-regulation of harmful Internet content", *Information & Communications Technology Law* 2005, Vol. 14, No. 2, 146.

417 Latzer, Michael, "Trust in the industry – Trust in the users: self-regulation and self-help in the context of digital media content in the EU", Report for working group 3 of the Expert Conference on European media policy "More trust in content – The potential of co- and self-regulation in digital media", Leipzig, 9–11.05.2007, retrieved from http://www.leipzig-eu2007.de/en/downloads/dokumente.asp (on 21.05.2008), 61.

they think is suitable for their children. While this is undoubtedly a positive development – certainly from the point of view of the protection of freedom of expression – it does require parents and teachers to actually take up their responsibility.

C. *Illustrations*

TECHNICAL TOOLS TO PROTECT CHILDREN – Many technical options exist to protect children against harmful digital media content. A significant number of these technical tools primarily focus on Internet content. What follows is a brief overview of the most common systems that are currently available.

C.1. *Filtering*

FILTERING INAPPROPRIATE CONTENT – Filtering has always been a part of our everyday life.[418] Everyone, consciously or unconsciously, filters content. Whether it is by selecting one particular newspaper to read everyday or by opting to go watch one movie and not another one, a filtering process takes place. Today's technical innovations, however, enable parents to consciously apply filtering systems to television content (by means of the V-chip in the United States, for instance (*supra*), or through options provided by digital television menus)[419]

---

[418] LAMBERS, Rik, "Code and speech. Speech control through network architecture", in DOMMERING, Egbert and ASSCHER, Lodewijk (eds), *Coding regulation: essays on the normative role of information technology*, The Hague, TMC Asser Press, 105.

[419] Regarding digital television, available mechanisms can vary from blocking access to specific channels, to filtering certain content on the basis of labels or classifications (e.g., sexual or violent images) or barring the on-demand function. The Commission already emphasised filtering possibilities for digital television in: COMMISSION OF THE EUROPEAN COMMUNITIES, Communication from the Commission to the Council, the European Parliament, the Economic and Social Committee and the Committee of the Regions, Principles and guidelines for the Community's audiovisual policy in the digital age, COM (1999) 657 final, 14.12.1999. See also: OFCOM, Ofcom's response to the Byron review – Annex 3: TV content regulation and child protection: policy, practice and user tools, 30.11.2007, retrieved from http://www.ofcom.org.uk/research/telecoms/reports/byron/annex3.pdf (on 04.07.2008), 15–18.

and (fixed and mobile)[420] Internet content.[421, 422] The use of filtering tools is a prime example of the shift away from top-down state control. Filtering technologies present a way of transferring control of and responsibility for managing harmful content from governments, regulatory agencies, and supervisory bodies to end users, primarily parents.[423, 424]

---

420 For more information on filtering on mobile phones: cf. EUROPEAN COMMISSION, Consultation paper: Child safety and mobile phone services, 25.07.2006, retrieved from http://ec.europa.eu/information_society/activities/sip/public_consultation/index_en.htm (on 25.07.2006).

421 For more information on Internet content filtering, cf. ROSENBERG, Richard, "Controlling access to the Internet: the role of filtering", *Ethics and Information Technology* 2001, Vol. 3, No. 1, 35–54; AKDENIZ, Yaman, "Who watches the watchmen? The role of filtering software in Internet content regulation", 101–121, in: MÖLLER, Christian and AMOUROUX, Arnaud (eds), *The media freedom Internet cookbook*, Vienna, OSCE, 2004, 274 p., retrieved from http://www.osce.org/publications/rfm/2004/12/12239_89_en.pdf (on 29.02.2008); D'UDEKEM-GEVERS, Marie and POULLET, Yves, "Internet content regulation: concerns from a European use empowerment perspective about Internet content regulation: an analysis of some recent statements – Part II", *Computer Law & Security Report* 2002, Vol. 18, No. 1, 11–23; PCMLP, Parental control in a converged communications environment: self-regulation, technical devices and meta-information (Final report for the DVB Regulatory Group), 2000, retrieved from http://ec.europa.eu/comm/avpolicy/docs/reg/minors/dvbgroup.pdf (on 11.06.2008); INTERNET SAFETY TECHNICAL TASK FORCE, Enhancing child safety & online technologies: final report of the Internet safety technical task force to the Multi-State working group on social networking of State Attorneys General of the United States, 31.12.2008, retrieved from http://cyber.law.harvard.edu/publications/2009/ISTTF_Final_Report (on 20.01.2010); DEIBERT, Ronald, PALFREY, John, ROHOZINSKI, Rafal, and ZITTRAIN, Jonathan (eds), *Access denied: the practice and policy of global Internet filtering*, Cambridge, MIT Press, 2008, 449 p.; AUSTRALIAN COMMUNICATIONS AND MEDIA AUTHORITY, Developments in Internet filtering technologies and other measures for promoting online safety – Second annual report to the Minister for Broadband, Communications and the Digital Economy, April 2009, retrieved from http://www.acma.gov.au/webwr/_assets/main/lib310554/developments_in_internet_filters_2ndreport.pdf (on 20.01.2010).

422 Internet content filtering has been described as follows: "*Internet content filtering refers to the use of computer hardware or software to screen content and control users' access to that content. Most commonly, it is used to exclude from access content that is deemed to be objectionable or that falls into certain predetermined categories of content deemed to be inappropriate for a given user*": ACMA, Developments in internet filtering technologies and other measures for promoting online safety, 2007, retrieved from http://www.acma.gov.au/webwr/_assets/main/lib310554/developments_in_internet_filters_1streport.pdf (on 13.06.2008).

423 BERTELSMANN FOUNDATION, Self-regulation of Internet Content, 1999, retrieved from http://www.cdt.org/speech/BertelsmannProposal.pdf (on 12.06.2008).

424 Put another way, filtering promotes parental bottom-up control rather than top-down censorship by state agencies. Cf.: COMMISSION OF THE EUROPEAN COMMUNITIES, Communication to the European Parliament, the Council, the Economic and Social Committee

Filtering has also been used to implement both legislative[425] and alternative[426] regulatory strategies.

FILTERING AND THE EU – At the EU level, filtering has been advocated as a tool to deal with harmful Internet content since the first documents related to this issue appeared. The Green Paper on the protection of minors and human dignity, the Communication on illegal and harmful content and the 1998 Recommendation all suggested the use of filtering to address the issue of harmful content. Later documents confirmed this trend.[427] Commissioner REDING also voiced her belief in filtering to protect minors against harmful content when she stated that "*[the Commission] firmly believes that rating and labelling of content combined with media literacy and technological solutions, such as user controlled filtering, are key tools to address these important issues*".[428] The same trend was also noticeable at the Council of Europe level.[429]

---

and the Committee of the Regions, Illegal and harmful content on the Internet, COM (1996) 487 final, 16.10.1996. Also on the subject of filter technology, in the case *Ashcroft v. American Civil Liberties Union et al.*, S. Ct. No. 03–218, slip opinion at 9, 15 (June 29, 2004), the U.S. Supreme Court stated that "*[f]ilters impose selective restrictions on speech at the receiving end, not universal restrictions at the source. [...] Promoting filter use does not condemn as criminal any category of speech, and so the potential chilling effect is eliminated, or at least much diminished*".

425 In France, for instance, access providers are legally obliged to inform their subscribers of the existence of technical tools which allow for the restriction or selection of access to certain content, and to offer them one of these tools. This leaves the final decision to the end user. Article 43–7 *Loi n° 86–1067 du 30 septembre 1986 relative à la liberté de communication* [*Act regarding the freedom of communication*], J.O.R.F. 01.10.1986, retrieved from http://www.legifrance.gouv.fr/affichTexte.do?cidTexte=LEGITEXT000006068930&dateTexte=20090105 (on 05.01.2009) [in French].

426 The UK Code of conduct for mobile operators, for instance, offers the opportunity to apply a filter to mobile content (cf. *supra*).

427 For instance: EUROPEAN PARLIAMENT AND COUNCIL Recommendation 2006/952/EC of 20 December 2006 on the protection of minors and human dignity and on the right of reply in relation to the competitiveness of the European audiovisual and on-line information services industry, *OJ* 27.12.2007, *L* 378, 72.

428 REDING, Viviane, Freedom of the media, effective co-regulation and media literacy: cornerstones for an efficient protection of minors in the European Union, Speech at the ICRA Roundtable Brussels 'Mission Impossible', Brussels, 14.06.2006, retrieved from http://europa.eu.int/rapid/pressReleasesAction.do?reference=SPEECH/06/374&type=HTML&aged=0&language=EN&guiLanguage=en (on 15.06.2006).

429 Cf. COUNCIL OF EUROPE (COMMITTEE OF MINISTERS), Recommendation Rec(2001)8 on self-regulation concerning cyber content (self-regulation and user protection against illegal or harmful content on new communications and information services), 05.09.2001, retrieved from https://wcd.coe.int/ViewDoc.jsp?id=220387&Site=COE&BackColorInternet=DBDCF2&BackColorIntranet=FDC864&BackColorLogged=FDC864 (on 24.04.2007);

Different filtering systems – There are various kinds of filtering systems. The five most common systems are 'white-list' filtering, 'black-list' filtering,[430] filtering based on neutral labelling, keyword filtering and image analysis filtering. The first category blocks all content except content that has been considered appropriate and consequently been put on a 'white list'.[431] Such a mechanism is highly restrictive since it prevents access to any website that has not been put on this 'white list'.[432] The second category blocks access to content that has been deemed inappropriate (for instance, because of violent or sexual content) and has been put on a 'black list'. Such lists need to be updated constantly in order for the system to remain effective.[433, 434] Thirdly,

---

Council of Europe (Committee of Ministers), Declaration on freedom of communications on the Internet, 28.05.2003, retrieved from https://wcd.coe.int/rsi/common/renderers/rend_standard.jsp?DocId=37031&SecMode=1&SiteName=cm&Lang=en (on 24.04.2007); Council of Europe (Committee of Ministers), Recommendation CM/Rec(2008)6 on measures to promote the respect for freedom of expression and information with regard to Internet filters, 26.03.2008, retrieved from https://wcd.coe.int/ViewDoc.jsp?Ref=CM/Rec(2008)6&Language=lanEnglish&Ver=original&BackColorInternet=9999CC&BackColorIntranet=FFBB55&BackColorLogged=FFAC75 (on 31.03.2008).

430 White-list and black-list filtering are systems that work on the basis of 'URL filtering'.

431 Commission of the European Communities, Communication to the European Parliament, the Council, the Economic and Social Committee and the Committee of the Regions, Illegal and harmful content on the Internet, COM (1996) 487 final, 16.10.1996, retrieved from http://europa.eu.int/ISPO/legal/en/internet/communic.html (on 27.07.2006), 20. Certain Internet browsers provide parents with the opportunity to enter such a white list (e.g. Internet Explorer).

432 A type of white-list filtering is 'a walled garden', which entails a closed space being created in which children can freely navigate. Their Internet use is limited to that space. Specialised kids browsers are another example of 'white-list' filtering. An example of such a kid-friendly browser is 'KidZui': cf. The Wall Street Journal (Walter S. Mossberg), KidZui's parent plan lets children explore in safe corner of Web, 20.03.2008, retrieved from http://online.wsj.com/article/SB120597536349250547.html (on 31.03.2008). Cf. also Council of Europe (Committee of Ministers), Recommendation CM/REC(2009)5 on measures to protect children against harmful content and behaviour and to promote their active participation in the new information and communications environment, 08.07.2009, retrieved from https://wcd.coe.int/ViewDoc.jsp?id=1470045&Site=CM (on 20.01.2010), which recommends the use of "*safe and secure spaces for children on the Internet*".

433 Commission of the European Communities, Green Paper on the protection of minors and human dignity in audiovisual and information services, COM (1996) 483 final, 16.10.1996, 19.

434 While it falls not within the scope of this thesis to make recommendations on the best choice of filtering systems, in our opinion, the use of filtering tools to protect children should be strongly linked to age. Whereas 'walled gardens' or 'white-list' filtering systems can be particularly suitable for very young children, they are not necessarily appropriate for older children, who need to learn how to navigate the web in a responsible way. Cf. also: Ofcom, Ofcom's response to the Byron review – Statement, 27.03.2008, retrieved

there are systems which filter content on the basis of labelling (added to certain websites by the content providers themselves or by third parties). Parents can then instruct the filter to block content according to the labels they think are appropriate or not.[435] A fourth type of filtering system works on the basis of keywords. Such systems block content on the basis of keywords that are selected (for instance, sex, breast, etc.). Finally, certain filters use image analysis to block certain content. These systems are primarily used to block sexual images, as they automatically (attempt to) detect nudity.

Criticism – Filtering technologies, however, have been the subject of significant criticism due to their possible 'over-inclusiveness' or 'under-inclusiveness', their lack of accountability,[436] and the ease of circumvention.[437] The complaint most often levelled at filtering tools is that they are either over- or under-inclusive.[438] In other words, a number of filters block words that are inoffensive in the given context (for instance, 'breast' cancer), while other material that can be considered offensive is not flagged or filtered at all.[439]

---

from http://www.ofcom.org.uk/research/telecoms/reports/byron/byron_review.pdf (on 04.07.2008), 68–69.

[435] Such systems are, for instance, built into Internet browsers (e.g. Microsoft Internet Explorer: cf. http://www.microsoft.com/windows/ie/ie6/using/howto/security/contentadv/config.mspx, or the Apple Operating System: cf. http://www.apple.com/macosx/features/parentalcontrols.html).

[436] McIntyre, TJ and Scott, Colin, "Internet filtering: rhetoric, legitimacy, accountability and responsibility", in: Brownsword, Roger and Yeung, Karen (eds), *Regulating technologies: legal futures, regulatory frames and technological fixes*, Oxford, Hart Publishing, 2008, 111.

[437] See, for instance, Akdeniz, Yaman, "Who watches the watchmen? The role of filtering software in Internet content regulation", 101–121, in: Möller, Christian and Amouroux, Arnaud (eds), *The media freedom Internet cookbook*, Vienna, OSCE, 2004, 274 p., retrieved from http://www.osce.org/publications/rfm/2004/12/12239_89_en.pdf (on 29.02.2008); Ofcom, Ofcom's response to the Byron Review – Annex 2: Current tools and approaches to protecting children from harmful content online, 30.11.2007, retrieved from http://www.ofcom.org.uk/research/telecoms/reports/byron/annex2.pdf (on 04.07.2008), 18–19.

[438] Cf. Heins, Marjorie, Cho, Christina and Feldman, Ariel, Internet Filters – A public policy report, Brennan Center for Justice at NYU School of Law, 2006, retrieved from http://www.fepproject.org/policyreports/filters2.pdf (on 22.05.2006).

[439] In 2005, the European Commission commissioned a benchmarking study aimed at objectively assessing filtering software and services that are currently available. In 2008, the final report of the study was published: Deloitte et al., Safer Internet: Protecting our children on the net using content filtering and parental control techniques – Test and benchmark of products and services to voluntarily filter Internet content for children between 6 and 16 years, Study commissioned by the European Union, 2008, retrieved from http://ec.europa.eu/information_society/activities/sip/docs/project_reports/sip_bench_2008_synthe-

This issue is problematic with respect to the fundamental right to freedom of expression.[440] We will examine this in the next part of this study. Nonetheless, if filtering software is not seen as an infallible remedy to protect minors against harmful content, but as an empowerment tool which provides parents with the possibility to decide for themselves what content their children can and cannot see, it can be a very useful instrument.[441]

C.2. *Rating and labelling*

Rating and protection of minors – In order to be able to make a rational and well-balanced decision about which content is appropriate for children, rating, labelling and classification mechanisms are invaluable. This decision can either be made consciously by parents each time a child watches a film or programme, or can be made by a preset filtering system. Content rating has played a role in the protection of minors for a long time.[442] In every

---

sis_report_en.pdf (on 22.12.2008). Although the three-year study found that it witnessed some significant evolutions in filtering technology, for instance, both accuracy and convenience have improved, it also identified new challenges, for example with respect to user-generated content and social networking. However, according to the study, "*filtering tools are capable of filtering potentially harmful content without seriously degrading the Internet experience of the youngsters*" (p. 6).

440 Cf. Council of Europe (Committee of Ministers), Recommendation CM/Rec(2008)6 on measures to promote the respect for freedom of expression and information with regard to Internet filters, 26.03.2008, retrieved from https://wcd.coe.int/ViewDoc.jsp?Ref=CM/Rec(2008)6&Language=lanEnglish&Ver=original&BackColorInternet=9999CC&BackColorIntranet=FFBB55&BackColorLogged=FFAC75 (on 31.03.2008). See also: Weitzner, Daniel, "Yelling 'filter' on the crowded Net: the implications of user control technologies", in: Price, Monroe (ed.), *The V-chip debate: content filtering from television to the internet*, Mahwah NJ, Lawrence Erlbaum Associates, 1998, 214.

441 It is important to stress that users should apply filters on a voluntary basis (*infra*, Part 2, Chapter 1). Cf. The organization for security and co-operation in Europe & Reporters sans Frontières, Joint declaration on guaranteeing media freedom on the Internet, 17–18.06.2005, retrieved from https://www.osce.org/documents/rfm/2005/06/15239_en.pdf (on 13.06.2008); Council of Europe (Committee of Ministers), Recommendation Rec(2001)8 on self-regulation concerning cyber content (self-regulation and user protection against illegal or harmful content on new communications and information services), 05.09.2001, retrieved from https://wcd.coe.int/ViewDoc.jsp?id=220387&Site=COE&BackColorInternet=DBDCF2&BackColorIntranet=FDC864&BackColorLogged=FDC864 (on 24.04.2007). Governments, on the other hand, should promote, rather than mandate and enforce, the use of filters: cf. Möller, Christian and Amouroux, Arnaud (eds), *The media freedom Internet cookbook*, Vienna, OSCE, 2004, 19.

442 For more sociological information on ratings cf., for instance: Greenberg, Bradley S. and Rampoldi-Hnilo, Lynn, "Child and parent responses to the age-based and content-based television ratings", in: Singer, Dorothy G. and Singer, Jerome, L., *Handbook of children*

European Member State, for instance, a film classification regime is part of the regulatory framework. In the United States, television programmes are rated according to the TV parental guidelines.[443] The guidelines provide age ratings which can be used to filter content by means of the V-chip (*supra*).[444] The Dutch cross-media *Kijkwijzer* system, which was described above as an illustration of a co-regulatory system (*supra*), also functions on the basis of age classification and content labelling. With respect to Internet content, rating and labelling is not as evident, given the enormous amounts of information available on the World Wide Web. However, efforts were already undertaken in the mid-1990s to set up a content rating standard. The W3C Consortium developed PICS (Platform for Internet Content Selection),[445] "*a standardised machine-readable format for describing content in an HTML file*",[446] and the Internet Content Rating Association created a rating system[447, 448] based on a vocabulary that functions on PICS.[449] Subsequently, filtering software which

and the media, Thousand Oaks, Sage Publications, 2001, 621–634; Cantor, Joanne, Harrison, Kristen and Krcmar, Marina, "Ratings and advisories: implications for the new ratings system for television", 179–211, in: Hamilton, James T. (ed.), *Television violence and public policy*, Ann Arbor, The University of Michigan Press, 1998, 394 p.

443 For more information, cf. http://www.tvguidelines.org/index.htm. See also: Hamilton, James T., "Who will rate the ratings?", 133–156, in: Price, Monroe (ed.), *The V-chip debate: content filtering from television to the internet*, Mahwah NJ, Lawrence Erlbaum Associates, 1998, 363 p.

444 See also: Heins, Marjorie, "Three questions about television ratings", 47–58, in: Price, Monroe (ed.), *The V-chip debate: content filtering from television to the internet*, Mahwah NJ, Lawrence Erlbaum Associates, 1998, 363 p.

445 For more information, cf. http://www.w3.org/PICS/. Cf. also: Lessig, Lawrence, "What things regulate speech: CDA 2.0 vs. filtering", *Jurimetrics* 1998, Vol. 38, No. 4, 658 *et seq.*; PCMLP, Parental control in a converged communications environment: Self-regulation, technical devices and meta-information (Final report for the DVB Regulatory Group), 2000, retrieved from http://ec.europa.eu/comm/avpolicy/docs/reg/minors/dvbgroup.pdf (on 11.06.2008), 31 *et seq.*; Martin, Dianne, "An alternative to government regulation and censorship: content advisory systems for interactive media", 179–194, in: Price, Monroe (ed.), *The V-chip debate: content filtering from television to the internet*, Mahwah, Lawrence Erlbaum Associates, 1998, 363 p.

446 PCMLP, Parental control in a converged communications environment: Self-regulation, technical devices and meta-information (Final report for the DVB Regulatory Group), 2000, retrieved from http://ec.europa.eu/comm/avpolicy/docs/reg/minors/dvbgroup.pdf (on 11.06.2008), 6.

447 For more information, cf. http://www.fosi.org/icra/.

448 The Internet Explorer browser, for instance, uses the ICRA rating system.

449 At the moment, ICRA primarily uses a more recently developed standard, i.e., RDF (Resource Description Framework), also a W3C recommendation. For more information, cf. http://www.w3.org/RDF/.

can read these ratings can be used to filter out content that parents consider inappropriate. The system, however, requires that content providers themselves rate their content by means of a questionnaire: one can wonder how many content providers actually do rate their content.[450] The system is thus by no means foolproof. Finally, labelling also plays an important role when it comes to videogames.[451] The video game sector is unique since it is the only sector in which a pan-European labelling system is operative. The Pan-European Game Information (PEGI) system, based on the Dutch '*Kijkwijzer*' system, provides off- and on-line video games with an age recommendation and a content description.[452]

Different rating mechanisms – Different types of rating or labelling mechanisms exist. Kirsh distinguishes between evaluative systems, descriptive systems and hybrid systems.[453] The first category consists of systems which provide parents with advice on which content might be considered

---

[450] ICRA, for instance, does not provide any statistics on its website. Lambers has criticised the system: "*At first sight PICS was a fine initiative, aside from the more general objections against filtering expressed before. It would bring about empowerment of the user and keep censorship out of the hands of the state. Or so it was thought, because until now it has not been much of a success and it is questionable if it ever will be: as a system for end-users, or as a governmental tool, for that matter*": Lambers, Rik, "Code and speech. Speech control through network architecture", in: Dommering, Egbert and Asscher, Lodewijk (eds), *Coding regulation: essays on the normative role of information technology*, The Hague, TMC Asser Press, 124.

[451] Cf. Council Resolution of 1 March 2002 on the protection of consumers, in particular young people, through the labelling of certain video games and computer games according to the age group, 2002/C 65/02, *OJ* 14.03.2002, *C* 65, 2.

[452] For more information: http://www.pegi.info and http://www.pegionline.eu/en/index/. See also: European Commission, Background report on cross media rating and classification and age verification solutions, Safer Internet Forum Luxembourg, 25–26.09.2008, retrieved from http://ec.europa.eu/information_society/activities/sip/docs/pub_consult_age_rating_sns/reportageverification.pdf (on 19.11.2008); Reding, Viviane, Self regulation applied to interactive games: success and challenges, speech at the ISFE Expert Conference, Brussels, 26.06.2007, retrieved from http://europa.eu/rapid/pressReleasesAction.do?reference=SPEECH/07/429&type=HTML&aged=0&language=EN&guiLanguage=en (on 22.05.2008); Reding, Viviane, Video games: let's go for PEGI Plus, Speech at the Annual Conference Interactive Software Federation of Europe, Brussels, 07.05.2008, retrieved from http://ec.europa.eu/commission_barroso/reding/docs/speeches/2008/brussels-20080507.pdf (on 21.05.2008); Byron, Tanya, Safer children in a digital world: the report of the Byron review, 27.03.2008, retrieved from http://www.dfes.gov.uk/byronreview/ (on 04.07.2008), 163 *et seq*.

[453] Kirsch, Steven J., *Children, adolescents and media violence: a critical look at the research*, Thousand Oaks CA, Sage Publications, 2006, 300 *et seq*.

inappropriate, by means of age-based recommendations or cautionary warnings. The second category of systems provides details on the specific content of the material that is being rated. Such systems, for instance, describe material as containing violence, sexual images or swearing. Hybrid systems combine evaluative and descriptive ratings. The Dutch *Kijkwijzer* system (*supra*) is an example of a hybrid rating system.

The future of ratings – It has been argued that the continually growing number of content delivery methods makes it increasingly difficult to rate content on an *ex ante* basis.[454] Labelling all content circulating on the Internet indeed seems a Sisyphean task. Hence, *ex post* methods with efficient consumer complaint mechanisms may be considered more appropriate in the future.[455, 456] Although EU policy documents have already called for the establishment of a system of common descriptive symbols,[457] such a uni-

454 Olsberg / SPI et al., Empirical study on the practice of the rating of films distributed in cinemas, television, DVD and videocassettes in the EU and EEA Member States: Final report, Study commissioned by the European Commission, May 2003, retrieved from http://ec.europa.eu/avpolicy/docs/library/studies/finalised/studpdf/rating_finalrep2.pdf, (on 22.12.2008), 110.

455 Olsberg / SPI et al., Empirical study on the practice of the rating of films distributed in cinemas, television, DVD and videocassettes in the EU and EEA Member States: Final report, Study commissioned by the European Commission, May 2003, retrieved from http://ec.europa.eu/avpolicy/docs/library/studies/finalised/studpdf/rating_finalrep2.pdf, (on 22.12.2008), 111. See also: Reding, Viviane, Minors and media: towards a more effective protection, speech at the Workshop of scientists in the field of protection of minors on media violence, self-regulation and media literacy, Brussels, 10.09.2003, retrieved from http://www.ebu.ch/CMSimages/en/INFOEN_090_tcm6–8328.pdf (on 13.06.2008).

456 An example might be YouTube, where videos can be flagged as 'inappropriate' by users/viewers (because they consider the content sexual, violent or repulsive, hateful or abusive, a harmful dangerous act, or spam, or because the content infringes their rights). The YouTube community guidelines state that "*we review the video to determine whether it violates our Terms of Use – flagged videos are not automatically taken down by the system. If we remove your video after reviewing it, you can assume that we removed it purposefully, and you should take our warning notification seriously*" (retrieved from http://www.youtube.com/t/community_guidelines (on 04.07.3008).

457 European Parliament and Council Recommendation 2006/952/EC of 20 December 2006 on the protection of minors and human dignity and on the right of reply in relation to the competitiveness of the European audiovisual and on-line information services industry, *OJ* 27.12.2007, *L* 378, 72. For a similar appeal in the UK, cf. Ofcom, Ofcom's strategy and priorities for the promotion of media literacy – A statement, 2004, retrieved from http://www.ofcom.org.uk/consult/condocs/strategymedialit/ml_statement/strat_prior_statement.pdf (on 13.06.2008), section 6: Common labelling of audiovisual materials, 11.

form system across Europe might seem unfeasible because of the differences in cultural sensitivities from Member State to Member State.[458] However, given the border-crossing nature of the new media, an agreement on which symbols or categories of age groups to use throughout the European Union would already be an improvement. The implementation could then still be tailored to the local needs. Inspiration could be drawn from the Dutch *Kijkwijzer* system and the Pan-European Game Information System (PEGI) for video games (*supra*).[459]

Trustmark – In this context, it can be noted that the Council of Europe has advocated the development of a pan-European trustmark for labelling systems of online content.[460] A number of criteria are proposed: (1) adherence to human rights principles and standards, including the right to provide for effective means of recourse and remedy (for example, the possibility to re-assess labelling when users and/or creators of online content claim that content has been incorrectly labelled; (2) provision and use of labelling systems on a voluntary basis, both by creators/authors and users; (3) inadmissibility of any form of censorship of content; (4) respect for the editorial independence of media and media-like online content services; and (5) regular review of the labelled content.

C.3. *Parental monitoring and notification software*

Monitoring and Notification – Another tool for parents to exercise some form of control over their children's Internet use is software that allows parents to check their child's online behaviour or software that notifies parents of certain actions undertaken by their children on the Internet. Monitoring

---

458 In 2008, a public consultation was launched by the European Commission: European Commission, Public consultation: Age verification, cross media rating and classification, online social networking, June 2008, retrieved from http://ec.europa.eu/information_society/activities/sip/docs/pub_consult_age_rating_sns/pc_2008_info_questions_en.pdf (on 17.06.2008). On the feasibility of a pan-European rating system, cf. also: Füg, Oliver Carsten, "Content ratings harmonization and the protection of minors in the European Information Society", 165–186, in: Ward, David (ed.), *The European Union and the culture industries: regulation and the public interest*, Aldershot, Ashgate, 2008, 264 p.

459 Palzer, Carmen, "Horizontal rating of audiovisual content in Europe. An alternative to multi-level classification?", *Iris Plus* 2003, No. 10, 2–8.

460 Council of Europe (Committee of Ministers), Recommendation CM/REC(2009)5 on measures to protect children against harmful content and behaviour and to promote their active participation in the new information and communications environment, 08.07.2009, retrieved from https://wcd.coe.int/ViewDoc.jsp?id=1470045&Site=CM (on 20.01.2010).

software keeps a 'log' of children's Internet usage: it is able to generate an overview of which websites they visited, which e-mails or instant messages they sent, and even which words they were typing.[461] Such software often also allows parents to restrict the amount of time children can spend on the Internet. Notification software warns parents of certain actions of their children on the Internet, such as, for example, the creation of a MySpace page.[462] Parents can then, for instance, check if their children have registered with the correct age and if they have revealed personal details on their page.

PRIVACY ISSUES – Monitoring children's Internet behaviour has sometimes been compared to parents reading their children's private diaries. It is evident that such mechanisms raise some serious privacy concerns. The compliance of such technologies with fundamental rights will be examined in the second part of this study.

C.4. *Identification mechanisms*

IDENTIFICATION AND AGE VERIFICATION MECHANISMS – In real life, children are often prevented from accessing inappropriate material based on their appearance. A shopkeeper, for instance, will (in most cases) be able to tell that a ten-year-old child has not reached the appropriate age to buy cigarettes, pornography or weapons. In the online world, of course, this facial identification mechanism is lacking. Hence, preventing children from being confronted with harmful online content by limiting their access to such content needs to happen by means of online identification mechanisms, ranging

[461] THIERER, Adam, "Parental controls and online child protection: a survey of tools and methods", July 2007, retrieved from http://www.pff.org/parentalcontrols/Parental%20Controls%20&%20Online%20Child%20Protection%20%5BVersion%202.2%5D.pdf (on 18.01.2008). See also: WEEKES, Russel B., "Cyber-zoning a mature domain: the solution to preventing inadvertent access to sexually explicit content on the Internet", *Virginia Journal of Law and Technology* 2003, Vol. 8, No. 4, retrieved from http://www.vjolt.net/vol8/issue1/v8i1_a04-Weekes.pdf (on 16.06.2008), 14–15.

[462] NET FAMILY NEWS (Anne COLLIER), A look at MySpace software for parents, 12.01.2007, retrieved from http://www.netfamilynews.org/nl0701specialreport.html (on 13.06.2008).

from the provision of credit card details[463] to digital certificates,[464] online identity tokens and electronic identity cards.[465, 466]

Illustration: use of the e-ID – An illustration of the use of an identification mechanism to protect minors against online harm is 'SaferChat', a Belgian government initiative in cooperation with the Belgian Internet Service Providers Association.[467] This public-private partnership established a system that requires the use of a child's electronic identity card to gain access to a 'safe' chatroom ('safe' in this instance means that only children will be pres-

[463] As discussed above, in the United States, legislation was enacted to protect minors from harmful content. Both the CDA and COPA (*supra*) relied on the verification of the user's identity, for instance, by requiring a credit card or debit account number. Cf. also Lessig, Lawrence, "What things regulate speech: CDA 2.0 vs. filtering", *Jurimetrics* 1998, Vol. 38, No. 4, 647 *et seq.*; Nunziato, Dawn C., Technology and pornography, The George Washington University Law School Public Law and Legal Theory Working Paper No. 324, retrieved from http://papers.ssrn.com/sol3/papers.cfm?abstract_id=1003394 (on 11.01.2007), 1–2. For Australian legislation based on access controls and age verification, cf. ACMA, Restricted access systems declaration, 2007, retrieved from http://www.acma.gov.au/WEB/STANDARD/pc=PC_310905 (on 16.06.2008).

[464] Digital certificates have been defined as "*digital objects cryptographically signed by a certification authority, a widely trusted entity that verifies an individual or organizational identity before issuing a certificate*": Lessig, Lawrence and Resnick, Paul, "Zoning speech on the Internet: a legal and technical model", *Michigan Law Review* 1999, Vol. 98, No. 2, 406. And Lessig, Lawrence, "What things regulate speech: CDA 2.0 vs. Filtering", *Jurimetrics* 1998, Vol. 38, No. 4, 649: "*Digital certificates are encrypted digital objects that make it possible for the holder of the certificate to make credible assertions about himself*".

[465] The Council of Europe, for instance, encouraged states to use "*conditional access tools by content and service providers with regard to content harmful to minors, such as age-verification systems, personal identification codes, passwords, encryption and decoding systems or access through cards with an electronic code*": Council of Europe (Committee of Ministers), Recommendation Rec(2001)8 on self-regulation concerning cyber content (self-regulation and user protection against illegal or harmful content on new communications and information services), 05.09.2001, retrieved from https://wcd.coe.int/ViewDoc.jsp?id=220387&Site=COE&BackColorInternet=DBDCF2&BackColorIntranet=FDC864&BackColorLogged=FDC864 (on 24.04.2007).

[466] For recent reports on age verification solutions, cf. European Commission, Background report on cross media rating and classification and age verification solutions, Safer Internet Forum Luxembourg, 25–26.09.2008, retrieved from http://ec.europa.eu/information_society/activities/sip/docs/pub_consult_age_rating_sns/reportageverification.pdf (on 19.11.2008); Australian Communications and media authority, Developments in Internet filtering technologies and other measures for promoting online safety – Second annual report to the Minister for Broadband, Communications and the Digital Economy, April 2009, retrieved from http://www.acma.gov.au/webwr/_assets/main/lib310554/developments_in_internet_filters_2ndreport.pdf (on 20.01.2010).

[467] For more information [in Dutch and French], see: http://www.saferchat.be/.

ent in this chatroom, and hence no adults with possible bad intentions). All children above the age of twelve received a free card reader in an attempt to promote this feature. In order to verify the age of a person wanting to access a particular 'safe' chatroom, the National Registry identification number embedded in the electronic identity card is used.[468] However, even apart from serious privacy concerns (which will be examined in the next part of this study), the system has not proven successful at all.

Age verification and social networking – The debate regarding age verification has been revived over the past couple of years subsequent to the rise in popularity of social networks.[469] Although this debate focuses mostly on preventing contact between children and sexual predators, it has also provided an opportunity to evaluate current age verification systems. The results have not been positive. It has been claimed that age verification is not feasible,[470] nor effective.[471] On top of these practical issues, there are

---

[468] Commissie voor de bescherming van de persoonlijke levenssfeer [*Commission for privacy protection*], Advies met betrekking tot het ontwerp van koninklijk besluit betreffende het elektronisch identiteitsdocument voor Belgische kinderen onder de twaalf jaar [*Recommendation regarding the proposal for Royal Decree with respect to the electronic identity document for Belgian children under the age of twelve*], 06.09.2006, retrieved from http://www.privacycommission.be/nl/docs/Commission/2006/advies_33_2006.pdf (on 02.10.2006) [in Dutch].

[469] In 2008, a public consultation was launched by the European Commission: European Commission, Public consultation: Age verification, cross media rating and classification, online social networking, June 2008, retrieved from http://ec.europa.eu/information_society/activities/sip/docs/pub_consult_age_rating_sns/pc_2008_info_questions_en.pdf (on 17.06.2008).

[470] The most important problem is that there are few official reliable records that can be consulted to check children's identity. Children do not have credit cards or driving licenses, and are not included in other databases such as voter records (primarily a U.S. phenomenon). One could argue that, for instance, in Belgium, the e-ID or the social security card could be used. However, serious privacy issues are linked to the use of these documents (*infra*, Part 2, Chapter 2).

[471] Financial Times, Out of MySpace, 16.10.2007, retrieved from http://www.ft.com/cms/s/0/37d523fe-7c12-11dc-be7e-000779fd2ac.html?nclick_check=1 (on 14.01.2008, no longer available); The Wall Street Journal (Emily Steel and Julia Angwin), MySpace receives more pressure to limit children's access to site, 23.06.2006, retrieved from http://online.wsj.com/public/article/SB115102268445288250-YRxkt0rTsyyf1QiQf2EPBYSf7iU_20070624.html?mod=tff_main_tff_top (on 16.06.2008); USA Today (Anick Jesdanun), Age verification at social-network sites could prove difficult, 14.07.2008, retrieved from http://www.usatoday.com/tech/news/internetprivacy/2006-07-17-age-check-proves-difficult_x.htm (on 16.06.2008); Thierer, Adam, "Social networking and age verification: many hard questions; no easy solutions", Progress on Point 14.5, March 2007, retrieved from http://papers.ssrn.com/sol3/papers.cfm?abstract_id=976936 (on 16.06.2008), 13 *et*

also significant concerns regarding fundamental rights such as freedom of expression and privacy (*infra*).[472] THIERER has argued that even if these concerns could be remedied, "*[p]erfect age verification is a quixotic objective*". He warned not to provide parents with a false sense of security, nor to drive young people away from mainstream websites – which are accountable to a certain degree – towards offshore sites.[473]

C.5. *Domain names*

ATTEMPTS TO CREATE ONLINE 'RED LIGHT DISTRICTS'... – There have been two different attempts at protecting minors against harmful content by means of domain names. On the hand, it has been suggested to create a top level domain '.xxx' with which all websites with sexually oriented content could be labelled. The creation of such a domain would facilitate filtering of adult content. Significant criticism, however, was directed at the plan.[474] One of the weak points, for instance, is that the system would rely on the goodwill of adult content providers, since moving to the new '.xxx' domain would be voluntary.[475] Consequently, up until now, the domain has not been officially created.[476]

---

seq.; OFCOM, Ofcom's response to the Byron review – Statement, 27.03.2008, retrieved from http://www.ofcom.org.uk/research/telecoms/reports/byron/byron_review.pdf (on 04.07.2008), 65–66.

472 THIERER, Adam, "Social networking and age verification: many hard questions; no easy solutions", Progress on Point 14.5, March 2007, retrieved from http://papers.ssrn.com/sol3/papers.cfm?abstract_id=976936 (on 16.06.2008), 3.

473 THIERER, Adam, "Social networking and age verification: many hard questions; no easy solutions", Progress on Point 14.5, March 2007, retrieved from http://papers.ssrn.com/sol3/papers.cfm?abstract_id=976936 (on 16.06.2008), 3.

474 BBC NEWS, Net porn plan labelled 'obscene', 03.06.2005, retrieved from http://news.bbc.co.uk/1/hi/technology/4606125.stm (on 13.06.2008); BERNERS-LEE, Tim, "New Top Level Domains .mobi and .xxx considered harmful", 2004, retrieved from http://www.w3.org/DesignIssues/TLD (on 13.06.2008).

475 BBC NEWS, Plan for .xxx porn domain dropped, 11.05.2006, retrieved from http://news.bbc.co.uk/2/hi/technology/4760459.stm (on 13.06.2008); NET CONSUMERS, Policy document: the use of rating systems, website quality assurance schemes and options for domain names, 2002, retrieved from http://www.net-consumers.org/policy/domain.htm#three (on 13.06.2008).

476 BBC NEWS, Plan for .xxx porn domain dropped, 11.05.2006, retrieved from http://news.bbc.co.uk/2/hi/technology/4760459.stm (on 13.06.2008); ICANN, Board rejects .xxx domain application, 30.03.2007, retrieved from http://www.icann.org/en/announcements/announcement-30mar07.htm (on 22.12.2008).

...and safe havens – On the other hand, reversing the logic above, the creation of a '.kid' domain, which would gather child-friendly websites, has also been suggested.[477] This idea was particularly controversial since it has been argued that such a domain attracts adults with questionable intentions.[478] Moreover, a similar domain has been established in the United States,[479] without much success.[480]

D. *Interim conclusion*

Not a panacea – As the Internet Safety Technical Task Force concluded:

> *Technology can play a helpful role, but there is no one technological solution or specific combination of technological solutions to the problem of online safety for minors.*[481]

There is an array of technical tools that could be employed in the battle against harmful media (and especially Internet) content. Filtering, combined with rating or labelling, is most often included in regulatory strategies

[477] The idea was first launched in the United States with the enactment of the *Dot Kids Implementation and Efficiency Act of 2002* (retrieved from http://thomas.loc.gov/cgi-bin/query/D?c107:1:./temp/~c1078vCBTm::), and then copied in Europe, in the proposals for the 2006 Recommendation on the protection of minors. Cf. European Parliament, Report on the proposal for a recommendation of the European Parliament and of the Council on the protection of minors and human dignity and the right of reply in relation to the competitiveness of the European audiovisual and information services industry, A6–0244/2005, 19.07.2006, retrieved from http://www.europarl.europa.eu/sides/getDoc.do?pubRef=-//EP//NONSGML+REPORT+A6–2005–0244+0+DOC+PDF+V0//EN&language=EN (on 05.07.2007), Explanatory memorandum, IV. 1, 22 and 30; and European Parliament and Council Recommendation 2006/952/EC of 20 December 2006 on the protection of minors and human dignity and on the right of reply in relation to the competitiveness of the European audiovisual and on-line information services industry, *OJ* 27.12.2007, *L* 378, 72. So far, however, no concrete actions in Europe have been taken regarding such a domain.

[478] Net Consumers, Policy document: the use of rating systems, website quality assurance schemes and options for domain names, 2002, retrieved from http://www.net-consumers.org/policy/domain.htm#three (on 13.06.2008).

[479] For more information, cf. http://www.kids.us/content_policy/content.html.

[480] Reuters (Andy Sullivan), PluggedIn: Not much to do in kids' online domain, 03.06.2005, retrieved from http://massis.lcs.mit.edu/telecom-archives/TELECOM_Digest_Online2005–1/4801.html (on 20.12.2008).

[481] Internet safety technical task force, Enhancing child safety & online technologies: final report of the Internet safety technical task force to the Multi-State working group on social networking of State Attorneys General of the United States, 31.12.2008, retrieved from http://cyber.law.harvard.edu/publications/2009/ISTTF_Final_Report (on 20.01.2010), 6.

related to the protection of minors. Other tools are slightly less common, but available nonetheless. We have noted that, with respect to almost all technical tools, there are often fundamental rights concerns: it is important to be reminded of the fact that any use of technology to advance a public policy goal needs to comply with the broader legal framework. This issue will be analysed in depth in the next part of this study.

User empowerment – It is also imperative to re-emphasise the fact that the use of certain technical tools, especially when their use is decided upon by parents or teachers, provides great opportunities with respect to user empowerment. This trend implies that control over which content can be accessed lies in the hands of the user, and not the government. Yet, for user empowerment techniques to be reasonably effective, it is essential that 'users' – primarily parents – are not only aware of these techniques, but are also able and prepared to use them in a efficient way. This is where the next type of regulatory tools – i.e., supporting mechanisms – comes into play.

2.3.6. *Regulatory tools: Supporting mechanisms*

Supporting mechanisms – In recent years, policymakers have devoted more and more attention to what we call 'supporting mechanisms' in the struggle to protect minors against harmful media content. As experience with digital technologies increases, the idea that media literacy, education and awareness campaigns are indispensable to effectively protect minors has grown. Such supporting mechanisms have been advocated extensively at the European level,[482] and are, hence, regular components of recent regulatory strategies.

Media literacy – For the past few years, media literacy has been one of the buzzwords of media policy. Although this concept is certainly not limited to new digital technologies,[483] the complexity of these new technologies has

[482] By the European Union (*infra*) as well as the Council of Europe, for instance: Council of Europe (Committee of Ministers), Recommendation CM/REC(2009)5 on measures to protect children against harmful content and behaviour and to promote their active participation in the new information and communications environment, 08.07.2009, retrieved from https://wcd.coe.int/ViewDoc.jsp?id=1470045&Site=CM (on 20.01.2010).

[483] "*Media literacy relates to all media, including television and film, radio and recorded music, print media, the Internet and other new digital communication technologies*": European Commission, "What is media literacy?", retrieved from http://ec.europa.eu/avpolicy/media_literacy/index_en.htm (on 17.07.2008). On media literacy in traditional media, cf., for instance, McCannon, Bob, "Media literacy: What? Why? How?", 322–365, in: Strasburger, Victor C. and Wilson, Barbara J., *Children, adolescents & the media*, Thousand Oaks, Sage Publications, 2002, 539 p.

amplified the importance of media literacy, which has been defined as "*the ability to access the media, to understand and to critically evaluate different aspects of the media and media contents and to create communications in a variety of contexts*".[484, 485] The new information and communication technologies present difficulties on different levels. The fact that these technologies are user-centric – and thus provide more control to users[486] – implies that more knowledge and 'literacy' is required to process information in an adequate way.[487] Although the significance of media literacy is not limited to the protection of minors against harmful content,[488] this public policy goal, is, however, still of vital importance.[489] Most parents (and teachers) are not as

---

[484] Commission of the European Communities, Communication from the Commission to the European Parliament, the Council, the European Economic and Social Committee and the Committee of the Regions "A European approach to media literacy in the digital environment", COM (2007) 833 final, 20.12.2007, 3. For more information on the concept of media literacy, cf. Celot, Paolo (ed.), Study on assessment criteria for media literacy levels: A comprehensive view of the concept of media literacy and an understanding of how media literacy levels in Europe should be assessed, Study commissioned by the European Commission, October 2009, retrieved from http://ec.europa.eu/avpolicy/media_literacy/docs/studies/eavi_study_assess_crit_media_lit_levels_europe_finrep.pdf (on 21.01.2010).

[485] Art Silverblatt developed a more detailed and comprehensive definition: "*Media literacy emphasises the following elements: a critical thinking skill that allows audiences to develop independent judgments about media content; an understanding of the process of mass communication; an awareness of the impact of media on the individual and society; the development of strategies with which to discuss and analyse media usages; an awareness of media content as a 'text' that provides insight into our contemporary culture and ourselves; the cultivation of an enhanced enjoyment, understanding, and appreciation of media content; and in the case of media communicators, the ability to produce effective responsible media messages*": as quoted in: Strasburger, Victor C. and Wilson, Barbara J., *Children, adolescents & the media*, Thousand Oaks, Sage Publications, 2002, 438.

[486] When (analogue) television was the prime medium, a limited number of broadcasters offered a limited number of programmes in a linear schedule, over which the user could not exercise any control. Although media literacy was also, without a doubt, required then as well (in terms of content), today's digital media consumption presents other (and more complicated) challenges.

[487] For more information, cf. "Raising media and Internet literacy: activities, projects and resources", in: Carlsson, Ulla (ed.), *Regulation, awareness, empowerment. Young people and harmful media content in the digital age*, Göteborg, The International Clearinghouse on Children, Youth and Media, 2006, 155 *et seq.*

[488] Cf. Commission of the European Communities, Communication from the Commission to the European Parliament, the Council, the European Economic and Social Committee and the Committee of the Regions, "A European approach to media literacy in the digital environment", COM (2007) 833 final, 20.12.2007, 3–4.

[489] Buckingham, David, "Children and new media", in: Lievrouw, Leah A. and Livingstone, Sonia, *Handbook of new media – Social shaping and social consequences of ICTs*, London, Sage Publications, 2006, 87: "*Simply providing children with technology is not*

technically skilled as their children and often feel uncomfortable when using these new technologies.[490] Children, on the other hand, are confronted with an enormous amount of information coming from countless sources all over the world. Media literacy can help both parents and children to cope with these challenges. As the 2007 Audiovisual Media Services Directive puts it:

> *Media-literate people are able to exercise informed choices, understand the nature of content and services and take advantage of the full range of opportunities offered by new communications technologies. They are better able to protect themselves and their families from harmful or offensive material.*[491]

MEDIA LITERACY, EDUCATION AND THE EU – The European Commission has paid an increasing amount of attention to the topic of media literacy in the past couple of years.[492, 493] In 2006, a Media Literacy Expert Group[494] was set up and a public consultation was launched,[495] which resulted in a

---

enough: we have to enable them to develop the intellectual and cultural competencies that are required to select, interpret and utilize it. Despite the optimism of some advocates, children do not automatically know how to use new media technology, let alone evaluate what it provides". For research on children's media literacy, cf. OFCOM, Media literacy audit, Report on media literacy among children, 02.05.2006 retrieved from www.ofcom.org.uk/advice/media_literacy/medlitpub/medlitpubrss/children/ (on 16.06.2008). Also OFCOM, Ofcom's response to the Byron review – Statement, 27.03.2008, retrieved from http://www.ofcom.org.uk/research/telecoms/reports/byron/byron_review.pdf (on 04.07.2008), 55 *et seq*.

[490] BBC NEWS, Net-illiterate 'failing children', 28.04.2005, retrieved from http://news.bbc.co.uk/1/hi/uk/4490879.stm (on 17.06.2008); THE GUARDIAN (Alexandra SMITH), Teachers lack knowledge on Internet safety, report reveals, 10.05.2006, retrieved from http://education.guardian.co.uk/schools/story/0,,1771667,00.html (on 17.06.2008); CNET NEWS (Stefanie OLSEN), Parents shaky about kids' safety online, 10.08.2006, retrieved from http://www.news.com/2009-1025_3-6104028.html (on 11.01.2008).

[491] Recital 37 AVMS Directive (*infra*).

[492] Support for media literacy and education is not limited to Europe. In the United States a number of initiatives have also been taken. Cf. for instance: THIERER, Adam, "Rep. Bean's 'Safer NET act': an education-based approach to online safety", Progress on Point 14.3, February 2007, retrieved from http://papers.ssrn.com/sol3/papers.cfm?abstract_id=975507 (on 17.06.2008); and THIERER, Adam, "Parents have many tools to combat objectionable media content", Progress on Point 13.9, April 2006, retrieved from http://www.pff.org/issues-pubs/pops/pop13.9contenttools.pdf (on 06.07.2006).

[493] HELBERGER, Natali, "The Media-Literate Viewer", in: VAN EIJK, Nico and HUGENHOLTZ, Bernt (eds), *Dommering-bundel: Opstellen over informatierecht aangeboden aan prof. mr. E.J. Dommering*, Amsterdam, Otto Cramwinckel Uitgever, 2008, 141.

[494] For more information, cf. http://ec.europa.eu/avpolicy/media_literacy/expert_group/index_en.htm.

[495] RAPID, Making sense of today's media content: Commission begins public media literacy consultation, IP/06/1326, 06.10.2006, retrieved from http://europa.eu.int/rapid/press

Communication on A European approach to media literacy in the digital environment.[496] This Communication listed all initiatives that had already been taken, provided an overview of best practices and called on Member States to take action.[497] One of these actions the Commission proposed was to "*develop and implement codes of conduct and, as appropriate, co-regulatory frameworks in conjunction with all interested parties at national level, and promote self-regulatory initiatives*".[498] Commissioner REDING made it very clear that media literacy is one of the cornerstones of the protection of minors:

> *The Commission has not only proposed legislation laying down rules for audiovisual service providers: it firmly believes that rating and labelling of content combined with media literacy and technological solutions, such as user controlled filtering, are key tools to address these important issues.*[499]

Provisions regarding media literacy were also included in the 2007 Audiovisual Media Services Directive (*infra*)[500] and the 2006 Recommendation on

---

ReleasesAction.do?reference=IP/06/1326 (on 12.10.2006). For results of this consultation, cf. http://ec.europa.eu/avpolicy/media_literacy/consultation/index_en.htm.

[496] COMMISSION OF THE EUROPEAN COMMUNITIES, Communication from the Commission to the European Parliament, the Council, the European Economic and Social Committee and the Committee of the Regions "A European approach to media literacy in the digital environment", COM (2007) 833 final, 20.12.2007; RAPID, Media literacy: do people really understand how to make the most of blogs, search engines or interactive TV?, IP/07/1970, 20.12.2007, retrieved from http://www.europa.eu/rapid/pressReleasesAction.do?reference=IP/07/1970&format=HTML&aged=0&language=EN&guiLanguage=en (on 16.01.2007).

[497] One of the Member States which devotes a significant amount of attention to media literacy is the United Kingdom. For more on Ofcom's strategy cf.: http://www.ofcom.org.uk/advice/media_literacy/ and OFCOM, Ofcom's response to the Byron review – Annex 2: current tools and approaches to protecting children from harmful content online, 30.11.2007, retrieved from http://www.ofcom.org.uk/research/telecoms/reports/byron/annex2.pdf (on 04.07.2008), 47–54.

[498] COMMISSION OF THE EUROPEAN COMMUNITIES, Communication from the Commission to the European Parliament, the Council, the European Economic and Social Committee and the Committee of the Regions "A European approach to media literacy in the digital environment", COM (2007) 833 final, 20.12.2007, 9. For an example of a self-regulatory initiative, cf. VODAFONE, Teachtoday.eu: ICT industry alliance launches TeachToday initiative, retrieved from http://www.vodafone.com/start/media_relations/news/group_press_releases/2007/ict_industry_alliance.html (17.06.2008).

[499] REDING, Viviane, Freedom of the media, effective co-regulation and media literacy: cornerstones for an efficient protection of minors in the European Union, Speech at the ICRA Roundtable Brussels 'Mission Impossible', Brussels, 14.06.2006, retrieved from http://europa.eu.int/rapid/pressReleasesAction.do?reference=SPEECH/06/374&type=HTML&aged=0&language=EN&guiLanguage=en (on 15.06.2006).

[500] Recital 8 and 37 and article 26 AVMS Directive (*infra*). See also: HELBERGER, Natali, "From eyeball to creator – Toying with audience empowerment in the Audiovisual Media Service Directive", *Entertainment Law Review* 2008, No. 6, 128–137.

the protection of minors and human dignity (*supra*).[501] In an Annex to this latter document a list of possible actions concerning media literacy was put forward. Several of these actions emphasised the importance of education, not only aimed at children, but also at teachers and parents.[502] There can be no doubt that media literacy and media education[503] will play a key role in future strategies that aim to protect minors against harmful content.[504]

AWARENESS – A similar role is reserved for awareness actions and campaigns. Creating awareness of challenges posed by new digital technologies and of possible solutions is indispensable to achieve an optimal result. Parents who are not Internet-savvy, for instance, may have the impression that, whereas there are dangers in the outside world, the home environment is a safe environment, not thinking about the doors that are opened to the outside world by means of an Internet connection.[505] If citizens are not aware of the issues that are posed and of steps they can undertake to remedy these

---

501 Recital 13, I.2.a and Annex II 2006 Recommendation (*supra*).

502 Annex II 2006 Recommendation (*supra*): "*(a) continuing education of teachers and trainers, in liaison with child protection associations, on using the Internet in the context of school education so as to maintain awareness of the possible risks of the Internet with particular regard to chatrooms and fora; (b) introduction of specific Internet training aimed at children from a very early age, including sessions open to parents; (c) an integrated educational approach forming part of school curricula and media literacy programmes, so as to provide information on using the Internet responsibly*".

503 For more on media education: FRECHETTE, Julie, "Cyber-censorship or cyber-literacy? Envisioning cyber-learning through media education", 149–171, in: BUCKINGHAM, David and WILLETT, Rebekah, *Digital generations: children, young people and new media*, Mahwah NJ, Lawrence Erlbaum Associates, 2006, 337 p.; BYRON, Tanya, Safer children in a digital world: the report of the Byron review, 27.03.2008, retrieved from http://www.dfes.gov.uk/byronreview/ (on 04.07.2008), Chapter 5; OFCOM, Ofcom's response to the Byron review – Annex 2: Current tools and approaches to protecting children from harmful content online, 30.11.2007, retrieved from http://www.ofcom.org.uk/research/telecoms/reports/byron/annex2.pdf (on 04.07.2008), 44–47.

504 UNESCO, Media education – A kit for teachers, students, parents and professionals (ed. Divina FRAU-MEIGS), Paris, L'exprimeur, 2006, retrieved from http://unesdoc.unesco.org/images/0014/001492/149278E.pdf (on 09.01.2007): "*[...] the entities for media regulation are moving away from notions of censorship to lay the emphasis on the preparation and the participation of consumers and users. Media education is often considered as an essential dimension, if not the best filter*". See also: COUNCIL OF EUROPE (GROUP OF SPECIALISTS ON HUMAN RIGHTS IN THE INFORMATION SOCIETY), Young people, well-being and risk on-line (abridged), Study by Rachel O'CONNELL and Jo BRYCE, 25.04.2006, retrieved from http://www.coe.int/t/dghl/standardsetting/media/doc/H-Inf(2006)005_en.pdf (on 30.05.2006).

505 ETSI, Human Factors (HF); Specification and guidelines for service providers on the provision of information services to young children under twelve years of age, ETSI DTS/HF 102 745, 2008, retrieved from http://portal.etsi.org/stfs/STF_HomePages/STF323/DTS%20102745v6b.doc (on 07.04.2008), 29.

issues, the dream of a safer digital environment for children is an illusionary one. Several EU policy documents have stressed the importance of awareness campaigns. The 2006 Recommendation on the protection of minors and human dignity, for instance, encouraged Member States to improve the level of awareness among parents, teachers and trainers, to organise national campaigns aimed at citizens, involving all communications media, to provide information on using the Internet responsibly and to distribute information packs on possible risks of the Internet.[506] Awareness has been and still is one of the key ingredients of the Safer Internet Programmes (*supra*) as well.[507] It has been argued that in order to raise awareness and empower young people the Internet should be used. As Commissioner Reding proposed:

> *Because our children are online, we need to meet them online. In 2008, 75% of youngsters visited a social networking site. So we have to use social networking to raise awareness regarding internet risks and solutions.*[508]

Conclusion – Just as is the case with technical tools, supporting mechanisms such as media literacy, education and awareness campaigns aim to empower parents, teachers and children. On the one hand, parents have a responsibility with respect to their children's media usage. The complexity of today's media environment, however, is challenging for parents (and teachers). In order to enable them to responsibly guide their children, it is necessary, first, that they are aware of the dangers and, second, that they have the skills to deal with these dangers. On the other hand, children need to be as aware and educated as their parents. Without awareness, education and media literacy, any attempt, regulatory or not, to protect minors against harmful content is doomed to fail.

---

506 I.2.a and Annex II 2006 Recommendation (*supra*).

507 Parliament and Council of the European Communities, Decision No 276/1999/EC of the European Parliament and Council adopting a multiannual Community action plan on promoting safer use of the Internet by combating illegal and harmful content on the global networks, 25.01.1999, *OJ* 06.02.1999, *L* 33, 1; Parliament and Council of the European Communities, Decision No 854/2005/EC of the European Parliament and of the Council establishing a multiannual Community Programme on promoting safer use of the Internet and new online technologies, 11.05.2005, *OJ* 11.06.2005, *L* 149, 1; Commission of the European Communities, Proposal for a Decision of the European Parliament and of the Council establishing a multiannual Community programme on protecting children using the Internet and other communication technologies, COM (2008) 106 final, 27.02.2008.

508 Reding, Viviane, How can we empower youngsters to stay safe online? Innovative solutions in Europe, Speech at the World Childhood Foundation Seminar, Stockholm, 17 September 2009, retrieved from http://ec.europa.eu/commission_barroso/reding/docs/speeches/2009/stockholm-170909.pdf (on 21.01.2010).

2.4. Conclusion

Traditional regulation and alternative regulation – In this chapter, we first tried to sketch the broader context in which the use of ARIs is situated. After having briefly explored the concept of regulation, we focused on a particular element of this concept, i.e., the involvement of different actors in the regulatory process. We found that over the past couple of decades, there was a shift from traditional command-and-control regulation to more decentred forms of regulation. It was thought that these latter forms of regulation could provide an answer to a number of drawbacks that command-and-control regulation suffers from, especially in complex sectors such as the information- and communication sector. The added value of decentred, more open, alternative instruments is their receptivity to the involvement of other actors than the government in the regulatory process. The field of protecting minors against harmful content is one area in which this characteristic was – and still is – considered to be promising.

ARIs and policymaking – The second part of this chapter focused on the alternative regulation discourse in European policy documents. First, we concentrated on the general 'Better Regulation'-trend at the European Union level. We found that the use of ARIs such as self-regulation and co-regulation was often incorporated into strategies designed to achieve more efficient and improved regulation. This relatively abstract trend also appeared in the media sector. First self-regulation and, later, co-regulation, were put forward as promising regulatory instruments, especially given the rising popularity of the Internet. However, neither at the general, nor at sector level, were these concepts approached in a uniform or consistent way. This resulted in the creation of an array of notions and definitions, each with a different nuance.

Self-regulation, co-regulation and regulatory tools – In the third part of this chapter, we tried to elucidate the concepts of self- and co-regulation by means of overviews of definitions, literature, research results and illustrations. We learned that the distinguishing characteristic is the intensity of the level of involvement of the different actors. We described a number of criteria that can be used to assess this level of involvement, but we also emphasised that strict categorisations of regulatory instruments are not as important as their compliance with normative requirements and the legal framework. Finally, we also devoted some attention to the use of regulatory tools. These tools, such as technology and supporting mechanisms, often are a significant element of an alternative regulatory strategy, and hence their use also needs to respect the broader legal framework.

Legal framework – The legal framework that surrounds the use of ARIs is central to the topic of this study. The use of these kinds of instruments does not occur in a legal vacuum. On the contrary, there are fundamental rights and other legal requirements that need to be respected when creating, implementing and enforcing alternative regulatory instruments. The next part of the study will, first, provide an overview of the legal framework, and, second, check the compliance of the use of ARIs with this legal framework.

Part II

Chapter 1

Legal Framework ('*de lege lata*')

1.1. Introduction

Situation – The first part of this study has provided an overview and analysis of the two building blocks which are crucial to the research topic of this study, i.e., the protection of minors against harmful content, on the one hand, and the concept of alternative regulatory instruments (ARIs), on the other. The opening chapter of this part first discussed the three constitutive elements of the issue of protecting minors against harmful digital media content – 'digital media content', 'minor' and 'harmful content' – and then examined the difficulties that have arisen with respect to this issue and the use of traditional legislation. We concluded that, clearly, a broader regulatory framework was needed and, subsequently, explored the policy history at the EU level (starting from 1996), which demonstrated that, indeed, increasing attention was drawn to the use of self- and co-regulation as tools to effectively protect minors against harmful content. The second chapter of the first part then explored the concepts of regulation and alternative regulation in policy documents and academic literature, and provided an overview and analysis of different ARIs, i.e., self- and co-regulation (possibly accompanied by the use of regulatory tools, such as technology and supporting mechanisms).

The second part of this study contains, in this first chapter, a description and analysis of the legal framework for the protection of minors against harmful content and the use of ARIs. Subsequently, in the second chapter, from this framework, the relevant provisions will be selected, and the compliance of the use of ARIs to protect minors against harmful content with these legal provisions will be assessed.

Legal framework – This chapter thus presents the broader legal framework for the protection of minors against harmful content, as well as the use of ARIs to achieve this public interest goal. This is because, in order to be able to correctly assess the delicate issues related to the protection of minors against harmful content, as well as the compliance of the use of ARIs with existing legislative requirements, it is necessary to gain a clear insight into this broader legal framework.

Different sets of regulation – This chapter examines five sets of regulation in turn. First, a brief overview is given of the development and different sources of children's fundamental rights. Second, specific and very important fundamental rights, i.e., the right to freedom of expression, the right to privacy and rights relating to procedural guarantees (the right to a fair trial and the right to an effective remedy), are discussed in greater detail. Third, different aspects of the (direct and indirect) regulation of content are studied; this includes a closer examination of the new Audiovisual Media Services Directive, and elements of the e-Commerce Directive. Fourth, legislation with respect to the internal market and competition is briefly introduced. Finally, several general legislative principles and requirements, such as proportionality, subsidiarity and article 288 para. 3 TFEU [ex 249 EC Treaty], are clarified.

Delineation – Again, we would like to stress that we have chosen to carry out the research into our topic at the European level. Hence, the framework which is presented is the European legal and regulatory framework (Council of Europe and European Union). Of course, other, for instance, national, legal provisions are possibly relevant to the use of ARIs in order to protect minors against harmful content. However, these provisions fall outside of the scope of this study.

1.2. Human Rights – Children's rights

Introduction – Over the past hundred years, awareness of the fact that children are individuals worthy of respect has slowly grown. From the beginning of the 20th century onwards, efforts have been made internationally to attribute a number of fundamental rights not only to adults, but to children as well.[1] This development culminated in 1989 with the creation of the United Nations Convention on the Rights of the Child (UNCRC, *infra*).

[1] Verhellen, Eugeen, *Convention on the Rights of the Child: background, motivation, strategies, main themes*, Antwerpen, Garant, 2006, 16.

Human rights also applicable to children – Today, it is accepted that fundamental human rights are applicable to children as well. The creation of the UNCRC (*infra*) has been instrumental in the identification and promotion of children's rights, and has caused a "*qualitative transformation of the status of children as the holders of rights*".[2] It is of crucial importance to have an understanding of the legal framework surrounding fundamental human rights, and more specifically children's rights, when dealing with a sensitive issue such as the protection of minors against harmful media content.

History of children's human rights – The development of international law on the rights of the child, parallel to general human rights law, has traditionally been divided into three phases. First, it was acknowledged by the international community that all individuals, children included, needed to be legally protected at the international level.[3] In the second phase, specific substantive rights were granted to individuals, both adults and children.[4] A final phase saw the realisation that, for individuals to benefit from their rights, it is necessary for them to have access to the necessary procedures to claim these rights.[5] The two latter phases were not as easily achieved for children as for adults. The adoption of the UNCRC, however, is considered to have been of the utmost importance in strengthening the approach to children's rights.[6]

Sources at international and European level – Apart from the UNCRC, a number of other international and European documents deal with the issue of children's rights, either directly or indirectly. These documents, as well as several general human rights documents, will be briefly analysed in the following section.

---

[2] Innocenti Insight (Philip Alston and John Tobin), Laying the foundations for children's rights – An independent study of some key legal and institutional aspects of the impact of the Convention on the Rights of the Child, 2005, retrieved from http://www.unicef-icdc.org/publications/pdf/ii_layingthefoundations.pdf (on 15.05.2.2007), ix.

[3] Van Bueren, Geraldine, *The international law on the rights of the child*, Dordrecht, Martinus Nijhoff Publishers, 1995, 1.

[4] Van Bueren, Geraldine, *The international law on the rights of the child*, Dordrecht, Martinus Nijhoff Publishers, 1995, 1.

[5] Van Bueren, Geraldine, *The international law on the rights of the child*, Dordrecht, Martinus Nijhoff Publishers, 1995, 1; for more on the actual implementation of the international rights of the child, see pages 378–422.

[6] Van Bueren, Geraldine, *The international law on the rights of the child*, Dordrecht, Martinus Nijhoff Publishers, 1995, 1.

1.2.1. *International*

A. *United Nations Convention on the Rights of the Child*

Legal framework – The United Nations Convention on the Rights of the Child (UNCRC),[7] adopted by the UN General Assembly on 20 November 1989,[8] provides the international legal framework for children's rights.[9] The Convention has so far been ratified by 193 countries,[10, 11] making it the most widely accepted international law instrument.[12] It came into force in 1990

[7] United Nations, Convention on the Rights of the Child, 20.11.1989, retrieved from http://www.unhchr.ch/html/menu3/b/k2crc.htm (on 12.09.2006) [hereinafer: UNCRC].

[8] Previous international documents on children's rights were: "Declaration on the Rights of Child", adopted by the League of Nations in 1924, and the 1959 "UN Declaration on the Rights of Child", which was adopted unanimously by the General Assembly of the United Nations on 20 November 1959, retrieved from http://www.unhchr.ch/html/menu3/b/25.htm (on 14.09.2006). For a detailed overview cf. Van Bueren, Geraldine, *The international law on the rights of the child*, Dordrecht, Martinus Nijhoff Publishers, 1995, 6–12.

[9] See also: Commission of the European Communities, Commission Staff working document accompanying the Communication from the Commission Towards an EU strategy on the rights of the child, Impact assessment, COM (2006) 367 final, SEC (2006) 888, 04.07.2006, retrieved from http://register.consilium.europa.eu/pdf/en/06/st12/st12107-ad01.en06.pdf (on 29.08.2006), 6: "*The UNCRC provides a coherent and comprehensive framework against which to evaluate legislation, policy, structures and actions*".

[10] Note that the United States has up until now not ratified the UNCRC. See: Office of the United Nations High Commissioner for Human Rights, Ratification, declarations and reservations, retrieved from http://www2.ohchr.org/english/bodies/ratification/11.htm#reservations (on 12.09.2006).

[11] The importance of ratifying the UNCRC was stressed again in the United Nations Millennium Declaration: United Nations General Assembly, United Nations Millennium Declaration, 55th session, 18.09.2000, retrieved from http://www.un.org/millennium/declaration/ares552e.htm (on 29.08.2006): "*We resolve therefore [...] to encourage the ratification and full implementation of the Convention on the Rights of the Child and its optional protocols on the involvement of children in armed conflict and on the sale of children, child prostitution and child pornography*". Furthermore, a special UN General Assembly's Special Session on Children highlighted the global commitment to children's rights: United Nations, *A world fit for children*, Millennium Development Goals Special Session on children, Documents, 2002, retrieved from http://www.unicef.org/publications/files/A_World_Fit_for_Children_072808.pdf (on 13.09.2006).

[12] Kilkelly, Ursula, "The best of both worlds for children's rights? Interpreting the European Convention on Human Rights in the light of the UN Convention on the Rights of the Child", *Human Rights Quarterly* 2001, Vol. 23, 310; Innocenti Insight (Philip Alston and John Tobin), Laying the foundations for children's rights – An independent study of some key legal and institutional aspects of the impact of the Convention on the Rights of the Child, 2005, retrieved from http://www.unicef-icdc.org/publications/pdf/ii_layingthefoundations.pdf (on 15.05.2.2007), ix.

and its provisions, asserting the fundamental rights children can exercise,[13] are legally binding[14] for the signatories.[15, 16] The actual implementation of the provisions of the UNCRC is left to the discretion of the countries,[17] but the principles enshrined in the Convention are considered the key guidelines that

---

[13] Commission of the European Communities, Commission Staff working document accompanying the Communication from the Commission Towards an EU strategy on the rights of the child, Impact assessment, COM (2006) 367 final, SEC (2006) 888, 04.07.2006, retrieved from http://register.consilium.europa.eu/pdf/en/06/st12/st12107-ad01.en06.pdf (on 29.08.2006), 6: "*It clearly enshrines in international law children's right to protection, provision and participation*". See also: Ruxton, Sandy, *What about us? Children's rights in the European Union? Next Steps*, Brussels, The European Children's Network, 2005, 7: "*The Convention provides a solid and ostensibly shared understanding of obligations towards human beings under the age of 18 years*".

[14] ECJ, Parliament v. Council, C-540/03, 27.06.2006, para. 37: "*The Court has already had occasion to point out that the International Covenant on Civil and Political Rights is one of the international instruments for the protection of human rights of which it takes account in applying the general principles of Community law […]. That is also true of the Convention on the Rights of the Child referred to above which, like the Covenant, binds each of the Member States*". See also: Verhellen, Eugeen, *Convention on the Rights of the Child: background, motivation, strategies, main themes*, Antwerpen, Garant, 2006, 84 and 147; Meuwese, Stan, Blaak, Mirjam and Kaandorp, Majorie (eds), *Handboek Internationaal Jeugdrecht* [*International Youth Law Handbook*], Nijmegen, Ars Aequi Libri, 2005, 3 [in Dutch].

[15] Kilkelly, Ursula, "The best of both worlds for children's rights? Interpreting the European Convention on Human Rights in the light of the UN Convention on the Rights of the Child", *Human Rights Quarterly* 2001, Vol. 23, 315.

[16] There is, however, no consensus on the direct effect of the UNCRC. Cf. for instance: Verhellen, Eugeen, *Convention on the Rights of the Child: background, motivation, strategies, main themes*, Antwerpen, Garant, 2006, 84–86; Meuwese, Stan, Blaak, Mirjam and Kaandorp, Majorie (eds), *Handboek Internationaal Jeugdrecht* [*International Youth Law Handbook*], Nijmegen, Ars Aequi Libri, 2005, 4 [in Dutch].

[17] However, the Committee on the Rights of the Child does emphasise that it "*welcomes the inclusion of sections on the rights of the child in national constitutions, reflecting key principles in the Convention, which helps to underline the key message of the Convention – that children alongside adults are holders of human rights*": United Nations Committee on the Rights of the Child, General measures of implementation of the Convention on the Rights of the Child (arts. 4, 42 and 44, para. 6), General comment No. 5, 27.11.2003, retrieved from http://www.unhchr.ch/tbs/doc.nsf/898586b1dc7b4043c1256a450044f331/3bba808e47bf25a8c1256db400308b9e/$FILE/G0345514.pdf (on 14.09.2006), 7. In Belgium in 2000, article 22bis was added to the Constitution. This article explicitly stipulates that "*every child has the right to respect of his or her moral, physical, mental and sexual integrity*". Furthermore, since December 2008 this article specified further that "*Any child has the right to express his opinion in all matters of concern to him; this opinion will be taken into account in accordance with his age and judgment. Any child has the right to measures and services that advance his development. The interest of the child is the first consideration regarding any decision that concerns the child […]*".

need to be taken into account when establishing children's rights policies.[18] The UNCRC thus functions as a comprehensive framework against which legislative or policy proposals should be evaluated.[19] The European Court of Justice has repeatedly acknowledged the Convention and has emphasised that it takes the Convention into account when applying the general principles of Community law.[20]

'Child' as an active subject of rights – The Convention is applicable to "*every human being below the age of eighteen years unless under the law applicable to the child, majority is attained earlier*".[21] An essential characteristic of the UNCRC is the belief that children are not merely vulnerable victims; on the contrary, in the spirit of the Convention, they must be recognised as social actors who need support in their gradual transition to adulthood.[22, 23] Hence, as Ruxton argues, the Convention not only acknowledges the vulnerability of children in certain situations, but also emphasises their capacities and strengths as rights holders.[24] The Committee on the Rights of the Child[25] has repeatedly stressed that, still too often, children are not treated as subjects of rights.[26]

---

[18] Commission of the European Communities, Commission Staff working document accompanying the Communication from the Commission Towards an EU strategy on the rights of the child, Impact assessment, COM (2006) 367 final, SEC (2006) 888, 04.07.2006, retrieved from http://register.consilium.europa.eu/pdf/en/06/st12/st12107–ad01.en06.pdf (on 29.08.2006), 6.

[19] Ruxton, Sandy, *What about us? Children's rights in the European Union? Next Steps*, Brussels, The European Children's Network, 2005, 28.

[20] ECJ, Dynamic Medien v. Avides Media AG, C-244/06, 14.02.2008, para. 39; ECJ, Parliament v. Council, C-540/03, 27.06.2006, para. 37.

[21] Article 1 UNCRC. Cf. *supra:* Part 1, Chapter 1.

[22] Ruxton, Sandy, *What about us? Children's rights in the European Union? Next Steps*, Brussels, The European Children's Network, 2005, 17.

[23] The formal phrasing "*the exercise by the child of the rights recognized in the present Convention*" in article 5, for instance, is an expression of the fact that a child is an active subject of rights (Hodgkin, Rachel and Newell, Peter, *Implementation handbook for the Convention on the Rights of the Child*, New York, Unicef, 2002, 85).

[24] Ruxton, Sandy, *What about us? Children's rights in the European Union? Next Steps*, Brussels, The European Children's Network, 2005, 105.

[25] The Committee on the Rights of the Child is the body of independent experts that monitors implementation of the Convention on the Rights of the Child by its State parties. For more information: cf.. http://www2.ohchr.org/english/bodies/crc/index.htm (last retrieved on 12.12.2008).

[26] For instance: United Nations Committee on the Rights of the Child, CRC/C/15/Add.17, 07.02.1994, retrieved from http://www.unhchr.ch/tbs/doc.nsf/(Symbol)/f1713d27ca8644ca4125615100388669?Opendocument (on 26.11.2008); United Nations Committee on the Rights of the Child, CRC/C/15/Add.44, 27.11.1995, retrieved from http://

Key principles – In general, it has been suggested that the UNCRC embodies four basic principles upon which the interpretation of the other articles can be based.[27] These four key principles are:

- Article 2: **Non-discrimination**: protection against all forms of discrimination
- Article 3: The **best interests of the child** as a primary[28] consideration:
  - The interpretation of the best interests of the child cannot trump or override any of the other rights ensured by other provisions on the UNCRC.[29]
  - This general principle can also be considered relevant to media regulation, as the article "*emphasizes that governments and public and private bodies must ascertain the impact on children of their actions, in order to ensure that the best interests of the child are a primary consideration, giving proper priority to children and building child-friendly societies*".[30] Hence, the best interests of the child should also be taken into account with respect to the development of media policy.

www.unhchr.ch/tbs/doc.nsf/(Symbol)/0d05ba579bd44515412562dd003c8695?Opendocument (on 26.11.2008); United Nations Committee on the Rights of the Child, CRC/C/15/Add.105, 24.08.1999, retrieved from http://www.unhchr.ch/tbs/doc.nsf/(Symbol)/545ce3a12d1e386c80256797003d5ad8?Opendocument (on 26.11.2008); United Nations Committee on the Rights of the Child, CRC/C/15/Add.150, 21.02.2001, retrieved from http://www.unhchr.ch/tbs/doc.nsf/(Symbol)/82f20503b2732d3ac12569ee00302483?Opendocument (on 26.11.2008).

[27] Committee on the Rights of the Child, General measures of implementation of the Convention on the Rights of the Child (arts. 4, 42 and 44, para. 6), General comment No. 5, 27.11.2003, retrieved from http://www.unhchr.ch/tbs/doc.nsf/898586b1dc7b4043c1256a450044f331/3bba808e47bf25a8c1256db400308b9e/$FILE/G0345514.pdf (on 14.09.2006), 4. See also: Ruxton, Sandy, *What about us? Children's rights in the European Union? Next Steps*, Brussels, The European Children's Network, 2005, 16 ("*Together they form a child rights perspective. These principles constitute a vision of the child as an individual, whose integrity must be respected*"); Office of the United Nations High Commissioner for Human Rights, Fact Sheet No.10 (Rev.1), The Rights of the Child: I. A landmark for children and their rights – Universal and forward-looking principles, 1993, retrieved from http://www.ohchr.org/Documents/Publications/FactSheet10Rev.1en.pdf (on 14.09.2006).

[28] This has been taken to indicate that the bests interests of the child are not always the only factor to consider; competing human rights interests, for instance, between children and adults can arise (Hodgkin, Rachel and Newell, Peter, *Implementation handbook for the Convention on the Rights of the Child*, New York, Unicef, 2002, 43). This is the case when dealing with the protection of minors against harmful media content.

[29] Hodgkin, Rachel and Newell, Peter, *Implementation handbook for the Convention on the Rights of the Child*, New York, Unicef, 2002, 39.

[30] Hodgkin, Rachel and Newell, Peter, *Implementation handbook for the Convention on the Rights of the Child*, New York, Unicef, 2002, 39.

  - This principle also implies the creation of mechanisms to assess the impact of government actions on children, and to effectively take these results into account when shaping the policy.[31]
  - Furthermore, the article requires states to ensure the necessary protection and care for the child (para. 2) when individual parents are unable or unwilling to protect the child.[32] In these cases, the state needs to function as a safety net. It could be argued that this requirement justifies government involvement in protecting minors against harmful new media content.
- Article 6: The right to **life, survival and development**
- Article 12: The right to **express an opinion** and to have that opinion taken into account; in any matter of procedure affecting the child, the child's view needs to be given due weight (cf. *infra*).

Categories of rights – The UNCRC is a comprehensive instrument,[33] and groups rights specifically created for children, as well as child-specific versions of general fundamental rights. Traditionally, three categories of rights are distinguished:

Table 6: Categories of rights in the UNCRC

Survival & development rights	5, 6, 7, 8, 9, 10, 14, 18, 20, 22, 23, 24, 25, 26, 27, 28, 29, 30, 31, 40	The right to life and to have the most basic needs met (e.g., an adequate standard of living, shelter, nutrition, medical treatment), and the rights that enable children to reach their fullest potential (e.g., education, play and leisure, cultural activities, access to information and freedom of thought, conscience and religion)
Participation rights	12, 13, 14, 15, 16, 17	Rights that allow children to take an active role in their communities (e.g., the freedom to express opinions; to have a say in matters affecting their own lives; to join associations)
Protection rights	11, 19, 20, 21, 22, 32, 33, 34, 35, 36, 37, 38, 39, 40, 41	Rights that are essential for safeguarding children and adolescents from all forms of abuse, neglect and exploitation (e.g., special care for refugee children; protection against involvement in armed conflict, child labour, sexual exploitation, torture and drug abuse)

Source: http://www.unicef.org/crc/index_30177.html and http://www.hrea.org/learn/guides/children.html.

[31] Hodgkin, Rachel and Newell, Peter, *Implementation handbook for the Convention on the Rights of the Child*, New York, Unicef, 2002, 43.

[32] Hodgkin, Rachel and Newell, Peter, *Implementation handbook for the Convention on the Rights of the Child*, New York, Unicef, 2002, 47.

[33] Kilkelly, Ursula, "The best of both worlds for children's rights? Interpreting the European Convention on Human Rights in the light of the UN Convention on the Rights of the Child", *Human Rights Quarterly* 2001, Vol. 23, 311.

The UNCRC and harmful new media content – Articles of particular interest to the protection of children against harmful new media content are articles 12 (the right to express an opinion and to have that opinion taken into account), 13 (the right to freedom of expression and to obtain and impart information), 14 (the right to freedom of conscience, thought and religion), 15 (the right to freedom of association and peaceful assembly), 16 (the right to protection from interference with privacy, family, home and correspondence), 17 (access to information and material from a diversity of national and international sources), 19 (the right to protection from all forms of violence, injury, abuse, neglect or exploitation), 31 (the right to participate in leisure, cultural and artistic activities), 34 (the right to protection from sexual exploitation) and 36 (the right to protection from all other harmful forms of exploitation).

Children's participation – Article 12 of the UNCRC embodies the vision that children should have the opportunity to act as active participants in the promotion, protection and monitoring of their rights.[34] More specifically, the article stipulates that children who are capable of forming their own views have the right to express those views freely in all matters affecting the child (para. 1).[35] Furthermore, these views must be respected. It has been argued that within the scope of this article, "*child friendly and accessible spaces for children to express themselves should be developed, for example using technology such as (mobile) telephones and the internet*".[36] The importance of children themselves participating in the media has also been emphasised by the Committee on the Rights of the Child.[37] In this context, it can be noted that the rise of the Internet and linked media innovations, such as weblogs and social networks, have considerably lowered the traditional threshold for

[34] This principle applies to all measures adopted by Governments to implement the Convention: Ruxton, Sandy, *What about us? Children's rights in the European Union? Next Steps*, Brussels, The European Children's Network, 2005, 129.

[35] Article 24 of the Charter of Fundamental Rights (*cf. infra*) is the EU equivalent, albeit it is formulated less strongly ("*They may express their views freely. Such views shall be taken into consideration on matters which concern them in accordance with their age and maturity*").

[36] Ruxton, Sandy, *What about us? Children's rights in the European Union? Next Steps*, Brussels, The European Children's Network, 2005, 33.

[37] United Nations Committee on the Rights of the Child, Report on the eleventh session, CRC/C/50, 22.03.2006, retrieved from http://www.unhchr.ch/tbs/doc.nsf/898586b1dc7b4043c1256a450044f331/36686733b8cbf2eac1256333004ed6e4/$FILE/G9611831.pdf (on 22.09.2006), 81; United Nations Committee on the Rights of the Child, Report on the thirteenth session, CRC/C/57, 31.10.1996, retrieved from http://www.unhchr.ch/tbs/doc.nsf/898586b1dc7b4043c1256a450044f331/5a7331a09a8b4f3fc1256404003d10bd/$FILE/G9618895.pdf (on 22.09.2006), 40 *et seq.*

self-expression. The new media landscape could in this context thus be considered conducive to the implementation of the UNCRC.[38]

FREEDOM OF EXPRESSION – Article 13 confirms the child-specific version[39] of the (general) right to freedom of expression[40] "*which includes the freedom to seek, receive and impart information and ideas of all kinds, regardless of frontiers, either orally, in writing or in print, in the form of art, or through any other media of the child's choice*".[41] In the past, it was not considered self-evident or obvious that children could appeal to the right to freely express themselves.[42] Hence, the inclusion of this right in the Convention provides some welcome clarity. The article has a broad scope of application, which certainly extends to the Internet as well as any other (future) medium. Moreover, and as mentioned above, these new media provide children with greater

---

[38] UNITED NATIONS COMMITTEE ON THE RIGHTS OF THE CHILD, Report on the thirteenth session, CRC/C/57, 31.10.1996, retrieved from http://www.unhchr.ch/tbs/doc.nsf/898586b1dc7b4043c1256a450044f331/5a7331a09a8b4f3fc1256404003d10bd/$FILE/G9618895.pdf (on 22.09.2006), 42.

[39] KILKELLY, Ursula, "The best of both worlds for children's rights? Interpreting the European Convention on Human Rights in the light of the UN Convention on the Rights of the Child", *Human Rights Quarterly* 2001, Vol. 23, 311.

[40] Similar articles are article 19 Universal Declaration of Human Rights, article 19 International Covenant of Civil and Political Rights, and article 10 European Convention on Human Rights and Fundamental Freedoms (cf. *infra*). Belgium formulated the following reservation with respect to article 13 UNCRC: "*Articles 13 and 15 shall be applied by the Belgian Government within the context of the provisions and limitations set forth or authorized by said Convention in articles 10 and 11 of the European Convention for the Protection of Human Rights and Fundamental Freedoms of 4 November 1950*". This entails that the restrictions on the freedom of expression are interpreted in a slightly wider manner.

[41] The United Nations Committee on the Rights of the Child has stressed that it is not sufficient to just include the 'general' right to freedom of expression applicable to everyone in a country's constitution. It is necessary, according to the Committee, to also expressly incorporate the child's right to freedom of expression in legislation. See for instance: UNITED NATIONS COMMITTEE ON THE RIGHTS OF THE CHILD, General Guidelines for Periodic Reports, CRC/C/58, 20.11.1996, retrieved from http://www.unhchr.ch/tbs/doc.nsf/(Symbol)/CRC.C.58.En?Opendocument (on 25.09.2006): "*States parties are requested to provide information on the measures adopted to ensure that the civil rights and freedoms of children set forth in the Convention, in particular those covered by articles 7, 8, 13 to 17 and 37 (a), are recognized by law specifically in relation to children and implemented in practice, including by administrative and judicial bodies, at the national, regional and local levels, and where appropriate at the federal and provincial levels*".

[42] MEUWESE, Stan, BLAAK, Mirjam and KAANDORP, Majorie (eds), *Handboek Internationaal Jeugdrecht* [*International Youth Law Handbook*], Nijmegen, Ars Aequi Libri, 2005, 19 [in Dutch].

possibilities to express themselves.[43] Finally, it is necessary to note that this fundamental right can only be restricted if this is provided by law and necessary "*for respect of the rights or reputations of others, or for the protection of national security or of public order, or of public health or morals*" (para. 2).[44]

Freedom of thought, conscience and religion – Article 14, which requires States to respect the right of the child to freedom of thought, conscience and religion,[45] has also been argued to be linked with article 12 and article 13. The practical implementation of the freedom of thought aspect in particular, is intertwined with the above-mentioned articles. Forming and formulating thoughts requires access to information. Contrary to article 13, which addresses children directly ("*The child shall have the right to freedom of expression*"), article 14 is aimed at the state parties, who need to ensure the children's right. No restrictions on the freedom of thought are allowed.[46, 47]

Freedom of association – Another important (participation) right is the right to freedom of association and peaceful assembly, provided in article 15.[48] This right can only be limited in conformity with the law and if it is deemed necessary in a democratic society in the interests of national security

---

[43] In this context, the Voices of Youth website (http://www.unicef.org/voy/index.php) – a UNICEF initiative – and its discussion forum (http://www.unicef.org/voy/speakout/speakout.php) in particular, can be mentioned.

[44] These grounds for restrictions are identical to the grounds listed in article 19 para. 3 of the International Covenant of Civil and Political Rights. For more on possible restrictions on freedom of expression, cf. *infra*.

[45] This right is also expressed in article 18 of the Universal Declaration on Human Rights, article 18 of the International Covenant on Civil and Political Rights, and article 9 of the European Convention on Human Rights and Fundamental Freedoms.

[46] Hodgkin, Rachel and Newell, Peter, *Implementation handbook for the Convention on the Rights of the Child*, New York, Unicef, 2002, 195.

[47] However, there is no consensus on this issue. For example, Meuwese, Blaak and Kaandorp argue that restrictions are allowed. According to these authors, the third paragraph – which contains possible grounds for exception – applies to the freedom of thought as well (although it is formulated as follows: "*Freedom to manifest one's religion or beliefs may be subject only to such limitations as are prescribed by law and are necessary to protect public safety, order, health or morals, or the fundamental rights and freedoms of others*"): Meuwese, Stan, Blaak, Mirjam and Kaandorp, Majorie (eds), *Handboek Internationaal Jeugdrecht* [*International Youth Law Handbook*], Nijmegen, Ars Aequi Libri, 2005, 131 [in Dutch].

[48] Equivalents in other human rights treaties are article 20 of the Universal Declaration on Human Rights, article 22 of the International Covenant on Civil and Political Rights, and article 11 of the European Convention on Human Rights and Fundamental Freedoms. The Belgian government made the same reservation as for article 13, cf. *supra*.

or public safety, public order, the protection of public health or morals, or the protection of the rights and freedoms of others (para. 2). New social network technology could be a tool to forward the realisation of this right.

Right to privacy – Equally important as the previous rights, is the child's right to privacy, formulated in article 16 of the Convention.[49] According to this article, children cannot be subjected to any arbitrary or unlawful interference – by state authorities or by others (e.g., private organisations)[50] – with their privacy, family, home or correspondence, nor to unlawful attacks on their honour and reputation. Moreover, it is clearly stated that the law should protect a child against such interference. The right to privacy is directed at the child itself and is to be protected in all situations.[51] In the new media environment, privacy issues could, for instance, arise with respect to identification mechanisms developed to help protecting minors from harmful content. Furthermore, monitoring a child's use of the Internet and other new media, for instance, with the help of software, could be considered in conflict with the child's right to privacy. Finally, parents may neither, according to article 16, interfere with their child's correspondence. There is no reason to limit the application of this article to 'paper' correspondence, so monitoring e-mail conversations could be proscribed as well.

Access to good-quality media – A crucial article for the protection of minors against harmful new media content is article 17.[52] This article requires states to ensure that children have access to "*information and material from a diversity of national and international sources, especially those aimed at the promotion of his or her social, spiritual and moral well-being and physical and mental health*",[53] since access to a wide diversity of information is a pre-

[49] Again, this is a child-specific 'translation' of the general right to privacy, which is granted to everyone by, *inter alia*, article 12 Universal Declaration on Human Rights, article 17 International Covenant on Civil and Political Rights, and article 8 European Convention on Human Rights and Fundamental Freedoms.

[50] Hodgkin, Rachel and Newell, Peter, *Implementation handbook for the Convention on the Rights of the Child*, New York, Unicef, 2002, 216.

[51] Hodgkin, Rachel and Newell, Peter, *Implementation handbook for the Convention on the Rights of the Child*, New York, Unicef, 2002, 213; Meuwese, Stan, Blaak, Mirjam and Kaandorp, Majorie (eds), *Handboek Internationaal Jeugdrecht* [*International Youth Law Handbook*], Nijmegen, Ars Aequi Libri, 2005, 141 [in Dutch].

[52] The European Court of Justice has also referred to this article in a case concerning potential harmful new media content: ECJ, Dynamic Medien v. Avides Media AG, C-244/06, 14.02.2008, para. 40.

[53] A general discussion on 'The child and the media' was held by the Committee on the Rights of the Child on the 7th of October 1996. A report of this discussion was included

requisite for the exercise of other fundamental rights, most importantly the right to freedom of expression.[54] States are thus incited to pursue a proactive policy which stimulates the cultural, educational and informational potential of media with respect to children.[55] However, while the UNCRC promotes children's access to media, it also encourages the development of guidelines to protect children from harmful material. On the one hand, the Internet and other new media technologies enable children to access a huge variety of educational material[56] and cultural opportunities, as "*powerful tool*[s] *that can help to meet children's rights under the UNCRC (e.g., to participation,*

in the Report on the thirteenth session: United Nations Committee on the Rights of the Child, Report on the thirteenth session, CRC/C/57, 31.10.1996, retrieved from http://www.unhchr.ch/tbs/doc.nsf/898586b1dc7b4043c1256a450044f331/5a7331a09a8b4f3fc1256404003d10bd/$FILE/G9618895.pdf (on 22.09.2006). Following this discussion, an informal Working Group was set up (CRC/C/57, p. 45). This Working Group met twice (*cf.* United Nations Committee on the Rights of the Child, CRC/C/66, 06.06.1997, retrieved from http://www.unhchr.ch/tbs/doc.nsf/898586b1dc7b4043c1256a450044f331/b27bf9857a55819d802564f3003b10ee/$FILE/G9717203.pdf (on 26.11.2008), 51; United Nations Committee on the Rights of the Child, CRC/C/79, 27.07.1998, retrieved from http://www.unhchr.ch/tbs/doc.nsf/898586b1dc7b4043c1256a450044f331/a505a81ff8dcaf89802566d6003b6298/$FILE/G9817376.pdf (on 26.11.2008), 46) and was also involved with the development of 'The Oslo Challenge', a call for action, addressed to "*everyone engaged in exploring, developing, monitoring and participating in the complex relationship between children and the media*". This document elaborates on ways to effectively implement articles 12, 13 and especially 17 UNCRC: "*The Oslo challenge signals to governments, the media, the private sector, civil society in general and young people in particular that Article 17 of the Convention on the Rights of the Child, far from isolating the child/media relationship, is an entry point into the wide and multi-faceted world of children and their rights – to education, freedom of expression, play, identity, health, dignity and self-respect, protection – and that in every aspect of child rights, in every element of the life of a child, the relationship with children and the media plays a role*" (cf. http://www.mediawise.org.uk/files/uploaded/Oslo%20Challenge.pdf).

[54] Meuwese, Stan, Blaak, Mirjam and Kaandorp, Majorie (eds), *Handboek Internationaal Jeugdrecht* [*International Youth Law Handbook*], Nijmegen, Ars Aequi Libri, 2005, 144–145 [in Dutch].

[55] Voorhoof, Dirk, "Media(recht) en kinder(recht)en" ["*Media(law) and children('s rights*"], Deel 1, 1.9., update 1995, in: Verhellen, Eugeen (ed.), *Kinderrechtengids (KIDS): Commentaren, regelgeving, rechtspraak en nuttige informatie over de maatschappelijke en juridische positie van het kind* [*Guide to children's rights: Comments, regulation, case law and useful information about the social and legal status of the child*], Gent, Mys en Breesch, 1994, 30 [in Dutch].

[56] Article 17 (a) emphasises the importance of disseminating information and material of social and cultural benefit to the child and in accordance with the spirit of article 29, which is related to education.

information and freedom of expression)".[57] However, on the other hand, these technologies have also lowered the threshold of access to illegal and harmful material (cf. *supra*).

It has been argued that the word 'guidelines', used in article 17 UNCRC, indicates a preference for voluntary, rather than legislative constraints.[58] However, the Committee on the Rights of the Child has recommended to "*enact special* legislation *to protect children from harmful information, in particular from television programmes and films containing brutal violence and pornography*" (own emphasis).[59] This attitude is not limited to traditional media: the Committee is concerned about new media, such as the Internet, as well.[60]

Regardless of the medium, it is of the utmost importance that the developed guidelines are in accordance with article 13 (*supra*) and article 18 of the UNCRC. First, any restriction imposed by such a guideline on a child's freedom of expression needs to adhere to the conditions of article 13 para. 2 (*supra*). Secondly, article 18 para. 1 recalls the primary responsibility of parents for the upbringing and development of the child. In the same spirit, article 5 as well is – in our view – especially relevant when dealing with harmful content (although this article is not traditionally mentioned in this context).[61] Article 5 refers to the responsibilities, rights and duties of parents

---

[57] Ruxton, Sandy, *What about us? Children's rights in the European Union? Next Steps*, Brussels, The European Children's Network, 2005, 109.

[58] Hodgkin, Rachel and Newell, Peter, *Implementation handbook for the Convention on the Rights of the Child*, New York, Unicef, 2002, 236. See also: United Nations Committee on the Rights of the Child, Report on the thirteenth session, CRC/C/57, 31.10.1996, retrieved from http://www.unhchr.ch/tbs/doc.nsf/898586b1dc7b4043c1256a450044f331/5a7331a09a8b4f3fc1256404003d10bd/$FILE/G9618895.pdf (on 22.09.2006), 44.

[59] United Nations Committee on the Rights of the Child, Concluding observations of the Committee on the Rights of the Child: Cambodia, CRC/C/15/Add.128, 28.06.2000, retrieved from http://www.unhchr.ch/tbs/doc.nsf/(Symbol)/30dce34798ef39f480256900003397ac?Opendocument (on 27.09.2006), para. 36; United Nations Committee on the Rights of the Child, Concluding observations of the Committee on the Rights of the Child: Marshall Islands, CRC/C/15/Add.139, 16.10.2000, retrieved from http://www.unhchr.ch/tbs/doc.nsf/(Symbol)/e91ea24ff52b434ac125697a00339c0c?Opendocument (on 27.09.2006), para. 34–35.

[60] "*The Committee is concerned that no legislation exists to protect children from being exposed to violence and pornography through video movies and other modern technologies, most prominently, the Internet*": United Nations Committee on the Rights of the Child, Concluding observations of the Committee on the Rights of the Child: Luxembourg, CRC/C/15/Add.92, 24.06.1998, retrieved from http://www.unhchr.ch/tbs/doc.nsf/(Symbol)/62258a94c261c9318025662400376374?Opendocument (on 27.09.2006), para. 30.

[61] However, Hodgkin and Newell do stress the link with articles 12 and 13: "*In fact, parents are particularly well placed to build the capacity of children to intervene in a growing man-*

(or other persons legally responsible for the child), to offer, in a manner consistent with the evolving capacities of the child, appropriate direction and guidance to the child when exercising his or her rights.[62] This provision could be interpreted as implying that parents have a responsibility to (do their best to) support their children in their approach to new media.[63] Ultimately, parents or other carers are the only persons who will be able to monitor their children's actual media use.[64] However, according to article 18 para. 2, States must "*render appropriate assistance to parents and legal guardians in the performance of their child-rearing responsibilities*". An example of this 'assistance' or, otherwise put, the 'duty of care' of the state,[65] could be the provision of adequate information by States to parents about the dangers of certain media content to which their children can be exposed.[66]

ner in the different stages of decision, to prepare them for responsible life in a free society, informing them, giving the necessary guidance and direction, while assuring children the right to express views freely and to give those views due weight" (Hodgkin, Rachel and Newell, Peter, *Implementation handbook for the Convention on the Rights of the Child*, New York, Unicef, 2002, 92).

62 For more details on parental responsibility, cf. Couzens, Meda, "Autonomy rights versus parental autonomy", 419–439, in: Alen, Andre et al. (eds), *The UN Children's rights Convention: theory meets practice* (Proceedings of the International Interdisciplinary Conference on Children's Rights, 18– Ghent, 19.05.2006, Belgium), Antwerpen, Intersentia, 2007, 658 p.

63 The United Nations General Assembly has also touched upon the responsibilities of parents *et al.* in this respect: "*19. Encourage measures to protect children from violent or harmful web sites, computer programmes and games that negatively influence the psychological development of children, taking into account the responsibilities of the family, parents, legal guardians and caregivers*": United Nations General Assembly, Resolution A world fit for children, A/RES/S-27/2, 11.10.2002, retrieved from http://www.unicef.org/specialsession/docs_new/documents/A-RES-S27–2E.pdf (on 27.09.2006), 16.

64 Hodgkin, Rachel and Newell, Peter, *Implementation handbook for the Convention on the Rights of the Child*, New York, Unicef, 2002, 236. On parental guidance of children's media use, cf. Van den Bulck, Jan and Van den Bergh, Bea, "Parental media guidance, communication and self-concept in pre-adolescents", 151–174, in: Van den Bergh, Bea and Van den Bulck, Jan (eds), *Children and media: multidisciplinary approaches*, Leuven, Garant, 2000, 235 p.

65 Voorhoof, Dirk, "Media(recht) en kinder(recht)en" ["*Media(law) and children('s rights*"], Deel 1, 1.9., update 1995, in: Verhellen, Eugeen (ed.), *Kinderrechtengids (KIDS): Commentaren, regelgeving, rechtspraak en nuttige informatie over de maatschappelijke en juridische positie van het kind* [*Guide to children's rights: Comments, regulation, case law and useful information about the social and legal status of the child*], Gent, Mys en Breesch, 1994, 8 [in Dutch].

66 Hodgkin, Rachel and Newell, Peter, *Implementation handbook for the Convention on the Rights of the Child*, New York, Unicef, 2002, 236.

Right to participate in leisure, culture and art – Linked with article 17 is article 31, which refers to the right of the child to rest and leisure, to engage in play and recreational activities appropriate to the age of the child, and to participate freely in cultural life and the arts. The media can play an important role in the realisation of this right.[67] New media technologies can facilitate access to cultural and artistic activities. Innovative developments, such as on-line gaming, can also be placed under this heading. However, it has been argued that the formula "*appropriate to the age of the child*" implies that protection against certain television programmes or computer games might be desirable.[68]

Violence, Abuse, Sexual or other harmful exploitation, Child-pornography – Three articles can be linked to illegal (media) content rather than harmful content. Article 19 requires the protection of the child from all forms of physical or mental violence, injury, abuse, neglect, maltreatment or exploitation, including sexual abuse. Furthermore, article 34 obliges states to take measures to prevent the inducement or coercion of a child to engage in any unlawful sexual activity, the exploitative use of children in prostitution or other unlawful sexual practices, and the exploitative use of children in pornographic performances and materials (i.e., child pornography). Online child pornography has been a growing concern over the past decade. Hence, in 2000 the Optional Protocol to the Convention of the Rights of the Child on the sale of children, child prostitution and child pornography was drafted. This Protocol complements article 34 and is also applicable to the dissemination of child pornography via the Internet.[69] Finally, article 36 calls for protection against all other forms of exploitation prejudicial to any aspects of the child's welfare. The scope of this article is very broad, and can, for instance,

---

[67] Hodgkin, Rachel and Newell, Peter, *Implementation handbook for the Convention on the Rights of the Child*, New York, Unicef, 2002, 231.

[68] Hodgkin, Rachel and Newell, Peter, *Implementation handbook for the Convention on the Rights of the Child*, New York, Unicef, 2002, 470; Meuwese, Stan, Blaak, Mirjam and Kaandorp, Majorie (eds), *Handboek Internationaal Jeugdrecht* [*International Youth Law Handbook*], Nijmegen, Ars Aequi Libri, 2005, 260 [in Dutch].

[69] United Nations, Optional Protocol to the Convention on the Rights of the Child on the sale of children, child prostitution and child pornography, A/RES/54/263, 25.05.2000, retrieved from http://www2.ohchr.org/english/law/crc-sale.htm (on 12.12.2008). Article 2 of the Protocol defines 'child pornography' as "*any representation, by whatever means, of a child engaged in real or simulated explicit sexual activities or any representation of the sexual parts of a child for primarily sexual purposes*". This technology-neutral definition ensures the possibility to apply the Protocol to online child-pornography images.

include the protection of the child against abuse by the media,[70] or – as has been argued by RUXTON – against pornography.[71]

IMPLEMENTATION AND ENFORCEMENT – The UNCRC does not contain an actual enforcement mechanism.[72] Children cannot file complaints,[73] therefore the Convention cannot be tested in specific cases by the courts.[74] However, the UNCRC does have a symbolic function[75] and a strong moral force.[76] Additionally, the UN Committee on the Rights of the Child monitors the implementation of the UNCRC and issues critical remarks or recommendations.[77] It is then up to the national governments to take these into account. Hence, the Committee's role is "*advisory and non-adversial in nature and its success relies on diplomacy rather than legal sanction*".[78] To help countries to implement the UNCRC in an adequate manner, the Committee on the Rights of the Child has issued a number of implementation guidelines:[79]

---

70 HODGKIN, Rachel and NEWELL, Peter, *Implementation handbook for the Convention on the Rights of the Child*, New York, Unicef, 2002, 535.

71 RUXTON, Sandy, *What about us? Children's rights in the European Union? Next Steps*, Brussels, The European Children's Network, 2005, 105.

72 KILKELLY, Ursula, "The best of both worlds for children's rights? Interpreting the European Convention on Human Rights in the light of the UN Convention on the Rights of the Child", *Human Rights Quarterly* 2001, Vol. 23, 309. For more on the implementation of UNCRC cf. VAN BUEREN, Geraldine, *The international law on the rights of the child*, Dordrecht, Martinus Nijhoff Publishers, 1995, 378–422.

73 MEUWESE, Stan, BLAAK, Mirjam and KAANDORP, Majorie (eds), *Handboek Internationaal Jeugdrecht* [*International Youth Law Handbook*], Nijmegen, Ars Aequi Libri, 2005, 19 [in Dutch].

74 BAINHAM, Andrew, *Children – the modern law*, Bristol, Family Law, 2005, 67. It is useful however to stress the fact that supranational courts, such as the European Court of Justice, for instance, do refer to the UNCRC in its caselaw: cf. *infra*.

75 VAN BUEREN, Geraldine, *The international law on the rights of the child*, Dordrecht, Martinus Nijhoff Publishers, 1995, xx.

76 KILKELLY, Ursula, "The best of both worlds for children's rights? Interpreting the European Convention on Human Rights in the light of the UN Convention on the Rights of the Child", *Human Rights Quarterly* 2001, Vol. 23, 310.

77 KILKELLY, Ursula, "The best of both worlds for children's rights? Interpreting the European Convention on Human Rights in the light of the UN Convention on the Rights of the Child", *Human Rights Quarterly* 2001, Vol. 23, 309.

78 KILKELLY, Ursula, "The best of both worlds for children's rights? Interpreting the European Convention on Human Rights in the light of the UN Convention on the Rights of the Child", *Human Rights Quarterly* 2001, Vol. 23, 309.

79 COMMITTEE ON THE RIGHTS OF THE CHILD, General measures of implementation of the Convention on the Rights of the Child (arts. 4, 42 and 44 para. 6), General comment No. 5, 27.11.2003, retrieved from http://www.unhchr.ch/tbs/doc.nsf/898586b1dc7b4043c1256a450044f331/3bba808e47bf25a8c1256db400308b9e/$FILE/G0345514.pdf (on 14.09.2006).

- Legislation needs to be fully compatible with the UNCRC.
- The general measures set out in Articles 2 (non-discrimination, (3) 1 (best interests of the child) and 12 (the right to express views) must be implemented.
- Comprehensive national strategies or plans of action for children, built on the Framework of the Convention must be developed.
- Governments need to coordinate to ensure effective implementation.
- The implementation should be monitored through child impact assessment and evaluation.
- Sufficient and reliable data on children must be collected and disaggregated to enable identification of discrimination and/or disparities in the realisation of rights.
- Resources for children in national and other budgets must be identified and analysed.
- All those involved in the implementation process must have access to training and capacity-building.
- Co-operation with civil society, including children themselves, is encouraged.
- International cooperation to implement the Convention is encouraged.
- Independent human rights institutions must be established to independently monitor progress towards implementation.

B. *International Covenant on Civil and Political Rights and International Covenant on Economic, Social and Cultural Rights*

International Bill of Human Rights – Together with the Universal Declaration on Human Rights,[80] the International Covenant on Civil and Political Rights[81] and International Covenant on Economic, Social and Cultural Rights[82] constitute the International Bill of Human Rights.[83] The latter

See also: Ruxton, Sandy, *What about us? Children's rights in the European Union? Next Steps*, Brussels, The European Children's Network, 2005, 28. Office of the United Nations High Commissioner for Human Rights, Fact Sheet No.10 (Rev.1), The Rights of the Child, 1993, retrieved from http://www.ohchr.org/Documents/Publications/FactSheet10Rev.1en.pdf (on 14.09.2006).

[80] The Universal Declaration was adopted in 1948: United Nations, Universal Declaration on Human Rights, 10.12.1948, retrieved from http://www.unhchr.ch/udhr/lang/eng.htm (on 15.05.2007). Cf. *infra*.

[81] United Nations, International Covenant on Civil and Political Rights, 16.12.1966, retrieved from http://www.ohchr.org/english/law/ccpr.htm (on 15.05.2007) [hereinafter: ICCPR].

[82] United Nations, International Covenant on Economic, Social and Cultural Rights, 16.12.1966, retrieved from http://www.ohchr.org/english/law/cescr.htm (on 15.05.2007) [hereinafter: ICESCR].

[83] Office of the United Nations High Commissioner for Human Rights, International law: The International Bill of Human Rights, retrieved from http://www.ohchr.org/english/law/ (on 15.05.2007); Nowak, Manfred, *U.N. Covenant on Civil and Political Rights – CCPR Commentary*, Kehl, N.P. Engel, 2005, XIX.

covenants were signed in 1966 and entered into force in 1976. On the basis of articles 2 para. 1 ICCPR and 2 para. 2 ICESCR, it is generally accepted that both covenants are also applicable to children.[84]

ICCPR – The International Covenant on Civil and Political Rights (ICCPR),[85] which entered into force in 1976, applies to all individuals without distinction of any kind (for instance: race, colour, sex, language, religion, political or other opinion, national or social origin, property, birth or other status).[86, 87] Hence, it can be deduced that children[88] as well can appeal to the rights included in the ICCPR,[89] such as the right to freedom of expression.[90]

---

84 Belgische Senaat, Herziening van titel II van de Grondwet, om nieuwe bepalingen in te voegen die de bescherming van de rechten van het kind op morele, lichamelijke, geestelijke en seksuele integriteit verzekeren [*Review of Title II of the Constitution, to insert new provisions which guarantee the protection of the rights of the child to moral, physical psychological and sexual integrity*], Report by Mrs. Taelman, 2–21/4, 13.01.2000, retrieved from http://www.senate.be/www/?MIval=/publications/viewPub.html&COLL=S&LEG=2&NR=21&VOLGNR=4&LANG=nl (on 02.10.2006) [in Dutch]; Joseph, Sarah, Schultz, Jenny and Castan, Melissa, *The International Covenant on Civil and Political Rights – Cases, materials and commentary*, Oxford, Oxford University Press, 2004, 622; Van Bueren, Geraldine, *The international law on the rights of the child*, Dordrecht, Martinus Nijhoff Publishers, 1995, 19–21.

85 For a detailed analysis of the ICCPR cf. Nowak, Manfred, *U.N. Covenant on Civil and Political Rights – CCPR Commentary*, Kehl, N.P. Engel, 2005, 1277 p.; Joseph, Sarah, Schultz, Jenny and Castan, Melissa, *The International Covenant on Civil and Political Rights – Cases, materials and commentary*, Oxford, Oxford University Press, 2004, 985 p.

86 Article 2 para. 1 ICCPR.

87 'Age' is not explicitly mentioned as a criterion, but it is accepted that age is covered by the phrase "*other status*": Nowak, Manfred, *U.N. Covenant on Civil and Political Rights – CCPR Commentary*, Kehl, N.P. Engel, 2005, 47.

88 The ICCPR contains no provision which determines under what age a person is considered a 'minor' or a 'child'. It is up to the States to determine this age: United Nations Human Rights Committee, General comment No. 17: Rights of the Child (Article 24), 35th session, 07.04.1989, retrieved from http://www.unhchr.ch/tbs/doc.nsf/(Symbol)/cc0f1f8c391478b7c12563ed004b35e3?Opendocument (on 15.05.2007).

89 This was confirmed by the Human Rights Committee: United Nations Human Rights Committee, General comment No. 17: Rights of the Child (article 24), 35th session, 07.04.1989, retrieved from http://www.unhchr.ch/tbs/doc.nsf/(Symbol)/cc0f1f8c391478b7c12563ed004b35e3?Opendocument (on 15.05.2007): "*In this connection, the Committee points out that the rights provided for in article 24 are not the only ones that the Covenant recognizes for children and that, as individuals, children benefit from all of the civil rights enunciated in the Covenant*"; Joseph, Sarah, Schultz, Jenny and Castan, Melissa, *The International Covenant on Civil and Political Rights – Cases, materials and commentary*, Oxford, Oxford University Press, 2004, 625.

90 Article 19 ICCPR.

Furthermore, there are also specific references to children in the ICCPR.[91] An important article in this context is article 24, which provides that "*every child shall have, without any discrimination as to race, colour, sex, language, religion, national or social origin, property or birth, the right to such measures of protection as are required by his status as a minor, on the part of his family, society and the State*".[92] These 'measures' are not specified by the Covenant and, hence, each State may decide which steps it takes to protect children.[93] Some scholars suggest that the UNCRC may be used to interpret article 24 ICCPR.[94] The Human Rights Committee has emphasised that the measures, even though mainly meant to guarantee that minors fully enjoy the rights included in the ICCPR, may also be economic, social and cultural.[95] It could thus be argued that action undertaken in the field of harmful media content could fall under article 24 ICCPR.[96]

ICESCR – The International Covenant on Economic, Social and Cultural Rights (ICESCR) also entered into force in 1976 and is also applicable to children as well as adults.[97] This can be deduced from article 2 para. 2

[91] The European Court of Justice has referred to the ICCPR with respect to the protection of the rights of the child: cf. ECJ, Dynamic Medien v. Avides Media AG, C-244/06, 14.02.2008, para. 39.

[92] Other articles related to children, but less relevant to the topic of this study, are articles 6, 10, 14, 18 and 23.

[93] United Nations Human Rights Committee, General comment No. 17: Rights of the Child (article 24), 35th session, 07.04.1989, retrieved from http://www.unhchr.ch/tbs/doc.nsf/(Symbol)/cc0f1f8c391478b7c12563ed004b35e3?Opendocument (on 15.05.2007. Also Nowak, Manfred, *U.N. Covenant on Civil and Political Rights – CCPR Commentary*, Kehl, N.P. Engel, 2005, 547.

[94] Nowak, Manfred, *U.N. Covenant on Civil and Political Rights – CCPR Commentary*, Kehl, N.P. Engel, 2005, 548; Joseph, Sarah, Schultz, Jenny and Castan, Melissa, *The International Covenant on Civil and Political Rights – Cases, materials and commentary*, Oxford, Oxford University Press, 2004, 649.

[95] United Nations Human Rights Committee, General comment No. 17: Rights of the Child (Article 24), 35th session, 07.04.1989, retrieved from http://www.unhchr.ch/tbs/doc.nsf/(Symbol)/cc0f1f8c391478b7c12563ed004b35e3?Opendocument (on 15.05.2007).

[96] Cf. United Nations Human Rights Committee, General comment No. 17: Rights of the Child (Article 24), 35th session, 07.04.1989, retrieved from http://www.unhchr.ch/tbs/doc.nsf/(Symbol)/cc0f1f8c391478b7c12563ed004b35e3?Opendocument (on 15.05.2007: "*In the cultural field, every possible measure should be taken to foster the development of their personality and to provide them with a level of education that will enable them to enjoy the rights recognized in the Covenant, particularly the right to freedom of opinion and expression*".

[97] For more details on the ICESCR cf. Sepúlveda, Magdalena, *The nature of the obligations under the International Covenant on Economic, Social and Cultural Rights*, Antwerpen, Intersentia, 2003, 477 p.

ICESCR which asserts that States guarantee that the rights included in the Covenant will be exercised without discrimination of any kind.[98] Although not explicitly mentioned, 'age' has been regarded as a potential ground for discrimination.[99] A number of articles are related to children.[100] Article 10, for instance, provides that "*special measures of protection and assistance should be taken on behalf of all children and young persons without any discrimination for reasons of parentage or other conditions*".[101] This article, however, mostly relates to economic and social exploitation of children. With respect to culture, article 15 states that everyone has the right to participate in cultural life. No specific provisions with respect to the protection of minors in media are made. However, the explicit reference to cultural rights is important and could be interpreted as related to children's use of media.

1.2.2. *Council of Europe*

Human rights tradition – The Council of Europe (CoE) has a long-standing tradition of promoting human rights. The most important document in this field is undoubtedly the Convention on the protection of Human Rights and Fundamental Freedoms (*infra*).[102] Apart from general documents regarding the protection of human rights, the Council of Europe has also issued a number of more specific documents related to the safeguarding of

[98] Article 2 para. 2 ICESCR. Cf. Belgische Senaat, Herziening van titel II van de Grondwet, om nieuwe bepalingen in te voegen die de bescherming van de rechten van het kind op morele, lichamelijke, geestelijke en seksuele integriteit verzekeren [*Review of Title II of the Constitution, to insert new provisions which guarantee the protection of the rights of the child to moral, physical psychological and sexual integrity*], Report by Mrs. Taelman, 2-21/4, 13.01.2000, retrieved from http://www.senate.be/www/?MIval=/publications/viewPub.html&COLL=S&LEG=2&NR=21&VOLGNR=4&LANG=nl (on 02.10.2006) [in Dutch].

[99] Sepúlveda, Magdalena, *The nature of the obligations under the International Covenant on Economic, Social and Cultural Rights*, Antwerpen, Intersentia, 2003, 392.

[100] Articles 10, 12 and 13 ICESCR.

[101] Article 10 para. 3 ICESCR.

[102] Council of Europe, Convention for the Protection of Human Rights and Fundamental Freedoms, CETS No. 005, 04.11.1950, Rome, retrieved from http://conventions.coe.int/Treaty/en/Treaties/Html/005.htm (on 12.02.2007).

fundamental human rights in the (new) media environment,[103] as well as documents concerning children's rights.[104]

A. *European Convention on the protection of Human Rights and Fundamental Freedoms*

ECHR – The European Convention on the protection of Human Rights and Fundamental Freedoms (ECHR)[105] is one of the most important human rights instruments in Europe. The Convention was adopted in 1950 and is ratified by 47 countries. The ECHR has been incorporated into most of these countries' national legislation and, hence, is binding as part of their legal systems.[106] Its application is supervised by the European Court of Human Rights.[107]

Scope of application – The ECHR requires State Parties secure the rights and freedoms of "*everyone within their jurisdiction*".[108] Given the broadness of this description, children can be considered to be included in the scope

[103] Two conventions that can be mentioned in this area are the Cybercrime Convention (Council of Europe, Convention on Cybercrime, ETS No. 185, 23.11.2001, Budapest, retrieved from http://conventions.coe.int/Treaty/EN/Treaties/Html/185.htm (on 13.03.2007)) and the Transfrontier Television Convention (Council of Europe, European Convention on Transfrontier Television, ETS No. 132, 05.05.1989, Strasbourg, as amended by ETS. No. 171, 01.03.2002, retrieved from http://conventions.coe.int/Treaty/EN/Treaties/Html/132.htm (on 16.05.2007)). The Cybercrime Convention will not be discussed here as it mainly deals with illegal content. The Transfrontier Television Convention will be referred to *infra*.

[104] For instance: Council of Europe, Convention on the Protection of Children against Sexual Exploitation and Sexual Abuse, CETS No. 201, 25.10.2007, Lanzarote, retrieved from http://conventions.coe.int/Treaty/EN/treaties/Html/201.htm (on 14.01.2008).

[105] Council of Europe, Convention for the Protection of Human Rights and Fundamental Freedoms, CETS No. 005, 04.11.1950, Rome, retrieved from http://conventions.coe.int/Treaty/en/Treaties/Html/005.htm (on 12.02.2007) [hereinafter: ECHR].

[106] Macovei, Monica, *Freedom of expression – A guide to the implementation of Article 10 of the European Convention of Human Rights (Human rights handbooks, No. 2)*, Strasbourg, Council of Europe, 2004, 5.

[107] The European Court of Human Rights has had to issue relatively few judgments related to children. One important case brought before the Court – *Handyside v. the United Kingdom* – related to the protection of minors from potentially harmful content. This case is discussed in the next section. (*infra*): European Court of Human Rights, Handyside v. the United Kingdom, 07.12.1976. Cf. also Buquicchio-De Boer, Maud, "Children and the European Convention on Human Rights", in: Matscher, Franz and Petzold, Herbert (eds), *Protecting human rights: the European dimension (Studies in honour of Gérard J. Wiarda)*, Cologne, Carl Heymanns Verlag KG, 1988, 86.

[108] Article 1 ECHR.

of application.[109] This is, however, certainly not evident from the text itself, since there is no explicit provision which grants special protection to children.[110] Only two articles refer to children, i.e., article 5 para. 1 (d) concerning detention of minors, and article 6 para. 1 regarding the exception, in the interests of juveniles, to the public pronouncement of judgments. Yet, it has been argued that this limited occurrence of specific children's rights in the ECHR does not automatically diminish its potential for the protection of children's rights.[111]

USING THE UNCRC TO INTERPRET CHILDREN'S RIGHTS UNDER THE ECHR – Ursula KILKELLY argues that the UNCRC (*supra*) can be used to interpret children's rights under the ECHR.[112] She argues that this is possible because of the broadness of the ECHR's provisions, which allow them to be interpreted in an "*expansive and imaginative way*", and because of the fact that

---

[109] VOORHOOF, Dirk, "Media(recht) en kinder(recht)en" ["*Media(law) and children's rights*"], Deel 1, 1.9., update 1995, in: VERHELLEN, Eugeen (ed.), *Kinderrechtengids (KIDS): Commentaren, regelgeving, rechtspraak en nuttige informatie over de maatschappelijke en juridische positie van het kind* [*Guide to children's rights: Comments, regulation, case law and useful information about the social and legal status of the child*], Gent, Mys en Breesch, 1994, 20 [in Dutch]; KILKELLY, Ursula, "The best of both worlds for children's rights? Interpreting the European Convention on Human Rights in the light of the UN Convention on the Rights of the Child", *Human Rights Quarterly* 2001, Vol. 23, 314; BELGISCHE SENAAT, Herziening van titel II van de Grondwet, om nieuwe bepalingen in te voegen die de bescherming van de rechten van het kind op morele, lichamelijke, geestelijke en seksuele integriteit verzekeren [*Review of Title II of the Constitution, to insert new provisions which guarantee the protection of the rights of the child to moral, physical psychological and sexual integrity*], Report by Mrs. Taelman, 2–21/4, 13.01.2000, retrieved from http://www.senate.be/www/?MIval=/publications/viewPub.html&COLL=S&LEG=2&NR=21&VOLGNR=4&LANG=nl (on 02.10.2006) [in Dutch].

[110] BUQUICCHIO-DE BOER, Maud, "Children and the European Convention on Human Rights", in: MATSCHER, Franz and PETZOLD, Herbert (eds), *Protecting human rights: the European dimension (Studies in honour of Gérard J. Wiarda)*, Cologne, Carl Heymanns Verlag KG, 1988, 73. See also: VERHELLEN, Eugeen, *Convention on the Rights of the Child: background, motivation, strategies, main themes*, Antwerpen, Garant, 2006, 133.

[111] KILKELLY, Ursula, "The best of both worlds for children's rights? Interpreting the European Convention on Human Rights in the light of the UN Convention on the Rights of the Child", *Human Rights Quarterly* 2001, Vol. 23, 311. BUQUICCHIO-DE BOER, Maud, "Children and the European Convention on Human Rights", in: MATSCHER, Franz and PETZOLD, Herbert (eds), *Protecting human rights: the European dimension (Studies in honour of Gérard J. Wiarda)*, Cologne, Carl Heymanns Verlag KG, 1988, 89: "*The foregoing survey has attempted to show that in spite of the absence of an express provision enshrining children's rights, the Convention is not ineffective as regards their protection*".

[112] KILKELLY, Ursula, "The best of both worlds for children's rights? Interpreting the European Convention on Human Rights in the light of the UN Convention on the Rights of the Child", *Human Rights Quarterly* 2001, Vol. 23, 316.

the ECHR is considered a living instrument that must be interpreted in an evolutive way so as to remain relevant to the current legal and social circumstances.[113] One of the elements upon which such an interpretation can be based is the body of international human rights law, for instance, treaties and conventions.[114] In this context, she points out that the European Court of Human Rights has referred to the UNCRC "*with increasing frequency and with significant effect*".[115, 116] KILKELLY also argues that the use of the UNCRC, which – contrary to the ECHR – contains a number of very detailed child-specific rights, as an interpretive tool has a considerable positive effect on the application of the general rights included in the ECHR to children.[117]

FREEDOM OF EXPRESSION AND PRIVACY – The fundamental rights to freedom of expression (article 10 ECHR), to privacy (article 8 ECHR) and to an effective remedy (article 13 ECHR) are of particular relevance to this study. These rights are analysed in greater detail *infra*.

B. *European Social Charter*

ECONOMIC AND SOCIAL COMPLEMENT TO THE ECHR – In 1961, the Council of Europe adopted the European Social Charter (ESC), which entered into force in 1965,[118] and was revised in 1996.[119] Specifically with respect to chil-

---

113 KILKELLY, Ursula, "The best of both worlds for children's rights? Interpreting the European Convention on Human Rights in the light of the UN Convention on the Rights of the Child", *Human Rights Quarterly* 2001, Vol. 23, 313.

114 KILKELLY, Ursula, "The best of both worlds for children's rights? Interpreting the European Convention on Human Rights in the light of the UN Convention on the Rights of the Child", *Human Rights Quarterly* 2001, Vol. 23, 313.

115 KILKELLY, Ursula, "The best of both worlds for children's rights? Interpreting the European Convention on Human Rights in the light of the UN Convention on the Rights of the Child", *Human Rights Quarterly* 2001, Vol. 23, 309.

116 E.g., EUROPEAN COURT OF HUMAN RIGHTS, Keegan v. Ireland, 26.05.1994: reference to article 7 UNCRC; EUROPEAN COURT OF HUMAN RIGHTS, A v. the United Kingdom, 23.09.1998: reference to article 19 and 37 UNCRC; EUROPEAN COURT OF HUMAN RIGHTS, T. and V. v. the United Kingdom, 16.12.1999: reference to the UNCRC as a relevant international text.

117 KILKELLY, Ursula, "The best of both worlds for children's rights? Interpreting the European Convention on Human Rights in the light of the UN Convention on the Rights of the Child", *Human Rights Quarterly* 2001, Vol. 23, 326.

118 COUNCIL OF EUROPE, European Social Charter, CETS No. 35, 18.10.1961, Turin, retrieved from http://conventions.coe.int/Treaty/Commun/QueVoulezVous.asp?NT=035&CM=8&DF=07/11/2005&CL=ENG (on 21.05.2007).

119 COUNCIL OF EUROPE, European Social Charter (revised), CETS No. 163, 03.05.1996, Strasbourg, retrieved from http://conventions.coe.int/Treaty/Commun/QueVoulezVous.asp?NT=163&CM=7&DF=26/10/2005&CL=ENG (on 21.05.2007).

dren, the ESC states in Part 1, 7 that "*children and young persons have the right to a special protection against the physical and moral hazards to which they are exposed*". The corresponding article 7 (in Part 2) contains a number of conditions related to the working conditions of children (minimum age, holiday, working hours, wage, etc.). Furthermore, article 17 (Part 2) asserts that "*children and young persons have the right to appropriate social, legal and economic protection*". More precisely, they have the right to grow up in an environment which encourages the full development of their personality and of their physical and mental capacities. To this aim, certain measures must be taken by the signatories. These include, for instance, measures to ensure that children and young persons, taking account of the rights and duties of their parents, have the care, the assistance, the education and the training they need (in particular by providing for the establishment or maintenance of institutions and services sufficient and adequate for this purpose); measures to protect children and young persons against negligence, violence or exploitation; measures to provide protection and special aid by the state for children and young persons temporarily or definitively deprived of their family's support; and measures to provide to children and young persons a free primary and secondary education, as well as to encourage regular attendance at schools.[120] It could be assumed that certain measures taken to achieve one of these goals could relate to the media environment.

C. *Documents related to human rights and the information society*

Human rights and the Internet – The Council of Europe has been paying attention to the issue of human rights with respect to new information and communication networks since the mid-1990s. From 1999 onwards, different recommendations and declarations have been issued. Most of these documents have the same objectives: guaranteeing respect for human rights, fostering freedom of expression,[121] and contributing to a more democratic information society.[122] The protection of minors from harmful content often is an element of this aspiration (*infra*).

---

[120] Council of Europe, European Social Charter (revised), CETS No. 163, 03.05.1996, Strasbourg, retrieved from http://conventions.coe.int/Treaty/Commun/QueVoulezVous.asp?NT=163&CM=7&DF=26/10/2005&CL=ENG (on 21.05.2007), Part 2, article 17.

[121] For more details on the protection of freedom of expression in the information society cf. *infra*.

[122] Council of Europe (Committee of Ministers), Declaration on a European policy for new information technologies, 07.05.1999, retrieved from https://wcd.coe.int/ViewDoc.jsp?id=448133&Site=CM&BackColorInternet=9999CC&BackColorIntranet=FFBB55&BackColorLogged=FFAC75 (on 24.04.2007); Council of Europe (Standing committee on transfrontier television), Statement (2002)1 on human dignity and the

Documents – It has been stressed repeatedly that the ECHR remains fully valid in the new information society.[123] In this context, with respect to the protection of the freedom of expression (*infra*), the Council of Europe has time and again stated that Internet content should not be restricted to a greater extent than other means of content delivery.[124] Another recurring theme throughout CoE documents is the important role that is attributed to the private sector, sometimes in partnership with the public sector, to help achieve these goals.[125] The idea of building self-[126] and co-regulation

fundamental rights of others, 12–13.09.2002, retrieved from http://www.coe.int/t/dghl/standardsetting/media/T-TT/T-TT(2006)012rev_en.asp#TopOfPage (on 24.04.2007); Council of Europe, Democracy, human rights and the rule of law in the Information Society, Contribution by the Council of Europe to the 2nd Preparatory Committee for the World Summit on the Information Society, 07.12.2002, retrieved from http://www.coe.int/t/e/integrated_projects/democracy/02_activities/04_w.s.i.s/90IP1(2002)27.asp (on 24.04.2007); Council of Europe (Committee of Ministers), Declaration on human rights and the rule of law in the Information Society, 13.05.2005, retrieved from https://wcd.coe.int/ViewDoc.jsp?Ref=CM(2005)56&Sector=secCM&Language=lanEnglish&Ver=final&BackColorInternet=9999CC&BackColorIntranet=FFBB55&BackColorLogged=FFAC75 (on 19.05.2008); Council of Europe (Committee of Ministers), Recommendation CM/Rec(2007)11 on promoting freedom of expression and information in the new information and communications environment, 26.09.2007, retrieved from https://wcd.coe.int/ViewDoc.jsp?Ref=CM/Rec(2007)11&Language=lanEnglish&Ver=original&Site=CM&BackColorInternet=9999CC&BackColorIntranet=FFBB55&BackColorLogged=FFAC75 (on 26.03.2008).

[123] Council of Europe (Committee of Ministers), Declaration on human rights and the rule of law in the Information Society, 13.05.2005, retrieved from https://wcd.coe.int/ViewDoc.jsp?Ref=CM(2005)56&Sector=secCM&Language=lanEnglish&Ver=final&BackColorInternet=9999CC&BackColorIntranet=FFBB55&BackColorLogged=FFAC75 (on 19.05.2008).

[124] Council of Europe, Democracy, human rights and the rule of law in the Information Society, Contribution by the Council of Europe to the 2nd Preparatory Committee for the World Summit on the Information Society, 07.12.2002, retrieved from http://www.coe.int/t/e/integrated_projects/democracy/02_activities/04_w.s.i.s/90IP1(2002)27.asp (on 24.04.2007); Council of Europe (Committee of Ministers), Declaration on freedom of communication on the Internet, 28.05.2003, retrieved from https://wcd.coe.int/rsi/common/renderers/rend_standard.jsp?DocId=37031&SecMode=1&SiteName=cm&Lang=en (on 19.05.2008).

[125] Council of Europe, Human rights guidelines for Internet Service Providers – Developed by the Council of Europe in co-operation with the European Internet Service Providers Association (EuroISPA), July 2008, retrieved from http://www.coe.int/t/dghl/standardsetting/media/Doc/H-Inf(2008)009_en.pdf (on 10.10.2008).

[126] Council of Europe (Committee of Ministers), Recommendation Rec(2001)8 on self-regulation concerning cyber content (self-regulation and user protection against illegal or harmful content on new communications and information services), 05.09.2001, retrieved from https://wcd.coe.int/ViewDoc.jsp?id=220387&Site=COE&BackColorInternet=DBDCF2&BackColorIntranet=FDC864&BackColorLogged=FDC864 (on 24.04.2007).

frameworks to ensure the continuing respect for human rights is maintained throughout the different recommendations and declarations.[127] This is consistent with the fact that partnerships and cooperation between governments, civil society, the private sector and international organisations were increasingly put forward as the correct approach to adopt.[128] A final aspect worth mentioning is the increasing number of references to the importance of media literacy and user empowerment in the more recent documents.[129]

D. *Documents related specifically to children's rights*

Council of Europe and Children's rights – The Council of Europe has paid attention to the issue of children's rights in different – both general and specific – documents. The most relevant and recent texts are briefly commented upon in this section.[130]

---

127 Council of Europe, Democracy, human rights and the rule of law in the Information Society, Contribution by the Council of Europe to the 2nd Preparatory Committee for the World Summit on the Information Society, 07.12.2002, retrieved from http://www.coe.int/t/e/integrated_projects/democracy/02_activities/04_w.s.i.s/90IP1(2002)27.asp (on 24.04.2007).

128 Council of Europe (Committee of Ministers), Declaration on human rights and the rule of law in the Information Society, 13.05.2005, retrieved from https://wcd.coe.int/ViewDoc.jsp?Ref=CM(2005)56&Sector=secCM&Language=lanEnglish&Ver=final&BackColorInternet=9999CC&BackColorIntranet=FFBB55&BackColorLogged=FFAC75 (on 19.05.2008).

129 Cf. *infra*.

130 Earlier (directly or indirectly) relevant texts issued by the Committee of Ministers were: Council of Europe (Committee of Ministers), Recommendation Rec(91)11 concerning sexual exploitation, pornography, and prostitution of, and trafficking in children and young adults, 09.09.1991, retrieved from https://wcd.coe.int/com.instranet.InstraServlet?command=com.instranet.CmdBlobGet&InstranetImage=572467&SecMode=1&DocId=597998&Usage=2 (on 12.12.2008); Council of Europe (Committee of Ministers), Recommendation Rec(97)19 on the portrayal of violence in the electronic media, 30.10.1997, retrieved from https://wcd.coe.int/com.instranet.InstraServlet?command=com.instranet.CmdBlobGet&InstranetImage=568198&SecMode=1&DocId=582650&Usage=2 on (12.12.2008); Council of Europe (Committee of Ministers), Recommendation Rec(98)8 on children's participation in family and social life, 18.09.1998, retrieved from https://wcd.coe.int/com.instranet.InstraServlet?command=com.instranet.CmdBlobGet&InstranetImage=532375&SecMode=1&DocId=486272&Usage=2 (on 12.12.2008). The Parliamentary Assembly has also issued documents with respect to children's rights, for instance Council of Europe (Parliamentary Assembly), Rec (2002) 1551 Building a twenty-first century society with and for children: follow-up to the European strategy for children (Recommendation 1286 (1996)), 26.03.2002, retrieved from http://assembly.coe.int/main.asp?Link=/documents/adoptedtext/ta02/erec1551.htm (on 01.06.2007).

European Convention on the exercise of children's rights – The European Convention on the exercise of children's rights,[131] which entered into force in 2000,[132] centres around the fact that the rights and best interests of children should be promoted and that, to that end, children should have the opportunity to exercise their rights. Hence, the Convention mostly focuses on the procedural rights that should be attributed to children. Examples of such rights are the right to express their views in proceedings (cf. article 12 UNCRC) and the right to appoint special representatives in proceedings. Judicial authorities and appointed representatives must also adhere to a number of requirements (e.g., the judicial authorities must act speedily and the representatives must provide all relevant information to the child). The Convention can be seen as a supplement to the UNCRC.[133]

The 'Building a Europe for and with children' Programme – The 2005 Warsaw summit put forward an action plan in the field of children's rights.[134] The three-year programme is being implemented through two main lines of action, which both deal with media and cyberspace: the promotion of children's rights and the protection of children from violence.[135] The programme is set up to effectively promote the rights of the child and to fully comply with the obligations of the UNCRC.[136]

Relevant Council of Europe recommendations – In 2006, two recommendations which are relevant to this study were issued by the Committee of Ministers. The first, the Recommendation on empowering children in the

---

131 Council of Europe, European Convention on the exercise of children's rights, ETS No. 160, 25.01.1996, Strasbourg, retrieved from http://conventions.coe.int/Treaty/en/Treaties/Html/160.htm (on 01.06.2007).

132 Belgium, for instance, has not yet signed the Convention.

133 Council of Europe, Explanatory report to the European Convention on the exercise of children's rights, retrieved from http://conventions.coe.int/Treaty/EN/Reports/HTML/160.htm (on 01.06.2007).

134 Council of Europe (Ministers' Deputies), Warsaw Summit Action Plan, CM(2005)80 final, Warsaw, 17.05.2005, retrieved from http://www.coe.int/t/dcr/summit/20050517_plan_action_en.asp (on 30.05.2006).

135 Council of Europe, Building a Europe for and with children, Description, retrieved from http://www.coe.int/t/transversalprojects/children/BriefDescription/Default_en.asp (on 21.05.2007). For general information concerning the programme cf. http://www.coe.int/T/TransversalProjects/Children/ (last retrieved on 21.05.2007).

136 Council of Europe (Ministers' Deputies), Warsaw Summit Action Plan, CM(2005)80 final, Warsaw, 17.05.2005, retrieved from http://www.coe.int/t/dcr/summit/20050517_plan_action_en.asp (on 30.05.2006).

new information and communications environment,[137] is a detailed document which focuses on the concept of 'risk of harm' from content and behaviour in the new information and communications environment (*supra*), and on positive measures, such as empowerment, education and literacy, to counter this risk. The second Recommendation on policy to support positive parenting[138] is a more general document, but could also be useful for approaching the issue of protecting children against harmful content. The objective of the Recommendation is to "*make states recognize the importance of parental responsibilities and the necessity of providing the parents with sufficient support in meeting their responsibilities in bringing up their children*".[139] Positive parenting is defined in the appendix to the Recommendation as "*parental behaviour based on the best interests of the child that is nurturing, empowering, non-violent and provides recognition and guidance which involves setting of boundaries to enable the full development of the child*".[140] The concept is valuable and fits in with the growing trend towards empowerment of parents and children.[141] Two other aspects that are clearly emphasised in the Recommendation are the importance of recognising that a child is a person with rights (including the right to be protected and to participate, to express his/her views, to be heard and to be heeded) on the one hand, and the fact that parents have prime responsibility for their child, subject to the child's best interests, on the other.[142] The explanatory report clarifies that parenting in

[137] Council of Europe (Committee of Ministers), Recommendation Rec(2006)12 on empowering children in the new information and communications environment, 27.09.2006, retrieved from https://wcd.coe.int/ViewDoc.jsp?id=1041181&Site=CM&BackColorInternet=9999CC&BackColorIntranet=FFBB55&BackColorLogged=FFAC75 (on 12.12.2008).

[138] Council of Europe (Committee of Ministers), Recommendation Rec(2006)19 on policy to support positive parenting, 13.12.2006, retrieved from https://wcd.coe.int/ViewDoc.jsp?id=1073507&BackColorInternet=9999CC&BackColorIntranet=FFBB55&BackColorLogged=FFAC75 (on 12.12.2008).

[139] Council of Europe (Ministers' Deputies), Draft recommendation Rec(2006)... to member states on policy to support positive parenting – Explanatory report, 27.11.2006, retrieved from https://wcd.coe.int/ViewDoc.jsp?id=1067853&BackColorInternet=9999CC&BackColorIntranet=FFBB55&BackColorLogged=FFAC75 (on 01.06.2007).

[140] Council of Europe (Committee of Ministers), Recommendation Rec(2006)19 on policy to support positive parenting, 13.12.2006, retrieved from https://wcd.coe.int/ViewDoc.jsp?id=1073507&BackColorInternet=9999CC&BackColorIntranet=FFBB55&BackColorLogged=FFAC75 (on 12.12.2008), Appendix.

[141] Also cf. *infra*.

[142] Council of Europe (Committee of Ministers), Recommendation Rec(2006)19 on policy to support positive parenting, 13.12.2006, retrieved from https://wcd.coe.int/ViewDoc.jsp?id=1073507&BackColorInternet=9999CC&BackColorIntranet=FFBB55&BackColorLogged=FFAC75 (on 12.12.2008).

the best interests of the child implies that parents must have the well-being and development of the child as their main concern, and that they need to raise their children in ways that enable them to achieve their best at home, in school, with friends and in the community.[143] It could be argued that one of the aspects of achieving this goal relates to providing guidance with respect to their children's media use. A final important recommendation is the Recommendation on measures to protect children against harmful content and behaviour and to promote their active participation in the new information and communications environment.[144] This recommendation emphasises that whereas the right to freedom of expression is a primary objective of the Council of Europe, at the same time states also have a legitimate right, and even an obligation, to protect children from content which is unsuitable or inappropriate.

Committee of Ministers declaration – In September 2007, the Committee of Ministers issued a Declaration on protecting the dignity, security and privacy of children on the Internet.[145] The motivation for this declaration was found in the fears that have arisen as a result of children's increasing online presence and the fact that social networking and user-generated content trends result in vast amounts of available information about children and their online activities. Moreover, children often do not realise that once the information (for instance, photos or film clips) has been put online, it is almost impossible to retract this information. Hence, the Committee of Ministers declared that "*other than in the context of law enforcement, there should be no lasting or permanently accessible record of the content created by children on the Internet which challenges their dignity, security and privacy or otherwise renders them vulnerable now or at a later stage in their lives*" and invited "*member states together, where appropriate, with other relevant stakeholders, to explore the feasibility of removing or deleting such content,*

[143] Council of Europe (Ministers' Deputies), Draft recommendation Rec(2006)...to member states on policy to support positive parenting – Explanatory report, 27.11.2006, retrieved from https://wcd.coe.int/ViewDoc.jsp?id=1067853&BackColorInternet=9999CC&BackColorIntranet=FFBB55&BackColorLogged=FFAC75 (on 01.06.2007).

[144] Council of Europe (Committee of Ministers), Recommendation CM/REC(2009)5 on measures to protect children against harmful content and behaviour and to promote their active participation in the new information and communications environment, 08.07.2009, retrieved from https://wcd.coe.int/ViewDoc.jsp?id=1470045&Site=CM (on 20.01.2010).

[145] Committee of Ministers, Declaration on protecting the dignity, security and privacy of children on the Internet, 20.02.2008 retrieved from https://wcd.coe.int/ViewDoc.jsp?Ref=Decl(20.02.2008)&Language=lanEnglish&Ver=0001&BackColorInternet=9999CC&BackColorIntranet=FFBB55&BackColorLogged=FFAC75 (on 26.03.2008).

including its traces (logs, records and processing), within a reasonably short period of time".[146]

1.2.3. *European Union*

European Union and children's rights – The European Union has also been active in the field of promoting children's rights. References to children's rights have been included in different treaties and in the recent EU Charter on Fundamental Rights. Furthermore, in 2006, the European Commission launched the Communication Toward an EU strategy on the rights of the child.

A. *EU Treaties*

Limited reference to children in EU Treaties – The EU Treaties barely include references to children and their rights.[147] This is not so surprising given the traditional focus of the Treaties on the citizen as a 'worker'.[148] Until recently (cf. *infra*), the concept of the child as a subject of rights and an active participant in society was not put into practice at the European Union level. It was argued that the absence of an explicit legal basis implied that there could not be a coherent strategy on children's rights.[149] With the adoption of the Lisbon Treaty, the creation of the Charter of Fundamental Rights and the 2006 Commission Communication 'Towards an EU strategy on the rights of the child (cf. *infra*), however, steps towards such a basis were taken.

---

[146] Committee of Ministers, Declaration on protecting the dignity, security and privacy of children on the Internet, 20.02.2008 retrieved from https://wcd.coe.int/ViewDoc.jsp?Ref=Decl(20.02.2008)&Language=lanEnglish&Ver=0001&BackColorInternet=9999CC&BackColorIntranet=FFBB55&BackColorLogged=FFAC75 (on 26.03.2008). Cf. *infra* with respect to the right to anonymity.

[147] Commission of the European Communities, Commission Staff working document accompanying the Communication from the Commission Towards an EU strategy on the rights of the child, Impact assessment, COM (2006) 367 final, SEC (2006) 888, 04.07.2006, retrieved from http://register.consilium.europa.eu/pdf/en/06/st12/st12107-ad01.en06.pdf (on 29.08.2006), 12 (footnote 29).

[148] Ruxton, Sandy, *What about us? Children's rights in the European Union? Next Steps*, Brussels, The European Children's Network, 2005, 19; Commission of the European Communities, Commission Staff working document accompanying the Communication from the Commission Towards an EU strategy on the rights of the child, Impact assessment, COM (2006) 367 final, SEC (2006) 888, 04.07.2006, retrieved from http://register.consilium.europa.eu/pdf/en/06/st12/st12107-ad01.en06.pdf (on 29.08.2006), 16.

[149] Ruxton, Sandy, *What about us? Children's rights in the European Union? Next Steps*, Brussels, The European Children's Network, 2005, 26.

Amsterdam Treaty – The first explicit reference to children in a Treaty text was introduced by the Amsterdam Treaty in article 29 of the previous Treaty on the European Union.[150] This article contains a reference to the prevention of offences against children.[151] The Amsterdam Treaty also introduced a number of other articles in the Treaty establishing the European Community (TEC) which are indirectly related to children's rights, such as article 13 TEC [currently article 19 TFEU] (which inserts a non-discrimination clause, with 'age' as one of the criteria), article 137 TEC [currently article 153 TFEU] (which provides a basis for combating social exclusion) and article 152 TEC [currently article 168 TFEU] (which presents a legal basis for ensuring that EU citizens receive a high level of protection of health in the definition and implementation of all Community policies and activities).[152] In more general terms, the Amsterdam Treaty also reaffirmed the European Union's commitment to the recognition of fundamental rights in Community Law (through the insertion of article 6 (2) into the TEU [currently article 6 para. 3 TEU]).

Lisbon Treaty – However, the Lisbon Treaty[153] creates an actual legal framework for children's rights at the EU level. The new article 3 para. 5 of the TEU, as introduced by article 1(4) of the Treaty of Lisbon, states that the Union "*shall combat [...] discrimination and shall promote [...] protection of the rights of the child*", and clarifies that "*in its relations with the wider world, the Union shall [...] contribute to [...] the protection of human rights, in particular the rights of the child*". The creation of this legal basis was welcomed by children rights advocates.[154]

---

150 Commission of the European Communities, Commission Staff working document accompanying the Communication from the Commission Towards an EU strategy on the rights of the child, Impact assessment, COM (2006) 367 final, SEC (2006) 888, 04.07.2006, retrieved from http://register.consilium.europa.eu/pdf/en/06/st12/st12107-ad01.en06.pdf (on 29.08.2006), 12. See also: Verhellen, Eugeen, *Convention on the Rights of the Child: background, motivation, strategies, main themes*, Antwerpen, Garant, 2006, 141. Note that this reference has not been included in the TEU, as amended by the Treaty of Lisbon.

151 Article 1 para. 11 Treaty of Amsterdam.

152 Commission of the European Communities, Commission Staff working document accompanying the Communication from the Commission Towards an EU strategy on the rights of the child, Impact assessment, COM (2006) 367 final, SEC (2006) 888, 04.07.2006, retrieved from http://register.consilium.europa.eu/pdf/en/06/st12/st12107-ad01.en06.pdf (on 29.08.2006), 12.

153 Treaty of Lisbon amending the Treaty on European Union and the Treaty establishing the European Community, 13.12.2007, *OJ* 17.12.2007, *C* 306, 1.

154 European Children's Network, The new EU Reform Treaty – What is the impact on children's rights?, 03.12.2007, retrieved from http://www.crin.org/docs/Briefing_EURONET_EU_Reform_Treaty_Nov_07_Final.pdf (on 23.01.2008).

B. *Charter of Fundamental Rights of the European Union*

Charter of Fundamental Rights and children – The Charter of Fundamental Rights of the European Union,[155] adopted in 2000, was considered another significant step towards recognising children as actual rights holders. Apart from a number of articles that are relevant to children with respect to specific issues,[156] the Charter also includes an article specifically dedicated to children's rights:

---

[155] European Union, Charter of Fundamental Rights of the European Union, *OJ* 18.12.2000, *C* 364, 1, retrieved from http://eur-lex.europa.eu/LexUriServ/site/en/oj/2000/c_364/c_36420001218en00010022.pdf (on 12.03.2007). Although fundamental rights were already part of the European Union legal framework (cf. article 6 para. 3 TEU: "*Fundamental rights, as guanteed by the European Convention for the Protection of Human Rights and Fundamental Freedoms and as they result from the constitutional traditions common to the Member States, shall constitute general principles of Community law*"), it was considered "*necessary to strengthen the protection of fundamental rights in the light of changes in society, social progress and scientific and technological developments by making those rights more visible in a Charter*" (preamble Charter, para. 4). The European Commission has stated that "*[t]he Charter of Fundamental Rights, independently of its legal status, may be seen as a particularly authentic expression of fundamental rights guaranteed as general principles of law*": Commission of the European Communities, Commission Staff working document accompanying the Communication from the Commission Towards an EU strategy on the rights of the child, Preliminary inventory of EU actions affecting children's rights, COM (2006) 367 final, SEC (2006) 889, 04.07.2006, retrieved from http://register.consilium.europa.eu/pdf/en/06/st12/st12107-ad02.en06.pdf (on 29.08.2006), 3. For more information on the Charter, cf. Tridimas, Takis, *The general principles of EU law*, Oxford, Oxford University Press, 2006, 356–369.

[156] For instance, article 32 on the prohibition of child labour and protection of young people at work, and article 14 on the right to education. In total, the European Commission considers 19 out of the 50 articles applicable to children and young people: Rapid, 25 May: Commission's actions in favour of children and young people, MEMO/05/171, 25.05.2005, retrieved from http://europa.eu/rapid/pressReleasesAction.do?reference=MEMO/05/171&format=HTML&aged=1&language=EN&guiLanguage=en (on 12.12.2008). It has also been argued that on the basis of articles 20 ("*Everyone is equal before the law*") and 21 ("*Any discrimination based on any ground such as sex, race, colour, ethnic or social origin, genetic features, language, religion or belief, political or any other opinion, membership of a national minority, property, birth, disability, age or sexual orientation shall be prohibited*"), all rights included in the Charter are applicable to children: Commission of the European Communities, Commission Staff working document accompanying the Communication from the Commission Towards an EU strategy on the rights of the child, Impact assessment, COM (2006) 367 final, SEC (2006) 888, 04.07.2006, retrieved from http://register.consilium.europa.eu/pdf/en/06/st12/st12107-ad01.en06.pdf (on 29.08.2006), 13.

> Article 24:
> 1. *Children shall have the right to such protection and care as is necessary for their well-being. They may express their views freely. Such views shall be taken into consideration on matters which concern them in accordance with their age and maturity.*
> 2. *In all actions relating to children, whether taken by public authorities or private institutions, the child's best interests must be a primary consideration.*

ARTICLE 24 – This article provides, for the first time in EU history, a clear and solid legal basis for considering children not only as vulnerable beings who need protection, but also as "*independent and autonomous rights holders*".[157,158] Inspiration was clearly drawn from the UNCRC. In the first paragraph of article 24, the substance of article 12 UNCRC is rephrased, and in the second paragraph, reference is made to a concept which is of the utmost importance in the UNCRC as well, i.e., the 'best interests of the child'. It has been argued that the introduction of this concept in the EU legal framework indicates "*a significant step towards 'child-proofing' of European Union legislation policy*".[159] This has been confirmed in a Commission Communication which makes it a requirement that, as part of the normal decision-making procedures, any proposal for legislation and any draft instrument must first be scrutinised for compatibility with the Charter of Fundamental Rights.[160] It is important,

---

157 COMMISSION OF THE EUROPEAN COMMUNITIES, Commission Staff working document accompanying the Communication from the Commission Towards an EU strategy on the rights of the child, Impact assessment, COM (2006) 367 final, SEC (2006) 888, 04.07.2006, retrieved from http://register.consilium.europa.eu/pdf/en/06/st12/st12107-ad01.en06.pdf (on 29.08.2006), 13; COMMISSION OF THE EUROPEAN COMMUNITIES, Commission Staff working document accompanying the Communication from the Commission Towards an EU strategy on the rights of the child, Preliminary inventory of EU actions affecting children's rights, COM (2006) 367 final, SEC (2006) 889, 04.07.2006, retrieved from http://register.consilium.europa.eu/pdf/en/06/st12/st12107-ad02.en06.pdf (on 29.08.2006), 3.

158 The European Court of Justice also refers to article 24 of the Charter with respect to the protection of children's rights: ECJ, Dynamic Medien v. Avides Media AG, C-244/06, 14.02.2008, para. 41.

159 COMMISSION OF THE EUROPEAN COMMUNITIES, Commission Staff working document accompanying the Communication from the Commission Towards an EU strategy on the rights of the child, Impact assessment, COM (2006) 367 final, SEC (2006) 888, 04.07.2006, retrieved from http://register.consilium.europa.eu/pdf/en/06/st12/st12107-ad01.en06.pdf (on 29.08.2006), 13; RUXTON, Sandy, *What about us? Children's rights in the European Union? Next Steps*, Brussels, The European Children's Network, 2005, 21.

160 COMMISSION OF THE EUROPEAN COMMUNITIES, Communication from the Commission Compliance with the Charter of Fundamental Rights in Commission legislative proposals – Methodology for systematic and rigorous monitoring, COM (2005) 172 final, 27.04.2005. This Communication proposes a 'methodology for systematic and rigorous monitoring',

however, to note that up until late 2007 the Charter was still not legally binding.[161] This does not alter the fact, however, that the Charter, and specifically article 24 – despite being more limited than the UNCRC – were an important step forward in the development of a coherent EU strategy with respect to children's rights.

LEGALLY BINDING – However, the Lisbon Treaty does attribute the same legal force to the Charter of Fundamental Rights as the other Treaties.[162, 163] It also provides for a number of amendments to the Charter. Article 24, for instance, is enlarged to include a third paragraph relating to the right of children to maintain a relationship with their parents.[164] Children's rights organisations greeted the elevation of the legal status of the Charter with approval.[165]

C. *EU strategy on the rights of the child*

COMMISSION COMMUNICATION – In July 2006, the Commission issued a Communication titled Toward an EU strategy on the rights of the child.[166] Its aim is to establish a "*comprehensive EU strategy to effectively promote and*

built around six important actions: systematic departmental monitoring of respect for fundamental rights at the preparatory and interdepartmental consultation stages, taking fundamental rights into account in impact assessments, taking fundamental rights into account in the explanatory memorandum, following-up by the Group of Commissioners on the internal monitoring of respect for fundamental rights, monitoring respect for fundamental rights in the work of the legislature, and publicising the internal monitoring of fundamental rights.

161 RUXTON, Sandy, *What about us? Children's rights in the European Union? Next Steps*, Brussels, The European Children's Network, 2005, 22.

162 RAPID, Charter of Fundamental Rights: the Presidents of the Commission, European Parliament and Council sign and solemnly proclaim the Charter in Strasbourg, IP/07/1916, 12.12.2007, retrieved from http://europa.eu/rapid/pressReleasesAction.do?reference=IP/07/1916&format=HTML&aged=0&language=EN&guiLanguage=en (on 23.01.2008).

163 Article 6 para. 1 TEU states: "*1. The Union recognises the rights, freedoms and principles set out in the Charter of Fundamental Rights of the European Union of 7 December 2000, as adapted at Strasbourg, on 12 December 2007, which shall have the same legal value as the Treaties*".

164 Charter of Fundamental Rights of the European Union (as amended by the Treaty of Lisbon), *OJ* 14.12.2007, *C* 303, 1.

165 EUROPEAN CHILDREN'S NETWORK, The new EU Reform Treaty – What is the impact on children's rights?, 03.12.2007, retrieved from http://www.crin.org/docs/Briefing_EURONET_EU_Reform_Treaty_Nov_07_Final.pdf (on 23.01.2008).

166 COMMISSION OF THE EUROPEAN COMMUNITIES, Communication from the Commission Towards an EU strategy on the rights of the child, COM (2006) 367 final, 04.07.2006.

safeguard the rights of the child in the European Union's internal and external policies and to support Member States' efforts in this field".[167] The Communication fits into the broader legal framework with respect to children's rights[168] and expresses the priority the Commission gives to this issue.[169] In this context, the Commission emphasises that children benefit from the full range of human rights and stresses that it is vital to recognise children's rights as a self-standing set of concerns.

COMPETENCE AND OBLIGATIONS – According to the Communication, the *general* competence of the European Union in the area of children's rights is based on article 6 TEU,[170] which states that fundamental rights must be respected in whatever action the EU takes in accordance with its competences. Furthermore, the EU can act in *particular* fields to safeguard and promote children's rights. In addition, the respect for children's rights not only entails a general obligation to refrain from acts violating these rights, but also implies that the EU must take them into account "*wherever relevant in the conduct of its own policies under the various legal bases of the Treaties*".[171, 172] The Commission clarifies that any such action – by means of legislation, soft-law, financial assistance or political dialogue – needs to respect the general

[167] It was clarified that children are considered to be "*persons below the age of 18, as in the UNCRC*".

[168] Such as the UNCRC, the ECHR and the Charter of Fundamental Rights of the European Union: cf. *supra*.

[169] See for instance: COMMISSION OF THE EUROPEAN COMMUNITIES, Strategic objectives 2005–2009, Europe 2010: A partnership for European renewal, prosperity, solidarity and security, COM (2005) 12 final, 26.01.2005, 9: "*A particular priority must be effective protection of the rights of children, both against economic exploitation and all forms of abuse, with the Union acting as a beacon to the rest of the world*".

[170] Article 6 para. 3 TEU: cf. footnote 155.

[171] COMMISSION OF THE EUROPEAN COMMUNITIES, Communication from the Commission Towards an EU strategy on the rights of the child, COM (2006) 367 final, 04.07.2006), 3.

[172] In 2008, the Article 29 Data Protection Working Party issued a working document on the protection of children's personal data (also with respect to new communication technologies) in the framework of the EU strategy on the rights of the child, cf. ARTICLE 29 DATA PROTECTION WORKING PARTY, Working document 1/2008 on the protection of children's personal data (General guidelines and the special case of schools), 18.02.2008, retrieved from http://ec.europa.eu/justice_home/fsj/privacy/docs/wpdocs/2008/wp147_en.pdf (on 05.03.2008). A year later, in February 2009, an opinion on this subject was adopted: ARTICLE 29 DATA PROTECTION WORKING PARTY, Opinion 2/2009 on the protection of children's personal data (General guidelines and the special case of schools), 11.02.2009, retrieved from http://ec.europa.eu/justice_home/fsj/privacy/docs/wpdocs/2009/wp160_en.pdf (on 18.05.2009).

principles of subsidiarity and proportionality, and must not infringe on the competence of Member States.

Action undertaken – According to the Communication, the EU has already undertaken action in different policy fields related to children's rights, such as child trafficking and prostitution, violence against children, discrimination, child poverty, social exclusion, child labour, health and education.[173] To address these issues more effectively in the future, the Communication also puts forward seven specific objectives: (1) capitalising on existing activities while addressing urgent needs, (2) addressing priorities for future EU action, (3) mainstreaming children's rights in EU actions, (4) establishing efficient coordination and consultation mechanisms, (5) enhancing capacity for and expertise in children's rights, (6) communicating more effectively on children's rights, and (7) promoting the rights of the child in external relations.[174] To attain these objectives, a number of action points are suggested: for instance, the collection of data on children's rights, the establishment of a European Forum for the Rights of the Child, the appointment of a Commission Coordinator for the Rights of the Child, the development of a web-based discussion and work platform, and the provision of information on children's rights in a child-friendly manner. No specific mention of children's rights in the media environment is made in the Communication itself.[175] It can, of course, be considered logical that other issues such as poverty, health and basic well-being take precedence over media related issues. However, the topic has not totally escaped notice. In the impact assessment document, the establishment of a 'Permanent Childhood and Adolescence Intergovernmental Group' is mentioned. One of the issues this Group is urged to address is the growing number of transnational phenomena that have a negative impact on children, such as illegal and dangerous information on the Internet. Furthermore, in a second annex to the Commission Communication, which lists all EU actions affecting children's rights, 'Media

[173] Commission of the European Communities, Communication from the Commission Towards an EU strategy on the rights of the child, COM (2006) 367 final, 04.07.2006, 6.

[174] It has been suggested – before the Communication was actually approved – that the document was "*likely to be a significant advance for children's rights at EU level, setting out both a long-term vision for the future, and also concrete practical measures that can be taken in the short-to-medium term*": Ruxton, Sandy, *What about us? Children's rights in the European Union? Next Steps*, Brussels, The European Children's Network, 2005, 26.

[175] There is one point of action regarding online child pornography: the Commission proposes to support the banking sector and credit card companies to combat the use of credit cards when purchasing sexual images of children on the Internet: Commission of the European Communities, Communication from the Commission Towards an EU strategy on the rights of the child, COM (2006) 367 final, 04.07.2006, 7.

and Internet' is a separate topic.[176] Within this context, reference is made to the Television without Frontiers Directive (*infra*), the Council Recommendation on the protection of minors and human dignity (*supra*), the consultation document on child safety and mobile phone services, and the Safer Internet Plus Programme (*supra*).[177, 178] Emphasis is put on the two sides of the Internet-coin. On the one hand, according to the Commission, the Internet makes available "*an enormous range of educational materials and cultural opportunities, and is a powerful tool that can help to meet children's rights under the CRC (e.g. to participation, information and freedom of expression)*".[179] However, at the same time, children can be confronted with harmful or illegal images on the Internet.

PROGRESS – The Commission reported on its progress in April 2008.[180] It stated in its press release that a number of actions proposed in the Commu-

[176] COMMISSION OF THE EUROPEAN COMMUNITIES, Commission Staff working document accompanying the Communication from the Commission Towards an EU strategy on the rights of the child, Preliminary inventory of EU actions affecting children's rights, COM (2006) 367 final, SEC (2006) 889, 04.07.2006, retrieved from http://register.consilium.europa.eu/pdf/en/06/st12/st12107–ad02.en06.pdf (on 29.08.2006), 15–18.

[177] COMMISSION OF THE EUROPEAN COMMUNITIES, Commission Staff working document accompanying the Communication from the Commission Towards an EU strategy on the rights of the child, Preliminary inventory of EU actions affecting children's rights, COM (2006) 367 final, SEC (2006) 889, 04.07.2006, retrieved from http://register.consilium.europa.eu/pdf/en/06/st12/st12107–ad02.en06.pdf (on 29.08.2006), 15–18. Two documents related to illegal content are also mentioned: the Council Decision on combating child pornography on the Internet, and a proposed Commission Communication on reserving the number range beginning with '116' for harmonised European services, including child helplines and hotlines for missing and sexually exploited children.

[178] A number of instruments and initiatives specifically focused on advertising, such as the Ad hoc Roundtable on advertising, the Directive on misleading advertising, the Directive on unfair commercial practices, the Television without Frontiers Directive, and an EU study on the impact of advertising on children (2001), were also mentioned: COMMISSION OF THE EUROPEAN COMMUNITIES, Commission Staff working document accompanying the Communication from the Commission Towards an EU strategy on the rights of the child, Preliminary inventory of EU actions affecting children's rights, COM (2006) 367 final, SEC (2006) 889, 04.07.2006, retrieved from http://register.consilium.europa.eu/pdf/en/06/st12/st12107–ad02.en06.pdf (on 29.08.2006), 15–16.

[179] COMMISSION OF THE EUROPEAN COMMUNITIES, Commission Staff working document accompanying the Communication from the Commission Towards an EU strategy on the rights of the child, Preliminary inventory of EU actions affecting children's rights, COM (2006) 367 final, SEC (2006) 889, 04.07.2006, retrieved from http://register.consilium.europa.eu/pdf/en/06/st12/st12107–ad02.en06.pdf (on 29.08.2006), 17.

[180] RAPID, Follow-up to the EU strategy on the rights of the child, MEMO/08/231, 10.04.2008, retrieved from http://europa.eu/rapid/pressReleasesAction.do?reference=MEMO/08/231&format (on 07.07.2008).

nication had already been launched. One of the actions mentioned related to the establishment of a system to stop payments by means of a credit card or electronic payment of images of sexual abuse of children on the Internet.[181]

Parliament resolution – Inspired by the Commission Communication, the European Parliament issued its own Resolution Towards an EU strategy on the rights of the child,[182] aimed at strengthening and completing the Commission's strategy. Contrary to the Commission's Communication, the Parliament did pay much attention to media-related issues. Aside from some points concerning the fight against (Internet) child pornography and the sexual abuse of children via the Internet, a number of recommendations were made related to harmful media content. The Parliament called for a prohibition on the broadcasting of harmful images and content and the marketing of violent video games.[183] Furthermore, support was expressed for the Safer Internet Plus Programme, the implementation of a framework for the safer use of mobile telephones by young people and children, the creation of a uniform classification and labelling system in the EU for the sale and distribution of audiovisual content and videogames intended for minors and the PEGI system (i.e., a pan-European classification scheme for videogames).[184] Finally, the Parliament emphasised that "*greater consideration is needed to review the mass media's unrestricted right of access to children and the right of the child to access the mass media without restriction*".[185]

---

181 See also footnote 175.

182 European Parliament, Resolution Towards an EU strategy on the rights of the child, 2007/2093 (INI), 16.01.2008, retrieved from http://www.europarl.europa.eu/sides/getDoc.do?pubRef=-//EP//TEXT+TA+P6–TA-2008–0012+0+DOC+XML+V0//EN (on 21.01.2008).

183 European Parliament, Resolution Towards an EU strategy on the rights of the child, 2007/2093 (INI), 16.01.2008, retrieved from http://www.europarl.europa.eu/sides/getDoc.do?pubRef=-//EP//TEXT+TA+P6–TA-2008–0012+0+DOC+XML+V0//EN (on 21.01.2008), recital 63.

184 European Parliament, Resolution Towards an EU strategy on the rights of the child, 2007/2093 (INI), 16.01.2008, retrieved from http://www.europarl.europa.eu/sides/getDoc.do?pubRef=-//EP//TEXT+TA+P6–TA-2008–0012+0+DOC+XML+V0//EN (on 21.01.2008), recitals 63–66.

185 European Parliament, Resolution Towards an EU strategy on the rights of the child, 2007/2093 (INI), 16.01.2008, retrieved from http://www.europarl.europa.eu/sides/getDoc.do?pubRef=-//EP//TEXT+TA+P6–TA-2008–0012+0+DOC+XML+V0//EN (on 21.01.2008), recital 67.

1.2.4. *Concluding remark*

Children's rights: a multidimensional debate – The adoption of the UNCRC has dispelled any remaining doubts on whether fundamental rights are applicable to children. We have noted that the debate surrounding these children's rights is multidimensional. On the one hand, children should not merely be seen as victims, but as strong and often competent social actors, but, on the other hand, with respect to certain aspects of their lives their vulnerability is undeniable, and, hence, guidance and support is required. The scope of this guidance and support will, of course, vary according to the age and the level of development of the child.[186]

Restrictions on children's rights – The question which then arises of course, as Voorhoof points out, is to what extent the government, schools and parents (exercising their parental authority) can impose restrictions on the fundamental rights exercised by children.[187] In this context, Voorhoof refers to the vertical and horizontal effect of the exercise of children's fundamental rights. The vertical effect relates to interferences by the government, the horizontal effect concerns interferences by parents or educators. Whereas restrictions on fundamental rights by governments often need to adhere to strict requirements put down in treaties or legislation (for instance, article 10 para. 2 ECHR, *infra*), the situation is less clear with respect to restrictions imposed by parents or educators. The acceptance of a horizontal effect with respect to children's rights entails that not all restrictions by parents and educators, for instance with respect to a child's right to freedom of expression, are acceptable, and furthermore, that governments have a 'duty of care' to create the basic conditions for children to be able to exercise their rights in an efficient and meaningful manner.[188] This debate on the relation between

---

[186] Voorhoof, Dirk, "Media(recht) en kinder(recht)en" ["*Media(law) and children's rights*"], Deel 1, 1.9., update 1995, in: Verhellen, Eugeen (ed.), *Kinderrechtengids (KIDS): Commentaren, regelgeving, rechtspraak en nuttige informatie over de maatschappelijke en juridische positie van het kind* [*Guide to children's rights: Comments, regulation, case law and useful information about the social and legal status of the child*], Gent, Mys en Breesch, 1994, 15 [in Dutch].

[187] Voorhoof, Dirk, "Media(recht) en kinder(recht)en" ["*Media(law) and children's rights*"], Deel 1, 1.9., update 1995, in: Verhellen, Eugeen (ed.), *Kinderrechtengids (KIDS): Commentaren, regelgeving, rechtspraak en nuttige informatie over de maatschappelijke en juridische positie van het kind* [*Guide to children's rights: Comments, regulation, case law and useful information about the social and legal status of the child*], Gent, Mys en Breesch, 1994, 15 [in Dutch].

[188] Detrick, Sharon, *A commentary on the United Nations Convention on the Rights of the Child*, The Hague, Martinus Nijhoff Publishers, 1999, 31; Voorhoof, Dirk, "Media(recht)

children's exercise of their fundamental rights and parental responsibility is very complex one, in which both elements will need to be balanced against each other.[189] Restrictions on children's rights and their legitimacy will be examined in greater detail in the next chapter.

1.3. Human Rights: freedom of expression, privacy and procedural guarantees

Fundamental human rights – With respect to the protection of children from harmful media content, two important (substantive) human rights are of the utmost importance, i.e., the right to freedom of expression and the right to privacy. Although the right to privacy is a vital right, which often comes into play with respect to children's online (or mobile) presence, this topic could (and should) be the subject of further research. Hence in this section, the right to privacy is discussed only briefly, and the main focus is on the right to freedom of expression. Finally, two rights relating to procedural guarantees, the right to a fair trial and the right to an effective remedy, are also discussed briefly, because of their relevance to the use of ARIs.

1.3.1. *Freedom of expression*

A. *Article 10 ECHR*

Principle and sources – Freedom of expression is a fundamental right in any democratic society, "*one of the basic conditions for its progress and for the development of every man*".[190] This fundamental right is expressed in a

en kinder(recht)en" ["*Media(law) and children's rights*"], Deel 1, 1.9., update 1995, in: Verhellen, Eugeen (ed.), *Kinderrechtengids (KIDS): Commentaren, regelgeving, rechtspraak en nuttige informatie over de maatschappelijke en juridische positie van het kind* [*Guide to children's rights: Comments, regulation, case law and useful information about the social and legal status of the child*], Gent, Mys en Breesch, 1994, 15–16 [in Dutch]. For more details on the 'horizontal effect', for instance, in the context of the ECHR: *infra*.

189 Voorhoof, Dirk, "Media(recht) en kinder(recht)en" ["*Media(law) and children's rights*"], Deel 1, 1.9., update 1995, in: Verhellen, Eugeen (ed.), *Kinderrechtengids (KIDS): Commentaren, regelgeving, rechtspraak en nuttige informatie over de maatschappelijke en juridische positie van het kind* [*Guide to children's rights: Comments, regulation, case law and useful information about the social and legal status of the child*], Gent, Mys en Breesch, 1994, 31 [in Dutch].

190 European Court of Human Rights, Perna v. Italy, 06.05.2003, para. 39.

number of international,[191] European and national[192] legislative texts.[193] At the European level, the core provision guaranteeing this right is article 10 of the ECHR (*supra*):[194]

> 1. *Everyone has the right to freedom of expression. This right shall include freedom to hold opinions and to receive and impart information and ideas without interference by public authority and regardless of frontiers. This article shall not prevent States from requiring the licensing of broadcasting, television or cinema enterprises.*

[191] The two most important international sources are article 19 of the 1948 Universal Declaration on Human Rights ("*Everyone has the right to freedom of opinion and expression; this right includes freedom to hold opinions without interference and to seek, receive and impart information and ideas through any media and regardless of frontiers*": United Nations, Universal Declaration on Human Rights, 10.12.1948, retrieved from http://www.unhchr.ch/udhr/lang/eng.htm (on 15.05.2007)) and Article 19 of the 1966 International Covenant on Civil and Political Rights ("*Everyone shall have the right to hold opinions without interference. 2. Everyone shall have the right to freedom of expression; this right shall include freedom to seek, receive and impart information and ideas of all kinds, regardless of frontiers, either orally, in writing or in print, in the form of art, or through any other media of his choice. 3. The exercise of the rights provided for in paragraph 2 of this article carries with it special duties and responsibilities. It may therefore be subject to certain restrictions, but these shall only be such as are provided by law and are necessary: (a) For respect of the rights or reputations of others; (b) For the protection of national security or of public order (ordre public), or of public health or morals*": United Nations, International Covenant on Civil and Political Rights, 16.12.1966, retrieved from http://www.unhchr.ch/html/menu3/b/a_ccpr.htm (on 15.05.2007)). Belgium has made reservations with respect to article 19 ICCPR, of which the Belgian government has stated that it "*shall be applied […] in the context of the provisions and restrictions set forth or authorized in articles 10 and 11 of the Convention for the Protection of Human Rights and Fundamental Freedoms*". Reservations can be found at http://www.unhchr.ch/html/menu3/b/treaty5_asp.htm (last retrieved on 12.03.2007). For a comparison of these international sources with article 10 ECHR, cf. Voorhoof, Dirk, "Vrijheid van meningsuiting" ["*Freedom of expression*"], in: Vande Lanotte, Johan and Haeck, Yves, *Handboek EVRM: Deel II: Artikelsgewijze commentaar (Volume I)* [*ECHR: Part II: Commentary on the articles*], Antwerpen, Intersentia, 2004, 950 *et seq.* [in Dutch].

[192] In Belgium, the relevant provisions are articles 19, 25 and 150 of the Constitution.

[193] For more information on the legal concept of freedom of expression, cf. for instance: Barendt, Eric, *Freedom of speech*, Oxford, Oxford University Press, 2005, 526 p.

[194] The importance of this article has been affirmed in Council of Europe (Committee of Ministers), Declaration on freedom of expression and information, 29.04.1982, retrieved from https://wcd.coe.int/com.instranet.InstraServlet?command=com.instranet.CmdBlobGet&InstranetImage=601273&SecMode=1&DocId=675536&Usage=2 (on 12.12.2008).

2. *The exercise of these freedoms, since it carries with it duties and responsibilities, may be subject to such formalities, conditions, restrictions or penalties as are prescribed by law and are necessary in a democratic society, in the interests of national security, territorial integrity or public safety, for the prevention of disorder or crime, for the protection of health or morals, for the protection of the reputation or the rights of others, for preventing the disclosure of information received in confidence, or for maintaining the authority and impartiality of the judiciary.*

As discussed above, the ECHR is an initiative of the Council of Europe. However, it is part of the legal framework of the European Union due to article 6 para. 3 TEU. Hence, article 10 ECHR is also of the utmost importance in the EU legislative framework. The European Court of Justice has confirmed this fundamental rights theory on several occasions, for instance:

> *With regard to Article 10 of the European Convention on Human Rights, [...] it must first be pointed out that, as the Court has consistently held, fundamental rights form an integral part of the general principles of law, the observance of which it ensures. For that purpose the Court draws inspiration from the constitutional traditions common to the Member States and from the guidelines supplied by international treaties for the protection of human rights on which the Member States have collaborated or of which they are signatories (see, in particular, the judgment in Case C-4/73 Nold v Commission [1974] ECR 491, paragraph 13). The European Convention on Human Rights has special significance in that respect (see in particular Case C-222/84 Johnston v Chief Constable of the Royal Ulster Constabulary [1986] ECR 1651, paragraph 18). It follows that, as the Court held in its judgment in Case C-5/88 Wachauf v Federal Republic of Germany [1989] ECR 2609, paragraph 19, the Community cannot accept measures which are incompatible with observance of the human rights thus recognized and guaranteed.*[195]

The right to freedom of expression is, at the EU level, also included in the Charter of Fundamental Rights of the European Union (*supra*), and more specifically in article 11.[196]

[195] ECJ, Elliniki Radiophonia Tiléorassi AE and Panellinia Omospondia Syllogon Prossopikou v. Dimotiki Etairia Pliroforissis and Sotirios Kouvelas and Nicolaos Avdellas and others, C-260/89, 18.06.1991.

[196] "*1. Everyone has the right to freedom of expression. This right shall include freedom to hold opinions and to receive and impart information and ideas without interference by public authority and regardless of frontiers. 2. The freedom and pluralism of the media shall be respected*": European Union, Charter of Fundamental Rights of the European Union, *OJ* 18.12.2000, *C* 364, 1.

ARTICLE 10 ECHR – Freedom of expression includes the freedom to hold opinions and to receive and impart information and ideas without interference by any public authority, and regardless of frontiers. This fundamental right encompasses two facets: States need to not only refrain from interfering with the freedom of expression of their citizens (passive),[197] but they also might have to ensure that the freedom of expression of these citizens is not too restricted by private persons or organisations (active 'duty to care').[198] In this respect, the European Court of Human Rights has stated that

> *[g]enuine, effective exercise of this freedom [of expression] does not depend merely on the State's duty not to interfere, but may require positive measures of protection, even in the sphere of relations between individuals.*[199]

Ensuring pluralism and diversity of media output is also part of this active duty to care.[200]

SCOPE OF PROTECTION – The scope of application of article 10 ECHR is very broad and extends to any expression regardless of its content, its form (any word, picture, image or action to express an idea,[201] etc.),[202] its disseminator, or the type of medium used.[203] Furthermore, it not only protects information

---

197 The wording "*interference by public authority*" does not preclude an indirect horizontal effect: VOORHOOF, Dirk, "Vrijheid van meningsuiting" ["*Freedom of expression*"], in: VANDE LANOTTE, Johan and HAECK, Yves, *Handboek EVRM: Deel II: Artikelsgewijze commentaar (Volume I)* [*ECHR: Part II: Commentary on the articles*], Antwerpen, Intersentia, 2004, 922 [in Dutch].

198 VOORHOOF, Dirk, "Vrijheid van meningsuiting" ["*Freedom of expression*"], in: VANDE LANOTTE, Johan and HAECK, Yves, *Handboek EVRM: Deel II: Artikelsgewijze commentaar (Volume I)* [*ECHR: Part II: Commentary on the articles*], Antwerpen, Intersentia, 2004, 925 [in Dutch]. See for instance: EUROPEAN COURT OF HUMAN RIGHTS, Özgür Gündem v. Turkey, 16.03.2000, para. 42–43.

199 EUROPEAN COURT OF HUMAN RIGHTS, Özgür Gündem v. Turkey, 16.03.2000, para. 42–43.

200 UYTTENDAELE, Caroline, *Openbare informatie – Het juridisch statuut in een convergerende mediaomgeving* [*Public information – The legal status in a converging media environment*], Antwerpen- Apeldoorn, Maklu, 2002; 169 [in Dutch].

201 VOORHOOF, Dirk, "Vrijheid van meningsuiting" ["*Freedom of expression*"], in: VANDE LANOTTE, Johan and HAECK, Yves, *Handboek EVRM: Deel II: Artikelsgewijze commentaar (Volume I)* [*ECHR: Part II: Commentary on the articles*], Antwerpen, Intersentia, 2004, 905 [in Dutch].

202 MACOVEI, Monica, *Freedom of expression – A guide to the implementation of Article 10 of the European Convention of Human Rights (Human rights handbooks, No. 2)*, Strasbourg, Council of Europe, 2004, 15.

203 MACOVEI, Monica, *Freedom of expression – A guide to the implementation of Article 10 of the European Convention of Human Rights (Human rights handbooks, No. 2)*, Strasbourg, Council of Europe, 2004, 7.

and ideas that are favourably received or deemed inoffensive, but also those that offend, shock or disturb.[204] Such are, as the Court repeats regularly, the demands of pluralism, tolerance and broadmindedness, since without conflicting information and ideas there would be no 'democratic society' at all.[205] Pornographic content, for instance, also falls within the scope of article 10.[206] However, one exception to this rule was made with respect to the dissemination of racism and the Nazi ideology.[207, 208] The justification for this exception can be found in article 17 ECHR which states that "*[n]othing in this Convention may be interpreted as implying for any State, group or person any right to engage in any activity or perform any act aimed at the destruction of any of the rights and freedoms set forth herein or at their limitation to a greater extent than is provided for in the Convention*". According to Macovei, this is an application of the 'theory of the paradox of tolerance': "*an absolute tolerance may lead to the tolerance of the ideas promoting intolerance, and the latter could then destroy the tolerance*".[209]

---

204 This doctrine was first put forward in the *Handyside* case (European Court of Human Rights, Handyside v. the United Kingdom, 7.12.1976, para. 49; see also European Court of Human Rights, Perna v. Italy, 06.05.2003, para. 39).

205 European Court of Human Rights, Handyside v. the United Kingdom, 7.12.1976, para. 49.

206 Hans-Bredow-Institut and EMR, Study on co-regulation measures in the media sector: Final report, Study commissioned by the European Commission, June 2006, retrieved from http://ec.europa.eu/avpolicy/docs/library/studies/coregul/final_rep_en.pdf (on 28.07.2006), 149.

207 European Court of Human Rights, Garaudy v. France, 24.06.2003: "*Accordingly, the Court considers that, in accordance with Article 17 of the Convention, the applicant cannot rely on the provisions of Article 10 of the Convention regarding his conviction for denying crimes against humanity*"; European Court of Human Rights, Gündüz v. Turkey, 04.12.2003: "*That being so, as a matter of principle it may be considered necessary in certain democratic societies to sanction or even prevent all forms of expression which spread, incite, promote or justify hatred based on intolerance (including religious intolerance), provided that any 'formalities', 'conditions', 'restrictions' or 'penalties' imposed are proportionate to the legitimate aim pursued*"; European Commission of Human Rights, Kühnen v. Germany, 12.05.1988.

208 Macovei, Monica, *Freedom of expression – A guide to the implementation of Article 10 of the European Convention of Human Rights (Human rights handbooks, No. 2)*, Strasbourg, Council of Europe, 2004, 7.

209 Macovei, Monica, *Freedom of expression – A guide to the implementation of Article 10 of the European Convention of Human Rights (Human rights handbooks, No. 2)*, Strasbourg, Council of Europe, 2004, 7.

Exceptions – However, the right to freely express ideas and opinions is not an absolute right. Restrictions[210] can be imposed if they are (1) prescribed by law, (2) introduced with a view to specified interests such as national security, territorial integrity or public safety, for the prevention of disorder or crime, for the protection of health or morals, for the protection of the reputation or the rights of others, for preventing the disclosure of information received in confidence, or maintaining the authority and impartiality of the judiciary, and (3) necessary in a democratic society.[211] The *first* requirement implies that the regulation (legislation, deontological code, implementing orders, etc.) must be adequately foreseeable, i.e., it must be phrased with sufficient precision so that individuals are able to anticipate the consequences which a given action may cause. Most importantly, the regulation must be constructed in such a way so that any interference by public authorities cannot occur arbitrarily.[212] The European Court of Human Rights considers whether rules satisfy this requirement in a rather flexible manner. Even rules issued by a non-state entity to which the state has delegated rule-making

[210] Article 10 para. 2 ECHR mentions "*formalities, conditions, restrictions or penalties*". This description covers a very wide range of measures, of which censorship prior to publication is considered the most dangerous: Macovei, Monica, *Freedom of expression – A guide to the implementation of Article 10 of the European Convention of Human Rights (Human rights handbooks, No. 2)*, Strasbourg, Council of Europe, 2004, 25.

[211] Article 10 para. 2 ECHR. Other human rights texts also contain possible restrictions on the freedom of expression. An interesting provision in this respect is article 13 American Convention on Human Rights (Inter-American Commission on Human Rights, American Convention on Human Rights, 22.11.1969, retrieved from http://www.cidh.oas.org/Basicos/English/Basic4.Amer.Conv.Ratif.htm (on 12.06.2007)): "*1. Everyone has the right to freedom of thought and expression. This right includes freedom to seek, receive, and impart information and ideas of all kinds, regardless of frontiers, either orally, in writing, in print, in the form of art, or through any other medium of one's choice; 2. The exercise of the right provided for in the foregoing paragraph shall not be subject to prior censorship but shall be subject to subsequent imposition of liability, which shall be expressly established by law to the extent necessary to ensure: a. respect for the rights or reputations of others; or b. the protection of national security, public order, or public health or morals; […] 4. Notwithstanding the provisions of paragraph 2 above, public entertainments may be subject by law to prior censorship for the sole purpose of regulating access to them for the moral protection of childhood and adolescence*". This last, explicit exception with respect to the protection of children and young people is especially interesting, and has no equivalent in European human rights legislation.

[212] Voorhoof, Dirk, "Vrijheid van meningsuiting" ["*Freedom of expression*"], in: Vande Lanotte, Johan and Haeck, Yves, *Handboek EVRM: Deel II: Artikelsgewijze commentaar (Volume I)* [*ECHR: Part II: Commentary on the articles*], Antwerpen, Intersentia, 2004, 968 [in Dutch].

authority can be considered 'law' for the purposes of the ECHR.[213] *Second*, the restriction must have a "*legitimate aim*" (*supra*). The protection of morals, for instance, is an aim which has been used to justify interferences with the freedom of expression intended to protect children.[214] The grounds upon which a restriction can be based are enumerated exhaustively in article 10 para. 2,[215] and are interpreted in a restrictive way by the European Court of Human Rights.[216] *Third* and most importantly,[217] the restriction has to be "*necessary in a democratic society*", which entails the existence of a "*pressing social need*". Even though a margin of appreciation is left to the states, the Court will always have the final word[218] and will evaluate whether the

---

213 Hans-Bredow-Institut and EMR, Study on co-regulation measures in the media sector: Final report, Study commissioned by the European Commission, June 2006, retrieved from http://ec.europa.eu/avpolicy/docs/library/studies/coregul/final_rep_en.pdf (on 28.07.2006), 151. Cf. also European Court of Human Rights, Barthold v. Germany, 25.03.1985, para. 46: "*The legal basis of the interference under consideration was provided by section 1 of the 1909 Act, section 8 (1) of the 1964 Act and Rule 7, paragraph (a), of the Rules of Professional Conduct, as applied by the Hanseatic Court of Appeal (see paragraph 22 above). Unlike the first two of these provisions, the third emanated from the Veterinary Surgeons' Council (see paragraphs 11 and 26 above) and not directly from parliament. It is nonetheless to be regarded as a 'law' within the meaning of Article 10 para. 2 (art. 10–2) of the Convention. The competence of the Veterinary Surgeons' Council in the sphere of professional conduct derives from the independent rule-making power that the veterinary profession – in company with other liberal professions – traditionally enjoys, by parliamentary delegation, in the Federal Republic of Germany (see notably the judgment of 9 May 1972 by the Federal Constitutional Court, Entscheidungen des Bundesverfassungsgerichts, vol. 33, pp. 125–171). Furthermore, it is a competence exercised by the Council under the control of the State, which in particular satisfies itself as to observance of national legislation, and the Council is obliged to submit its rules of professional conduct to the Land Government for approval (sections 8 (3) and 18 of the 1964 Act – see paragraphs 11 and 26 above)*".

214 European Court of Human Rights, Handyside v. the United Kingdom, 7.12.1976, *infra*.

215 "*National security, territorial integrity or public safety, for the prevention of disorder or crime, for the protection of health or morals, for the protection of the reputation or rights of others, for preventing the disclosure of information received in confidence, or for maintaining the authority and impartiality of the judiciary*".

216 For a number of examples, cf. Ovey, Clare, White, Robin and Jacobs, Francis, *Jacobs and White The European Convention on Human Rights*, Oxford, Oxford University Press, 2006, 317–334.

217 The former two requirements are less frequently considered problematic by the Court. Cf. also Voorhoof, Dirk, "Vrijheid van meningsuiting" ["*Freedom of expression*"], in: Vande Lanotte, Johan and Haeck, Yves, *Handboek EVRM: Deel II: Artikelsgewijze commentaar (Volume I)* [*ECHR: Part II: Commentary on the articles*], Antwerpen, Intersentia, 2004, 976 and 979 [in Dutch].

218 In *Handyside v. the United Kingdom*, the Court formulated this as follows: "*The domestic margin of appreciation thus goes hand in hand with a European supervision*" (European Court of Human Rights, Handyside v. the United Kingdom, 7.12.1976, para. 49).

concrete measure was "*proportionate to the legitimate aims pursued*",[219] and whether the reasons for justification presented by the national authorities are "*relevant and sufficient*". To this aim, the Court assesses interferences in the light of the case as a whole, including the content of statements that were made, the context, the consequences, the intentions, etc. It is important to note that the three qualitative conditions are interpreted in a strict manner.[220] Furthermore, the burden to prove that all three conditions are met lies with the state.[221]

B. *Freedom of expression and the information society*

Freedom of expression and the information society – Article 10 covers all means of dissemination of information, since any restriction imposed on the means necessarily interferes with the right to receive and impart information.[222, 223] Consequently, the Internet and any other existing and future communication technology fall within the scope of applicability of article 10 ECHR.[224] Different policy documents by various international and supranational organisations have pointed to the utmost importance of respecting freedom of expression (and for that matter, all rights enshrined in the ECHR) in the information age, regardless of new technological

---

[219] Voorhoof argues that this implies a double test. To begin with, the concrete consequences of a restrictive government interference are of importance: the more comprehensive, far-reaching or preventive a measure is, the more difficult it will be to justify. On the other hand, the gravity or severity of a conviction will also be an important element in the proportionality test. Cf. Voorhoof, Dirk, "Vrijheid van meningsuiting" ["*Freedom of expression*"], in: Vande Lanotte, Johan and Haeck, Yves, *Handboek EVRM: Deel II: Artikelsgewijze commentaar (Volume I)* [*ECHR: Part II: Commentary on the articles*], Antwerpen, Intersentia, 2004, 1024 [in Dutch].

[220] European Court of Human Rights, Perna v. Italy, 06.05.2003, para. 39: "*As set forth in Article 10, this freedom is subject to exceptions, which must, however, be construed strictly, and the need for any restrictions must be established convincingly*".

[221] Macovei, Monica, *Freedom of expression – A guide to the implementation of Article 10 of the European Convention of Human Rights (Human rights handbooks, No. 2)*, Strasbourg, Council of Europe, 2004, 30.

[222] European Court of Human Rights, Autronic AG v. Switzerland, 22.05.1990, para. 47; European Court of Human Rights, Murphy v. Ireland, 10.07.2003, para. 61.

[223] For more details on freedom of expression and traditional media such as press, broadcasting, film and video, cf. Barendt, Eric, *Freedom of speech*, Oxford, Oxford University Press, 2005, 129–136 (Theatre, film, and video censorship) and 416–450 (Freedom of speech in the media).

[224] For more details on freedom of expression and the Internet, cf. Barendt, Eric, *Freedom of speech*, Oxford, Oxford University Press, 2005, 451–474 and *infra*, Part 2, Chapter 2.

developments,[225] and governments have been incited to ensure that "*freedom of expression and information is fully respected with regard to Internet content with any restrictions not going beyond what is necessary in a democratic society*".[226] In addition, the European Commission and the Council of Europe have explicitly and repeatedly confirmed that the right to freedom of expression needs to be fully respected with regard to the issue of harmful (Internet) content and the protection of minors.[227]

---

225 Council of Europe documents: Council of Europe, Democracy, human rights and the rule of law in the Information Society, Contribution by the Council of Europe to the 2nd Preparatory Committee for the World Summit on the Information Society, 07.12.2002, retrieved from http://www.coe.int/t/e/integrated_projects/democracy/02_activities/04_w.s.i.s/90IP1(2002)27.asp (on 24.04.2007); Council of Europe (Committee of Ministers), Declaration on freedom of communication on the Internet, 28.05.2003, retrieved from https://wcd.coe.int/rsi/common/renderers/rend_standard.jsp?DocId=37031&SecMode=1&SiteName=cm&Lang=en (on 24.04.2007); Council of Europe (Standing committee on transfrontier television, Statement (2002)1 on human dignity and the fundamental rights of others, 12–13.09.2002, retrieved from http://www.coe.int/t/dghl/standardsetting/media/T-TT/T-TT(2006)012rev_en.asp#TopOfPage (on 24.04.2007); Council of Europe (Committee of Ministers), Recommendation CM/Rec(2007)11 on promoting freedom of expression and information in the new information and communications environment, 26.10.2007, retrieved from https://wcd.coe.int/ViewDoc.jsp?Ref=CM/Rec(2007)11&Language=lanEnglish&Ver=original&Site=CM&BackColorInternet=9999CC&BackColorIntranet=FFBB55&BackColorLogged=FFAC75 (on 14.01.2008); Council of Europe (Parliamentary Assembly), Recommendation 1882 (2009) The promotion of Internet and online media services appropriate for minors, 28 September 2009, retrieved from http://assembly.coe.int/Mainf.asp?link=/Documents/AdoptedText/ta09/EREC1882.htm (on 20 January 2010). EU documents: Commission of the European Communities, Communication from the Commission to the Council, the European Parliament, the European Economic and Social Committee and the Committee of the Regions, Towards a global partnership in the Information Society: Follow-up to the Tunis Phase of the World Summit on the Information Society (WSIS), COM (2006) 181 final, 27.04.2006, 2. Other documents: The organization for security and co-operation in Europe and Reporters sans Frontières, Joint declaration on guaranteeing media freedom on the Internet, 17–18.06.2005, retrieved from https://www.osce.org/documents/rfm/2005/06/15239_en.pdf (on 09.09.2008); UN Special Rapporteur on Freedom of Opinion and Expression, the OSCE Representative on Freedom of the Media and the OAS Special Rapporteur on Freedom of Expression, Joint declaration: International mechanisms for promoting freedom of expression, 21.12.2005, retrieved from http://www.osce.org/documents/rfm/2005/12/18636_en.pdf (on 09.09.2008).

226 Council of Europe, Democracy, human rights and the rule of law in the Information Society, Contribution by the Council of Europe to the 2nd Preparatory Committee for the World Summit on the Information Society, 07.12.2002, retrieved from http://www.coe.int/t/e/integrated_projects/democracy/02_activities/04_w.s.i.s/90IP1(2002)27.asp (on 24.04.2007).

227 Commission of the European Communities, Communication to the European Parliament, the Council, the Economic and Social Committee and the Committee of the

C. *Freedom of expression and children*

CHILDREN'S RIGHT TO FREEDOM OF EXPRESSION – As was discussed above, children are granted a right to freedom of expression as well, for instance, through article 13 UNCRC. However, again, this right is not absolute and can be restricted under certain conditions. It has been accepted that with respect to children, information that 'shocks, offends or disturbs' – usually an element of the right to freedom of expression (*supra*) – might be considered problematic.[228] This can be connected to article 17 UNCRC, which encourages the development of guidelines to protect children from harmful media material (*supra*).

DELICATE BALANCE – Finding an adequate balance between the freedom of expression and the protection of minors against harmful content is an extremely delicate issue. Trying to tackle content which is considered harmful to minors could result in unwanted side-effects on the freedom of expression of adults, who should be able to access such content freely. Therefore, States should act very cautiously in attempting to attain the normative goal of protecting children. Arbitrary restrictions on access to harmful content are not easily accepted by the European Court of Human Rights, given that the conditions of article 10 para. 2, which need to be fulfilled to legitimately interfere with the freedom of expression, are interpreted very strictly.[229] State legislation restricting the publication and distribution of allegedly harmful content could be perceived as a form of censorship.[230] However, States do

Regions, Illegal and harmful content on the Internet, COM (1996) 487, 16.10.1996, retrieved from http://ec.europa.eu/archives/ISPO/legal/en/internet/communic.html (on 25.03.2008); COMMISSION OF THE EUROPEAN COMMUNITIES, Green Paper on the protection of minors and human dignity in audiovisual and information services, COM (1996) 483 final, 16.10.1996, 12; COUNCIL OF EUROPE (COMMITTEE OF MINISTERS), Recommendation CM/REC(2009)5 on measures to protect children against harmful content and behaviour and to promote their active participation in the new information and communications environment, 08.07.2009, retrieved from https://wcd.coe.int/ViewDoc.jsp?id=1470045&Site=CM (on 20.01.2010).

228 VAN BUEREN, Geraldine, *The international law on the rights of the child*, Dordrecht, Martinus Nijhoff Publishers, 1995, 134. An example of such content is pornography. For more details on freedom of expression and pornography, cf. BARENDT, Eric, *Freedom of speech*, Oxford, Oxford University Press, 2005, 352–391.

229 This does not mean that there have not been cases in which the Court decided that certain restrictions, in the light of the protection of minors, were legitimate. See for instance *infra*: EUROPEAN COURT OF HUMAN RIGHTS, Handyside v. the United Kingdom, 7.12.1976.

230 MIFSUD BONNICI, J.P. and DE VEY MESTDAGH, C.N.J., "Right vision, wrong expectations: the European Union and self-regulation of harmful Internet content", *Information & Communications Technology Law*, Vol. 14, No. 2, June 2005, 136. In this context we can refer

have a certain margin of appreciation when imposing restrictions on the distribution of potentially harmful content.

Handyside v. the United Kingdom – In the 1976 *Handyside* case, for instance, the European Court of Human Rights decided that the United Kingdom authorities had not acted outside this margin of appreciation by punishing the publisher of *The Little Red Schoolbook* on the basis of the UK *Obscene Publications Acts (1959) (1964).*[231, 232] *The Little Red Schoolbook* was meant for children of twelve years old and more, and contained a twenty-six-page section on sex. A UK Magistrate's Court, upheld on appeal, had judged that certain passages of the book had a tendency to deprave and to corrupt children.[233] The European Court of Human Rights accepted that the interference by the UK public authorities (i.e., the applicant's criminal conviction, the seizure and subsequent forfeiture and destruction of the matrix and of hundreds of copies of the book)[234] was prescribed by law and legitimately aimed at the protection of morals.[235] The Court then evaluated whether the protection of morals in a democratic society necessitated the measures taken against the applicant. The Court argued that the book

> *included, above all in the section on sex and in the passage headed 'Be yourself' in the chapter on pupils (paragraph 32 above), sentences or paragraphs that young people at a critical stage of their development could have interpreted as an encouragement to indulge in precocious activities harmful for them or even to commit certain criminal offences. In these circumstances, despite the variety and the constant evolution in the United Kingdom of views on ethics and education,*

---

to the situation in the United States (cf. *supra*), where the Supreme Court found several attempts at protecting minors against harmful Internet content by means of legislation, such as the *Communications Decency Act of 1996* (CDA) and the *Children Online Protection Act of 1998* (COPA), to be too restrictive with respect to the freedom of expression.

231 *Obscene Publications Act* 1959, c.66 7_and_8_Eliz_2, retrieved from http://www.statutelaw.gov.uk/content.aspx?activeTextDocId=1128038 (on 05.01.2009); *Obscene Publications Act* 1964, c.74, retrieved from http://www.statutelaw.gov.uk/content.aspx?activeTextDocId=1169641 (on 05.01.2009).

232 European Court of Human Rights, Handyside v. the United Kingdom, 7.12.1976. Another decision concerning this Act, but in relation to a website, is European Court of Human Rights, Perrin v. the United Kingdom, 18.10.2005 (see *infra*), in which the Court declared the case to be inadmissible. The decision, however, contains several interesting statements concerning the protection of minors against digital harmful content (*infra*).

233 European Court of Human Rights, Handyside v. the United Kingdom, 7.12.1976, para. 34.

234 European Court of Human Rights, Handyside v. the United Kingdom, 7.12.1976, para. 43.

235 European Court of Human Rights, Handyside v. the United Kingdom, 7.12.1976, para. 44–46.

> *the competent English judges were entitled, in the exercise of their discretion, to think at the relevant time that the* Schoolbook *would have pernicious effects on the morals of many of the children and adolescents who would read it.*[236]

Interestingly, the Court explicitly stressed that "*the protection of the morals of the young*" is a legitimate purpose under article 10 para. 2 ECHR.[237] The Court concluded that the measures taken were indeed necessary in a democratic society and hence, that no breach of the requirements of article 10 para. 2 had been established *in casu.*[238] It has been argued that if the case was brought before the Court by an older child who claimed that his or her right to receive information was breached, the Court would have possibly approached the case with an emphasis on proportionality and may have concluded that a total prohibition of the book was disproportionate.[239]

Perrin v. the United Kingdom – Another application concerning the UK *Obscene Publications Acts* (*supra*), but in relation to a website, *Perrin v. the United Kingdom*, was declared inadmissible by the European Court of Human Rights.[240] Yet, the Court's decision still contains several interesting statements. A UK resident, Mr. Perrin, was convicted on the basis of the UK *Obscene Publications Acts (1959) (1964)* for running a website with obscene images.[241] He brought the case before the European Court of Human Rights claiming that his conviction violated article 10 ECHR, since it was, firstly, neither prescribed by law, nor, secondly, proportionate. With respect to the first claim, the Court found that the law in question did afford the applicant adequate protection against arbitrary interference. Regarding the second contention regarding the lack of proportionality, the Court found the arguments brought forward by the applicant ill-founded. First, the applicant had argued that prosecution on the basis of the *Obscene Publications Act* was unlikely to have any noteworthy impact on the protection of morals because similar material was accessible on other sites. The Court refuted this argument by

---

236 European Court of Human Rights, Handyside v. the United Kingdom, 7.12.1976, para. 52.

237 European Court of Human Rights, Handyside v. the United Kingdom, 7.12.1976, para. 52.

238 European Court of Human Rights, Handyside v. the United Kingdom, 7.12.1976, para. 59.

239 Van Bueren, Geraldine, *The international law on the rights of the child*, Dordrecht, Martinus Nijhoff Publishers, 1995, 135

240 European Court of Human Rights, Perrin v. the United Kingdom, 18.10.2005.

241 More specifically, people covered in faeces, coprophilia, coprophagia and men involved in fellatio: European Court of Human Rights, Perrin v. the United Kingdom, 18.10.2005.

stating that the fact that the Act may offer only limited protection to vulnerable citizens is no reason why a responsible government should abandon the attempt to protect them. Second, Mr. Perrin had contended that other measures, such as parental control software packages, would be more effective in achieving the objectives in question. Again, the Court did not agree, and stated that the existence of other measures did not render it disproportionate for a government to resort to criminal prosecution, particularly when these other measures had not been proven to be effective. Thirdly, the applicant had suggested that websites are seldom accessed by accident. The Court countered this argument by saying that the applicant's webpage was freely available to anyone surfing the Internet and moreover, that the content was the very type of material which might be sought out by young persons whom the national authorities were attempting to protect. To conclude, the Court pointed out that it would have been possible for the applicant to have prevented the harm, and therefore the conviction, by making sure that none of the photographs were available on the free preview page (where there were no age checks). Thus, although the case was ultimately declared 'inadmissible', the decision is still a useful indicator of the Court's position on the protection of minors against harmful digital media content.

D. *Concluding remarks*

Conclusion – Without a doubt, the right to freedom of expression is an essential element in the evaluation of any policy which attempts to protect children against harmful media content.[242] In this context, it is of the utmost importance to take into consideration the balance that needs to be aspired to between the child's right to freedom of expression, the adult's right to freedom of expression, and the child's right to be protected from potentially damaging content.

1.3.2. *Privacy*

A. *Privacy and children*

Delineation – Children can claim a right to privacy, as has been affirmed by article 16 of the UNCRC.[243] Children's privacy is often at risk in the digital

---

[242] *Infra*, Part 2, Chapter 2.

[243] Cf. also Article 29 Data Protection Working Party, Working document 1/2008 on the protection of children's personal data (General guidelines and the special case of schools), 18.02.2008, retrieved from http://ec.europa.eu/justice_home/fsj/privacy/docs/

information and communications environment,[244] for instance, when they are asked to transmit their personal details in exchange for a prize, or when identification and age verification tools are used to check their age before gaining access to a particular website.[245, 246] However, a full analysis of the issue of children and online privacy would lead us too far from the context of this study. Consequently, the following section is limited to a brief overview of the core legal framework concerning children and privacy.[247]

B. *Article 8 ECHR and the EU Privacy Directives*

Core ECHR provision – At the European level, one of the key provisions with respect to the fundamental right to privacy is article 8 ECHR, which has the same status as the principle of freedom of expression, and is also considered inherent in any truly democratic society.[248, 249] The importance attached to these two fundamental rights with respect to the issue of pro-

---

wpdocs/2008/wp147_en.pdf (on 05.03.2008), 2 and 4–5 and Article 29 Data Protection Working Party, Opinion 2/2009 on the protection of children's personal data (General guidelines and the special case of schools), 11.02.2009, retrieved from http://ec.europa.eu/justice_home/fsj/privacy/docs/wpdocs/2009/wp160_en.pdf (on 18.05.2009), 5.

244 A Belgian study, for instance, analysed the privacy policies and privacy statements of websites aimed at children and adolescents and found that a majority of these websites collects personal data of the young visitors without respecting their right to privacy: Walrave, Michel (ed.), Cyberkids' e-Privacy – Minderjarigen, minder rechten? (Privacy Paper Nr. 4) [*Kids' and Teens' e-Privacy at stake? An analysis of data processing and privacy statements on websites aimed at children and adolescents*], 2005, retrieved from http://www.e-privacy.be/PrivacyPaper4–Cyberkids-e-Privacy.pdf (on 14.06.2007) [in Dutch]. For a US study, cf. Pew Internet and American Life Project, Teens, privacy and online social networks – How teens manage their online identities and personal information in the age of MySpace, 18.04.2007, retrieved from http://www.pewinternet.org/pdfs/PIP_Teens_Privacy_SNS_Report_Final.pdf (on 23.04.2007).

245 Cf. *supra*, Part 1, Chapter 2.

246 Out-Law.com, Social networking site fined $ 1m for gathering children's data, 08.09.2006, retrieved from http://www.out-law.com/page-7279 (on 14.06.2007).

247 For a more detailed analysis, cf. Ovey, Clare, White, Robin and Jacobs, Francis, *Jacobs and White The European Convention on Human Rights*, Oxford, Oxford University Press, 2006, 241–299.

248 Commission of the European Communities, Green Paper on the protection of minors and human dignity in audiovisual and information services, COM (1996) 483 final, 16.10.1996.

249 The right to privacy is also included in articles 7 and 8 of the Charter of Fundamental Rights of the European Union. International equivalents are article 12 of the Universal Declaration of Human Rights and article 17 International Covenant on Civil and Political Rights.

tecting children is apparent from the following statement by the European Commission:

> *Before considering what rules and enforcement measures are applicable to protection of minors and human dignity, it must be emphasised that they are all subject to two fundamental principles that are inherent in any democratic society – freedom of expression and respect for privacy.*[250]

Article 8 ECHR reads as follows:

> 1. *Everyone has the right to respect for his private and family life, his home and his correspondence.*
> 2. *There shall be no interference by a public authority with the exercise of this right except such as is in accordance with the law and is necessary in a democratic society in the interests of national security, public safety or the economic well-being of the country, for the prevention of disorder or crime, for the protection of health or morals, or for the protection of the rights and freedoms of others.*

Again, the article protects an individual from interference by public authorities, but also entails a number of positive obligations for the State.[251] These positive obligations may "*involve the adoption of measures designed to secure respect for private life even in the sphere of the relations of individuals between themselves*" (*infra*, Chapter 2).[252]

Exceptions – Possible restrictions on the right to privacy, as provided for by article 8 para. 2 ECHR, are conceived similarly to article 10 para. 2. They need to be (1) in accordance with the law, (2) necessary in a democratic society and (3) in the interests of national security, public safety or the economic well-being of the country, for the prevention of disorder or crime, for the protection of health or morals, or for the protection of the rights and freedoms of others. Again, States are granted a certain margin of appreciation

[250] Commission of the European Communities, Green Paper on the protection of minors and human dignity in audiovisual and information services, COM (1996) 483 final, 16.10.1996. Along the same lines see: recital 4 Council Recommendation 98/560/EC of 24 September 1998 on the development of the competitiveness of the European audiovisual and information services industry by promoting national frameworks aimed at achieving a comparable and effective level of protection of minors and human dignity, *OJ* 07.10.1998, *L* 270, 48.

[251] Kilkelly, Ursula, *The right to respect for private and family life – A guide to the implementation of Article 8 of the European Convention on Human Rights (Human Rights Handbook, no. 1)*, Strasbourg, Council of Europe, 2001.

[252] European Court of Human Rights, X. and Y. v. the Netherlands, 26.03.1985, para. 23.

when establishing restrictions on the right to privacy.[253] KILKELLY observes that the margin of appreciation has been considered to be especially wide in areas such as child protection.[254]

EU PRIVACY DIRECTIVES – Additional important rules on privacy and the protection of personal data are laid down in the EU Data Protection Directive[255] and the EU Directive on Privacy and Electronic Communications.[256] Both these directives are applicable to the Internet[257] and pertain to adults as well as children.[258, 259] The Data Protection Directive – which is intended

253 KILKELLY, Ursula, *The right to respect for private and family life – A guide to the implementation of Article 8 of the European Convention on Human Rights (Human Rights Handbook, no. 1)*, Strasbourg, Council of Europe, 2001, 6.

254 KILKELLY, Ursula, *The right to respect for private and family life – A guide to the implementation of Article 8 of the European Convention on Human Rights (Human Rights Handbook, no. 1)*, Strasbourg, Council of Europe, 2001, 7.

255 EUROPEAN PARLIAMENT AND COUNCIL Directive 95/46/EC of 24 October 1995 on the protection of individuals with regard to the processing of personal data and on the free movement of such data, *OJ* 23.11.1995, *L* 281, 31.

256 EUROPEAN PARLIAMENT AND COUNCIL Directive 2002/58/EC of 12 July 2002 concerning the processing of personal data and the protection of privacy in the electronic communications sector (Directive on privacy and electronic communications), *OJ* 31.07.2002, *L* 201, 37.

257 ARTICLE 29 DATA PROTECTION WORKING PARTY, Working document WP 37, "Privacy on the Internet, an integrated EU approach to on-line data protection", 21.11.2000, retrieved from http://ec.europa.eu/justice_home/fsj/privacy/docs/wpdocs/2000/wp37en.pdf (on 27.03.2008), 46. An ECJ case relating to the processing of data on a webpage is ECJ, Bodil Lindqvist v. Sweden, C-101/01, 06.11.2003.

258 ARTICLE 29 DATA PROTECTION WORKING PARTY, Opinion 2/2009 on the protection of children's personal data (General guidelines and the special case of schools), 11.02.2009, retrieved from http://ec.europa.eu/justice_home/fsj/privacy/docs/wpdocs/2009/wp160_en.pdf (on 18.05.2009), 4 and 7. The Article 29 Data Protection Working Party clarifies that "*[i]n cases of conflicting interests, a solution can be sought by interpreting the Directives in accordance with the general principles of the UN Convention on the Rights of the Child, namely, the best interest of the child, and also by reference to the other legal instruments already mentioned*": ARTICLE 29 DATA PROTECTION WORKING PARTY, Opinion 2/2009 on the protection of children's personal data (General guidelines and the special case of schools), 11.02.2009, retrieved from http://ec.europa.eu/justice_home/fsj/privacy/docs/wpdocs/2009/wp160_en.pdf (on 18.05.2009), 19.

259 In the United States a specific law was enacted to protect children's privacy online: the 1998 Children's Online Privacy Protection Act (U.S. Code, Sec. 6501, retrieved from http://www.ftc.gov/ogc/coppa1.shtm (on 14.06.2007)). The Act aims to protect the privacy of children under the age of 13 by demanding parental consent for the gathering or use of any personal information of the children. For more on COPPA, cf. http://www.coppa.org/ (retrieved on 14.06.2007).

to encourage the free movement of personal data between Member States, while ensuring a high level of protection of the right to privacy – stipulates a number of essential safeguards that need to be adhered to when processing personal data. Article 6, for instance, requires that personal data must be: (a) processed fairly and lawfully; (b) collected for specified, explicit and legitimate purposes and not further processed in a way incompatible with those purposes; (c) adequate, relevant and not excessive in relation to the purposes for which they are collected and/or further processed; (d) accurate and, where necessary, kept up to date; and (e) kept in a form which permits identification of data subjects for no longer than is necessary for the purposes for which the data were collected or for which they are further processed. Furthermore, article 7 lists the grounds on the basis of which data may be processed; the unambiguous consent of the data subject is one of them. In the case where the data subject is a child, his or her representatives will need to give this consent, taking into account the best interests of the child.[260] Whenever personal data is processed, for instance, as part of a regulatory scheme to protect minors against harmful content (*infra*), it must be checked if these requirements are met.

C. *The right to anonymity*

Principle – In the sphere of privacy protection, it is generally accepted that individuals have a right to anonymity.[261] This right finds its origin in values such as individual autonomy and personal freedom, which are inherent to a

[260] Article 29 Data Protection Working Party, Opinion 2/2009 on the protection of children's personal data (General guidelines and the special case of schools), 11.02.2009, retrieved from http://ec.europa.eu/justice_home/fsj/privacy/docs/wpdocs/2009/wp160_en.pdf (on 18.05.2009), 4,5 and 9.

[261] For a detailed overview of the concept of anonymity and anonymous communication, cf. Ekker, Anton, *Anoniem communiceren: van drukpers tot weblog* [*Communicating anonymously: from printing press to weblog*], Den Haag, Sdu Uitgevers, 2006, 286 p. [in Dutch]; Nicoll, Chris, Prins, Corien and van Dellen, Miriam (eds), *Digital anonymity and the law: tensions and dimensions*, Den Haag, TMC Asser Press, 2003, 307 p. For a comparison with the extensive protection of anonymity as part of the freedom of expression under the First Amendment in the United States, cf. Ekker, Anton, *Anoniem communiceren: van drukpers tot weblog* [*Communicating anonymously: from printing press to weblog*], Den Haag, Sdu Uitgevers, 2006, 49–86 [in Dutch] and Froomkin, Michael, "Anonymity in the balance", 5–46, in: Nicoll, Chris, Prins, Corien and van Dellen, Miriam (eds), *Digital anonymity and the law: tensions and dimensions*, Den Haag, TMC Asser Press, 2003, 307 p.

democratic society.[262] Notwithstanding the fact that this right is not as such explicitly present in legislative documents, references have been made to it.[263] Specifically with respect to the Internet, the Council of Europe, for instance, has stated that "*in order to ensure protection against online surveillance and to enhance the free expression of information and ideas, member States should respect the will of users of the Internet not to disclose their identity*".[264] It has

---

262 Ekker, Anton, *Anoniem communiceren: van drukpers tot weblog* [*Communicating anonymously: from printing press to weblog*], Den Haag, Sdu Uitgevers, 2006, 12–13 [in Dutch]; McIntyre, Thomas, "Online anonymity: some legal issues", *Commercial Law Practitioner* 2004, April, 90; Article 29 Data Protection Working Party, Recommendation 3/97 Anonymity on the Internet, 03.12.1997, retrieved from http://ec.europa.eu/justice_home/fsj/privacy/docs/wpdocs/1997/wp6_en.pdf (on 18.05.2009), 5. Note that the right to anonymity is also connected – positively as well as negatively – to the right to freedom of expression; on the one hand, it can be assumed that in certain instances people will express their opinions more freely if their identity is not disclosed, on the other hand, it has also been argued, for instance by US Supreme Court Judge Scalia, that the right to privacy presents an obstacle to freedom of expression: cf. Mediapost (Wendy Davis), Scalia: free speech trumps privacy online, 01.05.2009, retrieved from http://www.mediapost.com/publications/?fa=Articles.showArticle&art_aid=105258 (on 26.05.2009). Pitt-Payne also refers to the potential conflict between freedom of information and the right to privacy: Pitt-Payne, Timothy, "Privacy versus freedom of information: is there a conflict?", *European Human Rights Law Review* 2003, Special Issue, 109–119.

263 PRIME, Framework text, 13.06.2005, retrieved from https://www.prime-project.eu/prime_products/reports/fmwk/pub_del_D14.1.a_ec_wp14.1_V4_final.pdf (on 27.03.2008), 121. See for instance: recital 9 European Parliament and Council Directive 2002/58/EC of 12 July 2002 concerning the processing of personal data and the protection of privacy in the electronic communications sector (Directive on privacy and electronic communications), *OJ* 31.07.2002, *L* 201, 37: "*objectives of minimising the processing of personal data and of using anonymous of pseudonymous data where possible*".

264 Council of Europe (Committee of Ministers), Declaration on freedom of communication on the Internet, 28.03.2003, retrieved from https://wcd.coe.int/rsi/common/renderers/rend_standard.jsp?DocId=37031&SecMode=1&SiteName=cm&Lang=en (on 19.05.2008), principle 7. Cf. also Council of Europe (Committee of Ministers), Recommendation Rec(99)5 for the protection of privacy on the Internet, 23.02.1999, retrieved from https://wcd.coe.int/com.instranet.InstraServlet?command=com.instranet.CmdBlobGet&InstranetImage=276580&SecMode=1&DocId=396826&Usage=2 (on 18.05.2009): "*Aware of the need to develop techniques which permit the anonymity of data subjects and the confidentiality of the information exchanged on information highways while respecting the rights and freedoms of others and the values of a democratic society*", and Commission of the European Communities, Communication to the European Parliament, the Council, the Economic and Social Committee and the Committee of the Regions, Illegal and harmful content on the Internet, COM (1996) 487: "*There are legitimate reasons why a user might want to remain anonymous (including fear of retaliation for views expressed or lack of confidence in the use to which his personal details might be put by the recipient). However, the legitimate need for anonymity should be reconciled with the principles of legal traceability*".

been deemed essential, and encouraged by European authorities in charge of the protection of privacy[265] that anonymous Internet access is supplied to users surfing or taking part in discussion fora.[266, 267]

Not absolute – However, this right to anonymity is not absolute.[268] At times, it is necessary to balance this right with other rights or legislative imperatives, as the European Court of Human Rights recently stated in *K.U. v. Finland*:[269]

> *Although freedom of expression and confidentiality of communications are primary considerations and users of telecommunications and Internet services must have a guarantee that their own privacy and freedom of expression will be respected, such guarantee cannot be absolute and must yield on occasion to other legitimate imperatives, such as the prevention of disorder or crime or the protection of the rights and freedoms of others.*[270]

According to the Court of Human Rights, in certain instances – *in casu* with respect to a grave infringement of a minor's right to privacy – identification

---

[265] Commissie voor de bescherming van de persoonlijke levenssfeer [*Commission for privacy protection*], Advies uit eigen beweging betreffende de bescherming van de persoonlijke levenssfeer van minderjarigen op het Internet [*Recommendation on the protection of privacy of minors on the Internet*], 16.09.2002, retrieved from http://www.internet-observatory.be/internet_observatory/pdf/advice_privacy_nl.pdf (on 14.10.2008) [in Dutch].

[266] Article 29 Data Protection Working Party, Working document WP 37, "Privacy on the Internet, an integrated EU approach to on-line data protection", 21.11.2000, retrieved from http://ec.europa.eu/justice_home/fsj/privacy/docs/wpdocs/2000/wp37en.pdf (on 27.03.2008), 53.

[267] PRIME, Framework text, 13.06.2005, retrieved from https://www.prime-project.eu/prime_products/reports/fmwk/pub_del_D14.1.a_ec_wp14.1_V4_final.pdf (on 27.03.2008), 121.

[268] Council of Europe (Committee of Ministers), Recommendation Rec(99)5 for the protection of privacy on the Internet, 23.02.1999, retrieved from https://wcd.coe.int/com.instranet.InstraServlet?command=com.instranet.CmdBlobGet&InstranetImage=276580&SecMode=1&DocId=396826&Usage=2 (on 18.05.2009): "*Complete anonymity may not be appropriate because of legal constraints*"; Voorhoof, Dirk, "Internet and the right of anonymity", Proceedings of the PCMLP 2008 Belgrade Conference on Regulation of Freedom of Expression on the Internet, Belgrade, 08–09.09.2008, *in press*.

[269] For more information on the facts of this case, cf. *infra* Part 2, Chapter 2 (2.2.1. B.2. Privacy and alternative regulatory instruments).

[270] European Court of Human Rights, K.U. v. Finland, 02.12.2008, para. 49. Also: Voorhoof, Dirk, "Recente arresten van het E.H.R.M. in verband met artikel 10 E.V.R.M. (vrijheid van meningsuiting en informatie)" ["*Recent judgments of the ECHR related to article 10 ECHR (freedom of expression and information)*"], November – December 2008, *Auteurs & Media* 2009, No. 1, *in press* [in Dutch].

measures might be justified, and moreover, might even be required.[271] In this context the Council of Europe has referred to the possibility for Member States to take measures "*in order to trace those responsible for criminal acts*".[272] Along the same lines, the Article 29 Data Protection Working Party stated:

> *Anonymity is not appropriate in all circumstances. Determining the circumstances in which the 'anonymity option' is appropriate and those in which it is not requires the careful balancing of fundamental rights, not only to privacy but also to freedom of expression, with other important public policy objectives such as the prevention of crime.*[273]

PROPORTIONALITY – It can be noted that *K.U. v. Finland* is a controversial decision. Notwithstanding the explicitly references of the Court to the fact that the right to anonymity must yield "*on occasion*" to other legitimate imperatives and to the graveness of the infringement in question, it might be wondered whether the European Court of Human Rights has not opened the door to a far-reaching reduction of anonymity on the Internet. It might be assumed that Member States who want to impose identification measures could find an argument in the judgment of the Court to adopt such measures in various circumstances. We would like to emphasise that the adoption of such measures always needs to comply with the principle of proportionality and should be restricted to "*what is necessary to protect a specific public interest in a democratic society*".[274]

---

[271] With respect to the right to anonymity and the possibility to impose identification measures linked to the liability of intermediaries regime in the e-Commerce Directive, cf. also *infra*, 1.4.4. Indirect content regulation: liability of intermediaries. There we also note that the clash between the right to anonymity and the imposition of identification requirements is currently a very controversial issue, for instance with respect to copyright and initiatives such as the Data Retention Directive.

[272] COUNCIL OF EUROPE (COMMITTEE OF MINISTERS), Declaration on freedom of communication on the Internet, 28.03.2003, retrieved from https://wcd.coe.int/rsi/common/renderers/rend_standard.jsp?DocId=37031&SecMode=1&SiteName=cm&Lang=en (on 19.05.2008), principle 7; VOORHOOF, Dirk, "Recente arresten van het E.H.R.M. in verband met artikel 10 E.V.R.M. (vrijheid van meningsuiting en informatie)" ["*Recent judgments of the ECHR related to article 10 ECHR (freedom of expression and information)*"], November – December 2008, *Auteurs & Media* 2009, No. 1, *in press* [in Dutch].

[273] ARTICLE 29 DATA PROTECTION WORKING PARTY, Recommendation 3/97 Anonymity on the Internet, 03.12.1997, retrieved from http://ec.europa.eu/justice_home/fsj/privacy/docs/wpdocs/1997/wp6_en.pdf (on 18.05.2009), 11.

[274] ARTICLE 29 DATA PROTECTION WORKING PARTY, Recommendation 3/97 Anonymity on the Internet, 03.12.1997, retrieved from http://ec.europa.eu/justice_home/fsj/privacy/docs/wpdocs/1997/wp6_en.pdf (on 18.05.2009), 11.

Children and anonymity – Finally, in this context we can refer to the Council of Europe's 2008 Declaration on protecting the dignity, security and privacy of children on the Internet,[275] which emphasised that traceability of children's activities may expose them to criminal, illegal and harmful behaviour (e.g. grooming, bullying, stalking). As a consequence, according to the Council of Europe, there should, other than in the context of law enforcement, "*be no lasting or permanently accessible record of the content created by children on the Internet which challenges their dignity, security and privacy or otherwise renders them vulnerable now or at a later stage in their lives*". We could consider this an expression of a child's right to anonymity.

D. *Concluding remark*

Protection of privacy – This brief overview demonstrated that the right to privacy is protected through general human rights instruments, as well as specific legislation. It is of crucial importance to take this legal framework into consideration when establishing mechanisms to protect children from harmful content in the digital media environment.

1.3.3. *Procedural guarantees*

Article 6 and article 13 ECHR – Finally, there are two human rights which provide certain procedural guarantees that could be relevant to the use of ARIs: the right to a fair trial (article 6 ECHR) and the right to an effective remedy (article 13 ECHR).

A. *Article 6 ECHR*

Right to a fair trial – Article 6 ECHR contains the right to a fair trial, which is essential in a democratic society.[276] The first paragraph stipulates that every individual "*in the determination of his civil rights and obligations or of any criminal charge against him, [...] is entitled to a fair and public*

---

[275] Council of Europe (Committee of Ministers), Declaration on protecting the dignity, security and privacy of children using the Internet, 20.02.2008, retrieved from https://wcd.coe.int/ViewDoc.jsp?Ref=Decl(20.02.2008)&Language=lanEnglish&Ver=0001&BackColorInternet=9999CC&BackColorIntranet=FFBB55&BackColorLogged=FFAC75 (on 19.09.2008).

[276] Harris, David, O'Boyle, Michael, Warbrick, Colin, Bates, Ed et al. (eds), *Harris, O'Boyle and Warbrick Law of the European Convention on human rights*, Oxford, Oxford University Press, 2009, 201.

hearing within a reasonable time by an independent and impartial tribunal established by law". In addition, the pronouncement of the judgment needs to be public, except in a number of circumstances (for instance, in the interest of juveniles). The second paragraph embodies a presumption of innocence and the third paragraph contains a non-exhaustive[277] list of rights, which – in criminal cases – are linked to the notion of 'fair trial'. In the following brief analysis we focus on the first paragraph and leave the second and third paragraph[278] out of consideration since criminal cases will be rare with respect to the protection of minors against harmful content.[279]

Scope of application – Article 6 ECHR is applicable, on the one hand, in criminal cases, and, on the other hand, in non-criminal cases where civil rights and obligations are at stake. With respect to the second field of application, the European Court of Human Rights has developed an autonomous interpretation of what is meant by the notion 'civil rights and obligations' (*infra*, Chapter 2). It is important to note that article 6 ECHR only comes into play when there is a dispute concerning such rights, which is real and serious and which relates to an actual right.[280] This can be a dispute between individuals or between an individual and the state.[281]

---

277 De Smet, Bart, Lathouwers, Jan et al., "Artikel 6: recht op eerlijk proces" ["*Article 6: right to fair trial*"], in: Vande Lanotte, Johan and Haeck, Yves, *Handboek EVRM: Deel II: Artikelsgewijze commentaar (Volume I)* [*ECHR: Part II: Commentary on the articles*], Antwerpen, Intersentia, 2004, 386 [in Dutch].

278 For a detailed overview of these paragraphs, cf. Harris, David, O'Boyle, Michael, Warbrick, Colin, Bates, Ed et al. (eds), *Harris, O'Boyle and Warbrick Law of the European Convention on human rights*, Oxford, Oxford University Press, 2009, 299–330; De Smet, Bart, Lathouwers, Jan et al., "Artikel 6: recht op eerlijk proces" ["*Article 6: right to fair trial*"], in: Vande Lanotte, Johan and Haeck, Yves, *Handboek EVRM: Deel II: Artikelsgewijze commentaar (Volume I)* [*ECHR: Part II: Commentary on the articles*], Antwerpen, Intersentia, 2004, 519–646 [in Dutch].

279 Of course this depends on the national legislation. If in a certain country the distribution of content harmful to minors is criminalised, a person may face a criminal charge when he distributes such content.

280 European Court of Human Rights, Van Marle and others v. the Netherlands, 26.06.1986, para. 32. De Smet, Bart, Lathouwers, Jan et al., "Artikel 6: recht op eerlijk proces" ["*Article 6: right to fair trial*"], in: Vande Lanotte, Johan and Haeck, Yves, *Handboek EVRM: Deel II: Artikelsgewijze commentaar (Volume I)* [*ECHR: Part II: Commentary on the articles*], Antwerpen, Intersentia, 2004, 388–390 [in Dutch]; Viering, Marc, *Het toepassingsgebied van artikel 6 EVRM* [*The scope of application of article 6 ECHR*], Zwolle, W.E.J. Tjeenk Willink, 1994, 72–83 [in Dutch].

281 De Smet, Bart, Lathouwers, Jan et al., "Artikel 6: recht op eerlijk proces" ["*Article 6: right to fair trial*"], in: Vande Lanotte, Johan and Haeck, Yves, *Handboek EVRM: Deel II: Artikelsgewijze commentaar (Volume I)* [*ECHR: Part II: Commentary on the articles*], Antwerpen, Intersentia, 2004, 388 [in Dutch].

Right of access to a court – Article 6 ECHR not only provides a number of procedural guarantees but also embodies the right of access to a court; access must be effective and can only be restricted when there is a legitimate aim and the restriction is proportional.[282] There is no explicit reference to the right of access in the text of article 6 para. 1 ECHR, but the European Court of Human Rights has noted in the *Golder v. the United Kingdom* case that this right "*constitutes an element which is inherent in the right stated by article 6 para. 1*".[283]

Fair, public hearing and public judgment – A first procedural requirement put forward by article 6 para. 1 ECHR is that of a fair and public hearing and a publicly pronounced judgment. The notion 'fair hearing' is rather general, and has been judged to encompass a number of specific rights, such as equality of arms, the right to a reasoned judgment, the right to a hearing in one's presence, the right to participate effectively at the hearing, freedom from self-incrimination, or the right to a hearing free from pre-trial publicity.[284] Furthermore, a hearing needs to be conducted in public. This requirement, however, is not absolute. Article 6 para. 1 ECHR stipulates that the press and the public may be excluded from all or part of the trial

> *in the interest of morals, public order or national security in a democratic society, where the interests of juveniles or the protection of the private life of the parties so require, or to the extent strictly necessary in the opinion of the court in special circumstances where publicity would prejudice the interests of justice.*

Not only the hearing must usually be carried out in public, the judgment as well needs to be pronounced publicly. Although no exceptions to this

---

[282] Mole, Nuala and Harby, Catharina, *The right to a fair trial: a guide to the implementation of Article 6 of the European Convention on Human Rights (Human rights handbooks, No. 3)*, Strasbourg, Council of Europe, 2006, 39; Harris, David, O'Boyle, Michael, Warbrick, Colin, Bates, Ed et al. (eds), *Harris, O'Boyle and Warbrick Law of the European Convention on human rights*, Oxford, Oxford University Press, 2009, 235–246. Also: De Smet, Bart, Lathouwers, Jan et al., "Artikel 6: recht op eerlijk proces" ["*Article 6: right to fair trial*"], in: Vande Lanotte, Johan and Haeck, Yves, *Handboek EVRM: Deel II: Artikelsgewijze commentaar (Volume I)* [*ECHR: Part II: Commentary on the articles*], Antwerpen, Intersentia, 2004, 489 *et seq.* [in Dutch].

[283] European Court of Human Rights, Golder v. the United Kingdom, 21.02.1975, para. 36.

[284] De Smet, Bart, Lathouwers, Jan et al., "Artikel 6: recht op eerlijk proces" ["*Article 6: right to fair trial*"], in: Vande Lanotte, Johan and Haeck, Yves, *Handboek EVRM: Deel II: Artikelsgewijze commentaar (Volume I)* [*ECHR: Part II: Commentary on the articles*], Antwerpen, Intersentia, 2004, 451–483 [in Dutch]; Harris, David, O'Boyle, Michael, Warbrick, Colin, Bates, Ed et al. (eds), *Harris, O'Boyle and Warbrick Law of the European Convention on human rights*, Oxford, Oxford University Press, 2009, 246–271.

requirement are included in article 6 para. 1 ECHR, the European Court of Human Rights has interpreted this obligation in a flexible manner.[285]

Reasonable time – A second requirement is that a hearing must occur within a reasonable time frame. Mole and Harby argue that the rationale behind this requirement is the guarantee that

> *within a reasonable time and by means of a judicial decision, an end is put to the insecurity into which a person finds himself/herself as to his/her civil law position or on account of a criminal charge against him/her: this is in the interest of the person in question as well as of legal certainty.*[286]

The reasonableness of the time frame will be assessed on a case-by-case basis taking into account a number of factors, such as the complexity of the case, the conduct of the applicant and the conduct of the authorities.[287] In this context we can note that states have a positive obligation to organise their judicial system in such a way that their courts can meet each of the requirements, including the obligation to hear cases within a reasonable time.[288]

Independent and impartial tribunal established by law – A third requirement – possibly the most relevant to our research subject – is that cases need to be dealt with by "*an independent and impartial tribunal established by law*". The European Court of Human Rights has acknowledged that a tribunal does not need to be "*a court of law of the classic kind, integrated within the standard judicial machinery of the country*".[289] However, what is considered essential is that the function of the body in question is "*to determine matters within its competence on the basis of rules of law, following proceedings conducted in a prescribed manner*".[290] In addition, the Court will assess the independent and impartial nature of the authority in order to decide upon its qualification. Finally, the 'tribunal' should be established

---

285 Harris, David, O'Boyle, Michael, Warbrick, Colin, Bates, Ed et al. (eds), *Harris, O'Boyle and Warbrick Law of the European Convention on human rights*, Oxford, Oxford University Press, 2009, 276.

286 Mole, Nuala and Harby, Catharina, *The right to a fair trial: a guide to the implementation of Article 6 of the European Convention on Human Rights (Human rights handbooks, No. 3)*, Strasbourg, Council of Europe, 2006, 25.

287 European Court of Human Rights, Pélissier and Sassi v. France, 25.03.1999, para. 67.

288 Harris, David, O'Boyle, Michael, Warbrick, Colin, Bates, Ed et al. (eds), *Harris, O'Boyle and Warbrick Law of the European Convention on human rights*, Oxford, Oxford University Press, 2009, 282.

289 European Court of Human Rights, Campbell and Fell v. the United Kingdom, 28.06.1984, para. 76.

290 European Court of Human Rights, Sramek v. Austria, 22.10.1984, para. 36.

by law. This has been interpreted as requiring a formal act of the legislature, which, however, may be limited to the establishment of the organisational framework for the judicial organisation.[291]

Concluding remark – This brief overview raises a number of questions that could be relevant to the use of ARIs. The applicability of article 6 ECHR to such instruments as well as the requirements for compliance with the right to a fair trial will be analysed in greater detail in the next chapter.

B. *Article 13 ECHR*

Article 13 ECHR – Another fundamental right that could raise difficulties – similarly to article 6 ECHR, not as much with respect to the protection of minors from harmful content, but especially with respect to the structure of ARIs – is the right to an effective remedy before a national authority, included in article 13 ECHR. The exact text of the article reads as follows:

> *Everyone whose rights and freedoms as set forth in this Convention are violated shall have an effective remedy before a national authority notwithstanding that the violation has been committed by persons acting in an official capacity.*

Article 13 ECHR concretises (along with article 5 paras. 4 and 5 and article 6 para. 1 ECHR)[292] the obligation for Contracting States to secure for everyone within their jurisdiction the Convention rights and freedoms included in article 1. It is also linked to article 35, which states that the Court may only deal with the matter after all domestic remedies have been exhausted.[293]

---

291 Kuijer, Martin, *The blindfold of Lady Justice: Judicial independence and impartiality in light of the requirements of article 6 ECHR*, Leiden, E.M. Meijers Instituut, 2004, 184.

292 For more details on the relation between these articles and article 13, cf. Cromheecke, Marc and Staelens, Valentina, "Artikel 13 – Recht op daadwerkelijke rechtshulp" ["*Article 13 – Right to an effective remedy*"], in: Vande Lanotte, Johan and Haeck, Yves, *Handboek EVRM: Deel II: Artikelsgewijze commentaar (Volume II)* [*ECHR: Part II: Commentary on the articles (Volume II)*], Antwerpen – Oxford, Intersentia, 2004, 81–86 [in Dutch]; Barkhuysen, Tom, *Artikel 13 EVRM: effectieve nationale rechtsbescherming bij schending van mensenrechten* [*Article 13 ECHR: effective domestic legal protection against human rights violations*], Lelystad, Uitgeverij Koninklijke Vermande, 1998, 177–191 [in Dutch].

293 Cromheecke, Marc and Staelens, Valentina, "Artikel 13 – Recht op daadwerkelijke rechtshulp" ["*Article 13 – Right to an effective remedy*"], in: Vande Lanotte, Johan and Haeck, Yves, *Handboek EVRM: Deel II: Artikelsgewijze commentaar (Volume II)* [*ECHR: Part II: Commentary on the articles (Volume II)*], Antwerpen – Oxford, Intersentia, 2004, 78–79 [in Dutch].

RIGHT TO AN EFFECTIVE REMEDY – Article 13, as its first part indicates, will normally be invoked in conjunction with another fundamental right expressed in the Convention (or in one of its protocols),[294] such as freedom of expression. It has been argued that a remedy should be available not only when an infringement of a Convention right has occurred by an action of the State, but also when the State has failed to comply with a positive obligation to act.[295] Notwithstanding the fact that article 13 ECHR will always be linked with a Convention right, the right to an effective remedy is an independent or autonomous right, in that it is not necessary that a violation of the Convention right in question needs to be established first.[296] Whether or not an actual violation took place, article 13 requires Contracting States to provide citizens with an effective remedy "*for the examination of the alleged violation*", provided that they have an arguable claim.[297] The European Court of Human Rights clarified the object of article 13 in the case *Kudla v. Poland*:

> *The object of article 13, as emerges from the travaux préparatoires, is to provide a means whereby individuals can obtain relief at national level for violations of their Convention rights before having to set in motion the international machinery of complaint before the Court.*[298]

---

[294] VAN DIJK, Pieter, VAN HOOF, Fried, VAN RIJN, Arjen and ZWAAK, Leo (eds), *Theory and practice of the European Convention on Human Rights*, Antwerpen, Intersentia, 2006, 998; CROMHEECKE, Marc and STAELENS, Valentina, "Artikel 13 – Recht op daadwerkelijke rechtshulp" ["*Article 13 – Right to an effective remedy*"], in: VANDE LANOTTE, Johan and HAECK, Yves, *Handboek EVRM: Deel II: Artikelsgewijze commentaar (Volume II)* [*ECHR: Part II: Commentary on the articles (Volume II)*], Antwerpen – Oxford, Intersentia, 2004, 80 [in Dutch].

[295] BARKHUYSEN, Tom, *Artikel 13 EVRM: effectieve nationale rechtsbescherming bij schending van mensenrechten* [*Article 13 ECHR: effective domestic legal protection against human rights violations*], Lelystad, Uitgeverij Koninklijke Vermande, 1998, 40–42 [in Dutch]. Cf. also *infra*, Part 2, Chapter 2.

[296] EUROPEAN COURT OF HUMAN RIGHTS, Klass and others v. Germany, 06.09.1978, para. 64; EUROPEAN COURT OF HUMAN RIGHTS, Boyle and Rice v. the United Kingdom, 27.04.1988, para. 52. For more details on the gradual acknowledgement of the autonomy of article 13 ECHR, cf. BARKHUYSEN, Tom, *Artikel 13 EVRM: effectieve nationale rechtsbescherming bij schending van mensenrechten* [*Article 13 ECHR: effective domestic legal protection against human rights violations*], Lelystad, Uitgeverij Koninklijke Vermande, 1998, 44–55 [in Dutch].

[297] EUROPEAN COURT OF HUMAN RIGHTS, Boyle and Rice v. the United Kingdom, 27.04.1988, para. 52: "*However, Article 13 (art. 13) cannot reasonably be interpreted so as to require a remedy in domestic law in respect of any supposed grievance under the Convention that an individual may have, no matter how unmeritorious his complaint may be: the grievance must be an arguable one in terms of the Convention*". See also: VAN DIJK, Pieter, VAN HOOF, Fried, VAN RIJN, Arjen and ZWAAK, Leo (eds), *Theory and practice of the European Convention on Human Rights*, Antwerpen, Intersentia, 2006, 1000–1001.

[298] EUROPEAN COURT OF HUMAN RIGHTS, Kudla v. Poland, 26.10.2000, para. 152.

The remedy which an individual, who has an arguable claim that his or her Convention rights were violated,[299] should be able to invoke, ought to either lead to the prevention of the suspected violation or, if appropriate, to the obtainment of adequate redress,[300] including compensation.[301] Hence, the violation should not only be terminated, but all consequences that have already occurred should be neutralised as well.[302] Although states are granted a certain discretion for how exactly they realise this obligation,[303] the European Court of Human Rights has repeatedly stressed that the remedy must be effective in practice as well as in law.[304] The evaluation of this 'effectiveness'

---

[299] Whether or not an individual has an 'arguable claim' is examined by the Court on the basis of the concrete facts and circumstances of the case, or on the basis of legitimate presumptions: CROMHEECKE, Marc and STAELENS, Valentina, "Artikel 13 – Recht op daadwerkelijke rechtshulp" ["*Article 13 – Right to an effective remedy*"], in: VANDE LANOTTE, Johan and HAECK, Yves, *Handboek EVRM: Deel II: Artikelsgewijze commentaar (Volume II)* [*ECHR: Part II: Commentary on the articles (Volume II)*], Antwerpen – Oxford, Intersentia, 2004, 94–95 [in Dutch]. For more details on the notion 'arguable claim' and its coincidence with the notion 'manifestly ill-founded' of article 35 para. 3, cf. *ibidem*, 97–99; BARKHUYSEN, Tom, *Artikel 13 EVRM: effectieve nationale rechtsbescherming bij schending van mensenrechten* [*Article 13 ECHR: effective domestic legal protection against human rights violations*], Lelystad, Uitgeverij Koninklijke Vermande, 1998, 57–71 [in Dutch].

[300] EUROPEAN COURT OF HUMAN RIGHTS, Silver and others v. the United Kingdom, 25.03.1983, para. 113.

[301] VAN DIJK, Pieter, VAN HOOF, Fried, VAN RIJN, Arjen and ZWAAK, Leo (eds), *Theory and practice of the European Convention on Human Rights*, Antwerpen, Intersentia, 2006, 1006. See also: EUROPEAN COURT OF HUMAN RIGHTS, Wille v. Liechtenstein, 28.10.1999, para. 75; EUROPEAN COURT OF HUMAN RIGHTS, Krasuski v. Poland, 14.06.2005, para. 65 ("*The effect of Article 13 is thus to require the provision of a domestic remedy to deal with the substance of an 'arguable complaint' under the Convention and to grant appropriate relief*"). OVEY and WHITE clarified that "*[t]he Court has said that the 'nature of the right at stake has implications for the type of remedy' which the State is required to provide. In some cases this must include the possibility of 'compensation for the non-pecuniary damage flowing from the breach' of the Convention*": OVEY, Clare and WHITE, Robin, *Jacobs and White The European Convention on Human Rights*, Oxford, Oxford University Press, 2006, 470.

[302] BARKHUYSEN, Tom, *Artikel 13 EVRM: effectieve nationale rechtsbescherming bij schending van mensenrechten* [*Article 13 ECHR: effective domestic legal protection against human rights violations*], Lelystad, Uitgeverij Koninklijke Vermande, 1998, 139 [in Dutch].

[303] EUROPEAN COURT OF HUMAN RIGHTS, Peck v. the United Kingdom, 28.01.2003, para. 99. BARKHUYSEN clarifies that the remedy can be an annulment, a withdrawal, an adaptation, a non-application, awarding compensation or sanctioning: BARKHUYSEN, Tom, *Artikel 13 EVRM: effectieve nationale rechtsbescherming bij schending van mensenrechten* [*Article 13 ECHR: effective domestic legal protection against human rights violations*], Lelystad, Uitgeverij Koninklijke Vermande, 1998, 118 and 139 [in Dutch].

[304] EUROPEAN COURT OF HUMAN RIGHTS, Wille v. Liechtenstein, 28.10.1999, para. 75. See also: EUROPEAN COURT OF HUMAN RIGHTS, Aksoy v. Turkey, 18.12.1996, para. 95:

will take the concrete circumstances and contextual factors into account. In this context, Barkhuysen clarified that 'effectiveness' contains several elements: the remedy must actually exist, must be accessible to the person whose rights have been violated and must be able to effectively and efficiently reach the goal (i.e., assessing the violation of a fundamental right and if necessary remedying this in the most efficient manner).[305] The government will be required to list the remedies that were available to the applicant and will need to demonstrate "*at least a prima facie case for their effectiveness*".[306] It is important to note, however, that a negative outcome for the applicant does not imply that a remedy is not 'effective'.[307]

Concluding remark – Within the scope of this study, the issue that is of the most interest is whether the use of ARIs could affect the right to an effective remedy. Thus, in the next chapter, we will examine the requirements ARIs need to fulfil in order to comply with article 13 ECHR.

1.4. Content regulation

1.4.1. *Introduction*

Media content regulation – Having analysed the general human rights-oriented regulatory framework, in this section, emphasis is put on the sector-specific regulation of media content. Other types of content regulation, such as intellectual property regulation, are not considered in the present analysis. Rather, mechanisms to regulate content *directly*, such as the Television without Frontiers Directive and the Audiovisual Media Services Directive, as well as methods to regulate content *indirectly*, such as the

"*Nevertheless, the remedy required by Article 13 (art. 13) must be 'effective' in practice as well as in law, in particular in the sense that its exercise must not be unjustifiably hindered by the acts or omissions of the authorities of the respondent State*".

305 For more details, cf. Barkhuysen, Tom, *Artikel 13 EVRM: effectieve nationale rechtsbescherming bij schending van mensenrechten* [*Article 13 ECHR: effective domestic legal protection against human rights violations*], Lelystad, Uitgeverij Koninklijke Vermande, 1998, 118 and 120–146 [in Dutch].

306 Ovey, Clare and White, Robin, *Jacobs and White The European Convention on Human Rights*, Oxford, Oxford University Press, 2006, 464.

307 European Court of Human Rights, Soering v. the United Kingdom, 07.07.1989, para. 122: "*The effectiveness of the remedy, for the purposes of Article 13 (art. 13), does not depend on the certainty of a favourable outcome [...]*".

e-Commerce Directive regime regarding the liability of intermediaries, are discussed.

Rationales for traditional content regulation – There used to be a number of reasons why it was considered necessary to regulate 'content', and especially audiovisual content.[308] The first reason was of a technical nature, i.e., spectrum scarcity.[309] Today, this rationale is not as vital as it was before, given the increasing digitisation of content distribution. Digital television and the Internet make it possible to distribute enormous amounts of information without major technical restrictions, as was the case when frequencies were essential. A second rationale to regulate content was the impact of the mass media on the viewer or user (*supra*).[310] Audiovisual media, in particular radio and television, were deemed to have "*a major influence on what citizens know, believe and feel, and play a crucial role in the transmission, development and even construction of cultural identities*".[311] Moreover,

> *the audiovisual media play a fundamental role in the development and transmission of social values. This is not simply because they influence to a large degree which facts about and which images of the world we encounter, but also because*

---

[308] Also *supra*.

[309] Tambini, Damien and Forgan, Liz, "Content", Communications White Paper, retrieved from http://www.communicationswhitepaper.gov.uk/cwp_consultation/contentregulation.pdf (18.12.2003, no longer available), 4; Goldberg, David, Prosser, Tony and Verhulst, Stefaan (eds), *Regulating the changing media: A comparative study*, Oxford, Oxford University Press, 1998, 16; Wetenschappelijke Raad voor het Regeringsbeleid, Focus op functies – Uitdagingen voor een toekomstbestendig mediabeleid [*Focus on functions – Challenges for a future proof media policy*], Amsterdam, Amsterdam University Press, 2005, retrieved from http://www.wrr.nl/dsc?c=getobject&s=obj&!sessionid=1o7p!cnhb9o!M9xXGwuyBPekM35UuYCWRZ1zyOvsfxauyo3h50uVxzYXp1K38HdW&objectid=2799&!dsname=default&isapidir=/gvisapi/ (on 27.07.2007), 41–42 [in Dutch].

[310] Cf. European Commission, Focus group 1: Regulation of audiovisual content, September 2004, retrieved from http://ec.europa.eu/avpolicy/docs/reg/modernisation/focus_groups/fg1_wp_en.pdf (on 13.07.2007): "*The justification for a sector specific regulation of television services lies within their 'pervasiveness', and the 'particular immediacy in the provision of audiovisual content'*"; Wetenschappelijke Raad voor het Regeringsbeleid, Focus op functies – Uitdagingen voor een toekomstbestendig mediabeleid [*Focus on functions – Challenges for a future proof media policy*], Amsterdam, Amsterdam University Press, 2005, retrieved from http://www.wrr.nl/dsc?c=getobject&s=obj&!sessionid=1o7p!cnhb9o!M9xXGwuyBPekM35UuYCWRZ1zyOvsfxauyo3h50uVxzYXp1K38HdW&objectid=2799&!dsname=default&isapidir=/gvisapi/ (on 27.07.2007), 42 [in Dutch].

[311] Commission of the European Communities, Communication from the Commission to the Council, the European Parliament, the Economic and Social Committee and the Committee of the Regions, Principles and guidelines for the Community's audiovisual policy in the digital age, COM (1999) 657 final, 14.12.1999, 8.

> *they provide concepts and categories – political, social, ethnic, geographical, psychological and so on – which we use to render these facts and images intelligible. They therefore help to determine not only what we see of the world but also how we see it.*[312]

The fact that thousands or millions of people watched the same programmes at the same time was considered a key factor for the necessity of content regulation. Today, this 'push'-model is slowly being overtaken by a model that relies more on 'pull' content. Users now have increasing control over their media use and can decide what, where and when they want to watch certain programmes. From this discussion, it may seem that the rationales for content regulation are not as relevant today as they were before. However, it cannot be denied that the different media still play a role of crucial importance in today's societies. Moreover, there still are a number of essential general interest objectives that justify the regulation of content, even in this digital era.[313]

General interest objectives of media content regulation – Since the rise of mass media, media content has always been regulated to a certain extent, either by social norms, or by laws and state regulations. Different objectives are at the origin of the regulation of content. These can be classified as 'positive' and 'negative' objectives.[314] 'Positive' goals include, for instance, ensuring freedom of expression, and promoting pluralism, cultural diversity and wide access to content. Examples of 'negative' objectives are the protection of minors against potentially harmful content, the protection of consumers, the protection of individuals' reputation, and the protection of public order and national security. Most, if not all, of these objectives have not been called into question by technical developments, and remain as significant in the digital era as they were in the context of traditional content

312 Commission of the European Communities, Communication from the Commission to the Council, the European Parliament, the Economic and Social Committee and the Committee of the Regions, Principles and guidelines for the Community's audiovisual policy in the digital age, COM (1999) 657 final, 14.12.1999, 7.

313 Commission of the European Communities, Communication from the Commission to the Council, the European Parliament, the Economic and Social Committee and the Committee of the Regions, Principles and guidelines for the Community's audiovisual policy in the digital age, COM (1999) 657 final, 14.12.1999, 11.

314 Hans-Bredow-Institut and EMR, Study on co-regulation measures in the media sector: Final report, Study commissioned by the European Commission, June 2006, retrieved from http://ec.europa.eu/avpolicy/docs/library/studies/coregul/final_rep_en.pdf (on 28.07.2006), 19; Tambini, Damien and Forgan, Liz, "Content", Communications White Paper, retrieved from http://www.communicationswhitepaper.gov.uk/cwp_consultation/contentregulation.pdf (18.12.2003, no longer available), 3.

regulation (e.g., press, radio and television).[315] The objective of protection of minors, which was acknowledged as a goal of European audiovisual policy from the outset,[316] is certainly as justified as it was before the upsurge of digital media.

EU MEDIA CONTENT REGULATION 'INTERNAL MARKET DRIVEN' – Aside from attaining certain public interest objectives (*supra*), media content regulation at the EU level has always been developed with internal market objectives (*infra*) in mind as well.[317] Freedom to provide services such as radio and television broadcasts, for instance, has, in this context, been considered crucial.[318] The internal market policy also indirectly contributes to the promotion of freedom of expression, since this fundamental right is dependent on the free circulation of information.[319]

CULTURE-DEPENDENCY – Content regulation differs from culture to culture. Every country has its own approach to what content is considered appropriate or inappropriate. Hence, there is no uniform European content policy.[320] At the EU and CoE levels, there are, however, a number of instruments which have been created with the intention of harmonising a number of content-related rules and regulations, such as the Television without Frontiers Directive, the Audiovisual Media Services Directive and the Convention on Transfrontier Television (*infra*).

CONTENT AND GENERAL CIVIL AND CRIMINAL LAW PRINCIPLES – Finally, it should not be forgotten that in a number of countries, certain general (civil and criminal) legislation, for instance relating to public decency, also

---

315 COMMISSION OF THE EUROPEAN COMMUNITIES, Communication from the Commission to the Council, the European Parliament, the Economic and Social Committee and the Committee of the Regions, Principles and guidelines for the Community's audiovisual policy in the digital age, COM (1999) 657 final, 14.12.1999, 2.

316 FÜG, Oliver C., "Save the children: the protection of minors in the Information Society and the Audiovisual Media Services Directive", *Journal of Consumer Policy* 2008, Vol. 31, No. 1, 46.

317 NIKOLINAKOS, Nikos, *EU competition law and regulation in the converging telecommunications, media and IT Sectors*, Alphen a/d Rijn, Kluwer Law International, 2006, 537–538.

318 Cf. Television without Frontiers and Audiovisual Media Services Directive: *infra*.

319 NIKOLINAKOS, Nikos, *EU competition law and regulation in the converging telecommunications, media and IT Sectors*, Alphen a/d Rijn, Kluwer Law International, 2006, 538.

320 HOLOUBEK, Michael (ed.), *Regulating content – European regulatory framework for the media and related creative sectors*, Alphen a/d Rijn, Kluwer Law International, 2007, 4.

influences the regulation of content.[321] In Belgium, for example, certain kinds of pornography may be considered illegal on the basis of article 383 of the Criminal Code. These national provisions, however, do not fall within the scope of this study. In what follows, the focus is on more specific (direct and indirect) forms of content regulation at the EU (and CoE) level.

1.4.2. *Regulation of audiovisual content*

AUDIOVISUAL CONTENT REGULATION – Regulation of audiovisual content has been harmonised at the EU level, as well as the CoE level. Over the past decades, more and more questions were raised about the viability of traditional content regulation in the changing media environment. This debate resulted in a number of regulatory developments.

A. *Television without Frontiers Directive*

TELEVISION WITHOUT FRONTIERS DIRECTIVE – Since 1989, the regulatory basis for protecting minors in television broadcasting has been embedded in the EU Council Directive on the coordination of certain provisions laid down by law, regulation or administrative action in Member States concerning the pursuit of television broadcasting activities, better-known as the Television without Frontiers Directive (TVWFD).[322] The Directive has been the cornerstone of audiovisual content regulation for almost twenty years. Its key elements were the free movement of television broadcasting services (based on the country of origin-principle), rules on events of major importance, the promotion, distribution and production of (European) programmes, provisions on advertising, teleshopping and sponsorship, stipulations on the protection of minors and human dignity, and a clause on the right of reply.[323]

---

[321] COMMISSION OF THE EUROPEAN COMMUNITIES, Green Paper on the protection of minors and human dignity in audiovisual and information services, COM (1996) 483 final, 16.10.1996, 15.

[322] COUNCIL Directive 89/552/EEC of 3 October 1989 on the coordination of certain provisions laid down by law, regulation or administrative action in Member States concerning the pursuit of television broadcasting activities, *OJ L* 298, 17.10.1989, 23, amended by EUROPEAN PARLIAMENT AND COUNCIL Directive 97/36/EC of 30 June 1997, *OJ L* 202, 30.07.1997, 60 [hereinafter: TVWFD].

[323] For comprehensive analyses of the TVWFD cf. AUBRY, Patrice, "The 'Television without Frontiers' Directive – Cornerstone of the European broadcasting policy", 2000, retrieved from http://www.obs.coe.int/online_publication/reports/TWF.pdf.en (on 09.07.2007); JONES, Clifford, "Television without Frontiers", in: EECKHOUT, Piet and TRIDIMAS, Takis, *Yearbook of European Law 1999–2000*, Oxford, Oxford University Press, 2000, 299–347;

The Directive was applicable to 'television broadcasting activities', defined as "*the initial transmission by wire or over the air, including that by satellite, in unencoded or encoded form, of television programmes intended for reception by the public. It includes the communication of programmes between undertakings with a view to their being relayed to the public*".[324]

PROTECTION OF CHILDREN IN THE TVWFD – Up until recently, the protection of minors in broadcasting services was regulated by article 22 TVWFD, which established both an absolute and a relative ban on programmes that might be considered harmful to children.[325] Programmes which might *seriously* impair the physical, mental or moral development of minors could not be broadcast. Although the TVWFD did not specify which content was considered to have such a seriously damaging effect,[326] it nevertheless provided some guidance by referring to two examples: pornography and gratuitous violence. It has been argued that the reference to these two examples was general enough to be understood by the national legislators.[327] Furthermore, it has also been suggested that the two categories mentioned constituted a minimum requirement; hence other categories of content could have been attributed the same qualification by Member States.[328] Programmes *likely* to impair the physical, mental or moral development of minors, on the other hand, could be broadcast if it was ensured, by selecting the time of the broadcast or by any technical measure, that minors in the area of transmission

---

NIKOLINAKOS, Nikos, *EU competition law and regulation in the converging telecommunications, media and IT Sectors*, Alphen a/d Rijn, Kluwer Law International, 2006, 698 p. (Chapter 14: EU audiovisual policy – Content regulation: 537–599); CASTENDYCK, Oliver, DOMMERING, Egbert and SCHEUER, Alexander (eds.), *European media law*, Kluwer Law International, 2007, 1416 p.

[324] Article 1 (a) TVWFD.

[325] As explained *supra*, there is no uniform EU-wide understanding of what content is potentially harmful for children. Each Member State interprets this concept according to its own cultural sensitivities.

[326] HEROLD identified the subsidiarity principle (*infra*) as the cause for a lack of definitions. She noted "*[t]his interpretation freedom points to the capacity of the country of origin mechanism as devised under the Directive to accommodate national sensitivities in the area of protecting minors*": HEROLD, Anna, "Country of origin principle in the EU market for audiovisual media services: consumer's friend or foe?", *Journal of Consumer Policy* 2008, Vol. 31, No. 1, 9.

[327] FÜG, Oliver C., "Save the children: the protection of minors in the Information Society and the Audiovisual Media Services Directive", *Journal of Consumer Policy* 2008, Issue 31, No. 1, 46–47.

[328] FÜG, Oliver C., "Save the children: the protection of minors in the Information Society and the Audiovisual Media Services Directive", *Journal of Consumer Policy* 2008, Issue 31, No. 1, 46–47.

would not normally hear or see such broadcasts. Moreover, when broadcast in unencoded form, such programmes needed to be preceded by an acoustic warning, or identified by a visual symbol throughout their duration.[329] Article 22b TVWFD stressed the importance of this chapter (Protection of minors and public order).[330] There were two other articles which were indirectly related to the issue of protecting minors in the audiovisual environment, i.e., articles 2 and 2a on the country of origin-principle and freedom of television broadcasting services.[331] In brief, these two articles implied that a broadcaster who met the requirements of one Member State (article 2) could provide its services throughout the European Union without having to comply with specific obligations of other Member States (article 2a para. 1). When a broadcast coming from another Member State, however, violated article 22 para. 1 or 2, a Member State was allowed, under certain

---

[329] An illustration of the implementation of article 22 can be found in the Ofcom Broadcasting Code: OFCOM, Broadcasting Code, October 2008, retrieved from http://www.ofcom.org.uk/tv/ifi/codes/bcode/bcode.pdf (on 19.10.2008). The framework it constructs for the protection of minors in television services is very detailed content-wise: as well as adopting the general terms of article 22, it also specifically deals with drugs, smoking, solvents and alcohol, violence and dangerous behaviour, offensive language, sex and nudity and, finally, exorcism, the occult and the paranormal. Moreover, it establishes a regime based on protection systems (mandatory PIN or other equivalent protection) for premium subscription and pay per view services and, a total ban on R18–rated films – meaning that such films can simply not be broadcast. The reasoning behind this was that "*those viewers that subscribe to premium subscription film services have accepted a greater share of responsibility for what is broadcast into the home (and therefore have particular responsibility to oversee children's access to material in this area)*". See OFCOM, Guidance notes Broadcasting Code section 1: Protecting the under18s, 2007, retrieved from http://www.ofcom.org.uk/tv/ifi/guidance/bguidance/guidance1.pdf (on 19.10.2008).

[330] Article 22b para. 2 (inserted in 1997) stipulated that the Commission, in cooperation with the Member States, should launch an investigation of the possible advantages and drawbacks of further measures with a view to facilitating the control exercised by parents or guardians over the programmes that minors may watch. In this study, attention needed to be brought to the potential of technical devices, filtering, rating systems and education and awareness. The study, titled *Study on parental control of television broadcasting*, was carried out by the University of Oxford (Centre for socio-legal studies): cf. PRICE, Monroe and VERHULST, Stefaan, *Parental control of television broadcasting*, Mahwah, Erlbaum, 2002, 314 p. A follow-up study, *Parental control in a converged communications environment – Self-regulation, technical devices and meta-information*, was commissioned by the DVB Regulatory Group: cf. KELLER, Daphne and VERHULST, Stefaan, Parental control in a converged communications environment. Self-regulation, technical devices and meta-information (Final report for the DVB regulatory group), October 2000, retrieved from http://ec.europa.eu/avpolicy/docs/reg/minors/dvbgroup.pdf (on 23.04.2007).

[331] For a detailed overview and the history of article 2 TVWFD, cf. FÜG, Oliver C., "Save the children: the protection of minors in the Information Society and the Audiovisual Media Services Directive", *Journal of Consumer Policy* 2008, Issue 31, No. 1, 49–52.

conditions, to derogate from article 2a para. 1.[332] Finally, a number of articles related to the protection of children against certain kinds of advertising (for instance, alcoholic beverages advertising, or advertising which may harm children's development).[333]

Evaluation – At the end of 2003, the Commission declared in its Communication on 'The future of European regulatory audiovisual policy' that the provisions laid down in the TVWFD on the protection of minors were "*satisfactory and adequate*".[334] This positive evaluation, however, did not alter the finding that the Directive was no longer suitable for the changed media environment. Watershed provisions such as, for instance, advanced by article 22 para. 2, are no longer as effective in the Internet setting, where information is available and accessible '24/7'.[335] Moreover, identical examples of audiovisual content were increasingly subject to divergent regulatory frameworks depending on the method of delivery.[336] This was perceived as creating a non-level playing field between 'traditional' broadcasters and providers of new media services.[337] The European Commission felt that this situation

---

[332] Article 2a para. 2 TVWFD.

[333] This will not be examined further in detail since advertising falls outside the scope of this analysis (cf. Part 1, Chapter 1).

[334] Commission of the European Communities, Communication from the Commission to the Council, the European Parliament, the European Economic and Social Committee and the Committee of the Regions, The future of European regulatory audiovisual policy, COM (2003) 784 final, 15.12.2003, 20. The fact that the TVWFD functioned effectively was reiterated a number of times, most recently in the sixth evaluation report: Commission of the European Communities, Sixth report from the Commission to the European Parliament, the Council, the European Economic and Social Committee and the Committee of the Regions on the application of Directive 89/552/EEC "Television without Frontiers", COM (2007) 452 final, 24.10.2007, retrieved from http://eur-lex.europa.eu/LexUriServ/site/en/com/2007/com2007_0452en01.pdf (on 14.01.2008).

[335] Ruxton, Sandy, *What about us? Children's rights in the European Union? Next Steps*, Brussels, The European Children's Network, 2005, 108; Commission of the European Communities, Green Paper on the protection of minors and human dignity in audiovisual and information services, COM (1996) 483 final, 16.10.1996, 15.

[336] For example: the exact same television programme can be watched when it is broadcast or after it has been downloaded (on-demand) from the Internet.

[337] Reding, Viviane, Audiovisual media services directive: the right instrument to provide legal certainty for Europe's media businesses in the next decade, Speech at the Seminar "Regulating the new media landscape", Brussels, 07.06.2006, retrieved from http://europa.eu.int/rapid/pressReleasesAction.do?reference=SPEECH/06/352&format=HTML&aged=0&language=EN&guiLanguage=en (on 12.07.2006): "*Keeping the TVWF Directive as it stands now would aggravate increasingly unjustifiable differences in regulatory treatment between the various forms of distribution of identical or similar content. 'Traditional' television broadcasting services would remain regulated on the basis of the regulatory approach*

created difficulties with respect to competition and legal certainty, and hence initiated a revision process.

B. *Revision process: from Television without Frontiers to Audiovisual Media Services*

Revision of the TVWFD – After an intensive preparation and consultation phase,[338] a first proposal for an 'Audiovisual Media Services Directive'[339] (AVMSD) was presented by the Commission in December 2005. The proposal aimed to create a comprehensive regulatory framework for any form of electronic delivery of audiovisual content by including non-linear services in the scope of the Directive and establishing a two-tier regulatory regime with both a basic (for all services, including non-linear services) and advanced set of obligations (for linear services).[340]

EU Council – In May 2006, the EU Council published a progress report in which it stated that, on the whole, delegations reacted favourably to the proposal, with only one delegation, with the support from another delegation – a safe guess might be the United Kingdom, backed by Slovakia – indicating clear opposition to the extension of the Directive's scope to non-linear services.[341] With respect to the protection of minors, the Council

of the 1980's and 1990's. With the current rules, non-linear service providers have to comply with different – often diverging – national rules applying to the new services. This bears the risk of closing markets for on-demand audiovisual services and creating or reinforcing monopolies. This is in my opinion not acceptable!".

338 A detailed chronology of events during this period, as well as documents regarding the modernisation of the TVWFD, are available on the EU Commission Audiovisual Policy website: http://ec.europa.eu/avpolicy/reg/history/index_en.htm (last retrieved on 13.12.2008). Cf. also Holoubek, Michael (ed.), *Regulating content – European regulatory framework for the media and related creative sectors*, Alphen a/d Rijn, Kluwer Law International, 2007, 121 *et seq*; Nikolinakos, Nikos, *EU competition law and regulation in the converging telecommunications, media and IT Sectors*, Alphen a/d Rijn, Kluwer Law International, 2006, 577 *et seq*.

339 Hereinafter: AVMSD.

340 Commission of the European Communities, Proposal for a Directive of the European Parliament and of the Council amending Council Directive 89/552/EEC on the coordination of certain provisions laid down by law, regulation or administrative action in Member States concerning the pursuit of television broadcasting activities, COM (2005) 646 final, 13.12.2005, 7 [hereinafter: 2005 Proposal AVMS Directive].

341 Council of the European Union, Progress report/exchange of views on Proposal for a directive of the European Parliament and of the Council amending Council directive 89/552/EEC on the coordination of certain provisions laid down by law, regulation or

observed broad support for the introduction of a common standard for the protection of minors for all audiovisual services.[342] An agreement on a general approach for the adoption of a new directive, broadly in line with the Commission proposal,[343] was reached in November 2006.[344]

European Parliament – The European Parliament finalised its first reading, based on the report of MEP Hieronymi, on 13 December 2006, exactly one year after the publication of the original proposal by the Commission.[345] Even though the European Parliament largely accepted the Commission's proposal, it proposed a number of amendments, for instance, with respect to the country of origin-principle, advertising and product placement, short reports, and pluralism.[346]

Last steps in the legislative procedure – During the informal Council of 12 February 2007, the European Council suggested that it was preparing the ground for the adoption of a common position on the Directive in May

administrative action in Member States concerning the pursuit of television broadcasting activities, No. 9134/06, Interinstitutional file 2005/0260 (COD), 10.06.2006, retrieved from http://register.consilium.europa.eu/pdf/en/06/st09/st09134.en06.pdf (on 10.07.2006), 2.

342 Council of the European Union, Progress report/exchange of views on Proposal for a directive of the European Parliament and of the Council amending Council directive 89/552/EEC on the coordination of certain provisions laid down by law, regulation or administrative action in Member States concerning the pursuit of television broadcasting activities, No. 9134/06, Interinstitutional file 2005/0260 (COD), 10.06.2006, retrieved from http://register.consilium.europa.eu/pdf/en/06/st09/st09134.en06.pdf (on 10.07.2006), 5.

343 European Commission, Audiovisual and media policies, Overview legislative proposal for an Audiovisual Media Services Directive, retrieved from http://ec.europa.eu/comm/avpolicy/reg/tvwf/modernisation/proposal_2005/index_en.htm (on 26.03.2007, no longer available).

344 Council of the European Union, Press release 2762nd Council meeting Education, Youth and Culture, Brussels, 13–14.11.2006, retrieved from http://www.consilium.europa.eu/ueDocs/cms_Data/docs/pressData/en/educ/91666.pdf (on 13.07.2007).

345 European Parliament, Legislative resolution on the proposal for a directive of the European Parliament and of the Council amending Council Directive 89/552/EEC on the coordination of certain provisions laid down by law, regulation or administrative action in Member States concerning the pursuit of television broadcasting activities, COM(2005)0646 – C6-0443/2005 – 2005/0260(COD), 13.12.2006, retrieved from http://www.europarl.europa.eu/sides/getDoc.do?pubRef=-//EP//TEXT+TA+P6-TA-2006-0559+0+DOC+XML+V0//EN (on 26.03.2007).

346 European Commission, Audiovisual and media policies, Overview legislative proposal for an Audiovisual Media Services Directive, retrieved from http://ec.europa.eu/comm/avpolicy/reg/tvwf/modernisation/proposal_2005/index_en.htm (on 26.03.2007, no longer available).

2007.[347] On 9 March 2007, the Commission unveiled a draft consolidated text for the AVMSD,[348] and as predicted, on 24 May 2007, a political agreement on a common position was reached by the Council and the European Parliament.[349] The adoption of the common position followed in October 2007,[350] and the European Parliament finished its second reading on 29 November 2007, approving the text without any amendments.[351]

Adoption – The AVMSD was adopted on 11 December 2007.[352] On the occasion of the finalisation of the review process, the Commission empha-

---

347 RAPID, Boosting the diversity of European TV- and on-demand services: Commission paves the way for the new Directive 'Audiovisual without Frontiers', IP/07/311, 09.03.2007, retrieved from http://europa.eu/rapid/pressReleasesAction.do?reference=IP/07/311&format=HTML&aged=0&language=EN&guiLanguage=en (on 26.03.2007).

348 European Commission, Audiovisual Media Services Directive: Draft consolidated amended version 2007, March 2007, retrieved from http://ec.europa.eu/information_society/newsroom/cf/itemlongdetail.cfm?item_id=2343 (on 26.03.2007) [hereinafter: Draft consolidated amended version].

349 Council and Parliament of the European Communities, Political agreement on common position AVMS Directive – Newly modified Commission proposal, 24.05.2007, retrieved from http://ec.europa.eu/avpolicy/docs/reg/modernisation/proposal_2005/avmsd_cons_may07_en.pdf (on 10.07.2007) [hereinafter: Proposal AVMS Directive May 2007].

350 Council of the European union, Common position (EC) No 18/2007 of 15 October 2007 adopted by the Council, acting in accordance with the procedure referred to in Article 251 of the Treaty establishing the European Community, with a view to the adoption of a Directive of the European Parliament and of the Council amending Council Directive 89/552/EEC on the coordination of certain provisions laid down by law, regulation or administrative action in Member States concerning the pursuit of television broadcasting activities, *OJ* 18.12.2007, *C* 307E, 1.

351 European Parliament, Legislative resolution on the Council common position for adopting a directive of the European Parliament and of the Council amending Council Directive 89/552/EEC on the coordination of certain provisions laid down by law, regulation or administrative action in Member States concerning the pursuit of television broadcasting activities, 10076/6/2007 – C6-0352/2007 – 2005/0260(COD), 29.11.2007, retrieved from http://www.europarl.europa.eu/oeil/FindByProcnum.do?lang=2&procnum=COD/2005/0260 (on 28.03.2008).

352 European Parliament and Council Directive 2007/65/EC of 11 December 2007 amending Council Directive 89/552/EEC on the coordination of certain provisions laid down by law, regulation or administrative action in Member States concerning the pursuit of television broadcasting activities, *OJ* 18.12.2007, *L* 332, 27; Rapid, Commission welcomes start of a new era for Europe's audiovisual media, IP/07/1809, 29.11.2007, retrieved from http://www.europa.eu/rapid/pressReleasesAction.do?reference=IP/07/1809&format=HTML&aged=0&language=EN&guiLanguage=en (on 16.01.2008). In April 2009, the Commission issued a proposal for a codified version of the AVMSD: Commission of the European Communities, Proposal for a Directive of the European Parliament and

sised that there would be "*less regulation, better financing for content and greater visibility to cultural diversity and the protection of minors*". Furthermore, Commissioner REDING asked Member States to proceed with a 'light touch' transposition of the Directive, i.e., to not add too many stricter national provisions, which would prevent their audiovisual industries from fully benefiting from the freedom brought by the AVMSD.[353]

C. *Audiovisual Media Services Directive*

SCOPE OF APPLICATION – The key change in the regulatory framework for audiovisual content is the extension of the scope of application of the AVMSD to 'audiovisual media services'; such a service is "*a service as defined by Articles 49 and 50 of the Treaty*[354] *which is under the editorial responsibility of a media service provider and the principal purpose of which is the provision of programmes in order to inform, entertain or educate, to the general public by electronic communications networks within the meaning of Article 2(a) of Directive 2002/21/EC of the European Parliament and of the Council*".[355, 356] Within this wide scope, the AVMSD distinguishes between linear ('push') and non-linear ('pull') services. Article 1 (g) defines a 'non-linear' or 'on-demand' audiovisual media service as an "*an audiovisual media service provided by a media service provider for the viewing of programmes*

of the Council on the coordination of certain provisions laid down by law, regulation or administrative action in Member States concerning the provision of audiovisual media services (Audiovisual Media Services Directive) (Codified version), COM (2009) 185 final, 21.04.2009.

353 REDING, Viviane, Le nouveau contexte des médias audiovisuels – Tendances et enjeux publics [*The new context of audiovisual media – Trends and public challenges*], Speech at the Colloque international pour les 10 ans du Conseil supérieur de l'audiovisuel de la Communauté française de Belgique, Brussels, 21.09.2007, retrieved from http://europa.eu/rapid/pressReleasesAction.do?reference=SPEECH/07/560 (on 14.01.2008) [in French]. Commissioner REDING reiterated this wish in December 2008. She also presented a table on the state of play on the implementation of the new Directive in EU Member States, from which could be deduced that the majority of countries had not yet transposed the AVMSD in December 2008: RAPID, Commission calls on Member States to rule with a light hand while updating TV rules in 2009, IP/08/2032, 18.12.2008, retrieved from http://europa.eu/rapid/pressReleasesAction.do?reference=IP/08/2032&format=HTML&aged=0&language=EN&guiLanguage=en (on 24.12.2008).

354 More specifically, services as defined by articles 56 and 57 TFEU [ex 49 and 50 EC Treaty], i.e., "*normally provided for remuneration*".

355 Article 1 (a) AVMSD.

356 Cf. also HOLOUBEK, Michael (ed.), *Regulating content – European regulatory framework for the media and related creative sectors*, Alphen a/d Rijn, Kluwer Law International, 2007, 18–21.

at the moment chosen by the user and at his individual request on the basis of a catalogue of programmes selected by the media service provider". 'Television broadcasting' (a linear audiovisual media service), on the other hand, is defined as "*an audiovisual media service provided by a media service provider for simultaneous viewing of programmes on the basis of a programme schedule*" (article 1 (e)).[357]

Opposition – Following the publication of the Commission's original proposal, heated arguments concerning the scope of application, and particularly the proposed regulation of non-linear services, surfaced at regular intervals. Governments, academics[358] and industry players voiced their opposition to the inclusion of non-linear services in the AVMSD.[359] Their main arguments were the ambiguity of the concepts as they were defined in the original pro-

[357] The European Court of Justice clarified the difference between a television broadcasting service (linear) and an information society service (non-linear) in ECJ, Mediakabel BV v. Commissariaat voor de Media, C-89/04, 02.06.2005.

[358] Molnar, Peter et al., Budapest declaration for freedom of the Internet, 15.06.2006, retrieved from http://www.edri.org/docs/BudapestDeclaration.pdf (on 27.06.2008); van Eijk, Nico, "The modernisation of the European Television without Frontiers Directive: unnecessary regulation and the introduction of internet governance", paper for the ITS 19th European Regional Conference, Istanbul, 02–05.09.2007, retrieved from http://www.itseurope.org/ITS%20CONF/istanbul2007/downloads/paper/29.08.2007_Eijk.pdf (on 27.06.2008).

[359] See for instance: The Times (Dan Sabbagh), Minister opposes EU plan to regulate Internet, 20.06.2006, retrieved from http://business.timesonline.co.uk/article/0,,13130-2001048,00.html (on 12.07.2006); The Guardian (Chris Tryhorn), Minister attacks EU media plans, 29.06.2006, retrieved from http://politics.guardian.co.uk/media/story/0,,1808895,00.html (on 12.07.2006); ZDNet UK (Tom Espiner), Government attacks EC's 'dangerous' online media plans, 29.06.2006, retrieved from http://news.zdnet.co.uk/internet/0,39020369,39277928,00.htm (on 12.07.2006); Audiovisual Stakeholders, Audiovisual Media Services Draft Directive: Opinions and recommendations from stakeholders in the UK, April 2006, retrieved from http://www.audiovisualstakeholders.org/AMS_Stakeholder_Paper_FINAL_April06.pdf (on 12.07.2006, no longer available); Intellect, TVWF will hamper competition and harm competitiveness, says hi-tech industry, 13.12.2005, retrieved from http://www.intellectuk.org/content/view/618/108/ (on 13.07.2007); EDRI, Newsletter 4.10: Draft Audiovisual Media Services Directive under criticism, 24.05.2006, retrieved from http://www.edri.org/edrigram/number4.10/audiovisual (on 29.05.2006); Ross, Patrick, "Regulation without Frontiers: Europe shows U.S. policymakers how not to embrace convergence", Progress Snapshot 1.15, September 2005, retrieved from http://www.pff.org/issues-pubs/ps/ps1.15frontiers.html (on 06.07.2006); Ross, Patrick, "Content Regulation without Frontiers: why the EU is indeed regulating the Internet", Progress Snapshot 1.24, December 2005, retrieved from http://www.pff.org/issues-pubs/ps/ps1.24eu.html (on 06.07.2006).

posal, and the legal uncertainty this would create.[360] Some even suggested that the proposal was inclined towards censorship.[361] Commissioner Reding, the EU primary protagonist, vehemently denied these accusations:

> *[...] I think it is necessary to correct a misperception with which some players try to influence the discussion. This Commission proposal is not about new restrictive provisions but about giving effect to the freedoms of the EC Treaty and about paving the way for a better exercise of the fundamental right of freedom of expression across the borders in the EU.*[362]

It also needs to be mentioned that in subsequent documents, much attention was paid to the clarification of the concepts used in the Directive. However, given the rapid technological developments over the past few years, it remains to be seen for how long these concepts will be valid.

Graduated regulation – An impact assessment of different possible strategies to revise the directive, carried out during the preparation process, had concluded that "*a comprehensive legislative framework, with graduated treatment of linear and non-linear audiovisual media services, would provide a*

---

[360] Audiovisual Stakeholders, Audiovisual Media Services Draft Directive: Opinions and recommendations from stakeholders in the UK, April 2006, retrieved from http://www.audiovisualstakeholders.org/AMS_Stakeholder_Paper_FINAL_April06.pdf (on 12.07.2006, no longer available), 3.

[361] IT Analysis (Bob McDowall), The Television without Frontiers Directive: another 'directive too far'?, 05.05.2006, retrieved from http://www.it-analysis.com/business/content.php?cid=8476 (on 12.07.2006); The Register (Mark Ballard), EU regulation attacked as censorship, 19.05.2006, retrieved from http://www.theregister.co.uk/2006/05/19/eu_censorship/ (on 12.07.2006).

[362] Reding, Viviane, Audiovisual media services directive: the right instrument to provide legal certainty for Europe's media businesses in the next decade, Speech at the Seminar "Regulating the new media landscape", Brussels, 07.06.2006, retrieved from http://europa.eu.int/rapid/pressReleasesAction.do?reference=SPEECH/06/352&format=HTML&aged=0&language=EN&guiLanguage=en (on 12.07.2006). See also: Reding, Viviane, Convergence and innovation, the new agenda for growth and jobs, Speech at the Meeting of the Council of Presidents of UNICE, Brussels, 21.03.2005, retrieved from http://europa.eu/rapid/pressReleasesAction.do?reference=SPEECH/05/190&format=HTML&aged=0&language=EN&guiLanguage=en (on 13.07.2007): "*I will only regulate this new market where absolutely necessary in the concerns of European citizens for diversity, quality, decency and safety from abusive uses*"; Reding, Viviane, Freedom of the media, effective co-regulation and media literacy: cornerstones for an efficient protection of minors in the European Union, Speech at the ICRA Roundtable Brussels 'Mission Impossible', Brussels, 14.06.2006, retrieved from http://europa.eu.int/rapid/pressReleasesAction.do?reference=SPEECH/06/374&type=HTML&aged=0&language=EN&guiLanguage=en (on 15.06.2006).

neutral or improved situation for a majority of stakeholders".[363] Hence, the AVMSD links separate sets of obligations to the two types of services: a basic set of (minimum) rules are applicable to all audiovisual media services (including non-linear services),[364] while linear services are also subject to a set of rules similar to those in the TVWFD, but which have been modernised.[365] According to the Commission, arguments in favour of lighter regulation of non-linear services are the choice and control the user can exercise and the – lesser – impact such services have on society (compared to linear services, *supra*).[366] The 'basic' rules (applicable to *all* services) range from identification[367] and non-discrimination[368] obligations to provisions with respect to audiovisual commercial communication ('advertising').[369, 370] However, there is a somewhat special category of articles that are only applicable to *non-linear* services: article 3h on the protection of minors (cf. *infra*) and article 3i on the promotion of production and access to European works for on-demand services. Provisions related to television broadcasting, finally, deal with exclusive rights and short news reports,[371] the promotion of distribution and productions of television programmes,[372] television advertising

363 Commission of the European Communities, Commission Staff working document *Annex to the* Proposal for a Directive of the European Parliament and of the Council amending Council Directive 89/552/EEC on the coordination of certain provisions laid down by law, regulation or administrative action in Member States concerning the pursuit of television broadcasting activities, Impact Assessment – Draft Audiovisual Media Services Directive, SEC (2005) 1625/2, 13.12.2005, retrieved from http://ec.europa.eu/avpolicy/docs/reg/modernisation/proposal_2005/newtwf_ia.pdf (on 26.11.2008), 4. For the impact assessment specifically with respect to the protection of minors, see 29–32.
364 Although article 3h and 3i are only applicable to non-linear services, cf. *infra*.
365 Proposal AVMS Directive May 2007, 3 and 16 (recitals 5 and 28).
366 Proposal AVMS Directive May 2007, 16 (recital 28).
367 Article 3a AVMSD.
368 Article 3b AVMSD.
369 Articles 3e–3g AVMSD.
370 Other articles relate to access to programmes for people with a visual or hearing disability (article 3c AVMSD), and the prohibition on media service providers to transmit cinematographic works outside periods agreed with the rights holders (article 3d AVMSD).
371 Articles 3j and 3k AVMSD.
372 Articles 4–9 AVMSD.

and teleshopping,[373] the protection of minors (*infra*),[374] and the right of reply.[375, 376]

Protection of minors in the AVMSD – As regards the protection of minors in the AVMSD, the broad consensus on the continued importance of this objective of public interest was evident during the preparatory stage.[377] It was – and is still – deemed necessary, by all parties involved, to establish rules to protect the physical, mental and moral development of minors in *all* audiovisual media services.[378] However, the Commission – correctly – emphasised that these rules need to be carefully balanced with the freedom of expression. An impact assesssment carried out in the preparatory phases of the revision of the TVWFD showed that the system favoured by the Commission (extension of the scope of application and graduated regulation) would have no negative impact whatsoever with respect to the protection of minors.[379]

---

373 Articles 10–20 AVMSD.

374 Article 22 AVMSD.

375 Article 23 AVMSD.

376 For a comprehensive analysis of the new directive, cf. Castendyck, Oliver, Dommering, Egbert and Scheuer, Alexander (eds.), *European media law*, Kluwer Law International, 2007, 1416 p. See also: Valcke, Peggy and Stevens, David, "Graduated regulation of 'regulatable' content and the European Audiovisual Media Services Directive – One small step for the industry and one giant leap for the legislator?", *Telematics & Informatics* 2007, Vol. 24, Issue 4, November 2007, 285–302. For the purpose of this book, the focus in this section is on the protection of minors and the impact of other (new) provisions on this topic.

377 The significance of protecting minors was repeatedly expressed in the numerous contributions the Commission received to the consultation. These contributions can be found at: http://ec.europa.eu/avpolicy/reg/history/consult/consultation_2003/contributions/index_en.htm (last retrieved on 14.12.2008). Cf. also an earlier Commission document which pronounced the protection of minors "*a policy objective valid for any kind of audiovisual services*": Commission of the European Communities, Communication from the Commission to the Council, the European Parliament, the European Economic and Social Committee and the Committee of the Regions, The future of European regulatory audiovisual policy, COM (2003) 784 final, 15.12.2003, 13.

378 Proposal AVMS Directive May 2007, 17 (recital 31): "*The availability of harmful content in audiovisual media services continue [sic] to be a concern for law-makers, industry and parents. […] It is therefore necessary to introduce rules to protect the physical, mental and moral development of minors as well as human dignity in all audiovisual media services, including audiovisual commercial communication*".

379 Commission of the European Communities, Commission Staff working document *Annex to the* Proposal for a Directive of the European Parliament and of the Council amending Council Directive 89/552/EEC on the coordination of certain provisions laid

Protection of minors non-linear services – With respect to non-linear services, article 3h AVMSD stipulates that Member States need to take "*appropriate measures to ensure that on-demand audiovisual media services provided by media services providers under their jurisdiction which might seriously impair the physical, mental or moral development of minors are only made available in such a way that ensures that minors will not normally hear or see such on-demand audiovisual media services*".[380] If one compares this article to the traditional approach of article 22 TVWFD (with respect to traditional broadcasting services, *supra*), it becomes clear that no restrictions are imposed on non-linear services which are *likely* to harm children. Clearly, the Commission only deems it necessary to provide safeguards with respect to *seriously* harmful content. And even with respect to such content, the Commission has stressed that this article does not constitute an absolute ban, but a "*requirement for protective measures (such as filters) to be put in place regarding the making available of 'seriously harmful' material*".[381] Other examples of such measures are the use of PINs and labelling.[382] This approach fits in with Commission policy in this field (*supra*, Part 1, Chapter 1).[383] It has been argued, however, that it is regrettable that no absolute prohibition of seriously harmful content for non-linear services was included in the Directive.[384]

---

down by law, regulation or administrative action in Member States concerning the pursuit of television broadcasting activities, Impact Assessment – Draft Audiovisual Media Services Directive, SEC (2005) 1625/2, 13.12.2005, retrieved from http://ec.europa.eu/avpolicy/docs/reg/modernisation/proposal_2005/newtwf_ia.pdf (on 26.11.2008), 29–32. Another impact assessment commissioned by the UK regulator Ofcom concluded that, with respect to the protection of minors, there would be significant social benefits for applying the basic tier of rules. This, however, would best be done through self- or co-regulation (*infra*): Indepen, Extension of the Television without Frontiers Directive – An impact assessment Final report for Ofcom, September 2005, retrieved from http://www.ofcom.org.uk/research/tv/twf/twfreport/twf.pdf (on 18.07.2007).

380 For the sake of comparison, in the original Commission proposal, the article (then 3d) was formulated as follows: "*Member States shall take appropriate measures to ensure that audiovisual media services under their jurisdiction are not made available in such a way that might seriously impair the physical, mental or moral development of minors*".

381 European Commission, Consultation paper: Child safety and mobile phone services, 25.07.2006, retrieved from http://ec.europa.eu/information_society/activities/sip/public_consultation/index_en.htm (on 25.07.2006), 25.

382 Recital 45 AVMSD.

383 For instance, reference is made to the 2006 Recommendation on the protection of minors and human dignity and the right of reply (*supra*, Part 1, chapter 1).

384 Ukrow, Jörg, "Chapter IIb Provisions applicable to on-demand audiovisual services", in: Castendyk, Oliver, Dommering, Egbert and Scheuer, Alexander (eds.), *European media law*, Alphen a/d Rijn, Kluwer Law International, 2008, 920.

Protection of minors linear services – With respect to linear audiovisual media services, article 22 TVWFD (*supra*) has been copied into the AVMSD. Hence, the same regulatory approach remains valid. The AVMSD also contains a number of provisions with respect to children and 'audiovisual commercial communication', for instance, with respect to advertising of alcohol or advertising which might harm the development of minors.[385]

Derogation possibilities – As regards the derogation possibilities linked to the country of origin-principle and the freedom of audiovisual media services (both with respect to linear[386] as well as non-linear services),[387] a Member States can restrict transmissions from other Member States for the sake of the protection of minors.[388] However, a number of conditions, which are different for linear and non-linear services, need to be fulfilled in order to be able to derogate from the country of origin-principle. Broadcasting derogations are only possible if a broadcast coming from another Member State "*manifestly, seriously and gravely infringes article 22 (1) or (2) and/or article 3(b)*" (article 2a para. 2). In addition to this requirement, a number of procedural conditions are stipulated in article 2a para. 2. These include: two prior infringements by the broadcaster in the past 12 months, written notification of the infringements and the proposed measures by the Member State to the broadcaster and the Commission, unsatisfactory consultations with the transmitting Member State and the Commission, and a persistence of the infringement. The conditions for derogation with respect to

---

385 These provisions are applicable to linear and non-linear services. They will not be examined in further detail since advertising falls outside the scope of this analysis.

386 Article 2a para. 2 AVMSD: "*In respect of television broadcasting, Member States may provisionally derogate from paragraph 1 if the following conditions are fulfilled: (a) a television broadcast coming from another Member State manifestly, seriously and gravely infringes Article 22(1) or (2) [...]*".

387 Article 2a para. 4 AVMSD: "*In respect of on-demand audiovisual media services, Member States may take measures to derogate from paragraph 1 in respect of a given service if the following conditions are fulfilled: (a) the measures are: (i) necessary for one of the following reasons: – public policy, in particular the prevention, investigation, detection and prosecution of criminal offences, including the protection of minors [...]*".

388 For a detailed overview, cf. Füg, Oliver C., "Save the children: the protection of minors in the Information Society and the Audiovisual Media Services Directive", *Journal of Consumer Policy* 2008, Issue 31, No. 1, 59–60. See also: Dommering, Egbert, "Article 2a AVMSD", 851–856, in: Castendyk, Oliver, Dommering, Egbert J. and Scheuer, Alexander (eds), *European media law*, Alphen a/d Rijn, Kluwer Law International, 2008, 1379 p.; Herold, Anna, "Country of origin principle in the EU market for audiovisual media services: consumer's friend or foe?", *Journal of Consumer Policy* 2008, Vol. 31, No. 1, 5–24.

non-linear services are different from – and less onerous than[389] – those for linear services. In this instance, Member States can derogate from the country of origin-principle if a non-linear service presents a serious and/or grave risk of prejudice to objectives of public policy – protection of minors included – the protection of public health, public security, or the protection of consumers (article 2a para. 4). The measures proposed by the derogating Member State need to be proportionate to the objectives mentioned. Unless there is real urgency,[390] a consultation between Member States first needs to be carried out. If this consultation does not result in a satisfactory solution, the first Member State can take measures if it has notified the Commission and the transmitting Member State. In any case, the Commission will examine the compatibility of the measures with Community law and will ask the Member State to cease the measures if the Commission finds that there is a problem of compliance. It is worth noting that the derogation conditions for non-linear services are exactly the same as those provided for 'information society services' in the e-Commerce Directive.[391]

Circumvention mechanism – Furthermore, Member States which have opted to adopt stricter rules than those included in the Directive (which is allowed under article 3 para. 1),[392] and who have come to the conclusion that "*a broadcaster under the jurisdiction of another Member State provides a television broadcast which is wholly or mostly directed towards its territory*", can take certain steps against those broadcasters. This 'anti-circumvention mechanism' – aimed at situations where the broadcaster circumvents the stricter rules imposed by the first Member State by broadcasting from another Member State, and, hence, is subject to the rules of that more lenient Member State – is only valid for linear services, and also requires a number of conditions to be fulfilled (article 3 paras 2–5).[393] First, article 3 para. 2 requires a

[389] Herold, Anna, "Country of origin principle in the EU market for audiovisual media services: consumer's friend or foe?", *Journal of Consumer Policy* 2008, Vol. 31, No. 1, 12.

[390] Article 2a para. 5 AVMSD.

[391] Article 3 para. 4–6 e-Commerce Directive (*infra*).

[392] Herold argues that "*[t]his faculty to go further in the requirements imposed on media service providers is a gesture towards the Member States, insofar as it leaves them a margin of regulatory control over the audiovisual media services under their jurisdiction. It is a laudable form of flexibility in an EU law instrument, but it does leave the door open to 'forum shopping' by media service providers who may be tempted to establish themselves in those Member States where the audiovisual standards are lower*": Herold, Anna, "Country of origin principle in the EU market for audiovisual media services: consumer's friend or foe?", *Journal of Consumer Policy* 2008, Vol. 31, No. 1, 7.

[393] For more details, cf. also: Dommering, Egbert, Scheuer, Alexander and Ader, Thorsten, "Article 3 AVMSD", 857–866, in: Castendyk, Oliver, Dommering, Egbert J. and Scheuer,

consultation procedure between the two Member States. If this consultation procedure does not have a satisfactory outcome, the first Member State may then take measures against the broadcaster who has "*established itself in the Member State having jurisdiction in order to circumvent the stricter rules, in the fields coordinated by this Directive, which would be applicable to it if it were established within the first Member State*" (article 3 para. 3).[394] The first Member State, however, may only take these measures if it has notified the Commission and the Member State in which the broadcaster is established, and if the Commission has decided that the measures are compatible with Community law (article 3 para. 4). The Commission has three months to decide whether the measures are in compliance with Community law and, if the decision is negative, the first Member State must not carry them out (article 3 para. 5). We mention this anti-circumvention mechanism here because it is conceivable the Member States opt to implement the protection of minors provision with respect to broadcasting in a stricter manner than required by the AVMSD.

IMPLEMENTATION: SELF- AND CO-REGULATION? – Article 3 para. 7, which states that Member States must encourage co- and self-regulatory regimes in the field coordinated by the Directive, has already been discussed above in Part 1, Chapter 2 (*supra*).[395, 396] To reiterate, this article clarifies that such regimes must be broadly accepted by the main stakeholders, and provide for effective enforcement. Furthermore, it was stressed that Member States

---

Alexander (eds), *European media law*, Alphen a/d Rijn, Kluwer Law International, 2008, 1379 p.; HEROLD, Anna, "Country of origin principle in the EU market for audiovisual media services: consumer's friend or foe?", *Journal of Consumer Policy* 2008, Vol. 31, No. 1, 5–24.

394 Recital 33 AVMSD refers to indicators such as the origin of the television advertising and/or subscription revenues, the main language of the service, or the existence of programmes or commercial communications targeted specifically at the public in the Member State where they are received to assess to which Member State a broadcast is directed.

395 Article 3 para. 7 AVMSD. In one of the studies carried out in the preparatory phase of the revision procedure, it was stressed that especially non-linear services can be regulated with the help of alternative regulatory instruments: "*The element of choice that is at the heart of these services make them more suitable to self- or co-regulation and user-based solutions like filters and trustmark accreditation*": RAND EUROPE (Edwin HORLINGS, Chris MARSDEN, Constantijn VAN ORANJE and Maarten BOTTERMAN), Contribution to impact assessment of the revision of the Television without Frontiers Directive, Study commissioned by the European Commission, 11.11.2005, retrieved from http://ec.europa.eu/dgs/information_society/evaluation/data/pdf/studies/s2004_01/tvwf_rand.pdf (on 10.07.2006), 32.

396 Also cf. PROSSER, Tony, "Self-regulation, Co-regulation and the Audio-Visual Media Services Directive", *Journal of Consumer Policy* 2008, Vol. 31, No. 1, 99–113.

should not feel obliged to set up such mechanisms. This last specification can be understood more clearly in the context of article 288 TFEU [ex 249 EC Treaty], which leaves Member States the choice of form and methods to implement directives. This article will be discussed *infra*.

Analysis protection of minors in the AVMS Directive – Notwithstanding conflicts between the different stakeholders regarding certain elements of the AVMSD, the agreement on the importance and necessity of protecting minors against harmful content was patently obvious throughout the legislative procedure. In our view, the inclusion of the protection of minors in the basic tier of obligations is a welcome signal in a time when anxiety about harmful content is still growing. However, one can wonder if the protection provided by article 3h AVMSD will be sufficient with regard to non-linear services. Although the justification for 'lighter' regulation, i.e., more choice and control, with respect to non-linear services might be well-founded vis-à-vis adults, this is less than certain with respect to children and young people. In an environment where parental supervision is increasingly complicated (for instance, with respect to content received on mobile phones), would it not have been wiser to opt for a greater harmonisation of the rules in this field?

The strength and effectiveness of the protection will ultimately depend on the implementation of the obligations related to the protection of minors. Article 3h AVMSD, however, is formulated in a rather vague way that lacks clarity regarding which measures will be considered 'appropriate' and, furthermore, who will be responsible for the implementation of these measures.[397] The only clue as to which regulatory method is preferred by the Commission, i.e., article 3 para. 7, is formulated and interpreted (cf. *supra*) in a rather noncommittal way. Hence, Member States have a wide range of regulatory possibilities at their disposal. However, if the Directive aims to achieve harmonised and successful results, the wording of this article might not be sufficiently clear. As it now stands, article 3 para. 7 is, in our view, more of a symbolic nature rather than a firm commitment. Furthermore, Member States, spurred on by industry, interest groups and parents, have already begun taking (self- as well as co-regulatory) initiatives to ensure the protection of minors against harmful new media content. In this respect, the AVMSD confirms rather than revolutionises current trends.

---

[397] Füg, Oliver C., "Save the children: the protection of minors in the Information Society and the Audiovisual Media Services Directive", *Journal of Consumer Policy* 2008, Issue 31, No. 1, 60.

AVMSD vs. Recommendation – A final remark concerns the scope of application of the 2006 Recommendation on the protection of minors[398] and its link with the AVMSD. Recital 19 of the 2006 Recommendation states that it covers "*audiovisual and online information services, made available to the public via fixed or mobile electronic networks*". Article 22 TVWFD is referred to as already having "*specifically addressed the question of the protection of minors and human dignity in television broadcasting services*".[399] Further along in the text, a number of measures are encouraged "*in addition to and consistent with existing legal and other measures regarding broadcasting services*".[400] In any case, in today's media landscape, where content circulates on different platforms, it seems imperative that both policy instruments, the AVMSD and the 2006 Recommendation, co-exist in a co-ordinated manner. It could be argued that the Commission's approach towards both instruments sometimes appears ambivalent, for instance, with respect to the regulatory methods that are emphasised. Both instruments have – at least partly – the same objective: protecting minors. Hence, the fact that the respective review processes have not been dealt with in a more harmonised manner, is regrettable.

D. *Council of Europe Convention on Transfrontier Television*

Council of Europe Convention on Transfrontier Television – The Council of Europe also has a history of regulating audiovisual content. The European Convention on Transfrontier Television (ECTT), adopted in the same year as the EU TVWFD, is the most important instrument in

[398] European Parliament and Council Recommendation 2006/952/EC of 20 December 2006 on the protection of minors and human dignity and on the right of reply in relation to the competitiveness of the European audiovisual and on-line information services industry, *OJ* 27.12.2007, *L* 378, 72; *supra*, Part 1, chapter 1.

[399] Recital 6 European Parliament and Council Recommendation 2006/952/EC of 20 December 2006 on the protection of minors and human dignity and on the right of reply in relation to the competitiveness of the European audiovisual and on-line information services industry, *OJ* 27.12.2007, *L* 378, 72.

[400] I.2. European Parliament and Council Recommendation 2006/952/EC of 20 December 2006 on the protection of minors and human dignity and on the right of reply in relation to the competitiveness of the European audiovisual and on-line information services industry, *OJ* 27.12.2007, *L* 378, 72.

this field.[401, 402] Both instruments' aim was similar, since the ECTT was also created to guarantee the unhindered transfrontier circulation of television programme services. The ECTT lays down a number of minimum rules as well, again mostly on topics similar to those incorporated in the TVWFD, such as the protection of certain individual rights, the responsibility of broadcasters in regard to programming matters, the European content of programming, advertising, teleshopping and sponsorship. The main difference between the ECTT and the TVWFD is their respective geographical scopes. The ECTT is ratified by thirty-one countries, a number of them non-EU members. Hence, the two instruments together "*deal with almost all cross-border broadcasts within, into or from wider Europe, thus addressing EU Member States, parties to the ECTT and/or third countries*".[403] Following the revision of the TVWFD, the Council of Europe is currently taking the initiative to revise the ECTT.[404] In this context, the Parliamentary Assembly drafted a Recommendation on The regulation of audio-visual media services

[401] Council of Europe, European Convention on Transfrontier Television, ETS No. 132, 05.05.1989, Strasbourg, retrieved from http://conventions.coe.int/Treaty/EN/Treaties/Html/132.htm (on 16.07.2007).

[402] On the interplay between both instruments, cf. Goerens, Pierre, "Interplay between relevant European legal instruments – ECTT and TVwF Directive: competition or complementarity?", 1–11, in: Nikoltchev, Susanne (ed.), *Audiovisual Media Services without Frontiers: Implementing the rules*, IRIS Special, Strasbourg, European Audiovisual Observatory, 2006, 76 p.

[403] Nikoltchev, Susanne (ed.), *Audiovisual Media Services without Frontiers: Implementing the rules*, IRIS Special, Strasbourg, European Audiovisual Observatory, 2006, i.

[404] Council of Europe (Drafting group on the revision of the European Convention on Transfrontier Television), Report, 29–30.03.2007, T-TT-GDR(2007)002, retrieved from http://www.coe.int/t/dghl/standardsetting/media/T-TT/T-TT-GDR(2007)002_en.asp#TopOfPage (on 17.07.2007). Cf. also: Council of Europe (Standing Committee on Transfrontier Television), Discussion document prepared by the Delegate of Poland on questions concerning the scope of the Convention, jurisdiction, freedom of conception and retransmission, the duties of the Parties of the Convention, advertising directed at a single Party and the abuse of rights granted by the Convention, 38th meeting, 31.03–01.04.2005, retrieved from http://www.coe.int/t/e/human_rights/media/2_transfrontier_television/texts_and_documents/2T-TT(2005)003_en.asp#TopOfPage (on 17.07.2007, no longer available); Council of Europe (Standing Committee on Transfrontier Television), Provisional agreement on the draft amendments to the ECTT, 43rd meeting, 12–14.11.2008, retrieved from http://www.coe.int/t/dghl/standardsetting/media/T-TT/T-TT(2008)003Prov_en.pdf (on 24.12.2008). Cf. also Commission of the European Communities, Sixth report from the Commission to the European Parliament, the Council, the European Economic and Social Committee and the Committee of the Regions on the application of Directive 89/552/EEC "Television without Frontiers", COM (2007) 452 final, 24.10.2007, retrieved from http://eur-lex.europa.eu/LexUriServ/site/en/com/2007/com2007_0452en01.pdf (on 14.01.2008): in this evaluation report the

in January 2009,[405] and the Standing Committee on Transfrontier Television adopted a provisional agreement on draft amendments to the ECTT in February 2009.[406] It seems that the revision of the ECTT will adopt a very similar approach to that of the AVMSD (for instance, by extending the scope of application to audiovisual media services, including on-demand services, and by encouraging self- and co-regulation).

ECTT AND PROTECTION OF MINORS FROM HARMFUL CONTENT – With respect to the protection of minors, article 7 para. 2 (dealing with the 'responsibilities of the broadcaster') stipulates that "*[a]ll items of programme services which are likely to impair the physical, mental or moral development of children and adolescents shall not be scheduled when, because of the time of transmission and reception, they are likely to watch them*". This article is comparable to article 22 para. 2 TVWFD/AVMSD (i.e., a relative ban on potentially harmful content). The current version of the ECTT thus contains no absolute ban on the dissemination of content that could seriously harm children. Article 6 para. 3 of the (provisional) revised version, however, contains (almost)[407] the same requirements as the AVMSD (an absolute ban for seriously impairing television programmes, a relative ban for television programmes which are likely to impair and a relative ban for seriously impairing on-demand services).[408]

EU Commission stressed that it wished "*to maintain the consistency that both institutions have fostered over many years between both instruments*".

405 Council of Europe (Parliamentary Assembly), Recommendation 1855 (2009) The regulation of audio-visual media services, 27.01.2009, retrieved from http://assembly.coe.int/Main.asp?link=/Documents/AdoptedText/ta09/EREC1855.htm#1 (on 28.05.2009).

406 Council of Europe (Standing Committee on Transfrontier Television), Provisional agreement on the draft amendments to the ECTT, 25–27.02.2009, retrieved from http://www.coe.int/t/dghl/standardsetting/media/T-TT/T-TT(2008)003Rev_en%20Agreements%20on%20amendts%20ECTT%20(2).asp#TopOfPage (on 28.05.2009); Council of Europe (Drafting group on the revision of the European Convention on Transfrontier Television), Draft explanatory report to the revised European Convention on Transfrontier Television updated following the consultation on 25–27 February 2009, 27.02.2009, retrieved from http://www.coe.int/t/dghl/standardsetting/media/T-TT/T-TT-GDR_2008_002Rev5_en%20Preliminary%20Draft%20Expl%20Rep%20ECTT.pdf (on 28.05.2009).

407 With respect to television programmes which are likely to impair the development of minors the article does not require an acoustic warning or the presence of a visual symbol.

408 Article 6 para. 3 Council of Europe (Standing Committee on Transfrontier Television), Provisional agreement on the draft amendments to the ECTT, 25–27.02.2009, retrieved from http://www.coe.int/t/dghl/standardsetting/media/T-TT/T-TT(2008)003Rev_en%20Agreements%20on%20amendts%20ECTT%20(2).asp#TopOfPage (on 28.05.2009).

The Standing Committee on Transfrontier Television has also issued several statements and recommendations on the protection of minors, for instance with respect to the protection of minors from pornographic programmes.[409] In this latter recommendation, the Committee re-emphasised the importance of the protection of minors against harmful programmes and expressed its concern about the increasing number of infringements of article 7 ECTT, especially "*with respect to free-to-air programme services containing pornographic content, which can be easily accessible by minors and seriously impair their development*".[410]

1.4.3. *Regulation of information society services: e-Commerce Directive*

E-COMMERCE DIRECTIVE – The e-Commerce Directive,[411] which dates from 2000, regulates a number of aspects of 'information society services'. Such services are defined as "*any service normally provided for remuneration, at a distance, by electronic means and at the individual request of a recipient of services*".[412] Certain content with which children are confronted on the Internet might fall under this definition. By adopting the e-Commerce Directive, the European legislator wished to provide a legal framework to ensure legal certainty, consumer confidence and the free movement of information society services.[413] It was emphasised that the Directive must "*ensure a high level of protection of objectives of general interest, in particular the protection of*

---

[409] COUNCIL OF EUROPE, Statement (2002)1 on human dignity and the fundamental rights of others, adopted by the Standing Committee on Transfrontier Television, retrieved from http://www.coe.int/t/dghl/standardsetting/media/T-TT/T-TT(2006)012rev_en.asp#TopOfPage (on 24.04.2007); COUNCIL OF EUROPE (STANDING COMMITTEE ON TRANSFRONTIER TELEVISION), Recommendation (04) 1 on the protection of minors from pornographic programmes, 11–12.10.2004, retrieved from http://www.coe.int/t/dghl/standardsetting/media/T-TT/T-TT(2004)011_en.asp#TopOfPage (on 24.04.2007).

[410] COUNCIL OF EUROPE (STANDING COMMITTEE ON TRANSFRONTIER TELEVISION), Recommendation (04) 1 on the protection of minors from pornographic programmes, 11–12.10.2004, retrieved from http://www.coe.int/t/dghl/standardsetting/media/T-TT/T-TT(2004)011_en.asp#TopOfPage (on 24.04.2007).

[411] EUROPEAN PARLIAMENT AND COUNCIL Directive 2000/31/EC of 8 June 2000 on certain legal aspects of information society services, in particular electronic commerce, in the Internal Market (Directive on electronic commerce), *OJ L* 178, 17.07.2000, 1[hereinafter: e-Commerce Directive].

[412] Article 2 e-Commerce Directive refers to Directive 98/34/EC of 22 June 1998 laying down a procedure for the provision of information in the field of technical standards and regulations, *OJ L* 21.07.1998, 204, 37, as amended by Directive 98/48/EC, *OJ L* 05.08.1998, 217, 18.

[413] Recitals 7–9 and article 1 e-Commerce Directive.

minors and human dignity, consumer protection and the protection of public health".[414] At the moment it remains to be seen how easy it will be to clearly distinguish between information society services and audiovisual media services (cf. *supra*) in practice.[415, 416] In this context, however, it can be noted that article 3 para. 4 AVMS Directive explains that in the case of conflict, the AVMS Directive will have priority over the e-Commerce Directive.

FREE MOVEMENT OF INFORMATION SOCIETY SERVICES AND EXCEPTION FOR THE PROTECTION OF MINORS – One of the cornerstones of the e-Commerce Directive is the country of origin-principle, which states that receiving Member States are not allowed to restrict the free movement of services originating from other Member States (article 3 para. 2 e-Commerce Directive) if these services adhere to the legislation of those latter Member States (article 3 para. 1 e-Commerce Directive). The Directive, however, also provides possibilities for deviation from this general principle. One of the grounds upon which such an exception can be justified is the protection of minors (article 3 para. 4 (a)(i) e-Commerce Directive). When the free movement of information society services is limited, however, a strict procedure, which is described in the last three paragraphs of article 3 e-Commerce Directive, must be followed. Hence, if restrictions are introduced on the basis of the protection of minors, this procedure has to be followed to the letter.

CODES OF CONDUCT – Article 16 e-Commerce Directive encourages the creation of codes of conduct for the protection of minors and human dignity.[417] In Belgium, in this context, a code of conduct was drawn up by the Internet

---

414 Recital 10 e-Commerce Directive.

415 For an earlier clarification of the difference between information society services and television broadcasting services, cf. ECJ, Mediakabel BV v. Commissariaat voor de Media, C-89/04, 02.06.2005.

416 Commissioner REDING already emphasised the complementarity between the two Directives: "*[The proposal for the AVMS Directive] complements other elements of Community legislation. This is especially true for the e-Commerce Directive which neither provides for measures relating to cultural and linguistic diversity nor for harmonised rules in some essential areas of public interest such as the protection of minors*": REDING, Viviane, Audiovisual media services directive: the right instrument to provide legal certainty for Europe's media businesses in the next decade, Speech at the Seminar "Regulating the new media landscape", Brussels, 07.06.2006, retrieved from http://europa.eu.int/rapid/pressReleasesAction.do?reference=SPEECH/06/352&format=HTML&aged=0&language=EN&guiLanguage=en (on 12.07.2006).

417 HOLOUBEK, Michael (ed.), *Regulating content – European regulatory framework for the media and related creative sectors*, Alphen a/d Rijn, Kluwer Law International, 2007, 125.

Service Providers Association.[418] This code, however, does not contain any specific provisions with respect to minors, although the ISPs do guarantee that they will make every effort to help combating unlawful and harmful acts on the Internet. Opting for codes of conduct can be seen as part of the trend to regulate new information- and communication technologies by means of self- and co-regulation.[419]

1.4.4. *Indirect content regulation: liability of intermediaries*

A. *Introduction*

Indirect form of content regulation – The liability of intermediaries is regulated at the EU level by the e-Commerce Directive.[420] At first sight, it might seem odd to discuss the regulatory regime for intermediaries in the context of content regulation. However, the regime might have an indirect impact on content regulation, and, hence, also on the regulation of the protection of minors against harmful content, because of the 'chilling effect' it arguably creates when perfectly legal content is taken down by intermediaries out of fear of being held liable. This liability regime, covering mere conduit, caching and hosting, is thus briefly analysed. However, it is necessary to keep in mind that the system focuses on (suspected) illegal content. The liability for content which is potentially harmful for children is not explicitly regulated. For certain types of content, general civil and criminal law might be applied. Despite this, though, the system does have an impact on the regulation of (legal, and possibly harmful) content.

Content provider – It is logical that the person who posts illegal digital content is directly liable. It may, however, prove difficult to get hold of the responsible content provider, as it is possible to act anonymously or under a pseudonym. Consequently, it was considered necessary to establish a system which determines under which conditions intermediaries can be held liable.

---

[418] Cf. www.ispa.be.

[419] Cf. *supra*, Part 1, chapter 2.

[420] In Belgium, the Directive was implemented by the Belgian Act of 11 March 2003 (Wet van 11 maart 2003 betreffende bepaalde juridische aspecten van de diensten van de informatiemaatschappij [*Act of 11 March 2003 with regard to certain legal aspects of services of the information society*], *BS* 17.03.2003 [in Dutch]).

B. *e-Commerce liability regime*[421]

EXEMPTIONS FROM LIABILITY – The e-Commerce Directive stipulates a horizontal and conditional exemption from (penal and civil) liability for certain service providers[422] for a wide range[423] of illegal information (copyright infringement, libel and defamation, child pornography, xenophobia, etc.) provided by a recipient of the service.[424] The exemptions from liability established in this Directive, however, are only applicable to cases where the activity of the information society service provider is limited to a mere technical functionality, i.e., the technical process of operating and giving access to a communication network over which information made available by third parties is transmitted or temporarily stored, for the sole purpose of making the transmission more efficient.[425] This activity has to be of a mere technical, automatic and passive nature, which entails that the Internet service provider has neither knowledge of nor control over the information which is transmitted or stored.[426] Three types of provision of information society services[427] can, under certain conditions, claim this exemption: mere conduit, caching and hosting.

MERE CONDUIT – Article 12 of the e-Commerce Directive stipulates that when an information society service is provided, and consists of the transmission in a communication network of information provided by a recipient of the service, or of the provision of access to a communication network, the

421 Parts of this description of the e-Commerce liability regime were inspired on: LIEVENS, Eva, WERKERS, Evi, LEFEVER, Katrien and VOLANIS, Nick, Legal report: applying the current regulatory framework to Virtual Individual Networks (WP2 – Deliverable 2.1), Research report IBBT ISBO VIN project, March 2007, 72 p., not published.

422 Defined as "*any natural or legal person providing an information society service*" in article 2 b) e-Commerce Directive.

423 BARCELO, Rosa-Juliá and KOELMAN, Kamiel, "Intermediary liability in the E-commerce Directive: so far so good, but it's not enough", *Computer Law & Security Report* 2000, No. 4, 231–239; DE PRETER, Christoph, "Wie heeft nog boodschap aan de boodschap? De aansprakelijkheid van tussenpersonen onder de wet elektronische handel" ["*Liability of intermediaries under the E-commerce Act*"], *Auteurs & Media* 2003, 258 [in Dutch].

424 Defined as "*any natural or legal person who, for professional ends or otherwise, uses an information society service, in particular for the purposes of seeking information or making it accessible*" in article 2 d) e-Commerce Directive.

425 Recital 42 e-Commerce Directive.

426 Recital 42 e-Commerce Directive.

427 'Information society services' are defined as "*any service normally provided for remuneration, at a distance, by means of electronic equipment for the processing (including digital compression) and storage of data, and at the individual request of a recipient of a service*": cf. article 2 e-Commerce Directive.

service provider is not liable for the information transmitted, on condition that the provider:

> *(a) does not initiate the transmission;*
> *(b) does not select the receiver of the transmission; and*
> *(c) does not select or modify the information contained in the transmission.*[428]

The acts of transmission and of provision of access as referred to above include the automatic, intermediate and transient storage of the information transmitted insofar as this takes place for the sole purpose of carrying out the transmission in the communication network, and provided that the information is not stored for any period longer than is reasonably necessary for the transmission.[429] Furthermore, the access or network provider may not in any way be involved with the information it transmits, nor modify that information. However, this does not cover manipulations of a technical nature which take place in the course of the transmission, as they do not alter the integrity of the information.[430] Of course, a service provider who deliberately collaborates with one of the recipients of its service in order to undertake illegal acts cannot benefit from the liability exemptions established for these activities.[431]

Caching – Article 13 of the e-Commerce Directive specifies that a service provider is not liable for the automatic, intermediate and temporary storage of information it transmits, performed for the sole purpose of making more efficient the information's onward transmission to other recipients of the service (upon their request), on condition that:

> *(a) the provider does not modify the information;*
> *(b) the provider complies with conditions on access to the information (i.e. secured information or information against remuneration);*
> *(c) the provider complies with rules regarding the updating of the information, specified in a manner widely recognised and used by industry (instructions concerning the storing of information on a cache server; updating or refreshing data on the server);*
> *(d) the provider does not interfere with the lawful use of technology, widely recognised and used by industry, to obtain data on the use of the information (the program of statistics keeping track of the number of visitors);*
> *(e) the provider acts expeditiously to remove or to disable access to the information it has stored upon obtaining actual knowledge of the fact that the*

428 Article 12 para. 1 e-Commerce Directive.
429 Article 12 para. 2 e-Commerce Directive.
430 Recital 43 e-Commerce Directive.
431 Recital 44 e-Commerce Directive.

> *information at the initial source of the transmission has been removed from the network, or access to it has been disabled, or that a court or an administrative authority has ordered such removal or disablement.*[432]

Hence, the service provider's activity must be limited to a technical, passive and automatic intervention. However, it also has to act instantaneously when it receives actual knowledge of the fact that the information at the initial source of the transmission has removed from the network, or access to it has been disabled, or that a court or an administrative authority has ordered such removal or disablement. Otherwise put, a positive obligation rests on the service provider.[433] Furthermore, again, the service provider cannot benefit from the exemption for caching when it has interfered with the transmitted information or when it deliberately collaborates with one of its service recipients to undertake illegal acts.[434]

HOSTING – Article 14 of the e-Commerce Directive states that where an information society service is provided, and consists of the storage of information provided by a recipient of the service, the service provider is not liable for the information stored at the request of a recipient of the service, on condition that:

> *(a) the provider does not have actual knowledge of illegal activity or information and, as regards claims for damages, is not aware of facts or circumstances from which the illegal activity or information is apparent; or*
> *(b) the provider, upon obtaining such knowledge or awareness, acts expeditiously to remove or to disable access to the information and if he acts according to the following procedure:*
> - *when the provider obtains actual knowledge of the illegal activity or information, he immediately reports it to the public prosecutor who takes action according to article 39bis of the Code of Criminal Procedure*
> - *as long as the public prosecutor has not made any decision with regard to the copying, disabling access and removing of stored data, the provider can only take measures as to prevent access to the information.*[435]

---

432 Article 13 para. 1 e-Commerce Directive.

433 IDE, Nicolas and STROWEL, Alain, "Responsabilité des intermédiaires: actualités législatives et jurisprudentielles" ["*Liability of intermediaries: legislative and jurisprudential news*"], 10.10.2000, retrieved from http://www.droit-technologie.org/2_1.asp?dossier_id=32&motcle=ide+strowel&mode=motamot (on 20.03.2007), 24 [in French]; IDE, Nicolas, STROWEL, Alain and VERHOESTRAETE, Florence, "La Directive du 8 juin 2000 sur le commerce électronique: un cadre juridique pour l'internet" ["*The directive of 8 June 2000 on electronic commerce: a legal framework for the Internet*"], *J.T.* 2001, 143 [in French].

434 Recitals 43 and 44 e-Commerce Directive.

435 Article 14 para. 1 e-Commerce Directive.

The exemption also depends on the level of knowledge and the legal actions with which the service provider is being confronted. When confronted with a criminal action, evidence has to be given that the Internet service provider has actual knowledge of the illegal information, for example, that he is aware that users are exchanging data to download works illegally on a discussion forum, or that links to racist websites, etc. are being posted.[436] When challenged with a civil action (claim for compensation), the mere knowledge of facts or circumstances which indicate the illegal character of the relevant information ('constructive knowledge') could thus pre-empt a claim to the exemption.

Several legal scholars distinguish between obvious illegal information, of which a provider is supposed to be aware (such as child pornography), and information which is not so clearly illegal (libel and defamation, for instance).[437] It has been argued that hosting providers have been unfairly burdened with the difficult task of judging themselves when a complaint is credible, or when a content provider is clearly surpassing certain limits, before undertaking action and expeditiously removing the information or disabling access to it.[438] This gives rise to the above mentioned 'chilling effect': in order not to be found liable, providers might remove content which is perfectly legal.[439] This possibility could seriously impact on the right to freedom of expression.

---

[436] Lodder, Arno, "Directive 2000/31/EC on certain legal aspects of information society services, in particular electronic commerce, in the Internal Market", in: Lodder, Arno and Kaspersen, Henrick (eds), *eDirectives: guide to European Union law on e-Commerce,* Den Haag, Kluwer Law International, 2002, 88.

[437] De Preter, Christoph, "Wie heeft nog boodschap aan de boodschap? De aansprakelijkheid van tussenpersonen onder de wet elektronische handel" ["*Liability of intermediaries under the E-commerce Act*"], *Auteurs & Media* 2003, 261–262 [in Dutch]; Barcelo, Rosa-Juliá, "On-line intermediary liability issues: comparing EU and US legal frameworks", *E.I.P.R.* 2000, 111; Ide, Nicolas, Strowel, Alain and Verhoestraete, Florence, "La Directive du 8 juin 2000 sur le commerce électronique: un cadre juridique pour l'internet" ["*The directive of 8 June 2000 on electronic commerce: a legal framework for the Internet*"], *J.T.* 2001, 133–145 [in French].

[438] Barcelo, Rosa-Juliá and Koelman, Kamiel, "Intermediary liability in the E-commerce Directive: so far so good, but it's not enough", *Computer Law & Security Report* 2000, No. 4, 231–239; Ide, Nicolas and Strowel, Alain, "Responsabilité des intermédiaires: actualités législatives et jurisprudentielles" ["*Liability of intermediaries: legislative and jurisprudential news*"], 10.10.2000, retrieved from http://www.droit-technologie.org/2_1.asp?dossier_id=32&motcle=ide+strowel&mode=motamot (on 20.03.2007), 43 [in French]; Montéro, Etienne, "La responsabilité des prestataires intermédiaires sur les réseaux" ["*The liability of intermediaries in networks*"], in: Montéro, Etienne (ed.), *Le commerce électronique européen sur les rails?* [*European e-commerce on the rails?*], Cahiers du CRID, Brussel, Bruylant, 2001, 289–290 [in French].

[439] Council of Europe (Council of Ministers), Declaration on freedom of communications on the Internet, 28.05.2003, retrieved from https://wcd.coe.int/rsi/common/

No general obligation to monitor – Notwithstanding article 14, article 15 e-Commerce Directive confirms that Internet service providers do not have a general obligation to monitor.[440] After all, it is considered an impossible task for Internet service providers to monitor all information which is being stored or transmitted to search for illegal activities. Yet, article 15 does not mean that an Internet service provider cannot voluntarily perform spontaneous acts of (editorial) control, or use filters, etc., for example, because it wants to protects its image or promote its services as being, for instance, 'child-friendly'. In these circumstances, however, private censorship is lurking behind the corner,[441] and the Internet service provider runs the risk of losing its exemption when an active instead of a passive role is assumed. Article 15 also does not affect the ability of courts or administrative authorities to issue injunctions such as orders requiring the termination or prevention of any infringement, including the removal of illegal information or the disabling of access to such content, or orders in accordance with national legislation, for instance, in specific cases.[442] Member States can also require service providers, who host information provided by recipients, to exercise duties of care which can reasonably be expected from them and which are stipulated in national law, in order to uncover and prevent certain types of illegal activities.[443] It is also important to note that the second paragraph

renderers/rend_standard.jsp?DocId=37031&SecMode=1&SiteName=cm&Lang=en (on 24.04.2007): "*Member States should, however, exercise caution imposing liability on service providers for not reacting to such a notice. Questions about whether certain material is illegal are often complicated and best dealt with by the courts. If service providers act too quickly to remove content after a complaint is received, this might be dangerous from the point of view of freedom of expression and information. Perfectly legitimate content might thus be suppressed out of fear of legal liability*".

440 Article 15 e-Commerce Directive.

441 Barcelo, Rosa-Juliá, "On-line intermediary liability issues: comparing EU and US legal frameworks", *E..I.P.R.* 2000, 110–111; Montéro, Etienne, "La responsabilité des prestataires intermédiaires sur les réseaux" ["*The liability of intermediaries in networks*"], in: Montéro, Etienne (ed.), *Le commerce électronique européen sur les rails?* [*European e-commerce on the rails?*], Cahiers du CRID, Brussel, Bruylant, 2001, 279 [in French].

442 Article 12 para. 3, articles 13 para. 2 and 14 para. 3 e-Commerce Directive, recitals 45 and 47.

443 Recital 48; Demoulin, Marie and Jacquemin, Hervé, "Bespreking van de wetten betreffende de diensten van de informatiemaatschappij" ["*Review of the acts regarding the information society services*"], retrieved from http://www.internet-observatory.be/internet_observatory/pdf/legislation/cmt/law_be_2003-03-11_cmt_nl.pdf (on 20.03.2007) [in Dutch]; De Preter, Christoph, "Wie heeft nog boodschap aan de boodschap? De aansprakelijkheid van tussenpersonen onder de wet elektronische handel" ["*Liability of intermediaries under the E-commerce Act*"], *Auteurs & Media* 2003, 258 [in Dutch]; Ide, Nicolas, Strowel, Alain and Verhoestraete, Florence, "La Directive du 8 juin 2000 sur le commerce électronique: un cadre juridique pour l'internet" ["*The directive of*

of article 15 specifies that, notwithstanding the absence of a general obligation to monitor, Member States "*may establish obligations for information society service providers promptly to inform the competent public authorities of alleged illegal activities undertaken or information provided by recipients of their service, or obligations to communicate to the competent authorities, at their request, information enabling the identification of recipients of their service with whom they have storage agreements*".[444]

C. *Issues of concern*

ISPs and chilling effect – The fact that providers not only have to respect and guard the right to freedom of expression and information, but also have the duty to expeditiously take down allegedly infringing material, is questionable because of, once again, the risk of the 'chilling effect'. It can be rightfully argued that the guarding of constitutional rights should not be left to private companies, since they do not have enough legal knowledge to judge whether an infringement has taken place, especially when the material is not evidently illegal.[445, 446] For reasons of legal certainty and European harmonisation, it would thus have been useful to put forward a number of indicators to take into account when judging the admissibility and (il)legitimate nature of a

8 June 2000 on electronic commerce: a legal framework for the Internet"], *J.T.* 2001, 141 [in French]; Verbiest, Thibault and Wéry, Etienne (eds), *Le droit de l'internet et de la société de l'information* [*Law of the Internet and the Information Society*], Brussels, Larcier, 2001, 231 [in French].

[444] Article 15 para. 2 e-Commerce Directive.

[445] Barcelo, Rosa-Juliá and Koelman, Kamiel, "Intermediary liability in the E-commerce Directive: so far so good, but it's not enough", *Computer Law & Security Report* 2000, No. 4, 231–239; Barcelo, Rosa-Juliá, "On-line intermediary liability issues: comparing EU and US legal frameworks", *E.I.P.R.* 2000, 111; Montéro, Etienne, "La responsabilité des prestataires intermédiaires sur les réseaux" ["*The liability of intermediaries in networks*"], in: Montéro, Etienne (ed.), *Le commerce électronique européen sur les rails?* [*European e-commerce on the rails?*], Cahiers du CRID, Brussel, Bruylant, 2001, 229–230 [in French].

[446] The Organization for Security and Co-operation in Europe and Reporters sans Frontières, Joint declaration on guaranteeing media freedom on the Internet, 17–18.06.2005, retrieved from https://www.osce.org/documents/rfm/2005/06/15239_en.pdf (on 09.09.2008): "*A technical service provider must not be held responsible for the mere conduit or hosting of content unless the hosting provider refuses to obey a court ruling. A decision on whether a website is legal or illegal can only be taken by a judge, not by a service provider. Such proceedings should guarantee transparency, accountability and the right to appeal*".

request for takedown. A clear 'notice-takedown-putback' procedure,[447] such as the one included in the US Digital Millennium Copyright Act (DMCA),[448] has the advantage of providing content providers whose legal content has been taken down with a means to react.[449] The ultimate decision then lies with judicial authorities who are competent to decide on the legality of the content in question.

INTERPLAY ARTICLES 14 AND 15 – Furthermore, the combination of articles 14 and 15 can lead to a situation in which a provider that takes it upon himself to exercise a very limited form of control (for instance, because it wants to offer a child-friendly service) could lose his exemption from liability.[450] Some clarification would also be welcome in this context, and especially in the context of the protection of minors. In a document such as

---

[447] US COPYRIGHT OFFICE, The Digital Millennium Copyright Act of 1998: summary, December 1998, retrieved from http://www.copyright.gov/legislation/dmca.pdf (on 26.05.2009): "*In order to protect against the possibility of erroneous or fraudulent notifications, certain safeguards are built into section 512. Subsection (g)(1) gives the subscriber the opportunity to respond to the notice and takedown by filing a counter notification. In order to qualify for the protection against liability for taking down material, the service provider must promptly notify the subscriber that it has removed or disabled access to the material. If the subscriber serves a counter notification complying with statutory requirements, including a statement under penalty of perjury that the material was removed or disabled through mistake or misidentification, then unless the copyright owner files an action seeking a court order against the subscriber, the service provider must put the material back up within 10–14 business days after receiving the counter notification*".

[448] For more details on the DCMA, cf. KOELMAN, Kamiel, "Online intermediary liability", in: HUGENHOLTZ, Bernt (ed.), *Copyright and electronic commerce: legal aspects of copyright management*, The Hague, Kluwer Law International, 2000, 7–57.

[449] LIEVENS, Eva, VALCKE, Peggy and STEVENS, David, "Vrijheid van meningsuiting", [Freedom of expression], in: DE CORTE, Rogier (ed.), *Praktijkboek Recht & Internet* [*Book of practice law & the Internet*], Brugge, Vanden Broele, 2005, 58 [in Dutch]. Cf. also: RORIVE, Isabelle and FRYDMAN, Benoît, "Regulating Internet content through intermediaries in Europe and the USA", *Droit et Nouvelles Technologies*, 19.03.2003, retrieved from http://www.droit-technologie.org/dossier-92/regulating-internet-content-through-intermediaries-in-europe-and-the-u.html (on 23.03.2007).

[450] This issue was also mentioned in the Byron report: BYRON, Tanya, Safer children in a digital world: the report of the Byron review, 27.03.2008, retrieved from http://www.dfes.gov.uk/byronreview/ (on 04.07.2008), 84–85: "*In discussion with the Byron Review team, several industry stakeholders said they were sometimes hesitant about taking proactive steps to tackle the existence of harmful and inappropriate content online, or to publicise steps that they were taking, for fears around liability*", and "*Some companies interviewed by the Byron Review expressed concern that efforts to automatically scan the content hosted on their site could be interpreted by a court as meaning that they have actual knowledge of all the content they host, meaning that they would lose their protection from liability under the E-Commerce Directive. In particular, it has been suggested that some companies might not*

the Recommendation on the protection of minors and human dignity,[451] for instance, the online information services industry is encouraged to develop filtering systems. At the moment, however, it is unclear how exactly this should be reconciled with the liability exemption regime. In any case, it has been argued that filtering at the level of the service provider is unacceptable (*infra*).[452]

Identification by intermediaries v. content providers' right to anonymity – A last issue of concern relates to the possibility provided in article 15 para. 2 e-Commerce Directive for Member States to establish obligations for intermediaries[453] to pass on identification data to the competent authorities. The question which arises is in which circumstances such obligations can imposed, and furthermore, what impact this has on the right to privacy and more specifically the right to anonymity of content providers.[454] First, we can wonder whether Member States can only impose identification obligations with respect to illegal activities or whether this would also be possible with respect to the publication of harmful content. Whereas the first obligation included in article 15 para. 2 e-Commerce Directive ("*obligations for information society providers promptly to inform the competent pub-*

(publicly) scan for harmful and inappropriate content because of fears around being sued or prosecuted for hosting material that is defamatory or breaches copyrights".

451 *Supra*, Part 1, chapter 1.

452 UN Special Rapporteur on Freedom of Opinion and Expression, the OSCE Representative on Freedom of the Media and the OAS Special Rapporteur on Freedom of Expression, Joint declaration: International mechanisms for promoting freedom of expression, 21.12.2005, retrieved from http://www.osce.org/documents/rfm/2005/12/18636_en.pdf (on 25.07.2007): "*Filtering systems which are not end-user controlled – whether imposed by a government or commercial service provider – are a form of prior-censorship and cannot be justified*".

453 From the text of article 15 para. 2 e-Commerce Directive it can be inferred that this obligation can only be imposed on hosting providers, since the wording "*enabling the identification of recipients of their service with whom they have storage agreements*" is used. It has been noted that the rationale for this restriction to hosting providers is unclear: Ekker, Anton, *Anoniem communiceren: van drukpers tot weblog* [*Communicating anonymously: from printing press to weblog*], Den Haag, Sdu Uitgevers, 2006, 184.

454 For an overview, cf. Ekker, Anton, *Anoniem communiceren: van drukpers tot weblog* [*Communicating anonymously: from printing press to weblog*], Den Haag, Sdu Uitgevers, 2006, 175–231 [in Dutch]; also Voorhoof, Dirk, "Internet and the right of anonymity", Proceedings of the PCMLP 2008 Belgrade Conference on Regulation of Freedom of Expression on the Internet, Belgrade, 08–09.09.2008, *in press*. Please note that liability issues in the sphere of user-generated content are the subject of a current F.W.O.-research project at the Interdisciplinary Centre for Law & ICT. Within this project issues such as the liability of intermediaries, identification obligations and the right of anonymity of content providers are studied in greater detail.

lic authorities of alleged illegal activities undertaken or information provided by recipients of their service") explicitly refers to 'alleged illegal activities', no such specification is provided with respect to identification obligations. Hence, in theory and based on a grammatical analysis, it would be possible to argue that Member States could impose such obligations with respect to harmful content. However, when article 15 para. 2 e-Commerce Directive is read as an exception on the first paragraph ("*Member States shall not impose a general obligation on providers, when providing the services convered by Articles 12, 13 and 14, to monitor the information which they transmit or store, nor a general obligation actively to seek facts or circumstances indicating illegal activity*"), which needs to be interpreted restrictively, it would seem more likely that the obligation to pass on identification data should be restricted to illegal activities.

Furthermore, in this respect, the clash between an individual's right to anonymity and the removal of this anonymity by the provision of identification data by intermediaries – who hold the technical key to an individual's identity – is a controversial issue, for instance in the sphere of copyright protection,[455] or with respect to data retention.[456] We briefly discussed the right to anonymity *supra* and noted there that although in certain instances individuals have the right not to disclose their identity,[457] this is not an absolute right. The right to anonymity may need to be weighed against other

455 ECJ, Promusicae v. Telefónica de España SAU, C-275/06, 29.01.2008; Werkers, Evi and Coudert, Fanny, "Promusicae versus Telefónica: auteursrecht en recht op privacy in de weegschaal gelegd" ["*Promusicae versus Telefónica: copyright and right to privacy put in the balance?*"], *Auteurs & Media* 2008, No. 4, 249–263 [in Dutch]; Coudert, Fanny and Werkers, Evi, "In the aftermath of the Promusicae case: how to strike the balance?", *International Journal of Law and Information Technology* 2008, Advanced access: retrieved from http://ijlit.oxfordjournals.org/cgi/content/full/ean015v1?maxtoshow=&HITS=10&hits=10&RESULTFORMAT=&fulltext=werkers&searchid=1&FIRSTINDEX=0&resourcetype=HWCIT (on 15.05.2009).

456 European Parliament and Council Directive 2006/24/EC of 15 March 2006 on the retention of data generated or processed in connection with the provision of publicly available electronic communications services or of public communications networks and amending Directive 2002/58/EC, *OJ* 13.04.2006, *L* 105, 54; Goemans, Caroline and Dumortier, Jos, "Enforcement Issues – Mandatory retention of traffic data in the EU: possible impact on privacy and on-line anonymity", 161–183, in: Nicoll, Chris, Prins, Corien and van Dellen, Miriam (eds), *Digital anonymity and the law: tensions and dimensions*, Den Haag, TMC Asser Press, 2003, 307 p.; Kosta, Eleni and Dumortier, Jos, "The Data Retention Directive and the principles of European data protection legislation", *Medien und Recht International* 2007, No. 3, 130–136.

457 For examples, cf. Voorhoof, Dirk, "Internet and the right of anonymity", Proceedings of the PCMLP 2008 Belgrade Conference on Regulation of Freedom of Expression on the Internet, Belgrade, 08–09.09.2008, *in press*.

fundamental rights or objectives of public interest and should, for instance, not be used as a cover for avoiding liability for criminal acts.[458] In this context, the European Court of Human Rights decided recently in the case *K.U. v. Finland* that with respect to a grave infringement of an individual's right (*in casu* a minor's right to privacy) the actual identification and prosecution of the offender was the only option to achieve an effective protection of the victim.[459] We would like to emphasise that proportionality is a very important guiding principle regarding the balancing exercise that needs to be carried out. In our opinion, even if article 15 para. 2 e-Commerce Directive would in theory allow Member States to impose identification obligations with respect to harmful content, it is highly doubtful whether this would be proportional to the content provider's right to privacy.[460]

1.5. Internal market and competition

1.5.1. *Internal market principles*

Internal market principles and content – As was already mentioned above, internal market principles can, at the EU level, play an important role with respect to content.[461] In the TVWFD, as well as the AVMSD,[462] the free movement of broadcasting or audiovisual media services was, and still is, one of the cornerstones of the regulatory framework. The same is true with respect to the e-Commerce Directive for information society services.[463]

Free movement of services – The transfrontier movement of services which fall outside of the scope of both these regimes is covered by the general

---

458 Voorhoof, Dirk, "Recente arresten van het E.H.R.M. in verband met artikel 10 E.V.R.M. (vrijheid van meningsuiting en informatie)" ["*Recent judgments of the ECHR related to article 10 ECHR (freedom of expression and information)*"], November – December 2008, *Auteurs & Media* 2009, No. 1, *in press* [in Dutch].

459 European Court of Human Rights, K.U. v. Finland, 02.12.2008, paras 46–50 (for more information on the facts of this case, cf. *infra* Part 2, Chapter 2 (2.2.1. B.2. Privacy and alternative regulatory instruments).

460 Cf. Ekker, Anton, "Noot onder KU t. Finland" ["*Note under KU v. Finland*"], *Mediaforum* 2009, No. 2, 70–71 [in Dutch].

461 For a detailed overview of the internal market principles of the 'free movement of goods' and the 'free movement of services', cf. Woods, Lorna, *Free movement of goods and services within the European Community*, Aldershot, Ashgate, 2004, 307 p.

462 *Supra.*

463 *Supra.*

rules of the internal market, and more specifically, by the freedom to provide services, laid down in article 56 *et seq.* TFEU [ex 49 *et seq.* EC Treaty].[464, 465] Restrictions on the free movement of services are only allowed "*in specific circumstances where these are justified by overriding reasons of general interest, for instance on grounds of public policy, public security or public health; and where they are proportionate*".[466] It could be argued that the protection of minors against harmful content is an 'overriding reason of general interest'. If Member States were to enact restrictions for this reason, they should be strictly proportional to this aim, and no other less restrictive measures of equivalent effect should be available.[467]

Free movement of goods – Issues cannot only arise with respect to services, but to goods as well (for instance import of DVDs). The principles regarding the free movement of goods are embedded in articles 34 to 36 TFEU [ex 28 to 30 EC Treaty]. Articles 34 and 35 TFEU [ex 28 and 29 EC Treaty] prohibit quantitative restrictions on import and all measures having equivalent effect between Member States. Article 36 TFEU [ex 30 EC Treaty] clarifies that articles 34 and 35 TFEU [ex 28 and 29 EC Treaty] do not preclude "*prohibitions or restrictions on imports, exports or goods in transit justified on grounds of public morality, public policy or public security; the protection of health and life of humans, animals or plants; the protection of national treasures possessing artistic, historic or archaeological value; or the protection of industrial and commercial property*", provided that they do not "*constitute a means of arbitrary discrimination or a disguised restriction*

---

464 Article 56 TFEU [ex 49 EC Treaty] states "*Within the framework of the provisions set out below, restrictions on freedom to provide services within the Community shall be prohibited in respect of nationals of Member States who are established in a State of the Community other than that of the person for whom the services are intended. The Council may, acting by a qualified majority on a proposal from the Commission, extend the provisions of the Chapter to nationals of a third country who provide services and who are established within the Community*".

465 Commission of the European Communities, Green Paper on the protection of minors and human dignity in audiovisual and information services, COM (1996) 483 final, 16.10.1996, 21–22.

466 European Commission, Internal market – General principles Freedom to provide services, retrieved from http://ec.europa.eu/internal_market/services/principles_en.htm (on 26.07.2007). See also: Commission of the European Communities, Green Paper on the protection of minors and human dignity in audiovisual and information services, COM (1996) 483 final, 16.10.1996, 21–22.

467 Commission of the European Communities, Green Paper on the protection of minors and human dignity in audiovisual and information services, COM (1996) 483 final, 16.10.1996, 21–22.

on trade between Member States". Again, the protection of minors against harmful content could be classified as a ground of public morality (or even a measure to protect the health of humans).

Internal market and ARIs – In the next chapter, the aspects of both the free movement of services and of goods that are relevant to the use of ARIs to protect minors against harmful content will be examined in greater detail.

1.5.2. *Competition rules*

Competition rules and ARIs – Different policy documents which can be situated in the 'Better Regulation' discourse (*supra*), such as the Better Legislation Action Plan and the Interinstitutional Agreement on Better Lawmaking, have emphasised that ARIs cannot interfere with the rules on competition. These rules are a fundamental part of the EU legislative framework and aim to guarantee fair and open competition, which in turn "*encourages companies to provide consumers products that consumers want [; i]t encourages innovation, and pushes down prices*".[468] Contrary to the internal market legislation (*supra*), which is primarily directed at the Member States, the competition rules mainly target undertakings.

Key provisions – The two key provisions are articles 101 and 102 TFEU [ex 81 and 82 EC Treaty].[469] The former article contains a prohibition on anti-competitive agreements between undertakings; the latter prohibits an undertaking from abusing a dominant position. A final article which might be of relevance to the use of ARIs is article 106 TFEU [ex 86 EC Treaty], which concerns possible problematic relationships between Member States and undertakings in the field of competition. In the next chapter, the competition rules will be analysed in greater detail: the most relevant aspects with respect to the use of ARIs will be identified and potential difficulties regarding the interference of ARIs with the competition rules will be analysed.

---

468 European Commission, Competition – Antitrust, retrieved from http://ec.europa.eu/comm/competition/antitrust/overview_en.html (on 27.11.2008).

469 The complete "*framework for competition law, applicable to undertakings, public enterprises and States*" is formed by articles 101 to 109 TFEU [ex 81 to 89 EC Treaty], supplemented by secondary legislation and soft law devices (Arnull, Anthony et al., *Wyatt and Dashwood's European Union law*, London, Sweet & Maxwell, 2006, 970). However, articles 101, 102 and 106 TFEU [ex 81, 82 and 86 EC Treaty] are the most relevant with respect to the use of ARIs. Hence, we will limit our analysis to these articles, and the relevant case-law of the ECJ, which has played an essential role in the development of the competition rules.

1.6. General EU legislative principles and requirements

Introduction – This chapter concludes with some insights into a number of general EU legislative principles[470] and requirements which are important to the subject of this study, and which will be studied in greater detail in the next chapter. Proportionality and subsidiarity are two important EU principles which are, for instance, often referred to in documents regarding Better Regulation policy (*supra*).[471] Article 288 TFEU [ex 249 EC Treaty], on the other hand, deals with requirements concerning the implementation of EU directives. Since directives sometimes impose obligations on Member States with respect to the protection of minors against harmful media content (e.g., the Audiovisual Media Services Directive, *supra*), it is essential to be aware of the conditions with which the regulatory measures – possibly self- or co-regulatory measures – taken to implement these obligations need to comply.

1.6.1. *Proportionality*

Cornerstone – The principle of proportionality is one of the cornerstones of modern, democratically governed states.[472] It represents an idea of "*fairness which has strengthened the protection of individual rights at both the national and supranational level*".[473] Moreover, not only is proportionality a general principle of EU law[474] to which both Community and national measures need to adhere,[475] it is also an important element of the article 10 para. 2 ECHR test, which is used to check the compliance of regulatory measures

---

470 For details on what constitutes a 'general principle of law', cf. Emiliou, Nicholas, *The principle of proportionality in European law: a comparative study*, London, Kluwer Law International, 1996, 115–133.

471 Cf. *supra*, footnote 66, Part 1, Chapter 2.

472 For more details on the origin, function and precise scope of the proportionality principle, cf. Emiliou, Nicholas, *The principle of proportionality in European law: a comparative study*, London, Kluwer Law International, 1996, 288 p.

473 Emiliou, Nicholas, *The principle of proportionality in European law: a comparative study*, London, Kluwer Law International, 1996, 1.

474 Craig, Paul and de Búrca, Gráinne, *EU law: Text, cases, and materials*, Oxford University Press, Oxford, 2007, 544; Kapteyn, Paul and VerLoren van Themaat, Pieter, *Introduction to the law of the European Communities – From Maastricht to Amsterdam*, London, Kluwer Law International, 1998, 147.

475 Tridimas, Takis, *The general principles of EU law*, Oxford, Oxford University Press, 2006, 137; Emiliou, Nicholas, *The principle of proportionality in European law: a comparative study*, London, Kluwer Law International, 1996, 134 *et seq.*

with the fundamental right to freedom of expression.[476] The principle has been incorporated into the Treaty on the European Union[477] and in the Protocol on the application of the principles of subsidiarity and proportionality (added by the Treaty of Amsterdam).[478]

WHAT IS PROPORTIONALITY? – Proportionality entails that any "*action undertaken must be proportionate to its objectives*",[479] or as the ECJ[480] formulates it: "*it is necessary to verify whether the means which [a provision of Community law] employs are appropriate to achieve the objective pursued and whether or not they go beyond what is necessary to achieve it*".[481] The principle of proportionality fulfils three functions in EU law: it is used to assess Community measures,[482] to review national measures which affect fundamental freedoms,[483] and, as provided by article 5 TEU, to govern "*the exercise by the*

[476] As well as other fundamental rights such as, for instance, privacy (cf. article 8 para. 2 ECHR). With respect to fundamental rights generally, cf. also article 52 Charter of Fundamental Rights of the European Union (Charter of Fundamental Rights of the European Union, *OJ* 18.12.2000, *C* 364, 1, retrieved from http://eur-lex.europa.eu/LexUriServ/site/en/oj/2000/c_364/c_36420001218en00010022.pdf (on 12.03.2007)): "*Any limitation on the exercise of the rights and freedoms recognised by this Charter must be provided for by law and respect the essence of those rights and freedoms. Subject to the principle of proportionality, limitations may be made only if they are necessary and genuinely meet objectives of general interest recognised by the Union or the need to protect the rights and freedoms of others*".

[477] Article 5 para. 4 TEU: "*Under the principle of proportionality, the content and form of Union action shall not exceed what is necessary to achieve the objectives of the Treaties*".

[478] Protocol (No. 30) on the application of the principles of subsidiarity and proportionality, 02.10.1997, *OJ* 10.11.1997, *C* 340, 105. The protocol describes the application of the principles of subsidiarity and proportionality on Community action. Cf. also EUROPEAN COUNCIL, Presidency conclusions – Annex 1: Overall approach to the application by the Council of the subsidiarity principle and article 3b of the Treaty on the European Union, 11–12.12.1992, Edinburgh, retrieved from http://www.europarl.europa.eu/summits/edinburgh/a1_en.pdf (on 14.07.2008).

[479] TRIDIMAS, Takis, *The general principles of EU law*, Oxford, Oxford University Press, 2006, 136.

[480] For more details on the development of the case-law concept, cf. USHER, John, *General principles of EC law*, London-New York, Longman, 1998, 40–44.

[481] ECJ, Roquette Frères SA v. Office national interprofessionnel des céréales (ONIC), C-47/86, 30.06.1987, para. 19.

[482] CRAIG, Paul and DE BÚRCA, Gráinne, *EU law: Text, cases, and materials*, Oxford University Press, Oxford, 2007, 547–549.

[483] USHER, John, *General principles of EC law*, London-New York, Longman, 1998, 47–51; CRAIG, Paul and DE BÚRCA, Gráinne, *EU law: Text, cases, and materials*, Oxford University Press, Oxford, 2007, 549–551; TRIDIMAS, Takis, *The general principles of EU law*, Oxford, Oxford University Press, 2006, 193–241; EMILIOU, Nicholas, *The principle of proportionality in European law: a comparative study*, London, Kluwer Law International, 1996, 166–169.

Community of its legislative competence".[484] In this context, it can be noted that proportionality is also one of the principles which play an important role in the Better Regulation discourse, since one of the motivations for promoting the use of alternative regulatory instruments is the fact that, based on proportionality (and subsidiarity, *infra*), the EU should make sure that its actions do not go beyond what is necessary.[485]

Proportionality test – To check the compliance of a certain measure with the principle of proportionality, a multi-step test is undertaken.[486] Some scholars argue that two steps need to be taken, others suggest that the test implies three steps. The two-step test checks for suitability as well as necessity,[487] while the three-step test verifies if the measure in question is (1) objectively suitable (or appropriate) to achieve the desired end, (2) necessary to achieve this end, and (3) proportionate *stricto sensu*, i.e., it does not impose a burden that is excessive in relation to the objective desired.[488] Tridimas pointed out that

> *the tripartite test has received some judicial support, but in practice the Court does not distinguish in its analysis between the second and the third test. Also, it will be shown, in some cases the Court finds that a measure is compatible with proportionality without searching for less restrictive alternatives or even where such alternatives seem to exist. The essential characteristic of the principle is that the Court performs a balancing exercise between the objectives pursued by the measure in issue and its adverse effects on individual freedom.*[489]

---

[484] Tridimas, Takis, *The general principles of EU law*, Oxford, Oxford University Press, 2006, 137.

[485] Recital 16 European Parliament, Council, and Commission, Interinstitutional agreement on better law-making, 2003/C 321/01, *OJ* 31.12.2003, *C* 321, 1.

[486] For a detailed overview, cf. Emiliou, Nicholas, *The principle of proportionality in European law: a comparative study*, London, Kluwer Law International, 1996, 171–194.

[487] Tridimas, Takis, *The general principles of EU law*, Oxford, Oxford University Press, 2006, 139.

[488] For example: ECJ, The Queen v. Minister of Agriculture, Fisheries and Food and Secretary of State for Health, ex parte: Fedesa and others, C-331/88, 13.11.1990, summary para. 2: "*In accordance with the principle of proportionality, which is one of the general principles of Community law, the lawfulness of the prohibition of an economic activity is subject to the condition that the prohibitory measures are appropriate and necessary in order to achieve the objectives legitimately pursued by the legislation in question, it being understood that when there is a choice between several appropriate measures recourse must be had to the least onerous, and the disadvantages caused must not be disproportionate to the aims pursued*".

[489] Tridimas, Takis, *The general principles of EU law*, Oxford, Oxford University Press, 2006, 139. Along the same lines, Craig and de Búrca suggest that "*the reality is that the ECJ will consider stage three when an applicant addresses an argument concerning this stage of the inquiry. It may not do so where no such specific argument has been raised, more specifically*

It is important to note that the strictness of the test applied by the Court depends on the interests that are at stake. When Community measures are reviewed, and, hence, a private interest versus a public interest is at the centre of the review, the Court will carry out a 'manifestly inappropriate' test.[490] This means that the Court will only disapprove of a measure if it is manifestly inappropriate to attain its goal.[491] If, on the other hand, national measures are under review and, consequently, the focus is on a Community interest versus a national interest, the review will most often be based on the 'necessity' and 'least restrictive alternative' test.[492] In this case, the Court will examine if the national measure is necessary to reach a legitimate objective and if that aim cannot be realised by less restrictive means.[493]

Proportionality and freedom of expression – As has been mentioned *supra* with respect to the fundamental right to freedom of expression, any restriction or limit on this right needs to be (1) prescribed by law, (2) introduced with a view to specified interests, and (3) necessary in a democratic society. One of the elements that is checked when verifying this third condition is the proportionality of the measure.[494] Of course, when creating mechanisms to protect children, this principle will have to be taken into account if these mechanisms limit the freedom of expression of adults (*infra*).

1.6.2. *Subsidiarity*

Concept and legal base – Proportionality and subsidiarity, although not identical, are closely linked and complementary principles.[495] Similar to the

where the case can be resolved at one of the earlier stages. Moreover, in some cases the ECJ may distinguish stages two and three of the inquiry, in others it may in effect 'fold' stage three of the inquiry back into stage two": Craig, Paul and de Búrca, Gráinne, *EU law: Text, cases, and materials*, Oxford University Press, Oxford, 2007, 545.

490 Tridimas, Takis, *The general principles of EU law*, Oxford, Oxford University Press, 2006, 138. For more on this test, cf. Tridimas, Takis, *The general principles of EU law*, Oxford, Oxford University Press, 2006, 142–149.

491 Tridimas, Takis, *The general principles of EU law*, Oxford, Oxford University Press, 2006, 138.

492 Tridimas, Takis, *The general principles of EU law*, Oxford, Oxford University Press, 2006, 138 and 209 *et seq.*

493 Tridimas, Takis, *The general principles of EU law*, Oxford, Oxford University Press, 2006, 138.

494 Barendt, Eric, *Freedom of speech*, Oxford, Oxford University Press, 2005, 65.

495 Emiliou, Nicholas, *The principle of proportionality in European law: a comparative study*, London, Kluwer Law International, 1996, 140; Tridimas, Takis, *The general principles of*

proportionality principle, the principle of subsidiarity[496] has been incorporated into the Treaty on the European Union[497] and into the Protocol on the application of the principles of subsidiarity and proportionality.[498] The Treaty on the European Union specifies that subsidiarity entails that the action will only be undertaken at the EU level if the objectives of that action cannot be appropriately reached by the Member States, "*but can rather, by reason of the scale or effects of the proposed action, be better achieved at Union level*".[499] The Protocol stipulates that the subsidiarity principle "*allows Community action within the limits of its powers to be expanded where circumstances so require, and conversely, to be restricted or discontinued where it is no longer justified*".[500]

EU law, Oxford, Oxford University Press, 2006, 176–177. Both principles have been often mentioned in the Better Regulation documents (*supra*).

496 On the origins of this principle, cf. Kapteyn, Paul and VerLoren van Themaat, Pieter, *Introduction to the law of the European Communities – From Maastricht to Amsterdam*, London, Kluwer Law International, 1998, 135; Carozza, Paolo, "Subsidiarity as a structural principle of international human rights law", *American Journal of International Law* 2003, Vol. 97, 40–42; Barber, Nicholas, "The limited modesty of subsidiarity", *European Law Journal* 2005, Vol. 11, No. 3, 309–311.

497 Article 5 para. 3 TEU.

498 Protocol (No. 30) on the application of the principles of subsidiarity and proportionality, 02.10.1997, *OJ* 10.11.1997, *C* 340, 105. Cf. also European Council, Presidency conclusions – Annex 1: Overall approach to the application by the Council of the subsidiarity principle and article 3b of the Treaty on the European Union, 11–12.12.1992, Edinburgh, retrieved from http://www.europarl.europa.eu/summits/edinburgh/a1_en.pdf (on 14.07.2008).

499 Article 5 para. 3 TEU. Along the same lines: recital 5 Protocol (No. 30) on the application of the principles of subsidiarity and proportionality, 02.10.1997, *OJ* 10.11.1997, *C* 340, 105. This recital also provides a number of guidelines that need to be used to check whether Community action is the best option: "*the issue under consideration has transnational aspects which cannot be satisfactorily regulated by action by Member States; actions by Member States alone or lack of Community action would conflict with the requirements of the Treaty (such as the need to correct distortion of competition or avoid disguised restrictions on trade or strengthen economic and social cohesion) or would otherwise significantly damage Member States' interests; action at Community level would produce clear benefits by reason of its scale or effects compared with action at the level of the Member States*". This test has been dubbed the 'comparative efficiency' test: Craig, Paul and de Búrca, Gráinne, *EU law: Text, cases, and materials*, Oxford University Press, Oxford, 2007, 103; Steiner, Josephine, Woods, Lorna and Twigg-Flesner, Christian, *EU law*, Oxford, Oxford University Press, 50.

500 Recital 3 Protocol (No. 30) on the application of the principles of subsidiarity and proportionality, 02.10.1997, *OJ* 10.11.1997, *C* 340, 105.

PROPORTIONALITY VERSUS SUBSIDIARITY – EMILIOU makes a clear distinction between the two principles. He argues that while "*subsidiarity constitutes a limitation of Community powers towards Member States*", proportionality "*provides a criterion whereby the intensity of a Community measure can be measured*".[501] Furthermore, according to him,

> *proportionality goes a step further than subsidiarity. Subsidiarity is concerned with the question whether Community action is required at all. If Community action is not required then there is a breach of the principle of subsidiarity. On the other hand, proportionality comes into place when the decision has been made that a particular EC measure is required. In other words, subsidiarity is concerned with the question who is responsible for introducing the measure in question. From this point of view, proportionality complements the principle of subsidiarity and takes it one step further.*[502]

TRIDIMAS pointed out two other differences. He observed that while subsidiarity only applies in areas in which the Community does not have an exclusive competence,[503] the proportionality principle is also relevant to areas where the Community has exclusive competences.[504] A second difference pointed out by TRIDIMAS is found on a more practical level. He noted that contrary to the principle of proportionality, which is considered very important in case law, the subsidiarity principle "*has had virtually no impact as a ground for review or as a rule of interpretation in the case law of the ECJ or the CFI*".[505] According to TRIDIMAS, the reason for this is the fact that proportionality has a "*human rights ancestry*", whereas subsidiarity is foremost a political principle (which, however, carries an important symbolic significance).[506, 507]

---

501 EMILIOU, Nicholas, *The principle of proportionality in European law: a comparative study*, London, Kluwer Law International, 1996, 140.

502 EMILIOU, Nicholas, *The principle of proportionality in European law: a comparative study*, London, Kluwer Law International, 1996, 140.

503 Recital 3 Protocol (No. 30) on the application of the principles of subsidiarity and proportionality, 02.10.1997, *OJ* 10.11.1997, *C* 340, 105. See also: CRAIG, Paul and DE BÚRCA, Gráinne, *EU law: Text, cases, and materials*, Oxford University Press, Oxford, 2007, 101.

504 TRIDIMAS, Takis, *The general principles of EU law*, Oxford, Oxford University Press, 2006, 176.

505 TRIDIMAS, Takis, *The general principles of EU law*, Oxford, Oxford University Press, 2006, 183.

506 BARBER, Nicholas, "The limited modesty of subsidiarity", *European Law Journal* 2005, Vol. 11, No. 3, 308.

507 TRIDIMAS, Takis, *The general principles of EU law*, Oxford, Oxford University Press, 2006, 183. See also: KAPTEYN, Paul and VERLOREN VAN THEMAAT, Pieter, *Introduction to the law of the European Communities – From Maastricht to Amsterdam*, London, Kluwer Law International, 1998, 139.

REMARK – Interestingly, the Protocol on the application of the principles of subsidiarity and proportionality mentions that where appropriate, and without overlooking the need for suitable enforcement, "*Community measures should provide Member States with alternative ways to achieve the objectives of the measures*". Although the Protocol does not further clarify what is meant exactly by this provision, we could assume, recalling the Better Regulation documents, that alternative regulatory methods (*supra*) are referred to.

1.6.3. *Article 288 para. 3 TFEU [ex 249 EC Treaty]*

IMPLEMENTATION OF DIRECTIVES – Finally, we turn our attention to one of the articles of the TFEU which will need to be examined in greater detail in the next chapter. Article 288 para. 3 TFEU [ex 249 EC Treaty] stipulates that directives "*shall be binding, as to the result to be achieved, upon each Member State to which it is addressed, but shall leave to the national authorities the choice of form and methods*".[508] The fact that the choice of form and methods is left to the national authorities can be considered as an expression of the principle of subsidiarity.[509] It has been argued that the reason for leaving this choice to the Member States is twofold: to respect the sovereignty of the Member States, and to allow Member States to take into account national sensitivities and particular circumstances.[510]

CHOICE OF FORM AND METHODS – Importantly, PRECHAL has stressed that this "*choice is limited to the* kind *of measures to be taken; their* content *is entirely determined by the directive at issue*".[511] However, the freedom to choose the form and methods of implementation is not absolute. The ECJ has developed a substantial body of case law in which the exact scope of article 288 para. 3 TFEU [ex 249 EC Treaty] has been clarified. In the case *Commission v. Germany*, the Court clarified that the manner in which a directive is implemented needs to

---

[508] Article 288 para. 3 TFEU [ex 249 EC Treaty]. This was repeated in Recital 6 Protocol (No. 30) on the application of the principles of subsidiarity and proportionality, 02.10.1997, *OJ* 10.11.1997, *C* 340, 105.

[509] HANS-BREDOW-INSTITUT AND EMR, Study on co-regulation measures in the media sector: Final report, Study commissioned by the European Commission, June 2006, retrieved from http://ec.europa.eu/avpolicy/docs/library/studies/coregul/final_rep_en.pdf (on 28.07.2006), 153; LENAERTS, Koen, VAN NUFFEL, Piet and BRAY, Robert (ed.), *Constitutional law of the European Union*, London, Sweet & Maxwell Limited, 2005, 766.

[510] PRECHAL, Sacha, *Directives in EC law*, Oxford, Oxford University Press, 2005, 73.

[511] PRECHAL, Sacha, *Directives in EC law*, Oxford, Oxford University Press, 2005, 73 [original emphasis].

> *guarantee that the national authorities will in fact apply the directive fully and that, where the directive is intended to create rights for individuals [their] legal position […] is sufficiently precise and clear and the persons concerned are made fully aware of their rights and, where appropriate, afforded the possibility of relying on them before the national courts.*[512]

In the case *Commission v. Italy*, the Court formulated it as follows:

> *the provisions of directives must be implemented with unquestionable binding force, and the specificity, precision and clarity necessary to satisfy the requirements of legal certainty.*[513]

The compliance with these requirements is checked on a case-by-case basis.[514] Significantly, the ECJ has stressed that the transposition of a directive into national legislation does not inevitably and in every circumstance necessitate the adoption of an explicit and specific law.[515] A general legal context may be adequate provided that it guarantees "*the full application of the directive in a sufficiently clear and precise manner*".[516]

Article 288 para. 3 TFEU [ex 249 EC Treaty] and alternative regulatory instruments – The question that interests us the most in the framework of this study is whether alternative regulatory instruments are considered appropriate instruments to implement a directive. If one of the requirements proposed by the ECJ is that the implementing measures need to be legally binding, what scope is left for the use of alternative regulatory instruments? And what about the prerequisite that it should be possible for citizens to rely upon the implementing measures in court? If alternative regulatory instruments are an option, which kind of alternative regulatory instruments would be preferred? And to what extent can the European Union mandate or encourage the use of alternative regulatory instruments

512 ECJ, Commission of the European Communities v. Federal Republic of Germany, C-29/84, 23.05.1985, summary para. 1.

513 ECJ, Commission v. Italy, C-159/99, 17.05.2001, para. 32. See also: ECJ, Commission v. France, C-225/97, 19.05.1999, para. 37.

514 Prechal, Sacha, *Directives in EC law*, Oxford, Oxford University Press, 2005, 75.

515 ECJ, Commission of the European Communities v. Federal Republic of Germany, C-29/84, 23.05.1985, summary para. 1; ECJ, Commission of the European Communities v. Federal Republic of Germany, C-131/88, 28.02.1991, para. 6 ("*the transposition of a directive into domestic law does not necessarily require that its provisions be incorporated formally and verbatim in express, specific legislation*"); ECJ, Commission v. Italy, C-363/85, 09.04.1987, para. 7.

516 ECJ, Commission of the European Communities v. Federal Republic of Germany, C-131/88, 28.02.1991, para. 6; ECJ, Commission v. Italy, C-363/85, 09.04.1987, para. 7. See also: Prechal, Sacha, *Directives in EC law*, Oxford, Oxford University Press, 2005, 77.

for the implementation of directives? These issues will be examined more thoroughly in the next chapter.

1.7. Conclusion

Broader legal background – The aim of this chapter was twofold. The first goal was to sketch the broader legal background to the case-study of this study, the protection of minors against harmful digital content and the use of alternative regulatory instruments to achieve this goal; in order to achieve balanced and efficient regulation of this issue it is crucial to be aware of the legal context.

This descriptive-analytical outline focused on five areas. The starting point was the attribution of human rights to children at the international and supranational (EU and CoE) level. We found that, at these different levels, the importance of children's human rights greatly increased over the past decades. At the international level, the UNCRC functions as the international legal framework, which recognises that children, on the one hand, can invoke human rights, such as the freedom of expression and the right to privacy, but, on the other hand, also need to be protected, for instance, against harmful content. We observed that both the ECJ and the ECHR refer to the UNCRC in cases where children's rights are at stake. At the Council of Europe level, different documents – sometimes directly, sometimes indirectly – refer to the importance of children' rights, generally as well as specifically, in the context of the new information and communication environment. Furthermore, at the EU level, we noted that although the earlier Treaties only contained limited references to children's rights, the Charter of Fundamental Rights (article 24) as well as the Lisbon Treaty have since created a legal framework for children's rights (new article 3 TEU). In addition, the EU established a 'Strategy on the rights of the child'. Many of these documents, like the UNCRC, attempt to achieve a delicate balance between ensuring that children can exercise their fundamental rights, while, on the other hand, protecting them against harmful influences.

Second, in the area of the protection of minors against harmful content, we noted that human rights, such as freedom of expression and privacy, are of vital importance. Regulatory measures taken to protect minors cannot interfere with these human rights unless certain requirements are fulfilled, and need to delicately balance this protection with the freedom of expression and privacy of adults as well as children. Furthermore, we observed that a number of essential procedural guarantees, such as the right to a fair trial (article 6 ECHR) and the right to an effective remedy (article 13 ECHR), are also part of the human rights framework, and, hence, need to be respected.

Third, we examined different content rules which are significant both for the protection of minors against harmful content as well as the use of ARIs, such as the TVWFD and AVMSD with respect to audiovisual content, and the e-Commerce Directive with respect to information society services. Both the TVWFD and the AVMSD contain provisions with respect to the protection of minors against harmful content (the former with respect to broadcasting services, the latter with respect to linear as well as non-linear services). The AVMSD also proposes that Member States use self- and co-regulatory instruments to achieve the objectives included in the directive. In addition, the TVWFD and AVMSD, as well as the e-Commerce Directive, allow Member States to derogate from the free movement of broadcasting services, linear and non-linear services, and information society services, to protect minors. Moreover, the e-Commerce Directive also encourages the creation of codes of conduct for the protection of minors and human dignity. We also considered the liability of intermediaries regime of the e-Commerce Directive, and found that this regime could be, in certain circumstances, interpreted as indirectly regulating content.

Fourth, we briefly discussed the basic elements of the internal market principles (the free movement of services and goods), directed at Member States, and competition principles, directed at undertakings, both of which can be relevant to the use of ARIs to protect minors against harmful content.

Finally, we explored a number of general EU legislative principles and requirements relevant to our case-study, such as proportionality (which is important for testing that measures do not go beyond the goal they want to achieve), subsidiarity (of which the use of ARIs could be considered an expression), and article 288 para. 3 TFEU [ex 249 EC Treaty] (which contains requirements to which the implementation of directives needs to adhere).

Preparation for the next chapter – The second objective of this chapter was to lay the ground for the legal compliance check of the use of ARIs to protect minors from harmful content with the broader legal framework, which will be performed in the next chapter. All legal elements that, at first sight, could be of importance to the use of ARIs in the field of the protection of minors against harmful content have been listed and briefly described. In the next chapter, we will build further on this list of relevant provisions by checking the compliance of the use of self-regulation and co-regulation (with or without the use of technological tools) with this legal framework. This compliance check aims to answer the question at the centre of this book: i.e., are there legal obstacles (at the European level) to the use of alternative regulatory methods to protect minors against digital harmful content? The most important legal obstacles will be thoroughly analysed and, afterwards, recommendations will be made as to the future use of these ARIs.

Chapter 2

Using ARIs to Protect Minors from Harmful Content: Compliance with the Legal Framework

2.1. Introduction

Overview – After the presentation and clarification of the issue of protecting minors against harmful digital content, and a conceptual analysis of alternative regulatory instruments (ARIs) in the first part of this study, the first chapter of this second part provided a descriptive-analytical overview of the legal framework for the use of such instruments in order to achieve the policy goal of protecting minors against harmful content.

Question – The question which logically follows from these previous chapters is the following: are there legal obstacles which prevent the use of ARIs in this field? Furthermore, are these obstacles, if there are any, the same for the different kinds of ARIs?[1] In short, this chapter examines which conditions the use of ARIs will need to fulfil in order to be in compliance with the legal framework at the European level (European Union as well as Council of Europe). As mentioned above, we have chosen to carry out this analysis at the European level since these general supranational rules need to be respected by a significant number of countries. Of course, in every country there will be additional national rules that need to be respected, but

---

[1] In our analysis we will refer to the concepts of self- and co-regulation to clarify which level of government involvement may have an impact on the applicability of or compliance with certain legal provisions. We can recall that self-regulation entails no or a minimal level of government involvement, co-regulation involves a combination of state and non-state involvement. However, we would like to emphasise, as we did in Part 1, Chapter 2, that, since the level of government involvement may vary widely, it may not be easy (nor necessary) to put a specific label on any given ARI. The references to self- and co-regulation are thus only meant as a guideline; further assessment will need to occur on a case-by-case basis.

the variation of these rules according to country and culture – especially in our field of research – entails a far too extended scope of analysis within the framework of this study. Ultimately, the aim of our analysis is to provide a number of recommendations for the future use of ARIs for the protection of minors against harmful content, which can then also be of use in other fields (*infra*, Conclusion).

Existing lacuna – Although a preliminary analysis of the legal framework with which the use of ARIs needs to comply was carried out by the HBI and EMR with respect to co-regulatory instruments,[2] a detailed analysis of applicable legal provisions for all ARIs (including those supported by the use of technology) has been lacking. All too often, relevant legal provisions are not taken into account when creating and structuring ARIs. This, however, stands in stark contrast with the fact that the use of these ARIs does not occur in a legal vacuum.

Normative concerns – The use of ARIs to protect minors against harmful content can potentially raise a number of normative concerns – at a national as well as supranational level – stemming from constitutions, conventions, laws, jurisprudence and soft law instruments.[3] Since a fully comprehensive study of all of these provisions cannot be undertaken within the scope of this study, we have identified four groups of legal provisions at the European level, which are, in our view, the most relevant with respect to the use of ARIs for the protection of minors from harmful content. In succession, we examine potential obstacles posed by human rights provisions (CoE), internal market legislation (EU), competition rules (EU) and article 288 TFEU [ex 249 EC Treaty] regarding the requirements that are imposed with respect to the implementation of directives (EU).

Specificity of analysis – However, it should be noted that it has not been the intent to provide a comprehensive analysis of the legal provisions in question – most of which have already been discussed at great length and in great detail in the academic literature. Instead, we have focused on those elements that are relevant, and potentially problematic, in light of the use of ARIs, especially to protect minors against harmful content.

---

2 Hans-Bredow-Institut and EMR, Study on co-regulation measures in the media sector: Final report, Study commissioned by the European Commission, June 2006, retrieved from http://ec.europa.eu/avpolicy/docs/library/studies/coregul/final_rep_en.pdf (on 28.07.2006).

3 Prosser, Tony, "Self-regulation, Co-regulation and the Audio-Visual Media Services Directive", *Journal of Consumer Policy* 2008, Vol. 31, No. 1, 112.

2.2. Evaluation of different alternative regulatory instruments: compliance with the legal framework

2.2.1. *Human rights*

Cornerstone – Fundamental or constitutional rights are the cornerstone of democratic legal systems. It is hence of the utmost importance that ARIs respect these rights.[4] This is even more crucial in delicate matters, such as the protection of minors against harmful content, in which a balance needs to be found between different goals of public interest.

Concerns – From the very beginnings of the increasing fascination with the use of ARIs, warnings have been issued about the compatibility of using such systems with safeguarding certain fundamental rights. The delegation of regulatory power to non-state bodies where fundamental rights are – potentially – at stake has thus always been regarded with scepticism. In this context, it has been argued that the state should remain the primary guarantor of human rights.[5] It can also be recalled that in the first documents broaching co-regulation, such as the White Paper on European Governance, the European Commission stressed that co-regulation should not be used in cases where fundamental rights are called into question.[6] The rationale behind this was, of course, the concern that private actors should not decide upon the scope of regulations which could restrict fundamental rights.[7] However,

---

[4] O'Connell and Bryce refer to the necessity of 'human rights proofing' all key actions, decisions and technologies affecting the Information Society: O'Connell, Rachel and Bryce, Jo, Children and young people in on-line and related off-line environments: Promoting well-being and minimising risk of harm, Study commissioned by the Council of Europe, not published, 86.

[5] Council of Europe, Pan-European forum on "Human rights in the Information Society: responsible behaviour by key actors", Strasbourg, 12–13.09.2005, retrieved from http://www.coe.int/t/dghl/standardsetting/media/doc/ForumStbgSept2005Report_en.asp#TopOfPage (on 25.04.2007) (under heading 'Harmful content' and 'Risk of harm'); McGonagle, Tarlach, "The potential for practice of an intangible idea", in: Nikoltchev, Susanne (ed.), *Co-regulation of the media in Europe*, IRIS Special, Strasbourg, European Audiovisual Observatory, 2003, 18.

[6] Commission of the European Communities, European Governance – A White Paper, COM (2001) 428 final, 25.07.2001, 21.

[7] Craufurd Smith, Rachael, "European Community media regulation in a converging environment", in: Shuibhne, Niamh Nic (ed.), *Regulating the internal market*, Cheltenham, Edward Elgar, 2006, 135. In this context, Craufurd Smith also referred to article 52 Charter of Fundamental Rights of the European Union which states that "*[a]ny limitation on the exercise of the rights and freedoms recognised by this Charter must be provided for by*

since the adoption of the White Paper in 2001, it has been argued that the unsuitability of the use of co-regulation in situations where fundamental rights are at stake should not be interpreted quite so strictly.[8] Moreover, it has also been suggested that collaboration between the state, industry and civil society could safeguard certain fundamental rights in a more complete way.[9] Hence, a mixture of concerns as well as opportunities regarding the interplay of ARIs and human rights can be discerned.

Analysis – In the following section, this complex balancing exercise between safeguarding an adequate level of protection of a number of fundamental rights and taking advantage of the positive aspects of the use of ARIs, while minimising its negative features, is analysed in greater detail. We have opted to focus on four fundamental rights: first, freedom of expression, second, the right to privacy and, finally, two rights which provide procedural guarantees, i.e., the right to a fair trial and the right to an effective remedy. The first two rights are especially important for the information and communication sector as well as the protection of minors against harmful content; the latter rights are particularly relevant with respect to the structure of ARIs.

---

law and respect the essence of those rights and freedoms" (Charter of Fundamental Rights of the European Union, *OJ* 18.12.2000, *C* 364, 1).

[8] Hans-Bredow-Institut and EMR, Study on co-regulation measures in the media sector: Final report, Study commissioned by the European Commission, June 2006, retrieved from http://ec.europa.eu/avpolicy/docs/library/studies/coregul/final_rep_en.pdf (on 28.07.2006), 174; Rand Europe (Chris Marsden, Stephen Simmons and Jonathan Cave), Options for effectiveness of Internet self- and co-regulation – Inception report, Study commissioned by the European Commission, 30.04.2007, retrieved from http://ec.europa.eu/dgs/information_society/evaluation/data/pdf/studies/s2006_05/inception_final.pdf (on 08.01.2008), 37; Poullet, Yves, "Technologies de l'information et de la communication et 'co-régulation': une nouvelle approche?" ["*Information and communication technologies and 'co-regulation': a new approach?*"], *Droit et Nouvelles Technologies*, 27.05.2004, retrieved from http://www.droit-technologie.org/upload/dossier/doc/120-1.pdf (on 29.11.2008), 11 [in French]. See also: *supra* Part 1 Chapter 2.

[9] Council of Europe, Pan-European forum on "Human rights in the Information Society: responsible behaviour by key actors", Strasbourg, 12–13.09.2005, retrieved from http://www.coe.int/t/dghl/standardsetting/media/doc/ForumStbgSept2005Report_en.asp#TopOfPage (on 25.04.2007) (under heading 'Harmful content' and 'Risk of harm').

A. *Freedom of expression*

A.1. *General principle*

FUNDAMENTAL PRINCIPLE – Article 10 ECHR stipulates that everyone has the "*freedom to hold opinions and to receive and impart information and ideas without interference by public authority and regardless of frontiers*". As mentioned in the previous chapter, however, equally important is the fact that the fundamental right to freedom of expression is not absolute.[10] Restrictions, i.e., "*formalities, conditions, restrictions or penalties*",[11] such as the seizure of published material, criminal sanctions[12] or labelling used to filter content,[13] can be allowed, but only if certain – strictly interpreted[14] – conditions are fulfilled.[15] Interferences with freedom of expression by public authorities thus need to be prescribed by law, must pursue a legitimate aim (such as the protection of morals, which is the aim most suitable in the field of protecting minors against harmful content), and has to be necessary in a

---

[10] Article 10 para. 2. ECHR.

[11] Article 10 para. 2. ECHR.

[12] OVEY, Clare and WHITE, Robin, *Jacobs and White The European Convention on Human Rights*, Oxford, Oxford University Press, 2006, 318–319.

[13] HANS-BREDOW-INSTITUT AND EMR, Study on co-regulation measures in the media sector: Final report, Study commissioned by the European Commission, June 2006, retrieved from http://ec.europa.eu/avpolicy/docs/library/studies/coregul/final_rep_en.pdf (on 28.07.2006), 149.

[14] COUNCIL OF EUROPE, *Freedom of expression in Europe: case-law concerning article 10 of the European Convention on Human Rights*, Strasbourg, Council of Europe Publishing, 2007, 9; VAN DIJK, Pieter, VAN HOOF, Fried, VAN RIJN, Arjen and ZWAAK, Leo (eds), *Theory and practice of the European Convention on Human Rights*, Antwerpen, Intersentia, 2006, 793; VOORHOOF, Dirk, "Vrijheid van meningsuiting" ["*Freedom of expression*"], in: VANDE LANOTTE, Johan and HAECK, Yves, *Handboek EVRM: Deel II: Artikelsgewijze commentaar (Volume I)* [*ECHR: Part II: Commentary on the articles*], Antwerpen, Intersentia, 2004, 967 [in Dutch].

[15] With respect to Internet content, cf., for instance, COUNCIL OF EUROPE (COMMITTEE OF MINISTERS), Recommendation CM/Rec(2008)6 on measures to promote the respect for freedom of expression and information with regard to Internet filters, 26.03.2008, retrieved from https://wcd.coe.int/ViewDoc.jsp?Ref=CM/Rec(2008)6&Language=lanEnglish&Ver=original&BackColorInternet=9999CC&BackColorIntranet=FFBB55&BackColorLogged=FFAC75 (on 31.03.2008): "*Aware that any intervention by member states that forbids access to specific Internet content may constitute a restriction on freedom of expression and access to information in the online environment and that such a restriction would have to fulfil the conditions in Article 10, paragraph 2, of the European Convention on Human Rights and the relevant case-law of the European Court of Human Rights*".

democratic society.[16] Three main issues can be raised: first, whether the fact that article 10 ECHR targets interferences by 'public authorities' presents problems with respect to the use of ARIs, second, whether there are particular difficulties with respect to the three conditions of article 10 para. 2 ECHR, and third, whether there are specific issues related to the use of self-regulation and technology in the human rights context.

A.2. *Infringement by 'public authorities'*

PUBLIC AUTHORITIES? – A first issue regarding the relationship between the use of ARIs and article 10 ECHR centres around the fact that this article deals with interferences with freedom of expression by 'public authorities'.[17] A public authority has been interpreted as "*any authority exercising public power and duties or being in the public service, such as courts, prosecutors' offices, police, any law-enforcement body, intelligence services, central or local councils, government departments, army decision-making bodies, [or] public professional structures*".[18]

WHAT ABOUT SELF- OR CO-REGULATORY BODIES? – Of course, in the case of ARIs, the potential interference of the freedom of expression will often – depending on the structure of the ARIs in question – originate from a non-state body. Hence, the question is whether article 10 ECHR is at all applicable when restrictions are part of a self-regulatory or co-regulatory scheme. Of course, the answer to this question will depend on the level of government involvement in the scheme. If the restrictive measures do stem from a state actor (for instance, in a co-regulatory scheme), or from an actor which can be considered – according to the circumstances – as a 'public authority', then the applicability of article 10 ECHR will not be questioned.[19] In the case *Casado Coca v. Spain*, for instance, the European Court of Human Rights decided that the Barcelona Bar Council was, according to Spanish law, a

[16] Article 10 para. 2. ECHR.

[17] Article 10 para. 1 ECHR: "*This right includes the freedom to hold opinions and to receive and impart information and ideas without interference by a public authority and regardless of frontiers*".

[18] MACOVEI, Monica, *Freedom of expression – A guide to the implementation of Article 10 of the European Convention of Human Rights (Human rights handbooks, No. 2)*, Strasbourg, Council of Europe, 2004, 30.

[19] See also: HANS-BREDOW-INSTITUT AND EMR, Study on co-regulation measures in the media sector: Final report, Study commissioned by the European Commission, June 2006, retrieved from http://ec.europa.eu/avpolicy/docs/library/studies/coregul/final_rep_en.pdf (on 28.07.2006), 150.

public law corporation, and, moreover, that the purpose of the Bar Council served the public interest, and that the penalty imposed by the Bar Council had been upheld in national courts.[20] Hence, the Court decided that there was in fact an interference by a public authority and, consequently, article 10 ECHR was considered applicable.[21] In the case of a purely self-regulatory scheme or 'soft' co-regulatory scheme with a low degree of government involvement, however, this would probably not be the case.

A.3. *Freedom of expression and horizontal effect*

Article 10 ECHR applicable between private actors? – At this point, a second question can be raised, i.e., to what extent the Convention is applicable to relations between private or non-state actors.[22] A hesitant answer can be found in the 'horizontal effect'[23] or '*Drittwirkung*' theory.[24] The legal basis for this theory is article 1 ECHR, which states that "*[t]he High Contracting Parties shall secure to everyone within their jurisdiction the rights and freedoms defined in Section I of this Convention*". The European Court of Human Rights developed this theory further, and has, in some instances,

---

[20] European Court of Human Rights, Casado Coca v. Spain, 24.02.1994, para. 39. See also: van Dijk, Pieter, van Hoof, Fried, van Rijn, Arjen and Zwaak, Leo (eds), *Theory and practice of the European Convention on Human Rights*, Antwerpen, Intersentia, 2006, 783–784.

[21] For instance: European Court of Human Rights, Casado Coca v. Spain, 24.02.1994, para. 39. See also: Hans-Bredow-Institut and EMR, Study on co-regulation measures in the media sector: Final report, Study commissioned by the European Commission, June 2006, retrieved from http://ec.europa.eu/avpolicy/docs/library/studies/coregul/final_rep_en.pdf (on 28.07.2006), 150.

[22] Clapham, Andrew, "The 'Drittwirkung' of the Convention", in: MacDonald, Ronald Saint John, Matscher, Franz and Petzold, Herbert, *The European system for the protection of human rights*, Dordrecht, Martinus Nijhoff Publishers, 1993, 163.

[23] Voorhoof, Dirk, *Critical perspectives on the scope and interpretation of Article 10 of the European Convention on Human Rights (Mass media files No. 10)*, Strasbourg, Council of Europe Press, 1995, 59–60; Voorhoof, Dirk, "Co-regulation and European basic rights", Presentation at the Expert Conference on Media Policy "More trust in content – The potential of self- and co-regulation in digital media", Leipzig, 9–11.05.2007, retrieved from http://www.leipzig-eu2007.de/en/downloads/dokumente.asp (on 03.09.2008).

[24] Clapham describes the origin of the notion: "*The word* Drittwirkung *originates from a doctrinal debate in Germany and means 'third-party effect'. It refers to the possible application of the German Basic Law in cases where both parties are private parties. The 'third party' refers to the party outside the classic individual / State relationship who is affected by the constitutional norms*": Clapham, Andrew, "The 'Drittwirkung' of the Convention", in: MacDonald, Ronald Saint John, Matscher, Franz and Petzold, Herbert, *The European system for the protection of human rights*, Dordrecht, Martinus Nijhoff Publishers, 1993, 165 (original emphasis).

accepted that article 10 ECHR can be invoked in horizontal relations, or in other words between individuals, particularly "*where a State had taken or failed to take certain measures*".[25] In the *Fuentes Bobo v. Spain* case, for instance, the Court acknowledged that "*a positive obligation can rest with the authorities to protect the freedom of expression against infringements, even by private persons*".[26] Furthermore, in *VGT Verein v. Tierfabriken*, the Court stated that "*in addition to the primarily negative undertaking of a State to abstain from interference in Convention guarantees, 'there may be positive obligations inherent' in such guarantees*".[27] Hence, the Court reasoned that "*[t]he responsibility of a State may then be engaged as a result of not observing its obligation to enact domestic legislation*".[28]

It is very difficult, however, to make general assumptions about the application of horizontal effect with respect to ARIs, since there is no consensus on its scope.[29] The European Court of Human Rights has even explicitly stated that it does not wish "*to elaborate a general theory concerning the extent to which the Convention guarantees should be extended to relations between private individuals inter se*".[30]

Scope *Drittwirkung* – Van Dijk et al. distinguish two interpretations of the *Drittwirkung* concept. A first – rather broad – view implies that human rights provisions apply not only to relations between private actors and public authorities, but to legal relations between private parties as well.[31] A second – more narrow – view suggests that *Drittwirkung* only entails that individuals can enforce human rights provisions against other individuals.[32] As complaints directly aimed at an individual (instead of a state) cannot be brought before the European Court of Human Rights, at best, this second interpretation suggests an 'indirect horizontal effect' stemming from national law.[33] Hence, if the rights included in the Convention are recognised in a

---

25 van Dijk, Pieter, van Hoof, Fried, van Rijn, Arjen and Zwaak, Leo (eds), *Theory and practice of the European Convention on Human Rights*, Antwerpen, Intersentia, 2006, 784.

26 European Court of Human Rights, Fuentes Bobo v. Spain, 29.02.2000. See also: van Dijk, Pieter, van Hoof, Fried, van Rijn, Arjen and Zwaak, Leo (eds), *Theory and practice of the European Convention on Human Rights*, Antwerpen, Intersentia, 2006, 784–785.

27 European Court of Human Rights, VGT Verein v. Tierfabriken, 28.06.2001, para. 45.

28 European Court of Human Rights, VGT Verein v. Tierfabriken, 28.06.2001, para. 45.

29 van Dijk, Pieter, van Hoof, Fried, van Rijn, Arjen and Zwaak, Leo (eds), *Theory and practice of the European Convention on Human Rights*, Antwerpen, Intersentia, 2006, 28.

30 European Court of Human Rights, VGT Verein v. Tierfabriken, 28.06.2001, para. 46.

31 van Dijk, Pieter, van Hoof, Fried, van Rijn, Arjen and Zwaak, Leo (eds), *Theory and practice of the European Convention on Human Rights*, Antwerpen, Intersentia, 2006, 29.

32 van Dijk, Pieter, van Hoof, Fried, van Rijn, Arjen and Zwaak, Leo (eds), *Theory and practice of the European Convention on Human Rights*, Antwerpen, Intersentia, 2006, 29.

33 Voorhoof, Dirk, "Vrijheid van meningsuiting" ["*Freedom of expression*"], in: Vande

state's national law as having direct effect, individuals can – between themselves – invoke these rights before national courts.[34] If a decision in such a case is in conflict with the Convention, the issue can then be brought before the European Court of Human Rights.[35]

However, even if a state does not acknowledge the direct effect of the rights and freedoms included in the Convention, the Court has, in certain cases, acknowledged that states nevertheless have a positive obligation to protect their citizens against violations of their fundamental rights by other citizens and can, furthermore, be held responsible for the lack of such protection.[36] In *Appleby and others v. the United Kingdom*, for instance, the Court held that

> *The applicants were stopped from setting up a stand and distributing leaflets in the Galleries by Postel, the private company which owned the shopping centre. The Court does not find that the authorities bear any direct responsibility for this restriction on the applicants' freedom of expression. It is not persuaded that any element of State responsibility can be derived from the fact that a public development corporation transferred the property to Postel or that this was done with ministerial permission. The issue to be determined is whether the respondent State has failed in any positive obligation to protect the exercise of the applicants' Article 10 rights from interference by others – in this case, the owner of the Galleries.*[37]

Lanotte, Johan and Haeck, Yves, *Handboek EVRM: Deel II: Artikelsgewijze commentaar (Volume I)* [*ECHR: Part II: Commentary on the articles*], Antwerpen, Intersentia, 2004, 922–923 [in Dutch]; van Dijk, Pieter, van Hoof, Fried, van Rijn, Arjen and Zwaak, Leo (eds), *Theory and practice of the European Convention on Human Rights*, Antwerpen, Intersentia, 2006, 29.

[34] van Dijk, Pieter, van Hoof, Fried, van Rijn, Arjen and Zwaak, Leo (eds), *Theory and practice of the European Convention on Human Rights*, Antwerpen, Intersentia, 2006, 30.

[35] Clapham, Andrew, "The 'Drittwirkung' of the Convention", in: MacDonald, Ronald Saint John, Matscher, Franz and Petzold, Herbert, *The European system for the protection of human rights*, Dordrecht, Martinus Nijhoff Publishers, 1993, 198; Voorhoof, Dirk, "Vrijheid van meningsuiting" ["*Freedom of expression*"], in: Vande Lanotte, Johan and Haeck, Yves, *Handboek EVRM: Deel II: Artikelsgewijze commentaar (Volume I)* [*ECHR: Part II: Commentary on the articles*], Antwerpen, Intersentia, 2004, 922–923 [in Dutch].

[36] For instance: European Court of Human Rights, Fuentes Bobo v. Spain, 29.02.2000, para. 38; European Court of Human Rights, Özgür Gündem v. Turkey, 16.03.2000, paras 42–43; European Court of Human Rights, VGT Verein v. Tierfabriken, 28.06.2001, para. 45. See also: van Dijk, Pieter, van Hoof, Fried, van Rijn, Arjen and Zwaak, Leo (eds), *Theory and practice of the European Convention on Human Rights*, Antwerpen, Intersentia, 2006, 30; Voorhoof, Dirk, "Vrijheid van meningsuiting" ["*Freedom of expression*"], in: Vande Lanotte, Johan and Haeck, Yves, *Handboek EVRM: Deel II: Artikelsgewijze commentaar (Volume I)* [*ECHR: Part II: Commentary on the articles*], Antwerpen, Intersentia, 2004, 923 and 925–927 [in Dutch].

[37] European Court of Human Rights, Appleby and others v. the United Kingdom, 06.05.2003, para. 41.

Furthermore, even when a state 'outsources' regulation, for instance to alternative regulatory bodies, this positive obligation to secure the Convention rights remains valid.[38]

Horizontal effect and ARIs – Considering this – rather vague – theory of 'horizontal effect' or *Drittwirkung*, it is possible to suppose that the European Court of Human Rights would not automatically assume that article 10 ECHR is not applicable because a case concerns non-state bodies involved in self- or co-regulatory schemes. The Court will asses the applicability of article 10 ECHR based on the exact circumstances of the case, and will pay, of course, particular attention to the level of government involvement.

A.4. *Restrictions on freedom of expression and their justification*

Fulfilling the conditions of article 10 para. 2 ECHR – If it has been accepted that article 10 ECHR is applicable in a given situation, however, a further potential hurdle is found in its second paragraph. When an alternative regulatory system is devised to protect minors against harmful content, almost always the right to freedom of expression will be limited to a certain extent.[39] It is possible that such a system only limits the freedom of expression of children, but it is also conceivable it even affects adults. In both cases the conditions of article 10 para. 2 ECHR (*supra*) will need to be fulfilled.

Legitimate aim – The second condition, i.e., the pursuance of a legitimate aim, will in the majority of cases not be a significant hurdle, given that the European Court of Human Rights has judged the protection of minors to be a legitimate aim (under the umbrella of the 'protection of morals' or the 'protection of the rights of others').[40]

Prescription by law – Difficulties could, however, arise with respect to the first condition, i.e., prescription by law. Usually, this condition is assumed to

---

[38] Voorhoof, Dirk, "Co-regulation and European basic rights", Presentation at the Expert Conference on Media Policy "More trust in content – The potential of self- and co-regulation in digital media", Leipzig, 9–11.05.2007, retrieved from http://www.leipzig-eu2007.de/en/downloads/dokumente.asp (on 03.09.2008).

[39] Council of Europe (Committee of Ministers), Recommendation CM/REC(2009)5 on measures to protect children against harmful content and behaviour and to promote their active participation in the new information and communications environment, 08.07.2009, retrieved from https://wcd.coe.int/ViewDoc.jsp?id=1470045&Site=CM (on 20.01.2010).

[40] European Court of Human Rights, Handyside v. the United Kingdom, 7.12.1976, *Publ. Eur. Court H.R.*, Series, A, Vol. 24, para. 52.

be fulfilled when there is a written and public law adopted by a Parliament.[41] However, the European Court of Human Rights has accepted other forms of 'law', such as common-law rules or principles of international law, as satisfying the requirement.[42] To qualify as 'law', the Court requires that the 'legal' basis for the interference is accessible and foreseeable. It provided further clarification in the *Sunday Times v. the United Kingdom* case:

> *Firstly, the law must be adequately accessible: the citizen must be able to have an indication that is adequate in the circumstances of the legal rules applicable to a given case. Secondly, a norm cannot be regarded as a 'law' unless it is formulated with sufficient precision to enable the citizen to regulate his conduct: he must be able – if need be with appropriate advice – to foresee, to a degree that is reasonable in the circumstances, the consequences which a given action may entail. Those consequences need not be foreseeable with absolute certainty: experience shows this to be unattainable. Again, whilst certainty is highly desirable, it may bring in its train excessive rigidity and the law must be able to keep pace with changing circumstances. Accordingly, many laws are inevitably couched in terms which, to a greater or lesser extent, are vague and whose interpretation and application are questions of practice.*[43]

Additionally, the Court has clarified in a number of cases that it is essential that the 'law' in question "*afford[s] a measure of legal protection against arbitrary interferences by public authorities with the rights guaranteed by the Convention*".[44] In order to avoid arbitrariness, the measures which interfere

---

[41] Macovei, Monica, *Freedom of expression – A guide to the implementation of Article 10 of the European Convention of Human Rights (Human rights handbooks, No. 2)*, Strasbourg, Council of Europe, 2004, 30. Macovei explained this further: "*[f]reedom of expression is such an important value that its restriction should always receive the democratic legitimacy which is only given by the parliamentary debates and vote*" (p. 31).

[42] European Court of Human Rights, Sunday Times v. the United Kingdom, 26.04.1979, para. 47; European Court of Human Rights, Groppera Radio AG and others v. Switzerland, 28.03.1990, para. 68. See also: Macovei, Monica, *Freedom of expression – A guide to the implementation of Article 10 of the European Convention of Human Rights (Human rights handbooks, No. 2)*, Strasbourg, Council of Europe, 2004, 30.

[43] European Court of Human Rights, Sunday Times v. the United Kingdom, 26.04.1979, para. 49.

[44] European Court of Human Rights, Glas Nadezhda and Elenkov v. Bulgaria, 11.10.2007, para. 46; European Court of Human Rights, Meltex Ltd and Mesrop Movsesyan v. Armenia, 17.06.2008, para. 81. Cf. also: Voorhoof, Dirk, "Recente arresten van het E.H.R.M. in verband met het artikel 10 E.V.R.M. (vrijheid van meningsuiting en informatie)" ["*Recent judgments of the ECHR related to article 10 ECHR (freedom of expression and information)*"], September-October 2007, *Auteurs & Media* 2007, No. 6, 597–606 [in Dutch]; Voorhoof, Dirk, "Recente arresten van het E.H.R.M. in verband met het artikel 10 E.V.R.M. (vrijheid van meningsuiting en informatie)" ["*Recent judgments of the ECHR related to article 10 ECHR (freedom of expression and information)*"], June 2008, *Auteurs & Media* 2008, No. 4, 314–318 [in Dutch].

with the right to freedom of expression should adhere to a number of procedural guarantees.[45] Hence, decisions of regulatory bodies need to be duly reasoned and open to judicial review and procedures need to be open and transparent.[46] This is an element that will need to be taken into account when ARIs are structured.

In the case of ARIs – especially with respect to self-regulatory instruments, but sometimes also with regard to co-regulatory systems – often no clear legal basis is available. In the case of *Barthold v. Germany*, the European Court of Human Rights specified that an interference with a person's freedom of expression "*must have some basis in domestic law, which itself must be adequately accessible and be formulated with sufficient precision to enable the individual to regulate his conduct, if need be with appropriate advice*".[47] This specific case is relevant to the use of ARIs since, *in casu*, the question was asked if the 'Rules of Professional Conduct of the Hamburg Veterinary Surgeons' Council' could be considered as 'prescribed by law'. The Court decided that although these rules did not emanate directly from Parliament, but from the Veterinary Surgeons Council,

> *[they are] nonetheless to be regarded as a 'law' within the meaning of article 10 para. 2 (art. 10–2) of the Convention. The competence of the Veterinary Surgeons' Council in the sphere of professional conduct derives from the independent rule-making power that the veterinary profession – in company with other liberal professions – traditionally enjoys, by parliamentary delegation, in the Federal Republic of Germany [...].*[48]

Hence, it seems that, in certain circumstances, the Court accepts the delegation of a degree of 'rule-making power' to a non-state body, and acknowledges its decisions to have a 'law-like' status. However, in this specific case, the Court noted that

---

[45] It can be noted that the European Court of Human Rights has also pointed to the importance of certain 'procedural guarantees' (such as the fact that decision-making bodies need issue 'informed decisions', on the basis of an acceptable assessment of the facts) under the condition of 'necessity in a democratic society' (*infra*). Cf. European Court of Human Rights, Steur v. the Netherlands, 28.10.2003; European Court of Human Rights, Veraart v. the Netherlands, 30.11.2006. For more on procedural guarantees, cf. article 6 ECHR (*infra*).

[46] European Court of Human Rights, Glas Nadezhda and Elenkov v. Bulgaria, 11.10.2007, paras 50–51; European Court of Human Rights, Meltex Ltd and Mesrop Movsesyan v. Armenia, 17.06.2008, para. 81.

[47] European Court of Human Rights, Barthold v. Germany, 25.03.1985, para. 45. See also: European Court of Human Rights, Silver and others v. the United Kingdom, 25.03.1983, paras 85–88.

[48] European Court of Human Rights, Barthold v. Germany, 25.03.1985, para. 46.

> *[f]urthermore, it is a competence exercised by the Council under the control of the State, which in particular satisfies itself as to observance of national legislation, and the Council is obliged to submit its rules of professional conduct to the Land Government for approval [...].*[49]

This statement demonstrates that the Court actually demands a considerable degree of government involvement: not only the control which the state retains over the Council, but also the required approval of the rules by the German government, were evaluated positively by the Court. Hence, it could certainly be questioned whether pure self-regulatory measures, with no or a very limited degree of government involvement, would be accepted by the Court as being 'prescribed by law'.

NECESSARY IN A DEMOCRATIC SOCIETY – The fulfilment of the third required condition, i.e., the necessity of the interference in a democratic society, is, again, very much dependent on the concrete circumstances of each case. The European Court of Human Rights will check whether the interference is proportional, whether the reasons for justification are relevant and sufficient,[50] and whether there is a pressing social need for the interference.[51] With respect to the use of ARIs to protect minors from harmful content, the Court will thus have to verify whether the restriction imposed on the freedom of expression by the ARI (provided it has fulfilled the two previous conditions) is proportional to the aim of protecting minors against harmful content, and whether there is a pressing social need for this restriction. Given that the European Court of Human Rights has up until now not judged a case in which an infringement of article 10 ECHR by means of such an ARI was at issue, it is very hard to predict which restrictions embodied in ARIs would be considered by the Court as necessary in a democratic society. In each case, the Court will take the concrete circumstances into account. Hence, only general assumptions can be made with regard to the balancing test which the Court will carry out.

For instance, it can be assumed that the Court will not accept regulatory methods to protect children which significantly restrict adults' rights to freedom of expression (for instance, by preventing adult access to

---

[49] EUROPEAN COURT OF HUMAN RIGHTS, Barthold v. Germany, 25.03.1985, para. 46.

[50] VAN DIJK, Pieter, VAN HOOF, Fried, VAN RIJN, Arjen and ZWAAK, Leo (eds), *Theory and practice of the European Convention on Human Rights*, Antwerpen, Intersentia, 2006, 775.

[51] EUROPEAN COURT OF HUMAN RIGHTS, Observer and Guardian v. the United Kingdom, 26.11.1991, para. 57. See also: COUNCIL OF EUROPE, Freedom of expression in Europe: COUNCIL OF EUROPE, *Freedom of expression in Europe: case-law concerning article 10 of the European Convention on Human Rights*, Strasbourg, Council of Europe Publishing, 2007, 9.

content which is legal, but considered harmful to minors),[52] since such mechanisms could be argued to be disproportional.[53] Furthermore, the availability of less restrictive alternative measures could also play a significant role in the assessment of proportionality.[54] In this context, we can learn from the US case law (discussed *supra*, in Part 1, Chapter 1) which considered that both the *Communications Decency Act* and the *Child Online Protection Act*, aimed at protecting minors, restricted the freedom of expression of adults in a disproportional manner, and that the use of filtering systems, for example, could possibly be a less restrictive alternative.[55] A final factor which may also play a role in the assessment of proportionality by the Court is whether the stringency of the measures or severity of any penalties could lead to a 'chilling effect'.[56] This implies that if the measures are too restrictive or if certain liabilities are imposed,[57] people will not be as forthcoming in expressing their thoughts and ideas as would be usual or natural.

A.5. *Freedom of expression and self-regulation*

PRIVATE ACTORS – It is a fact that private actors or intermediaries, such as Internet Service Providers (ISPs), mobile telephony providers or search engine operators, play a far greater role in the new information and com-

---

[52] BIRNHACK, Michael and ROWBOTTOM, Jacob, "Shielding children: the European way", *Chicago-Kent Law Review* 2004, Issue 79, 195.

[53] For instance: COMMISSION OF THE EUROPEAN COMMUNITIES, Communication to the European Parliament, the Council, the Economic and Social Committee and the Committee of the Regions, Illegal and harmful content on the Internet, COM (1996) 487 final: "*One general conclusion is that any regulatory action intended to protect minors should not take the form of an unconditional prohibition of using the Internet to distribute certain content that is available freely in other media*".

[54] KÜHLING, Jürgen, "Fundamental rights", in: VON BOGDANDY, Armin and BAST, Jürgen (eds), *Principles of European constitutional law*, Oxford, Hart Publishing, 2006, 537 ("*no other means available which were equally efficient but less onerous*").

[55] For issues related to filtering, cf. *infra*.

[56] For more on the US origins of this concept, cf. SCHAUER, Frederick, "Fear, risk and the First Amendment: Unravelling the chilling effect", *Boston University Law Review* 1978, Vol. 58, Issue 5, 685–732.

[57] Cf., for instance, the liability regime in the e-Commerce Directive (*supra*, Part 2, Chapter 1). See also: VALCKE, Peggy and DOMMERING, Egbert, "e-Commerce Directive", in: CASTENDYK, Oliver, DOMMERING, Egbert J. and SCHEUER, Alexander (eds), *European media law*, Alphen a/d Rijn, Kluwer Law International, 2008, 1099; RORIVE, Isabelle and FRYDMAN, Benoît, "Regulating Internet content through intermediaries in Europe and the USA", *Droit et Nouvelles Technologies*, 19.03.2003, retrieved from http://www.droit-technologie.org/dossier-92/regulating-internet-content-through-intermediaries-in-europe-and-the-u.html (on 23.03.2007).

munication environment compared to the traditional media landscape, which was dominated by a much more limited number of broadcasters and newspaper publishers (*supra*). Those private 'new media' actors are often indispensable points of access to the new communication technologies and, hence, as the Council of Europe pointed out: "*their role is a prerequisite for enabling and empowering users to access the benefits of the information society, in particular to seek and impart information and ideas, to create and to access knowledge and education*".[58] However, this also means that these private actors have the power to restrict access to the services they provide, for instance, by removing, filtering or blocking content. These restrictions carried out by private actors may thus have a significant impact on the freedom of expression. Special mention can be made of search engine operators.[59] It is impossible to imagine life (or at least certain aspects of life) today without search engines. van Eijk argues that "*[s]earch engines are becoming the most important gateway used to find content: research shows that the average user considers them to be the most important intermediary in their search for content*".[60] Search engines can play a role with respect to harmful content as well, not only because they provide access to such content,[61] but also because

[58] Council of Europe, Human rights guidelines for Internet Service Providers – Developed by the Council of Europe in co-operation with the European Internet Service Providers Association (EuroISPA), July 2008, retrieved from http://www.coe.int/t/dghl/standardsetting/media/Doc/H-Inf(2008)009_en.pdf (on 10.10.2008), 3.

[59] The legal issues surrounding search engines are currently a controversial topic. It is not possible to provide a detailed analysis of these issues within the scope of this thesis. For more details, cf. Nikoltchev, Susanne (ed.), *Searching for audiovisual content*, IRIS Special, Strasbourg, European Audiovisual Observatory, 2008, 90 p. (especially the contributions by Valcke, Peggy, "In search of the audiovisual search tools in the EU regulatory frameworks", 65–76; Schulz, Wolfgang, "Regulating search engines? On the use of self- and co-regulation in the field of Internet search", 79–86 and van Hoboken, Joris, "Freedom of expression implications for the governance of search", 49–62); van Eijk, Nico, "Search engines: seek and ye shall find? The position of search engines in law", *Iris Plus* 2006, No. 2, 2–8; van Hoboken, Joris, "Legal space for innovative ordering: on the need to update selection intermediary liability in the EU", *International Journal of Communications Law & Policy* 2009, Issue 13, Winter, 49–69; Jakubowicz, Karl, "A new notion of media?", Background text, 1st Council of Europe Conference of Ministers responsible for media and new communications services: A new notion of media?; Reykjavik, 28–29.05.2009, retrieved from http://www.ministerialconference.is/media/images/a_new_notion_of_media_web_version.df (on 27.05.2009), 33.

[60] van Eijk, Nico, "Search engines, the new bottleneck for content access", paper for the ITS 19th European Regional Conference, Istanbul, 02–05.09.2007, retrieved from http://www.ivir.nl/publications/vaneijk/Paper_SearchEngines_ITS_2007.pdf (on 28.05.2009), 2.

[61] Schulz, Wolfgang, "Regulating search engines? On the use of self- and co-regulation in the field of Internet search", in: Nikoltchev, Susanne (ed.), *Searching for audiovisual content*, IRIS Special, Strasbourg, European Audiovisual Observatory, 2008, 81.

they might restrict access to such content by eliminating such content from the search results.

Private censorship – One of the fears that has frequently been voiced over the past decade is that restrictions on the freedom to expression by private actors, for instance by means of filtering or blocking schemes, in fact amount to private censorship.[62] As was mentioned above, according to article 10 ECHR, states or 'public authorities' are prevented from interfering with the freedom of expression of their citizens if no serious justifications can be put forward. However, we have also found that the applicability of article 10 ECHR is not as straightforward with respect to private actors (cf. *supra*: horizontal effect). Hence, if questionable actions by private actors do not fall within the remit of article 10 ECHR, the protection of fundamental rights is at stake. Schemes in which private actors carry the full responsibility for filtering, labelling or blocking content, for instance, to protect minors from harmful content, have therefore been regarded with scepticism by many commentators. Just as state censorship cannot be tolerated, nor should private censorship. Distinguishing between what is illegal and what is harmful is a very difficult and delicate issue that should not be left to private companies.[63] In this context, the Council of Europe stated in its Human Rights Guidelines for Internet Service Providers that ISPs which provide access services, hosting, applications or content, should not be "*expected to advise on what content or behaviours are illegal and/or harmful*".[64] Furthermore, with respect to ISPs which offer hosting, applications or content, the Council of Europe stressed that

> *[i]n respect of filtering, blocking or removal of illegal content, you should do so only after a verification of the illegality of the content, for instance by contacting the competent law enforcement authorities. Acting without first checking and*

[62] Noorlander, Peter, "Freedom of expression and Internet regulation", in: Hardy, Christiane and Möller, Christian (eds), *Spreading the Word on the Internet: 16 Answers to 4 Questions (Reflections on Freedom of the Media and the Internet Amsterdam Conference, June 2003)*, Vienna, OSCE, 2003, retrieved from http://www.osce.org/publications/rfm/2003/06/12245_103_en.pdf (on 23.04.2007), 110.

[63] Noorlander, Peter, "Freedom of expression and Internet regulation", in: Hardy, Christiane and Möller, Christian (eds), *Spreading the Word on the Internet: 16 Answers to 4 Questions (Reflections on Freedom of the Media and the Internet Amsterdam Conference, June 2003)*, Vienna, OSCE, 2003, retrieved from http://www.osce.org/publications/rfm/2003/06/12245_103_en.pdf (on 23.04.2007), 110–111.

[64] Council of Europe, Human rights guidelines for Internet Service Providers – Developed by the Council of Europe in co-operation with the European Internet Service Providers Association (EuroISPA), July 2008, retrieved from http://www.coe.int/t/dghl/standardsetting/media/Doc/H-Inf(2008)009_en.pdf (on 10.10.2008), paras 16 and 24.

> *verifying may be considered as an interference with legal content and with the rights and freedoms of those creating, communicating and accessing such content, in particular the right to freedom of expression and information.*[65]

It is clear that the Council of Europe intended to say very little and very much at the same time with this statement. The theory that ISPs should take the utmost care in dealing with alleged illegal content – which can actually be illegal, but can also be 'simply' harmful – might, however, in practice, prove to be challenging. It is, for instance, not very clear what exactly is meant by 'contacting the competent law enforcement authorities'. How far should ISPs go to achieve a satisfactory answer to the question whether certain content is illegal? Most often, only a court will be able to decide upon the legality or illegality of certain content. Furthermore, if we recall the liability regime imposed by the EU e-Commerce Directive (*supra*, Part 2, Chapter 1), the issue only becomes more complicated, since this regime requires, for instance, hosting providers who have an actual knowledge of illegal content to block access to that content. As noted above, this, again, can potentially result in a 'chilling effect', given that this regime encourages ISPs to err on the side of caution by taking down content which is not illegal.[66] Hence, we can conclude that the e-Commerce regime and the Council of Europe guidelines do not seem to be on the same wavelength.

Requirements – At the very least, private companies who are involved in schemes related to filtering and blocking harmful content, should employ transparent procedures[67] and be very open about the criteria they use when deciding upon the potential harmfulness of content.[68] Again, we can refer to

---

[65] Council of Europe, Human rights guidelines for Internet Service Providers – Developed by the Council of Europe in co-operation with the European Internet Service Providers Association (EuroISPA), July 2008, retrieved from http://www.coe.int/t/dghl/standardsetting/media/Doc/H-Inf(2008)009_en.pdf (on 10.10.2008), para. 21.

[66] Also: McIntyre, TJ and Scott, Colin, "Internet filtering: rhetoric, legitimacy, accountability and responsibility", in: Brownsword, Roger and Yeung, Karen (eds), *Regulating technologies: legal futures, regulatory frames and technological fixes*, Oxford, Hart Publishing, 2008, 122.

[67] Tambini, Damien and Forgan, Liz, "Content", Communications White Paper, retrieved from http://www.communicationswhitepaper.gov.uk/cwp_consultation/contentregulation.pdf (18.12.2003, no longer available); Livingstone, Sonia and Haddon, Leslie, *EU Kids Online: Final report*, 2009, retrieved from http://www.lse.ac.uk/collections/EUKidsOnline/Reports/EUKidsOnlineFinalReport.pdf (on 21.01.2010): "*Self-regulatory provision in improving children's safety online is to be welcomed and supported, although it is not always transparent or independently evaluated*".

[68] It should be noted that awareness of the importance of complying with such guarantees, especially when fundamental rights are at stake, does exist, also within the industry. In

the Council of Europe Guidelines which specify that ISPs providing hosting, applications and content should "*[m]ake sure that any filtering or blocking of services carried out is legitimate, proportional and transparent to [their] customers*".[69] Furthermore, they should

> *inform [their] customers of any filtering or blocking software installed on [their] servers that may lead to a removal or inaccessibility of content as well as the nature of filtering that takes place (form of filtering, general criteria used to filter, reasons for applying filters).*[70]

Concluding remark – Given the dangers of private censorship, self-regulatory schemes in which only private actors are in control of removing, filtering or blocking content are not ideal to protect minors from harmful content. Especially with respect to such a delicate normative goal, balanced co-regulatory schemes, in which the government,[71] and hence, the public interest, is represented to a greater extent, might be more suitable.

A.6. *Freedom of expression and technology*

Concerns regarding the use of technology – Linked to the previous issue are the difficulties that can arise with respect to the use of technology and freedom of expression. Although technology has often been hailed as the answer to anxiety regarding minors' exposure to harmful content (*supra*), significant concerns related to the protection of freedom of expression, for

---

this context we can refer to the 'Global Network Initiative', a multi-stakeholder group of companies, civil society organizations (including human rights and press freedom groups), investors and academics, who drafted a number of principles and implementation guidelines on making sure that the rights to freedom of expression and privacy are respected within the ICT sector. For more information, cf. Global Network Initiative, Core commitments, retrieved from http://www.globalnetworkinitiative.org/index.php (on 28.05.2009).

[69] Council of Europe, Human rights guidelines for Internet Service Providers – Developed by the Council of Europe in co-operation with the European Internet Service Providers Association (EuroISPA), July 2008, retrieved from http://www.coe.int/t/dghl/standardsetting/media/Doc/H-Inf(2008)009_en.pdf (on 10.10.2008), para. 20.

[70] Council of Europe, Human rights guidelines for Internet Service Providers – Developed by the Council of Europe in co-operation with the European Internet Service Providers Association (EuroISPA), July 2008, retrieved from http://www.coe.int/t/dghl/standardsetting/media/Doc/H-Inf(2008)009_en.pdf (on 10.10.2008), para. 20.

[71] Without overlooking, of course, the requirements of article 10 para. 2 ECHR with respect to restrictions imposed on the freedom of expression by public authorities.

adults as well as children, can be identified. This is especially the case with respect to filtering. As the Council of Europe put it:

> *Noting that the voluntary and responsible use of Internet filters (products, systems and measures to block or filter Internet content) can promote confidence and security on the Internet for users, in particular children and young people, while also aware that the use of such filters can impact on the right to freedom of expression and information, as protected by Article 10 of the European Convention on Human Rights.*[72]

Filtering – The use of filters restricts access to certain content, such as material considered harmful to minors. Such filters, however, give rise to a number of free speech concerns.

A first issue concerning filtering, which is linked with the previous section regarding private censorship, relates to the filtering process: who is in control of this process, and which criteria are used? In order to uphold a high level of freedom of expression, it is necessary, first, that the user (parent or child) knows that content is being filtered, second, that the organisation in charge of the filtering (for instance, a private company) uses transparent methods to filter content (*supra*), third, that the criteria used to classify content as harmful are made public to the user, and finally, that there is a procedure which allows wrongfully filtered content to be accessed.[73] If these requirements are not respected, the threat of arbitrary censorship lurks around the corner.[74]

Second, as was mentioned *supra* (Part 1, Chapter 2), filters have often been found to be over- or under-inclusive.[75] McIntyre and Scott note

---

[72] Council of Europe (Committee of Ministers), Recommendation CM/Rec(2008)6 on measures to promote the respect for freedom of expression and information with regard to Internet filters, 26.03.2008, retrieved from https://wcd.coe.int/ViewDoc.jsp?Ref=CM/Rec(2008)6&Language=lanEnglish&Ver=original&BackColorInternet=9999CC&BackColorIntranet=FFBB55&BackColorLogged=FFAC75 (on 31.03.2008).

[73] Council of Europe (Committee of Ministers), Recommendation CM/Rec(2008)6 on measures to promote the respect for freedom of expression and information with regard to Internet filters, 26.03.2008, retrieved from https://wcd.coe.int/ViewDoc.jsp?Ref=CM/Rec(2008)6&Language=lanEnglish&Ver=original&BackColorInternet=9999CC&BackColorIntranet=FFBB55&BackColorLogged=FFAC75 (on 31.03.2008), Appendix to Recommendation CM/Rec (2008) 6: Guidelines. Also: McIntyre, TJ and Scott, Colin, "Internet filtering: rhetoric, legitimacy, accountability and responsibility", in: Brownsword, Roger and Yeung, Karen (eds), *Regulating technologies: legal futures, regulatory frames and technological fixes*, Oxford, Hart Publishing, 2008, 117–120.

[74] Akdeniz, Yaman, "Who watches the watchmen? The role of filtering software in Internet content regulaticon", in: Möller, Christian and Amouroux, Arnaud (eds), *The media freedom Internet cookbook*, Vienna, OSCE, retrieved from http://www.osce.org/publications/rfm/2004/12/12239_89_en.pdf (on 29.02.2008), 110.

[75] Akdeniz, Yaman, "Who watches the watchmen? The role of filtering software in Internet content regulation", in: Möller, Christian and Amouroux, Arnaud (eds), *The media freedom*

in this respect that since filters are applied automatically, without human intervention, "*[t]here is no scope for argument, no exercise of discretion and (depending on the code) all users are treated alike*".[76] They argue that this leads to a disproportional 'all or nothing approach' (for instance, when an entire website is blocked because of offending material on one page, or, as we mentioned above, by blocking everything related to 'breasts', including valuable information about 'breast cancer').[77] Such an approach may pose legitimacy problems, since conduct is inhibited "*beyond what was intended*",[78] and, moreover, has a significant impact on the freedom of expression of the child. In this context, the Council of Europe recently encouraged Member States to cooperate with the private sector and civil society in order to create 'intelligent filters' that "*take more account of the context in which the information is provided (for example by differentiating between harmful content itself and unproblematic references to it, such as may be found on scientific websites)*".[79] If, on the other hand, filters are under-inclusive, they do not function effectively and will not achieve their goal, i.e., ensuring that children are not confronted with harmful material.

Third, attention must be drawn to the fact that as well as protecting minors, the freedom of expression of adults needs to be respected as well. This raises questions as to who should choose to use a filtering system with respect to harmful content,[80] and at what level such a system should

Internet cookbook, Vienna, OSCE, retrieved from http://www.osce.org/publications/rfm/2004/12/12239_89_en.pdf (on 29.02.2008), 108–109.

[76] McIntyre, TJ and Scott, Colin, "Internet filtering: rhetoric, legitimacy, accountability and responsibility", in: Brownsword, Roger and Yeung, Karen (eds), *Regulating technologies: legal futures, regulatory frames and technological fixes*, Oxford, Hart Publishing, 2008, 115.

[77] McIntyre, TJ and Scott, Colin, "Internet filtering: rhetoric, legitimacy, accountability and responsibility", in: Brownsword, Roger and Yeung, Karen (eds), *Regulating technologies: legal futures, regulatory frames and technological fixes*, Oxford, Hart Publishing, 2008, 115.

[78] McIntyre, TJ and Scott, Colin, "Internet filtering: rhetoric, legitimacy, accountability and responsibility", in: Brownsword, Roger and Yeung, Karen (eds), *Regulating technologies: legal futures, regulatory frames and technological fixes*, Oxford, Hart Publishing, 2008, 117.

[79] Council of Europe (Committee of Ministers), Recommendation CM/Rec(2008)6 on measures to promote the respect for freedom of expression and information with regard to Internet filters, 26.03.2008, retrieved from https://wcd.coe.int/ViewDoc.jsp?Ref=CM/Rec(2008)6&Language=lanEnglish&Ver=original&BackColorInternet=9999CC&BackColorIntranet=FFBB55&BackColorLogged=FFAC75 (on 31.03.2008), Appendix to Recommendation CM/Rec (2008) 6: Guidelines.

[80] It might be useful to note that, according to the Council of Europe, nationwide filtering measures could be allowed for illegal content (child pornography might be an example), again if certain conditions are fulfilled. Not only should such measures comply with article 10 para. 2 ECHR, but they should also concern specific and clearly identifiable content, a competent national authority should have taken a decision on the illegality of the content,

operate. In our opinion, in order to safeguard the right to freedom of expression, users should be allowed to apply filters on a voluntary basis,[81] since filtering interferes to a significant extent with the free flow of content. Setting up filtering systems, aimed at harmful content, at server level, with no choice for the user to apply this filter, is unacceptable. Filters should be operated at user level, or if they are set up at server level,[82] users should be able to decide freely whether they want to apply them and should have the option to configure the filters to their preferences. Governments, on the other hand, should promote, rather than mandate and enforce the use of filters aimed at harmful content.[83]

Concluding remark – The use of technology, such as content filters, to protect minors from harmful material can be valuable and empower users, provided that the use of the technological tool in question is transparent,

---

and the decision can be reviewed by an independent and impartial tribunal or regulatory body. Cf. Council of Europe (Committee of Ministers), Recommendation CM/Rec(2008)6 on measures to promote the respect for freedom of expression and information with regard to Internet filters, 26.03.2008, retrieved from https://wcd.coe.int/ViewDoc.jsp?Ref=CM/Rec(2008)6&Language=lanEnglish&Ver=original&BackColorInternet=9999CC&BackColorIntranet=FFBB55&BackColorLogged=FFAC75 (on 31.03.2008), Appendix to Recommendation CM/Rec (2008) 6: Guidelines.

81 Cf. also: The organization for security and co-operation in Europe and Reporters sans Frontières, Joint declaration on guaranteeing media freedom on the Internet, 17–18.06.2005, retrieved from https://www.osce.org/documents/rfm/2005/06/15239_en.pdf (on 09.09.2008); Council of Europe (Committee of Ministers), Recommendation Rec(2001)8 on self-regulation concerning cyber content (self-regulation and user protection against illegal or harmful content on new communications and information services), 05.09.2001, retrieved from https://wcd.coe.int/ViewDoc.jsp?id=220387&Site=COE&BackColorInternet=DBDCF2&BackColorIntranet=FDC864&BackColorLogged=FDC864 (on 24.04.2007); UN Special Rapporteur on Freedom of Opinion and Expression, the OSCE Representative on Freedom of the Media and the OAS Special Rapporteur on Freedom of Expression, Joint declaration: International mechanisms for promoting freedom of expression, 21.12.2005, retrieved from http://www.osce.org/documents/rfm/2005/12/18636_en.pdf (on 09.09.2008), 1–2.

82 For more information on filtering at ISP level: cf. Australian Computer Society, Technical observations on ISP based filtering of the Internet, 2009, retrieved from https://www.acs.org.au/attachments/2009/ispfilteringoct09.pdf (on 21.02.2009).

83 Möller, Christian and Amouroux, Arnaud (eds), *The media freedom Internet cookbook*, Vienna, OSCE, 2004, retrieved from http://www.osce.org/publications/rfm/2004/12/12239_89_en.pdf (on 29.02.2008), 19; Akdeniz, Yaman, "Who watches the watchmen? The role of filtering software in Internet content regulation", in: Möller, Christian and Amouroux, Arnaud (eds), *The media freedom Internet cookbook*, Vienna, OSCE, retrieved from http://www.osce.org/publications/rfm/2004/12/12239_89_en.pdf (on 29.02.2008), 114.

effective, proportional and legitimate.[84] Any use of filtering systems by public authorities, or self- or co-regulatory bodies with a similar status (cf. *supra*), must adhere to article 10 para. 2 ECHR. In other words, the use of these filtering systems will need to be prescribed by law, have a legitimate aim, and be necessary in a democratic society.

A.7. *Concluding remarks*

In the previous paragraphs, the main difficulties regarding the protection of the freedom of expression (of children as well as adults) when ARIs are used were discussed.

First, we focused on the question whether article 10 ECHR is applicable when the infringement is committed by a self-regulatory or co-regulatory body (as opposed to a 'public authority'). Two scenarios were touched upon. On the one hand, we observed that, in certain circumstances, depending in particular on the level of government involvement, a co-regulatory body might be considered a 'public authority' and, hence, article 10 ECHR could be applied. On the other hand, if this were not the case, for instance, because the level of government involvement is not high enough, we examined whether article 10 ECHR can also be applied between individuals. We found that, according to the – rather vague – 'horizontal effect' theory, where national law accepts the direct effect of the Convention articles, individuals can, in certain circumstances, invoke article 10 ECHR before the national courts to challenge other individuals. Moreover, even when this is not the case, the European Court of Human Rights has judged that, again in certain circumstances, a positive obligation may rest on public authorities to guarantee that the freedom of expression of their citizens is not infringed upon by private actors. We can thus conclude that, depending on the concrete structure of a given ARI, it is certainly not ruled out from the start that article 10 ECHR is not applicable, and, hence, any restriction on the freedom of expression imposed by a self- or co-regulatory body will need to fulfill the requirements included in article 10 para. 2 ECHR.

Second, we considered these requirements imposed by article 10 para. 2 ECHR. While the second condition, i.e., a legitimate aim, will, in the area of the protection of minors against harmful content, in all probability, not pose significant problems, the first and third condition could prove challenging

[84] Council of Europe (Committee of Ministers), Recommendation CM/Rec(2008)6 on measures to promote the respect for freedom of expression and information with regard to Internet filters, 26.03.2008, retrieved from https://wcd.coe.int/ViewDoc.jsp?Ref=CM/Rec(2008)6&Language=lanEnglish&Ver=original&BackColorInternet=9999CC&BackColorIntranet=FFBB55&BackColorLogged=FFAC75 (on 31.03.2008), Appendix to Recommendation CM/Rec (2008) 6: Guidelines.

with respect to the use of ARIs. As for the first condition, measures imposed by self- or co-regulatory bodies will need to be considered to have a 'law-like' status in order to adhere to the first condition (prescription by law). Therefore, the measures need to be accessible and foreseeable. Furthermore, we found that the European Court of Human Rights requires a rather high level of government involvement in order for measures to be qualified as equivalent to law. Hence, in our view, pure self-regulatory measures will not be adequate. Measures springing from a co-regulatory structure, however, depending on the circumstances (for instance, the degree of control the government retains) may be considered acceptable. As for the third condition, measures that are part of an alternative regulatory scheme will need to be 'necessary in a democratic society', and, thus proportional. Again, this will depend on the actual rationale, structure and implementation of the measures in question. With respect to this condition in particular, a balancing test will be carried out. The different interests at stake – the protection of minors against harmful content, and the protection of the freedom of expression of adults – will thus need to be weighed.

Finally, we addressed the difficulties linked to the freedom of expression that may arise, first, with respect to self-regulatory schemes and, second, with respect to technology. With regard to the former issue, i.e., the involvement of private actors in the restriction of access to content which may be considered harmful to children, we noted the danger of private censorship. It has been frequently argued that decisions on whether content can be considered harmful or illegal should not be left to private actors. This is especially relevant with respect to the issue of protecting minors against harmful content, since the line between harmful, but legal, and illegal content can be very fine. We concluded that ARIs in which private actors are solely in control of access to content may pose a real danger to the protection of the freedom of expression. Hence, in our view, co-regulatory schemes in which certain guarantees are provided by a state body might be more appropriate in the delicate field of protection of minors. Finally, we broached the subject of the impact of the use of technology on the freedom of expression. We chose to focus on the use of filtering, since this technological tool has been often put forward as especially useful to protect minors from being exposed to harmful material. The use of filtering tools is certainly not unproblematic with respect to children's as well as adults' right to freedom of expression. Again, we noted several issues of concern: first, the danger of arbitrary censorship, second, the risk of over- and under-inclusiveness, and finally, the unacceptability of using filters at a level which is not the user level. We concluded that, in any case, when the use of technological tools, which restrict access to content, is imposed by public authorities or self- or co-regulatory bodies with the same status, this should be done in a proportional manner, and moreover, with respect to the second paragraph of article 10 ECHR.

B. *Privacy*

Issues of interest – Without a doubt, children's 'digital' privacy is a relevant[85] – and often problematic – issue. Given the fact that this issue is very broad – in fact, several separate theses could be dedicated to this topic – here we only briefly touch upon a few points of interest. As mentioned in the previous chapter, it is possible that ARIs do not sufficiently take children's privacy into account. However, given that the right to privacy is a fundamental right included in the ECHR as well as in specific legislation (*supra*), all self- or co-regulatory mechanisms, possibly functioning with the help of technological tools, and all actors involved with these mechanisms, need to respect all relevant legal provisions.[86] We would like to emphasise that we have chosen to approach this issue from the point of view of the user, *in casu* the child. Privacy concerns with respect to other actors (for instance, content providers, which we briefly touched upon in the previous chapter in the context of the liability regime) remain outside of the scope of the present analysis.

B.1. *General principle*

Fundamental right to privacy – As mentioned in the previous chapter, the right to privacy has been included in a number of legal provisions. For children's privacy, the cornerstone article is article 16 UNCRC. Other sources are article 8 ECHR and specific EU directives, such as the Data Protection Directive and the Directive on Privacy and Electronic Communications.[87]

---

[85] Cf. Article 29 Data Protection Working Party, Opinion 2/2009 on the protection of children's personal data (General guidelines and the special case of schools), 11.02.2009, retrieved from http://ec.europa.eu/justice_home/fsj/privacy/docs/wpdocs/2009/wp160_en.pdf (on 18.05.2009), 5 ("*As a human being, the child has a right to privacy*"); Committee of Ministers, Declaration of the Committee of Ministers on protecting the dignity, security and privacy of children using the Internet, 20.02.2008, retrieved from https://wcd.coe.int/ViewDoc.jsp?Ref=Decl(20.02.2008)&Language=lanEnglish&Ver=0001&BackColorInternet=9999CC&BackColorIntranet=FFBB55&BackColorLogged=FFAC75 (on 19.09.2008). See also: *supra*: Part 2, Chapter 1.

[86] With respect to ISPs, cf. Council of Europe, Human rights guidelines for Internet Service Providers – Developed by the Council of Europe in co-operation with the European Internet Service Providers Association (EuroISPA), July 2008, retrieved from http://www.coe.int/t/dghl/standardsetting/media/Doc/H-Inf(2008)009_en.pdf (on 10.10.2008), paras 27–33.

[87] Cf. *supra*, Part 2, Chapter 1.

B.2. *Privacy and alternative regulatory instruments*

Article 8 ECHR and ARIs – At the European level, one of the most important foundations for the right to privacy is article 8 ECHR. This article is similar to article 10 in that its second paragraph also offers 'public authorities' the possibility of limiting the basic right to privacy, provided that certain conditions are fulfilled (i.e., such measures need to be in accordance with the law and necessary in a democratic society, as well as pursuing a legitimate interest, such as the protection of health or morals).[88] In fact, when it comes to the relationship between ARIs and privacy, the questions that are raised are rather similar to the ones which surfaced with respect to article 10 ECHR: first, can article 8 ECHR be applied to acts of private actors (who are involved in the functioning of ARIs aimed at protecting minors against harmful content), and, second, how is the reference to 'the law' (as in the first condition of article 8 para. 2 ECHR) interpreted?

Acts of private actors – With respect to the first question, it can be observed that in the context of article 8 ECHR, the European Court of Human Rights has often referred to positive obligations of the state to protect an individual's privacy.[89] In *X. and Y. v. the Netherlands*, for instance, the Court stated:

> *The Court recalls that although the object of Article 8 (art. 8) is essentially that of protecting the individual against arbitrary interference by the public authorities, it does not merely compel the State to abstain from such interference: in addition to this primarily negative undertaking, there may be positive obligations inherent in an effective respect for private or family life (see the Airey judgment of*

[88] For more details on the two-stage test incorporated in article 8 ECHR, cf. Kilkelly, Ursula, *The right to respect for private and family life – A guide to the implementation of Article 8 of the European Convention on Human Rights (Human Rights Handbook, no. 1)*, Strasbourg, Council of Europe, 2001, 8 *et seq.*

[89] van Dijk, Pieter, van Hoof, Fried, van Rijn, Arjen and Zwaak, Leo (eds), *Theory and practice of the European Convention on Human Rights*, Antwerpen, Intersentia, 2006, 739; Clapham, Andrew, "The 'Drittwirkung' of the Convention", in: MacDonald, Ronald Saint John, Matscher, Franz and Petzold, Herbert, *The European system for the protection of human rights*, Dordrecht, Martinus Nijhoff Publishers, 1993, 181. See also: Kilkelly, Ursula, *The right to respect for private and family life – A guide to the implementation of Article 8 of the European Convention on Human Rights (Human Rights Handbook, no. 1)*, Strasbourg, Council of Europe, 2001, 20: "*Thus, as well as the negative obligation not to interfere arbitrarily with a person's family and private life, home and correspondence, the State may also have to act affirmatively to respect the wide of personal interests set out in the provision*".

> *9 October 1979, Series A no. 32, p. 17, para. 32). These obligations may involve the adoption of measures designed to secure respect for private life even in the sphere of the relations of individuals between themselves.*[90]

The actual adoption of such measures by the state depends on an assessment of the reasonable balance that needs to be reached between the competing interests of the individual and the community, and on the margin of appreciation of the state.[91] In a recent case, *K.U. v. Finland*,[92] the European Court of Human Rights specified, for instance, that notwithstanding this margin of appreciation, "*effective deterrence against grave acts, where fundamental values and essential aspects of private life are at stake, requires efficient criminal-law provisions*".[93] The case dealt with an advertisement on a dating site, placed by unknown persons, in the name of a 12-year-old boy without his knowledge. This advertisement included the age of the boy, a description of his physical characteristics, a link to his website which contained a picture and a telephone number, and a statement that he was seeking an intimate relationship with a boy.[94] At the time of the facts it was not possible according to Finnish legislation to obtain the identity of the person who placed the advertisement from the Internet provider.[95] The Court considered the applicability of article 8 ECHR indisputable,[96] and emphasised that "*[c]hildren and other vulnerable individuals are entitled to State protection, in the form of effective deterrence, from such grave types of interference with essential aspects of their private lives*".[97] The fact that no effective steps could be taken to identify and prosecute the person who placed the advertisement, and thus the failure by the Finnish government to fulfil its positive obligation to provide a framework of protection, led the Court to decide that article 8 ECHR had been violated.[98] Although the Court's decision has raised some controversy (*supra*), this case is interesting because it shows that the Court

---

[90] European Court of Human Rights, X. and Y. v. the Netherlands, 26.03.1985, para. 23.

[91] Kilkelly, Ursula, *The right to respect for private and family life – A guide to the implementation of Article 8 of the European Convention on Human Rights (Human Rights Handbook, no. 1)*, Strasbourg, Council of Europe, 2001, 21; van Dijk, Pieter, van Hoof, Fried, van Rijn, Arjen and Zwaak, Leo (eds), *Theory and practice of the European Convention on Human Rights*, Antwerpen, Intersentia, 2006, 740.

[92] Cf. also *supra*, Part 2, Chapter 1: Privacy and Indirect content regulation: liability of intermediaries.

[93] European Court of Human Rights, K.U. v. Finland, 02.12.2008, paras 42–43.

[94] European Court of Human Rights, K.U. v. Finland, 02.12.2008, para. 7.

[95] European Court of Human Rights, K.U. v. Finland, 02.12.2008, para. 40.

[96] European Court of Human Rights, K.U. v. Finland, 02.12.2008, para. 41.

[97] European Court of Human Rights, K.U. v. Finland, 02.12.2008, para. 46.

[98] European Court of Human Rights, K.U. v. Finland, 02.12.2008, paras 49–50.

takes into account the vulnerability of children and the existence of positive obligations when their privacy is interfered with.

We can conclude that, depending on the circumstances, a certain horizontal effect of article 8 ECHR is conceivable.[99]

IN ACCORDANCE WITH THE LAW – As to the second question, regarding the interpretation of the word 'law', the findings are quite similar to the ones related to article 10 ECHR: the interference in question "*must have a legal basis*", "*must be sufficiently precise and contain a measure of protection against arbitrariness by public authorities*", and must be "*foreseeable*".[100] Non-binding guidelines, for instance, are not considered sufficient.[101] Thus, again, the assessment of whether article 8 ECHR will be applicable with respect to restrictions imposed by self- or co-regulatory bodies will depend on the concrete circumstances of each case.

B.3. *Privacy and technology*

CHILDREN'S PRIVACY AND TECHNOLOGICAL TOOLS – The opposition between a child's best interest – for instance, to protect him or her from harmful content – and his or her privacy rights is an issue that is often raised when technological tools are used. In Part 1, Chapter 2, for instance, we noted the existence of parental monitoring and notification software. This software is often installed by parents who have their child's best interest in mind, i.e., to protect them from receiving unwanted content or from making too many personal details available; but at the same time, of course, this has an impact on their children's right to privacy. In this respect, we could also refer to article 8 ECHR which requires respect for an individual's correspondence as well. If it is assumed that parental monitoring software also keeps track of children's e-mails and msn-conversations – which could be interpreted as correspondence[102] – their right to uninterrupted and uncensored

---

[99] VAN DIJK, Pieter, VAN HOOF, Fried, VAN RIJN, Arjen and ZWAAK, Leo (eds), *Theory and practice of the European Convention on Human Rights*, Antwerpen, Intersentia, 2006, 743.

[100] KILKELLY, Ursula, *The right to respect for private and family life – A guide to the implementation of Article 8 of the European Convention on Human Rights (Human Rights Handbook, no. 1)*, Strasbourg, Council of Europe, 2001, 25.

[101] KILKELLY, Ursula, *The right to respect for private and family life – A guide to the implementation of Article 8 of the European Convention on Human Rights (Human Rights Handbook, no. 1)*, Strasbourg, Council of Europe, 2001, 25–26.

[102] KILKELLY, Ursula, *The right to respect for private and family life – A guide to the implementation of Article 8 of the European Convention on Human Rights (Human Rights Handbook, no. 1)*, Strasbourg, Council of Europe, 2001, 20.

communications with others[103] could be at stake.[104] With respect to content filtering and blocking systems, the right to privacy could also be at stake both for children and adults.[105] The European Data Protection Supervisor, for instance, pointed out that

> *filtering, especially in its most recent developments using identity management, can function on the basis of given criteria, including personal data such as the age of the individual connected to the network (to prevent access by adults or children to specified content), the content of the information and traffic data linked with the identity of the author of the information. Depending on the way this personal information will – automatically – be processed, the individuals concerned could face consequences with regard to their right to communicate online.*[106]

Hence, when using filtering and content blocking tools, the impact this has on individuals' privacy needs to be taken into account.[107] One important

---

[103] Kilkelly, Ursula, *The right to respect for private and family life – A guide to the implementation of Article 8 of the European Convention on Human Rights (Human Rights Handbook, no. 1)*, Strasbourg, Council of Europe, 2001, 19.

[104] Furthermore, although this might be one step too far, one could wonder whether content filtering and the tracking and monitoring of children's behaviour could be possibly put on the same footing as 'telephone tapping' or 'use of covert technological devices to intercept private communications', issues that have often been the subject of cases brought before the European Court of Human Rights under article 8 ECHR. Cf. Kilkelly, Ursula, *The right to respect for private and family life – A guide to the implementation of Article 8 of the European Convention on Human Rights (Human Rights Handbook, no. 1)*, Strasbourg, Council of Europe, 2001, 12.

[105] European Data Protection Supervisor, Opinion of the European Data Protection Supervisor on the proposal for a decision of the European Parliament and of the Council establishing a multiannual Community programme on protecting children using the Internet and other communication technologies, 23.06.2008, retrieved from http://www.edps.europa.eu/EDPSWEB/webdav/site/mySite/shared/Documents/Consultation/Opinions/2008/08-06-23_Children_Internet_EN.pdf (on 25.06.2008), 8: "*These actions should be developed without overlooking the fact that the protection of children takes place within an environment where the rights of others might be at stake*".

[106] European Data Protection Supervisor, Opinion of the European Data Protection Supervisor on the proposal for a decision of the European Parliament and of the Council establishing a multiannual Community programme on protecting children using the Internet and other communication technologies, 23.06.2008, retrieved from http://www.edps.europa.eu/EDPSWEB/webdav/site/mySite/shared/Documents/Consultation/Opinions/2008/08-06-23_Children_Internet_EN.pdf (on 25.06.2008), 6.

[107] European Data Protection Supervisor, Opinion of the European Data Protection Supervisor on the proposal for a decision of the European Parliament and of the Council establishing a multiannual Community programme on protecting children using the Internet and other communication technologies, 23.06.2008, retrieved from http://www.edps.europa.eu/EDPSWEB/webdav/site/mySite/shared/Documents/Consultation/Opinions/2008/08-06-23_Children_Internet_EN.pdf (on 25.06.2008), 8: "*Any initiative of collecting, blocking or reporting information should only be taken in the respect of the*

observation that needs to be made here relates to the relationships at stake in each particular case: technological tools can be used in private relationships, for instance, by parents to protect their children, as part of self- or co-regulatory strategies (with varying levels of government involvement), or as part of a government enforcement policy. It is important to know the nature of these relationships to assess the correct legal consequences.

ARTICLE 8 ECHR – Hence, in relationships between private individuals, for instance, article 8 ECHR will only be applicable if the Court accepts a certain horizontal effect. We can refer to the theory examined *supra* (cf. freedom of expression and horizontal effect). In this context, it is important to note that to fully exercise their rights, children often need to rely on legal representatives.[108] In most cases, children or minors will be represented by their parents or guardians (based also on article 8 ECHR on the respect for family life,[109] which encompasses a wide range of parental rights and responsibilities with respect to care and custody of minor children).[110] The European Court of Human Rights, however, has held that minors have the right to file a complaint in their own name without being represented, especially in cases where the relationship between the child and his or her parent or guardian is questioned.[111] Interestingly, with respect to children's privacy, the Article 29 Data Protection Working Party stated that

> *the representative's status [does not have] any absolute or unconditional priority over the child's – because the child's best interest can sometimes confer upon them rights relating to data protection which may override the wishes of parents or other legal representatives. Nor does the need for representation imply that children should not, from a certain age, be consulted on matters relating to them.*[112]

fundamental rights of all individuals involved and in compliance with the data protection legal framework".

[108] ARTICLE 29 DATA PROTECTION WORKING PARTY, Opinion 2/2009 on the protection of children's personal data (General guidelines and the special case of schools), 11.02.2009, retrieved from http://ec.europa.eu/justice_home/fsj/privacy/docs/wpdocs/2009/wp160_en.pdf (on 18.05.2009), 5.

[109] Article 8 para. 1 ECHR: "*Everyone has the right to respect for his private and family life, his home and his correspondence*".

[110] EUROPEAN COURT OF HUMAN RIGHTS, Nielsen v. Denmark, 28.11.1988, para. 61.

[111] VAN DIJK, Pieter, VAN HOOF, Fried, VAN RIJN, Arjen and ZWAAK, Leo (eds), *Theory and practice of the European Convention on Human Rights*, Antwerpen, Intersentia, 2006, 52; OVEY, Clare and WHITE, Robin, *Jacobs and White The European Convention on Human Rights*, Oxford, Oxford University Press, 2006, 483; VANDE LANOTTE, Johan and HAECK, Yves, *Handboek EVRM: Deel 1 Algemene beginselen* [*ECHR Handbook: Part 1 General principles*], Antwerpen, Intersentia, 2005, 495 [in Dutch].

[112] ARTICLE 29 DATA PROTECTION WORKING PARTY, Opinion 2/2009 on the protection of

In matters relating to privacy and the use of technological tools to protect minors, the interests of parents and children are sometimes incompatible. In such circumstances, much will depend on the age of the child in question. Tracking a six year old's Internet behaviour is quite different from monitoring a sixteen year old's e-mail correspondence. In each particular case the competing interests, i.e., the desire to protect a child from harmful content and the child's right to privacy, will therefore have to be balanced.

In cases where the use of technological tools is imposed by authorities or self- or co-regulatory bodies with a similar status, compliance with article 8 para. 2 ECHR is required.

EU LEGISLATION – In addition, specific legislation, such as the Data Protection Directive and the Directive on Privacy and Electronic Communications (*supra*, Part 2, Chapter 1)[113] will also need to be complied with. A detailed analysis of these directives, however, falls outside of the scope of this study.

CASE-STUDY: 'SAFER CHAT' – Privacy concerns can also arise with respect to age verification or identification mechanisms.[114] This was, for instance, the case with respect to the Belgian 'Safer Chat' case-study, already briefly described in Part 1, Chapter 2. 'Safer Chat' was an initiative of the government in cooperation with the Belgian Internet Service Providers Association. This public-private – or co-regulatory – partnership established a system that requires the use of a child's electronic identity card to gain access to a 'safe' chatroom ('safe' in this instance meaning that only children are present in this chatroom excluding adults with bad intentions). In order to verify the age of a person wanting to access a particular 'safe' chatroom, the National Registry identification number embedded in the electronic identity card was used.[115]

---

children's personal data (General guidelines and the special case of schools), 11.02.2009, retrieved from http://ec.europa.eu/justice_home/fsj/privacy/docs/wpdocs/2009/wp160_en.pdf (on 18.05.2009), 5.

[113] The scope of application as well as the key provisions of these directives were briefly clarified in the previous chapter.

[114] Cf. also: KILKELLY, Ursula, *The right to respect for private and family life – A guide to the implementation of Article 8 of the European Convention on Human Rights (Human Rights Handbook, no. 1)*, Strasbourg, Council of Europe, 2001, 13. Similar concerns have been voiced in the United States: THE NEW YORK TIMES (Brad STONE), Online age verification for children brings worries, retrieved from http://www.nytimes.com/2008/11/16/business/16ping.html?_r=1&scp=7&sq=children%20internet&st=cse (on 28.11.2008).

[115] COMMISSIE VOOR DE BESCHERMING VAN DE PERSOONLIJKE LEVENSSFEER [*COMMISSION FOR PRIVACY PROTECTION*], Advies met betrekking tot het ontwerp van koninklijk besluit betreffende het elektronisch identiteitsdocument voor Belgische kinderen onder de twaalf

In Belgium, the Federal Public Service for Information and Communication Technology (Fedict) requested and obtained authorisation from the Privacy Commission to use this National Registry number to verify the ages of children. The Commission decided that the purposes of the system submitted by Fedict, which reserves access to certain Internet services for persons of a certain age, were *specified, explicit and legitimate* (as required by article 4, para. 1, 2° Act on the processing of personal data, which transposes the Data Protection Directive). Contributing to this decision was the fact that the Commission considered 'enabling safe internet use for minors' a task of public interest. Furthermore, the Commission deemed the use of the National Registry number *proportional* (as required by article 4, para. 1, 3° Act on the processing of personal data). In our view, it could be argued, however, that the use of children's National Registry identification numbers is too intrusive (and therefore *not* proportional). In the regime proposed by Fedict, children would be identifiable every time they log onto a certain chatroom, due to the fact that when using the electronic identity card not only the National Registry number (which reveals the exact date of birth and the sex), but also the name of the child is transmitted. This contradicts the fact that, actually, only one attribute of their identity, i.e., that they are under a certain age, is needed to grant access to the 'safe' chatroom. In 2001, the Belgian Privacy Commission did stress the importance of using means to control age that intrude as little as possible into someone's private sphere in their Recommendation on the protection of privacy of minors on the Internet.[116] In the Privacy Commission's decision related to 'Safer Chat', however, little of this opinion seemed to be applied. Keeping article 6 of the Data Protection Directive (*supra*, Part 2, Chapter 1) in mind, in our view, age verification mechanisms should identify a child as 'a child', and not as a particular child.[117] However, at the moment, the Belgian e-ID card does not offer the possibility

jaar [*Recommendation regarding the proposal for Royal Decree with respect to the electronic identity document for Belgian children under the age of twelve*], 06.09.2006, retrieved from http://www.privacycommission.be/nl/docs/Commission/2006/advies_33_2006.pdf (on 02.10.2006) [in Dutch].

[116] Commissie voor de bescherming van de persoonlijke levenssfeer [*Commission for privacy protection*], Advies uit eigen beweging betreffende de bescherming van de persoonlijke levenssfeer van minderjarigen op het Internet [*Recommendation on the protection of privacy of minors on the Internet*], 16.09.2002, retrieved from http://www.internet-observatory.be/internet_observatory/pdf/advice_privacy_nl.pdf (on 14.10.2008) [in Dutch].

[117] Cf. also: PCMLP, Parental control in a converged communications environment: Self-regulation, technical devices and meta-information (Final report for The DVB Regulatory Group), 2000, retrieved from http://ec.europa.eu/comm/avpolicy/docs/reg/minors/dvb-group.pdf (on 11.06.2008), 29.

to select only one attribute of someone's identity, which is probably the reason why the Privacy Commission relented and, valuing the protection of children in these safer chatrooms higher than their privacy, allowed the use of National Registry numbers. It should be noted, however, that the system never was successful and that, apparently, it is no longer operational.[118]

B.4. *Concluding remarks*

Privacy issues – Although we would like to stress again that issues regarding privacy have only been briefly touched upon in this study, we have tried to indicate a number of problems that could arise in the relationship between the right to privacy and the use of ARIs, with or without the use of technological tools.

Article 8 ECHR – We noted that with respect to article 8 ECHR – the cornerstone of the right to privacy at the European level – issues similar to those regarding article 10 ECHR could be detected (*supra*). Article 8 ECHR prevents public authorities from interfering with their citizens' right to privacy, unless the three conditions of its second paragraph are fulfilled. Again, in the case of self- and co-regulatory bodies, the concrete circumstances will need to be examined in order to decide whether the article is applicable. In our opinion, however, this will be more likely if there is a certain level of government involvement.

Technological tools – Furthermore, from the 'Safer Chat' case-study, we can deduce that initiatives that aim to protect minors in the digital environment and which use technological tools must be structured in a careful manner, and take privacy rights into account. Although the balance that needs to be sought is indeed a very delicate one, it is nevertheless important to be aware of the different rights that are at stake since, all too often, children's right to privacy is overlooked.

---

[118] ZDNet.be (Pieterjan Van Leemputten), Veilige kinderchatbox volledig geflopt [*Safe children's chat box flopped completely*], 24.06.2008, retrieved from http://www.zdnet.be/news.cfm?id=87256 (on 16.12.2008) [in Dutch]. References to the system, however, can still be found on other websites, such as for instance: http://www.kidcity.be/page.php?house=kidclub&category=saferchat_desc&id=17180&par=26551 (last retrieved on 16.12.2008), but it is not clear whether the system is actually used.

C. *Right to a fair trial*

C.1. *General principle and delineation*

Right to a fair trial – In the previous chapter we noted that aside from 'substantive rights', such as freedom of expression and privacy, certain procedural rights also need to be respected. A first right that might be of importance to the use of ARIs is the right to a fair trial included in article 6 ECHR, the first paragraph of which stipulates that "*[i]n the determination of his civil rights and obligations or of any criminal charge against him, everyone is entitled to a fair and public hearing within a reasonable time by an independent and impartial tribunal established by law*".

Delineation – Article 6 ECHR is drawn up in an elaborate manner (*supra*) and contains many different elements, not all of which relevant to our research subject. We have thus opted to focus on a limited number of aspects, i.e., the scope of application concerning civil rights, requirements related to the notion 'tribunal' and its independence and impartiality, and the fairness and publicness of a hearing. We have chosen not to examine the requirements related to criminal charges in greater detail, since matters related to harmful content will not often give rise to such charges.[119]

C.2. *Scope of application*

Interpretation of 'civil rights' – First of all, it is necessary to determine whether ARIs in the field of the protection of minors against harmful content can fall within the scope of application of article 6 ECHR. This article stipulates that the right to a fair trial can be invoked by an individual "*in the determination of his civil rights and obligations*" ("*or of any criminal charge against him*"). The Court has never provided an abstract definition of which rights it considers to fall under the notion 'civil rights and obligations',[120] but it has constructed an autonomous Convention meaning of the notion on a case-by-case basis.[121] In *Benthem v. the Netherlands*, for instance, the Court

[119] As was mentioned *supra*, this, of course, depends on the national legislation. If legislation criminalises the distribution of content harmful to minors, a person may face a criminal charge when he distributes such content.

[120] European Court of Human Rights, Benthem v. the Netherlands, 23.10.1985; para. 35.

[121] Lemmens, Paul, Geschillen over burgerlijke rechten en verplichtingen: het toepassingsgebied van de artikelen 6, lid 1, van het Europees Verdrag over de rechten van de mens en 14, lid 1, van het Internationaal Verdrag inzake burgerrechten en politieke rechten [*Disputes over civil rights and obligations: the scope of application of the articles 6, para. 1, of*

has clarified that the decisive factor is the character of the right. The Court stated:

> *Article 6 (art. 6) does not cover only "private-law disputes in the traditional sense, that is disputes between individuals or between an individual and the State to the extent that the latter had been acting as a private person, subject to private law," and not "in its sovereign capacity" [...]. Accordingly, "the character of the legislation which governs how the matter is to be determined... and that of the authority which is invested with jurisdiction in the matter... are... of little consequence": the latter may be an "ordinary court, [an] administrative body, etc." [...]. "Only the character of the right at issue is relevant" [...].*[122]

Lemmens has argued that the notion 'civil rights' should not be interpreted restrictively.[123]

Convention rights? – It has been assumed that substantive Convention rights, such as the rights to freedom of expression and privacy, may fall within the scope of article 6 ECHR.[124] Hence, when ARIs lead to an interference with an individual's right to freedom of expression or privacy and

---

the European Convention on human rights and 14, para. 1, of the International Covenant on Civil and Political Rights], PhD Thesis (promotor: Prof. dr. Jan De Meyer), 1987, 17 and 130–133 [in Dutch]; Kuijer, Martin, *The blindfold of Lady Justice: Judicial independence and impartiality in light of the requirements of article 6 ECHR*, Leiden, E.M. Meijers Instituut, 2004, 118; Harris, David, O'Boyle, Michael, Warbrick, Colin, Bates, Ed et al. (eds), *Harris, O'Boyle and Warbrick Law of the European Convention on human rights*, Oxford, Oxford University Press, 2009, 212. Also: European Court of Human Rights, König v. Germany, 28.06.1978, para. 88.

122 European Court of Human Rights, Benthem v. the Netherlands, 23.10.1985; para. 34.

123 Lemmens, Paul, Geschillen over burgerlijke rechten en verplichtingen: het toepassingsgebied van de artikelen 6, lid 1, van het Europees Verdrag over de rechten van de mens en 14, lid 1, van het Internationaal Verdrag inzake burgerrechten en politieke rechten [*Disputes over civil rights and obligations: the scope of application of the articles 6, para. 1, of the European Convention on human rights and 14, para. 1, of the International Covenant on Civil and Political Rights*], PhD Thesis (promotor: Prof. dr. Jan De Meyer), 1987, 204 [in Dutch].

124 Harris, David, O'Boyle, Michael, Warbrick, Colin, Bates, Ed et al. (eds), *Harris, O'Boyle and Warbrick Law of the European Convention on human rights*, Oxford, Oxford University Press, 2009, 211 and 217–218; Kuijer, Martin, *The blindfold of Lady Justice: Judicial independence and impartiality in light of the requirements of article 6 ECHR*, Leiden, E.M. Meijers Instituut, 2004, 538; Lemmens, Paul, Geschillen over burgerlijke rechten en verplichtingen: het toepassingsgebied van de artikelen 6, lid 1, van het Europees Verdrag over de rechten van de mens en 14, lid 1, van het Internationaal Verdrag inzake burgerrechten en politieke rechten [*Disputes over civil rights and obligations: the scope of application of the articles 6, para. 1, of the European Convention on human rights and 14, para. 1, of the International Covenant on Civil and Political Rights*], PhD Thesis (promotor: Prof. dr. Jan De Meyer), 1987, 178 [in Dutch].

moreover to a dispute concerning this interference,[125] article 6 ECHR may come into play.

C.3. *The notion 'tribunal established by law'*

TRIBUNAL – When it has been established that article 6 ECHR is applicable, it is necessary to examine whether recourse to an 'alternative regulatory body' which exercises functions which are determinative of civil rights,[126] might be considered as satisfying the requirement of a trial before a 'tribunal established by law'. The European Court of Human Rights described a 'tribunal' as being

> *characterised in the substantive sense of the term by its judicial function, that is to say determining matters within its competence on the basis of rules of law and after proceedings conducted in a prescribed manner. It must also satisfy a series of further requirements – independence, in particular of the executive; impartiality; duration of its members' terms of office; guarantees afforded by its procedure – several of which appear in the text of Article 6 § 1.*[127]

Tribunals must be capable to take legally binding decisions, and its members should usually be professional judges.[128] The latter requirement, however, is not an absolute one.[129] In addition, the definition put forward by the Court also points to the requirements of independence and impartiality. Hence, to determine whether a body can be considered a 'tribunal', which would then need to meet the requirements of independence and impartiality, the Court already assesses the independent and impartial character of the body.[130]

---

[125] Cf. *supra*, Part 2, Chapter 1, where it was noted that article 6 ECHR is only applicable if there is a (real and serious) dispute concerning a right or obligation.

[126] MOLE, Nuala and HARBY, Catharina, *The right to a fair trial: a guide to the implementation of Article 6 of the European Convention on Human Rights (Human rights handbooks, No. 3)*, Strasbourg, Council of Europe, 2006, 30.

[127] EUROPEAN COURT OF HUMAN RIGHTS, Cyprus v. Turkey, 10.05.2001, para. 233.

[128] HARRIS, David, O'BOYLE, Michael, WARBRICK, Colin, BATES, Ed et al. (eds), *Harris, O'Boyle and Warbrick Law of the European Convention on human rights*, Oxford, Oxford University Press, 2009, 286.

[129] HARRIS, David, O'BOYLE, Michael, WARBRICK, Colin, BATES, Ed et al. (eds), *Harris, O'Boyle and Warbrick Law of the European Convention on human rights*, Oxford, Oxford University Press, 2009, 286.

[130] KUIJER notes that "*[t]he (slightly bizarre) consequence thereof is that the requirements of independence and impartiality are already of some importance within the framework of determination whether or not a national authority is a 'tribunal' within the meaning of Article 6 ECHR*": KUIJER, Martin, *The blindfold of Lady Justice: Judicial independence and impartiality in light of the requirements of article 6 ECHR*, Leiden, E.M. Meijers Instituut, 2004, 177.

ESTABLISHED BY LAW – Article 6 para. 1 ECHR also refers to the fact that a tribunal needs to be "*established by law*". This requirement finds its origin in the idea that the organisation of the judiciary should not be left to the executive, but should be based on a law, issued by the legislature.[131] However, it has been clarified that being 'established by law' "*does not mean that every detail of the court system must be spelt out in legislation: provided that the basic rules concerning its organization and jurisdiction are set out by legislation, particular matters may be left to the executive acting by way of delegated legislation and subject to judicial review to prevent illegal or arbitrary action*".[132] KUIJER notes that in order to establish whether a tribunal has been established by law, the interpretation of the Court of the notion 'prescribed by law' in the second paragraph of articles 8 and 10 ECHR (*supra*) has also been taken into account.[133]

ALTERNATIVE REGULATORY BODIES AS TRIBUNALS? – Whether or not an alternative regulatory body will satisfy these requirements will of course depend on the exact structure and function of the body, and the procedural guarantees it provides. It has been argued that the Court's requirements are relatively strict.[134] Hence, it can be assumed that self-regulatory bodies will not meet the standards put forward by the Court and that it is doubtful whether co-regulatory bodies could be classified as 'tribunals'. If, however, a co-regulatory body would live up to the standards upheld by the Court, the body in question needs to fulfil all procedural requirements put forward by article 6 ECHR.[135]

DOCTRINE OF FULL REVIEW – If a dispute over a civil right occurs and the alternative regulatory body does not meet the requirements of article 6

---

131 KUIJER, Martin, *The blindfold of Lady Justice: Judicial independence and impartiality in light of the requirements of article 6 ECHR*, Leiden, E.M. Meijers Instituut, 2004, 183; VAN DIJK, Pieter, VAN HOOF, Fried, VAN RIJN, Arjen and ZWAAK, Leo (eds), *Theory and practice of the European Convention on Human Rights*, Antwerpen, Intersentia, 2006, 623.

132 HARRIS, David, O'BOYLE, Michael, WARBRICK, Colin, BATES, Ed et al. (eds), *Harris, O'Boyle and Warbrick Law of the European Convention on human rights*, Oxford, Oxford University Press, 2009, 297.

133 KUIJER, Martin, *The blindfold of Lady Justice: Judicial independence and impartiality in light of the requirements of article 6 ECHR*, Leiden, E.M. Meijers Instituut, 2004, 185–186.

134 KUIJER, Martin, *The blindfold of Lady Justice: Judicial independence and impartiality in light of the requirements of article 6 ECHR*, Leiden, E.M. Meijers Instituut, 2004, 175.

135 MOLE, Nuala and HARBY, Catharina, *The right to a fair trial: a guide to the implementation of Article 6 of the European Convention on Human Rights (Human rights handbooks, No. 3)*, Strasbourg, Council of Europe, 2006, 30.

para. 1 ECHR, the dispute must be "*subject to subsequent control by a judicial body that has full jurisdiction*".[136] This is required by the 'doctrine of full review', which the European Court of Human Rights has developed specifically with respect to administrative and disciplinary authorities, who do not always comply with the requirements of article 6 ECHR.[137, 138] In such instances, as KUIJER puts it

> *The Court simply requires that domestic law provides for the possibility to have all aspects (both legal and factual) of the judgment by the disciplinary or administrative tribunal (which does not itself meet the requirements of Article 6 ECHR) reviewed by a judicial institution, which does fully comply with the requirements of Article 6 ECHR.*[139]

The same reasoning could be applied to decisions of alternative regulatory bodies. The availability of such a full judicial review will thus have to be taken into account when ARIs are established.

C.4. *Procedural guarantees*

INDEPENDENCE AND IMPARTIALITY – A 'tribunal' needs to be independent and impartial.[140] These requirements are usually considered jointly by the Court. First, the 'independence' requirement aims to guarantee that the tribunal and its members are "*independent of the executive and also of the parties*".[141] Interestingly, MOLE and HARBY point out that cases in which the independence requirement is brought up usually relate to decisions of

---

136 EUROPEAN COURT OF HUMAN RIGHTS, Pfarrmeier v. Austria, 23.10.1995, para. 38. DE SMET, Bart, LATHOUWERS, Jan et al., "Artikel 6: recht op eerlijk proces" ["*Article 6: right to fair trial*"], in: VANDE LANOTTE, Johan and HAECK, Yves, *Handboek EVRM: Deel II: Artikelsgewijze commentaar (Volume I)* [*ECHR: Part II: Commentary on the articles*], Antwerpen, Intersentia, 2004, 484–485 [in Dutch].

137 KUIJER, Martin, *The blindfold of Lady Justice: Judicial independence and impartiality in light of the requirements of article 6 ECHR*, Leiden, E.M. Meijers Instituut, 2004, 133.

138 Please note that the European Court of Human Rights does not display the same 'mildness' with respect to 'classic' courts: KUIJER, Martin, *The blindfold of Lady Justice: Judicial independence and impartiality in light of the requirements of article 6 ECHR*, Leiden, E.M. Meijers Instituut, 2004, 136–137.

139 KUIJER, Martin, *The blindfold of Lady Justice: Judicial independence and impartiality in light of the requirements of article 6 ECHR*, Leiden, E.M. Meijers Instituut, 2004, 134.

140 For a detailed study of 'independence' and 'impartiality' in this context, cf. KUIJER, Martin, *The blindfold of Lady Justice: Judicial independence and impartiality in light of the requirements of article 6 ECHR*, Leiden, E.M. Meijers Instituut, 2004, 497 p.

141 EUROPEAN COURT OF HUMAN RIGHTS, Le Compte, Van Leuven and De Meyere v. Belgium, 23.06.1981, para. 55.

non-judicial bodies.[142] The European Court of Human Rights has clarified in *Campbell and Fell v. the United Kingdom* how independence is assessed:

> *In determining whether a body can be considered to be 'independent' – notably of the executive and of the parties to the case [...] –, the Court has had regard to the manner of appointment of its members and the duration of their term of office [...], the existence of guarantees against outside pressures [...] and the question whether the body presents an appearance of independence [...].*[143]

Second, impartiality requires that "*the court is not biassed with regard to the decision to be taken, does not allow itself to be influenced by information from outside the court room, by popular feeling or by any pressures whatsoever, but bases its opinion on objective arguments on the ground of what has been put forward at the trial*".[144] The requirement encompasses two aspects: impartiality needs to ensure that not only there has not been an actual bias by a judge (subjective or personal impartiality), but also that there is no legitimate doubt that there was partiality (objective or structural partiality).[145]

Right to a fair hearing – The trial or hearing conducted by the 'tribunal' also needs to be fair. In *Kraska v. Switzerland* the European Court of Human Rights clarified that the effect of article 6 para. 1 ECHR is to place tribunals

> *under a duty to conduct a proper examination of the submissions, arguments and evidence adduced by the parties, without prejudice to its assessment of whether they are relevant to its decision.*[146]

As we have noted in the previous chapter, other rights have been found to be linked to the need for a 'fair hearing'. These include, for instance, equality of arms, the right to a reasoned judgment, the right to a hearing in one's presence, the right to participate effectively at the hearing, freedom from self-incrimination, or the right to a hearing free from pre-trial publicity. We

---

[142] Mole, Nuala and Harby, Catharina, *The right to a fair trial: a guide to the implementation of Article 6 of the European Convention on Human Rights (Human rights handbooks, No. 3)*, Strasbourg, Council of Europe, 2006, 30.

[143] European Court of Human Rights, Campbell and Fell v. the United Kingdom, 28.06.1984, para. 78.

[144] van Dijk, Pieter, van Hoof, Fried, van Rijn, Arjen and Zwaak, Leo (eds), *Theory and practice of the European Convention on Human Rights*, Antwerpen, Intersentia, 2006, 614.

[145] Harris, David, O'Boyle, Michael, Warbrick, Colin, Bates, Ed et al. (eds), *Harris, O'Boyle and Warbrick Law of the European Convention on human rights*, Oxford, Oxford University Press, 2009, 284; De Smet, Bart, Lathouwers, Jan et al., "Artikel 6: recht op eerlijk proces" ["*Article 6: right to fair trial*"], in: Vande Lanotte, Johan and Haeck, Yves, *Handboek EVRM: Deel II: Artikelsgewijze commentaar (Volume I)* [*ECHR: Part II: Commentary on the articles*], Antwerpen, Intersentia, 2004, 498 [in Dutch].

[146] European Court of Human Rights, Kraska v. Switzerland, 19.04.1993, para. 30.

would like to highlight the right to a reasoned judgment. The right embodies the principle that a judicial decision should state clear and complete reasons and that the arguments of the decision-making body should be legally valid and convincing.[147] We can recall that the European Court of Human Rights has also considered this a decisive factor in assessing whether an interference with the right to freedom of expression is 'prescribed by law' (article 10 para. 2 ECHR, *supra*).

Right to a public hearing – It has been noted that the requirement of a public hearing often raises problems for bodies "*that are not 'classic' courts within the ordinary court system but that are competent to adjudicate upon [...] a person's civil rights or obligations*", such as, for instance, disciplinary bodies.[148] Harris et al. argue that the failure to meet the requirement of a public hearing may be remedied if the decision of the body is "*subject to review by a judicial body that has full jurisdiction, on the law and the facts and that does provide a public hearing*".[149]

C.5. *Concluding remark*

Article 6 ECHR and ARIs – ARIs should respect article 6 ECHR when an individual's (civil) rights are at stake. This might for instance be the case when his or her rights to freedom of expression or privacy are interfered with by an ARI in the field of the protection of minors against harmful content. If such an ARI provides a possibility to raise this issue with an alternative regulatory body, it must be assessed whether or not such a body could be qualified as a 'tribunal established by law'. If this is the case, all requirements put forward by article 6 ECHR (such as independence, impartiality, right to a public hearing, a reasonable time limit, etc.) will need to be fulfilled. If certain requirements are not fulfilled, according to the doctrine of full review an opportunity for judicial review (by a tribunal with full jurisdiction) must be provided. If the alternative regulatory body cannot be qualified as a 'tribunal', judicial review will need to be available in any case. However, such a body

---

[147] Kuijer, Martin, *The blindfold of Lady Justice: Judicial independence and impartiality in light of the requirements of article 6 ECHR*, Leiden, E.M. Meijers Instituut, 2004, 167.

[148] Harris, David, O'Boyle, Michael, Warbrick, Colin, Bates, Ed et al. (eds), *Harris, O'Boyle and Warbrick Law of the European Convention on human rights*, Oxford, Oxford University Press, 2009, 271.

[149] Harris, David, O'Boyle, Michael, Warbrick, Colin, Bates, Ed et al. (eds), *Harris, O'Boyle and Warbrick Law of the European Convention on human rights*, Oxford, Oxford University Press, 2009, 271.

might still need to comply with certain procedural guarantees, for instance under article 10 para. 2 ECHR (*supra*)[150] or article 13 ECHR (*infra*).

D. *Right to an effective remedy*

ARTICLE 13 ECHR – A final fundamental right that needs to be examined with respect to the use of ARIs, is the right to an effective remedy before a national authority for anyone who claims that his or her rights or freedoms under the ECHR have been violated, laid down in article 13 ECHR.[151]

D.1. *General principle*

RIGHT TO AN EFFECTIVE REMEDY – As noted in the previous chapter, the right to an effective remedy is an autonomous right, but one that is invoked when another fundamental right of the ECHR, for instance, freedom of expression, is allegedly violated. In such a case, the remedy should either lead to the prevention of the suspected violation or, if appropriate, to the obtainment of adequate redress, including compensation, and should be effective in practice as well as in law. The effectiveness of a remedy will be assessed on the basis of the concrete circumstances of the case.

ARTICLE 13 AND CHILDREN – It is interesting to note CROMHEECKE and STAELENS' observation that children themselves do not have the right to an effective remedy.[152] In relation to this, they refer to the European Court of Human Rights case, *Margareta and Roger Andersson v. Sweden*, in which the Court stated that

---

[150] Cf. EUROPEAN COURT OF HUMAN RIGHTS, Glas Nadezhda and Elenkov v. Bulgaria, 11.10.2007, paras 50–51; EUROPEAN COURT OF HUMAN RIGHTS, Meltex Ltd and Mesrop Movsesyan v. Armenia, 17.06.2008, para. 81.

[151] RENUCCI, Jean-François, *Introduction to the European Convention on Human Rights – The rights guaranteed and the protection mechanism*, Strasbourg, Council of Europe Publishing, 2005, 69.

[152] CROMHEECKE, Marc and STAELENS, Valentina, "Artikel 13 – Recht op daadwerkelijke rechtshulp" ["*Article 13 – Right to an effective remedy*"], in: VANDE LANOTTE, Johan and HAECK, Yves, *Handboek EVRM: Deel II: Artikelsgewijze commentaar (Volume II)* [*ECHR: Part II: Commentary on the articles (Volume II)*], Antwerpen – Oxford, Intersentia, 2004, 90–91 [in Dutch]. See also: BARKHUYSEN, Tom, *Artikel 13 EVRM: effectieve nationale rechtsbescherming bij schending van mensenrechten* [*Article 13 ECHR: effective domestic legal protection against human rights violations*], Lelystad, Uitgeverij Koninklijke Vermande, 1998, 72–73 [in Dutch].

> *[i]t was common ground that Article 13 (art. 13) did not require that a 12 year-old child be able to institute and conduct such proceedings on his own; it was sufficient for the purposes of this provision that a legal representative was able to do so on the child's behalf.*[153]

Hence, as can be deduced from this case, article 13 ECHR is complied with if a legal representative of a child, who is involved in a violation of Convention rights, has recourse to a remedy.

D.2. *Article 13 ECHR and alternative regulatory instruments*

ARTICLE 13 AND ARIs – When it comes to ARIs, the question arises whether remedies provided by alternative regulatory bodies qualify as 'remedies before a national authority'. In this context, OVEY and WHITE have clarified that it is not a strict requirement that remedies are judicial. They argue that ombudsman procedures and other non-judicial remedies could also be considered adequate.[154] It is interesting to note as well that the European Court of Human Rights does not require the national authority to be a judicial authority in the strict sense.[155] However, in such a case, the Court will assess the "*powers and procedural guarantees an authority possesses*" when it determines whether a remedy can be considered effective.[156] The Court will, for instance, check whether the 'national authority' is independent, impartial and provides certain minimal procedural guarantees.[157] Such a national authority should be competent to receive a complaint, to investigate the merits of the complaint and to take binding decisions regarding the provision of redress.[158]

---

[153] EUROPEAN COURT OF HUMAN RIGHTS, Margareta and Roger Andersson v. Sweden, 25.02.1992, para. 101.

[154] OVEY, Clare and WHITE, Robin, *Jacobs and White The European Convention on Human Rights*, Oxford, Oxford University Press, 2006, 463.

[155] EUROPEAN COURT OF HUMAN RIGHTS, Klass and others v. Germany, 06.09.1978, para. 67; EUROPEAN COURT OF HUMAN RIGHTS, Kudla v. Poland, 26.10.2000, para. 157. See also: VAN DIJK, Pieter, VAN HOOF, Fried, VAN RIJN, Arjen and ZWAAK, Leo (eds), *Theory and practice of the European Convention on Human Rights*, Antwerpen, Intersentia, 2006, 1006.

[156] EUROPEAN COURT OF HUMAN RIGHTS, Kudla v. Poland, 26.10.2000, para. 157.

[157] CROMHEECKE, Marc and STAELENS, Valentina, "Artikel 13 – Recht op daadwerkelijke rechtshulp" ["*Article 13 – Right to an effective remedy*"], in: VANDE LANOTTE, Johan and HAECK, Yves, *Handboek EVRM: Deel II: Artikelsgewijze commentaar (Volume II)* [*ECHR: Part II: Commentary on the articles (Volume II)*], Antwerpen – Oxford, Intersentia, 2004, 121 [in Dutch].

[158] BARKHUYSEN, Tom, *Artikel 13 EVRM: effectieve nationale rechtsbescherming bij schending van mensenrechten* [*Article 13 ECHR: effective domestic legal protection against human rights violations*], Lelystad, Uitgeverij Koninklijke Vermande, 1998, 143 [in Dutch].

Effective remedies provided by self- or co-regulatory bodies? – An interesting case in this respect is *Peck v. the United Kingdom*,[159] in which the European Court of Human Rights found that a violation of article 8 ECHR had taken place when CCTV images of the applicant were made public through the media. The applicant had also claimed that article 13 was violated as, according to him, no remedy regarding this infringement of his right to privacy was available. The respondent (the UK government) argued that (aside from other remedies)[160] the applicant had been able to assert and vindicate his claims before the Broadcasting Standards Commission (BSC), the Independent Television Commission (ITC) and the Press Complaints Commission (PCC),[161] bodies which could be considered to be self- or co-regulatory.[162] The Court, however, decided that these bodies could not provide an effective remedy for the applicant:

> *The Court finds that the lack of legal power of the commissions to award damages to the applicant means that those bodies could not provide an effective remedy to him. It notes that the ITC's power to impose a fine on the relevant television company does not amount to an award of damages to the applicant. While the applicant was aware of the Council's disclosures prior to the Yellow Advertiser article of February 1996 and the BBC broadcasts, neither the BSC nor the PCC had the power to prevent such publications or broadcasts.*[163]

Hence, a violation of article 13 was asserted by the Court.

Impact on the use of ARIs – From this judgment we could deduce that – dependent, of course, on the concrete circumstances of each case – if alterna-

---

[159] European Court of Human Rights, Peck v. the United Kingdom, 28.01.2003.

[160] European Court of Human Rights, Peck v. the United Kingdom, 28.01.2003, para. 95.

[161] European Court of Human Rights, Peck v. the United Kingdom, 28.01.2003, para. 94. Regarding the status of the remedies provided by these bodies, the respondent stated that they "*accepted that it was not intended that the media commissions should provide a 'legal remedy, in the sense of making pecuniary compensation available to an aggrieved individual who may have been injured by an infringement of the relevant codes'. However, they contended that article 13 did not require in every case 'a court' or that a pecuniary award be available*" (para. 94).

[162] Hans-Bredow-Institut and EMR, Study on co-regulation measures in the media sector: Final report, Study commissioned by the European Commission, June 2006, retrieved from http://ec.europa.eu/avpolicy/docs/library/studies/coregul/final_rep_en.pdf (on 28.07.2006), 147–149; Voorhoof, Dirk, "Recente arresten van het E.H.R.M. in verband met het artikel 10 E.V.R.M. (vrijheid van meningsuiting en informatie)" ["*Recent judgments of the ECHR related to article 10 ECHR (freedom of expression and information)*"], March–May 2003, *Auteurs & Media* 2003, No. 3, 233 [in Dutch].

[163] European Court of Human Rights, Peck v. the United Kingdom, 28.01.2003, para. 109.

tive regulatory bodies are involved in the protection of Convention rights, such as the freedom of expression, in the framework of a system to protect minors from harmful content, the availability of remedies should be carefully considered.[164] Although the European Court of Human Rights has up until now not dealt with such cases, it would not be unimaginable that an adult, for instance, would claim that his or her freedom of expression has been restricted by a self- or co-regulatory scheme to protect minors against harmful content, and that he or she would seek to remedy this infringement by appealing to an alternative regulatory body.[165] The fact that the European Court of Human Rights would not automatically assume that such bodies are not classifiable as 'national authorities' is an important finding, and one that should be taken into account when self- and/or co-regulatory models are established that could conflict with the freedom of expression. However, it will, again, depend on the circumstances of the case whether the remedy provided will comply with the – rather high –standards used by the Court to assess the effectiveness of a remedy. If the Court considers that a remedy provided by a self- or co-regulatory body is not adequate, other remedies (such as for instance before national courts) need to be available.

D.3. *Horizontal effect of article 13 ECHR*

ARTICLE 13 AND INDIRECT *DRITTWIRKUNG* – A final observation that can be made with respect to article 13 and ARIs concerns the final part of the article, i.e., "*notwithstanding that the violation has been committed by persons acting in an official capacity*". Although it is usually assumed that this sentence is directed at laws that provide public officials with immunity from human

[164] Cf. also: CRAUFURD SMITH, Rachael, "European Community media regulation in a converging environment", in: SHUIBHNE, Niamh Nic (ed.), *Regulating the internal market*, Cheltenham, Edward Elgar, 2006, 139: "*where private actors are involved in the application and enforcement of co-regulatory agreements, provision should be made, depending on the circumstances, for a right of appeal or review to a court of law*".

[165] We would like to stress the intrinsic link between the protection of minors from harmful content and the fundamental right to freedom of expression (cf. *supra*). In our view, this link justifies our assessment of the significance of article 13 ECHR to the use of ARIs; this in contrast to the conclusion of the HBI/EMR study that the relevance of article 13 ECHR is restricted to co-regulatory models designed to protect rights that are granted by the ECHR, which, according to them, was not the case with the co-regulatory systems they assessed (notwithstanding the fact that these models mostly dealt with the protection of minors and advertising). Cf. HANS-BREDOW-INSTITUT AND EMR, Study on co-regulation measures in the media sector: Final report, Study commissioned by the European Commission, June 2006, retrieved from http://ec.europa.eu/avpolicy/docs/library/studies/coregul/final_rep_en.pdf (on 28.07.2006), 148–149.

rights infringements, it has also been suggested that this phrase could imply that "*an effective legal remedy within the meaning of Article 13 must also, and a fortiori, be furnished when the violation has been committed by a private individual, raising the possibility of indirect Drittwirkung of the Convention rights between citizens*".[166] However, at the same time it has been argued that this should be confined to cases where a positive obligation exists to safeguard individuals against serious violations committed by other individuals, as, for instance, related to article 2 (right to life) or article 3 (protection from torture and other inhuman or degrading treatment or punishment).[167] Nevertheless, the European Court of Human Rights did acknowledge in *Plattform Ärtze für das Leben v. Austria* that the applicability of article 13 was linked to article 11, which – according to the Court – "*sometimes requires positive measures to be taken, even in the sphere of relations between individuals, if need be*".[168] It is thus not inconceivable that in the context of article 10 ECHR (freedom of expression), the applicability of article 13 to relations between individuals would be considered possible as well.

D.4. *Article 6 and article 13 ECHR*

Interplay right to a fair trial and right to an effective remedy – We have noted in the previous chapter that article 6 ECHR implicitly embodies the right of access to a court. When a Convention right is at stake article 6 ECHR and article 13 ECHR might thus overlap in certain instances. When the Convention right at issue can be considered a 'civil right', article 6 ECHR is deemed to provide a stricter guarantee.[169] In cases where article 6 ECHR

---

[166] van Dijk, Pieter, van Hoof, Fried, van Rijn, Arjen and Zwaak, Leo (eds), *Theory and practice of the European Convention on Human Rights*, Antwerpen, Intersentia, 2006, 1024. See also: Ovey, Clare and White, Robin, *Jacobs and White The European Convention on Human Rights*, Oxford, Oxford University Press, 2006, 470: "*It has been argued that [the words] also show that the scope of the Convention is not limited to persons exercising public authority*".

[167] van Dijk, Pieter, van Hoof, Fried, van Rijn, Arjen and Zwaak, Leo (eds), *Theory and practice of the European Convention on Human Rights*, Antwerpen, Intersentia, 2006, 1024.

[168] European Court of Human Rights, Plattform Ärtze für das Leben v. Austria, 21.06.1988, para. 32.

[169] Lemmens, Paul, Geschillen over burgerlijke rechten en verplichtingen: het toepassingsgebied van de artikelen 6, lid 1, van het Europees Verdrag over de rechten van de mens en 14, lid 1, van het Internationaal Verdrag inzake burgerrechten en politieke rechten [*Disputes over civil rights and obligations: the scope of application of the articles 6, para. 1, of the European Convention on human rights and 14, para. 1, of the International Covenant on Civil and Political Rights*], PhD Thesis (promotor: Prof. dr. Jan De Meyer), 1987, 178

is not applicable (because the Convention right falls outside of the scope of the notion 'civil right' as interpreted by the Court), article 13 ECHR does of course still apply,[170] and hence, the procedural safeguards required by the European Court of Human Rights under this article, such as independence and impartiality, will apply nonetheless.[171] Finally, we can note that once an individual has had access to a court and judgment has been issued (and hence article 6 ECHR has been complied with), he can still invoke article 13 ECHR in order to obtain redress.[172]

D.5. *Concluding remarks*

Article 13 ECHR and ARIs – Article 13 ECHR complements the other rights and freedoms guaranteed by the Convention. If an individual's rights are interfered with, the protection of these rights would be ineffective if no effective remedy before a national authority is available. With respect to the use of ARIs, we found that, although the European Court of Human

[in Dutch]; Harris, David, O'Boyle, Michael, Warbrick, Colin, Bates, Ed et al. (eds), *Harris, O'Boyle and Warbrick Law of the European Convention on human rights*, Oxford, Oxford University Press, 2009, 245–246. Also: European Court of Human Rights, Håkansson and Sturesson v. Sweden, 21.02.1990, para. 69; European Court of Human Rights, Philis v. Greece, 27.08.1991, para. 67; European Court of Human Rights, De Geouffre de la Pradelle v. France, 16.12.1992, para. 37.

170 Lemmens, Paul, Geschillen over burgerlijke rechten en verplichtingen: het toepassingsgebied van de artikelen 6, lid 1, van het Europees Verdrag over de rechten van de mens en 14, lid 1, van het Internationaal Verdrag inzake burgerrechten en politieke rechten [*Disputes over civil rights and obligations: the scope of application of the articles 6, para. 1, of the European Convention on human rights and 14, para. 1, of the International Covenant on Civil and Political Rights*], PhD Thesis (promotor: Prof. dr. Jan De Meyer), 1987, 178 [in Dutch].

171 Mole, Nuala and Harby, Catharina, *The right to a fair trial: a guide to the implementation of Article 6 of the European Convention on Human Rights (Human rights handbooks, No. 3)*, Strasbourg, Council of Europe, 2006, 14; van Dijk, Pieter, van Hoof, Fried, van Rijn, Arjen and Zwaak, Leo (eds), *Theory and practice of the European Convention on Human Rights*, Antwerpen, Intersentia, 2006, 538. For a more detailed overview of the relationship between article 6 and article 13 ECHR, cf. Kuijer, Martin, *The blindfold of Lady Justice: Judicial independence and impartiality in light of the requirements of article 6 ECHR*, Leiden, E.M. Meijers Instituut, 2004, 110–115.

172 Lemmens, Paul, Geschillen over burgerlijke rechten en verplichtingen: het toepassingsgebied van de artikelen 6, lid 1, van het Europees Verdrag over de rechten van de mens en 14, lid 1, van het Internationaal Verdrag inzake burgerrechten en politieke rechten [*Disputes over civil rights and obligations: the scope of application of the articles 6, para. 1, of the European Convention on human rights and 14, para. 1, of the International Covenant on Civil and Political Rights*], PhD Thesis (promotor: Prof. dr. Jan De Meyer), 1987, 178 [in Dutch].

Rights does not require remedies to be judicial, nor national authorities to be judicial authorities in the strict sense, the Court will assess whether the 'authorities' in question are independent, impartial and provide certain procedural guarantees. Furthermore, from the *Peck v. the United Kingdom* case, we learned that the Court does not necessarily exclude bodies which can be classified as self- or co-regulatory. However, in any case, the Court will assess on the basis of the concrete circumstances whether the available remedies are effective. Finally, we observed that, at least in theory, it could be possible that an indirect horizontal effect could be attributed to article 13 ECHR, for instance, in combination with article 10 ECHR. This would mean that when a violation of Convention rights has been committed by an individual (or, an entity which would not fulfil the criteria to be considered a public authority, which could be the case in self-regulatory schemes), an effective remedy would also need to be available.

E. *Interim conclusion: ARIs and fundamental rights*

Human rights issues – The aim of this section was to examine whether there are legal obstacles to the use of ARIs to protect minors against harmful content from a human rights point of view, and more specifically, from the point of view of the rights embedded in the ECHR. We distinguished two categories of fundamental rights which could be affected: first, the substantive rights to freedom of expression and privacy, and, second, the procedural rights to a fair trial and to an effective remedy.

Articles 8 and 10 – When self- or co-regulatory schemes are designed to protect minors from harmful material, it is possible that restrictions are imposed on the freedom of expression of children as well adults, as well as on children's right to privacy. The question is then whether articles 8 and 10 ECHR, which prevent public authorities from interfering with their citizens' respective rights unless certain conditions are fulfilled, are applicable. Different issues, which are similar with respect to both articles, have been identified.

First, we established whether self- or co-regulatory bodies can be considered 'public authorities'. We found that although the Court would not automatically dismiss such bodies, much will depend on the concrete circumstances of the case, in particular on the level of government involvement. Hence, co-regulatory bodies would have a greater chance of being classified as having the same status as a public authority than self-regulatory bodies. If a body is considered to have such a status, articles 8 and 10 ECHR are applicable. This means that restrictions imposed by such bodies need to comply with the conditions of the second paragraph of both articles (*infra*).

Second, we then examined whether articles 8 and 10 ECHR could be applied even when the bodies in question would not be classified as 'public authorities'. This led us to a brief exploration of the theory of horizontal effect, which implies that, in certain circumstances, these articles can be invoked in relations between private actors, and furthermore, that, in certain cases, states have been considered by the European Court of Human Rights to have a positive obligation to ensure that private individuals do not interfere with the fundamental rights of other individuals. The applicability of articles 8 and 10 ECHR to ARIs which involve bodies who cannot be classified as being 'a public authority' is thus not *a priori* excluded. Of course, much will depend on the concrete circumstances of each case.

Third, if a self- or co-regulatory scheme imposes restrictions on the fundamental rights in question, this can only be allowed if the conditions of the second paragraph of, respectively, articles 8 or 10 ECHR are fulfilled. We established that whereas the need for a legitimate aim, *in casu* the protection of minors, will in all probability not pose problems, the two other conditions required closer examination. First, restrictions imposed by self- or co-regulatory schemes will not always be prescribed by a law. However, we found that the European Court of Human Rights has not always required the legal basis for a restriction to be included in a law *stricto sensu*: other instruments can be attributed a law-like status on the condition that they are accessible and foreseeable. The *Barthold v. Germany* case clarified, for instance, that rules of professional conduct could be attributed such a status. However, we observed that in that particular case, the level of government involvement was rather high. Hence, it is likely that the Court would not be as tolerant with respect to ARIs in which there is no or a very minimal level of government involvement. Second, restrictions imposed by ARIs should be 'necessary in a democratic society'. To fulfil this condition, the restriction must be proportional, the reasons for justification need to be relevant and sufficient, and a pressing social need must be present. The competing interests, i.e., the protection of minors against harmful content and the right to freedom of expression or privacy, will therefore be balanced on a case-by-case basis.

Fourth, we briefly explored the specific human rights difficulties that could arise with respect to the use of self-regulation and technology. First, we noted that the fact that only private actors are involved in schemes which restrict access to content might raise free speech concerns. Private actors should not decide upon the illegality or harmfulness of content, since this could lead to private censorship. Hence, with respect to a delicate issue such as the protection of minors against harmful content, it might be advisable to require a certain degree of government involvement. Second, we examined the use of filtering (in the context of freedom of expression) and the use of identification mechanisms (in the context of privacy). We found that, although the use of technology might be valuable and empowering, it carries considerable dangers, for instance regarding arbitrary censorship or infringements on the right to privacy. Hence, the use of such tools should be carefully considered, and should, above all, be proportional.

Procedural guarantees – A second category of rights that need to be respected when using ARIs to protect minors against harmful content are procedural rights. First, we studied article 6 ECHR which establishes a right to a fair and public hearing before an independent and impartial tribunal established by law when a dispute concerning an individual's civil rights (or a criminal charge) arises. We found that article 6 ECHR may be applicable with respect to a dispute concerning an individual's right to freedom of expression or privacy, and that if such a dispute can be brought before an alternative regulatory body, an assessment will need to be made whether this body can be qualified as a tribunal. If this is the case – and we established that we doubt whether an alternative regulatory body could live up to the rather strict standards put forward by the Court – the body in question should adhere to the procedural guarantees included in article 6 ECHR (of course, unless exceptions are accepted). If the body fails to do so, the Court might not consider this unacceptable if an opportunity for judicial review is provided for. When the alternative regulatory body cannot be considered 'a tribunal', judicial review will need to be available anyhow. This will need to be taken into account when ARIs are set up.

To conclude this section, we examined article 13 ECHR which requires the availability of an effective remedy before a national authority. We learned that the European Court of Human Rights does not *a priori* exclude self- or co-regulatory bodies from being classified as a 'national authority', and, furthermore, that it will decide on the basis of the facts of each case whether the remedies provided by such bodies can be considered effective. We can deduce from the *Peck v. the United Kingdom* case that the Court maintains rather high standards; the possibility of only imposing a fine instead of damages, for instance, did not constitute a satisfactory remedy. This might be problematic in the case of many self- or co-regulatory schemes, and, hence, other remedies would need to be foreseen. Finally, we also briefly considered the possibility that article 13 ECHR has a certain horizontal effect, and, hence, that also when private individuals (or, for instance, self-regulatory bodies) commit an infringement of the Convention rights, a remedy should be available.

Protection or no protection? – Overall, we can conclude that the key question which should be posed with respect to the use of ARIs to protect minors from harmful content is whether the measures or systems in question fall within the scope of the relevant articles of the ECHR. If the answer to this question be affirmative (because, for instance, the bodies in question qualify as 'public authorities' or because the theory of horizontal effect is considered applicable), any restrictions will be closely examined and, hence, the protection of the fundamental rights to freedom of expression and privacy will be guaranteed. However, if the answer be negative, the ECHR protection will not be guaranteed. In that case, it must be examined if there are, for instance, national (constitutional) provisions which could be invoked instead.

Importance of procedural guarantees – In addition, we would like to stress the importance of procedural guarantees. When important rights are at stake, when decisions are made that might interfere with such rights, the least that can be expected from the decision-making body is adherence to certain procedural safeguards, such as independence, impartiality and transparency (for instance by means of reasoned decisions). Furthermore, such decisions must be disputable. Compliance with such guarantees is not only essential for an ARI to be credible, it also ensures that the rights that are at stake are protected in an adequate manner.

Importance of fundamental rights – To conclude this section, we would like to emphasise that it is not possible to overstress the significance of respecting the fundamental rights of freedom of expression and privacy when trying to protect minors against harmful content. Finding the right balance between the competing values is very delicate and will therefore need to be carefully considered when establishing ARIs in this field, whatever their shape or form.

2.2.2. *Internal market legislation*

Legal framework – In this second section, we move from the Council of Europe level to the EU level. As we have seen in the previous chapter, internal market principles, which are the cornerstone of a large part of EU legislation,[173] may be of importance when it comes to content. The general (e.g., articles 34, 36 and 56 TFEU [ex 28, 30 and 49 EC Treaty]) as well specific legal provisions (e.g., AVMS Directive, e-Commerce Directive) which deal with the free movement of services and goods may, hence, also be relevant with respect to the use of ARIs in the field of protecting minors against

[173] For more details on the history of the internal market, cf. Gormley, Laurence W., "The internal market: history and evolution", 14–28, in: Shuibhne, Niamh Nic (ed.), *Regulating the internal market*, Cheltenham, Edward Elgar, 2006, 370 p.

harmful content,[174] since ARIs in this field could potentially limit these fundamental freedoms. This concern has also been expressed at the EU level, for instance, in the Interinstitutional Agreement on Better Lawmaking (*supra*), in which it was stressed that alternative regulatory methods should not have a negative impact on the unity of the EU market.[175]

A. *Free movement of goods*

A.1. *General principles*

Articles 34 to 36 TFEU [ex 28 to 30 EC Treaty] – When using ARIs to protect minors against harmful content, issues could arise with respect to the free movement of goods.[176] As was briefly described in the previous chapter, the key principles of this internal market freedom are included in articles 34 to 36 TFEU [ex 28 to 30 EC Treaty]. These articles have direct effect,[177] which means that individuals can invoke them in national courts.[178] In general, the first two articles prohibit quantitative restrictions and measures having an equivalent effect on imports (article 34 TFEU [ex 28 EC Treaty]), and quantitative restrictions and measures having an equivalent effect on exports (article 35 TFEU [ex 29 EC Treaty]). Although both articles are similar in many ways, their interpretation by the ECJ has not always been identical.[179] A close examination of these differences, however, is beyond the scope of this

[174] Cf., for instance, in the field of environmental law: Commission of the European Communities, Communication from the Commission to the Council and to the European Parliament on environmental agreements, COM (1996) 561 final, 27.11.1996, 14: "*Environmental Agreements shall not create barriers to the smooth functioning of the internal market*".

[175] European Parliament, Council, and Commission, Interinstitutional Agreement on Better Law-making, 2003/C 321/01, *OJ* 31.12.2003, *C* 321, para. 17.

[176] ECJ, Commission of the European Communities v. Italian Republic, C-7/68, 10.12.1968.

[177] ECJ, Iannelli & Volpi SpA v. Ditta Paolo Meroni, C-74/76, 22.03.1977, para. 17.

[178] Woods, Lorna, *Free movement of goods and services within the European Community*, Aldershot, Ashgate, 2004, 29.

[179] For instance, with respect to article 35 TFEU [ex 29 EC Treaty], the ECJ chose not to follow the 'indistinctly applicable' measures approach it developed in the context of article 34 TFEU [ex 28 EC Treaty]. Cf. Woods, Lorna, *Free movement of goods and services within the European Community*, Aldershot, Ashgate, 2004, 100 *et seq*. For more details on export of goods (and services), cf. Roth, Wulf-Henning, "Export of goods and services within the single market: reflections on the scope of articles 29 and 49 EC", 33–48, in: Tridimas, Takis and Nebbia, Paolisa (eds), *European Union law for the twenty-first century: rethinking the new legal order*, Oxford, Hart Publishing, 2004, 465 p.; Roth, Wulf-Henning and Oliver, Peter, "The internal market and the four freedoms", *Common Market Law Review* 2004, Volume 41, 419–421.

study.[180] Therefore, in what follows we will focus on article 34 TFEU [ex 28 EC Treaty] (imports, except where it is stated otherwise). The third article (article 36 TFEU [ex 30 EC Treaty]) then puts the prohibition elaborated in the previous articles into perspective by providing a number of exceptions, i.e., prohibitions or restrictions on imports, exports or goods in transit justified on grounds of public morality, public policy or public security; the protection of health and life of humans, animals or plants; the protection of national treasures possessing artistic, historic or archaeological value; or the protection of industrial and commercial property; provided that they do not constitute a means of arbitrary discrimination or a disguised restriction on trade between Member States.

Scope of article 34 and 35 TFEU [28 and 29 EC Treaty] – The scope of both articles 34 and 35 TFEU [ex 28 and 29 EC Treaty] is not limited to goods of European origin. Article 28 para. 2 TFEU [ex 23 EC Treaty] states that these articles apply to "*products originating in Member States and to products coming from third countries which are in free circulation in Member States*". Article 29 TFEU [ex 24 EC Treaty] then clarifies that "*products coming from a third country shall be considered to be in free circulation in a Member State if the import formalities have been complied with and any customs duties or charges having equivalent effect which are payable have been levied in that Member State, and if they have not benefited from a total or partial drawback of such duties or charges*". Articles 34 and 35 TFEU [ex 28 and 29 EC Treaty], however, only relate to transactions between Member States; neither relations with third countries nor intrastate transactions are covered.[181]

A.2. *Conceptual elements*

Goods – Goods have been defined by the ECJ as "*products which can be valued in money and which are capable, as such, of forming the subject matter of commercial transactions*".[182] Woods observed that in relation to media content, the distinction between goods and services can sometimes seem artificial: broadcasting is considered a service whereas videos and films, for instance, on DVD (which might contain the same content as broadcasting),

---

[180] For more details, cf. Oliver, Peter, *Free movement of goods in the European Community under articles 28 to 30 of the EC Treaty*, London, Sweet and Maxwell, 2003, 138–145.

[181] Woods, Lorna, *Free movement of goods and services within the European Community*, Aldershot, Ashgate, 2004, 21–22.

[182] ECJ, Commission of the European Communities v. Italian Republic, C-7/68, 10.12.1968.

are classified as goods.[183] Hence, the ECJ puts the emphasis on the transmission method, instead of the content. In this context, WOODS noted that the potential for inconsistencies only increases with the rise of intangible products, such as software and music accessed and bought via the Internet.[184]

QUANTITATIVE RESTRICTIONS AND MEASURES HAVING EQUIVALENT EFFECT – Article 34 TFEU [ex 28 EC Treaty] targets two types of measures: quantitative restrictions and measures having equivalent effect.[185, 186] The first notion refers to 'non-tariff barriers to trade',[187] and has been defined in the *Geddo* case as "*measures which amount to a total or partial restraint of, according to the circumstances, imports, exports or goods in transit*".[188] Examples range from total prohibitions (for instance, the prohibition of any importation of pornographic articles into a Member State)[189] *to quotas* (for instance,

[183] WOODS, Lorna, *Free movement of goods and services within the European Community*, Aldershot, Ashgate, 2004, 27–28.

[184] WOODS, Lorna, *Free movement of goods and services within the European Community*, Aldershot, Ashgate, 2004, 28.

[185] Note that – contrary to cases regarding competition provisions – the ECJ has always rejected the application of a *de minimis* rule with respect to quantitative restrictions and measures having equivalent effect: OLIVER, Peter, *Free movement of goods in the European Community under articles 28 to 30 of the EC Treaty*, London, Sweet and Maxwell, 2003, 99; WOODS, Lorna, *Free movement of goods and services within the European Community*, Aldershot, Ashgate, 2004, 49 and 55.

[186] Within the scope of this book, the issues regarding the distinction between discriminatory and 'indistinctly applicable' measures will not be considered. For more details: WOODS, Lorna, *Free movement of goods and services within the European Community*, Aldershot, Ashgate, 2004, 93–97; OLIVER, Peter, *Free movement of goods in the European Community under articles 28 to 30 of the EC Treaty*, London, Sweet and Maxwell, 2003, 111–133. Neither will the principle of mutual recognition (i.e., the principle that a product lawfully put on the market in one Member State must be permitted to enter the markets of the other Member States), which was put forward in the *Cassis de Dijon* case, be studied in detail. For more details: SNELL, Jukka, *Goods and services in EC Law – A study of the relationship between the freedoms*, Oxford, Oxford University Press, 2002, 55–56, 126 and 183–184; HATZOPOULOS, Vassilis and Do, Thien Uyen, "The case law of the ECJ concerning the free provisions of services: 2000–2005", *Common Market Law Review* 2006, Vol. 43, 979–986; ARMSTRONG, Kenneth A., "Mutual recognition", 225–267, in: BARNARD, Catherine and SCOTT, Joanne, *The law of the single European market*, Oxford, Hart Publishing, 2002, 414 p.

[187] Measures such as customs duties, discriminatory taxation and similar measures are discussed in other articles of the Treaty, for instance articles 28 TFEU [ex 23 EC Treaty], 30 TFEU [ex 25 EC Treaty] and 110 *et seq.* TFEU [ex 90 EC Treaty].

[188] ECJ, Riseria Luigi Geddo v. Ente Nazionale Risi, C-2/73, 12.07.1973, para. 7.

[189] ECJ, Regina v. Maurice Donald Henn and John Frederick Ernest Darby, C-34/79, 14.12.1979, para. 13.

restrictions by reference to percentages of national production).[190] The second type of measures are 'measures having equivalent effect', commonly shortened to MEQR.

Dassonville – An interpretation of what constitutes a MEQR was first put forward by the ECJ in the important *Dassonville* case, which stated that "*all trading rules enacted by Member States which are capable of hindering, directly or indirectly, actually or potentially, intra-Community trade are to be considered as measures having an effect equivalent to quantitative restrictions*".[191] This broad definition focuses on the effect of a measure.[192] Examples that fall under its scope are thus measures that delay, complicate or increase costs of the sale of imported goods, measures that impose origin marking requirements on imports, or packaging and labelling requirements.[193] Interestingly, Woods noted that the notion 'rules enacted' does not necessarily refer to legislative acts; administrative acts, court decisions and non-binding or indirect expressions of government policy have all also been found to fall within its scope.[194] Oliver indicated, moreover, that the financing of a scheme or

---

[190] Oliver, Peter, *Free movement of goods in the European Community under articles 28 to 30 of the EC Treaty*, London, Sweet and Maxwell, 2003, 89; Woods, Lorna, *Free movement of goods and services within the European Community*, Aldershot, Ashgate, 2004, 49.

[191] ECJ, Procureur du Roi v. Benoît and Gustave Dassonville, C-8/74, 11.07.1974, para. 5.

[192] Oliver, Peter, *Free movement of goods in the European Community under articles 28 to 30 of the EC Treaty*, London, Sweet and Maxwell, 2003, 102; Woods, Lorna, *Free movement of goods and services within the European Community*, Aldershot, Ashgate, 2004, 53.

[193] Woods, Lorna, *Free movement of goods and services within the European Community*, Aldershot, Ashgate, 2004, 57 *et seq.* Cf. also: Article 2, para. 3 Commission Directive 70/50/EEC of 22 December 1969 based on the provisions of Article 33 (7), on the abolition of measures which have an effect equivalent to quantitative restrictions on imports and are not covered by other provisions adopted in pursuance of the EEC Treaty, *OJ* 19.01.1970, *L* 13, 29. For a comprehensive overview of measures falling within the scope of article 34 TFEU [ex 28 EC Treaty], cf. Oliver, Peter, *Free movement of goods in the European Community under articles 28 to 30 of the EC Treaty*, London, Sweet and Maxwell, 2003, 158–204.

[194] Woods, Lorna, *Free movement of goods and services within the European Community*, Aldershot, Ashgate, 2004, 54. See also: Oliver, Peter, *Free movement of goods in the European Community under articles 28 to 30 of the EC Treaty*, London, Sweet and Maxwell, 2003, 96. Oliver refers to Commission Directive 70/50/EEC of 22 December 1969 based on the provisions of Article 33 (7), on the abolition of measures which have an effect equivalent to quantitative restrictions on imports and are not covered by other provisions adopted in pursuance of the EEC Treaty, *OJ* 19.01.1970, *L* 13, 29 – a directive adopted during the transitional period to clarify which MEQR Member States were required to abolish – which stated: "*[…] 'measures' means laws, regulations, administrative provisions, administrative practices, and all instruments issuing from a public authority, including recommendations; […] 'administrative practices' means any standard and regularly followed*

project could also constitute 'a measure'.[195] Hence, measures taken by co-regulatory bodies, depending on the degree of government involvement, would probably not be ruled out *a priori.*

KECK – An important restriction on the broad *Dassonville* definition was put forward by the ECJ in the *Keck* case.[196] In this case – partially reversing earlier case law – the ECJ held that

> *the application to products from other Member States of national provisions restricting or prohibiting certain selling arrangements is not such as to hinder directly or indirectly, actually or potentially, trade between Member States within the meaning of the Dassonville judgment [...], so long as those provisions apply to all relevant traders operating within the national territory and so long as they affect in the same manner, in law and in fact, the marketing of domestic products and of those from other Member States.*[197]

It is therefore important to note that such 'selling arrangements' (e.g., rules on when goods may be sold such as for instance, concerning trading on Sundays) should not be confused with 'rules that lay down requirements to be met by goods'[198], such as labelling, which do fall under the free movement of goods provisions.[199] As we will see *infra* with the *Dynamic Medien v. Avides*

---

procedure of a public authority; whereas 'recommendations' means any instruments issuing from a public authority which, while not legally binding on the addressees thereof, cause them to pursue a certain conduct".

[195] OLIVER, Peter, *Free movement of goods in the European Community under articles 28 to 30 of the EC Treaty*, London, Sweet and Maxwell, 2003, 98.

[196] ROTH, Wulf-Henning and OLIVER, Peter, "The internal market and the four freedoms", *Common Market Law Review* 2004, Volume 41, 413–414; SNELL, Jukka and ANDENAS, Mads, "Exploring the outer limits: restrictions on the free movement of goods and services", 69–139, in: ANDENAS, Mads and ROTH, Wulf-Henning, *Services and free movement in EU law*, Oxford, Oxford University Press, 2002, 466 p.

[197] ECJ, Criminal proceedings against Bernard Keck and Daniel Mithouard (References for a preliminary ruling: Tribunal de grande instance de Strasbourg – France), cases C-267/91 and C-268/91, 24.11.1993, para. 16.

[198] ECJ, Criminal proceedings against Bernard Keck and Daniel Mithouard (References for a preliminary ruling: Tribunal de grande instance de Strasbourg – France), cases C-267/91 and C-268/91, 24.11.1993, para. 15.

[199] ROTH and OLIVER explained the rationale behind this distinction as follows: "*Although it is couched in formal categories – the so-called 'product rules' and 'selling arrangements' – the real motivation behind this distinction lies in the different effect of these rules on the internal market. Product regulations tend to hinder or impede access to the market, whereas selling arrangements typically leave such access unimpeded. When and where access to the market is not hampered, the discrimination standard suffices to guarantee undistorted competition*": ROTH, Wulf-Henning and OLIVER, Peter, "The internal market and the four

Media case, the inclusion of labelling requirements within the scope of article 34 TFEU [ex 28 EC Treaty] could be relevant to schemes that attempt to protect minors against harmful content.

ARTICLE 36 TFEU [EX 30 EC TREATY]: DEROGATION – As mentioned *supra*, article 36 TFEU [ex 30 EC Treaty] provides the Member States with the possibility to derogate from articles 34 and 35 TFEU [ex 28 and 29 EC Treaty] in favour of other policy objectives, such as, for instance, 'public morality' or the 'protection of health and life of humans'. The ECJ, however, has repeatedly stressed that any derogation must be interpreted strictly,[200] and that the list of possible justification grounds is exhaustive.[201]

PROTECTION OF CHILDREN – In this context, the ECJ has already confirmed that the protection of children (for instance, against information and materials injurious to their well-being) is a legitimate interest which can justify a restriction on the free movement of goods.[202] Moreover, public morality, under which the protection of children against harmful content will most likely fall, is a domain in which Member States have a definite margin of discretion, given the fact that there are different moral views held across Member States and, hence, no uniform, standardised European conception exists.[203]

freedoms", *Common Market Law Review* 2004, Volume 41, 411–412. See also: WOODS, Lorna, *Free movement of goods and services within the European Community*, Aldershot, Ashgate, 2004, 64; OLIVER, Peter, *Free movement of goods in the European Community under articles 28 to 30 of the EC Treaty*, London, Sweet and Maxwell, 2003, 124. Cf. also *infra*: ECJ, Dynamic Medien v. Avides Media AG, C-244/06, 14.02.2008, in which the ECJ held that the labelling requirements did not constitute a selling arrangement.

200 ECJ, W. J. G. Bauhuis v. The Netherlands State, C-46/76, 25.01.1977, para. 12; ECJ, Commission of the European Communities v. Ireland, C-113/80, 17.06.1981, para. 7.

201 ECJ, Commission of the European Communities v. Ireland, C-113/80, 17.06.1981, para. 7; ECJ, Commission of the European Communities v. Italian Republic, C-95/81, 09.06.1982, para. 27.

202 ECJ, Dynamic Medien v. Avides Media AG, C-244/06, 14.02.2008, paras 42–43. Cf. also *infra*. In this judgment, the ECJ referred to the several international human rights instruments (e.g., the UNCRC) before acknowledging the protection of the child as a legitimate interest (paras 39–42).

203 ECJ, Dynamic Medien v. Avides Media AG, C-244/06, 14.02.2008, para. 44. Note that in this judgment the ECJ did not explicitly categorise the protection of children under 'public morality'.

Mandatory requirements – In addition, it is necessary to note that in the *Cassis de Dijon* judgment the ECJ held that

> *[o]bstacles to movement within the Community resulting from disparities between the national laws relating to the marketing of the products in question must be accepted insofar as those provisions may be recognized as being necessary in order to satisfy mandatory requirements relating in particular to the effectiveness of fiscal supervision, the protection of public health, the fairness of commercial transactions and the defence of the consumer.*[204]

This approach by the ECJ has been dubbed the 'rule of reason' approach. In short, by adopting this approach, the ECJ tries to balance common market interests with public interest goals in areas where no harmonised Community approach existed. Since the *Cassis de Dijon* judgment, other 'mandatory requirements' have been accepted by the ECJ: for instance, the protection of the environment, the improvement of working conditions, and the maintenance of press diversity.[205] There is no clear consensus in the academic literature, however, on what status should be attributed to these 'mandatory requirements'. Although these arguments are beyond the scope of this study, in brief, it can be observed that while a first theory argues that these requirements are an inherent part of article 34 TFEU [ex 28 EC Treaty], and are only relevant with respect to indistinctly applicable measures, a second theory suggests that the mandatory requirements must be interpreted as an addition to the justification grounds enumerated in article 36 TFEU [ex 30 EC Treaty].[206]

No discrimination or disguised restrictions – The second sentence of article 36 TFEU [ex 30 EC Treaty] further specifies that any justified restriction cannot constitute a means of arbitrary discrimination or a disguised restriction on trade between Member States. Furthermore, in its case law, the ECJ has found restrictions to be justified "*only if they are suitable for securing the attainment of the objective pursued and do not go beyond what is neces-*

---

[204] ECJ, Rewe-Zentral AG v. Bundesmonopolverwaltung für Branntwein, C-120/78, 20.02.1979, para. 8. See also: Woods, Lorna, *Free movement of goods and services within the European Community*, Aldershot, Ashgate, 2004, 68–69.

[205] Oliver, Peter, *Free movement of goods in the European Community under articles 28 to 30 of the EC Treaty*, London, Sweet and Maxwell, 2003, 216. Mandatory requirements have not been, in contrast to the justification for article 36 TFEU [ex 30 EC Treaty], listed in an exhaustive manner: Woods, Lorna, *Free movement of goods and services within the European Community*, Aldershot, Ashgate, 2004, 130.

[206] Oliver, Peter, *Free movement of goods in the European Community under articles 28 to 30 of the EC Treaty*, London, Sweet and Maxwell, 2003, 216–217.

sary in order to attain it".[207] This amounts to a suitability and necessity test, which, in turn, is part of a general proportionality test.[208]

A.3. *Member States, individuals and responsibility*

INTERPRETATION OF 'MEMBER STATE' – The provisions regarding the free movement of goods target 'Member State actions'.[209] An examination of the relationship between the free movement of goods and the use of ARIs should thus first consider how this notion is interpreted and what Member State actions are considered to fall under articles 34 and 35 TFEU [ex 28 and 29 EC Treaty]. Are only 'government' measures in the strict sense targeted, or can actions of non-governmental bodies such as co-regulatory bodies also be covered by the principles regarding free movement of goods? It has been argued that the ECJ has adopted a broad interpretation of the notion 'Member State'.[210] The ECJ clarified, for instance, that "*[a]rticle [34, ex 28] of the Treaty may apply to measures adopted by all authorities of the Member State, be they central authorities, the authorities of a federal state, or other territorial authorities*".[211] Furthermore, measures from the executive as well as the legislature or the judiciary fall within the scope of articles 34 to 36 TFEU [ex 28 to 30 EC Treaty].[212] With respect to non-governmental bodies, the opinion of the ECJ is less clear. When an association's foundations have a totally private and voluntary character, however, article 34 TFEU [ex 28 EC Treaty]

---

207 ECJ, Omega Spielhallen- und Automatenaufstellungs-GmbH v. Oberbürgermeisterin der Bundesstadt Bonn, C-36/02, 14.10.2004, para. 14; ECJ, International Transport Workers' Federation, Finnish Seamen's Union v. Viking Line ABP, OÜ Viking Line Eesti, C-438/05, 11.12.2007, para. 75; ECJ, Dynamic Medien v. Avides Media AG, C-244/06, 14.02.2008, para. 42.

208 SNELL, Jukka, *Goods and services in EC Law – A study of the relationship between the freedoms*, Oxford, Oxford University Press, 2002, 196. See also *supra*, Part 2, Chapter 1.

209 MACGOWAN, Nicholas and QUINN, Mary, "Could article 30 impose obligations on individuals?", *European Law Review* 1987, Volume 12, Issue 3, 163–178; SNELL, Jukka, "Private parties and the free movement of goods and services", in: ANDENAS, Mads and ROTH, Wulf-Henning (eds), *Services and free movement in EU law*, Oxford, Oxford University Press, 2002, 211.

210 OLIVER, Peter, *Free movement of goods in the European Community under articles 28 to 30 of the EC Treaty*, London, Sweet and Maxwell, 2003, 58; SNELL, Jukka, "Private parties and the free movement of goods and services", in: ANDENAS, Mads and ROTH, Wulf-Henning (eds), *Services and free movement in EU law*, Oxford, Oxford University Press, 2002, 219.

211 ECJ, Aragonesa de Publicidad Exterior SA and Publivía SAE v. Departamento de Sanidad y Seguridad Social de la Generalitat de Cataluña, C-1/90, 25.07.1991, para. 8.

212 OLIVER, Peter, *Free movement of goods in the European Community under articles 28 to 30 of the EC Treaty*, London, Sweet and Maxwell, 2003, 58–59.

will in all probability not be applicable.[213] This is because the ECJ requires at least 'support of the public authorities', as stated in the case *Apple and Pear Development Council*:

> *As the Court held in its judgment of 24 November 1982 in case 249/81 [...], a publicity campaign to promote the sale and purchase of domestic products may, in certain circumstances, fall within the prohibition contained in article [28, ex 30] of the Treaty, if the campaign is supported by the public authorities. In fact, a body such as the development council, which is set up by the government of a Member State and is financed by a charge imposed on growers, cannot under Community Law enjoy the same freedom as regards the methods of advertising used as that enjoyed by producers themselves or producers' associations of a voluntary character.*[214] [N.B. Articles refer to articles prior to the adoption of the Treaty of Lisbon]

Furthermore, it has been argued that measures taken by bodies created or approved by government or bodies to which national legislative bodies have delegated powers[215] could fall under the free movement of goods provisions.[216] SNELL observed that

> *[...] the involvement of private bodies does not make Article [28, ex 30] inapplicable if the State can be seen as the source of the measure. This is the case if the State uses a controlled private body as a medium through which the measure is brought into effect.*[217] [N.B. Articles refer to articles prior to the adoption of the Treaty of Lisbon]

---

[213] SNELL, Jukka, "Private parties and the free movement of goods and services", in: ANDENAS, Mads and ROTH, Wulf-Henning (eds), *Services and free movement in EU law*, Oxford, Oxford University Press, 2002, 220.

[214] ECJ, Apple and Pear Development Council v. K.J. Lewis Ltd and others, C-222/82, 13.12.1983, para. 17.

[215] ECJ, The Queen v. Royal Pharmaceutical Society of Great Britain, ex parte Association of Pharmaceutical Importers and others, C-266 and 267/87, 18.05.1989, para. 15: "*measures adopted by a professional body on which national legislation had conferred powers of that nature may, if they are capable of affecting trade between Member States, constitute 'measures' within the meaning of Article [34, ex 28] of the Treaty*". See also: ECJ, Ruth Hünermund and others v. Landesapothekerkammer Baden-Württemberg, C-292/92, 15.12.1993, paras 14–16.

[216] LANE, Robert, "The internal market and the individual", in: SHUIBHNE, Niamh Nic (ed.), *Regulating the internal market*, Cheltenham, Edward Elgar, 2006, 263; WOODS, Lorna, *Free movement of goods and services within the European Community*, Aldershot, Ashgate, 2004, 37.

[217] SNELL, Jukka, "Private parties and the free movement of goods and services", in: ANDENAS, Mads and ROTH, Wulf-Henning (eds), *Services and free movement in EU law*, Oxford, Oxford University Press, 2002, 219.

Woods concluded that, in this respect, the 'form' of the body is not the decisive factor. Instead, the nature of the powers exercised, especially "*whether they are compulsory or backed up by legislation*", must be considered when deciding on the applicability of articles 34 to 36 TFEU [ex 28 to 30 EC Treaty].[218] Snell indicated that direct or indirect financing by the State of a body that takes measures could also entail the applicability of the free movement of goods provisions.[219] Roth and Oliver summarised as follows:

> *The Court rightly applies the four freedoms not only to measures of the Member States and their subdivisions, but also to public enterprises and to private organisations to which state powers are delegated, or which are set up, staffed and perhaps financed by the State. In such cases which are characterized by an intermingling of the public and the private sphere, the application of the four freedoms seems to be necessary, for the simple reason that strategies of evading the application of the four freedoms should be forestalled at the outset.*[220]

From the above mentioned literature and case law, we can deduce that a certain level of government involvement in a private body – ranging from rather limited to extensive – is required if its measures are to fall under the free movement of goods provisions. Bodies in which there is no or very little government involvement will therefore probably fall outside their scope. However, it remains possible that such bodies would instead fall under EU competition principles (*infra*).

Applicability to individuals – A next – related – question, potentially relevant to self- or co-regulatory schemes, is whether articles 34 and 35 TFEU [ex 28 and 29 EC Treaty] could also apply to actions of individuals. We found that it is generally accepted that, in principle, this is not the case.[221]

---

[218] Woods, Lorna, *Free movement of goods and services within the European Community*, Aldershot, Ashgate, 2004, 37. Woods advocated a coherent approach to determine the boundary between public and private bodies, since inconsistencies could lead to either an overlap or a gap given the interrelationship between the free movement of goods provisions and the competition provisions (p. 38).

[219] Snell, Jukka, "Private parties and the free movement of goods and services", in: Andenas, Mads and Roth, Wulf-Henning (eds), *Services and free movement in EU law*, Oxford, Oxford University Press, 2002, 220.

[220] Roth, Wulf-Henning and Oliver, Peter, "The internal market and the four freedoms", *Common Market Law Review* 2004, Volume 41, 425.

[221] Woods, Lorna, *Free movement of goods and services within the European Community*, Aldershot, Ashgate, 2004, 29. However, Woods advances some arguments that could support the contrary (p. 30–35). One exception that is often put forward relates to intellectual property rights. There is, however, no clear consensus on whether the ECJ actually considers these 'private measures' to fall within the scope of articles 34 to 36 TFEU [ex 28 to 30 EC Treaty]. For a detailed overview of this issue: cf. Snell, Jukka, "Private parties and

In this context, the ECJ stated in the *Vlaamse reisbureaus* case that "*[...] articles [34, ex 28] and [35, ex 29] of the Treaty concern only public measures and not the conduct of undertakings*".[222] In this context, the academic literature and ECJ case law have repeatedly stressed the distinction between actions of Member States, which fall under the free movement of goods provisions, and actions of private parties, which fall under the competition provisions.[223] In the *Van de Haar* case, for instance, the ECJ observed that whereas

> *article [81, ex 85] of the Treaty belongs to the rules on competition which are addressed to undertakings and associations of undertakings and which are intended to maintain effective competition in the common market [...] [a]rticle [28, ex 30], on the other hand, belongs to the rules which seek to ensure the free movement of goods and, to that end, to eliminate measures taken by Member States which might in any way impede such free movement.*[224] [N.B. Articles refer to articles prior to the adoption of the Treaty of Lisbon]

A similar observation was made in the *Bayer v. Süllhöfer* case:

> *[...] articles [28 et seq., ex 30 et seq.] form part of the rules intended to ensure the free movement of goods and to eliminate for that purpose any measures of Member States likely to form, in any way, a barrier thereto. Agreements between undertakings, on the other hand, are governed by the rules on competition in Article [81, ex 85] et seq. of the Treaty, whose aim is to maintain effective competition within the common market.*[225] [N.B. Articles refer to articles prior to the adoption of the Treaty of Lisbon]

the free movement of goods and services", in: ANDENAS, Mads and ROTH, Wulf-Henning (eds), *Services and free movement in EU law*, Oxford, Oxford University Press, 2002, 213–218; VAN DEN BOGAERT, Stefaan, "Horizontality: the Court attacks?", 123–152, in: BARNARD, Catherine and SCOTT, Joanne, *The law of the single European market*, Oxford, Hart Publishing, 2002, 414 p.

[222] ECJ, ASBL Vereniging van Vlaamse Reisbureaus v. ASBL Sociale Dienst van de Plaatselijke en Gewestelijke Overheidsdiensten, C-311/85, 01.10.1987, para. 30.

[223] LANE, Robert, "The internal market and the individual", in: SHUIBHNE, Niamh Nic (ed.), *Regulating the internal market*, Cheltenham, Edward Elgar, 2006, 253: "*Internal market rules are for the Member States, for public authorities; competition rules are for individuals*". LANE observed, however, that "*the boundary between the two fields is beginning to break down, allowing a degree of haemorrhaging of principles between them*" (p. 254). See also: MACGOWAN, Nicholas and QUINN, Mary, "Could article 30 impose obligations on individuals?", *European Law Review* 1987, Volume 12, Issue 3, 163–178; ROTH, Wulf-Henning and OLIVER, Peter, "The internal market and the four freedoms", *Common Market Law Review* 2004, Volume 41, 423.

[224] ECJ, Criminal proceedings against Jan van de Haar and Kaveka de Meern BV, C-177 and 178/2, 05.04.1984, paras 11 and 12.

[225] ECJ, Bayer AG and Maschinenfabrik Hennecke GmbH v. Heinz Süllhöfer, C-65/86, 27.09.1988, para. 11.

MEMBER STATE RESPONSIBILITY – However, even if actions taken by private individuals are not directly subject to the free movement of goods provisions, Member States can be held responsible for actions taken by their citizens.[226] In the *Commission v. France* case (also dubbed the *Angry Farmers* case),[227] for instance, the ECJ held that

> *[a]rticle [28, ex 30] therefore requires the Member States not merely themselves to abstain from adopting measures or engaging in conduct liable to constitute an obstacle to trade but also, when read with Article 5 of the Treaty, to take all necessary and appropriate measures to ensure that that fundamental freedom is respected on their territory.*[228] [N.B. Articles refer to articles prior to the adoption of the Treaty of Lisbon]

Hence, if self- or co-regulatory bodies do not fulfil the conditions to be considered a public body, Member States could still be held responsible if measures taken by these bodies seriously infringe the fundamental right to free movement of goods. It can be noted, however, that the ECJ case law on Member State responsibility for actions by private parties is not very clear: it is, for instance, uncertain which private measures Member States should act upon. SNELL has also pointed out that situations in which private parties exercise their fundamental rights might be particularly problematic.[229] In such circumstances, the fulfilment of two rights, the right to free movement of goods and the fundamental right in question – for instance, the freedom of expression – will need to be balanced.

---

226 LANE, Robert, "The internal market and the individual", in: SHUIBHNE, Niamh Nic (ed.), *Regulating the internal market*, Cheltenham, Edward Elgar, 267; SNELL, Jukka, "Private parties and the free movement of goods and services", in: ANDENAS, Mads and ROTH, Wulf-Henning (eds), *Services and free movement in EU law*, Oxford, Oxford University Press, 2002, 236 *et seq.*

227 A year after this judgment, a Council Regulation was adopted that provided the Commission with an intervention mechanism for situations where a Member State fails to take measures when actions of private parties threaten the free movement of goods: COUNCIL Regulation (EC) No 2678/98 of 7 December 1998 on the functioning of the internal market in relation to the free movement of goods among the Member States, *OJ* 12.12.1998, *L* 337, 8.

228 ECJ, Commission of the European Communities v French Republic, C-265/95, 09.12.1997, para. 32.

229 SNELL, Jukka, "Private parties and the free movement of goods and services", in: ANDENAS, Mads and ROTH, Wulf-Henning (eds), *Services and free movement in EU law*, Oxford, Oxford University Press, 2002, 239.

A.4. *Application of theory in practice: Dynamic Medien v. Avides Media*

Factual elements – In the context of the free movement of goods, an interesting judgment of the ECJ was delivered in February 2008. The *Dynamic Medien v. Avides Media* case dealt with the question whether articles 34 to 36 TFEU [ex 28 to 30 EC Treaty] (in conjunction with the e-Commerce Directive)[230] preclude national rules which "*prohibit the sale and transfer by mail order of image storage media which have not been examined or classified by the competent authority for the purpose of protecting young persons and which does [sic] not bear a label from that authority indicating the age from which they may be viewed*".[231] This is a question which could be relevant to all (alternative) regulatory schemes which involve the labelling or rating of content. The national rules *in casu* were a number of articles of the German *Jugendschutzgesetz*, which deal with sale (by mail order) of image storage media to young persons.[232] In short, article 12 *Jugendschutzgesetz* stipulates that all kinds of image storage media containing, for instance, films or games, may only be made publicly accessible to children or adolescents if they have been authorised for that person's age range and labelled by the highest authority of the *Land* or by a voluntary self-regulation body (or if they are information, educational or training programmes, labelled by the supplier as 'information programmes' or 'educational programmes').[233] If these image storage media have not been labelled or have been labelled 'not suitable for young persons', they may not be offered, transferred or otherwise made accessible to a child or adolescent, nor be offered or transferred in retail trade outside of commercial premises, in kiosks or in other sales outlets which customers do not usually enter, nor by mail order.[234] Mail order is defined in the *Jugendschutzgesetz* as "*any transaction for consideration carried out by means of the ordering and dispatch of a product by postal or electronic means without personal contact between the supplier and the purchaser or without technical or other safeguards to ensure that the product is not dispatched to children or adolescents*".[235] The case itself concerned the importation of Japanese cartoons called 'Animes' in DVD or video cassette format from the United Kingdom to Germany by mail order via Internet.

[230] *Supra*, Part 2, Chapter 1.

[231] ECJ, Dynamic Medien v. Avides Media AG, C-244/06, 14.02.2008, para. 16.

[232] *Jugendschutzgesetz* [*Protection of young persons Act*], vom 23. Juli 2002 (BGBl. I S 2730 ff., 2003 I S. 476), retrieved from http://www.kjm-online.de/public/kjm/downloads/juschg%20081128.pdf (on 05.01.2009) [in German].

[233] Article 12 para. 1 *Jugendschutzgesetz.*

[234] Article 12 para. 3 *Jugendschutzgesetz.*

[235] Article 1 para. 4 *Jugendschutzgesetz.*

These cartoons were rated by the BBFC (British Board of Film Classification) as suitable only for audiences aged fifteen years and over, but they were not labelled by any German authority. A case was brought before a German court, the *Landgericht Koblenz*, by a competitor of the seller and this Court referred a number of questions to the ECJ for a preliminary ruling.

ECJ JUDGMENT – The ECJ confirmed, in its first phase of analysis, that the German national rules – which were found to be applicable not only to suppliers established on German territory but also to suppliers established in other Member States – "*constitute a measure having equivalent effect to quantitative restrictions within the meaning of Article [34, ex 28] EC, which in principle is incompatible with the obligations arising from that article unless it can be objectively justified*".[236] In a second phase, the ECJ examined whether the fact that the German rules aimed at protecting children against harmful material could satisfy the requirements of an exception under article 36 TFEU [ex 30 EC Treaty]. Although the ECJ confirmed that the protection of children against such content undoubtedly constitutes a legitimate interest, it stressed that measures implemented to achieve this interest need to be suitable, and may not go beyond what is necessary in order to attain it.[237] The ECJ concluded that the measures were indeed suitable to attain the objective in question, and found that they did not go beyond what is necessary, since the *Jugendschutzgesetz* does not preclude all forms of marketing of unchecked image storage media.[238] However, one important condition was postulated by the Court: the examination procedure, necessary to label the content in accordance with German law, should be one which "*is readily accessible, can be completed within a reasonable period, and, if it leads to a refusal, the decision of refusal must be open to challenge before the courts*".[239] In the present case, the measures were found to fulfil this condition.

PROPORTIONALITY – Interestingly, the ECJ stressed that measures laid down by one State to protect the rights of children do not have to correspond to a 'common conception' shared by all Member States as regards to the level

[236] ECJ, Dynamic Medien v. Avides Media AG, C-244/06, 14.02.2008, paras 21 and 35.

[237] ECJ, Dynamic Medien v. Avides Media AG, C-244/06, 14.02.2008, para. 46.

[238] ECJ, Dynamic Medien v. Avides Media AG, C-244/06, 14.02.2008, para. 48: it is still "*permissible to import and sell such image storage media to adults by way of distribution channels involving personal contact between the supplier and the purchaser, which thus ensures that children do not have access to the image storage media concerned*".

[239] ECJ, Dynamic Medien v. Avides Media AG, C-244/06, 14.02.2008, para. 50.

of protection and related regulatory details.[240] Hence, there is a margin of discretion for Member States – which often hold varying moral or cultural views – in determining the exact scope of fundamental values and the appropriate level of protection (*in casu* the protection of minors).[241] Furthermore, the ECJ emphasised that "*the mere fact that a Member State has opted for a system of protection which differs from that adopted by another Member State cannot affect the assessment of the proportionality of the national provisions enacted to that end*".[242] It is worth keeping this clarification in mind when dealing with cases where the protection of minors is put forward as a justification for interferences with the free movement of goods (or in fact, generally, with respect to interferences with Community law).

Conclusion – From the *Dynamic Medien v. Avides Media* case, we can gather a number of points. First of all, the case demonstrates that a system such as the German one, which can be classified as co-regulatory (cf. *supra*, Part 1, Chapter 2), aimed at protecting minors from harmful content, can interfere with the free movement of goods as provided for in articles 34 and 35 TFEU [ex 28 and 29 EC Treaty]. Second, the case shows that such systems with this aim can be justified under article 36 TFEU [ex 30 EC Treaty] if the measures they are implementing are suitable for attaining the aim, and if they do not go beyond what is necessary. This will depend largely on the actual structure and organisation of alternative regulatory systems and, hence, this will need to be examined on a case-by-case basis. Third, there is the interesting condition the ECJ puts forward with respect to the labelling procedure, i.e., that it must be readily accessible, can be completed within a reasonable time frame, and must be appealable. Again, the fulfilment of these conditions will depend on the specifics of each system. However, it might be sensible to take these requirements, put forward by the ECJ, into account when creating an alternative regulatory system. This is especially the case with regard to the final requirement, i.e., the possibility to challenge decisions by an alternative regulatory body before a court (cf. procedural guarantees, *supra*), which might be one that would most often be lacking.

---

[240] ECJ, Dynamic Medien v. Avides Media AG, C-244/06, 14.02.2008, para. 44. Cf. also ECJ, Omega Spielhallen- und Automatenaufstellungs-GmbH v. Oberbürgermeisterin der Bundesstadt Bonn, C-36/02, 14.10.2004, para. 37: "*It is not indispensable in that respect for the restrictive measure issued by the authorities of a Member State to correspond to a conception shared by all Member States as regards the precise way in which the fundamental right or legitimate interest in question is to be protected*".

[241] ECJ, Dynamic Medien v. Avides Media AG, C-244/06, 14.02.2008, para. 44.

[242] ECJ, Dynamic Medien v. Avides Media AG, C-244/06, 14.02.2008, para. 49.

B. *Free movement of services*

B.1. *General principles*

ARTICLES 56, 57 AND 52 TFEU [EX 49, 50 AND 46 EC TREATY] – Aside from concerns regarding the free movement of goods, issues could also arise with respect to the free movement of services. The key principles concerning the free movement of services are articles 56, 57 and 52 TFEU [ex 49, 50 and 46 EC Treaty]. According to article 56 [ex 49 EC Treaty], which has direct effect,[243] "*restrictions on freedom to provide services within the Union shall be prohibited in respect of nationals of Member States who are established in a Member State other than that of the person for whom the services are intended*". It has been accepted that article 56 TFEU [ex 49 EC Treaty] is applicable to the import as well as export of services.[244] Article 57 TFEU [ex 50 EC Treaty] further clarifies that "*services shall be considered to be 'services' within the meaning of the Treaties where they are normally provided for remuneration, in so far as they are not governed by the provisions relating to freedom of movement for goods, capital and persons*". More specifically, activities of an industrial or commercial character, and the activities of craftsmen or of the professions, fall under the notion 'services'. Again, the TFEU has provided a possibility of derogation. Article 52 TFEU [ex 46 EC Treaty] (embedded in the chapter on the right of establishment, but declared applicable to the chapter concerning services by article 62 TFEU [ex 55 EC Treaty]) allows "*provisions laid down by law, regulation or administrative action providing for special treatment for foreign nationals on grounds of public policy, public security or public health*".

B.2. *Scope*

SERVICES – It has proven difficult to describe the exact meaning of the notion 'services'. Although a few clues can be found in article 57 TFEU [ex 50 EC Treaty] (*supra*), these are not exhaustive.[245] Article 57 TFEU [ex 50 EC Treaty] suggests, first of all, that a service needs to be economic in nature. To fulfil

---

[243] SNELL, Jukka, *Goods and services in EC Law – A study of the relationship between the freedoms*, Oxford, Oxford University Press, 2002, 54.

[244] ROTH, Wulf-Henning, "Export of goods and services within the single market: reflections on the scope of articles 29 and 49 EC", in: TRIDIMAS, Takis and NEBBIA, Paolisa (eds), *European Union law for the twenty-first century: rethinking the new legal order*, Oxford, Hart Publishing, 2004, 42.

[245] WOODS, Lorna, *Free movement of goods and services within the European Community*, Aldershot, Ashgate, 2004, 159.

this requirement, the existence of an economic link between provider and recipient is sufficient; neither direct payment nor monetary remuneration is mandatory.[246] Second, this article excludes services which fall under provisions linked to freedom of goods, capital and persons. Hence, the scope of article 56 TFEU [ex 49 EC Treaty] is in part defined by elimination. The main criterion to separate goods from services is the intangible nature of the latter. This distinction is, of course, not always self-evident; if goods and services form an inseparable unity, the ECJ will decide which provisions are applicable based on the "*main focus of the activity*".[247] An example from the media sector put forward by Böttcher and Castendyk is video-on-demand, with regard to which they argue that "*the focus of activities is not on the trade in goods, which is only incidental to the provision of services but on the transmission of data*".[248] If it is not possible to make a distinction, the applicability of both articles 34 and 56 TFEU [ex 28 and 49 EC Treaty] will be examined by the Court, who will decide on the most suitable qualification.[249] A further

246 Hatzopoulos, Vassilis and Do, Thien Uyen, "The case law of the ECJ concerning the free provisions of services: 2000–2005", *Common Market Law Review* 2006, Vol. 43, 947; Woods, Lorna, *Free movement of goods and services within the European Community*, Aldershot, Ashgate, 2004, 165. Woods uses the example of free-to-air commercial television to demonstrate that direct payment nor monetary remuneration is required. Cf. also: ECJ, Bond van Adverteerders and others v. The Netherlands State, C-352/85, 26.04.1988, para. 16: "*Firstly, the cable network operators are paid, in the form of the fees which they charge their subscribers, for the service which they provide for the broadcasters. It is irrelevant that the broadcasters generally do not themselves pay the cable network operators for relaying their programmes. Article [57, ex 50] does not require the service to be paid for by those for whom it is performed. Secondly, the broadcasters are paid by the advertisers for the service which they perform for them in scheduling their advertisements*". Böttcher and Castendyk also observed that, generally, the transmission of television programmes and commercial communications is provided for remuneration; whether Internet services are provided for remuneration will need to be examined on a case-by-case basis: Böttcher, Kathrin and Castendyk, Oliver, "Part III Community policies, Title III Free movement of persons, services and capital, Chapter 3 Services", in: Castendyk, Oliver, Dommering, Egbert J. and Scheuer, Alexander (eds), *European media law*, Alphen a/d Rijn, Kluwer Law International, 2008, 105.

247 Böttcher, Kathrin and Castendyk, Oliver, "Part III Community policies, Title III Free movement of persons, services and capital, Chapter 3 Services", in: Castendyk, Oliver, Dommering, Egbert J. and Scheuer, Alexander (eds), *European media law*, Alphen a/d Rijn, Kluwer Law International, 2008, 100.

248 Böttcher, Kathrin and Castendyk, Oliver, "Part III Community policies, Title III Free movement of persons, services and capital, Chapter 3 Services", in: Castendyk, Oliver, Dommering, Egbert J. and Scheuer, Alexander (eds), *European media law*, Alphen a/d Rijn, Kluwer Law International, 2008, 100.

249 Böttcher, Kathrin and Castendyk, Oliver, "Part III Community policies, Title III Free movement of persons, services and capital, Chapter 3 Services", in: Castendyk, Oliver,

prerequisite for the applicability of article 56 TFEU [ex 49 EC Treaty] is a trans-border element in the provision of the services in question.[250] In this context, Woods has identified four possible scenarios:

1. the service provider moves to another Member State;
2. the service recipient moves to another Member State;
3. both provider and recipient move to another Member State;
4. the service itself moves (for instance broadcasting[251] or telecommunications services).[252]

Hence, both the import and export of services falls within the scope of article 56 TFEU [ex 49 EC Treaty],[253] contrary to the free movement of goods, where imports and exports are dealt with in two different articles.

Restrictions – Article 56 TFEU [ex 49 EC Treaty] was designed to eliminate all sorts of restrictions on the free movement of services. It is thus not surprising that much case law has been devoted to exploring what sorts of restrictions could fall within the scope of this article. One of the most pertinent questions in this area – and one that parallels the discussions surrounding the free movement of goods provisions – concerns the applicability of article 56 TFEU [ex 49 EC Treaty], not only to directly discriminatory measures, but also to 'indistinctly applicable' measures. This question was addressed by the ECJ in the *Säger* case:

> *It should first be pointed out that Article [49, ex 59] of the Treaty requires not only the elimination of all discrimination against a person providing services on the ground of his nationality but also the abolition of any restriction, even if it applies without distinction to national providers of services and to those of other Member States, when it is liable to prohibit or otherwise impede the activities*

Dommering, Egbert J. and Scheuer, Alexander (eds), *European media law*, Alphen a/d Rijn, Kluwer Law International, 2008, 101.

[250] However, the ECJ has not always interpreted the need for a transborder element in a restrictive manner: cf. Hatzopoulos, Vassilis and Do, Thien Uyen, "The case law of the ECJ concerning the free provisions of services: 2000–2005", *Common Market Law Review* 2006, Vol. 43, 944–946.

[251] For more details: cf. Böttcher, Kathrin and Castendyk, Oliver, "Part III Community policies, Title III Free movement of persons, services and capital, Chapter 3 Services", in: Castendyk, Oliver, Dommering, Egbert J. and Scheuer, Alexander (eds), *European media law*, Alphen a/d Rijn, Kluwer Law International, 2008, 106–107.

[252] Woods, Lorna, *Free movement of goods and services within the European Community*, Aldershot, Ashgate, 2004, 164.

[253] Woods, Lorna, *Free movement of goods and services within the European Community*, Aldershot, Ashgate, 2004, 164.

> *of a provider of services established in another Member State where he lawfully provides similar services.*[254] [N.B. Articles refer to articles prior to the adoption of the Treaty of Lisbon]

A detailed examination of this and other questions would, however, lead us too far from the focus of this study.[255] Suffice to say that the scope of article 56 TFEU [ex 49 EC Treaty] has been interpreted in a broad manner:[256] "*any national rule which has the effect of making the provision of services between Member States more difficult than the provision of services purely within one Member State*" falls within its scope.[257]

Articles 62 and 52 TFEU [ex 55 and 46 EC Treaty]: derogation – As is the case with other fundamental rights and freedoms, derogations from the free movement of services provisions may be allowed, provided that they are justified on grounds of public policy, public security or public health.[258] Again, any restriction on the free movement of services needs to be strictly interpreted and must be proportional.[259] Clarifications on the potential scope of derogations are found not only in case law, but also in a directive which

254 ECJ, Manfred Säger v. Dennemeyer & Co. Ltd, C-76/90, 25.07.1991, para. 12.

255 For more details, cf. Snell, Jukka, *Goods and services in EC Law – A study of the relationship between the freedoms*, Oxford, Oxford University Press, 2002, 60–65; Woods, Lorna, *Free movement of goods and services within the European Community*, Aldershot, Ashgate, 2004, Chapters 10 and 11. See also: Snell, Jukka and Andenas, Mads, "Exploring the outer limits: restrictions on the free movement of goods and services", 69–139, in: Andenas, Mads and Roth, Wulf-Henning, *Services and free movement in EU law*, Oxford, Oxford University Press, 2002, 466 p.

256 Woods, Lorna, *Free movement of goods and services within the European Community*, Aldershot, Ashgate, 2004, 216. For more details on interpretations by the ECJ of the concept 'services', cf. Hatzopoulos, Vassilis and Do, Thien Uyen, "The case law of the ECJ concerning the free provisions of services: 2000–2005", *Common Market Law Review* 2006, Vol. 43, 924–956.

257 ECJ, Raymond Kohll v. Union des caisses de maladie, C-158/96, 28.04.1998, para. 33; ECJ, Jessica Safir v. Skattemyndigheten i Dalarnas Län, formerly Skattemyndigheten i Kopparbergs Län, C-118/96, 28.04.1998, para. 23.

258 Article 52 TFEU [ex 46 EC Treaty] (a provision of the Chapter on Right of establishment), declared applicable to the free movement of services by article 62 TFEU [ex 55 EC Treaty]. The fact that there are fewer grounds for derogation mentioned in article 52 TFEU [ex 46 EC Treaty] than in article 36 TFEU [ex 30 EC Treaty] has not been considered very significant. Neither has the lack of a reference to the prohibition of "*arbitrary discrimination or a disguised restriction on trade between Member States*" (second sentence article 36 TFEU [ex 30 EC Treaty]) in article 52 TFEU [ex 46 EC Treaty] been considered important. Cf. Snell, Jukka, *Goods and services in EC Law – A study of the relationship between the freedoms*, Oxford, Oxford University Press, 2002, 175 and 181.

259 Snell, Jukka, *Goods and services in EC Law – A study of the relationship between the freedoms*, Oxford, Oxford University Press, 2002, 174; Woods, Lorna, *Free movement of goods and services within the European Community*, Aldershot, Ashgate, 2004, 231.

implemented article 53 TFEU [ex 46 EC Treaty]. Directive 64/221[260] is applicable to "*any national of a Member State who resides in or travels to another Member State of the Community, either in order to pursue an activity as an employed or self-employed person, or as a recipient of services*", as well as "*to the spouse and to members of the family who come within the provisions of the regulations and directives adopted in this field in pursuance of the Treaty*".[261] Hence, its scope of application covers only a part of the scope of application of the free movement of services provisions. One of the clarifications the Directive provides is that (parallel to the free movement of goods) a ground for derogation cannot be invoked to service economic ends.[262] Notwithstanding the fact that Directive 64/221 attempted to shed some light on the scope of derogation,[263] no clear-cut definitions or descriptions of the notions 'public policy, public security or public health' were, however, given. For situations which do not fall within the scope of the Directive (for instance, when services themselves travel across borders),[264] of course articles 52 and 62 TFEU [ex 46 and 55 EC Treaty] remain applicable.[265] Interestingly, the ECJ has stated that private individuals as well may rely on the derogation grounds of public policy, public security or public health:

> *There is nothing to preclude individuals from relying on justifications on grounds of public policy, public security or public health. Neither the scope nor the content of those grounds of justification is in any way affected by the public or private nature of the rules in question.* [266]

---

[260] Council Directive 64/221/EEC of 25 February 1964 on the co-ordination of special measures concerning the movement and residence of foreign nationals which are justified on grounds of public policy, public security or public health, *OJ* 04.04.1964, *L* 56, 850.

[261] Article 1 paras 1 and 2 Council Directive 64/221/EEC of 25 February 1964 on the co-ordination of special measures concerning the movement and residence of foreign nationals which are justified on grounds of public policy, public security or public health, *OJ* 04.04.1964, *L* 56, 850.

[262] Article 2 para. 2 Council Directive 64/221/EEC of 25 February 1964 on the co-ordination of special measures concerning the movement and residence of foreign nationals which are justified on grounds of public policy, public security or public health, *OJ* 04.04.1964, *L* 56, 850.

[263] For instance, in an Annex to the Directive a number of diseases which might endanger public health or which might threaten public policy or public security are listed.

[264] Woods, Lorna, *Free movement of goods and services within the European Community*, Aldershot, Ashgate, 2004, 232 and 237.

[265] In this context it can, for instance, be observed that the notion 'public policy' is interpreted in a broad manner (e.g., as encompassing public morality). Woods, Lorna, *Free movement of goods and services within the European Community*, Aldershot, Ashgate, 2004, 238.

[266] ECJ, Union royale belge des sociétés de football association ASBL v. Jean-Marc Bosman, Royal club liégeois SA v. Jean-Marc Bosman and others and Union des associations européennes de football (UEFA) v. Jean-Marc Bosman, C-415/93, 15.12.1995, para. 86.

Note that this judgment related to free movement of persons (workers). However, as the ECJ often uses the same principles regarding the four freedoms (free movement of goods, services, persons and capital), the possibility for private parties to rely on the grounds for derogation might be considered applicable to the free movement of goods and services as well, notwithstanding the fact that article 52 TFEU [ex 46 EC Treaty] speaks of "*provisions laid down by law, regulation or administrative action*". Snell has pointed out that the significance of the difference in wording in this respect between article 36 TFEU [ex 30 EC Treaty] and article 52 TFEU [ex 46 EC Treaty] is uncertain.[267]

A final observation relates to the possibility of non-discriminatory measures, which could still fall within the scope of article 56 TFEU [ex 49 EC Treaty], to be justified on grounds of public interest.[268] A number of such 'grounds of public interest'[269] have been accepted by the ECJ, for instance consumer protection, public morality, and cultural policy objectives.[270] It is plausible that the protection of minors could be considered a ground of public interest as well. However, whether the Treaty or the ECJ 'rule of reason' approach is relied upon, any restriction on the free movement of services will still need to stand the proportionality test, meaning that the restriction cannot go beyond what is necessary to reach the goal of public interest and is proportional to this goal.[271]

---

267 Snell, Jukka, *Goods and services in EC Law – A study of the relationship between the freedoms*, Oxford, Oxford University Press, 2002, 172–173.

268 O'Leary, Síofra and Fernández-Martín, José M., "Judicially-created exceptions to the free provision of services", 163–195, in: Andenas, Mads and Roth, Wulf-Henning (eds), *Services and free movement in EU law*, Oxford, Oxford University Press, 2002, 466 p.; Woods, Lorna, *Free movement of goods and services within the European Community*, Aldershot, Ashgate, 2004, 249. Cf. also with respect to free movement of goods, *supra*.

269 In the *De Agostini* case, the ECJ spoke of "*overriding requirements of general public importance*" (in relation to goods as well as services): ECJ, Konsumentombudsmannen (KO) v. De Agostini (Svenska) Förlag AB (C-34/95) and TV-Shop i Sverige AB (C-35/95 and C-36/95), C-34–35–36/95, 09.07.1997, paras 45 and 52.

270 Woods, Lorna, *Free movement of goods and services within the European Community*, Aldershot, Ashgate, 2004, 249.

271 Woods, Lorna, *Free movement of goods and services within the European Community*, Aldershot, Ashgate, 2004, 254. See also: ECJ, Bond van Adverteerders and others v. The Netherlands State, C-352/85, 26.04.1988, para. 36: "*As an exception to a fundamental principle of the Treaty, article [52, ex 46] of the Treaty must be interpreted in such a way that its effects are limited to that which is necessary in order to protect the interests which it seeks to safeguard*".

B.3. *Applicability to actions of private parties*

Free movement of services and private parties – Contrary to the provisions regarding goods, the ECJ has accepted that the free movement of services provisions have a certain horizontal effect.[272] Although the Member States are the primary addressees of article 56 TFEU [ex 49 EC Treaty] (even though they are not explicitly mentioned),[273] actions of private individuals can also fall within the scope of the provision. In the *Walrave and Koch* case the ECJ held that

> *Prohibition of such discrimination does not only apply to the action of public authorities but extends likewise to rules of any other nature aimed at regulating in a collective manner gainful employment and the provision of services. [...] The abolition as between Member States of obstacles to freedom of movement for persons and to freedom to provide services, which are fundamental objectives of the Community contained in article 3 (c) of the Treaty, would be compromised if the abolition of barriers of national origin could be neutralized by obstacles resulting from the exercise of their legal autonomy by associations or organizations which do not come under public law. [...] Although the third paragraph of article [50, ex 60], and articles 62 [abolished] and [53, ex 64], specifically relate, as regard the provision of services, to the abolition of measures by the state, this fact does not defeat the general nature of the terms of article [49, ex 59], which makes no distinction between the source of the restrictions to be abolished.*[274] [N.B. Articles refer to articles prior to the adoption of the Treaty of Lisbon]

Notwithstanding the fact that the Court did not explicitly declare article 56 TFEU [ex 49 EC Treaty] applicable to all private measures – the measures

---

[272] Woods, Lorna, *Free movement of goods and services within the European Community*, Aldershot, Ashgate, 2004, 185–186.

[273] Snell, Jukka, "Private parties and the free movement of goods and services", in: Andenas, Mads and Roth, Wulf-Henning (eds), *Services and free movement in EU law*, Oxford, Oxford University Press, 2002, 222.

[274] ECJ, B.N.O. Walrave and L.J.N. Koch v. Association Union cycliste internationale, Koninklijke Nederlandsche Wielren Unie and Federación Española Ciclismo, C-36/74, 12.12.1974, paras 17–18 and 20. Later cases were, for instance: ECJ, Eberhard Haug-Adrion v. Frankfurter Versicherungs-AG, C-251/83, 13.12.1984; ECJ, Union royale belge des sociétés de football association ASBL v. Jean-Marc Bosman, Royal club liégeois SA v. Jean-Marc Bosman and others and Union des associations européennes de football (UEFA) v. Jean-Marc Bosman, C-415/93, 15.12.1995; ECJ, Christelle Deliège v. Ligue francophone de judo et disciplines associées ASBL, Ligue belge de judo ASBL, Union européenne de judo (C-51/96) and François Pacquée (C-191/97), C-51/96 and C-191/97, 11.04.2000 ; ECJ, Roman Angonese v. Cassa di Risparmio di Bolzano SpA, C-281/98, 06.06.2000. Cf. Van Den Bogaert, Stefaan, "Horizontality: the Court attacks?", 123–152, in: Barnard, Catherine and Scott, Joanne, *The law of the single European market*, Oxford, Hart Publishing, 2002, 414 p.

in question often had a collective nature[275] – the Court's acceptance that private measures can fall within the scope of article 56 TFEU [ex 49 EC Treaty] has gone much further than in the case of free movement of goods.[276] SNELL has noted that the ECJ sometimes does not even deem it essential to scrutinise the link between the measure taken by the private party and the Member State (as it routinely does with respect to free movement of goods provisions).[277] Hence, we can deduce that measures taken by a co-regulatory body and even a self-regulatory body[278] could possibly fall within the scope of the free movement of services provisions.

MEMBER STATE RESPONSIBILITY – It is accepted that Member States can be held responsible for actions taken by private parties with respect to the free movement of services as well.[279] SNELL argues that there is "*simply no reason to treat the failure of a Member State to take measures against, for instance demonstrators preventing foreign doctors from operating in an abortion clinic, any differently from a similar failure affecting the free movement of goods*".[280] Hence, similar to our conclusion with respect to the free movement of goods

275 SNELL, Jukka, *Goods and services in EC Law – A study of the relationship between the freedoms*, Oxford, Oxford University Press, 2002, 141–143. Cf. also: ECJ, Jyri Lehtonen, Castors Canada Dry Namur-Braine ASBL v. Fédération Royale Belge des Sociétés de Basket-ball ASBL (FRBSB), C-176/96, 13.04.2000, para. 35.

276 It should be noted that conclusions drawn from cases that relate to free movement of workers (such as ECJ, Roman Angonese v. Cassa di Risparmio di Bolzano SpA, C-281/98, 06.06.2000) are often considered applicable to free movement of services, without much explanation. For more details cf. VAN DEN BOGAERT, Stefaan, "Horizontality: the Court attacks?", 123–152, in: BARNARD, Catherine and SCOTT, Joanne, *The law of the single European market*, Oxford, Hart Publishing, 2002, 414 p.

277 SNELL, Jukka, "Private parties and the free movement of goods and services", in: ANDENAS, Mads and ROTH, Wulf-Henning (eds), *Services and free movement in EU law*, Oxford, Oxford University Press, 2002, 226.

278 This was explicitly considered a possibility by ROTH and OLIVER. They have stated: "*One has to acknowledge that, although this kind of argument subjects private organizations to the exigencies of the internal market despite their autonomy, the fact remains that the instruments of self-regulation may exert the same impact on the persons concerned as measures taken by public authorities. The applications of the freedoms – as prohibitions of even-handed restrictions and of discriminatory measures – may derive its justification from the quasi-legislative character of the regulations of private organizations*": ROTH, Wulf-Henning and OLIVER, Peter, "The internal market and the four freedoms", *Common Market Law Review* 2004, Volume 41, 425.

279 SNELL, Jukka, "Private parties and the free movement of goods and services", in: ANDENAS, Mads and ROTH, Wulf-Henning (eds), *Services and free movement in EU law*, Oxford, Oxford University Press, 2002, 237.

280 SNELL, Jukka, *Goods and services in EC Law – A study of the relationship between the freedoms*, Oxford, Oxford University Press, 2002, 154.

provisions, it is not inconceivable that Member States would be held responsible for measures taken by self- or co-regulatory bodies. However, it has been pointed out that the actions in question need to be sufficiently serious for Member States to be obliged to intervene in the first place.[281] Yet, this will, of course, depend to a significant extent on the factual circumstances.

B.4. *Free movement of services and the media sector*

FREE MOVEMENT OF MEDIA SERVICES – The free movement of services is certainly relevant in the media sector. The ECJ repeatedly confirmed that broadcasting services, for instance, fall within the scope of article 56 TFEU [ex 49 EC Treaty].[282] BÖTTCHER and CASTENDYK argue, in this context, that the free movement of services provisions cover "*any form of electromagnetic transmission of information across frontiers, including terrestrial and direct satellite broadcasting and transmission via cable; Internet, multimedia and telecommunications services are also covered*".[283] Interestingly, the ECJ held in the *ERT* case that restrictions on the free movement of television services must also be appraised in the light of the fundamental right to freedom of expression.[284] In fact, any restriction must be evaluated in the light of existing fundamental rights.[285]

SPECIFIC LEGISLATION REGARDING FREE MOVEMENT OF SERVICES – There are a number of fields which the European Union considered necessary to harmonise across Member States. In the fields of audiovisual media services and

---

[281] SNELL, Jukka, *Goods and services in EC Law – A study of the relationship between the freedoms*, Oxford, Oxford University Press, 2002, 154–155.

[282] ECJ, Giuseppe Sacchi (Reference for a preliminary ruling: Tribunale civile e penale di Biella – Italy), C-155/73, 30.04.1974, para. 6: "*In the absence of express provision to the contrary in the Treaty, a television signal must, by reason of its nature, be regarded as provision of services*"; ECJ, Procureur du Roi v. Marc J.V.C. Debauve and others, C-52/79, 18.03.1980, para. 8: "*The broadcasting of television signals, including those in the nature of advertisements, comes, as such, within the rules of the Treaty relating to services*".

[283] BÖTTCHER, Kathrin and CASTENDYK, Oliver, "Part III Community policies, Title III Free movement of persons, services and capital, Chapter 3 Services", in: CASTENDYK, Oliver, DOMMERING, Egbert J. and SCHEUER, Alexander (eds), *European media law*, Alphen a/d Rijn, Kluwer Law International, 2008, 91.

[284] ECJ, Elliniki Radiophonia Tiléorassi AE and Panellinia Omospondia Syllogon Prossopikou v. Dimotiki Etairia Pliroforissis and Sotirios Kouvelas and Nicolaos Avdellas and others, C-260/89, 18.06.1991, summary para. 6.

[285] BÖTTCHER, Kathrin and CASTENDYK, Oliver, "Part III Community policies, Title III Free movement of persons, services and capital, Chapter 3 Services", in: CASTENDYK, Oliver, DOMMERING, Egbert J. and SCHEUER, Alexander (eds), *European Media Law*, Alphen a/d Rijn, Kluwer Law International, 2008, 118–199.

information society services – both relevant to the subject of this study – the AVMSD and e-Commerce Directive[286] were thus adopted, which also contain provisions regarding the free movement of audiovisual media services and information society services respectively.[287] Both directives establish a country of origin-principle which implies that Member States are not allowed to restrict the free movement of services originating from other Member States (article 3 para. 2 e-Commerce Directive and article 2a AMVSD) if these services adhere to the legislation of those latter Member States (article 3 para.1 e-Commerce Directive and article 2 AVMSD).[288] Both directives, however, allow for derogation from this general principle. One of the grounds upon which such an exception can be justified is the protection of minors (article 3 para. 4 (a)(i) e-Commerce Directive, and article 2a para. 2 (a) and para. 4 AVMSD). If Member States opt to introduce restrictions on the free movement of information society services or audiovisual media services, they need

[286] For more information on the e-Commerce Directive, cf. Valcke, Peggy and Dommering, Egbert, "e-Commerce Directive", 1081–1107, in: Castendyk, Oliver, Dommering, Egbert J. and Scheuer, Alexander (eds), *European media law*, Alphen a/d Rijn, Kluwer Law International, 2008, 1379 p.

[287] European Parliament and Council Directive 2007/65/EC of 11 December 2007 amending Council Directive 89/552/EEC on the coordination of certain provisions laid down by law, regulation or administrative action in Member States concerning the pursuit of television broadcasting activities, *OJ* 18.12.2007, *L* 332, 27; European Parliament and Council Directive 2000/31/EC of 8 June 2000 on certain legal aspects of information society services, in particular electronic commerce, in the Internal Market (Directive on electronic commerce), *OJ L* 178, 17.07.2000, 1 (also *supra*, Part 2, Chapter 1). There are other directives which could also be considered of interest to media services (for instance, the Misleading and Comparative Advertising Directives: Council Directive 84/450/EEC of 10 September 1984 relating to the approximation of the laws, regulations and administrative provisions of the Member States concerning misleading advertising, *OJ 19.9.1984, L 250, 17;* European Parliament and Council Directive 97/55/EC of 6 October 1997 amending Directive 84/450/EEC concerning misleading advertising so as to include comparative advertising, *OJ 23.10.1997, L 290, 18)*, but which will not be examined within the scope of this book.

[288] With respect to broadcasting, cf. ECJ, Commission of the European Communities v. Kingdom of Belgium, C-11/95, 10.09.1996, para. 34: "*It follows, first, that it is solely for the Member State from which television broadcasts emanate to monitor the application of the law of the originating Member State applying to such broadcasts and to ensure compliance with Directive 89/552, and, second, that the receiving Member State is not authorized to exercise its own control in that regard*". See also: Dommering, Egbert, "Article 2a AVMSD", in: Castendyk, Oliver, Dommering, Egbert J. and Scheuer, Alexander (eds), *European media law*, Alphen a/d Rijn, Kluwer Law International, 2008, 854: "*[The principle of Country of Origin] means that home State Control prevails in the coordinated area and that the receiving country may only derogate from the principle in non coordinated areas in case a compelling general interest of a non economical nature is at stake*".

to follow a strict procedure, which is described in the last three paragraphs of article 3 e-Commerce Directive and article 2a AVMSD. The European Commission[289] will closely examine the proportionality of the measures taken. The Member State which has opted to derogate from the free movement of services on the basis of a public interest will have to prove that this interest was not adequately protected in the country of origin.[290, 291]

HIERARCHY – A few remarks can be made regarding the hierarchy of applicable principles. First, it is important to note that – according to the '*lex specialis derogat legi generali*' principle – if rules applicable to specific services, such as for instance, audiovisual media services and information society services, have been harmonised by legally valid secondary legislation, these harmonised rules prevail over the general free movement of services provisions.[292] In this context, BÖTTCHER and CASTENDYK have noted that with respect to areas that have been fully harmonised, Member States cannot impose more stringent rules unless this has been explicitly allowed by the harmonisation legislation.[293] However, in this case, such stricter rules must be in accordance with the general free movement of services provisions.[294] Second, it must be noted that in the case of conflict between the AVMSD and the e-Commerce

289 And later, in case of a dispute, the ECJ.

290 DOMMERING, Egbert, "Article 2 AVMSD", in: CASTENDYK, Oliver, DOMMERING, Egbert J. and SCHEUER, Alexander (eds), *European media law*, Alphen a/d Rijn, Kluwer Law International, 2008, 849.

291 However, with respect to the AVMSD, DOMMERING has argued that such derogation measures may not relate to the substance or 'core' of Chapter IIa and b of the AVMSD (DOMMERING, Egbert, "Article 2a AVMSD", in: CASTENDYK, Oliver, DOMMERING, Egbert J. and SCHEUER, Alexander (eds), *European media law*, Alphen a/d Rijn, Kluwer Law International, 2008, 854). We assume that DOMMERING refers to, for instance, blanket restrictions or derogatory measures which run counter to the essence of the free movement of services. *De facto* derogatory measures taken vis-à-vis specific services should remain possible, provided that the procedure of article 2 para. 4 is adhered to.

292 BÖTTCHER, Kathrin and CASTENDYK, Oliver, "Part III Community policies, Title III Free movement of persons, services and capital, Chapter 3 Services", in: CASTENDYK, Oliver, DOMMERING, Egbert J. and SCHEUER, Alexander (eds), *European media law*, Alphen a/d Rijn, Kluwer Law International, 2008, 95.

293 Such as, for instance, by article 3 para. 1 AVMSD: "*Member States shall remain free to require media service providers under their jurisdiction to comply with more detailed or stricter rules in the fields coordinated by this Directive provided that such rules are in compliance with Community law*".

294 BÖTTCHER, Kathrin and CASTENDYK, Oliver, "Part III Community policies, Title III Free movement of persons, services and capital, Chapter 3 Services", in: CASTENDYK, Oliver, DOMMERING, Egbert J. and SCHEUER, Alexander (eds), *European media law*, Alphen a/d Rijn, Kluwer Law International, 2008, 95.

Directive, the AVMSD prevails (unless otherwise provided for).[295] Finally, of course, services which do not fall within the scope of the AVMSD or the e-Commerce Directive will continue to be governed by the general free movement of services provisions.

C. *Interim conclusion*

Relevance of internal market legislation for ARIs – We can conclude from the above analysis that ARIs in the field of protecting minors against harmful content could fall within the scope of the EU internal market rules. First, measures which are part of an alternative regulatory scheme can, as we have seen with respect to the *Dynamic Medien* case, impose restrictions on the free movement of goods and services. Second, although the internal market rules are primarily addressed to Member States, we found that this does not *a priori* exclude their application to measures taken by alternative regulatory bodies. With respect to the free movement of goods, we established that the ECJ interprets the notion 'Member State' in a broad manner. Depending on the level of government involvement, in our view, certain co-regulatory bodies (for instance, bodies to which national legislators have delegated powers) could, hence, be considered as falling within the scope of the free movement provisions. With respect to ARIs with no or a very limited degree of government involvement, this would probably not be the case, as the scope of articles 34 to 36 TFEU [ex 28 to 30 EC Treaty] does not extend to individuals or private parties (for instance, within the framework of a self-regulatory scheme). However, when actions of private individuals interfere with the free movement of goods, it is possible that Member States will be held responsible for these actions. Unfortunately, the case law in this area is rather vague. With respect to the free movement of services, on the other hand, the ECJ has explicitly confirmed that actions of private parties could fall within the scope of article 56 TFEU [ex 49 EC Treaty]. In addition, also with regard to services, Member States could be held responsible for actions of private actors which seriously restrict the free movement of these services.

[295] Article 3 para. 8 AVMSD. For more details on the relationship between the AVMSD and the e-Commerce Directive, cf. Dommering, Egbert, Scheuer, Alexander and Ader, Thorsten, "Article 3 AVMSD", in: Castendyk, Oliver, Dommering, Egbert J. and Scheuer, Alexander (eds), *European media law*, Alphen a/d Rijn, Kluwer Law International, 2008, 863–866.

Derogation and proportionality – We can thus conclude that when establishing ARIs to protect minors against harmful content, care should be taken that they do not restrict the free movement of services or goods. However, it would be possible to invoke the rationale behind such measures – i.e., the protection of minors – as a ground for derogation. Still, even if the ECJ would accept this, the measure in question would need to be proportional. Both with respect to the free movement of goods and of services, proportionality is an essential element when the Court decides whether a restriction can be allowed, notwithstanding its effect on Community trade. To assess a restriction, the ECJ will balance different interests, i.e., the Community interest in trade versus another general interest. Although the ECJ has not applied the proportionality test in a consistent manner,[296] in most of the cases, two key questions are examined: is the (restrictive) measure suitable to achieve the goal of public interest (suitability), and does the measure go beyond what is necessary to achieve this goal (necessity)?[297] Whereas the first test asks whether the measure aims to achieve an actual general interest goal (and hence prevents measures that "*ostensibly seek to protect a general interest but in reality have a protectionist purpose*"),[298] the second test examines whether there are alternative means to achieve the goal in question which are less restrictive for intra-Community trade.[299] Here, we might recall the *Dynamic Medien* case, in which the ECJ clarified that, with respect to measures which aim to protect minors against harmful content, the proportionality test will take into account the Member State's margin of discretion in this field. Given the diversity in views across the EU on the appropriate level of protection for children and young people, the mere fact that Member States have chosen a different level of protection will not lead to the automatic conclusion that the measures in question are not proportional.

---

[296] Snell, Jukka, *Goods and services in EC Law – A study of the relationship between the freedoms*, Oxford, Oxford University Press, 2002, 195–196.

[297] Cf. *supra*, Part 2, Chapter 1. As we have noted in the previous chapter, it is sometimes argued that a third question, that of 'true proportionality', needs to be considered. See also: cf. Snell, Jukka, *Goods and services in EC Law – A study of the relationship between the freedoms*, Oxford, Oxford University Press, 2002, 200–212 and 224: "*The Court has on occasion indicated its willingness to assess the true proportionality of national measures both in the field of goods and services. However, in recent years the Court seems to have steered away from overtly examining the true proportionality, but has consistently engaged in a marginal review of costs and benefits under the guise of the necessity test*".

[298] Snell, Jukka, *Goods and services in EC Law – A study of the relationship between the freedoms*, Oxford, Oxford University Press, 2002, 198.

[299] Snell, Jukka, *Goods and services in EC Law – A study of the relationship between the freedoms*, Oxford, Oxford University Press, 2002, 196–200.

2.2.3. *Competition rules*

RELEVANCE – As we briefly noted in the previous chapter, different policy documents, as well as the academic literature, have highlighted that the use of ARIs cannot affect the principles of competition.[300] Competition issues can be raised by self-regulation (for instance, when self-regulatory systems lead to the formation of cartels,[301] or where there are agreements which hin-

[300] For instance: COMMISSION OF THE EUROPEAN COMMUNITIES, Communication from the Commission to the Council and to the European Parliament on environmental agreements, COM (1996) 561 final, 27.11.1996, 15; COMMISSION OF THE EUROPEAN COMMUNITIES, Communication to the European Parliament, the Council, the Economic and Social Committee and the Committee of the Regions – The convergence of the telecommunications, media and information technology sectors, and the implications for regulation, Results of the public consultation on the Green Paper COM (97) 623, COM (1999) 108 final, 10.03.1999; COMMISSION OF THE EUROPEAN COMMUNITIES, Communication from the Commission Action Plan "Simplifying and improving the regulatory environment", COM (2002) 278 final, 05.06.2002, 13; COMMISSION OF THE EUROPEAN COMMUNITIES, Communication from the Commission to the European Parliament, the Council, the Economic and Social Committee and the Committee of the Regions of 17 July 2002 on environmental agreements at Community level within the framework of the Action Plan on the 'Simplification and improvement of the regulatory environment', COM (2002) 412 final, 17.07.2002, 8; Commission of the European Communities, Communication from the Commission to the European Parliament, the Council, the Economic and Social Committee and the Committee of the Regions of 17 July 2002 on environmental agreements at Community level within the framework of the Action Plan on the 'Simplification and improvement of the regulatory environment', COM (2002) 412 final, 17.07.2002, 8–9; EUROPEAN PARLIAMENT, COUNCIL, AND COMMISSION, Interinstitutional agreement on better law-making, 2003/C 321/01, *OJ* 31.12.2003, *C* 321, para. 17; VAN DEN BERGH, Roger, "Self-regulation of the medical and legal professions: remaining barriers to competition and EC-law", Paper prepared for the Conference "Pressure groups, self-regulation and enforcement mechanisms", Milan, 10–11.01.1997, retrieved from http://www.feem.it/NR/rdonlyres/DDA14FEC-D4FD-4022-9616-6105FDE83755/529/3197.pdf (30.10.2008); VEDDER, Hans, "Voluntary agreements and competition law", Working Paper Fondazione Eni Enrico Mattei, No. 79, 2000, retrieved from http://www.feem.it/NR/rdonlyres/FC5A9109-6763-4D72-B01E-A99C97874999/672/7900.pdf (on 30.10.2008); STEYGER, Elies, "European Community law and the self-regulatory capacity of society", *Journal of Common Market Studies* 1993, Vol. 31, No. 2, 173; HEUKELS, Ton, "Alternatieve implementatietechnieken en art. 189, lid 3 EEG: grondslagen en ontwikkelingen" [*Alternative implementation techniques and art. 189, para. 3 EEC: foundations and developments*], *NTB* 1993, Vol. 1, 72 [in Dutch].

[301] VERSCHUUREN, Jonathan, "EC environmental law and self-regulation in the Member States: in search of a legislative framework", *Yearbook of European Environmental Law* 2000, Vol. 1, 112; PROSSER, Tony, "Self-regulation, Co-regulation and the Audio-Visual Media Services Directive", *Journal of Consumer Policy* 2008, Vol. 31, No. 1, 103 (who, in this respect, refers to "*'club-like' restrictive practices which effectively closed markets to outsiders*").

der market entry, for example, by requiring undertakings to join an alternative regulatory association), but also with respect to co-regulation (mostly because the self-regulatory or non-state element could infringe existing competition rules).

COMPETITION PRINCIPLES – Guaranteeing open and fair competition, which should lead to the lowering of prices and an increased choice for consumers,[302] is one of the cornerstones of EU policy.[303] Whereas the internal market principles (*supra*) are essentially addressed at the Member States, the competition rules target undertakings and companies. The two key provisions are articles 101 and 102 TFEU [ex 81 and 82 EC Treaty].[304] The former article is directed at anti-competitive agreements between undertakings; the latter prohibits an undertaking's abuse of its dominant position.[305] A final article which might be of relevance to the use of ARIs is article 106 TFEU [ex 86 EC Treaty],

[302] EUROPEAN COMMISSION, EU competition policy and the consumer, 2004, retrieved from http://ec.europa.eu/comm/competition/publications/consumer_en.pdf (on 21.10.2008).

[303] Cf. article 3 para. 1 (b) TFEU [ex 3 para. 1 (g) EC Treaty]: *The Union shall have exclusive competence in the following areas: [...] (b) the establishing of competition rules necessary for the functioning of the internal market*", and article 119 TFEU [ex 4 EC Treaty]: "*For the purposes set out in Article 3 of the Treaty on European Union, the activities of the Member States and the Union shall include, as provided in the Treaties, the adoption of an economic policy which is based on the close coordination of Member States' economic policies, on the internal market and on the definition of common objectives, and conducted in accordance with the principle of an open market economy with free competition*". Cf. also: Protocol (No. 27) on the internal market and competition; AMTENBRINK, Fabian and VAN DE GRONDEN, Johan, "Economisch recht en het Verdrag van Lissabon I: mededinging en interne markt" ["*Economic law and the Treaty of Lisbon I: competition and internal market*"], *SEW* 2008, No. 9, 323–329 [in Dutch].

[304] The complete "*framework for competition law, applicable to undertakings, public enterprises and States*", is formed by articles 101 to 109 TFEU [ex 81 to 89 EC Treaty], supplemented by secondary legislation and soft law devices (ARNULL, Anthony et al., *Wyatt and Dashwood's European Union law*, London, Sweet & Maxwell, 2006, 970). However, articles 101, 102 and 106 TFEU [ex 81, 82 and 86 EC Treaty] are the most relevant with respect to the use of ARIs. Hence, we will limit our analysis to these articles, as well as the relevant case-law of the ECJ, which has played an essential role in the development of the competition rules.

[305] Again, we would like to reiterate that within the scope of this book it is not our aim to provide a comprehensive legal analysis of articles 101 and 102 TFEU [ex 81 and 82 EC Treaty]. The focus is rather on the aspects most relevant to the issue at hand, i.e., the use of ARIs. For a detailed analysis, cf. WHISH, Richard, *Competition law*, Oxford, Oxford University Press, 2009, 1006 p.; ARNULL, Anthony et al., *Wyatt and Dashwood's European Union law*, London, Sweet & Maxwell, 2006, 965–1080; ROTH, Peter and ROSE, Vivien (eds), *Bellamy & Child European Community law of competition*, Oxford, Oxford University Press, 2008, 1679 p.; TOTH, Akos (ed.), *The Oxford Encyclopaedia of European Community law – Volume III: competition law and policy*, Oxford, Oxford University Press, 2008, 832 p.

which deals with the interplay between Member States and undertakings in the field of competition.

A. *Article 101 TFEU [ex 81 EC Treaty]*

A.1. *General principle*

ARTICLE 101 TFEU [EX 81 EC TREATY] – Article 101 TFEU [ex 81 EC Treaty] forbids and declares void any agreement between undertakings, any decision by associations of undertakings and any concerted practice which distorts competition and affects trade between Member States (paras 1 and 2). However, the first two paragraphs can be declared inapplicable if pro-competitive benefits outweigh the anti-competitive effects (para. 3). In order to assess the relevance of article 101 TFEU [ex 81 EC Treaty] to the use of ARIs, the different constitutive elements, such as 'undertaking' and 'agreement' first need to be analysed in greater depth.

A.2. *Undertaking*

ECONOMIC ACTIVITY – The question that interests us most in this context is whether a self- or co-regulatory body could be classified as an undertaking.[306] The TFEU does not contain a definition of 'undertaking'.[307] However, the concept has been clarified in Community court judgments. The ECJ, for instance, has repeatedly described an undertaking as "*any entity engaged in an economic activity, regardless of its legal status and the way in which it is financed*",[308] taking into account that an economic activity has been defined as "*any activity consisting of offering goods and services on [sic] a given*

[306] For a comprehensive analysis of the concept of undertaking, cf. TOTH, Akos (ed.), *The Oxford Encyclopaedia of European Community law – Volume III: competition law and policy*, Oxford, Oxford University Press, 2008, 757–767.

[307] ELSPAß, Mathias and KETTNER, Moira, "Rules on competition – Rules applying to undertakings", in: CASTENDYK, Oliver, DOMMERING, Egbert J. and SCHEUER, Alexander (eds), *European media law*, Alphen a/d Rijn, Kluwer Law International, 2008, 127; ARNULL, Anthony et al., *Wyatt and Dashwood's European Union law*, London, Sweet & Maxwell, 2006, 973.

[308] ECJ, Klaus Höfner and Fritz Elser v. Macrotron GmbH, C-41/90, 23.04.1991, para. 21; ECJ, J.C.J. Wouters, J.W. Savelbergh, Price Waterhouse Belastingadviseurs BV v. Algemene Raad van de Nederlandse Orde van Advocaten, C-309/99, 19.02.2002, para. 46. Please note that within the scope of this book, we do not focus on the 'single economic entity' doctrine. For more details, cf. WHISH, Richard, *Competition law*, Oxford, Oxford University Press, 2009, 91–95; ROTH, Peter and ROSE, Vivien (eds), *Bellamy & Child European Community law of competition*, Oxford, Oxford University Press, 2008, 103–107.

market".[309] On the other hand, in the *Wouters* case, the Court clarified that the EU competition rules do not apply to any "*activity which, by its nature, its aim and the rules to which it is subject does not belong to the sphere of economic activity [...], or which is connected with the exercise of the powers of a public authority*".[310]

FURTHER CLARIFICATIONS – The word 'economic' in the ECJ's description of the notion 'undertaking' does not require, however, that a body pursues profits,[311] nor does it exclude bodies which "*exist[...] for a non-economic purpose but engage[...] in certain operations of a commercial nature*".[312] Nor is a service excluded because it is provided free of charge.[313] In addition, neither the ownership – public or private – nor the legal form of the undertaking – even individuals or entities without a legal personality can qualify – matters.[314] The CFI, for instance, held that "*a body governed by private law which set up a certification system for crane-hire firms to which affiliation is optional*", and which independently establishes the criteria which the certified firms must satisfy and issues certificates only on payment of a subscription, could be classified as an undertaking. This was because these features demonstrated that the body in question was engaged in an economic activity.[315] Moreover, in certain circumstances, depending on the – economic or purely public

---

309 ECJ, Commission of the European Communities v. Italian Republic, C-35/96, 18.06.1998, para. 36; ECJ, Pavel Pavlov and others v. Stichting Pensioenfonds Medische Specialisten, Joined Cases C-180–184/98, 12.09.2000, para. 75; ECJ, J.C.J. Wouters, J.W. Savelbergh, Price Waterhouse Belastingadviseurs BV v. Algemene Raad van de Nederlandse Orde van Advocaten, C-309/99, 19.02.2002, para. 47.

310 ECJ, J.C.J. Wouters, J.W. Savelbergh, Price Waterhouse Belastingadviseurs BV v. Algemene Raad van de Nederlandse Orde van Advocaten, C-309/99, 19.02.2002, para. 57.

311 WHISH, Richard, *Competition law*, Oxford, Oxford University Press, 2009, 84; ROTH, Peter and ROSE, Vivien (eds), *Bellamy & Child European Community law of competition*, Oxford, Oxford University Press, 2008, 93. See also: ECJ, Heintz van Landewyck SARL and others v. Commission of the European Communities, C-209 to 215 and 218/78, 29.10.1980, summary para. 10: "*Article [101, ex 81] (1) of the EC Treaty also applies to non-profit-making associations in so far as their own activities or those of the undertakings belonging to them are calculated to produce the results which it aims to suppress*".

312 ARNULL, Anthony et al., *Wyatt and Dashwood's European Union law*, London, Sweet & Maxwell, 2006, 974.

313 ROTH, Peter and ROSE, Vivien (eds), *Bellamy & Child European Community law of competition*, Oxford, Oxford University Press, 2008, 95.

314 TOTH, Akos (ed.), *The Oxford Encyclopaedia of European Community law – Volume III: competition law and policy*, Oxford, Oxford University Press, 2008, 759–760.

315 CFI, Stichting Certificatie Kraanverhuurbedrijf (SCK) and Federatie van Nederlandse Kraanbedrijven (FNK) v. Commission of the European Communities, T-213/95 and T-18/96, 22.10.1997, paras 121–122.

interest – nature of their activities, public authorities can also be considered undertakings.[316] Whish, for instance, has observed that "*bodies entrusted by the State with particular tasks and quasi-governmental bodies which carry on economic activities*" have already been qualified as undertakings. However, when the activity exercised is a "*task in the public interest which forms part of the essential functions of the State*" and "*its nature, its aim and the rules to which it is subject with the exercise of powers [...] are typically those of a public authority*", the public authority will not be considered an undertaking.[317]

Associations of undertakings – Furthermore, it can be noted that associations of undertakings also play a role in competition law (cf. *infra*, decisions of associations of undertakings). Again, this notion is broadly interpreted, and ranges from trade associations, non-profit-making associations, professional associations and de facto associations to "*industry-wide associations having statutory legal personality and entrusted with certain statutory duties, including quality control, whose members appointed by the relevant Minister, even if their decisions are made binding on the whole industry by acts of the public authorities*".[318] With respect to associations of undertakings, the ECJ made an interesting observation in the *Wouters* case. In order to clarify when measures are considered measures of an association of undertakings and when such measures are considered state measures, it distinguished between two approaches:

> *The first is that a Member State, when it grants regulatory powers to a professional association, is careful to define the public-interest criteria and the essential principles with which its rules must comply and also retains its power to adopt decisions in the last resort. In that case the rules adopted by the professional association remain State measures and are not covered by the Treaty rules applicable to undertakings. [...] The second approach is that the rules adopted by the professional association are attributable to it alone. Certainly, in so far as Article [81, ex 85](1) of the Treaty applies, the association must notify those rules to*

316 Whish, Richard, *Competition law*, Oxford, Oxford University Press, 2009, 85; Toth, Akos (ed.), *The Oxford Encyclopaedia of European Community law – Volume III: competition law and policy*, Oxford, Oxford University Press, 2008, 761.

317 ECJ, Diego Calì & Figli Srl v. Servizi ecologici porto di Genova SpA (SEPG), C-343/95, 18.03.1997, paras 22–23. Also, public authorities are not considered undertakings "*when they act in the performance of their sovereign or administrative functions*": Roth, Peter and Rose, Vivien (eds), *Bellamy & Child European Community law of competition*, Oxford, Oxford University Press, 2008, 95.

318 Toth, Akos (ed.), *The Oxford Encyclopaedia of European Community law – Volume III: competition law and policy*, Oxford, Oxford University Press, 2008, 286. See also: Whish, Richard, *Competition law*, Oxford, Oxford University Press, 2009, 103.

the Commission.[319] [N.B. Articles refer to articles prior to the adoption of the Treaty of Lisbon]

Hence, the actual degree of involvement of the state will be crucial in determining whether an association of undertakings could be made subject to article 101 TFEU [ex 81 EC Treaty].

Self- or co-regulatory bodies – From the previous paragraphs, it is possible to deduce that self- as well as co-regulatory bodies could be classified as 'undertakings' or possibly even as 'an association of undertakings', for instance, in the case of a content rating association of which industry players are members. Although the activities performed by the self- or co-regulatory body need in that case to be economic – which might not be self-evident if the sole purpose of the body is to protect minors – we have noted that the notion 'economic' is interpreted in a broad manner. The most crucial element in deciding whether self- or co-regulatory bodies might be qualified as 'undertakings', will, of course, be the actual level of government involvement in the schemes, as well as the nature of the tasks that are performed (economic or public interest, *supra*). With respect to co-regulatory instruments – more than with respect to self-regulatory instruments – it will not always be easy to determine whether the measures taken can be attributed to the Member State or to an undertaking. The concrete structure of the co-regulatory instruments will thus be decisive. For instance, in the case of the *Kijkwijzer* system, which was discussed in Part 1, Chapter 1, as an illustration of co-regulation, it is not inconceivable that NICAM – the co-regulatory body – might be considered an undertaking, since it functions with a considerable degree of autonomy, and the government involvement largely consists of supervision and co-funding.

A.3. *Agreements*

General – Article 101 para. 1 TFEU [ex 81 EC Treaty] prohibits "*all agreements between undertakings, decisions by associations of undertakings and concerted practices which may affect trade between Member States and which have as their object or effect the prevention, restriction or distortion of competition within the common market*".[320] The purpose of this provision is to

[319] ECJ, J.C.J. Wouters, J.W. Savelbergh, Price Waterhouse Belastingadviseurs BV v. Algemene Raad van de Nederlandse Orde van Advocaten, C-309/99, 19.02.2002, paras 68 and 69.

[320] Article 101 para. 1 TFEU [ex 81 EC Treaty].

protect market competition so as to increase consumer welfare and guarantee an efficient allocation of resources.[321]

Types of agreements targeted – The notions 'agreement', 'decision by associations of undertakings' and 'concerted practices', while they have not been defined in the Treaty, have been broadly interpreted by the Court.[322]

Agreements – In order to qualify as an 'agreement', it is not necessary that an arrangement is legally binding.[323] The European Court of First Instance (CFI) has indicated that what is needed is "*a concurrence of wills between at least two parties, the form in which it is manifested being unimportant as long as it constitutes the faithful expression of the parties' intention*".[324] Hence, an informal, only morally binding agreement, such as a 'gentlemen's agreement', or even an oral agreement, might be considered an agreement capable of falling within the ambit of article 101 para. 1 TFEU [ex 81 EC Treaty].[325]

Decisions of associations of undertakings – A second category targeted by article 101 para. 1 TFEU [ex 81 EC Treaty] consists of 'decisions of associations of undertakings'. Resolutions made by trade associations, or binding codes of conduct of associations, for instance, could fall within this category.[326] Again, it is not required that such decisions be legally binding.[327]

---

321 Commission Notice Guidelines on the application of Article 81 (3) of the Treaty, 2004/C 101/8, *OJ* 27.04.2004, *C* 101, 97, recital 13.

322 Whish, Richard, *Competition law*, Oxford, Oxford University Press, 2009, 97.

323 Arnull, Anthony et al., *Wyatt and Dashwood's European Union law*, London, Sweet & Maxwell, 2006, 996; Roth, Peter and Rose, Vivien (eds), *Bellamy & Child European Community law of competition*, Oxford, Oxford University Press, 2008, 108.

324 CFI, Bayer AG v. Commission of the European Communities, T-41/96, 26.10.2000, para. 69.

325 Roth, Peter and Rose, Vivien (eds), *Bellamy & Child European Community law of competition*, Oxford, Oxford University Press, 2008, 108.

326 Toth, Akos (ed.), *The Oxford Encyclopaedia of European Community law – Volume III: competition law and policy*, Oxford, Oxford University Press, 2008, 288; Whish, Richard, *Competition law*, Oxford, Oxford University Press, 2009, 102; Arnull, Anthony et al., *Wyatt and Dashwood's European Union law*, London, Sweet & Maxwell, 2006, 997; Roth, Peter and Rose, Vivien (eds), *Bellamy & Child European Community law of competition*, Oxford, Oxford University Press, 2008, 137–138. Cf. also: ECJ, J.C.J. Wouters, J.W. Savelbergh, Price Waterhouse Belastingadviseurs BV v. Algemene Raad van de Nederlandse Orde van Advocaten, C-309/99, 19.02.2002, para. 71; CFI, Institute of Professional Representatives before the European Patent Office v. Commission of the European Communities, T-144/99, 28.03.2001.

327 Arnull, Anthony et al., *Wyatt and Dashwood's European Union law*, London, Sweet & Maxwell, 2006, 998. Cf. for instance: ECJ, Heintz van Landewyck SARL and others v.

What is required is that the association is truly able to influence its members' conduct.[328] Furthermore, Whish has observed that the fact that a decision of an association of undertakings has been approved by a public authority does not lead to the inapplicability of article 101 TFEU [ex 81 EC Treaty].[329] However, in all probability, an association of undertakings would not be caught by article 101 in circumstances where it does exercise pure public interest functions, such as, for instance, regulatory supervision on behalf of the state.[330] It can also be noted that not only decisions of associations of undertakings, but also agreements between associations of undertakings, are prohibited by article 101 para. 1 TFEU [ex EC Treaty],[331] even if, according to Toth,

> *the associations are non-profit-making and, as such, are not involved in any economic activity, and even if the agreement is not legally binding on their members, insofar as the associations' own activities or those of the undertakings belonging to them are aimed at producing results which Art. 81 (1) prohibits.*[332] [N.B. Article refers to article prior to the adoption of the Treaty of Lisbon]

Concerted practices – 'Concerted practices' is the final type of collusive behaviour that is dealt with in article 101 para. 1 TFEU. The ECJ has defined a concerted practice as

> *a form of coordination between undertakings which, without having been taken to a stage where an agreement properly so called has been concluded, knowingly substitutes practical co-operation between them for the risks of competition.*[333]

Commission of the European Communities, C-209 to 215 and 218/78, 29.10.1980, paras 85–86, in which the Court held that although the recommendation in question was not a binding contract under national law, it nevertheless was "*a faithful expression of the applicant's intention to conduct themselves on the Belgian cigarette market in conformity with the terms of the recommendation*". See also: ECJ, NV IAZ International Belgium and others v. Commission of the European Communities, Joined cases 96–102, 104, 105, 108 and 110/82, 08.11.1983, para. 20: "*A recommendation, even if it has no binding effect, cannot escape article [101, ex 81] (1) where compliance with the recommendation by the undertakings to which it is addressed has an appreciable influence on competition in the market in question*".

328 Arnull, Anthony et al., *Wyatt and Dashwood's European Union law*, London, Sweet & Maxwell, 2006, 998.

329 Whish, Richard, *Competition law*, Oxford, Oxford University Press, 2009, 103.

330 Whish, Richard, *Competition law*, Oxford, Oxford University Press, 2009, 104.

331 Roth, Peter and Rose, Vivien (eds), *Bellamy & Child European Community law of competition*, Oxford, Oxford University Press, 2008, 138; Toth, Akos (ed.), *The Oxford Encyclopaedia of European Community law – Volume III: competition law and policy*, Oxford, Oxford University Press, 2008, 101.

332 Toth, Akos (ed.), *The Oxford Encyclopaedia of European Community law – Volume III: competition law and policy*, Oxford, Oxford University Press, 2008, 101.

333 ECJ, Imperial Chemical Industries Ltd. v. Commission of the European Communities,

This form of coordination implies, for instance, a coordinated course of action between competitors, the disclosure of an undertaking's policy to competitors, or even a unilateral disclosure of information.[334]

Adverse effect on competition – The agreements[335] targeted need to have an adverse effect on competition within the EU. More specifically, the agreements need to have as their object *or* effect[336] the prevention, restriction or distortion of competition. Concerning the first option, the Commission has clarified that "*restrictions of competition by* object *are those that by their very nature have the potential of restricting competition*".[337] On the other hand, agreements can also be prohibited if they have actual or potential restrictive *effects* on competition.[338] Both horizontal (between undertakings at the same level of supply) and vertical agreements (between undertakings operating at a different level of the production or distribution chain) can prevent, restrict or distort competition.[339] Article 101 para. 1 TFEU [ex 81 EC Treaty] contains five examples of restrictive agreements, such as, for instance, price

C-48/69, 14.07.1972, para. 64; ECJ, Commission of the European Communities v. Anic Partecipazioni SpA, C-49/92, 08.07.1999, para. 115. See also: ECJ, Coöperatieve Vereniging 'Suiker Unie' UA and others v. Commission of the European Communities, Joined cases 40–48, 50, 54–56, 111, 113, 114/73, 16.12.1975, para. 174: "*Although it is correct to say that this requirement of independence does not deprive economic operators of the right to adapt themselves intelligently to the existing and anticipated conduct of their competitors, it does however strictly preclude any direct or indirect contact between such operators, the object or effect whereof is either to influence the conduct on the market of an actual or potential competitor or to disclose to such a competitor the course of conduct which they themselves have decided to adopt or contemplate adopting on the market*".

334 Roth, Peter and Rose, Vivien (eds), *Bellamy & Child European Community law of competition*, Oxford, Oxford University Press, 2008, 120–124.

335 In what follows, the notion 'agreements' is used as a generic term that also includes decisions of associations of undertakings and concerted practices, unless indicated otherwise.

336 The notions 'object' and 'effect' should be read separately. If it has been determined that if an agreement has the object of restricting competition (interpreted as "*the objective meaning and purpose of the agreement considered in the economic context in which it is to be applied*"), there is no need to examine if the agreement also would have had anti-competitive effects. Whish, Richard, *Competition law*, Oxford, Oxford University Press, 2009, 116. See also: ECJ, Sandoz prodotti farmaceutici SpA v. Commission of the European Communities, C-277/87, 11.01.1990, summary para. 3.

337 Commission Notice Guidelines on the application of Article 81 (3) of the Treaty, 2004/C 101/8, *OJ* 27.04.2004, *C* 101, 97, recital 21 [original emphasis].

338 Commission Notice Guidelines on the application of Article 81 (3) of the Treaty, 2004/C 101/8, *OJ* 27.04.2004, *C* 101, 97, recital 24.

339 Roth, Peter and Rose, Vivien (eds), *Bellamy & Child European Community law of competition*, Oxford, Oxford University Press, 2008, 140–141. For more details on horizontal agreements: cf. Commission Notice Guidelines on the applicability of Article 81 of the EC Treaty to horizontal cooperation agreements, 2001/C 3/02, *OJ* 06.01.2001, *C* 3, 2. For more

fixing and market sharing. However, this list is not exhaustive, and evaluations will be carried out on a case-by-case basis. In order to assess a potentially adverse effect on competition, a number of factors will be taken into account including: the existing competition between undertakings, as well as the potential competition "*in the light of the structure of the market and the economic and legal context within which it functions*".[340]

Appreciable effects – Furthermore, the effects on competition need to be 'appreciable'.[341] This is an expression of the *de minimis* rule.[342] In 2001, the Commission issued a Notice on this *de minimis* theory,[343] which contains market share thresholds to help determine whether or not agreements should fall within the scope of article 101 TFEU [ex 81 EC Treaty].[344]

---

details on vertical agreements: cf. Commission Notice Guidelines on vertical restraints, 2000/C 291/01, *OJ* 13.10.2000, *C* 291, 1.

340 CFI, European Night Services Ltd (ENS), Eurostar (UK) Ltd, formerly European Passenger Services Ltd (EPS), Union internationale des chemins de fer (UIC), NV Nederlandse Spoorwegen (NS) and Société nationale des chemins de fer français (SNCF) v. Commission of the European Communities, Joined cases T-374, 375, 384 and 388/94, 15.09.1998, para. 137. See also: ECJ, David Meca-Medina and Igor Majcen v. Commission of the European Communities, C-519/04, 18.07.2006, para. 42: "*Next, the compatibility of rules with the Community rules on competition cannot be assessed in the abstract. […]. For the purposes of application of that provision to a particular case, account must first of all be taken of the overall context in which the decision of the association of undertakings was taken or produces its effects and, more specifically, of its objectives*". For more details, cf. Roth, Peter and Rose, Vivien (eds), *Bellamy & Child European Community law of competition*, Oxford, Oxford University Press, 2008, 166–171.

341 Arnull, Anthony et al., *Wyatt and Dashwood's European Union law*, London, Sweet & Maxwell, 2006, 1015; Whish, Richard, *Competition law*, Oxford, Oxford University Press, 2009, 117. See also: ECJ, Franz Völk v. S.P.R.L. Ets J. Vervaecke, C-5/69, 09.07.1969, para. 5/7 ("*Consequently an agreement falls outside the prohibition in article [101, ex 81] when it has only an insignificant effect on the markets, taking into the weak position which the persons concerned have on the market of the product in question*"); Commission Notice on agreements of minor importance which do not appreciably restrict competition under Article 81 (1) of the Treaty establishing the European Community (*de minimis*), 2001/C 368/07, *OJ* 22.12.2001, *C* 368, 13, recital 1.

342 Arnull, Anthony et al., *Wyatt and Dashwood's European Union law*, London, Sweet & Maxwell, 2006, 1015; Roth, Peter and Rose, Vivien (eds), *Bellamy & Child European Community law of competition*, Oxford, Oxford University Press, 2008, 178–187.

343 Commission Notice on agreements of minor importance which do not appreciably restrict competition under Article 81 (1) of the Treaty establishing the European Community (*de minimis*), 2001/C 368/07, *OJ* 22.12.2001, *C* 368, 13. For more details on this Notice, cf. Whish, Richard, *Competition law*, Oxford, Oxford University Press, 2009, 138–142.

344 Commission Notice on agreements of minor importance which do not appreciably restrict competition under Article 81 (1) of the Treaty establishing the European Community (*de minimis*), 2001/C 368/07, *OJ* 22.12.2001, *C* 368, 13, recital 2.

Influence on trade between Member States – Finally, the effects[345] of the agreements need to influence trade[346] between Member States. In this context, the crucial element is the "*diversion of trade flows from the pattern they would naturally follow in a unified market*".[347] In other words, "*there must be an impact on cross-border economic activity involving at least two Member States*".[348] This element could be of interest when self- or co-regulatory systems in the media sector, and especially in the field of protection of minors against harmful content, are at issue, since, still today, many of these systems are national, given cultural sensitivities.[349] However, the Court has accepted that, to fulfil this criterion, the parties to an agreement can be situated in just one Member State, as long as the agreement affects the flow of trade or the structure of competition.[350] This will, for instance, be the case if

[345] These effects may be "*direct or indirect, actual or potential*": Commission Notice Guidelines on the effect on trade concept contained in articles 81 and 82 of the Treaty, 2004/C 101/07, *OJ* 27.04.2004, *C* 101, recital 36.

[346] 'Trade' has been described in the Commission Notice as being "*not limited to traditional exchanges of goods and services across borders. It is a wider concept, covering all cross-border economic activity including establishment*": Commission Notice Guidelines on the effect on trade concept contained in Articles 81 and 82 of the Treaty, 2004/C 101/07, *OJ* 27.04.2004, *C* 101, recital 19.

[347] Arnull, Anthony et al., *Wyatt and Dashwood's European Union law*, London, Sweet & Maxwell, 2006, 1016. Cf. also: Commission Notice Guidelines on the effect on trade concept contained in Articles 81 and 82 of the Treaty, 2004/C 101/07, *OJ* 27.04.2004, *C* 101, 3.

[348] Commission Notice Guidelines on the effect on trade concept contained in Articles 81 and 82 of the Treaty, 2004/C 101/07, *OJ* 27.04.2004, *C* 101, 3, recital 21. For a thorough analysis of the concept, cf. Commission Notice Guidelines on the effect on trade concept contained in Articles 81 and 82 of the Treaty, 2004/C 101/07, *OJ* 27.04.2004, *C* 101, 3.

[349] Cf. Van den Bergh, Roger, "Self-regulation of the medical and legal professions: remaining barriers to competition and EC-law", Paper prepared for the Conference "Pressure groups, self-regulation and enforcement mechanisms", Milan, 10–11.01.1997, retrieved from http://www.feem.it/NR/rdonlyres/DDA14FEC-D4FD-4022–9616–6105FDE83755/529/3197.pdf (30.10.2008), 23 (with respect to the medical and legal professions, which are also largely local).

[350] ECJ, J.C.J. Wouters, J.W. Savelbergh, Price Waterhouse Belastingadviseurs BV v. Algemene Raad van de Nederlandse Orde van Advocaten, C-309/99, 19.02.2002, para. 95: "*As regards the question whether intra-Community trade is affected, it is sufficient to observe that an agreement, decision or concerted practice extending over the whole of the territory of a Member State has, by its very nature, the effect of reinforcing the partitioning of markets on a national basis, thereby holding up the economic interpenetration which the Treaty is designed to bring about*". See also: Commission Notice Guidelines on the effect on trade concept contained in Articles 81 and 82 of the Treaty, 2004/C 101/07, *OJ* 27.04.2004, *C* 101, 3, recital 78.

the existing scheme makes market entry for competitors from other Member States more difficult.

A.4. *Inapplicability of article 101 para. 1 TFEU [ex 81 EC Treaty]*

INAPPLICABILITY OF ARTICLE 101 PARA. 1 TFEU [ex art 81 EC TREATY] – There are a number of situations in which the prohibition contained in article 101 para. 1 TFEU [ex 81 EC Treaty] will be considered inapplicable. These situations will now be examined in turn.

ARTICLE 101 PARA. 3 TFEU [EX 81 EC TREATY] – The first situation allows for the possibility that agreements which affect competition in an adverse way nevertheless also have important economic advantages. Hence, article 101 para. 3 TFEU [ex 81 EC Treaty] contains a number of criteria with which agreements, decisions by associations of undertakings, or concerted practices need to comply in order to be granted an exemption from the first two paragraphs (*supra*).[351] Such agreements, decisions or concerted practices will be allowed if they

> *[contribute] to improving the production or distribution of goods or to promoting technical or economic progress, while allowing consumers a fair share of the resulting benefit, and [do] not: (a) impose on the undertakings concerned restrictions which are not indispensable to the attainment of these objectives; (b) afford such undertakings the possibility of eliminating competition in respect of a substantial part of the products in question.*[352, 353]

[351] Cf. also: COMMISSION Notice Guidelines on the application of Article 81 (3) of the Treaty, 2004/C 101/8, *OJ* 27.04.2004, *C* 101, 97.

[352] It can be noted that, until 2004, the power to grant individual exemptions fell within the competence of the Commission. From 2004 onwards, national courts and competition authorities may apply article 101 para. 3 TFEU [ex 81 EC Treaty] (articles 5 and 6 COUNCIL Regulation (EC) No 1/2003 of 16 December 2002 on the implementation of the rules on competition laid down in Articles 81 and 82 of the Treaty, *OJ* 04.01.2003, *L* 1, 1). However, block exemptions adopted under article 103 TFEU [ex 83 EC Treaty] still fall within the competence of the Commission. Cf. ARNULL, Anthony et al., *Wyatt and Dashwood's European Union law*, London, Sweet & Maxwell, 2006, 1018. For more details on block exemptions, cf. ROTH, Peter and ROSE, Vivien (eds), *Bellamy & Child European Community law of competition*, Oxford, Oxford University Press, 2008, 226–235.

[353] For more details on the four conditions, cf. ROTH, Peter and ROSE, Vivien (eds), *Bellamy & Child European Community law of competition*, Oxford, Oxford University Press, 2008, 200–226.

If all of these criteria have been, cumulatively,[354] fulfilled, it is deemed that the agreement actually enhances competition by offering cheaper or better products to consumers, and, hence, will be eligible for an exemption.[355, 356] Again, the proportionality principle plays an important role in this assessment.[357]

PUBLIC INTEREST CRITERIA? – The second situation involves the presence of a public interest. Usually, only positive *economic* effects are taken into account in the assessment of article 101 para. 3 TFEU [ex 81 EC Treaty].[358] Non-competition or public interest criteria (such as the protection of minors) are thus normally not considered. The Court has, however, on one occasion, taken such criteria into account as part of the 'overall context' of its decision, which consequently led the Court to decide that article 101 para. 1 TFEU [ex 81 EC Treaty], in this case, was inapplicable.[359] Although the judgment that adopted this latter approach, the *Wouters* case concerning deontological rules for the

---

[354] COMMISSION Notice Guidelines on the application of Article 81 (3) of the Treaty, 2004/C 101/8, *OJ* 27.04.2004, *C* 101, 97, recitals 34, 38 and 42.

[355] COMMISSION Notice Guidelines on the application of Article 81 (3) of the Treaty, 2004/C 101/8, *OJ* 27.04.2004, *C* 101, 97, recital 34.

[356] Please note that issues surrounding enforcement of article 101 TFEU [ex 81 EC Treaty], such as the application of article 101 para. 3 TFEU [ex 81 EC Treaty] by the European Commission, national courts and national competition authorities or block exemptions, fall outside of the scope of this book. For more details, cf. WHISH, Richard, *Competition law*, Oxford, Oxford University Press, 2009, 162–169 and 246–322.

[357] COMMISSION OF THE EUROPEAN COMMUNITIES, Communication from the Commission to the Council and to the European Parliament on environmental agreements, COM (1996) 561 final, 27.11.1996, 15.

[358] ARNULL, Anthony et al., *Wyatt and Dashwood's European Union law*, London, Sweet & Maxwell, 2006, 1019; WHISH, Richard, *Competition law*, Oxford, Oxford University Press, 2009, 152–156; VEDDER, Hans, "Voluntary agreements and competition law", Working Paper Fondazione Eni Enrico Mattei, No. 79, 2000, retrieved from http://www.feem.it/NR/rdonlyres/FC5A9109-6763-4D72-B01E-A99C97874999/672/7900.pdf (on 30.10.2008), 5.

[359] LENAERTS, Koen and VAN NUFFEL, Piet, *Europees recht in hoofdlijnen* [*Outline of European law*], Antwerpen, Maklu, 2008, 181 [in Dutch]; ARNULL, Anthony et al., *Wyatt and Dashwood's European Union law*, London, Sweet & MAXWELL, 2006, 1014 and 1019; WHISH, Richard, *Competition law*, Oxford, Oxford University Press, 2009, 127. See also: ECJ, J.C.J. Wouters, J.W. Savelbergh, Price Waterhouse Belastingadviseurs BV v. Algemene Raad van de Nederlandse Orde van Advocaten, C-309/99, 19.02.2002, para. 97; ECJ, David Meca-Medina and Igor Majcen v. Commission of the European Communities, C-519/04, 18.07.2006, para. 42–45. This has also been dubbed a 'rule of reason' approach, parallel to internal market case law (cf. *supra*). However, others have argued against the use of this notion. Cf. for instance: WHISH, Richard, *Competition law*, Oxford, Oxford University Press, 2009, 133.

legal profession,[360] was a controversial one, it has been argued that the same reasoning could be applied to other rules.[361] Yet, it is important to note that in the *Wouters* case, there was a mix of public and private elements: the legislation in question contained provisions regarding the regulation of the legal profession, but the actual implementation was left to a private law association of undertakings.[362] Hence, it might be conceivable that co-regulatory systems in the media sector could be found to fall outside of the scope of article 101 para. 1 TFEU [ex 81 EC Treaty] due to the pursuance of a legitimate objective or public interest. Whether the same would hold true for truly private or self-regulatory schemes could, however, be doubted.[363]

STATE COMPULSION – The third situation in which an undertaking can avoid the applicability of article 101 TFEU [ex 81 EC Treaty] (as well as article 102 TFEU [ex 82 EC Treaty], *infra*) is to argue that its conduct finds it origin in a national measure, i.e., a measure issued by the government.[364] This principle is applied in a restrictive manner.[365] The undertaking in question will only succeed in its claim if the national measure itself actually restricts competition and, hence, eliminates any possibility of competition.[366] If, despite the measure, the undertaking still enjoys commercial autonomy, then article 101 TFEU [ex 81 EC Treaty] may apply after all.[367] In this context, ROTH and ROSE have observed that

---

[360] ECJ, J.C.J. Wouters, J.W. Savelbergh, Price Waterhouse Belastingadviseurs BV v. Algemene Raad van de Nederlandse Orde van Advocaten, C-309/99, 19.02.2002.

[361] WHISH, Richard, *Competition law*, Oxford, Oxford University Press, 2009, 128.

[362] WHISH, Richard, *Competition law*, Oxford, Oxford University Press, 2009, 129.

[363] WHISH, Richard, *Competition law*, Oxford, Oxford University Press, 2009, 129.

[364] ROTH, Peter and ROSE, Vivien (eds), *Bellamy & Child European Community law of competition*, Oxford, Oxford University Press, 2008, 1033.

[365] TOTH, Akos (ed.), *The Oxford Encyclopaedia of European Community law – Volume III: competition law and policy*, Oxford, Oxford University Press, 2008, 292.

[366] TOTH, Akos (ed.), *The Oxford Encyclopaedia of European Community law – Volume III: competition law and policy*, Oxford, Oxford University Press, 2008, 292.

[367] ECJ, Commission of the European Communities and French Republic v. Ladbroke Racing Ltd, Joined cases C-359/95 P and C-379/95 P, 11.11.1997, paras 33–34: "*Articles [101, ex 81] and [102, ex 82] of the Treaty apply only to anti-competitive conduct engaged in by undertakings on their own initiative [...]. If anti-competitive conduct is required of undertakings by national legislation or if the latter creates a legal framework which itself eliminates any possibility of competitive activity on their part, Articles [101, ex 81] and [102, ex 82] do not apply. In such a situation, the restriction of competition is not attributable, as those provisions implicitly require, to the autonomous conduct of the undertakings [...]. Articles [101, ex 81] and [102, ex 82] may apply, however, if it is found that the national legislation does not preclude undertakings from engaging in autonomous conduct which prevents, restricts or distorts competition*".

> *an agreement or conduct which is not required by law may be caught by the competition rules even if it is done following consultation with the national authorities, or with their encouragement or approval, and even if it is later expressly ratified by national law.*[368]

It is worth keeping this in mind with respect to cases where the undertakings in question are alternative regulatory bodies.

A.5. *Delegation to private bodies*

Delegation of decision-making by the state – Related to the topic of state compulsion (*supra*) is another issue that could be of potential interest with respect to the relation between article 101 TFEU [ex 81 EC Treaty] and the use of ARIs. It concerns the finding of the ECJ that article 101 TFEU [ex 81 EC Treaty], in conjunction with articles 4 para. 3 TEU [ex 10 EC Treaty][369] and 3 para. 1 (b) TFEU [ex 3 para. 1 (g) EC Treaty],[370] entails that Member States cannot introduce or maintain in force measures which may make the application of the competition rules ineffective (this is also dubbed the 'useful effect doctrine').[371] This also includes situations where a Member State delegates decision-making responsibility to private economic actors.[372]

---

368 Roth, Peter and Rose, Vivien (eds), *Bellamy & Child European Community law of competition*, Oxford, Oxford University Press, 2008, 1033–1034.

369 Article 4 para. 3 TEU [ex 10 EC Treaty]: "*The Member States shall take any appropriate measure, general or particular, to ensure fulfilment of the obligations arising out of the Treaties or resulting from the acts of the institutions of the Union. The Member States shall facilitate the achievement of the Union's tasks and refrain from any measure which could jeopardise the attainment of the Union's objectives*".

370 Article 3 para. 1 (g) EC Treaty: "*[...] the activities of the Community shall include, as provided in this Treaty and in accordance with the timetable set out therein: [...] a system ensuring that competition in the internal market is not distorted*". Article 3 para. 1 (b) TFEU: "*The Union shall have exclusive competence in the following areas: [..] (b) the establishing of competition rules necessary for the functioning of the internal market*".

371 Schepel, Harm, "Delegation of regulatory powers to private parties under EC competition law: towards a procedural public interest test", *Common Market Law Review* 2002, 32; Arnull, Anthony et al., *Wyatt and Dashwood's European Union law*, London, Sweet & Maxwell, 2006, 1026; Vedder, Hans, "The democracy of competition – EC (Competition) law and the fine line between markets, public interests and (self-)regulation", Working Paper Annual Legal Research Network Conference, 2008, retrieved from http://papers.ssrn.com/sol3/papers.cfm?abstract_id=1282035 (on 30.10.2008), 13.

372 Lenaerts, Koen and Van Nuffel, Piet, *Europees recht in hoofdlijnen* [*Outline of European law*], Antwerpen, Maklu, 2008, 180 [in Dutch]; Arnull, Anthony et al., *Wyatt and Dashwood's European Union law*, London, Sweet & Maxwell, 2006, 1027; Commission of the European Communities, Communication from the Commission to the Council and to the European Parliament on environmental agreements, COM (1996) 561 final, 27.11.1996, 15. See also: ECJ, Pascal Van Eycke v. ASPA NV, C-267/86, 21.09.1988, para.

In such circumstances the Member States could be held liable,[373] unless the measures are justified by public interest considerations.[374] Advocate General LÉGER devised three criteria for assessing such a justification by a Member State:

> *The Court could find that a legislative or regulatory measure which reinforces the effects of an agreement, decision or concerted practice is compatible with Articles [10, ex 5] and [81, ex 85] of the Treaty provided that: (1) the public authorities of the Member State concerned exercise effective control over the content of the agreement, decision or concerted practice; (2) the State measure pursues a legitimate aim in the public interest, and (3) the State measure is proportionate to the aim which it pursues.*[375] [N.B. Articles refer to articles prior to the adoption of the Treaty of Lisbon]

Although this test has not been adopted by the ECJ, it nevertheless provides some useful clues as to the correct classification of certain measures (as state measures or measures attributable to undertakings).

LIABILITY – Hence, whether or not the state could be held liable will ultimately depend on the factual circumstances and the degree of government involvement.[376] Where an association acts on its own initiative and takes its decisions autonomously, as could be assumed with regard to a self-

16; ECJ, Criminal proceedings against Wolf W. Meng (Reference for a preliminary ruling: Kammergericht Berlin – Germany), C-2/91, 17.11.1993, para. 14, ECJ, Criminal proceedings against Manuele Arduino (Reference for a preliminary ruling: Pretore di Pinerolo – Italy), C-35/99, 19.02.2002, para. 35.

373 ARNULL, Anthony et al., *Wyatt and Dashwood's European Union law*, London, Sweet & Maxwell, 2006, 1028.

374 ARNULL, Anthony et al., *Wyatt and Dashwood's European Union law*, London, Sweet & Maxwell, 2006, 1029; VEDDER, Hans, "The democracy of competition – EC (Competition) law and the fine line between markets, public interests and (self-)regulation", Working Paper Annual Legal Research Network Conference, 2008, retrieved from http://papers.ssrn.com/sol3/papers.cfm?abstract_id=1282035 (on 30.10.2008), 17. See also: ECJ, Bundesanstalt für den Güterfernverkehr v. Gebrüder Reiff GmbH & Co. KG, C-185/91, 17.11.1993, summary.

375 ECJ, Criminal proceedings against Manuele Arduino (Reference for a preliminary ruling: Pretore di Pinerolo – Italy), C-35/99, Opinion Advocate General Léger, 10.07.2001, para. 91.

376 In this context, ROTH and ROSE observed that the ECJ has hardly ever found Member State measures to be illegal on the basis of articles 101 TFEU [ex 81 EC Treaty], article 4 para. 3 TEU [ex 10 EC Treaty] and article 3, para. 1 (b) TFEU [ex 3 para. 1 (g) EC Treaty]: ROTH, Peter and ROSE, Vivien (eds), *Bellamy & Child European Community law of competition*, Oxford, Oxford University Press, 2008, 1054.

regulatory scheme, article 101 TFEU [ex 81 EC Treaty], directed at undertakings or associations of undertakings, could be applied and the liability of the state will not be an issue. However, where there is an actual division of tasks between the public authorities and private associations (or co-regulatory bodies), which could be the case with respect to co-regulatory systems in the media sector, one should not exclude the possiblity that the state could be held liable as well. In this context, Toth observed that

> *Generally speaking, when a Member State in granting regulatory powers to a professional association, defines the public-interest criteria and the essential principles with which the rules must comply and also retains its power to adopt decisions in the last resort, the rules adopted by the association remain State measures and are not covered by the Treaty rules applicable to undertakings.*[377]

B. *Article 102 TFEU [ex 82 EC Treaty]*

Abuse of dominant position – The second pillar of the EC competition rules[378] is article 102 TFEU [ex 82 EC Treaty], which prohibits abusive behaviour by undertakings who have a dominant position in a market. In theory, it is possible that such an undertaking is part of a self- or co-regulatory scheme. Such a self- or co-regulatory body could, for instance, abuse its dominant position by impeding parallel imports or excluding competing products (for instance, on the basis of ratings). The ECJ has held that an undertaking with a dominant position has "*a special responsibility not to allow its conduct to impair genuine undistorted competition on the common market*".[379]

Relevant elements – Four elements must be satisfied for article 102 [ex 82 EC Treaty] to apply: (1) there must be one, or more, undertakings which have a dominant position (2) in the common market, or a substantial part of this market (3) that abuses its position, which leads to (4) an actual or

---

[377] Toth, Akos (ed.), *The Oxford Encyclopaedia of European Community law – Volume III: competition law and policy*, Oxford, Oxford University Press, 2008, 100.

[378] Articles 101 and 102 TFEU [ex 81 and 82 EC Treaty] are complementary provisions, which have the same goal: effective competition within the internal market (Toth, Akos (ed.), *The Oxford Encyclopaedia of European Community law – Volume III: competition law and policy*, Oxford, Oxford University Press, 2008, 290). In certain circumstances, both articles could apply simultaneously (Roth, Peter and Rose, Vivien (eds), *Bellamy & Child European Community law of competition*, Oxford, Oxford University Press, 2008, 914; Toth, Akos (ed.), *The Oxford Encyclopaedia of European Community law – Volume III: competition law and policy*, Oxford, Oxford University Press, 2008, 290).

[379] ECJ, NV Nederlandsche Banden Industrie Michelin v. Commission of the European Communities, C-322/81, 09.11.1983, para. 57.

potential effect on trade between the Member States.[380] The notions 'effect on trade' and 'undertaking' are interpreted in the same manner with regard to article 101 TFEU [ex 81 EC Treaty]. With respect to the latter notion, we should remind ourselves of the fact that neither public authorities, nor organisations which perform public interest activities that are part of the essential functions of the state, nor bodies performing non-economic activities in the exercise of powers typically belonging to public authorities, are considered undertakings.[381] In addition, it can be noted that the ECJ has judged that article 102 TFEU [ex 82 EC Treaty] can also apply to circumstances in which a number of undertakings together have a dominant position ('collective' or 'joint' dominance).[382] What is required in this situation is that the undertakings are "*linked in such a way that they adopt the same conduct on the market*" and that they "*should not compete against one another*".[383] In order to assess if an undertaking holds a dominant position in a substantial part of the market, both the geographic area in which the dominant position allegedly exists, and the product market in that area, will need to be considered.[384] A dominant position has been defined by the ECJ as

> *a position of economic strength enjoyed by an undertaking which enables it to hinder the maintenance of effective competition on the relevant market by allowing it to behave to an appreciable extent independently of its competitors and customers and ultimately of consumers.*[385]

Two factors are important in the assessment of a dominant position: the relevant (product and geographic) market, and the market power (indicated by market shares in combination with other factors such as the existence of barriers to entry). Although a detailed analysis of the actual dominance test,

---

380 Article 102 TFEU [ex 82 EC Treaty]. See also: Roth, Peter and Rose, Vivien (eds), *Bellamy & Child European Community law of vompetition*, Oxford, Oxford University Press, 2008, 917.

381 Toth, Akos (ed.), *The Oxford Encyclopaedia of European Community law – Volume III: competition law and policy*, Oxford, Oxford University Press, 2008, 291.

382 For more details on collective or joint dominance, cf. Roth, Peter and Rose, Vivien (eds), *Bellamy & Child European Community law of competition*, Oxford, Oxford University Press, 2008, 939–946; Toth, Akos (ed.), *The Oxford Encyclopaedia of European Community law – Volume III: competition law and policy*, Oxford, Oxford University Press, 2008, 303–307.

383 ECJ, DIP SpA v. Comune di Bassano del Grappa, LIDL Italia Srl v. Comune di Chioggia and Lingral Srl v. Comune di Chiogga, Joined cases C-140–142/94, 17.10.1995, paras 26 and 27.

384 Roth, Peter and Rose, Vivien (eds), *Bellamy & Child European Community law of competition*, Oxford, Oxford University Press, 2008, 919.

385 ECJ, NV Nederlandsche Banden Industrie Michelin v. Commission of the European Communities, C-322/81, 09.11.1983, summary para. 6.

would be beyond the scope of this study,[386] it is worth mentioning a final element, the abusive behaviour of the dominant undertaking.[387] Article 102 TFEU [ex 82 EC Treaty] contains a non-exhaustive list[388] of four examples of such behaviour, such as, for instance "*directly or indirectly imposing unfair purchase or selling prices or other unfair trading conditions*" or "*limiting production, markets or technical development to the prejudice of consumers*".[389] In practice, however, a careful assessment of the behaviour in question will be required. In this assessment, proportionality is an important criterion. As ROTH and ROSE put it:

> *in striving to improve its market position and pursue its legitimate interests, the dominant firm may employ only such measures as accord with 'commercial usage' in the market in question and are necessary to pursue those interests. It must not act in a way which foreseeably will limit competition more than is necessary.*[390]

EXEMPTION? – Unlike article 101 TFEU [ex 81 EC Treaty], article 102 TFEU [ex 82 EC Treaty] does not contain an explicit reference to the possibility of an exemption for what, at first sight, seems to be an abuse.[391] However,

386 For more details: cf. ROTH, Peter and ROSE, Vivien (eds), *Bellamy & Child European Community law of competition*, Oxford, Oxford University Press, 2008, 920–946; ARNULL, Anthony et al., *Wyatt and Dashwood's European Union law*, London, Sweet & Maxwell, 2006, 1047–1054; TOTH, Akos (ed.), *The Oxford Encyclopaedia of European Community law – Volume III: competition law and policy*, Oxford, Oxford University Press, 2008, 289–307.

387 Cf. ECJ, Hoffmann-La Roche & Co. AG v. Commission of the European Communities, C-85/76, 13.02.1979, para. 91: "*The concept of abuse is an objective concept relating to the behaviour of an undertaking in a dominant position which is such as to influence the structure of a market where, as a result of the very presence of the undertaking in question, the degree of competition is weakened and which, through recourse to methods different from those which condition normal competition in products or services on the basis of the transactions of commercial operators, has the effect hindering the maintenance of the degree of competition still existing in the market or the growth of that competition*".

388 ARNULL, Anthony et al., *Wyatt and Dashwood's European Union law*, London, Sweet & Maxwell, 2006, 1035.

389 For more details on the different forms of abuse, cf. ROTH, Peter and ROSE, Vivien (eds), *Bellamy & Child European Community law of competition*, Oxford, Oxford University Press, 2008, 954–1030; ARNULL, Anthony et al., *Wyatt and Dashwood's European Union law*, London, Sweet & Maxwell, 2006, 1058–1078.

390 ROTH, Peter and ROSE, Vivien (eds), *Bellamy & Child European Community law of competition*, Oxford, Oxford University Press, 2008, 948.

391 CFI, Atlantic Container Line AB et al. v. Commission of the European Communities, Joined Cases T-191/98 and T-212–214/98, 30.09.2003, para. 1109.

according to case law, in principle, dominant undertakings may provide an objective (economic) justification for their conduct.[392]

State compulsion and useful effect doctrine – We can briefly note that the rules with respect to the issues of state compulsion and useful effect doctrine (article 4 para. 3 TEU [ex 10 EC Treaty]) which we discussed above under article 101 TFEU [ex 81 EC Treaty] are also relevant to situations in which article 102 TFEU [ex 82 EC Treaty] is applicable.[393]

C. *Article 106 TFEU [ex 86 EC Treaty]*

Interplay between undertakings and Member States – A final article worth considering within the scope of this study is article 106 TFEU [ex 86 EC Treaty], given that this article also concerns the interplay between undertakings and the Member States. Article 106 para. 1 TFEU [ex 86 EC Treaty] is similar to article 4 para. 3 TEU [ex 10 EC Treaty] (*supra*) in that it forbids Member States, in the case of public undertakings and undertakings to which Member States have attributed special or exclusive rights, from enacting or maintaining in force any measures contrary to the Treaty rules, in particular the competition rules (articles 101 to 109 TFEU [ex 81 to 89 EC Treaty]). Article 106 para. 2 TFEU [ex 86 EC Treaty] prohibits the application of the competition rules to undertakings entrusted with the operation of services of general economic interest, or having the character of a revenue-producing monopoly, in so far as the application of such rules obstructs the performance, in law or in fact, of the particular tasks assigned to them.

Article 106 para. 1 TFEU [ex 86 EC Treaty] – The feature of the first paragraph relevant to this study is whether self- or co-regulatory bodies could be considered 'public undertakings' or 'undertakings to which Member States have attributed special or exclusive rights'. The Commission has defined 'public undertaking' as

> *any undertaking over which the public authorities may exercise, directly or indirectly, a dominant influence by virtue of their ownership of it, their financial participation therein, or the rules which govern it.*[394]

---

[392] ECJ, British Airways plc v. the Commission of the European Communities, C-95/04, 15.03.2007.

[393] For instance: ECJ, SA G.B.-INNO-B.M. v. Association des détaillants en tabac (ATAB), C-13/77, 16.11.1977.

[394] Article 2 (b) Commission Directive 2006/111/EC of 16 November 2006 on the transparency of financial relations between Member States and public undertakings as well as on financial transparency within certain undertakings, *OJ* 17.11.2006, *L* 318, 17.

It will depend on the concrete circumstances of the case whether or not a self- or co-regulatory body could be considered a 'public undertaking'. However, in our view, the qualification 'public undertaking' might in most cases be too far of a stretch, since a very strong degree of government involvement would be necessary. A second category of undertakings caught by article 101 para 1 TFEU [ex 81 EC Treaty] contains 'undertakings to which Member States have attributed special or exclusive rights' (also dubbed 'privileged undertakings').[395] Again, these notions are not clarified in the Treaty but have been defined by the Commission in the Transparency Directive:

> *exclusive rights means rights that are granted by a Member State to one undertaking through any legislative, regulatory or administrative instrument, reserving it the right to provide a service or undertake an activity within a given geographical area*; and
>
> *special rights means rights that are granted by a Member State to a limited number of undertakings, through any legislative, regulatory or administrative instrument, which, within a given geographical area:*
> *(i) limits to two or more the number of such undertakings, authorised to provide a service or undertake an activity, otherwise than according to objective, proportional and non-discriminatory criteria; or*
> *(ii) designates, otherwise than according to such criteria, several competing undertakings, as being authorized to provide a service or undertake an activity; or*
> *(iii) confers on any undertaking or undertakings, otherwise than according to such criteria, any legal or regulatory advantages which substantially affect the ability of any other undertaking to provide the same service or to operate the same activity in the same geographical area under substantially equivalent conditions.*[396]

Examples of exclusive rights relate, for instance, to the provision of recruitment services, waste management, and broadcasting.[397, 398] Whish has noted that to be qualified as an exclusive right, the State must have exercised a degree of discretion as to the attribution of the right.[399] Special rights, on the other hand, relate, for instance, to the operation of GSM radiotelephony networks.[400] In our view, however, the attribution by the government of the

---

[395] Whish, Richard, *Competition law*, Oxford, Oxford University Press, 2009, 222.

[396] Article 2 (f) and (g) Commission Directive 2006/111/EC of 16 November 2006 on the transparency of financial relations between Member States and public undertakings as well as on financial transparency within certain undertakings, *OJ* 17.11.2006, *L* 318, 17.

[397] ECJ, Elliniki Radiophonia Tiléorassi AE and Panellinia Omospondia Syllogon Prossopikou v. Dimotiki Etairia Pliroforissis and Sotirios Kouvelas and Nicolaos Avdellas and others, C-260/89, 18.06.1991, summary para. 4.

[398] Whish, Richard, *Competition law*, Oxford, Oxford University Press, 2009, 222.

[399] Whish, Richard, *Competition law*, Oxford, Oxford University Press, 2009, 223.

[400] Whish, Richard, *Competition law*, Oxford, Oxford University Press, 2009, 223.

competence to protect minors against harmful content to a self- or co-regulatory body will, in all probability, not be qualified as an exclusive or a special right.

ARTICLE 106 PARA. 2 TFEU [EX 86 EC TREATY] – The second paragraph of article 106 TFEU [ex 86 EC Treaty] permits an exemption from the competition rules with respect to 'undertakings entrusted with the operation of services of general economic interest', in cases where these rules would hinder the execution of the tasks assigned to them.[401, 402] Again, the question that interests us most is whether self- or co-regulatory bodies in the media sector, and more specifically, bodies which aim to protect minors against harmful content, could be considered 'undertakings entrusted with the operation of services of general economic interest'.[403] Two elements are important in this assessment. First of all, in order to fall within the remit of article 106 para. 2 TFEU [ex 86 EC Treaty], an act of a public authority is required for an undertaking to be 'entrusted' with the operation of services of general economic interest.[404] The ECJ has clarified that this act should not necessarily take the form of a legislative measure.[405] Second, the services in question must be 'of general economic interest'.[406] The Commission has defined this concept as "*market services which the Member States subject to specific public service obligations by virtue of a general interest criterion*".[407] Commonly given examples of such services relate to postal services, transport, energy

---

[401] The Commission considers article 106 para. 2 TFEU [ex 86 EC Treaty] "*the central provision for reconciling the Community objectives, including those of competition and internal market freedoms on the one hand, with the effective fulfilment of the mission of general economic interest entrusted by public authorities on the other hand*": COMMISSION OF THE EUROPEAN COMMUNITIES, Communication from the Commission Services of general interest in Europe, 2001/C 17/04, *OJ* 19.01.2001, *C* 17, 4, recital 10.

[402] Insofar as the means used to fulfil the object of general interest do not generate unnecessary distortions of trade: cf. last sentence of article 106 para. 2 TFEU [ex 86 EC Treaty] ("*The development of trade must not be affected to such an extent as would be contrary to the interest of the Community*").

[403] Assuming that being qualified as 'an undertaking having the character of a revenue-producing monopoly' is totally out of the question.

[404] ROTH, Peter and ROSE, Vivien (eds), *Bellamy & Child European Community law of competition*, Oxford, Oxford University Press, 2008, 1062–1063.

[405] ECJ, Commission of the European Communities v. French Republic, C-159/94, 23.10.1997, para. 66.

[406] Note that a 'Protocol on services of general interest' is attached to the Treaty of Lisbon (Treaty of Lisbon amending the Treaty on European Union and the Treaty establishing the European Community, 13.12.2007, *OJ* 17.12.2007, *C* 306, 1).

[407] COMMISSION OF THE EUROPEAN COMMUNITIES, Communication from the Commission Services of general interest in Europe, 2001/C 17/04, *OJ* 19.01.2001, *C* 17, 4, Annex II.

and telecommunications.[408] Public broadcasting has also been judged to fall within this category of services.[409] On the other hand, the Commission has specified that activities conducted by "*organisations performing largely social functions, which are not profit oriented and which are not meant to engage in industrial or commercial activity*", such as non-economic[410] activities of "*trade unions, political parties, churches and religious societies, consumer associations, learned societies, charities as well as relief and aid organisations*", will not fall within the remit of article 106 para. 2 TFEU [ex 86 EC Treaty].[411] In this light, it remains doubtful whether the bodies that are the focus of this study would be considered to fall within the scope of this article. In addition, one could wonder whether the required degree of government involvement ('entrusted by means of an act of public authority') would be considered too high for such bodies, certainly with respect to self-regulatory bodies.

D. *Interim conclusion*

In this section, we examined whether the use of ARIs could be problematic with respect to the competition rules. In order to provide an answer to this question, we explored the key legal provisions in this field, i.e., articles 101, 102 and 106 TFEU [ex 81, 82 and 86 EC Treaty]. First, given that these articles target measures taken by 'undertakings', we looked at whether alternative regulatory bodies could qualify as 'undertakings'. We found that this can be the case, provided that the activities the bodies engage in are of an economic nature. However, this notion ('economic') has been interpreted broadly, so the fact that the aim of the self- or co-regulatory body consists of the protection of minors against harmful content does not *a priori* rule

---

[408] WHISH, Richard, *Competition law*, Oxford, Oxford University Press, 2009, 234; ROTH, Peter and ROSE, Vivien (eds), *Bellamy & Child European Community law of competition*, Oxford, Oxford University Press, 2008, 1063.

[409] COMMISSION OF THE EUROPEAN COMMUNITIES, Communication from the Commission to the European Parliament, the Council, the European Economic and Social Committee and the Committee of the Regions – Accompanying the Communication on "A single market for 21st century Europe" – Services of general interest, including social services of general interest: a new European commitment, COM (2007) 725 final, 20.11.2007, 4. See also: ECJ, Giuseppe Sacchi (Reference for a preliminary ruling: Tribunale civile e penale di Biella – Italy), C-155/73, 30.04.1974, summary para. 8.

[410] Cf. also: ROTH, Peter and ROSE, Vivien (eds), *Bellamy & Child European Community law of competition*, Oxford, Oxford University Press, 2008, 1063 ("*Article [106, ex 86](2) does not, however, apply to non-economic services*"); COMMISSION OF THE EUROPEAN COMMUNITIES, Communication from the Commission Services of general interest in Europe, 2001/C 17/04, *OJ* 19.01.2001, *C* 17, 4, recital 28.

[411] COMMISSION OF THE EUROPEAN COMMUNITIES, Communication from the Commission Services of general interest in Europe, 2001/C 17/04, *OJ* 19.01.2001, *C* 17, 4, recital 30.

out any application of the competition rules. With respect to co-regulatory bodies, we noted that, under certain circumstances, bodies in which the government is involved, such as bodies entrusted by the State with particular tasks, can also be considered undertakings. In addition, self- or co-regulatory bodies could also qualify as 'associations of undertakings'. Of course, the exact qualification of the body will depend on the concrete circumstances of each case. But once this first hurdle is overcome, or in other words, the bodies in question are considered undertakings or associations of undertakings, this means that articles 101 or 102 TFEU [ex 81 and 82 EC Treaty] could be applicable to them.

With respect to article 101 TFEU [ex 81 EC Treaty], this means that all agreements, decisions or concerted practices by such bodies which adversely affect competition are prohibited. Hence, measures taken by alternative regulatory bodies should respect this prohibition. However, we found that there are three situations in which this prohibition will not be considered applicable. Apart from a possible exemption under article 101 para. 3 TFEU [ex 81 EC Treaty], Community Court case law as well as academic literature has confirmed that in the general assessment of the potential adverse effects of specific agreements under article 101 para. 1 TFEU [ex 81 EC Treaty], public interest criteria can be a taken into account, and could lead to an exemption to this paragraph. One could wonder, in this context, whether the protection of minors against harmful content could be accepted by the Court as such a criterion. A third way of avoiding the applicability of article 101 TFEU [ex 81 EC Treaty] is for an undertaking to argue that it took the measures in question on the basis of a rule imposed by a Member State that did not leave any room for commercial autonomy on behalf of the undertaking.

With respect to article 102 TFEU [ex 82 EC Treaty], alternative regulatory bodies that can be classified as an undertaking, and that have a (joint) dominant position, cannot abuse this position.

Second, we found that, with respect to both articles 101 and 102 TFEU [ex 81 and 82 EC Treaty], there can be an ambiguous relationship between Member States and undertakings. This might be especially relevant with respect to co-regulatory systems where it might not always be clear whether measures taken within the framework of such a system can be considered state measures or measures attributable to an undertaking. In this context, we examined the 'useful effect doctrine' theory put forward by the ECJ, which entails that on the basis of the competition principles included in articles 101 and 102 TFEU [ex 81 and 82 EC Treaty], in combination with articles 3 para. 1 (b) TFEU [ex 3 para. 1 (g) EC Treaty] and 4 para. 3 TFEU [ex 10 EC Treaty], Member States cannot be the source of measures which make the application of those principles ineffective. We noted that this theory also applies when Member States delegate certain regulatory powers to private bodies, a situation which could be relevant with respect to (self-) or co-regulatory bodies. Furthermore, we found that in such cases the Member State in question could be held liable, unless public interest considerations are put forward to justify the measures taken. The assessment of who will be considered responsible for the measures in question will depend on the concrete circumstances of each case, in particular the actual level of government involvement.

Finally, we examined whether article 106 TFEU [ex 86 EC Treaty], which also concerns the relationship between Member States and undertakings in the sphere of competition, might be of relevance to the use of ARIs. This article relates to public undertakings or undertakings which have been attributed special or exclusive rights (para. 1), or which are entrusted with the operation of services of general economic interest or which have the character of a revenue-producing monopoly (para. 2). We concluded, however, that self- or co-regulatory bodies which are involved in the protection of minors against harmful content would, in all probability, not fall within the scope of this article.

2.2.4. *Article 288 para. 3 TFEU [ex 249 EC Treaty]*

Requirements with respect to the implementation of Directives – The final legal provision, i.e., article 288 para. 3 TFEU [ex 249 EC Treaty], which we examine here in greater detail, slightly differs from the previous issues, since it does not relate to legal theories and principles, but deals with requirements that are imposed on the implementation of directives. However, this does not make this section less relevant, since the protection of minors against harmful content is an issue that has been included in directives, such as the Audiovisual Media Services Directive of 2007 (*supra*).

A. *General principle*

Choice of methods to implement directives – In the previous chapter, we briefly discussed article 288 para. 3 TFEU [ex 249 EC Treaty],[412] which attributes Member States a considerable margin of discretion with respect to the most appropriate method of implementation within their jurisdiction, as long as the actual result proposed by a directive is achieved.[413] This article is

[412] Article 288 para. 3 TFEU [ex 249 EC Treaty]: "*A directive shall be binding, as to the result to be achieved, upon each Member State to which it is addressed, but shall leave to the national authorities the choice of form and methods*".

[413] Please note that this section only concentrates on the aspects of article 288 para. 3 TFEU [ex 249 EC Treaty] which are relevant to the use of self-regulation and co-regulation as

a practical illustration of the general principle of subsidiarity (*supra*, Part 2, Chapter 1). We established that this article could be of importance to the use of ARIs, since it provides Member States with the option to choose the regulatory method they consider the most suitable or appropriate. In this context, we can also point to the Interinstitutional Agreement on Better Law-making, which recommends the use of self- and co-regulation.[414] Recital 13 of this Interinstitutional agreement refers to article 288 para. 3 TFEU [ex 249 EC Treaty], as well as certain provisions of the Protocol on the application of the principles of subsidiarity and proportionality.[415] It was stressed in the Interinstitutional agreement that

> *[i]n its proposals for directives, the Commission will ensure that a proper balance is struck between general principles and detailed provisions, in a manner that avoids excessive use of Community implementing measures.*[416]

National authorities – Article 288 para. 3 TFEU [ex 249 EC Treaty] clearly leaves the choice of form and methods to 'national authorities'. Prechal has noted that "*the choice of the competent authority is made within the framework of national constitutional law*".[417] The ECJ also clarified in the *Commission v. the Netherlands* case that Member States can delegate powers to domestic authorities, and, furthermore, that directives may be implemented by regional or local authorities.[418]

B. *Requirements*

Choice not absolute – However, the choice of form and methods is not unconditional. A number of requirements do need to be fulfilled. In the following paragraphs, we will analyse these requirements and try to draw conclusions as to the impact they have on the use of ARIs. Full effect and legal

implementation methods. For a comprehensive overview of other issues beyond the focus of this book, cf. Prechal, Sacha, *Directives in EC law*, Oxford, Oxford University Press, 2005, 349 p.

414 European Parliament, Council, and Commission, Interinstitutional agreement on better law-making, 2003/C 321/01, *OJ* 31.12.2003, *C* 321, 1. Cf. *supra*, Part 1, Chapter 2.

415 Protocol (No. 30) on the application of the principles of subsidiarity and proportionality, 02.10.1997, *OJ* 10.11.1997, *C* 340, 105. Cf. *supra*, Part 2, Chapter 1.

416 Recital 13 European Parliament, Council, and Commission, Interinstitutional agreement on better law-making, 2003/C 321/01, *OJ* 31.12.2003, *C* 321, 1.

417 Prechal, Sacha, *Directives in EC law*, Oxford, Oxford University Press, 2005, 74. See also: Brent, Richard, *Directives: rights and remedies in English and Community law*, London, LLP, 2001, 109.

418 ECJ, Commission of the European Communities v. Kingdom of the Netherlands, C-96/81, 25.05.1982, para. 12.

certainty are the cornerstones of the ECJ's case law regarding the implementation of directives.[419] Hence, although it is left to the Member States to pick the most appropriate implementation method, they are nevertheless obliged to take every measure necessary to ensure that the directive is fully effective,[420, 421] even when the Member State deems its "*own national provisions of better quality than the Community provisions*".[422] Furthermore, they need to guarantee that the implementing measures are sufficiently clear, precise, transparent,[423] publicised and accessible,[424] and are accompanied by effective judicial procedures so that individuals can assert their rights.

Content, nature and enforcement – To examine these requirements in greater detail, we adopt Prechal's distinction between requirements imposed on: the content of the directives which need to be implemented, the nature of the measures chosen to do so, and their application and enforcement in practice.[425]

---

419 Lenaerts, Koen and Van Nuffel, Piet, *Europees recht in hoofdlijnen* [*Outline of European law*], Antwerpen, Maklu, 2008, 463 [in Dutch]; Prechal, Sacha, *Directives in EC law*, Oxford, Oxford University Press, 2005, 75; Brent, Richard, *Directives: rights and remedies in English and Community law*, London, LLP, 2001, 111.

420 ECJ, Jean Noël Royer (Reference for a preliminary ruling: Tribunal de première instance de Liège – Belgium), C-48/75, 08.04.1976, para. 73; ECJ, Theresa Emmot v. Minister for Social Welfare and Attorney General, C-208/90, 25.07.1991, para. 18; ECJ, Commission of the European Communities v. Kingdom of Sweden, C-478/99, 07.05.2002, para. 15; ECJ, Commission of the European Communities v. French Republic, C-233/00, 26.06.2003, para. 75.

421 In this context, we can also refer to article 4 para. 3 TEU [ex 10 EC Treaty], cf. footnote 369. See also: ECJ, Sabine von Colson and Elisabeth Kamann v. Land Nordrhein-Westfalen, C-14/83, 10.04.1984, para. 26; ECJ, Commission of the European Communities v. Hellenic Republic, C-68/88, 21.09.1989, para. 23; Brent, Richard, *Directives: rights and remedies in English and Community law*, London, LLP, 2001, 131.

422 ECJ, Commission of the European Communities v. Republic of Austria, C-194/01, 29.04.2004, para. 25.

423 ECJ, Commission of the European Communities v. Grand Duchy of Luxemburg, C-220/94, 15.06.1995, para. 10.

424 ECJ, Commission of the European Communities v. Kingdom of Sweden, C-478/99, 07.05.2002, para. 12: "*In any event, in order to achieve the twofold objective pursued and to satisfy the requirements of legal certainty, it is essential for this list to be published as an integral part of the provisions of the Directive*".

425 Prechal, Sacha, *Directives in EC law*, Oxford, Oxford University Press, 2005, 76. Please note that issues concerning time limits for implementation and transitional measures do not fall within the scope of this book. For more details, cf. for instance: Brent, Richard, *Directives: rights and remedies in English and Community law*, London, LLP, 2001, 127–129; Prechal, Sacha, *Directives in EC law*, Oxford, Oxford University Press, 2005, 18–31.

B.1. *Content*

Clarity and precision – First of all, for the sake of legal certainty and predictability, the implementing measures must be clear and precise. In the case *Commission v. Greece*, the ECJ held that

> *the Court has consistently held that it is particularly important, in order to satisfy the requirement of legal certainty, that individuals should have the benefit of a clear and precise legal situation enabling them to ascertain the full extent of their rights and, where appropriate, to rely on them before the national courts.*[426]

The ECJ has clarified that a *verbatim* transposition of the directive's provisions is not necessary.[427] Nor will the passing of specific legislation always be essential;[428] existing general principles of constitutional or administrative law,[429] or even a general legal context may be sufficient,[430] provided it guarantees the full application of the directive's stipulations in an adequately clear

---

[426] ECJ, Commission of the European Communities v. Hellenic Republic, C-236/95, 19.09.1996, para. 13. Along the same lines: ECJ, Commission of the European Community v. Federal Republic of Germany, C-59/89, 30.05.1991, para. 18; ECJ, Commission of the European Communities v. Federal Republic of Germany, C-361/88, 30.05.1991, para. 15; ECJ, Commission of the European Communities v. Grand Duchy of Luxemburg, C-220/94, 15.06.1995, para. 10; ECJ, Commission of the European Communities v. Kingdom of the Netherlands, C-144/99, 10.05.2001, para. 17.

[427] ECJ, Commission of the European Communities v. Federal Republic of Germany, C-131/88, 28.02.1991, para. 6; ECJ, Commission of the European Community v. Federal Republic of Germany, C-59/89, 30.05.1991, para. 18; ECJ, Commission of the European Communities v. Federal Republic of Germany, C-361/88, 30.05.1991, para. 15. See also: Arnull, Anthony et al., *Wyatt and Dashwood's European Union law*, London, Sweet & Maxwell, 2006, 164.

[428] ECJ, Commission of the European Communities v. French Republic, C-296/01, 20.11.2003, para. 55.

[429] ECJ, Commission of the European Communities v. Federal Republic of Germany, C-29/84, 23.05.1985, para. 23; ECJ, Commission of the European Communities v. French Republic, C-296/01, 20.11.2003, para. 55.

[430] Lenaerts, Koen and Van Nuffel, Piet, *Europees recht in hoofdlijnen* [*Outline of European law*], Antwerpen, Maklu, 2008, 463–464 [in Dutch]. Prechal interprets a 'general legal context' rather in the following way: "*[t]hus the combination of existing (general) rules of national law, including general principles of constitutional or administrative law, and their application and interpretation, or the combination of general provisions and specific provisions enacted for the purposes of transposition of the directive may suffice, provided that the necessary clarity and precision is guaranteed and that there is no practical or theoretical risk of misapplying the rules*". She also points to the relevance of national case law in this context: Prechal, Sacha, *Directives in EC law*, Oxford, Oxford University Press, 2005, 77–81.

and precise manner.[431] With respect to this criterion, we might wonder if a self- or co-regulatory scheme could suffice. The fact that the ECJ refers to 'a legal context' might point to the fact that a minimum level of government involvement will be required, and, hence, that co-regulation would be preferred to self-regulation.

SPECIFIC METHODS IMPOSED BY THE DIRECTIVE – Furthermore, the freedom of Member States to choose the form and methods of implementation is limited by specific provisions of a directive. Hence, if the directive itself contains specific suggestions as to certain methods for achieving the result, Member States should take this into account.[432] However, whether or not a directive can oblige Member State to use a certain implementation method is a controversial issue on which neither academic literature nor case law provides a satisfactory answer.[433] We assume that whereas certain implementation methods, such as self- and co-regulation,[434] can specifically be allowed –

---

431 ECJ, Commission of the European Communities v. Federal Republic of Germany, C-131/88, 28.02.1991, para. 6: "*It should be pointed out first of all that according to the case-law of the Court (see, in particular, the judgment in Case 363/85 Commission v Italy [1987] ECR 1733), the transposition of a directive into domestic law does not necessarily require that its provisions be incorporated formally and verbatim in express, specific legislation; a general legal context may, depending on the content of the directive, be adequate for the purpose provided that it does indeed guarantee the full application of the directive in a sufficiently clear and precise manner so that, where the directive is intended to create rights for individuals, the persons concerned can ascertain the full extent of their rights and, where appropriate, rely on them before the national courts*". See also: ECJ, Commission of the European Communities v. Kingdom of Belgium, C-247/85, 08.07.1987, para. 9; ECJ, Commission of the European Community v. Federal Republic of Germany, C-59/89, 30.05.1991, para. 18; ECJ, Commission of the European Communities v. Federal Republic of Germany, C-361/88, 30.05.1991, para. 15.

432 BRENT, Richard, *Directives: rights and remedies in English and Community law*, London, LLP, 2001, 109; HANS-BREDOW-INSTITUT AND EMR, Study on co-regulation measures in the media sector: Final report, Study commissioned by the European Commission, June 2006, retrieved from http://ec.europa.eu/avpolicy/docs/library/studies/coregul/final_rep_en.pdf (on 28.07.2006), 156; HEUKELS, Ton, "Alternatieve implementatietechnieken en art. 189, lid 3 EEG: grondslagen en ontwikkelingen" ["*Alternative implementation techniques and art. 189, para. 3 EEC: foundations and developments*"], *NTB* 1993, Vol. 1, 60 [in Dutch].

433 In some instances, for instance, in the field of environmental law, the ECJ has decided that the specific methods of implementation proposed by a certain directive needed to be followed strictly: ECJ, Commission of the European Communities v. Federal Republic of Germany, C-184/97, 11.11.1999.

434 An example of such a directive provision is, for instance, article 4 para. 1 COUNCIL Directive 85/339/EEC of 27 June 1985 on containers of liquids for human consumption, *OJ* 06.07.1985, *L* 176, 18 (no longer in force). See also: AVMSD and footnote 484, *infra*.

and, hence, in such a case their use will not be contested by the ECJ[435] – it remains doubtful whether their use can be obliged.

B.2. *Nature*

Binding nature – Second, the ECJ has repeatedly held that measures must be implemented in a form that is legally binding.[436] Hence, in principle, binding national legislation or a precise legal framework will be required.[437] The ECJ, for instance, does not consider a draft national regulation,[438] or administrative practices, as appropriate implementing measures.[439] Yet, an implementation consisting of a legislative provision which serves as the basis for the adoption of administrative measures has been approved by the ECJ, on the express condition that these administrative measures be officially published, general in scope and capable of creating rights and obligations for individuals.[440]

In some instances, directives have been implemented by means of agreements, such as, for instance, in the field of labour law[441] or environmental

---

[435] Heukels, Ton, "Alternatieve implementatietechnieken en art. 189, lid 3 EEG: grondslagen en ontwikkelingen" ["*Alternative implementation techniques and art. 189, para. 3 EEC: foundations and developments*"], *NTB* 1993, Vol. 1, 60 [in Dutch].

[436] For instance: ECJ, Commission of the European Communities v. Federal Republic of Germany, C-131/88, 28.02.1991, para. 6.

[437] Prechal, Sacha, *Directives in EC law*, Oxford, Oxford University Press, 2005, 83.

[438] ECJ, Commission of the European Communities v. Grand Duchy of Luxemburg, C-221/94, 07.11.1996, para. 22.

[439] ECJ, Commission of the European Communities v. Federal Republic of Germany, C-131/88, 28.02.1991, para. 6: "*Mere administrative practices, which by their nature may be altered at the whim of the administration, may not be considered as constituting the proper fulfillment of the obligation deriving from that directive*".

[440] ECJ, Commission of the European Communities v. Kingdom of the Netherlands, C-339/87, 15.03.1990, summary para. 1.

[441] Cf. Treaty on the European Union, Protocol on social policy, Agreement on social policy concluded between the Member States of the European Community with the exception of the United Kingdom of Great Britain and Northern Ireland, *OJ* 29.07.1992, *C* 191, article 2 para. 4: "*A Member State may entrust management and labour, at their joint request, with the implementation of directives adopted pursuant to paragraphs 2 and 3. In this case, it shall ensure that, no later than the date on which a directive must be transposed in accordance with Article 189, management and labour have introduced the necessary measures by* agreement, *the Member State concerned being required to take any necessary measure enabling it at any time to be in a position to guarantee the results imposed by that directive*" [emphasis added]. Note that the Member State remains responsible for guaranteeing that the necessary agreements have been concluded. Cf. also: Commission of the European Communities, Communication concerning the application of the Agreement on social policy presented by the Commission to the Council and to the European Parliament, COM

law.[442] It has been noted that this often is problematic, given the voluntary nature of the agreements, non- or limited publicity, limited coverage and continuity, and enforcement intricacies.[443] However, the ECJ has accepted such agreements if the directive explicitly refers to them as a possible implementing measure (cf. also *infra*, AVMSD).[444]

Comparison: environmental agreements – The field of environmental law is interesting for comparative purposes. In 1996, the European Commission issued a Communication on environmental agreements.[445] With this Communication, the Commission aimed to "*promote and facilitate the use of effective and acceptable environmental agreements*" by providing guidelines[446] and a clear framework for the use of such agreements as an imple-

(93) 600 final, 14.12.1993, 4 and 30–31. This Communication clarified, amongst other things, that the Member States must set up procedures to deal, where necessary, with any shortcomings in the agreement implementing the directive (p. 31). In a way, this clarification can be considered as referring to the 'government safety net' that is often talked about with respect to co-regulation (cf. *supra*, Part 1, Chapter 2).

442 Prechal, Sacha, *Directives in EC law*, Oxford, Oxford University Press, 2005, 86. See also: Verschuuren, Jonathan, "EC environmental law and self-regulation in the Member States: in search of a legislative framework", *Yearbook of European Environmental Law* 2000, Vol. 1, 103–121.

443 Prechal, Sacha, *Directives in EC law*, Oxford, Oxford University Press, 2005, 86.

444 ECJ, Commission of the European Communities v. French Republic, C-255/93, 05.10.1994, paras 3, 4, 16–28.

445 Commission of the European Communities, Communication from the Commission to the Council and to the European Parliament on environmental agreements, COM (1996) 561 final, 27.11.1996. Note that this Communication did not deal with agreements at the Community level. In 2002, after the adoption of the Better Legislation Action Plan (*supra*, Part 1, Chapter 2), the Commission issued a new Communication which did address the possibilities to conclude environmental agreements at Community level. This Communication explicitly referred to self- and co-regulation. Cf. Commission of the European Communities, Communication from the Commission to the European Parliament, the Council, the Economic and Social Committee and the Committee of the Regions of 17 July 2002 on environmental agreements at Community level within the framework of the Action Plan on the 'Simplification and improvement of the regulatory environment', COM (2002) 412 final, 17.07.2002.

446 For instance, with respect to prior consultation with interested parties, a binding form, quantified and staged objectives, the monitoring of results, and the publication of the agreement and of the results obtained. Cf. also checklist for environmental agreements: Commission of the European Communities, Communication from the Commission to the Council and to the European Parliament on environmental agreements, COM (1996) 561 final, 27.11.1996, 3, 10–14 and 22. These guidelines were also set out in a Recommendation addressed to the Member States: Commission Recommendation 96/733/EC of 9 December 1996 concerning environmental agreements implementing Community directives, *OJ* 21.12.1996, *L* 333, 59–61.

mentation tool of Community directives.[447] The Communication considers agreements in this context a supplement to legislation and described these as either agreements between industry and public authorities on the achievement of environmental objectives, or unilateral commitments on the part of industry recognised by the public authorities.[448] Such agreements, in light of the definitions put forward in Part 1, Chapter 2, would probably rather be considered co-regulation instead of self-regulation, given the level of government involvement (government as an agreement partner or validator of agreements). In any case, the Communication clarified that, in some circumstances, binding agreements – which contain guarantees given by public authorities – may be considered an adequate implementation tool.[449] However, a distinction was made between directives which intend to create rights and obligations for individuals, and directives which require the setting up of general programmes or the achievement of general targets. Whereas agreements are not considered adequate to implement the former category of directive, binding (environmental) agreements could, according to the Commission, be an appropriate implementation tool for the latter type of directive. Furthermore, the Communication also suggested that directives might offer Member States the possibility to choose between agreements or national legislation as implementing measures. However, the Commission immediately added that this should be limited to "*clearly defined circumstances*" and made subject to "*expressly stated and verifiable conditions in order to ensure legal certainty and efficient enforcement of Community Directives throughout the Community*".[450] Moreover, even when agreements are opted for to implement a directive, the Communication emphasised that there should be a "*legislatory fall-back*" that provides "*an effective basis to prevent 'free-rider' profits and also a guarantee for compliance with Community legislation*".[451] In

[447] Commission of the European Communities, Communication from the Commission to the Council and to the European Parliament on environmental agreements, COM (1996) 561 final, 27.11.1996, 3 and 5.

[448] Commission of the European Communities, Communication from the Commission to the Council and to the European Parliament on environmental agreements, COM (1996) 561 final, 27.11.1996, 5.

[449] Commission of the European Communities, Communication from the Commission to the Council and to the European Parliament on environmental agreements, COM (1996) 561 final, 27.11.1996, 17.

[450] Commission of the European Communities, Communication from the Commission to the Council and to the European Parliament on environmental agreements, COM (1996) 561 final, 27.11.1996, 18.

[451] Commission of the European Communities, Communication from the Commission to the Council and to the European Parliament on environmental agreements, COM (1996) 561 final, 27.11.1996, 18.

addition, Member States would still be responsible for guaranteeing effective compliance with the agreement. These requirements point in the direction of (a rather strict type of) co-regulation. Finally, the Commission highlighted that implementing a directive by means of an (environmental) agreement is an option and not an obligation[452] (cf. also *supra* and *infra* AVMSD).

What can be deduced from this Communication is that, although its title refers to 'voluntary agreements', implementing a directive by means of pure self-regulation will not be considered satisfactory.[453] This is because a certain level of government involvement is required: the prerequisite that there must be a 'legislatory fall-back' especially points to the possible use of co-regulatory instead of self-regulatory systems.

B.3. *Application and enforcement*

Fully effective – Thirdly, the implementing measures cannot remain dead letter.[454] Practical application and effective enforcement are essential,[455] and when sanctions need to be implemented, they need to be effective, proportionate and dissuasive.[456, 457] Furthermore, effective judicial protection is of

---

[452] Commission of the European Communities, Communication from the Commission to the Council and to the European Parliament on environmental agreements, COM (1996) 561 final, 27.11.1996, 19.

[453] See also: Hans-Bredow-Institut and EMR, Study on co-regulation measures in the media sector: Final report, Study commissioned by the European Commission, June 2006, retrieved from http://ec.europa.eu/avpolicy/docs/library/studies/coregul/final_rep_en.pdf (on 28.07.2006), 175.

[454] Cf. also article 4 para. 3 TEU [ex 10 EC Treaty] (*supra*, footnote 369).

[455] Arnull, Anthony et al., *Wyatt and Dashwood's European Union law*, London, Sweet & Maxwell, 2006, 165; Prechal, Sacha, *Directives in EC law*, Oxford, Oxford University Press, 2005, 87. In this context we can also refer to article 4 para. 3 TEU [ex 10 EC Treaty] (*supra*, footnote 369). See also: ECJ, Sabine von Colson and Elisabeth Kamann v. Land Nordrhein-Westfalen, C-14/83, 10.04.1984, para. 26; ECJ, Commission of the European Communities v. Hellenic Republic, C-68/88, 21.09.1989, para. 23.

[456] Cf. ECJ, Criminal proceedings against Maria Amélia Nunes and Evangelina de Matos ((Reference for a preliminary ruling: Tribunal de Círculo do Porto – Portugal), C-186/98, 08.07.1999, para. 14 ("*The sanction provided for must be analogous to those applicable to infringements of national law of similar nature and importance, and must be effective, proportionate and dissuasive*"); ECJ, Commission of the European Communities v. Hellenic Republic, C-68/88, 21.09.1989, para. 24.

[457] Prechal described these criteria as follows: "*Arguably,* effective *should be understood in this context as producing the desired result, which is to compel observance of the terms and spirit of Community law,* proportionate *as referring to the relation between the nature of the offence committed and the sanction imposed laying down both a lower limit and an upper limit, and* dissuasive *as preventing disobedience of the Community law rules*": Prechal,

paramount importance.[458] In the *Johnston* case, the ECJ explicitly acknowledged that this is a general principle of law which "*underlies the constitutional traditions common to the Member States*", and which is also articulated in articles 6 and 13 ECHR (*supra*).[459] The principle entails that individuals who have been attributed rights by a directive thus need access to an effective judicial remedy.[460] Although the Member States are free to craft the procedural rules which individuals will be confronted with when asserting their rights created by the directive,[461] the ECJ has held that these rules "*cannot be less favourable than those relating to similar actions of a domestic nature*" (principle of equivalence).[462, 463] Nor should the adopted procedural rules make the exercise of rights too difficult or impossible in practice (principle of minimum protection).[464, 465] Furthermore, national courts "*are required to interpret their national law in the light of the wording and the purpose of the directive in order to achieve the result referred to in the third paragraph of article [288, ex 249]*".[466]

Sacha, *Directives in EC law*, Oxford, Oxford University Press, 2005, 91 [original emphasis]. See also: BRENT, Richard, *Directives: rights and remedies in English and Community law*, London, LLP, 2001, 115–118.

458 BRENT, Richard, *Directives: rights and remedies in English and Community law*, London, LLP, 2001, 133; PRECHAL, Sacha, *Directives in EC law*, Oxford, Oxford University Press, 2005, 91 and 142–145.

459 ECJ, Marguerite Johnston v. Chief Constable of the Royal Ulster Constabulary, C-222/84, 15.05.1986, para. 18.

460 BRENT, Richard, *Directives: rights and remedies in English and Community law*, London, LLP, 2001, 133.

461 ECJ, Cofidis SA v. Jean-Louis Fredout, C-473/00, 21.11.2002, para. 28.

462 BRENT, Richard, *Directives: rights and remedies in English and Community law*, London, LLP, 2001, 136.

463 ECJ, Rewe-Zentralfinanz eG and Rewe-Zentral AG v. Landwirtschaftskammer für das Saarland, C-33/76, 16.12.1976, para. 5.

464 BRENT, Richard, *Directives: rights and remedies in English and Community law*, London, LLP, 2001, 136.

465 ECJ, Rewe-Zentralfinanz eG and Rewe-Zentral AG v. Landwirtschaftskammer für das Saarland, C-33/76, 16.12.1976, para. 5. See also: SNYDER, Francis, "The effectiveness of European Community law: Institutions, processes, tools and techniques", *The Modern Law Review* 1993, 45; PRECHAL, Sacha, *Directives in EC law*, Oxford, Oxford University Press, 2005, 137–141.

466 ECJ, Sabine von Colson and Elisabeth Kamann v. Land Nordrhein-Westfalen, C-14/83, 10.04.1984, para. 26. For more details, cf. PRECHAL, Sacha, *Directives in EC law*, Oxford, Oxford University Press, 2005, chapter 8: Consistent interpretation.

B.4. *Liability in case of inadequate implementation*

MEMBER STATES' RESPONSIBILITY – As a result of the obligations imposed by article 288 para. 3 TFEU [ex 249 EC Treaty] as well as article 4 para. 3 TEU [ex 10 EC Treaty] (*supra*),[467] Member States will be held liable if a directive is not properly implemented.[468] Whereas the issues surrounding the liability of Member States in case of incorrect implementation are too numerous to be discussed in detail,[469] one element is noteworthy with respect to the use of ARIs. The ECJ has held that Member States cannot shirk their responsibility by attributing the blame to bodies to which they have delegated the implementation.[470] In this context, CRAUFURD SMITH has observed that

> *[t]his suggests that Member States must take effective measures to ensure, when they rely on private standard setting bodies to flesh out general European Community requirements, that those bodies comply with human rights standards, both procedurally and substantively. If not they risk Commission investigation*

[467] Cf. footnote 369.

[468] Procedures will be initiated on the basis of article 258 TFEU [ex 226 EC Treaty]: "*If the Commission considers that a Member State has failed to fulfil an obligation under the Treaties, it shall deliver a reasoned opinion on the matter after giving the State concerned the opportunity to submit its observations. If the State concerned does not comply with the opinion within the period laid down by the Commission, the latter may bring the matter before the Court of Justice of the European Union*".

[469] For more details, cf. PRECHAL, Sacha, *Directives in EC law*, Oxford, Oxford University Press, 2005, chapter 10: liability of the State in cases of inadequate implementation of directives. One of the most important ECJ cases in this field is the *Francovich* case: ECJ, Andrea Francovich and Danila Bonifaci and others v. Italian Republic, C-6/90 and C-9/90, 19.11.1991. See for instance: paras 39–41: "*Where, as in this case, a Member State fails to fulfil its obligation under the third paragraph of Article [288, ex 249] of the Treaty to take all the measures necessary to achieve the result prescribed by a directive, the full effectiveness of that rule of Community law requires that there should be a right to reparation provided that three conditions are fulfilled. The first of those conditions is that the result prescribed by the directive should entail the grant of rights to individuals. The second condition is that it should be possible to identify the content of those rights on the basis of the provisions of the directive. Finally, the third condition is the existence of a causal link between the breach of the State's obligation and the loss and damage suffered by the injured parties. Those conditions are sufficient to give rise to a right on the part of individuals to obtain reparation, a right founded directly on Community law*".

[470] ECJ, Commission of the European Communities v. Kingdom of Belgium, C-77/69, 05.05.1970, para. 15 ("*The liability of a Member State under article [258, ex 226] arises whatever the agency of the state whose action or inaction is the cause of the failure to fulfil its obligations, even in the case of a constitutionally independent institution*"); ECJ, Commission of the European Communities v. Kingdom of the Netherlands, C-96/81, 25.05.1982, para. 12. See also: STEYGER, Elies, "European Community law and the self-regulatory capacity of society", *Journal of Common Market Studies* 1993, Vol. 31, No. 2, 176.

> *and potential reference to the ECJ under Article 226 EC. It is also possible that an individual adversely affected by the action of a private body entrusted with fleshing out and implementing a directive might seek damages from the state under the principle established in the Francovich case.*[471] [N.B. Article refers to article prior to the adoption of the Treaty of Lisbon]

Hence, the fact that a Member State has delegated the actual implementation of a directive to an alternative regulatory body will not discharge this Member State from its responsibility under article 288 para. 3 TFEU [ex 249 EC Treaty].

Direct effect – In this context, a brief reference might be made to the potential direct effect[472] of a directive, which is a well-documented issue.[473] Although a thorough analysis of this topic would, again, lead us beyond the scope of this study, one element could be of importance to the analysis of the use of ARIs. In brief, the ECJ has held that directives can be considered to have direct effect if the provisions are unconditional and sufficiently precise, and if the Member State has not adequately implemented the directive's provisions (or if the rules are not correctly applied) and the implementation period has expired.[474] In this context – and of possible relevance to our research subject – the ECJ has held that

> *[u]nconditional and sufficiently precise provisions of a directive may be relied upon against organizations or bodies which are subject to the authority or control of the State or have special powers beyond those which result from the normal rules applicable in relations between individuals. They may in any event be relied upon against a body, whatever its legal form, which has been made responsible, pursuant to a measure adopted by the State, for providing a public service under*

---

471 Craufurd Smith, Rachel, "European Community media regulation in a converging environment", in: Shuibhne, Niamh Nic (ed.), *Regulating the internal market*, Cheltenham, Edward Elgar, 2006, 136–137.

472 Prechal defined the concept of direct effect as "*the obligation of a court or another authority to apply the relevant provision of Community law, either as a norm which governs the case or as a standard for legal review*": Prechal, Sacha, *Directives in EC law*, Oxford, Oxford University Press, 2005, 241.

473 Cf. Prechal, Sacha, *Directives in EC law*, Oxford, Oxford University Press, 2005, chapter 9: Direct effect of directives.

474 ECJ, Ursula Becker v. Finanzamt Münster-Innenstadt, C-8/81, 19.01.1982, para. 25: "*Thus, wherever the provisions of a directive appear, as far as their subject-matter is concerned, to be unconditional and sufficiently precise, those provisions may, in the absence of implementing measures adopted within the prescribed period, be relied upon as against any national provision which is incompatible with the directive or in so far as the provisions define rights which individuals are able to assert against the state*". See also: Prechal, Sacha, *Directives in EC law*, Oxford, Oxford University Press, 2005, 242–243.

> *the control of the State and has for that purpose special powers beyond those which result from the normal rules applicable in relations between individuals.*[475]

Examples of such organisations or bodies are tax authorities, local or regional authorities, constitutionally independent authorities responsible for the maintenance of public order, and safety and public authorities providing public health services.[476] Following the ECJ's description of the bodies in question, i.e.,

> *a body, whatever its legal form, which has been made responsible, pursuant to a measure adopted by the State, for providing a public service under the control of the State and has for that purpose special powers beyond those which result from the normal rules applicable in relations between individuals.*

We could assume that co-regulatory bodies might, in certain instances, be confronted with the direct effect of directives.

No horizontal direct effect – Yet, not all 'varieties' of direct effect have been accepted by the Court with respect to directives. A horizontal direct effect, for instance, which would offer individuals the possibility to invoke provisions of a directive against each other, has been rejected by the ECJ.[477]

C. *Article 288 TFEU [ex 249 EC Treaty] and ARIs*

Academic literature – A few academic commentators have expressed their opinion on the scope of article 288 para. 3 TFEU [ex 249 EC Treaty] linked to the use of ARIs. Craufurd Smith, for instance, observed in this respect that the fact that the obligations imposed by a directive are reached in

[475] *ECJ*, A. Foster and others v. British Gas plc., C-188/89, 12.07.1990, summary para. 1.

[476] *ECJ*, A. Foster and others v. British Gas plc., C-188/89, 12.07.1990, para. 19.

[477] ECJ, M. H. Marshall v. Southampton and South-West Hampshire Area Health Authority (Teaching), C-152/84, 26.02.1986, para. 48 ("*With regard to the argument that a directive may not be relied upon against an individual, it must be emphasized that according to article [288, ex 249] of the EEC Treaty the binding nature of a directive, which constitutes the basis for the possibility of relying on the directive before a national court, exists only in relation to 'each Member State to which it is addressed'. It follows that a directive may not of itself impose obligations on an individual and that a provision of a directive may not be relied upon as such against such a person*"); ECJ, Paola Faccini Dori v. Recreb Srl, C-91/92, 14.07.1994, summary para. 2 ("*The effect of extending that principle to the sphere of relations between individuals would be to recognize a power in the Community to enact obligations for individuals with immediate effect, whereas it has competence to do so only where it is empowered to adopt regulations. It follows that, in the absence of measures of transposition within the prescribed time-limit, an individual may not rely on a directive in order to claim a right against another individual and enforce such a right in a national court*").

practice does not absolve Member States of their duty to set up a legal framework which could ensure compliance at present and in the future.[478] Whereas she considered the use of self-regulation to implement directives problematic (in particular when the directive requires 'a legal framework'), she did suggest that co-regulation might be an acceptable mechanism to implement a directive.[479] She emphasised that

> *where codes developed by private actors are relied on to meet specific Community requirements, Commission v. Germany indicates that the standards must be sufficiently clear, must adequately reflect the Community objectives and have binding force. Moreover, individuals must be able to ascertain where to find such codes and their legal status should be readily apparent.*[480]

Both the academics carrying out the Study on co-regulation measures (*supra*, Part 1, Chapter 2) and Tony Prosser do believe that co-regulation could be considered as an implementation method.[481] The former also observed that if the implementation of a directive involves the use of co-regulation, but this co-regulatory system does not cover all addressees, the Member State has to provide state regulation for these addressees.[482] Furthermore, Steyger stressed that the Member State has the duty to intervene if the regulating organisation does not achieve the desired result.[483]

---

[478] Craufurd Smith, Rachel, "European Community media regulation in a converging environment", in: Shuibhne, Niamh Nic (ed.), *Regulating the internal market*, Cheltenham, Edward Elgar, 2006, 114.

[479] Craufurd Smith, Rachel, "European Community media regulation in a converging environment", in: Shuibhne, Niamh Nic (ed.), *Regulating the internal market*, Cheltenham, Edward Elgar, 2006, 114.

[480] Craufurd Smith, Rachel, "European Community media regulation in a converging environment", in: Shuibhne, Niamh Nic (ed.), *Regulating the internal market*, Cheltenham, Edward Elgar, 2006, 114–115.

[481] Hans-Bredow-Institut and EMR, Study on co-regulation measures in the media sector: Final report, Study commissioned by the European Commission, June 2006, retrieved from http://ec.europa.eu/avpolicy/docs/library/studies/coregul/final_rep_en.pdf (on 28.07.2006), 153–161; Prosser, Tony, "Self-regulation, Co-regulation and the Audio-Visual Media Services Directive", *Journal of Consumer Policy* 2008, Vol. 31, No. 1, 105.

[482] Hans-Bredow-Institut and EMR, Study on co-regulation measures in the media sector: Final report, Study commissioned by the European Commission, June 2006, retrieved from http://ec.europa.eu/avpolicy/docs/library/studies/coregul/final_rep_en.pdf (on 28.07.2006), 161. Along the same lines, see also: Steyger, Elies, "European Community law and the self-regulatory capacity of society", *Journal of Common Market Studies* 1993, Vol. 31, No. 2, 182.

[483] Steyger, Elies, "European Community law and the self-regulatory capacity of society", *Journal of Common Market Studies* 1993, Vol. 31, No. 2, 182.

Specific case: the AVMSD – The AVMSD states in its article 3 para. 7 that "*Member States shall encourage co- and/or self-regulatory regimes at national level in the fields coordinated by this Directive to the extent permitted by their legal systems*".[484] The AVMSD thus explicitly points to certain methods of implementation.[485] However, the use of the notion 'encourage' should be noted. Furthermore, recital 36 clarifies that Member States are not obliged to set up co- and/or self-regulatory regimes. These 'reservations' can be directly linked to article 288 para. 3 TFEU [ex 249 EC Treaty]. Given that this article is based on the principle of subsidiarity (as it leaves the decision on the most appropriate implementation method to the Member States), encouraging a particular method is probably as far as the EU authorities can go (*supra*).[486]

---

[484] The AVMSD is not the only directive in the media sector which contains references to the use of alternative regulatory instruments. Cf. for instance: Directive 2006/114/EC of the European Parliament and of the Council of 12 December 2006 concerning misleading and comparative advertising, *OJ* 27.12.2006, *L* 376, 21, article 6 ("*This Directive does not exclude the voluntary control, which Member States may encourage, of misleading or comparative advertising by self-regulatory bodies and recourse to such bodies by the persons or organisations referred to in the second subparagraph of Article 5(1) on condition that proceedings before such bodies are additional to the court or administrative proceedings referred to in that Article*"); e-Commerce Directive (*supra*), article 16 on codes of conduct ("*1. Member States and the Commission shall encourage: (a) the drawing up of codes of conduct at Community level, by trade, professional and consumer associations or organisations, designed to contribute to the proper implementation of Articles 5 to 15; (b) the voluntary transmission of draft codes of conduct at national or Community level to the Commission; (c) the accessibility of these codes of conduct in the Community languages by electronic means; (d) the communication to the Member States and the Commission, by trade, professional and consumer associations or organisations, of their assessment of the application of their codes of conduct and their impact upon practices, habits or customs relating to electronic commerce; (e) the drawing up of codes of conduct regarding the protection of minors and human dignity. 2. Member States and the Commission shall encourage the involvement of associations or organisations representing consumers in the drafting and implementation of codes of conduct affecting their interests and drawn up in accordance with paragraph 1(a). [...]*".

[485] We noted *supra* (Part 1, Chapter 2, 2.2.2. Media policy documents) that the AVMSD contains a rather ambivalent approach to the use of self- and co-regulation (cf. recital 36). We have assumed that co-regulation is the preferred instrument for implementation and that self-regulation will only be accepted as an implementation tool if it is accompanied by other measures and, hence, functions as a complement to other forms of regulation.

[486] Cf. also: Craufurd Smith, Rachel, "European Community media regulation in a converging environment", in: Shuibhne, Niamh Nic (ed.), *Regulating the internal market*, Cheltenham, Edward Elgar, 2006, 115; Hans-Bredow-Institut and EMR, Study on co-regulation measures in the media sector: Final report, Study commissioned by the European Commission, June 2006, retrieved from http://ec.europa.eu/avpolicy/docs/library/studies/coregul/final_rep_en.pdf (on 28.07.2006), 153: "*It could very well be argued that obliging the member states to use co-regulation as a binding instrument of directive*

D. *Interim conclusion*

Free, but conditional, choice – In the previous paragraphs, we discussed article 288 para. 3 TFEU [ex 249 EC Treaty] which, in accordance with the general principle of subsidiarity, leaves Member States to choose the most appropriate method to implement EU directives. Although the Member States are granted this margin of discretion, there are, however, a number of requirements which, nevertheless, need to be complied with in order to achieve a correct implementation. We found that any implementing measure needs to be, first, clear and precise, published and accessible, second, of a binding nature, and, third, effectively applied, enforced and accompanied by effective judicial protection. Certain nuances can also be mentioned. With respect to the first requirement, for instance, we noted that it is not required that actual legislation be drafted; a legal context could be considered sufficient. Furthermore, as regards the second requirement, i.e., the binding nature of implementing measures, we observed that a combination of a legal provision and other measures, or, certain agreements (in which both private actors and the government are involved) could be accepted. A final nuance which is of importance to the use of ARIs relates to the fact that the freedom of Member States to select implementation methods is curbed by the specific provisions of a directive. This means that if a directive specifies possible methods of implementation, such as, for example, self- and co-regulation (cf. AVMSD), this needs to be taken into account by the Member States and the use of these methods will be accepted by the ECJ. However, even though the ECJ's case law has not been very clear in this area, it is doubtful whether Member States could actually be obliged to use such implementation measures.

Implementation and ARIs – Generally speaking, article 288 para. 3 TFEU [ex 249 EC Treaty] thus does not impose insurmountable obstacles to the use of ARIs to implement a directive, provided that all requirements are respected. However, we can infer from the study of these requirements that self-regulation will, in all probability, not be considered a satisfactory method of implementation. The use of co-regulation, on the other hand, which entails a level of government involvement, will pose much less problems. We can conclude this section by referring to the fact that Member States are, and remain, responsible for the correct implementation of directives, even when they have delegated the implementation to co-regulatory bodies. They thus

implementation would form a violation of that principle and thus of art. 288 para. 3 TFEU [ex 249 EC Treaty]".

cannot escape liability by blaming these bodies for an incorrect implementation. Based on the theory of direct effect, however, under certain circumstances and in case of inadequate and late implementation, unconditional and sufficiently precise provisions of a directive may be relied upon against bodies which perform certain public service tasks under the control of the state.

2.3. Conclusion: ARIs and their compatibility with the European legal framework

No *a priori* exclusion, but various requirements – From the above analysis, we can, in general, conclude that there are no legal obstacles which *a priori* exclude the use of ARIs to protect minors against harmful content. However, there are various requirements which need to be taken into account in order for the ARIs in question to be in compliance with the European (EU and CoE) legal framework. The requirements of particular relevance to the use of ARIs can be summarised as follows:

> *Human rights: freedom of expression (article 10 ECHR)*
> If the alternative regulatory measures taken in the field of protecting minors against harmful content can be attributed to a body of a similar status to a public authority (this will depend on the level of government involvement; and will hence be more likely with respect to co-regulatory bodies), these measures cannot infringe the right of freedom to expression (which can be invoked by children as well as adults), unless they are prescribed by law (or an instrument with a law-like status), have a legitimate interest (which could be the protection of minors against harmful content), and are necessary in a democratic society (with an emphasis on proportionality).
>
> *Human rights: privacy (article 8 ECHR)*
> Likewise, these alternative regulatory measures attributable to a body of a similar status to a public authority, cannot infringe the right to privacy (which can be invoked by children as well as adults), unless they are in accordance with law (or an instrument with a law-like status), have a legitimate interest (which could be the protection of minors against harmful content), and are necessary in a democratic society (with an emphasis on proportionality).
>
> *Human rights: right to a fair trial (article 6 ECHR)*
> When a dispute arises concerning an individual's (civil) rights within the context of an ARI, this individual is entitled to a fair and public hearing by an independent and impartial tribunal established by law. If this hearing is held in front of an alternative regulatory body which can be qualified as a 'tribunal', all procedural safeguards provided in article 6 ECHR need to be in place. However, not complying with all of these requirements (for instance, the alternative regulatory body does not hold public hearings) may not be considered a breach

of the Convention if a full judicial review is available. Furthermore, in instances where the alternative regulatory body which cannot be considered a 'tribunal' judicial review always needs to be available when a dispute arises with respect to an individual's civil rights.

Human rights: right to an effective remedy (article 13 ECHR)
Alternative regulatory instruments must provide an effective remedy before a national authority in case of infringement of any fundamental right included in the European Convention on Human Rights (for instance, the right to freedom of expression, or privacy). Although the remedy does not need to be judicial in the strict sense, the authority in charge needs to be independent and impartial, and will need to provide minimal procedural guarantees. The remedy should be effective, and should either lead to the prevention of the suspected violation, or to the obtainment of appropriate redress, which could include the awarding of compensation or damages.

Internal market: free movement of goods and services (articles 34 to 36 TFEU [ex 28 to 30 EC Treaty] and articles 56, 57 and 52 TFEU [ex 49, 50 and 46 EC Treaty])
Measures taken in the framework of an alternative regulatory mechanism that can be attributed to a body with a status equivalent to that of a Member State (which could be the case with respect to alternative regulatory bodies, given that the notion 'Member State' is broadly interpreted, but will be more likely with respect to co-regulatory bodies), cannot interfere with the free movement of services or goods, unless these measures can be justified on the basis of a goal of public interest, such as the protection of minors against harmful content (cf. *Dynamic Medien* case), and, furthermore, if these measures are proportional.

We can also note here that, with respect to the free movement of services, the European Court of Justice has acknowledged that actions of private actors (which do not have the Member State-like status, such as, for instance, self-regulatory bodies) can potentially fall within the scope of the free movement of services provisions.

Competition (articles 101, 102, and 106 TFEU [ex 81, 82 and 86 EC Treaty])
If alternative regulatory measures taken to protect minors against harmful content can be attributed to undertakings or associations of undertakings, these measures are not permitted to constitute agreements with an adverse effect on competition (unless they are exempted under article 101 para. 3 TFEU [ex 81 EC Treaty], can be justified on the basis of a public interest criterion, or find their origin in a state measure), nor can they constitute abusive behaviour of a dominant position.

We observed that, occasionally, the relationship between Member States and undertakings can be ambiguous. Especially with respect to co-regulatory systems, it might not always be clear whether measures are attributable to a Member State or to an 'undertaking'. This matter will be dealt with by the Courts on a case-by-case basis.

In any case, Member States should not issue measures which render the application of the competition rules ineffective (articles 101 and 102 TFEU [ex 81 and 82 EC Treaty], in combination with articles 3 para. 1 (b) TFEU [ex 3 para. 1 (g) EC Treaty] and 4 para. 3 TFEU [ex 10 EC Treaty]). This principle also applies when Member States have delegated regulatory powers to private bodies. If the measures in question do infringe on the competition rules, Member States can be held liable, unless public interest considerations are put forward.

Implementation of directives (article 288 para. 3 TFEU [ex 249 EC Treaty])
If measures to protect minors against harmful content need to be taken in the context of a directive, the implementation methods, in principle freely chosen by the Member States, should be clear and precise (but a general legal context could suffice), should be of a binding nature (but certain agreements could sometimes be considered adequate), and should be effectively enforced and, hence, be accompanied by measures of effective judicial protection. Co-regulatory systems are probably more likely to fulfil these conditions than purely self-regulatory instruments. If a directive contains specific provisions (cf. AVMSD), these need to be taken into account. In this context, we have assumed that specific methods, such as self- and co-regulation can be encouraged or recommended, but doubt that they can actually be deemed obligatory.

It should be clear, finally, that Member States remain responsible for the correct implementation of a directive, even if they have delegated the implementation to alternative regulatory bodies.

COMPETING INTERESTS – As we have frequently stated throughout this chapter, the actual compliance of specific alternative regulatory systems with the legal framework will need to be considered on a case-by-case basis. In each case, the competing interests will need to be carefully balanced. ARIs which aim to protect minors against harmful content could possibly restrict other fundamental rights, freedoms and principles, especially the freedom of expression, the right to privacy, internal market legislation and competition rules. Yet, we have also seen that the protection of minors against harmful content is a goal of public interest which can, in many cases, be considered a possible justification to restrict the above mentioned fundamental rights and freedoms. However, measures which interfere with these rights and freedoms should not go beyond what is necessary to achieve this aim. Hence, in balancing the different interests at stake, proportionality will be a very important guiding principle.

OTHER LEGAL PROVISIONS – To conclude, we would like to draw attention to the fact that, of course, the legal provisions that were discussed in this chapter are not the only provisions with which alternative regulatory instruments need to comply. It is obvious that national legal frameworks, for instance, could impose certain restrictions on the use of self- and co-regulation. Furthermore, there might also be, at the international and EU levels, additional provisions which need to be taken into account. However, we chose the above mentioned provisions because of their direct relevance to the use of ARIs for the public interest goal of protecting minors against harmful content.

Concluding Remarks and Recommendations for the Future

1. Retrospective of the research undertaken

Retrospective – Before presenting our final conclusions, making a number of suggestions for the future and indicating a few issues which, in our opinion, require further research, we would first like to briefly look back on our research findings.

Part 1 – In the first part of this study, an in-depth analysis was performed of, on the one hand, the protection of minors against harmful digital content (Chapter 1), and, on the other hand, the concept of alternative regulatory instruments (ARIs) (Chapter 2), such as self- and co-regulation. A number of findings can be recalled:

1. Different trends, such as the emergence of new technologies (e.g., the Internet) and digitisation, have had a significant impact on the availability, accessibility and volume of content. Furthermore, convergence has led to the phenomenon of 'networked media', which implies that all kinds of media are produced, distributed, shared, managed and consumed through various networks in a converged manner. This has influenced media consumption patterns; content can now be accessed on an 'anywhere-anytime-anything' basis. Moreover, consumers and users can exercise much more control over their media consumption behaviour and, in addition, have a wide range of opportunities in terms of content production ('user generated content'). Aside from the many benefits that these evolutions have brought, however, concerns regarding children's exposure to harmful content – which have been around with respect to all media – are still justified, possibly even more than before.
2. There is no agreement in social science literature on the exact effects of media, and certainly not yet on the effects of new media. However, there seems to be a consensus that the confrontation with particular types of content may have a negative impact on a child's development. Based on

the 'precautionary principle', which implies that it is justified to err on the side of caution when there are certain – but not necessarily absolute – scientific indications of potential danger or harm in a certain area, this hesitant consensus on potential harmful media effects might be considered a sufficient trigger for regulation in this area.

3. 'Harmful content' is a concept that is difficult to grasp. There is no uniform interpretation of this concept, nor do legal definitions exist. Since 'harmful content' is a fluid concept which not only evolves continuously but is also culture dependent, the adoption of strict legal definitions would not even be desirable. Courts, however, have confirmed that the 'protection against harmful content' is a legitimate interest on the basis of which national measures can be taken. Notwithstanding the fact that in the area of harmful content, often references are made to illegal content, it is, however, absolutely necessary to differentiate between these two types of content, which require totally separate approaches. Contrary to illegal content, harmful content is content which is legal for adults to access, but which may harm vulnerable persons, such as children. Furthermore, we established that there is a whole array of potentially harmful content: sexual content, violence, information promoting anorexia, drugs and suicide, advertising and gambling, etc. Given that the concept of harmful content covers such a wide array of content, it is not surprising that regulation in this field is challenging. Especially interesting in this respect is the area of tension between harmful content and freedom of expression. On the one hand, protecting children from exposure to harmful content is a legitimate goal of public interest, but on the other hand, the freedom of expression of adults cannot be restricted in a disproportionate manner. Taking measures to protect minors against harmful content is thus a delicate exercise which should aspire to minimise spill-over restrictions to adults.
4. The fundamental legitimacy of the traditional policy goal of protecting minors against harmful content has not been called into question by the developments in the media sector. However, the 'new media' (such as the Internet) possess certain characteristics which significantly affect the use of traditional regulation or legislation to achieve this policy goal. First, the new media are decentralised and borderless. This stands in stark contrast to the use of traditional legislation which is usually confined to national territories. Hence, effective enforcement of legislation in this global and decentred environment is anything but obvious. Furthermore, the fast evolution of technology and the high degree of expertise that is required to regulate complex sectors clashes with the strict legislative processes and the limited level of knowledge of governments on specialised topics. Cooperation with private actors is thus needed. Moreover, whereas

before a limited number of media actors was controlled relatively easily by means of centralised regulation, the multiplicity of players which are active in the media environment today requires another – less unidirectional – approach. Linked to this issue is the fact that media are increasingly individual and present more opportunities for consumers to choose and control what content they want to access. This has been argued to undermine one of the traditional rationales of content regulation, which implied that the impact of mass media which are consumed at the same time by a large number of viewers (for instance, on television) is so significant that regulation is necessary. Finally, the variety of devices which can nowadays be used to access content require a technology-neutral or medium-independent regulatory approach. From all of these findings, it can be concluded that the use of traditional regulation or legislation is challenged in the digital media environment. In addition, there are issues regarding the balance that needs to be achieved between the protection of minors against harmful content and the right to freedom of expression. A brief look at certain initiatives to protect minors from harmful digital content in the United States showed that a legislative approach is problematic, given that it is very hard to delineate the scope of legislation in this field in a sufficiently careful manner. These findings, both the fact that various characteristics of the new information and communication networks clash with a number of features typical of legislation, and the fact that balanced legislation to protect minors against harmful content, especially in the new media environment, is very hard to achieve, have led to the conclusion that a broader regulatory framework in this area and this environment is needed.

5. At the EU level, from the mid-1990s onwards, policy makers realised that legislation might not be the most suitable means to achieve the policy goal of protecting minors in the digital media environment. This insight led to the exploration of the use of alternative regulatory instruments (ARIs). In a number of documents issued in 1996, practical instruments (such as parental control software, filtering technology and rating systems) and the use of self-regulation (for instance, by means of codes of conduct), were pushed forward as the instruments that would provide the solution. This trend peaked in 1998 with the adoption of the Recommendation on the protection of minors and human dignity. From 2001 onwards, increasing emphasis was put on the use of co-regulation; in 2003, this instrument was judged to be more flexible, adaptable and effective than legislation, in particular with respect to the sensitive issue of protecting minors. In later documents the emphasis shifted again, this time more towards awareness, information, media literacy and education. The same tendencies were noticeable in CoE documents. All documents also emphasised the impor-

tance of respecting fundamental rights and public interest considerations, the principles of the internal market and competition rules when using ARIs. However, what was not present in the studied policy documents, were clear and unambiguous descriptions or definitions of the proposed instruments.

6. We observed that the increasing references to the use of ARIs fitted in with the broader regulatory trend from centred to decentred forms of regulation. Over the past decades, the former type of regulation, also dubbed 'command-and-control regulation', which entails that the state performs all regulatory tasks (creation, implementation and monitoring, and enforcement), increasingly displayed a number of shortcomings, especially in complex sectors such as the media sector. Hence, decentred forms of regulation, which are much more open to the involvement of different actors in the regulatory process, grew in importance. It is this development which can also be credited with the growing enthusiasm for the use of self- and co-regulatory instruments in the media sector. This enthusiasm was also reflected in numerous international, EU and CoE policy documents, not only specifically with respect to the media sector, but also at a more general level within the framework of the 'Better Regulation' discourse. Again, we noted that the majority of documents which were issued on this topic did not contain clear characterisations or delineations of the concepts self- and co-regulation. Moreover, often the two notions were used in a very inconsistent manner: self-regulation was used where apparently co-regulation was meant or vice versa.
7. Self-regulation is a concept with a history, also in the media sector. When digital media, and especially the Internet, started to gain popularity, self-regulation was often put forward as the panacea to regulate these new media. There is, however, no uniform concept of self-regulation. We have assumed that self-regulation entails the creation, implementation and enforcement of rules by a group of actors with no – or at least minimal – involvement of actors that do not belong to this group (such as the government). Self-regulation has a number of assets (certainly in comparison with traditional legislation), such as its flexibility, adaptability, higher degree of expertise and greater incentives for compliance because of, on the one hand, the actors' involvement in the creation process, and, on the other hand, peer pressure. There are, however, also a significant number of drawbacks. These drawbacks, such as a lack of effective enforcement, a low level of transparency and accountability, the fact that private interests are put before public interests linked to the unaccountability of private actors to the public, and, as a result, the inadequate protection of fundamental rights, are particularly problematic with regard to a delicate issue such as the protection of minors.

8. Co-regulation is an instrument which consists of elements of state regulation and elements of self-regulation. Again, many interpretations of co-regulation exist. In an attempt to remedy this, the HBI and EMR study developed a balanced framework which contains a definition ("*a combination of non-state regulation and state regulation in such a way that a non-state regulatory system links up with state regulation*") and a number of criteria to identify co-regulatory systems. Furthermore, this study emphasised that sufficient incentives for the industry to participate, on the one hand, and proportional deterrents to enforce regulation, on the other hand, are indispensable to achieve a successful result. As a 'middle road' between the state and self-regulation, co-regulation combines the advantages of both these instruments (on the one hand, flexibility, fast adaptation, expertise and engagement of the industry, and, on the other hand, legal certainty, democratic guarantees and more efficient enforcement) while remedying their drawbacks (*supra*). Hence, co-regulation is considered to be a more refined instrument, and one that is especially suitable with respect to a delicate issue such as the protection of minors against harmful content. However, in order for co-regulatory mechanisms to actually offer the best of both worlds and not the worst, careful structuring is absolutely essential.
9. Following the conceptual analysis of both self- and co-regulation, we acknowledged that the obvious differentiating factor between the two ARIs is the intensity of the level of government involvement in a given system. Objectively establishing the required level of government involvement for each instrument, however, is unfeasible, since so many different nuances can be incorporated into ARIs (which, incidentally, is one of the assets of the use of ARIs). Furthermore, strict classifications of ARIs might, in our opinion, simply be irrelevant. We endorse the view that the different regulatory instruments can be situated along a 'regulatory continuum', differentiated by the level of intensity of involvement of different actors and the role they play in the different phases of the regulatory process (i.e., creation, implementation and enforcement). Far more important than strict classifications, is, in our view, the compliance of these different ARIs with the legal framework within which they function (*infra*).
10. To conclude the first part of this study, regulatory tools which are often a part of alternative regulatory strategies, such as technical tools and supporting mechanisms, were briefly looked into. First, the use of technology, such as filtering, has been advocated since the very first EU and CoE policy documents concerning the protection of minors against harmful content as the ultimate solution to the problem. However, whereas these technological tools have significant potential with respect to user

empowerment – i.e., the transfer of control over which content can be accessed from national authorities to the users themselves, or *in casu* to parents and teachers – these tools also display significant drawbacks, in particular with respect to fundamental rights. It is vital that the use of such tools complies with the broader legal framework. Second, in recent years, another type of regulatory tool, i.e., the use of supporting mechanisms such as education, media literacy, and awareness, has gained importance, since, gradually, it has become clear that regulation to protect minors against harmful content can never be foolproof. Hence, teaching parents and children how to cope with exposure to potentially harmful content is now frequently incorporated into regulatory strategies.

PART 2 – In the second part of this study, the focus narrowed to the legal framework which enfolds the use of ARIs to protect children from digital harmful content. The first chapter of this part aimed to provide a better understanding of the issues which are linked to our research subject, by presenting and briefly analysing five sets of regulation that are significant to both the protection of children against harmful content and the use of ARIs.

1. *Children's rights*
   Since the creation of the United Nations Convention on the Rights of the Child it has been accepted across the globe that children are entitled to a number of fundamental rights, such as the right to freedom of expression and the right to privacy. At the same time, this also entails that children sometimes need to be protected, for instance, against harmful content. Overall, children's rights have increasingly been awarded a significant place on the international as well as the supranational (CoE and EU) policy agenda. Aside from the possible application of the ECHR to children, the Council of Europe has, over the past decade, issued various documents concerning human rights in general, and children's rights in particular, also specifically with respect to the protection of these rights in the information society. The EU has been active in this field as well, laying down a legal basis for the protection of children's rights in the Charter of Fundamental Rights (article 24) as well as the Lisbon Treaty, and developing a conscious EU strategy on the rights of the child. A similar theme runs through the various documents at all levels: on the one hand, children are active subjects of rights who can invoke a number of fundamental rights, but, on the other hand, this also entails that sometimes they need to be safeguarded from harmful influences.

2. *Freedom of expression, right to privacy and procedural rights*
Four human rights are of particular relevance to the research subject of this study. First, the right to freedom of expression is closely related to the protection of minors from harmful content. It is possible that this right, which – without a doubt – can count on the same degree of protection with respect to traditional and new media, is restricted by measures which are taken to protect minors against harmful content. Hence, a conflict may arise between two competing interests: on the one hand, the freedom of expression of adults who are allowed to legally access harmful material, and on the other hand, the protection of minors against such material. An added competing interest might be the freedom of expression of children. Second, children's right to privacy can be at stake in the digital media environment, for instance, when identification mechanisms are used to prevent access to harmful content. Any restriction on this fundamental right needs to fulfil certain requirements, which are interpreted strictly. The two final human rights that are relevant are procedural rights. The right to a fair trial implies that an individual has the right to a fair and public hearing before an independent and impartial tribunal established by law, when a dispute concerning this individual's (civil) rights occurs. The right to an effective remedy entails that anyone who claims that his or her rights or freedoms under the ECHR have been violated has the right to an effective remedy before a national authority.

3. *Content regulation*
Although a number of rationales to regulate content are not as evident anymore in the digital environment, there are still a number of public interest objectives which justify content regulation regimes; one of these objectives is the protection of minors against harmful content. At the EU level, the framework for audiovisual content regulation is laid down in the 2007 Audiovisual Media Services Directive (which is the successor of the Television without Frontiers Directive). This directive contains provisions for the protection of minors against harmful content, both with respect to linear and non-linear services. Furthermore, the directive also encourages the use of self- and co-regulation in fields harmonised by the Directive (thus, for instance with respect to the protection of minors). At the CoE level, the Convention on Transfrontier Television (ECCT), which is currently being revised, also addresses the protection of minors. In addition to the AVMSD and the ECCT, the EU e-Commerce Directive, which deals with 'information society services', is another instrument which influences the regulation of content. Not only does this directive contain certain references to the protection of minors, it also sets up a

liability regime for intermediaries, that might 'indirectly' influence the regulation of content, since this regime can arguably result in a chilling effect on the freedom of expression when perfectly legal content is taken down by intermediaries out of fear of being held liable. Furthermore, this regime is unclear as to the possibilities for hosting providers to assume a proactive role in the protection of minors against harmful content, given that by assuming such a role, they might lose their exemption from liability.

4. *Internal market and competition*
Internal market principles, in particular the free movement of goods and services, can also play a role in the media sector. This entails that both sector-specific provisions, such as those related to the free movement of audiovisual media services in the AVMSD and information society services in the e-Commerce Directive, and general provisions, such as those related to the free movement of goods (articles 34 to 36 TFEU [ex 28 to 30 EC Treaty]) and services (articles 56 *et seq.* TFEU [ex 49 EC Treaty]), need to be respected when (alternative regulatory) measures to protect children from harmful material are taken. Furthermore, as stressed repeatedly in Better Regulation documents (*supra*), the use of ARIs cannot unduly interfere with EU competition principles. The two most important provisions in this field are articles 101 TFEU [ex 81 EC Treaty] – which prohibits anti-competitive agreements between undertakings – and 82 TFEU [ex 102 EC Treaty] – which forbids abusive behaviour by dominant undertakings.

5. *Proportionality, subsidiarity and article 288 para. 3 TFEU [ex 249 EC Treaty]*
Proportionality and subsidiarity are two general legislative principles which were mentioned repeatedly in the Better Regulation documents. The latter principle entails that measures should be taken at the level where the objectives of those measures can best be reached. The former principle requires that measures taken to achieve a certain goal need to be appropriate to reach this goal and should not go beyond what is necessary. The principle of proportionality, furthermore, is also of the utmost importance with respect to the assessment of restrictions on fundamental rights, such as the right to freedom of expression, or fundamental freedoms, such as the free movement of goods or services. Finally, article 288 para. 3 TFEU [ex 249 EC Treaty] contains general legislative requirements regarding the implementation of directives. This article is relevant to our research subject, since, as was clarified above, sometimes directives may impose certain obligations in the area of the protection of minors against harmful content. Article 288 para. 3 TFEU [ex 249 EC Treaty] stipulates

that Member States can choose the form and methods of implementation of directives (and could, thus, potentially, opt to use ARIs). This freedom of choice, however, is not absolute and is subject to certain restrictions.

The second chapter of the second part proceeded with an in-depth analysis of the requirements that are imposed by a selection of legal provisions listed in the previous chapter, on the use of ARIs to protect minors against harmful digital content. Based on the conclusions of this analysis, a checklist of potential difficulties can be compiled.

1. Human rights
   a. Freedom of expression (article 10 ECHR)
      - Is article 10 ECHR applicable when an infringement is committed by a self-regulatory or co-regulatory body (as opposed to a 'public authority')?
         - Depending, in particular, on the level of government involvement, an alternative regulatory body might be *considered a 'public authority'* and, hence, article 10 ECHR could be applied.
         - If, however, the level of government involvement is not high enough, in certain circumstances, *individuals or private actors* can – if the national legal system accepts the direct effect of the Convention articles – *invoke* article 10 ECHR before the national courts to challenge other individuals. This is an application of the 'horizontal effect' theory.
         - Even when this is not the case, the European Court of Human Rights has judged that, again in certain circumstances, a *positive obligation* may rest on public authorities to guarantee that the freedom of expression of their citizens is not infringed upon by private actors. Hence, in that case, public authorities should take measures to stop the interferences with the right to freedom of expression by the self- or co-regulatory body.
      - Can ARIs, which impose restrictions on the right to freedom of expression in order to protect minors from harmful digital content, fulfil the conditions of article 10 para. 2 ECHR?
         - *Legitimate aim*: the fulfilment of this condition will in the majority of cases not pose significant problems, since the protection of minors is a legitimate aim which can fall under the 'protection of morals' or the 'protection of the rights of others'.

- *Prescription by law*: to fulfil this condition, ARIs need to have a 'law-like' basis, which requires accessibility, foreseeability and a rather high level of government involvement.
- *Necessary in a democratic society*: to meet this requirement, ARIs need to be proportional, the reasons for the justification of the restriction need to be relevant and sufficient, and there has to be a pressing social need. The competing interests (the protection of minors against harmful content, and the protection of the freedom of expression) need to be accommodated.

▪ What is the impact of the use of (pure) self-regulation and the use of technology, in particular filtering, on the right to freedom of expression?

- ARIs in which private actors are solely in control of access to content may pose a danger to the protection of the freedom of expression, since this might amount to private censorship. Private actors, such as companies, should not decide upon what content is illegal or harmful. Furthermore, pure self-regulation might not fall within the remit of article 10 ECHR (unless an indirect horizontal effect or positive obligation by the state would be accepted, *supra*), and, hence, the safeguards contained in this article would not be applicable. Co-regulatory schemes in which certain guarantees are provided by a state body might thus be more appropriate in the delicate area of protection of minors.
- Several issues of concern can be distinguished with respect to filtering: first, the danger of arbitrary censorship, second, the risk of over- and under-inclusiveness, and finally, the unacceptability of using filters at a level which is not the user level. In any case, when the use of technological tools, which restrict access to content, is imposed by public authorities or self- or co-regulatory bodies with the same status, this should be done in a proportional manner, and moreover, with respect to the second paragraph of article 10 ECHR.

b. Privacy (article 8 ECHR)

▪ Is article 8 ECHR applicable when the infringement is committed by a self-regulatory or co-regulatory body (as opposed to a 'public authority')?

The analysis regarding this potential application with respect to article 10 ECHR is also valid with respect to article 8 ECHR (*supra*). One additional note that could be made is that the European Court of Human Rights has often referred to the positive obligation states have to protect an individual's right to privacy.

- Can ARIs, which impose restrictions on the right to privacy in order to protect minors from harmful digital content, fulfil the conditions of article 8 para. 2 ECHR?

  The analysis regarding this possibility with respect to freedom of expression is also valid with respect to the right to privacy (*supra*).

- What is the impact of the use of technology on the (child's) right to privacy?

  Parental control and monitoring software, content filtering and blocking systems, and age verifications systems might interfere with a child's right to privacy. Depending on who chooses to make use of these technological tools, there may be different legal consequences.

  If, on the one hand, parents make the voluntary decision to use such tools to protect their children, article 8 ECHR will only be applicable if a certain horizontal effect is accepted by the Court. It might be noted here that if it would come to a court case between a parent and a child (which is rather unlikely, but could occur in theory), this child will need to be represented in actions before the Court, usually by their parents or guardians. This might be problematic in cases where, as could occur *in casu*, the interests of parents and children clash. However, the European Court of Human Rights has judged that, in certain circumstances, minors have the right to file a complaint in their own name without being represented.

  On the other hand, in cases where the use of technological tools, which could have an impact on a child's privacy, is imposed by authorities or self- or co-regulatory bodies with a similar status, compliance with article 8 para. 2 ECHR is required.

c. Right to a fair trial (article 6 ECHR)

- Is article 6 ECHR applicable with respect to the use of ARIs to protect minors against harmful content?

  The applicability of article 6 ECHR is triggered by a dispute concerning an individual's civil rights. It has been accepted that the right to freedom of expression and the right to privacy – the two rights which will most often be interfered with when ARIs are used to protect minors from harmful content – may be considered civil rights. Hence, when such an ARI gives rise to a dispute concerning an individual's right to freedom of expression or privacy (or of course any other civil right), article 6 ECHR will be applicable.

- Can an alternative regulatory body be considered a 'tribunal established by law'?

  This could be the case if the European Court of Human Rights deems that the body is question is characterised by its judicial function, i.e., that it determines matters within its competence on the basis of rules of law and after proceedings conducted in a prescribed manner. Furthermore the Court will assess the body's independent and impartial character and will check whether other procedural guarantees are provided. We have argued that it is highly unlikely that a self-regulatory body will be considered to meet these standards. It may even be rather doubtful with respect to co-regulatory bodies. However, this will need to be assessed on a case-by-case basis.

- Which procedural guarantees, included in article 6 ECHR, do which alternative regulatory bodies need to comply with?

  There are two scenarios.

  - If the alternative regulatory body is considered a 'tribunal' then all procedural guarantees provided by article 6 ECHR (e.g., fair and public hearing, independence, impartiality, public judgment, reasonable time frame, etc.) need to be adhered to. However, if – because of the 'non-classic' nature of the decision-making body – not all requirements are complied with, the doctrine of full review could be considered applicable. This entails that the Court will accept this situation provided that a full judicial review is available.
  - If the alternative regulatory body in question cannot be considered a tribunal or if there is simply no possibility provided within the ARI to deal with a dispute concerning an individual's civil rights, the individual in question should have access to a tribunal that does comply with all procedural guarantees that are contained in article 6 ECHR.

d. Right to an effective remedy before a national authority (article 13 ECHR)

- Can remedies provided by an alternative regulatory body be considered as remedies before a 'national authority'?

  This could be the case if the European Court of Human Rights is of the opinion that the 'authorities' in question are independent and impartial, and provide certain procedural guarantees. It can be noted that the Court does not require remedies to be judicial, nor national authorities to be judicial authorities in the strict sense. The authorities in question, however, need to be competent to receive a complaint, to investigate the merits of the complaint and to take binding decisions regarding the provision of redress.

- When can remedies provided by an alternative regulatory body be considered effective?

  In theory, the remedy should either lead to the prevention of the suspected violation or, if appropriate, to the obtainment of adequate redress, including compensation, and should be effective in practice as well as in law. This will be considered by the European Court of Human Rights on a case-by-case basis. However, case-law has already demonstrated that the standards of the Court are rather high. In *Peck v. the United Kingdom*, the Court considered remedies provided by certain (alternative regulatory) bodies not effective because of their lack of legal power to award damages.

- Should there be an effective remedy before a national authority when an infringement is committed by a private actor (for instance, in a self-regulatory scheme)?

  It has been suggested that, in theory, the final part of article 13 ECHR ("*notwithstanding that the violation has been committed by persons acting in an official capacity*") could imply that an effective legal remedy must also be supplied when a violation has been committed by a private individual, according to the theory of indirect horizontal effect of the Convention rights between citizens.

2. Internal market legislation

   a. Free movement of goods

      - Can measures issued by alternative regulatory bodies fall within the scope of articles 34 to 36 TFEU [ex 28 to 30 EC Treaty] (which target 'Member State actions')?

      The ECJ has adopted a broad interpretation of the notion 'Member State'. Measures taken by bodies which are supported by the public authorities, by bodies created or approved by government or by bodies to which national legislative bodies have delegated powers, could possibly fall within the scope of articles 34 to 36 TFEU [ex 28 to 30 EC Treaty]. Hence, a certain level of government involvement is required. It is thus not inconceivable that co-regulatory bodies could be attributed a Member State like status.

- Can articles 34 to 36 TFEU [ex 28 to 30 EC Treaty] apply to actions of individuals (or, for instance, pure self-regulatory bodies)?

In principle, this is not the case. Here, the distinction between internal market principles, which are addressed at Member States, and competition principles, which are addressed at undertakings, can be referred to.

- Can Member States be held responsible for actions of individuals?

Member States could be held responsible if measures taken by private actors, such as, for instance, self- or co-regulatory bodies which can not be qualified as having a Member State like status, seriously infringe the fundamental right to free movement of goods. ECJ case-law in this area, however, is not very clear.

- Can ARIs which infringe the free movement of goods still be considered justified?

Yes, on the basis of article 36 TFEU [ex 30 EC Treaty] derogations can be allowed with respect to a number of justification grounds, such as public morality or the protection of health of humans. The protection of minors from harmful content is a legitimate interest which falls within the scope of article 36 TFEU [ex 30 EC Treaty]. However, measures that have been taken with this objective in mind still need to be proportional: the measures need to be suitable to reach the objective and they may not go beyond what is necessary to achieve this objective. The ECJ will consider this on a case-by-case basis and can impose specific conditions (for instance, that a labelling procedure should be readily accessible, can be completed within a reasonable time frame, and should be appealable; cf. *Dynamic Medien v. Avides Media*).

Furthermore, with respect to the protection of minors from harmful content, the ECJ has stated that, since there is no common conception of this legitimate interest throughout all Member States, the mere fact that a system of protection in one Member State differs from the system chosen in another Member State, cannot affect the assessment of the proportionality of the measures in question.

b. Free movement of services

- Can measures issued by alternative regulatory bodies fall within the scope of article 56 *et seq.* TFEU [ex 49 EC Treaty] (which are usually addressed to Member States)?

The analysis regarding the applicability of the free movement of goods provisions is also valid with respect to the free movement of services (*supra*).

- Can the free movement of services provisions apply to actions of individuals (or, for instance, pure self-regulatory bodies)?

Yes, the ECJ has accepted that the free movement of services provisions have a certain horizontal effect. Although the Member States are the primary addressees of article 56 TFEU [ex 49 EC Treaty] (even though they are not explicitly mentioned), actions of private individuals can, under certain circumstances, also fall within the scope of the provision.

- Can Member States be held responsible for actions of individuals?

It is accepted that Member States can be held responsible for actions taken by private parties with respect to the free movement of services as well. It has been pointed out, though, that the actions in question need to be sufficiently serious for Member States to be obliged to intervene in the first place.

- Can ARIs which infringe the free movement of services still be considered justified?

Yes, on the basis of articles 62 and 52 TFEU [ex 55 and 46 EC Treaty], derogations can be allowed on the basis of a number of justification grounds, such as public policy, public security or public health. Again, any restriction on the free movement of services needs to be strictly interpreted and must be proportional.

- Are there other provisions which need to be taken into account with respect to the free movement of services?

Yes, the AVMSD and e-Commerce Directive contain provisions regarding the free movement of audiovisual media services and information society services respectively. Both directives establish a country of origin-principle which implies that Member States are not allowed to restrict the free movement of services originating from other Member States (article 3 para. 2 e-Commerce Directive and article 2a AMVSD) if these services adhere to the legislation of those latter Member States (article 3 para. 1 e-Commerce Directive and article 2 AVMSD). Both directives, however, allow for derogation from this general principle. One of the grounds on the basis of which such an exception can be justified is the protection of minors (article 3 para. 4 (a)(i) e-Commerce Directive and article 2a para. 2 (a) and para. 4 AVMSD).

3. Competition rules

   a. General

      - Can alternative regulatory bodies be classified as 'undertakings' (or associations of undertakings)?

      In case-law, an undertaking has been defined as "*any entity engaged in an economic activity, regardless of its legal status and the way in which it is financed*". It is possible to assume that self- as well as co-regulatory bodies could be classified as 'undertakings' or possibly even as 'an association of undertakings'. Although the alternative regulatory bodies need in that case to perform 'economic activities' – which might not be self-evident if the sole purpose of the body is to protect minors – it can be noted that the notion 'economic' has also been interpreted in a broad manner. The most crucial element in deciding whether self- or co-regulatory bodies might be qualified as 'undertakings', will be the actual level of government involvement as well as the nature of the tasks performed (private interest or public interest). With respect to co-regulatory instruments – more than with respect to self-regulatory instruments – it might be difficult to determine whether the measures taken can be attributed to the Member State or to an undertaking. Bodies entrusted by the state with particular tasks and quasi-governmental bodies (which perform economic activities), for instance, have been qualified as undertakings. In any case, the concrete structure of the ARIs will be decisive.

      Alternative regulatory bodies might also be considered 'associations of undertakings', since this notion is also broadly interpreted. Again, this will be assessed on a case-by-case basis. When an association is granted regulatory powers by the state, who has defined the public interest criteria and the essential principles with which its rules must comply and who retains the power to adopt decisions in the last resort, for instance, its measures will not be attributed to the association but to the public authority.

   b. Article 101 TFEU [ex 81 EC Treaty]

      - When do measures taken by alternative regulatory bodies fall within the scope of article 101 para. 1 TFEU [ex 81 EC Treaty]?

        – When they are issued by bodies which can be classified as 'undertakings' or 'associations of undertakings': cf. previous question;
        – When they can be qualified as 'agreements', 'decisions of associations of undertakings' or 'concerted practices'. These notions have all been broadly interpreted. It is not necessary that such measures are legally binding. Even the fact that a decision of an association

of undertakings has been approved by a public authority does not lead to the inapplicability of article 101 TFEU [ex 81 EC Treaty];
- When they have an adverse effect on competition within the EU, or, in other words, when they have as their object or effect the prevention, restriction or distortion of competition; and
- When the effects on competition are appreciable and influence trade between Member States.

- When is article 101 para. 1 TFEU [ex 81 EC Treaty] not applicable to ARIs?

  - First, article 101 para. 3 TFEU [ex 81 EC Treaty] can provide an exemption if the measures which affect competition in an adverse way nevertheless also have important economic advantages. In order to profit from this exemption, four criteria need to be cumulatively fulfilled. The measures (1) should contribute to the improvement of the production or distribution of goods or to the promotion of technical or economic progress, (2) should allow consumers a fair share of the resulting benefit, (3) should not impose on the undertakings concerned restrictions which are not indispensable to the attainment of these objectives (proportionality), and (4) should not afford such undertakings the possibility of eliminating competition in respect of a substantial part of the products in question.
  - Second, it is possible that the ECJ, in its assessment of the applicability of article 101 para. 1 TFEU [ex 81 EC Treaty], is of the opinion that the presence of a public interest criterion leads to the inapplicability of article 101 para. 1 TFEU [ex 81 EC Treaty]. This, however, will be more likely if there is a certain mix of public and private elements (cf. the *Wouters* case).
  - Third, article 101 para. 1 TFEU [ex 81 EC Treaty] will not be applicable if the conduct of an alternative regulatory body is the result of a government measure, which actually restricts competition and, hence, eliminates any possibility of competition. If the measure in question, however, still leaves room for the body to exercise commercial autonomy, the competition rules will be applicable.

- What if Member States delegate decision-making power to private actors?

Article 101 TFEU [ex 81 EC Treaty], in conjunction with articles 4 para. 3 TFEU [ex 10 EC Treaty] and article 3 para. 1 (b) TFEU [ex 3 para. 1 (g) EC Treaty], entail that Member States cannot introduce or maintain in force measures which may make the application of the competition rules ineffective ('useful effect doctrine'). This also includes situations where a Member State delegates decision-making responsibility to private economic actors. In such circumstances the Member States could be held liable for anti-competitive measures, unless these measures are justified by public interest considerations and are proportional. Again, much will depend on the concrete circumstances, and in particular on the level of government involvement.

c. Article 102 TFEU [ex 82 EC Treaty]

- Could ARIs fall within the scope of article 102 TFEU [ex 82 EC Treaty]?

Yes, if four conditions are fulfilled: (1) one, or more, alternative regulatory bodies which can be qualified as undertakings (*supra*), and which have a dominant position, (2) in the common market, or a substantial part of this market, (3) abuse their position, which leads to (4) an actual or potential effect on trade between the Member States.

d. Article 106 TFEU [ex 86 EC Treaty]

- Could ARIs fall within the scope of article 106 TFEU [ex 86 EC Treaty]?

This will not be likely, since in our opinion, at least with respect to ARIs which aim to protect minors against harmful content, the alternative regulatory bodies will probably not be classified as 'public undertakings' or 'undertakings to which Member States have attributed special or exclusive rights', nor as 'undertakings entrusted with the operation of services of general economic interest', or 'having the character of a revenue-producing monopoly'.

4. Article 288 para. 3 TFEU [ex 249 EC Treaty]

- Can ARIs be used to implement directives?

Article 288 para. 3 TFEU [ex 249 EC Treaty] provides Member States with the freedom to choose the form and methods of implementation of a directive. However, this freedom is not absolute. A number of requirements need to be fulfilled.

- The implementing measures must be clear and precise (with a view to legal certainty). However, to achieve this, the ECJ has stated that it is not always necessary to adopt specific legislation; a general legal context might be sufficient.
- The implementing measures must have a (legally) binding nature. However, in specific circumstances, for instance, if a directive explicitly allows the use of agreements as an implementation tool or if

there is a combination of a legal provision with other measures, this requirement has been interpreted in a broad manner. Nevertheless, a certain level of government involvement seems to be required. This means that pure self-regulation will probably not be considered sufficient to implement a directive.
- The implementing measures must be practically applied and effectively enforced. Effective judicial protection is of paramount importance; hence, individuals who have been attributed rights by a directive need to be offered access to an effective 'judicial' remedy (cf. also *supra*, article 13 ECHR).

It was noted that it seems that a certain level of government involvement is required to adequately implement a directive. Hence, whereas pure self-regulatory instruments will probably not be accepted as an implementation tool (at least not if self-regulation is the only implementation method), co-regulatory mechanisms would pose significantly less problems.

- Can Member States escape their responsibility for non-implementation or incorrect implementation if they have delegated this implementation to other bodies (such as, for instance, alternative regulatory bodies)?

No, as a result of the obligations imposed by article 288 para. 3 TFEU [ex 249 EC Treaty] as well as article 4 para. 3 TEU [ex 10 EC Treaty], Member States will be held liable if a directive is not properly implemented, even when they have delegated the implementation to other bodies. In this context it might be noted that – based on the theory of direct effect – in case of inadequate and late implementation, unconditional and sufficiently precise provisions of a directive may be relied upon against organisations which are subject to the authority or control of the state or against bodies – whatever their legal form – which have been made responsible by means of a state measure, for providing a public service under the control of the state and have for that purpose special powers beyond those which result from the normal rules applicable in relations between individuals.

- Can the use of self- or co-regulation be made mandatory by a directive?

The freedom of Member States to choose the form and methods of implementation is limited by specific provisions of a directive. Hence, if a directive contains specific suggestions as to certain implementation methods, this should be taken into account. However, whether or not a directive can oblige Member State to use a certain implementation tool is a controversial issue on which neither academic literature nor case law provides a satisfactory answer. In our opinion, implementation methods can specifically be allowed by a directive; hence, if an explicit reference were made to self- or co-regulatory measures, their use will not be contested by the ECJ. It remains doubtful, however, whether their use could actually be imposed.

2. Conclusions

From the above listed research results, we can draw a number of conclusions.

ARIs and the legal framework – First of all, with respect to the research question at the heart of this study, we can conclude from the analysis of the relevant legal provisions that there are no legal obstacles which lead to an *a priori* or absolute exclusion of the use of ARIs to protect minors against harmful digital content. However, this general conclusion should be nuanced in two ways. On the one hand, as we specified above, there are a number of requirements which need to be taken into account in order for ARIs to comply with the legal framework. In the majority of cases, these requirements are linked to the protection of fundamental rights, freedoms or specific legislation. On the other hand, the applicability of certain provisions, typically those which are in theory addressed at states or governments, depends on the level of government involvement in ARIs.[1] This means that a number of provisions, such as, for instance, those relating to the protection of fundamental rights, will be more likely to apply when there is a degree of government involvement, as is common with respect to co-regulatory systems. Conversely, self-regulatory systems may fall outside of the protection of the legal framework (except, for instance, when theories, such as the 'horizontal effect' theory can be applied). In our opinion, this might be dangerous in a delicate area such as the one that is at the centre of this study.[2] Hence, to protect minors from exposure to harmful digital content, the use of co-regulatory systems, where there is an actual symbiosis between the involvement

[1] With respect to the level of government involvement that is required in order for certain legal provisions to be applicable, it might be noted that, up until now, both the European Court of Human Rights and the European Court of Justice have been very rarely faced with cases in which measures similar to ARIs (to protect minors from harmful content) were at issue. It can be assumed that as more ARIs are used, the chance that the Courts will have the opportunity to bring greater clarity to this matter will increase.

[2] We can frame this finding also within the current general 'malaise' with respect to self-regulation or regulation by the market or the sector (cf. for instance, the financial crisis). As a consequence, in different sectors, the calls for a renewed and more intense involvement of the government have recently grown louder.

of the government and other actors, and greater guarantees are provided as to the actual realisation of the policy objective, is preferable.

Categorisation of ARIs – Second, considering the above finding that the level of government involvement in regulatory systems often plays an important role with respect to the applicability of certain legal provisions, and, thus, the protection that is provided, it would be possible to conclude that strictly differentiated concepts of self- and co-regulation are needed. This would then stand in contrast to the suggestion put forward in the chapter that dealt with the conceptual analysis of ARIs (Part 1, Chapter 2), i.e., that strict categorisations of self- and co-regulation are irrelevant. However, we stand by that suggestion, since the level of government involvement in ARIs is, in our opinion, such a fluid given, that it would be impossible to rigidly delineate self- and co-regulation in such a way that the assessment of the applicability of certain legal provisions would suddenly be straightforward, and not depend anymore on the concrete circumstances. Although the conceptual framework put forward by the HBI/EMR study with respect to co-regulation might be helpful to differentiate between self- and co-regulatory systems, we do not believe that it can provide an answer to questions regarding the applicability of legal provisions.

Hence, in the context of this study, we propose to adopt a general concept of 'alternative regulatory instruments' (ARIs), which can be situated along the regulatory continuum. Thus, ARIs can lean towards 'self-regulation', where there is no government involvement (which will be very rare) or a very limited level of government involvement (such as, for instance, the encouragement of self-regulation, symbolic support or low-key cooperation with government agencies). Or, ARIs can incline towards 'co-regulation', where there is a higher degree of government involvement, which can vary widely – from soft varieties of co-regulation to more elaborate types of co-regulation. In any case, with respect to co-regulation, emphasis should be put on the actual involvement of the various actors in the different phases of the regulatory process (creation, implementation and monitoring, enforcement), and the cooperation between those different actors. In our view, this last element is another reason why co-regulation is more suitable to address the protection of minors against harmful content, since this is an issue where cooperation is a key element, given the shared responsibility of government, parents, teachers and industry (*infra*).

Structuring of ARIs – Third, we can conclude from the study of the relevant legal provisions that ARIs should be carefully structured. Legal restrictions and requirements, as were identified in the above analysis, should be taken into account. Attention should not only be paid to the respect for freedom of expression, but also to issues which may be more easily overlooked such as the respect for procedural guarantees and the provision of effective remedies (cf. article 6 and 13 ECHR and article 288 para. 3 TFEU [ex 249 EC Treaty], *supra*). However, we would like to note that although the broader legal framework needs to be taken into account when ARIs are set up, this should not lead to the adoption of inflexible or rigid instruments. It would certainly make no sense to force the use of ARIs in a similar straightjacket as the use of legislation.

Balancing competing interests and proportionality – Although we provided a checklist of legal requirements and potential difficulties, our analysis has shown that it is not possible to draw up a magic formula with which the use of ARIs should comply, since different legal provisions require assessment on a case-by-case basis. These assessments will often relate to the balancing of competing interests. In this context, we have observed that the protection of minors can often be raised as a ground of justification, for instance, with respect to restrictions on fundamental rights or freedoms. However, even if the protection of minors can be invoked to justify such restrictions, the measures in question will always need to be proportional. We have observed throughout our research that proportionality is indeed a key standard with respect to the use of ARIs to protect minors against harmful content (cf. checklist). Hence, it would be advisable to consider this general legislative principle carefully when ARIs are established: the measures in question should be suitable to attain the objective that is envisaged and should not go beyond what is necessary to achieve this objective. Such an *ex ante* evaluation could be of use in any sector where the use of ARIs is contemplated.

3. Recommendations and indications for future research

A. *Recommendations*

Impact assessment – In our opinion, choosing regulatory instruments to protect minors from harmful digital content should be the subject of a conscious and carefully considered decision-making process. Here, we can refer to a phenomenon which has gained importance over the past decade and which has also been mentioned within the Better Regulation discourse (*supra*),[3] i.e., 'regulatory impact assessments' (RIAs). The purpose of such

[3] Organisation for Economic Co-operation and Development, OECD Guiding principles for regulatory quality and performance, 2005, retrieved from http://www.oecd.org/

RIAs is to identify the regulatory objective (for instance, the protection of minors against harmful content), and the options to achieve these objectives (for instance, self- or co-regulation), and to assess the possible assets and drawbacks – or costs and benefits – of these options. We advocate carrying out a thorough RIA before adopting an ARI in the field of protecting minors against harmful digital content.

In 2008, the Rand study '*Options for effectiveness of Internet self- and co-regulation*' (cf. *supra*, Part 1, Chapter 2) carried out research into RIAs with respect to ARIs.[4] In our opinion, however, one caveat of the RIA framework that was developed by the study, is the compliance of (potential) ARIs with the broader legal framework. This should not be overlooked; the checklist provided *supra* could possibly be considered an impetus to take this issue more seriously. Especially regarding the protection of freedom of expression and the right to privacy we would like to urge policy makers to implement a 'human rights proofing' of every regulatory system that is adopted to protect minors against harmful content.

Regular evaluations – Furthermore, in order to achieve a high degree of efficiency on a long-term basis with respect to the protection of minors against harmful digital content by means of ARIs, it is of the utmost importance to regularly evaluate the functioning of these systems. One of the key elements of an efficient system, especially in a delicate area such as the one at issue, is credibility. To gain credibility, a system must function in an open, transparent and accountable manner. Regular evaluations should make sure that these standards are maintained and that the systems reach their objectives in an efficient way. Furthermore, ARIs must be sufficiently flexible so that they can be adapted quickly and easily according to the difficulties that might be uncovered by these evaluations.

---

dataoecd/19/51/37318586.pdf (on 28.12.2008), 4; Commission of the European Communities, European Governance – A White Paper, COM (2001) 428 final, 25.07.2001, 30; European Parliament, Council, and Commission, Interinstitutional agreement on better law-making, 2003/C 321/01, *OJ* 31.12.2003, *C* 321, recital 25, 27–30. See also: European Commission, Better Regulation – Impact assessment, retrieved from http://ec.europa.eu/governance/better_regulation/impact_en.htm (on 28.12.2008); Ofcom, Better policy making: Ofcom's approach to impact assessment, July 2005, retrieved from http://www.ofcom.org.uk/consult/policy_making/guidelines.pdf (on 28.12.2008).

4 Rand Europe (Jonathan Cave, Chris Marsden and Stephen Simmons), Options for effectiveness of Internet self- and co-regulation – Phase 3 (Final) Report, Study commissioned by the European Commission, 2008, retrieved from http://ec.europa.eu/dgs/information_society/evaluation/data/pdf/studies/s2006_05/final_report.pdf (on 30.05.2008). See also: Ofcom, Identifying appropriate regulatory solutions: principles for analysing self- and co-regulation: Statement, 10.12.2008, retrieved from http://www.ofcom.org.uk/consult/condocs/coregulation/statement/statement.pdf (on 30.12.2008).

Combination of tools – Aside from these 'procedural' recommendations, we can note that during our research we often felt a little anxious when thinking about the chance of ever finding a definite answer to the question: how can children best be protected against harmful digital content? At the end of our research it is clear that there is no definite answer, and that it is highly likely that there never will be a definite answer. What we did come to realise, however, is that the only way forward with respect to this issue is the combination of tools, such as, for instance, the enforcement of the broader legal framework (for example, with respect to children's rights), the use of ARIs, the carefully considered and proportional use of technological tools (*supra*), and – of particular importance – the incorporation of supporting mechanisms into regulatory strategies. We are convinced that without awareness, information, media literacy and education, the dream of a safer digital environment for children will always remain an illusionary one.

Shared responsibility – Connected to the previous paragraph is the fact that the achievement of the public policy goal of protecting minors against harmful content has always been subject to a shared responsibility by the different actors involved. From a legal perspective, this shared responsibility is based on the UNCRC, which explicitly refers to the responsibility of the government (article 3 para. 2 UNCRC: "*States Parties undertake to ensure the child such protection and care as is necessary for his or her well-being*") and parents (article 18 UNCRC: "*Parents or, as the case may be, legal guardians, have the primary responsibility for the upbringing and development of the child[; t]he best interests of the child will be their basic concern*"). Other involved actors are the industry and educators. If one of the actors does not take up his responsibility, any attempt to achieve the policy goal will irrevocably fail. It is a fact that regulation will never be foolproof. This has never been the case, and will never be the case. In the networked world we live in today, it is thus more important than ever that a multi-stakeholder approach is adopted in which all responsible actors, i.e., governments, industry, parents and educators, cooperate and take up their responsibilities.[5] We would

[5] Cf. also: Jakubowicz, Karl, "A new notion of media?", Background text, 1st Council of Europe Conference of Ministers responsible for media and new communications services: A new notion of media?, Reykjavik, 28–29.05.2009, retrieved from http://www.ministerialconference.is/media/images/a_new_notion_of_media_web_version.pdf (on 27.05.2009), 4; Millwood Hargrave, Andrea, Protecting children from harmful content, Report prepared for the Council of Europe's Group of Specialists on Human Rights in the Information Society, June 2009, retrieved from http://www.coe.int/t/dghl/standardsetting/media/Doc/H-Inf%282009%2913_en.pdf (on 21.01.2010).

like to emphasise in this context that any attempt to try to shift responsibility to one of the other actors is unhelpful and shows little courage.

B. *Indications for future research*

Future research – The research subject of this study is definitely one that is not set in stone. The issue still evolves and new challenges arise everyday. Hence, this study should certainly not be seen as a terminus, but rather as one stop on a long, and possibly never-ending journey. To conclude this study, we would thus like to pass on the baton and offer a few indications for further research.

Level of government involvement – First, we are convinced that more research into the structure of ARIs is needed, especially with respect to level of government involvement. As we have already stated, in our opinion, the involvement of government in ARIs which aim to protect minors against harmful content is advisable. However, the degree of involvement which could lead to a more efficient protection is difficult to determine in an objective way, since this, in the majority of cases, is dependent on a number of factors (such as, for instance, the culture or the sector). In this respect, we can note that if more ARIs will be used in the future, more data will be available on which level of government involvement leads to efficient systems. Not only our research subject would profit from further research into this topic, but other sectors in which ARIs can be used would benefit as well.

RIAs – Second, further research into tailored RIAs with respect to the use of ARIs would be of great value. Whereas research into RIAs and ARIs has already been carried out at an abstract level,[6] in our view, it is important to tailor general RIA principles to the specific needs and sensibilities of the normative goal and the potential ARIs in question. Attention for the legal framework in this context is essential.

Technology – Third, the use of technology to protect minors from digital harmful content is still to a certain extent shrouded in mystery. Further research into the assets and drawbacks of using technology in this field from a legal perspective (and not only from a technical or social science perspec-

[6] *Supra*, Rand Europe (Jonathan Cave, Chris Marsden and Stephen Simmons), Options for effectiveness of Internet self- and co-regulation – Phase 3 (Final) Report, Study commissioned by the European Commission, 2008, retrieved from http://ec.europa.eu/dgs/information_society/evaluation/data/pdf/studies/s2006_05/final_report.pdf (on 30.05.2008).

tive) should thus be encouraged. Especially the incorporation of the use of technological tools in alternative regulatory strategies, with specific attention to legal requirements such as respect for fundamental rights and proportionality, would benefit from additional research.

Other risks – Finally, and this brings us back to the first chapter of this study, concerns regarding the protection of minors in the networked and digital environment are certainly not limited to the issue of harmful content. Conduct- and contact-related risks, for instance, such as cyberbullying or issues linked to social networking websites, require urgent attention. The possibility of using ARIs to address these issues could in this context be the subject of future research.

Bibliography

1. Legislation & Policy documents

A. *International*

a. *United Nations*

i. *General documents*

Office of the United Nations High Commissioner for Human Rights, Fact Sheet No. 10 (Rev.1), The Rights of the Child, 1993, retrieved from http://www.ohchr.org/Documents/Publications/FactSheet10Rev.1en.pdf (on 14.09.2006)

——, International law: The International Bill of Human Rights, retrieved from http://www2.ohchr.org/english/law/ (on 15.05.2007)

——, Ratification, declarations and reservations, retrieved from http://www2.ohchr.org/english/bodies/ratification/11.htm#reservations (on 12.09.2006)

United Nations, Universal Declaration on Human Rights, 10.12.1948, retrieved from http://www.unhchr.ch/udhr/lang/eng.htm (on 15.05.2007)

——, International Covenant on Civil and Political Rights, 16.12.1966, retrieved from http://www.unhchr.ch/html/menu3/b/a_ccpr.htm (on 15.05.2007)

——, International Covenant on Economic, Social and Cultural Rights, 16.12.1966, retrieved from http://www.ohchr.org/english/law/cescr.htm (on 15.05.2007)

——, Convention of the Rights of the Child, 20.11.1989, retrieved from http://www.unhchr.ch/html/menu3/b/k2crc.htm (on 12.09.2006)

——, Report of the United Nations conference on environment and development (Rio de Janeiro, 3–14.06.1992), A/CONF.151/26 (Vol. I), 12.08.1992, retrieved from http://www.un.org/documents/ga/conf151/aconf15126–1annex1.htm (on 10.03.2008)

——, Optional Protocol to the Convention on the Rights of the Child on the sale of children, child prostitution and child pornography, A/RES/54/263, 25.05.2000, retrieved from http://www2.ohchr.org/english/law/crc-sale.htm (on 12.12.2008)

——, Durban Declaration and Programme for Action at the World Conference against Racism, Racial Discrimination, Xenophobia and Related Intolerance, 2001, retrieved from http://www.un.org/WCAR/durban.pdf (on 30.05.2008)

——, *A world fit for children*, Millennium Development Goals Special Session on children, Documents, 2002, retrieved from http://www.unicef.org/publications/files/A_World_Fit_for_Children_072808.pdf (on 13.09.2006)

United Nations General Assembly, United Nations Millennium Declaration, 55th session, 18.09.2000, retrieved from http://www.un.org/millennium/declaration/ares552e.htm (on 29.08.2006)

——, Resolution A world fit for children, A/RES/S-27/2, 11.10.2002, retrieved from http://www.unicef.org/specialsession/docs_new/documents/A-RES-S27–2E.pdf (on 27.09.2006)

United Nations Human Rights Committee, General comment No. 17: Rights of the Child (article 24), 35th session, 07.04.1989, retrieved from http://www.unhchr.ch/tbs/doc.nsf/(Symbol)/cc0f1f8c391478b7c12563ed004b35e3?Opendocument (on 15.05.2007)

ii. *United Nations Committee on the Rights of the Child*

United Nations Committee on the Rights of the Child, CRC/C/15/Add.17, 07.02.1994, retrieved from http://www.unhchr.ch/tbs/doc.nsf/(Symbol)/f1713d27ca8644ca4125615100388669?Opendocument (on 26.11.2008)

——, CRC/C/15/Add.44, 27.11.1995, retrieved from http://www.unhchr.ch/tbs/doc.nsf/(Symbol)/0d05ba579bd44515412562dd003c8695?Opendocument (on 26.11.2008)

——, Report on the thirteenth session, CRC/C/57, 31.10.1996, retrieved from http://www.unhchr.ch/tbs/doc.nsf/898586b1dc7b4043c1256a450044f331/5a7331a09a8b4f3fc1256404003d10bd/$FILE/G9618895.pdf (on 22.09.2006)

——, General Guidelines for Periodic Reports, CRC/C/58, 20.11.1996, retrieved from http://www.unhchr.ch/tbs/doc.nsf/(Symbol)/CRC.C.58.En?Opendocument (on 25.09.2006)

——, CRC/C/66, 06.06.1997, retrieved from http://www.unhchr.ch/tbs/doc.nsf/898586b1dc7b4043c1256a450044f331/b27bf9857a55819d802564f3003b10ee/$FILE/G9717203.pdf (on 26.11.2008)

——, Concluding observations of the Committee on the Rights of the Child: Luxembourg, CRC/C/15/Add.92, 24.06.1998, retrieved from http://www.unhchr.ch/tbs/doc.nsf/(Symbol)/62258a94c261c9318025662400376374?Opendocument (on 27.09.2006)

——, CRC/C/79, 27.07.1998, retrieved from http://www.unhchr.ch/tbs/doc.nsf/898586b1dc7b4043c1256a450044f331/a505a81ff8dcaf89802566d6003b6298/$FILE/G9817376.pdf (on 26.11.2008)

——, CRC/C/15/Add.105, 24.08.1999, retrieved from http://www.unhchr.ch/tbs/doc.nsf/(Symbol)/545ce3a12d1e386c80256797003d5ad8?Opendocument (on 26.11.2008)

——, Concluding observations of the Committee on the Rights of the Child: Cambodia, CRC/C/15/Add.128, 28.06.2000, retrieved from http://www.unhchr.ch/tbs/doc.nsf/(Symbol)/30dce34798ef39f480256900003397ac?Opendocument (on 27.09.2006)

——, Concluding observations of the Committee on the Rights of the Child: Marshall Islands, CRC/C/15/Add.139, 16.10.2000, retrieved from http://www.unhchr.ch/tbs/doc.nsf/(Symbol)/e91ea24ff52b434ac125697a00339c0c?Opendocument (on 27.09.2006)

——, CRC/C/15/Add.150, 21.02.2001, retrieved from http://www.unhchr.ch/tbs/doc.nsf/(Symbol)/82f20503b2732d3ac12569ee00302483?Opendocument (on 26.11.2008)

——, General measures of implementation of the Convention on the Rights of the Child (arts. 4, 42 and 44, para. 6), General comment No. 5, 27.11.2003, retrieved from http://www.unhchr.ch/tbs/doc.nsf/898586b1dc7b4043c1256a450044f331/3bba808e47bf25a8c1256db400308b9e/$FILE/G0345514.pdf (on 14.09.2006)

——, Report on the eleventh session, CRC/C/50, 22.03.2006, retrieved from http://www.unhchr.ch/tbs/doc.nsf/898586b1dc7b4043c1256a450044f331/36686733b8cbf2eac1256333004ed6e4/$FILE/G9611831.pdf (on 22.09.2006)

b. *OECD*

Organisation for Economic Co-operation and Development, Recommendation of the Council of the OECD on improving the quality of government regulation, OCDE/GD(95)95, 09.03.1995, retrieved from http://www.olis.oecd.org/olis/1995doc.nsf/LinkTo/NT000009E6/$FILE/PME5205.PDF (on 16.05.2008)

——, The OECD Report on regulatory reform, 1997, retrieved from http://www.oecd.org/dataoecd/17/25/2391768.pdf (on 09.04.2008)

——, Summary record of the BIAC/OECD Forum on Internet Content Self-regulation, 25.03.1998, retrieved from http://www.oecd.org/document/31/0,3343,fr_2649_34255_1893343_1_1_1_1,00.html (on 26.05.2008)
——, OECD Guiding principles for regulatory quality and performance, 2005, retrieved from http://www.oecd.org/dataoecd/19/51/37318586.pdf (on 28.12.2008)

c. *UNESCO*

Unesco, Media education – A kit for teachers, students, parents and professionals (ed. Divina Frau-Meigs), Paris, L'exprimeur, 2006, retrieved from http://unesdoc.unesco.org/images/0014/001492/149278E.pdf (on 09.01.2007)

d. *Other*

Ministerial Declaration of the Second International Conference on the North Sea, London, 24–25.11.1987, retrieved from http://www.seas-at-risk.org/1mages/1987%20London%20Declaration.pdf (on 11.03.2008)

B. *European Union*

Documents concerning EU law can be retrieved from http://eur-lex.europa.eu/en/index.htm

a. *Treaties*

Treaty on the European Union, Protocol on social policy, Agreement on social policy concluded between the Member States of the European Community with the exception of the United Kingdom of Great Britain and Northern Ireland, *OJ* 29.07.1992, *C* 191
Treaty of Lisbon amending the Treaty on European Union and the Treaty establishing the European Community, 13.12.2007, *OJ* 17.12.2007, *C* 306, 1
Consolidated version of the Treaty on European Union, *OJ* 09.05.2008, *C* 115, 13 [referred to as: TEU]
Consolidated version of the Treaty on the functioning of the European Union, *OJ* 09.05.2008, *C* 115, 47 [referred to as: TFEU]

b. *Charters & protocols*

Protocol (No. 30) on the application of the principles of subsidiarity and proportionality, 02.10.1997, *OJ* 10.11.1997, *C* 340, 105
Charter of Fundamental Rights of the European Union, *OJ* 18.12.2000, *C* 364, 1
Charter of Fundamental Rights of the European Union (as amended by the Treaty of Lisbon), *OJ* 14.12.2007, *C* 303, 1

c. *Directives*

Commission Directive 2006/111/EC of 16 November 2006 on the transparency of financial relations between Member States and public undertakings as well as on financial transparency within certain undertakings, *OJ* 17.11.2006, *L* 318, 17
Council Directive 64/221/EEC of 25 February 1964 on the co-ordination of special measures concerning the movement and residence of foreign nationals which are justified on grounds of public policy, public security or public health, *OJ* 04.04.1964, *L* 56, 850

COMMISSION Directive 70/50/EEC of 22 December 1969 based on the provisions of Article 33 (7), on the abolition of measures which have an effect equivalent to quantitative restrictions on imports and are not covered by other provisions adopted in pursuance of the EEC Treaty, *OJ* 19.01.1970, *L* 13, 29

COUNCIL Directive 84/450/EEC of 10 September 1984 relating to the approximation of the laws, regulations and administrative provisions of the Member States concerning misleading advertising, *OJ* 19.9.1984, *L* 250, 17

COUNCIL Directive 85/339/EEC of 27 June 1985 on containers of liquids for human consumption, *OJ* 06.07.1985, *L* 176, 18

COUNCIL Directive 89/552/EEC of 3 October 1989 on the coordination of certain provisions laid down by law, regulation or administrative action in Member States concerning the pursuit of television broadcasting activities, *OJ L* 298, 17.10.1989, 23, amended by EUROPEAN PARLIAMENT AND COUNCIL Directive 97/36/EC of 30 June 1997, *OJ L* 202, 30.07.1997, 60

EUROPEAN PARLIAMENT AND COUNCIL Directive 95/46/EC of 24 October 1995 on the protection of individuals with regard to the processing of personal data and on the free movement of such data, *OJ* 23.11.1995, *L* 281, 31

EUROPEAN PARLIAMENT AND COUNCIL Directive 97/55/EC of 6 October 1997 amending Directive 84/450/EEC concerning misleading advertising so as to include comparative advertising, *OJ* 23.10.1997, *L* 290, 18

EUROPEAN PARLIAMENT AND COUNCIL Directive 98/34/EC of 22 June 1998 laying down a procedure for the provision of information in the field of technical standards and regulations, *OJ L* 21.07.1998, 204, 37, as amended by EUROPEAN PARLIAMENT AND COUNCIL Directive 98/48/EC of 20 July 1998, *OJ L* 05.08.1998, 217, 18

EUROPEAN PARLIAMENT AND COUNCIL Directive 2000/31/EC of 8 June 2000 on certain legal aspects of information society services, in particular electronic commerce, in the Internal Market (Directive on electronic commerce), *OJ L* 178, 17.07.2000, 1

EUROPEAN PARLIAMENT AND COUNCIL Directive 2002/58/EC of 12 July 2002 concerning the processing of personal data and the protection of privacy in the electronic communications sector (Directive on privacy and electronic communications), *OJ* 31.07.2002, *L* 201, 37

EUROPEAN PARLIAMENT AND COUNCIL Directive 2006/24/EC of 15 March 2006 on the retention of data generated or processed in connection with the provision of publicly available electronic communications services or of public communications networks and amending Directive 2002/58/EC, *OJ* 13.04.2006, *L* 105, 54

EUROPEAN PARLIAMENT AND COUNCIL Directive 2007/65/EC of 11 December 2007 amending Council Directive 89/552/EEC on the coordination of certain provisions laid down by law, regulation or administrative action in Member States concerning the pursuit of television broadcasting activities, *OJ* 18.12.2007, *L* 332, 27

d. *Interinstitutional Agreements*

EUROPEAN PARLIAMENT, COUNCIL AND COMMISSION, Interinstitutional agreement on better law-making, *OJ* 31.12.2003, *C* 321, 1

e. *Regulations*

COUNCIL Regulation (EC) No 2678/98 of 7 December 1998 on the functioning of the internal market in relation to the free movement of goods among the Member States, *OJ* 12.12.1998, *L* 337, 8

COUNCIL Regulation (EC) No 1/2003 of 16 December 2002 on the implementation of the rules on competition laid down in Articles 81 and 82 of the Treaty, *OJ* 04.01.2003, *L* 1, 1

European Parliament and Council Regulation (EC) No 178/2002 of 28 January 2002 laying down the general principles and requirements of food law, establishing the European Food Safety Authority and laying down procedures in matters of food safety, *OJ* 01.02.2002, *L* 31, 1

f. *Framework decisions*

Council Framework Decision 2004/68/JHA of 22 December 2003 on combating the sexual exploitation of children and child pornography, *OJ* 20.01.2004, *L* 13, 13

g. *Recommendations*

Commission Recommendation 96/733/EC of 9 December 1996 concerning environmental agreements implementing Community directives, *OJ* 21.12.1996, *L* 333, 59

Council Recommendation 98/560/EC of 24 September 1998 on the development of the competitiveness of the European audiovisual and information services industry by promoting national frameworks aimed at achieving a comparable and effective level of protection of minors and human dignity, *OJ* 07.10.1998, *L* 270, 48

European Parliament and Council Recommendation 2006/952/EC of 20 December 2006 on the protection of minors and human dignity and on the right of reply in relation to the competitiveness of the European audiovisual and on-line information services industry, *OJ* 27.12.2007, *L* 378, 72

h. *Decisions*

Commission of the European Communities, Commission Decision of 28 February 2006 setting up a group of high-level regulatory experts, 2006/210/EC, *OJ* 15.03.2006, *L* 76, 3

Parliament and Council of the European Communities, Decision No 276/1999/EC of the European Parliament and of the Council adopting a multiannual Community action plan on promoting safer use of the Internet by combating illegal and harmful content on the global networks, 25.01.1999, *OJ* 06.02.1999, *L* 33, 1

——, Decision No 1151/2003/EC of the European Parliament and of the Council, amending Decision No 276/1999/EC adopting a Multiannual Community Action Plan on promoting safer use of the Internet by combating illegal and harmful content on global networks, 16.06.2003, *OJ* 01.07.2003, *L* 162, 1

——, Decision No 854/2005/EC of the European Parliament and of the Council establishing a multiannual Community Programme on promoting safer use of the Internet and new online technologies, 11.05.2005, *OJ* 11.06.2005, *L* 149, 1

Parliament and Council of the European Union, Decision No 1351/2008/EC of the European Parliament and of the Council establishing a multiannual Community programme on protecting children using the Internet and other communication technologies, 16.12.2008, *OJ 24.12.2008, L 348, 118*

i. *Notices*

Commission Notice on agreements of minor importance which do not appreciably restrict competition under Article 81 (1) of the Treaty establishing the European Community (*de minimis*), 2001/C 368/07, *OJ* 22.12.2001, *C* 368, 13

Commission Notice Guidelines on vertical restraints, 2000/C 291/01, *OJ* 13.10.2000, *C* 291, 1

Commission Notice Guidelines on the applicability of Article 81 of the EC Treaty to horizontal cooperation agreements, 2001/C 3/02, *OJ* 06.01.2001, *C* 3, 2

Commission Notice Guidelines on the effect on trade concept contained in Articles 81 and 82 of the Treaty, 2004/C 101/07, *OJ* 27.04.2004, *C* 101, 3
Commission Notice Guidelines on the application of Article 81 (3) of the Treaty, 2004/C 101/8, *OJ* 27.04.2004, *C* 101, 97

j. *Communications*

Commission of the European Communities, Communication concerning the application of the Agreement on social policy presented by the Commission to the Council and to the European Parliament, COM (93) 600 final, 14.12.1993
—, Communication to the Council and the European Parliament and to the Economic and Social Committee and the Committee of the Regions, Green Paper on the protection of minors and human dignity in audiovisual and information services, COM (1994) 347 final, 19.07.1994
—, Communication to the European Parliament, the Council, the Economic and Social Committee and the Committee of the Regions, Illegal and harmful content on the Internet, COM (1996) 487 final, 16.10.1996, retrieved from http://ec.europa.eu/archives/ISPO/legal/en/internet/communic.html (on 25.03.2008)
—, Communication to the Council and to the European Parliament on environmental agreements, COM (1996) 561 final, 27.11.1996
—, Communication to the Council, the European Parliament, the Economic and Social Committee and the Committee of the Regions, on the follow-up to the Green Paper on the protection of minors and human dignity in audiovisual and information services, including a Proposal for a Council Recommendation concerning the protection of minors and human dignity in audiovisual and information services, COM (1997) 570 final, 18.11.1997
—, Communication to the European Parliament, the Council, the Economic and Social Committeeand the Committee of the Regions – The convergence of the telecommunications, media and information technology sectors, and the implications for regulation, Results of the public consultation on the Green Paper COM (97) 623, COM (1999) 108 final, 10.03.1999
—, Communication to the Council, the European Parliament, and the Economic and Social Committee – Study on parental control of television broadcasting, COM (99) 371 final, 19.07.1999
—, Communication to the Council, the European Parliament, the Economic and Social Committee and the Committee of the Regions, Principles and guidelines for the Community's audiovisual policy in the digital age, COM (1999) 657 final, 14.12.1999
—, Communication on the precautionary principle, COM (2000) 1 final, 02.02.2000
—, Communication Services of general interest in Europe, 2001/C 17/04, *OJ* 19.01.2001, *C* 17, 4
—, Communication to the Council, the European Parliament, the Economic and Social Committee and the Committee of the Regions, Intermediate evaluation of the implementation of the multiannual Community action plan on promoting safer use of the Internet by combating illegal and harmful content on global networks, COM (2001) 690 final, 23.11.2001
—, Communication 'Simplifying and improving the regulatory environment', COM (2001) 726 final, 05.12.2001
—, Communication – European Governance: better lawmaking, COM (2002) 275 final, 05.06.2002

——, Communication Action Plan 'Simplifying and Improving the Regulatory Environment', COM (2002) 278 final, 05.06.2002
——, Communication to the European Parliament, the Council, the Economic and Social Committee and the Committee of the Regions of 17 July 2002 on environmental agreements at Community level within the framework of the Action Plan on the 'Simplification and improvement of the regulatory environment', COM (2002) 412 final, 17.07.2002
——, Communication to the Council, the European Parliament, the European Economic and Social Committee and the Committee of the Regions, concerning the evaluation of the Multiannual Community Action Plan on promoting safer use of the Internet and new online technologies by combating illegal and harmful content primarily in the area of the protection of children and minors, COM (2003) 653 final, 03.11.2003
——, Communication to the Council, the European Parliament, the European Economic and Social Committee and the Committee of the Regions, The future of European regulatory audiovisual policy, COM (2003) 784 final, 15.12.2003
——, Commission interpretative communication on certain aspects of the provisions on televised advertising in the 'Television without Frontiers' Directive, 2004/C 102/02, *OJ* 28.04.2004, *C* 102, 2
——, Strategic objectives 2005–2009, Europe 2010: A partnership for European renewal, prosperity, solidarity and security, COM (2005) 12 final, 26.01.2005
——, Communication to the Spring European Council Working together for growth and jobs: a new start for the Lisbon Strategy, COM (2005) 24 final, 02.02.2005
——, Communication to the Council and the European Parliament, Better regulation for growth and jobs in the European Union, COM (2005) 97 final, 16.03.2005
——, Communication Compliance with the Charter of Fundamental Rights in Commission legislative proposals – Methodology for systematic and rigorous monitoring, COM (2005) 172 final, 27.04.2005
——, Communication to the Council, the European Parliament, the European Economic and Social Committee and the Committee of the Regions: "i2010 – A European Information Society for growth and employment", COM (2005) 229 final, 01.06.2005
——, Communication to the European Parliament, the Council, the European Economic and Social Committee and the Committee of the Regions – Implementing the Community Lisbon programme: A strategy for the simplification of the regulatory environment, COM (2005) 535 final, 25.10.2005
——, Communication to the Council, the European Parliament, the European Economic and Social Committee and the Committee of the Regions, Towards a global partnership in the Information Society: Follow-up to the Tunis Phase of the World Summit on the Information Society (WSIS), COM (2006) 181 final, 27.04.2006
——, Communication Towards an EU strategy on the rights of the child, COM (2006) 367 final, 04.07.2006
——, Communication to the European Parliament pursuant to the second subparagraph of Article 251 (2) of the EC Treaty concerning the common position of the Council on the adoption of a Recommendation on the protection of minors and human dignity and on the right of reply in relation to the competitiveness of the European audiovisual and on-line information services industry, COM (2006) 546 final, 21.09.2006
——, Communication to the European Parliament, the Council, the European Economic and Social Committee and the Committee of the Regions, Communication, on the

implementation of the multiannual Community Programme on promoting safer use of the Internet and new online technologies (Safer Internet plus), COM (2006) 661 final, 06.11.2006
——, Communication to the European Parliament, the Council, the European Economic and Social Committee and the Committee of the Regions, Communication, Final evaluation of the implementation of the multiannual Community action plan on promoting safer use of the Internet by combating illegal and harmful content on global networks, COM (2006) 663 final, 06.11.2006
——, Communication to the European Parliament, the Council, the European Economic and Social Committee and the Committee of the Regions – A strategic review of Better Regulation in the European Union, COM (2006) 689 final, 14.11.2006
——, Communication to the European Parliament, the Council, the European Economic and Social Committee and the Committee of the Regions – Accompanying the Communication on "A single market for 21st century Europe" – Services of general interest, including social services of general interest: a new European commitment, COM (2007) 725 final, 20.11.2007
——, Communication to the European Parliament, the Council, the European Economic and Social Committee and the Committee of the Regions "A European approach to media literacy in the digital environment", COM (2007) 833 final, 20.12.2007
——, Communication to the European Parliament, the Council, the European Economic and Social Committee and the Committee of the Regions on Creative Content Online in the Single Market, COM (2007) 836 final, 03.01.2008
——, Communication to the European Parliament, the Council, the European Economic and Social Committee and the Committee of the Regions – Second strategic review of Better Regulation in the European Union, COM (2008) 32 final, 30.01.2008
——, Communication to the European Parliament, the Council, the European Economic and Social Committee and the Committee of the Regions on the protection of consumers, in particular minors, in respect of the use of video games, COM (2008) 207 final, 22.04.2008

k. *Political agreements*

Council of the European Union, Proposal for a Recommendation of the European Parliament and of the Council on the protection of minors and human dignity and on the right of reply in relation to the competitiveness of the European audiovisual and online information services industry – Political agreement, No. 8956/06, Interinstitutional file 2004/0117 (COD), Brussels, 11.05.2006, retrieved from http://register.consilium.europa.eu/pdf/en/06/st08/st08956.en06.pdf (on 30.05.2006)
Council and Parliament of the European Communities, Political agreement on common position AVMS Directive – Newly modified Commission proposal, 24.05.2007, retrieved from http://ec.europa.eu/avpolicy/docs/reg/modernisation/proposal_2005/avmsd_cons_may07_en.pdf (on 10.07.2007)

l. *Common positions*

Council of the European Union, Common Position (EC) No 24/2006 of 18 September 2006 adopted by the Council, acting in accordance with the procedure referred to in Article 251 of the Treaty establishing the European Community, with a view to adopting a Recommendation of the European Parliament and of the Council on the protection of minors and human dignity and on the right of reply in relation to the competitiveness of the European audiovisual and on-line information services industry, *OJ* 05.12.2006, *C* 295E, 48

——, Common position (EC) No 18/2007 of 15 October 2007 adopted by the Council, acting in accordance with the procedure referred to in Article 251 of the Treaty establishing the European Community, with a view to the adoption of a Directive of the European Parliament and of the Council amending Council Directive 89/552/EEC on the coordination of certain provisions laid down by law, regulation or administrative action in Member States concerning the pursuit of television broadcasting activities, *OJ* 18.12.2007, *C* 307E, 1

m. *Green Papers*

Commission of the European Communities, Green Paper on the protection of minors and human dignity in audiovisual and information services, COM (1996) 483 final, 16.10.1996

——, Green Paper on the convergence of the telecommunications, media and information technology sectors, and the implications for regulation, COM (1997) 623 final, 03.12.1997

n. *White Papers*

Commission of the European Communities, European Governance – A White Paper, COM (2001) 428 final, 25.07.2001

o. *Proposals*

Commission of the European Communities, Proposal for a Decision of the European Parliament and of the Council on establishing a multiannual Community programme on promoting safer use of the Internet and new online technologies, COM (2004) 91 final, 12.03.2004

——, Proposal for a recommendation of the European Parliament and of the Council on the protection of minors and human dignity and the right of reply in relation to the competitiveness of the European audiovisual and information services industry, COM (2004) 341 final, 30.04.2004

——, Proposal for a Directive of the European Parliament and of the Council amending Council Directive 89/552/EEC on the coordination of certain provisions laid down by law, regulation or administrative action in Member States concerning the pursuit of television broadcasting activities, COM (2005) 646 final, 13.12.2005

——, Amended proposal for a Recommendation of the European Parliament and of the Council on the protection of minors and human dignity and the right of reply in relation to the competitiveness of the European audiovisual and information services industry, COM (2006) 31 final, 20.01.2006

——, Proposal for a Decision of the European Parliament and of the Council establishing a multiannual Community programme on protecting children using the Internet and other communication technologies, COM (2008) 106 final, 27.02.2008

——, Proposal for a Directive of the European Parliament and of the Council on the coordination of certain provisions laid down by law, regulation or administrative action in Member States concerning the provision of audiovisual media services (Audiovisual Media Services Directive) (Codified version), COM (2009) 185 final, 21.04.2009

p. *Resolutions*

Council of the European Communities, Resolution of the Council and the Representatives of the Governments of the Member States, meeting within the Council of 17 February 1997 on illegal and harmful content on the Internet, *OJ* 06.03.1997, *C* 70, 1

Council Resolution on Community consumer policy 1999–2001, 28.06.1999, *OJ* 21.07.1999, *C* 206, 1

—— Resolution of 1 March 2002 on the protection of consumers, in particular young people, through the labelling of certain video games and computer games according to the age group, 2002/C 65/02, *OJ* 14.03.2002, *C* 65, 2

European Parliament, Resolution on the Commission Communication on illegal and harmful content on the Internet, A4–0098/97, 24.07.1997, retrieved from http://europa.eu.int/ISPO/legal/en/internet/98–97en.html (on 17.05.2006, no longer available)

——, Legislative resolution embodying Parliament's opinion on the proposal for a Council Recommendation concerning the protection of minors and human dignity in audiovisual and information services, *OJ* 01.06.1998, *C* 167, 128

——, Resolution on the Commission communication 'Study on Parental Control of Television Broadcasting', COM(1999) 371 – C5–0324/1999 – 1999/2210(COS), 05.10.2000, retrieved from http://www.europarl.europa.eu/omk/omnsapir.so/pv2?PRG=DOCPV&APP=PV2&LANGUE=EN&SDOCTA=7&TXTLST=1&POS=1&Type_Doc=RESOL&TPV=PROV&DATE=051000&PrgPrev=TYPEF@A5|PRG@QUERY|APP@PV2|FILE@BIBLIO00|NUMERO@258|YEAR@00|PLAGE@1&TYPEF=A5&NUMB=1&DATEF=001005 (on 26.05.2008)

——, Resolution on the evaluation report from the Commission to the Council and the European Parliament on the application of the Council Recommendation of 24 September 1998 concerning the protection of minors and human dignity, COM(2001) 106 – C5–0191/2001 –2001/2087(COS), 11.04.2002, *OJ* 29.05.2003, *C* 127 E, 671

——, Resolution on the Commission White Paper on European Governance, A5–0399/2001, 29.11.2001, *OJ* 27.06.2002, *C* 153 E, 314

——, Legislative resolution on the proposal for a recommendation of the European Parliament and of the Council on the protection of minors and human dignity and the right of reply in relation to the competitiveness of the European audiovisual and information services industry, COM(2004)0341 – C6–0029/2004 – 2004/0117(COD), 07.09.2005, *OJ* 17.8.2006, *C* 193 E, 217

——, Legislative resolution on the Council common position for adopting a recommendation of the European Parliament and of the Council on the protection of minors and human dignity and on the right of reply in relation to the competitiveness of the European audiovisual and online information services industry, 9577/1/2006 – C6–0313/2006 – 2004/0117(COD), 12.12.2006, retrieved from http://www.europarl.europa.eu/sides/getDoc.do?Type=TA&Reference=P6–TA-2006–0537&language=EN (on 26.03.2008)

——, Legislative resolution on the proposal for a directive of the European Parliament and of the Council amending Council Directive 89/552/EEC on the coordination of certain provisions laid down by law, regulation or administrative action in Member States concerning the pursuit of television broadcasting activities, COM(2005)0646 – C6–0443/2005 – 2005/0260(COD), 13.12.2006, retrieved from http://www.europarl.europa.eu/sides/getDoc.do?pubRef=-//EP//TEXT+TA+P6–TA-2006–0559+0+DOC+XML+V0//EN (on 26.03.2007)

——, Legislative resolution on the Council common position for adopting a directive of the European Parliament and of the Council amending Council Directive 89/552/EEC on the coordination of certain provisions laid down by law, regulation or administrative action in

Member States concerning the pursuit of television broadcasting activities, 10076/6/2007 – C6–0352/2007 – 2005/0260(COD), 29.11.2007, retrieved from http://www.europarl.europa.eu/oeil/FindByProcnum.do?lang=2&procnum=COD/2005/0260 (on 28.03.2008)

——, Resolution Towards an EU strategy on the rights of the child, 2007/2093 (INI), 16.01.2008, retrieved from http://www.europarl.europa.eu/sides/getDoc.do?pubRef=-//EP//TEXT+TA+P6–TA-2008–0012+0+DOC+XML+V0//EN (on 21.01.2008)

q. *Commission Staff Working Documents*

Commission of the European Communities, Commission working document Protection of minors and human dignity in audiovisual and information services: Consultations on the Green Paper, SEC (97) 1203, 13.06.1997

——, Commission Staff working paper Ex ante evaluation of Safer Internet Plus (2005–2008), SEC (2004) 148, retrieved from http://eur-lex.europa.eu/LexUriServ/LexUriServ.do?uri=CELEX:52004PC0091:EN:HTML (on 23.11.2006)

——, Commission Staff working document *Annex to the* Proposal for a Directive of the European Parliament and of the Council amending Council Directive 89/552/EEC on the coordination of certain provisions laid down by law, regulation or administrative action in Member States concerning the pursuit of television broadcasting activities, Impact Assessment – Draft Audiovisual Media Services Directive, SEC (2005) 1625/2, 13.12.2005, retrieved from http://ec.europa.eu/avpolicy/docs/reg/modernisation/proposal_2005/newtwf_ia.pdf (on 26.11.2008)

——, Commission Staff working document accompanying the Communication from the Commission Towards an EU strategy on the rights of the child, Impact assessment, COM (2006) 367 final, SEC (2006) 888, 04.07.2006, retrieved from http://register.consilium.europa.eu/pdf/en/06/st12/st12107–ad01.en06.pdf (on 29.08.2006)

——, Commission Staff working document accompanying the Communication from the Commission Towards an EU strategy on the rights of the child, Preliminary inventory of EU actions affecting children's rights, COM (2006) 367 final, SEC (2006) 889, 04.07.2006, retrieved from http://register.consilium.europa.eu/pdf/en/06/st12/st12107–ad02.en06.pdf (on 29.08.2006)

r. *Public Consultations*

European Commission, Consultation paper: Child safety and mobile phone services, 25.07.2006, retrieved from http://ec.europa.eu/information_society/activities/sip/public_consultation/index_en.htm (on 25.07.2006)

——, Summary of the results of the public consultation 'Child safety and mobile phone services', 2006, retrieved from http://ec.europa.eu/information_society/activities/sip/docs/public_consultation_mobile/public_consultation_rsults_en.pdf (on 11.03.2008)

——, Public consultation: Safer Internet and online technologies for children, 2007, retrieved from http://ec.europa.eu/information_society/activities/sip/docs/public_consultation_prog/pc_2007_info_en.pdf (on 02.04.2008)

——, Safer Internet and online technologies for children: Summary of the results of the online public consultation and 20–21 June 2007 Safer Internet Forum Report, January 2008, retrieved from http://ec.europa.eu/information_society/activities/sip/docs/public_consultation_prog/summary_report.pdf (on 09.01.2008)

——, Public consultation: Age verification, cross media rating and classification, online social networking, June 2008, retrieved from http://ec.europa.eu/information_society/activities/sip/docs/pub_consult_age_rating_sns/pc_2008_info_questions_en.pdf (on 17.06.2008)

——, Public consultation on online social networking – Summary report, November 2008, retrieved from http://ec.europa.eu/information_society/activities/sip/docs/pub_consult_age_rating_sns/summaryreport.pdf (on 19.11.2008)

s. *Reports*

Commission of the European Communities, Sixth report from the Commission to the European Parliament, the Council, the European Economic and Social Committee and the Committee of the Regions on the application of Directive 89/552/EEC "Television without Frontiers", COM (2007) 452 final, 24.10.2007, retrieved from http://eur-lex.europa.eu/LexUriServ/site/en/com/2007/com2007_0452en01.pdf (on 14.01.2008)

——, Working party on illegal and harmful content on the Internet – Report, presented to the Council on 28.11.1996, retrieved from http://europa.eu.int/ISPO/legal/en/internet/wpen.html (on 18.05.2006)

——, Commission report to the European Council: Better lawmaking 1998 A shared responsibility, COM (1998) 715 final, 01.12.1998, retrieved from http://aei.pitt.edu/926/01/subsidiarity_COM_98_715.pdf (on 14.05.2008)

——, Commission report to the European Council: Better lawmaking 1999, COM (1999) 562 final, 03.11.1999, retrieved from http://aei.pitt.edu/3541/01/000689_1.pdf (on 14.05.2008)

——, Evaluation report from the Commission to the Council and the European Parliament on the application of Council Recommendation of 24 September 1998 concerning the protection of minors and human dignity, COM (2001) 106 final, 27.02.2001, retrieved from http://ec.europa.eu/comm/avpolicy/docs/reg/minors/ermin_en.pdf (on 04.01.2006)

——, Interim report from the Commission to the Stockholm European Council: Improving and simplifying the regulatory environment, COM (2001) 130 final, 07.03.2001, retrieved from http://ec.europa.eu/fisheries/publications/factsheets/legal_texts/com_03_130_en.pdf (on 14.05.2008)

——, Second evaluation report from the Commission to the Council and the European Parliament on the application of Council Recommendation of 24 September 1998 concerning the protection of minors, COM (2003) 776 final, 12.12.2003, retrieved from http://eur-lex.europa.eu/LexUriServ/site/en/com/2003/com2003_0776en01.pdf (on 25.07.2006)

Council of the European Union, Progress report/exchange of views on Proposal for a directive of the European Parliament and of the Council amending Council directive 89/552/EEC on the coordination of certain provisions laid down by law, regulation or administrative action in Member States concerning the pursuit of television broadcasting activities, No. 9134/06, Interinstitutional file 2005/0260 (COD), 10.06.2006, retrieved from http://register.consilium.europa.eu/pdf/en/06/st09/st09134.en06.pdf (on 10.07.2006)

European Commission, Final report on the Content Online Platform, May 2009, retrieved from http://ec.europa.eu/avpolicy/docs/other_actions/col_platform_report.pdf (on 24.05.2009)

——, Background report on cross media rating and classification and age verification solutions, Safer Internet Forum Luxembourg, 25–26.09.2008, retrieved from http://ec.europa.eu/information_society/activities/sip/docs/pub_consult_age_rating_sns/reportageverification.pdf (on 19.11.2008)

European Parliament, Draft Report on the proposal for a recommendation on the protection of minors and human dignity and the right of reply in relation to the competitiveness of the European audiovisual and information services industry, 2004/0117 (COD), 14.03.2004, retrieved from http://www.europarl.europa.eu/meetdocs/2004_2009/documents/pr/547/547671/547671en.pdf (on 05.02.2007)

——, Report on the proposal for a decision of the European Parliament and of the Council on establishing a multiannual Community programme on promoting safer use of the Internet and new online technologies, A6–0033/2004, 18.11.2004, retrieved from http://www.europarl.europa.eu/omk/sipade3?PUBREF=-//EP//NONSGML+REPORT+A6–2004–0033+0+DOC+PDF+V0//EN&L=EN&LEVEL=2&NAV=S&LSTDOC=Y on (15.11.2006)

——, Draft report Marielle De Sarnez, Amendments 24–53, PE 355.734v01–00, 01.04.2005, retrieved from http://www.europarl.europa.eu/meetdocs/2004_2009/documents/am/561/561514/561514en.pdf (on 08.02.2007)

——, Report on the proposal for a recommendation of the European Parliament and of the Council on the protection of minors and human dignity and the right of reply in relation to the competitiveness of the European audiovisual and information services industry, A6–0244/2005, 19.07.2006, retrieved from http://www.europarl.europa.eu/sides/getDoc.do?pubRef=-//EP//NONSGML+REPORT+A6–2005–0244+0+DOC+PDF+V0//EN&language=EN (on 05.07.2007)

Internet working party, Interim report on initiatives in EU Member States with respect to combating illegal and harmful content on the Internet, 04.06.1997, retrieved from http://europa.eu.int/ISPO/legal/en/internet/wp2en-chap.html#1 (on 17.05.2006)

Mandelkern group on better regulation, Final Report, 13.11.2001, retrieved from http://ec.europa.eu/governance/impact/docs/key_docs/mandelkern_report_en.pdf (on 13.05.2008)

t. *Council conclusions and minutes*

European Council, Presidency conclusions, 11–12.12.1992, Edinburgh, retrieved from http://www.europarl.europa.eu/summits/edinburgh/a0_en.pdf (on 14.05.2008)

——, Presidency conclusions – Annex 1: Overall approach to the application by the Council of the subsidiarity principle and article 3b of the Treaty on the European Union, 11–12.12.1992, Edinburgh, retrieved from http://www.europarl.europa.eu/summits/edinburgh/a1_en.pdf (on 14.07.2008)

——, Presidency conclusions, 23–24.03.2000, Lisbon, retrieved from http://www.europarl.europa.eu/summits/lis1_en.htm (on 13.05.2008)

——, 2361st meeting of the Council (Culture), held in Luxembourg on 21.06.2001, 10308/01, retrieved from http://register.consilium.europa.eu/pdf/en/01/st10/10308en1.pdf (on 29.01.2007)

——, Draft minutes 2729th meeting of the Council of the European Union (Education, Youth and Culture), held in Brussels on 18–19 May 2006, 9547/06, retrieved from http://register.consilium.europa.eu/pdf/en/06/st09/st09547.en06.pdf (on 08.02.2007)

u. *Opinions*

European Economic and social committee, Opinion of the Economic and Social Committee on the 'Proposal for a Council Decision adopting a Multiannual Community Action Plan on promoting safe use of the Internet', 98/C 214/08, 29.04.1998, *OJ* 10.07.1998, *C* 214, 29

——, Opinion of the European Economic and Social Committee on the 'Proposal for a Decision of the European Parliament and of the Council on establishing a multiannual Community programme on promoting safer use of the internet and new online technologies', COM(2004) 91 final – 2004/0023 (COD), 16.12.2004, *OJ* 28/06/2005, *C* 157, 136

——, Opinion of the European Economic and Social Committee on the 'Proposal for a European Parliament and Council recommendation on the protection of minors and human dignity and the right of reply in relation to the competitiveness of the European audiovisual and information services industry', COM(2004) 341 final – 2004/0117 (COD), 09.02.2005, *OJ* 08.09.2005, *C* 221, 87

European Parliament, Opinion of the Committee on Civil Liberties, Justice and Home Affairs, for the Committee on Culture and Education on the 'Proposal for a recommendation of the European Parliament and of the Council on the protection of minors and human dignity and the right of reply in relation to the competitiveness of the European audiovisual and information services industry', 15.04.2005, retrieved from http://www.europarl.europa.eu/registre/commissions/libe/avis/2005/353374/LIBE_AD(2005)353374_EN.pdf (on 02.01.2006)

v. *Speeches*

Reding, Viviane, Minors and media: Towards a more effective protection, Speech at the Workshop of scientists in the field of the protection of minors on media violence, self-regulation and media literacy, Brussels, 10.09.2003, retrieved from http://europa.eu.int/rapid/pressReleasesAction.do?reference=SPEECH/03/400&format=HTML&aged=0&language=EN&guiLanguage=en (on 06.06.2008)

——, Convergence and innovation, the new agenda for growth and jobs, Speech at the Meeting of the Council of Presidents of UNICE, Brussels, 21.03.2005, retrieved from http://europa.eu/rapid/pressReleasesAction.do?reference=SPEECH/05/190&format=HTML&aged=0&language=EN&guiLanguage=en (on 13.07.2007)

——, The new Television without Frontiers Directive: the Commission proposal to boost Europe's audiovisual sector, Speech at the High level conference on the future of the television sector of the Association for Commercial Television (ACT), Brussels, 27.04.2006, retrieved from http://europa.eu/rapid/pressReleasesAction.do?reference=SPEECH/06/268&format=HTML&aged=0&language=EN&guiLanguage=en (on 21.05.2008)

——, Digital convergence: a whole new way of life, Speech at the Digital Lifestyle Exhibition, Brussels, 30.05.2006, retrieved from http://ec.europa.eu/commission_barroso/reding/docs/speeches/dle_20060530.pdf (on 31.07.2007)

——, Audiovisual media services directive: the right instrument to provide legal certainty for Europe's media businesses in the next decade, Speech at the Seminar "Regulating the new media landscape", Brussels, 07.06.2006, retrieved from http://europa.eu.int/rapid/pressReleasesAction.do?reference=SPEECH/06/352&format=HTML&aged=0&language=EN&guiLanguage=en (on 12.07.2006)

——, Freedom of the media, effective co-regulation and media literacy: cornerstones for an efficient protection of minors in the European Union, Speech at the ICRA Roundtable Brussels 'Mission Impossible', Brussels, 14.06.2006, retrieved from http://europa.eu.int/rapid/pressReleasesAction.do?reference=SPEECH/06/374&type=HTML&aged=0&language=EN&guiLanguage=en (on 15.06.2006)

——, Self regulation applied to interactive games: success and challenges, Speech at the ISFE Expert Conference, Brussels, 26.06.2007, retrieved from http://europa.eu/rapid/pressReleasesAction.do?reference=SPEECH/07/429&type=HTML&aged=0&language=EN&guiLanguage=en (on 22.05.2008)

——, Towards next generation media for the digital age?, Speech at the Conference organised by the IMPRESA Group and RADIO RENASCENCA on the Future of the Media, Lisbon, 17.07.2007, retrieved from http://ec.europa.eu/commission_barroso/reding/docs/speeches/lisbon_20070717.pdf (on 27.07.2007)

——, Le nouveau contexte des médias audiovisuels – Tendances et enjeux publics [*The new context of audiovisual media – Trends and public challenges*], Speech at the Colloque international pour les 10 ans du Conseil supérieur de l'audiovisuel de la Communauté française de Belgique, Brussels, 21.09.2007, retrieved from http://europa.eu/rapid/pressReleasesAction.do?reference=SPEECH/07/560 (on 14.01.2008) [in French]

——, Video games: let's go for PEGI Plus, Speech at the Annual Conference Interactive Software Federation of Europe, Brussels, 07.05.2008, retrieved from http://ec.europa.eu/commission_barroso/reding/docs/speeches/2008/brussels-20080507.pdf (on 21.05.2008)

——, How can we empower youngsters to stay safe online? Innovative solutions in Europe, Speech at the World Childhood Foundation Seminar, Stockholm, 17 September 2009, retrieved from http://ec.europa.eu/commission_barroso/reding/docs/speeches/2009/stockholm-170909.pdf (on 21.01.2010)

w. *Press releases*

i. *Council*

Council of the European Communities, Press release Telecommunications Council 1949, Brussels, 27.09.1996, No. 10259/96, Press No. 247, retrieved from http://www.consilium.europa.eu/ueDocs/cms_Data/docs/pressdata/en/trans/019a0005.htm (on 18.05.2006)

——, Press release Telecommunications Council 1972, Brussels, 28.11.1996, No. 12102/96, Press No. 344, retrieved from http://www.consilium.europa.eu/ueDocs/cms_Data/docs/pressdata/en/trans/019a0007.htm (on 18.05.2006)

Council of the European Union, Press release 2729th Council Meeting, Education, Youth and Culture, Brussels, 18–19.05.2006, retrieved from http://www.consilium.europa.eu/ueDocs/cms_Data/docs/pressData/en/educ/89661.pdf (on 29.05.2006)

——, Press release 2762nd Council meeting Education, Youth and Culture, Brussels, 13–14.11.2006, retrieved from http://www.consilium.europa.eu/ueDocs/cms_Data/docs/pressData/en/educ/91666.pdf (on 13.07.2007)

ii. *Rapid*

Rapid, 25 May: Commission's actions in favour of children and young people, MEMO/05/171, 25.05.2005, retrieved from http://europa.eu/rapid/pressReleasesAction.do?reference=MEMO/05/171&format=HTML&aged=1&language=EN&guiLanguage=en (on 12.12.2008)

——, Making sense of today's media content: Commission begins public media literacy consultation, IP/06/1326, 06.10.2006, retrieved from http://europa.eu.int/rapid/pressReleasesAction.do?reference=IP/06/1326 (on 12.10.2006)

——, Making the internet safer for children: Europe calls for determined action on "Safer Internet Day" 2007, IP/07/140, 06.02.2007, retrieved from http://www.europa.eu/rapid/pressReleasesAction.do?reference=IP/07/140&format=HTML&aged=0&language=EN&guiLanguage=en (on 07.02.2007)

——, Commission study points the way forward for better regulation of new media and the digital economy (press release on Safer Internet Day 2007), IP/07/138, 06.02.2007, retrieved from http://www.europa.eu/rapid/pressReleasesAction.do?reference=IP/07/138&format=HTML&aged=0&language=EN&guiLanguage=fr (on 07.02.2007)

——, Boosting the diversity of European TV- and on-demand services: Commission paves the way for the new Directive 'Audiovisual without Frontiers', IP/07/311, 09.03.2007, retrieved from http://europa.eu/rapid/pressReleasesAction.do?reference=IP/07/311&format=HTML&aged=0&language=EN&guiLanguage=en (on 26.03.2007)

——, Commission welcomes start of a new era for Europe's audiovisual media, IP/07/1809, 29.11.2007, retrieved from http://www.europa.eu/rapid/pressReleasesAction.do?reference=IP/07/1809&format=HTML&aged=0&language=EN&guiLanguage=en (on 16.01.2008)

——, Charter of Fundamental Rights: the Presidents of the Commission, European Parliament and Council sign and solemnly proclaim the Charter in Strasbourg, IP/07/1916, 12.12.2007, retrieved from http://europa.eu/rapid/pressReleasesAction.do?reference=IP/07/1916&format=HTML&aged=0&language=EN&guiLanguage=en (on 23.01.2008)

——, Media literacy: do people really understand how to make the most of blogs, search engines or interactive TV?, IP/07/1970, 20.12.2007, retrieved from http://www.europa.eu/rapid/pressReleasesAction.do?reference=IP/07/1970&format=HTML&aged=0&language=EN&guiLanguage=en (on 16.01.2007)

——, Follow-up to the EU strategy on the rights of the child, MEMO/08/231, 10.04.2008, retrieved from http://europa.eu/rapid/pressReleasesAction.do?reference=MEMO/08/231&format (on 07.07.2008)

——, Commission welcomes European Parliament's strong support for a new Safer Internet Programme, IP/08/1571, 22.10.2008, retrieved from http://europa.eu/rapid/pressReleases-Action.do?reference=IP/08/1571&format=HTML&aged=0&language=EN&guiLanguage=fr (on 26.11.2008)

——, EU adopts new Safer Internet Programme: € 55 million to make the Internet a safer place for children, IP/08/1899, 09.12.2008, retrieved from http://europa.eu/rapid/pressReleasesAction.do?reference=IP/08/1899&format=HTML&aged=0&language=EN&guiLanguage=en (on 20.12.2008)

——, Commission calls on Member States to rule with a light hand while updating TV rules in 2009, IP/08/2032, 18.12.2008, retrieved from http://europa.eu/rapid/pressReleasesAction.do?reference=IP/08/2032&format=HTML&aged=0&language=EN&guiLanguage=en (on 24.12.2008)

——, Commission calls on mobile operators to continue to improve child safety policies, IP/09/596, 20.04.2009, retrieved from http://europa.eu/rapid/pressReleasesAction.do?reference=IP/09/596&format=HTML&aged=0&language=EN&guiLanguage=en (on 28.05.2009)

x. *Miscellaneous*

i. *Parliament*

European Parliament, Draft Recommendation for second reading on the Council common position for adopting a recommendation of the European Parliament and of the Council on protection of minors and human dignity and the right of reply in relation to the competitiveness of the European audiovisual and online information services industry, 2004/0117(COD), 06.11.2006, retrieved from http://www.europarl.europa.eu/meetdocs/2004_2009/documents/pr/637/637009/637009en.pdf (on 28.11.2006)

——, Recommendation for second reading on the Council common position for adopting a recommendation of the European Parliament and of the Council on protection of minors and human dignity and the right of reply in relation to the competitiveness of the European audiovisual and online information services industry, A6-0433/2006, 29.11.2006, retrieved from http://www.europarl.europa.eu/sides/getDoc.do?pubRef=-//EP//NONSGML+REPORT+A6-2006-0433+0+DOC+PDF+V0//EN&language=EN (on 02.01.2006)

ii. *Council*

Council, Conclusions of 27 September 1999 on the role of self-regulation on the light of the development of new media services, 1999/C 283/02, *OJ* 06.10.1999, *C* 283, 3

iii. *Commission*

Commission of the European Communities, Learning in the information society – Action plan for a European education initiative (1996–1998), COM (1996) 471 final, 02.10.1996, retrieved from http://aei.pitt.edu/1200/01/education_gp_follow_COM_96_471.pdf (on 05.01.2009)

——, The Lisbon European Council – An agenda of economic and social renewal for Europe (Contribution of the European Commission to the special European Council in Lisbon), 23–24.03.2000, retrieved from http://ec.europa.eu/growthandjobs/pdf/lisbon_en.pdf (on 27.07.2007)

European Commission, EU competition policy and the consumer, 2004, retrieved from http://ec.europa.eu/comm/competition/publications/consumer_en.pdf (on 21.10.2008)

——, Focus group 1: Regulation of audiovisual content, September 2004, retrieved from http://ec.europa.eu/avpolicy/docs/reg/modernisation/focus_groups/fg1_wp_en.pdf (on 13.07.2007)

——, Eurobarometer Safer Internet, May 2006, retrieved from http://ec.europa.eu/information_society/activities/sip/docs/eurobarometer/eurobarometer_2005_25_ms.pdf (on 14.03.2008)

——, Better regulation: simply explained, 2006, retrieved from http://ec.europa.eu/governance/better_regulation/documents/brochure/br_brochure_en.pdf (on 14.05.2008)

——, Networked Media of the Future, October 2007, retrieved from ftp://ftp.cordis.europa.eu/pub/fp7/ict/docs/netmedia/networked-media-of-the-future_en.pdf (on 28.01.2008)

——, Audiovisual and media policies, Overview legislative proposal for an Audiovisual Media Services Directive, retrieved from http://ec.europa.eu/comm/avpolicy/reg/tvwf/modernisation/proposal_2005/index_en.htm (on 26.03.2007, no longer available)

——, Audiovisual Media Services Directive: Draft consolidated amended version 2007, March 2007, retrieved from http://ec.europa.eu/information_society/newsroom/cf/itemlongdetail.cfm?item_id=2343 (on 26.03.2007)

——, Eurobarometer Safer Internet for Children: Qualitative study in 29 European studies, May 2007, retrieved from http://ec.europa.eu/information_society/activities/sip/docs/eurobarometer/qualitative_study_2007/summary_report_en.pdf (on 14.03.2008)

——, Better Regulation – Impact assessment, retrieved from http://ec.europa.eu/governance/better_regulation/impact_en.htm (on 28.12.2008)

——, Internal market – General principles Freedom to provide services, retrieved from http://ec.europa.eu/internal_market/services/principles_en.htm (on 26.07.2007)

——, Competition – Antitrust, retrieved from http://ec.europa.eu/comm/competition/antitrust/overview_en.html (on 27.11.2008)

——, What is i2010?, retrieved from http://ec.europa.eu/information_society/eeurope/i2010/what_is_i2010/index_en.htm (on 27.07.2007)

——, "What is media literacy?", retrieved from http://ec.europa.eu/avpolicy/media_literacy/index_en.htm (on 17.07.2008)

——, What is social networking?, retrieved from http://ec.europa.eu/information_society/activities/sip/safety_tips/index_en.htm#1.1_what_is_social_networking (on 17.03.2008)

iv. *Article 29 Data Protection Working Party*

Article 29 Data Protection Working Party, Recommendation 3/97 Anonymity on the Internet, 03.12.1997, retrieved from http://ec.europa.eu/justice_home/fsj/privacy/docs/wpdocs/1997/wp6_en.pdf (on 18.05.2009)

——, Working document WP 37, "Privacy on the Internet, an integrated EU approach to on-line data protection", 21.11.2000, retrieved from http://ec.europa.eu/justice_home/fsj/privacy/docs/wpdocs/2000/wp37en.pdf (on 27.03.2008)

——, Working document 1/2008 on the protection of children's personal data (General guidelines and the special case of schools), 18.02.2008, retrieved from http://ec.europa.eu/justice_home/fsj/privacy/docs/wpdocs/2008/wp147_en.pdf (on 05.03.2008)

——, Opinion 2/2009 on the protection of children's personal data (General guidelines and the special case of schools), 11.02.2009, retrieved from http://ec.europa.eu/justice_home/fsj/privacy/docs/wpdocs/2009/wp160_en.pdf (on 18.05.2009)

v. *European Data Protection Supervisor*

European Data Protection Supervisor, Opinion of the European Data Protection Supervisor on the proposal for a decision of the European Parliament and of the Council establishing a multiannual Community programme on protecting children using the Internet and other communication technologies, 23.06.2008, retrieved from http://www.edps.europa.eu/EDPSWEB/webdav/site/mySite/shared/Documents/Consultation/Opinions/2008/08-06-23_Children_Internet_EN.pdf (on 25.06.2008)

vi. *Other*

Information Society Forum, Networks for people and their communities – Making the most of the information society in the European Union, First Annual Report to the European Commission from the Information Society Forum, June 1996, retrieved from http://europa.eu.int/ISPO/policy/isf/documents/rep-96/ISF-REPORT-96.html#ch4 (on 30.05.2006, no longer available)

C. *Council of Europe*

a. *Conventions*

Council of Europe, Convention for the Protection of Human Rights and Fundamental Freedoms, CETS No. 005, 04.11.1950, Rome, retrieved from http://conventions.coe.int/Treaty/en/Treaties/Html/005.htm (on 12.02.2007)

——, European Social Charter, CETS No. 35, 18.10.1961, Turin, retrieved from http://conventions.coe.int/Treaty/Commun/QueVoulezVous.asp?NT=035&CM=8&DF=07/11/2005&CL=ENG (on 21.05.2007)

——, European Convention on the exercise of children's rights, ETS No. 160, 25.01.1996, Strasbourg, retrieved from http://conventions.coe.int/Treaty/en/Treaties/Html/160.htm (on 01.06.2007)

——, Explanatory report to the European Convention on the exercise of children's rights, retrieved from http://conventions.coe.int/Treaty/EN/Reports/HTML/160.htm (on 01.06.2007)

——, European Social Charter (revised), CETS No. 163, 03.05.1996, Strasbourg, retrieved from http://conventions.coe.int/Treaty/Commun/QueVoulezVous.asp?NT=163&CM=7&DF=26/10/2005&CL=ENG (on 21.05.2007)

——, Convention on Cybercrime, ETS No. 185, 23.11.2001, Budapest, retrieved from http://conventions.coe.int/Treaty/EN/Treaties/Html/185.htm (on 13.03.2007)

——, European Convention on Transfrontier Television, ETS No. 132, 05.05.1989, Strasbourg, as amended by ETS. No. 171, 01.03.2002, retrieved from http://conventions.coe.int/Treaty/EN/Treaties/Html/132.htm (on 16.05.2007)

——, Convention on the Protection of Children against Sexual Exploitation and Sexual Abuse, CETS No. 201, 25.10.2007, Lanzarote, retrieved from http://conventions.coe.int/Treaty/EN/treaties/Html/201.htm (on 29.02.2008)
——, Explanatory report to the Convention on the Protection of Children against Sexual Exploitation and Sexual Abuse, retrieved from http://conventions.coe.int/Treaty/EN/Reports/Html/201.htm (on 29.02.2008)

b. *Declarations*

Council of Europe (Committee of Ministers), Declaration on freedom of expression and information, 29.04.1982, retrieved from https://wcd.coe.int/com.instranet.InstraServlet?command=com.instranet.CmdBlobGet&InstranetImage=601273&SecMode=1&DocId=675536&Usage=2 (on 12.12.2008)
——, Declaration on a European policy for new information technologies, 07.05.1999, retrieved from https://wcd.coe.int/ViewDoc.jsp?id=448133&Site=CM&BackColorInternet=9999CC&BackColorIntranet=FFBB55&BackColorLogged=FFAC75 (on 24.04.2007)
——, Declaration of freedom of communication on the Internet, 28.05.2003, retrieved from https://wcd.coe.int/rsi/common/renderers/rend_standard.jsp?DocId=37031&SecMode=1&SiteName=cm&Lang=en (on 19.05.2008)
——, Declaration on human rights and the rule of law in the Information Society, 13.05.2005, retrieved from https://wcd.coe.int/ViewDoc.jsp?Ref=CM(2005)56&Sector=secCM&Language=lanEnglish&Ver=final&BackColorInternet=9999CC&BackColorIntranet=FFBB55&BackColorLogged=FFAC75 (on 19.05.2008)
——, Declaration on protecting the dignity, security and privacy of children using the Internet, 20.02.2008, retrieved from https://wcd.coe.int/ViewDoc.jsp?Ref=Decl(20.02.2008)&Language=lanEnglish&Ver=0001&BackColorInternet=9999CC&BackColorIntranet=FFBB55&BackColorLogged=FFAC75 (on 19.09.2008)

c. *Recommendations*

Council of Europe (Committee of Ministers), Recommendation Rec(91)11 concerning sexual exploitation, pornography, and prostitution of, and trafficking in children and young adults, 09.09.1991, retrieved from https://wcd.coe.int/com.instranet.InstraServlet?command=com.instranet.CmdBlobGet&InstranetImage=572467&SecMode=1&DocId=597998&Usage=2 (on 12.12.2008)
—— (Committee of Ministers), Recommendation Rec(97)19 on the portrayal of violence in the electronic media, 30.10.1997, retrieved from https://wcd.coe.int/com.instranet.InstraServlet?command=com.instranet.CmdBlobGet&InstranetImage=568198&SecMode=1&DocId=582650&Usage=2 on (12.12.2008)
—— (Committee of Ministers), Recommendation Rec(98)8 on children's participation in family and social life, 18.09.1998, retrieved from https://wcd.coe.int/com.instranet.InstraServlet?command=com.instranet.CmdBlobGet&InstranetImage=532375&SecMode=1&DocId=486272&Usage=2 (on 12.12.2008)
—— (Committee of Ministers), Recommendation Rec(99)5 for the protection of privacy on the Internet, 23.02.1999, retrieved from https://wcd.coe.int/com.instranet.InstraServlet?command=com.instranet.CmdBlobGet&InstranetImage=276580&SecMode=1&DocId=396826&Usage=2 (on 18.05.2009)
—— (Committee of Ministers), Recommendation Rec(2001)8 on self-regulation concerning cyber content (self-regulation and user protection against illegal or harmful content on new communications and information services), 05.09.2001, retrieved from https://wcd

.coe.int/ViewDoc.jsp?id=220387&Site=COE&BackColorInternet=DBDCF2&BackColorIntranet=FDC864&BackColorLogged=FDC864 (on 24.04.2007)

—— (Parliamentary Assembly), Rec(2002)1551 Building a twenty-first century society with and for children: follow-up to the European strategy for children (Recommendation 1286 (1996)), 26.03.2002, retrieved from http://assembly.coe.int/main.asp?Link=/documents/adoptedtext/ta02/erec1551.htm (on 01.06.2007)

—— (Standing committee on transfrontier television), Recommendation (04) 1 on the protection of minors from pornographic programmes, 11–12.10.2004, retrieved from http://www.coe.int/t/dghl/standardsetting/media/T-TT/T-TT(2004)011_en.asp#TopOfPage (on 24.04.2007)

—— (Committee of Ministers), Recommendation Rec(2006)12 on empowering children in the new information and communications environment, 27.09.2006, retrieved from https://wcd.coe.int/ViewDoc.jsp?id=1041181&Site=CM&BackColorInternet=9999CC&BackColorIntranet=FFBB55&BackColorLogged=FFAC75 (on 12.12.2008)

—— (Committee of Ministers), Recommendation Rec(2006)19 on policy to support positive parenting, 13.12.2006, retrieved from https://wcd.coe.int/ViewDoc.jsp?id=1073507&BackColorInternet=9999CC&BackColorIntranet=FFBB55&BackColorLogged=FFAC75 (on 12.12.2008)

—— (Ministers' Deputies), Draft recommendation Rec(2006)… to member states on policy to support positive parenting – Explanatory report, 27.11.2006, retrieved from https://wcd.coe.int/ViewDoc.jsp?id=1067853&BackColorInternet=9999CC&BackColorIntranet=FFBB55&BackColorLogged=FFAC75 (on 01.06.2007)

—— (Committee of Ministers), Recommendation CM/Rec(2007)11 on promoting freedom of expression and information in the new information and communications environment, 26.09.2007, retrieved from https://wcd.coe.int/ViewDoc.jsp?id=1188541&Site=COE&BackColorInternet=DBDCF2&BackColorIntranet=FDC864&BackColorLogged=FDC864 (on 26.03.2008)

—— (Committee of Ministers), Recommendation CM/Rec(2008)6 on measures to promote the respect for freedom of expression and information with regard to Internet filters, 26.03.2008, retrieved from https://wcd.coe.int/ViewDoc.jsp?Ref=CM/Rec(2008)6&Language=lanEnglish&Ver=original&BackColorInternet=9999CC&BackColorIntranet=FFBB55&BackColorLogged=FFAC75 (on 31.03.2008)

—— (Parliamentary Assembly), Recommendation 1855 (2009) The regulation of audiovisual media services, 27.01.2009, retrieved from http://assembly.coe.int/Main.asp?link=/Documents/AdoptedText/ta09/EREC1855.htm#1 (on 28.05.2009)

—— (Committee of Ministers), Recommendation CM/REC(2009)5 on measures to protect children against harmful content and behaviour and to promote their active participation in the new information and communications environment, 08.07.2009, retrieved from https://wcd.coe.int/ViewDoc.jsp?id=1470045&Site=CM (on 20.01.2010)

—— (Parliamentary Assembly), Recommendation 1882 (2009) The promotion of Internet and online media services appropriate for minors, 28 September 2009, retrieved from http://assembly.coe.int/Mainf.asp?link=/Documents/AdoptedText/ta09/EREC1882.htm (on 20 January 2010)

d. *Statements*

Council of Europe (Standing committee on transfrontier television), Statement (2002)1 on human dignity and the fundamental rights of others, 12–13.09.2002, retrieved from http://www.coe.int/t/dghl/standardsetting/media/T-TT/T-TT(2006)012rev_en.asp#TopOfPage (on 24.04.2007)

e. *Research reports*

COUNCIL OF EUROPE (MEDIA DIVISION, DIRECTORATE GENERAL OF HUMAN RIGHTS), Public service media in the information society – Report prepared for the Council of Europe's Group of Specialists on Public Service Broadcasting in the Information Society by Christian S. NISSEN, February 2006, retrieved from http://www.coe.int/t/dghl/standardsetting/media/Doc/H-Inf(2006)003_en.pdf (on 30.05.2006)

—— (GROUP OF SPECIALISTS ON HUMAN RIGHTS IN THE INFORMATION SOCIETY), Young people, well-being and risk on-line (abridged), Study by Rachel O'CONNELL and Jo BRYCE, 25.04.2006, retrieved from http://www.coe.int/t/dghl/standardsetting/media/doc/H-Inf(2006)005_en.pdf (on 30.05.2006)

f. *Other*

COUNCIL OF EUROPE, Democracy, human rights and the rule of law in the Information Society, Contribution by the Council of Europe to the 2nd Preparatory Committee for the World Summit on the Information Society, 07.12.2002, retrieved from http://www.coe.int/t/e/integrated_projects/democracy/02_activities/04_w.s.i.s/90IP1(2002)27.asp (on 24.04.2007)

COUNCIL OF EUROPE AND EUROPEAN UNION, European Forum: Internet with a human face – a common responsibility, Warsaw, 26–27.03.2004, http://www.coe.int/t/dghl/standardsetting/media/Doc/MM-S-OD(2004)003_en.asp#TopOfPage (on 25.04.2007)

COUNCIL OF EUROPE (STANDING COMMITTEE ON TRANSFRONTIER TELEVISION), Discussion document prepared by the Delegate of Poland on questions concerning the scope of the Convention, jurisdiction, freedom of conception and retransmission, the duties of the Parties of the Convention, advertising directed at a single Party and the abuse of rights granted by the Convention, 38th meeting, 31.03–01.04.2005, retrieved from http://www.coe.int/t/e/human_rights/media/2_transfrontier_television/texts_and_documents/2T-TT(2005)003_en.asp#TopOfPage (on 17.07.2007, no longer available)

—— (MINISTERS' DEPUTIES), Warsaw Summit Action Plan, CM(2005)80 final, Warsaw, 17.05.2005, retrieved from http://www.coe.int/t/dcr/summit/20050517_plan_action_en.asp (on 30.05.2006)

——, Pan-European forum on "Human rights in the Information Society: responsible behaviour by key actors", Strasbourg, 12–13.09.2005, retrieved from http://www.coe.int/t/dghl/standardsetting/media/doc/forumstbgsept2005_EN.asp (on 25.04.2007)

——, Pan-European forum on "Human rights in the Information Society: empowering children and young people", Yerevan, 5–6.10.2006, retrieved from http://www.coe.int/t/e/human_rights/media/links/events/1GalREPORT_Yerevan_FrauMeigs_en.pdf (on 25.04.2007, no longer available)

—— (DRAFTING GROUP ON THE REVISION OF THE EUROPEAN CONVENTION ON TRANSFRONTIER TELEVISION), Report, 29–30.03.2007, T-TT-GDR(2007)002, retrieved from http://www.coe.int/t/dghl/standardsetting/media/T-TT/T-TT-GDR(2007)002_en.asp#TopOfPage (on 17.07.2007)

—— (VENICE COMMISSION), Report on self-regulation within the media in the handling of complaints, CDL(2008)039, 07.04.2008, retrieved from http://www.venice.coe.int/docs/2008/CDL(2008)039-e.asp (on 19.05.2008)

——, Human rights guidelines for Internet Service Providers – Developed by the Council of Europe in co-operation with the European Internet Service Providers Association (EuroISPA), July 2008, retrieved from http://www.coe.int/t/dghl/standardsetting/media/Doc/H-Inf(2008)009_en.pdf (on 10.10.2008)

——, Human rights guidelines for online games providers – Developed by the Council of Europe in co-operation with the Interactive Software Federation of Europe, July 2008, retrieved from http://www.coe.int/t/dghl/standardsetting/media/Doc/H-Inf(2008)008_en.pdf (on 17.12.2008)

—— (Standing Committee on Transfrontier Television), Provisional agreement on the draft amendments to the ECTT, 43rd meeting, 12–14.11.2008, retrieved from http://www.coe.int/t/dghl/standardsetting/media/T-TT/T-TT(2008)003Prov_en.pdf (on 24.12.2008)

—— (Standing Committee on Transfrontier Television), Provisional agreement on the draft amendments to the ECTT, 25–27.02.2009, retrieved from http://www.coe.int/t/dghl/standardsetting/media/T-TT/T-TT(2008)003Rev_en%20Agreements%20on%20amendts%20ECTT%20(2).asp#TopOfPage (on 28.05.2009)

—— (Drafting group on the revision of the European Convention on Transfrontier Television), Draft explanatory report to the revised European Convention on Transfrontier Television updated following the consultation on 25–27 February 2009, 27.02.2009, retrieved from http://www.coe.int/t/dghl/standardsetting/media/T-TT/T-TT-GDR_2008_002Rev5_en%20Preliminary%20Draft%20Expl%20Rep%20ECTT.pdf (on 28.05.2009)

——, Building a Europe for and with children, Description, retrieved from http://www.coe.int/t/transversalprojects/children/BriefDescription/Default_en.asp (on 21.05.2007)

D. *Belgium*

a. *Legislation*

Wet van 20 januari 1999 ter bescherming van het mariene milieu in de zeegebieden onder de rechtsbevoegdheid van België [*Law of 20 January 1999 on the protection of the marine environment in the seas under the legal competence of Belgium*], *BS* 12.03.1999 [in Dutch]

Decreet van 5 april 1999 houdende algemene bepalingen inzake milieubeleid [*Decree of 5 April 1999 holding general provisions regarding environmental policy*], *BS* 03.06.1995 (amended repeatedly) [in Dutch]

Wet van 11 maart 2003 betreffende bepaalde juridische aspecten van de diensten van de informatiemaatschappij [*Act of 11 March 2003 with regard to certain legal aspects of services of the information society*], *BS* 17.03.2003 [in Dutch]

b. *Preparatory documents*

Belgische Senaat, Herziening van titel II van de Grondwet, om nieuwe bepalingen in te voegen die de bescherming van de rechten van het kind op morele, lichamelijke, geestelijke en seksuele integriteit verzekeren [*Review of Title II of the Constitution, to insert new provisions which guarantee the protection of the rights of the child to moral, physical psychological and sexual integrity*], Proposal by Mrs. Nathalie de T'Serclaes, 2–21/1, 16.07.1999, retrieved from http://www.senate.be/www/?MIval=/publications/viewPub.html&COLL=S&LEG=2&NR=21&VOLGNR=1&LANG=nl (on 02.10.2006) [in Dutch]

——, Herziening van titel II van de Grondwet, om nieuwe bepalingen in te voegen die de bescherming van de rechten van het kind op morele, lichamelijke, geestelijke en seksuele integriteit verzekeren [*Review of Title II of the Constitution, to insert new provisions which guarantee the protection of the rights of the child to moral, physical psychological and sexual integrity*], Report by Mrs. Taelman, 2–21/4, 13.01.2000, retrieved from http://www.senate.be/www/?MIval=/publications/viewPub.html&COLL=S&LEG=2&NR=21&VOLGNR=4&LANG=nl (on 02.10.2006) [in Dutch]

c. *Documents Commission for privacy protection*

Commissie voor de bescherming van de persoonlijke levenssfeer [*Commission for privacy protection*], Advies uit eigen beweging betreffende de bescherming van de persoonlijke levenssfeer van minderjarigen op het Internet [*Recommendation on the protection of privacy of minors on the Internet*], 16.09.2002, retrieved from http://www.internet-observatory.be/internet_observatory/pdf/advice_privacy_nl.pdf (on 14.10.2008) [in Dutch]

——, Advies met betrekking tot het ontwerp van koninklijk besluit betreffende het elektronisch identiteitsdocument voor Belgische kinderen onder de twaalf jaar [*Recommendation regarding the proposal for Royal Decree with respect to the electronic identity document for Belgian children under the age of twelve*], 06.09.2006, retrieved from http://www.privacycommission.be/nl/docs/Commission/2006/advies_33_2006.pdf (on 02.10.2006) [in Dutch]

E. *United Kingdom*

a. *Acts*

Obscene Publications Act 1959, c.66 7_and_8_Eliz_2, retrieved from http://www.statutelaw.gov.uk/content.aspx?activeTextDocId=1128038 (on 05.01.2009)

Obscene Publications Act 1964, c.74 retrieved from http://www.statutelaw.gov.uk/content.aspx?activeTextDocId=1169641 (on 05.01.2009)

b. *Codes*

Ofcom, Guidance notes Broadcasting Code section 1: Protecting the under18s, 2007, retrieved from http://www.ofcom.org.uk/tv/ifi/guidance/bguidance/guidance1.pdf (on 19.10.2008)

——, Broadcasting Code, October 2008, retrieved from http://www.ofcom.org.uk/tv/ifi/codes/bcode/bcode.pdf (on 19.10.2008)

F. *Germany*

Jugendschutzgesetz [*Protection of young persons Act*], vom 23. Juli 2002 (BGBl. I S 2730 ff., 2003 I S. 476), retrieved from http://www.kjm-online.de/public/kjm/downloads/juschg%20081128.pdf (on 05.01.2009) [in German]

Jugendmedienschutz-Staatsvertrag [*Interstate Treaty on the protection of minors*], vom 10. bis 27.9.2002 (GBl. S. 93), zuletzt geändert durch Artikel 4 des Zehnten Staatsvertrages zur Änderung rundfunkrechtlicher Staatsverträge vom 19.12.2007 (GBI. S. 249), retrieved from http://www.kjm-online.de/public/kjm/downloads/2051_(2008)_2_jmstv_080901.pdf (on 05.01.2009) [in German]

G. *France*

Charte de l'environnement [*Charter of the environment*], 2004, retrieved from http://www.conseil-constitutionnel.fr/conseil-constitutionnel/francais/la-constitution/la-constitution-du-4-octobre-1958/charte-de-l-environnement-de-2004.5078.html547(on 11.03.2008) [in French]

Constitution [*French constitution*], 04.10.1958, retrieved from http://www.conseil-constitutionnel.fr/conseil-constitutionnel/francais/la-constitution/la-constitution-du-4-octobre-1958/texte-integral-de-la-constitution-de-1958.5074.html (on 11.03.2008) [in French]

Loi n° 86-1067 du 30 septembre 1986 relative à la liberté de communication [*Act regarding the freedom of communication*], J.O.R.F. 01.10.1986, retrieved from http://www.legifrance.gouv.fr/affichTexte.do?cidTexte=LEGITEXT000006068930&dateTexte=20090105 (on 05.01.2009) [in French]

H. *United States*

a. *Acts*

Communications Decency Act, Pub. L. No. 104–104, 110 Stat. 133
Child Online Protection Act, Pub. L. No. 105–227, 112 Stat. 2681–736
Children's Online Privacy Protection Act, Pub. L. No. 105–277, 112 Stat. 2681–728
Children's Internet Protection Act, Pub. L. No. 106–554, 114 Stat. 2763, 2763A-336
Broadcast Decency Enforcement Act, Pub. L. No. 109–235, 120 Stat. 491

b. *Bills*

Safeguarding America's Families by Enhancing and Reorganizing New and Efficient Technologies Act of 2007 (the *SAFER NET Act*), H.R. 1008, 110th Congress, retrieved from http://thomas.loc.gov/cgi-bin/query/D?c110:1:./temp/~c110Pufhnj:: (on 19.12.2008)

c. *Miscellaneous*

Administrative Conference of the United States, The use of audited self-regulation as a regulatory technique, Recommendation 94–1, 30.08.1994, retrieved from http://www.law.fsu.edu/library/admin/acus/305941.html (on 02.06.2008)
Inter-American Commission on Human Rights, American Convention on Human Rights, 22.11.1969, retrieved from http://www.cidh.oas.org/Basicos/English/Basic4.Amer.Conv.Ratif.htm (on 12.06.2007)
The White House, A framework for global electronic commerce, 01.07.1997, retrieved from http://www.technology.gov/digeconomy/framewrk.htm (on 26.05.2008, no longer available)
US Copyright Office, The Digital Millennium Copyright Act of 1998: summary, December 1998, retrieved from http://www.copyright.gov/legislation/dmca.pdf (on 26.05.2009)

I. *Australia*

Australian government, Review of the Operation of Schedule 5 to the Broadcasting Services Act 1992 – Report, 13.05.2004, retrieved from http://www.dcita.gov.au/__data/assets/pdf_file/10920/118872.pdf (on 28.07.2006, no longer available)
Broadcasting Services Amendment (Online Services) Act, No. 90, 1999, retrieved from http://www.comlaw.gov.au/comlaw/Legislation/Act1.nsf/0/6e2d62f72aacb92bca256f710082447e?OpenDocument&VIEWCAT=amending&COUNT=999&START=1 (on 05.01.2009)

2. Case law

A. *European Court of Justice*

EU case-law can be retrieved from the ECJ database: http://curia.europa.eu/en/content/juris/index.htm

ECJ, Commission of the European Communities v. Italian Republic, C-7/68, 10.12.1968
——, Franz Völk v. S.P.R.L. Ets J. Vervaecke, C-5/69, 09.07.1969
——, Commission of the European Communities v. Kingdom of Belgium, C-77/69, 05.05.1970
——, Imperial Chemical Industries Ltd. v. Commission of the European Communities, C- 48/69, 14.07.1972
——, Riseria Luigi Geddo v. Ente Nazionale Risi, C-2/73, 12.07.1973
——, Giuseppe Sacchi (Reference for a preliminary ruling: Tribunale civile e penale di Biella – Italy), C-155/73, 30.04.1974
——, Procureur du Roi v. Benoît and Gustave Dassonville, C-8/74, 11.07.1974
——, B.N.O. Walrave and L.J.N. Koch v. Association Union cycliste internationale, Koninklijke Nederlandsche Wielren Unie and Federación Española Ciclismo, C-36/74, 12.12.1974
——, Coöperatieve Vereniging 'Suiker Unie' UA and others v. Commission of the European Communities, Joined cases 40–48, 50, 54–56, 111, 113, 114/73, 16.12.1975
——, Jean Noël Royer (Reference for a preliminary ruling: Tribunal de première instance de Liège - Belgium), C-48/75, 08.04.1976
——, Rewe-Zentralfinanz eG and Rewe-Zentral AG v. Landwirtschaftskammer für das Saarland, C-33/76, 16.12.1976
——, W.J.G. Bauhuis v. The Netherlands State, C-46/76, 25.01.1977
——, Iannelli & Volpi SpA v. Ditta Paolo Meroni, C-74/76, 22.03.1977
——, SA G.B.-INNO-B.M. v. Association des détaillants en tabac (ATAB), C-13/77, 16.11.1977
——, Hoffmann-La Roche & Co. AG v. Commission of the European Communities, C-85/76, 13.02.1979
——, Rewe-Zentral AG v. Bundesmonopolverwaltung für Branntwein, C-120/78, 20.02.1979
——, Regina v. Maurice Donald Henn and John Frederick Ernest Darby, C-34/79, 14.12.1979
——, Procureur du Roi v. Marc J.V.C. Debauve and others, C-52/79, 18.03.1980
——, Heintz van Landewyck SARL and others v. Commission of the European Communities, C-209 to 215 and 218/78, 29.10.1980
——, Commission of the European Communities v. Ireland, C-113/80, 17.06.1981
——, Ursula Becker v. Finanzamt Münster-Innenstadt, C-8/81, 19.01.1982
——, Commission of the European Communities v. Kingdom of the Netherlands, C-96/81, 25.05.1982
——, Commission of the European Communities v. Italian Republic, C-95/81, 09.06.1982
——, NV IAZ International Belgium and others v. Commission of the European Communities, Joined cases 96–102, 104, 105, 108 and 110/82, 08.11.1983
——, NV Nederlandsche Banden Industrie Michelin v. Commission of the European Communities, C-322/81, 09.11.1983
——, Apple and Pear Development Council v. K.J. Lewis Ltd and others, C-222/82, 13.12.1983
——, Sabine von Colson and Elisabeth Kamann v. Land Nordrhein-Westfalen, C-14/83, 10.04.1984
——, Eberhard Haug-Adrion v. Frankfurter Versicherungs-AG, C-251/83, 13.12.1984
——, Commission of the European Communities v. Federal Republic of Germany, C-29/84, 23.05.1985
——, M.H. Marshall v. Southampton and South-West Hampshire Area Health Authority (Teaching), C-152/84, 26.02.1986
——, Marguerite Johnston v. Chief Constable of the Royal Ulster Constabulary, C-222/84, 15.05.1986

——, Commission v. Italy, C-363/85, 09.04.1987
——, Roquette Frères SA v. Office national interprofessionnel des céréales (ONIC), C-47/86, 30.06.1987
——, Commission of the European Communities v. Kingdom of Belgium, C-247/85, 08.07.1987
——, ASBL Vereniging van Vlaamse Reisbureaus v. ASBL Sociale Dienst van de Plaatselijke en Gewestelijke Overheidsdiensten, C-311/85, 01.10.1987
——, Bond van Adverteerders and others v. The Netherlands State, C-352/85, 26.04.1988
——, Pascal Van Eycke v. ASPA NV, C-267/86, 21.09.1988
——, Bayer AG and Maschinenfabrik Hennecke GmbH v. Heinz Süllhöfer, C-65/86, 27.09.1988
——, The Queen v. Royal Pharmaceutical Society of Great Britain, ex parte Association of Pharmaceutical Importers and others, C-266 and 267/87, 18.05.1989
——, Commission of the European Communities v. Hellenic Republic, C-68/88, 21.09.1989
——, Sandoz prodotti farmaceutici SpA v. Commission of the European Communities, C-277/87, 11.01.1990
——, Commission of the European Communities v. Kingdom of the Netherlands, C-339/87, 15.03.1990
——, A. Foster and others v. British Gas plc., C-188/89, 12.07.1990
——, The Queen v. Minister of Agriculture, Fisheries and Food and Secretary of State for Health, ex parte: Fedesa and others, C-331/88, 13.11.1990
——, Commission of the European Communities v. Federal Republic of Germany, C-131/88, 28.02.1991
——, Klaus Höfner and Fritz Elser v. Macrotron GmbH, C-41/90, 23.04.1991
——, Commission of the European Communities v. Federal Republic of Germany, C-361/88, 30.05.1991
——, Commission of the European Community v. Federal Republic of Germany, C-59/89, 30.05.1991
——, Elliniki Radiophonia Tiléorassi AE and Panellinia Omospondia Syllogon Prossopikou v. Dimotiki Etairia Pliroforissis and Sotirios Kouvelas and Nicolaos Avdellas and others, C-260/89, 18.06.1991
——, Aragonesa de Publicidad Exterior SA and Publivía SAE v. Departamento de Sanidad y Seguridad Social de la Generalitat de Cataluña, C-1/90, 25.07.1991
——, Theresa Emmot v. Minister for Social Welfare and Attorney General, C-208/90, 25.07.1991
——, Manfred Säger v. Dennemeyer & Co. Ltd, C-76/90, 25.07.1991
——, Andrea Francovich and Danila Bonifaci and others v. Italian Republic, C-6/90 and C-9/90, 19.11.1991
——, Criminal proceedings against Wolf W. Meng (Reference for a preliminary ruling: Kammergericht Berlin - Germany), C-2/91, 17.11.1993
——, Bundesanstalt für den Güterfernverkehr v. Gebrüder Reiff GmbH & Co. KG, C-185/91, 17.11.1993
——, Criminal proceedings against Bernard Keck and Daniel Mithouard (References for a preliminary ruling: Tribunal de grande instance de Strasbourg - France), cases C-267/91 and C-268/91, 24.11.1993
——, Paola Faccini Dori v. Recreb Srl, C-91/92, 14.07.1994
——, Commission of the European Communities v. French Republic, C-255/93, 05.10.1994
——, Commission of the European Communities v. Grand Duchy of Luxemburg, C-220/94, 15.06.1995

——, DIP SpA v. Comune di Bassano del Grappa, LIDL Italia Srl v. Comune di Chioggia and Lingral Srl v. Comune di Chiogga, Joined cases C-140–142/94, 17.10.1995
——, Union royale belge des sociétés de football association ASBL v. Jean-Marc Bosman, Royal club liégeois SA v. Jean-Marc Bosman and others and Union des associations européennes de football (UEFA) v. Jean-Marc Bosman, C-415/93, 15.12.1995
——, Commission of the European Communities v. Kingdom of Belgium, C-11/95, 10.09.1996
——, Commission of the European Communities v. Hellenic Republic, C-236/95, 19.09.1996
——, Commission of the European Communities v. Grand Duchy of Luxemburg, C-221/94, 07.11.1996
——, Diego Calì & Figli Srl v. Servizi ecologici porto di Genova SpA (SEPG), C-343/95, 18.03.1997
——, Konsumentombudsmannen (KO) v. De Agostini (Svenska) Förlag AB (C-34/95) and TV-Shop i Sverige AB (C-35/95 and C-36/95), C-34–35–36/95, 09.07.1997
——, Commission of the European Communities v. French Republic, C-159/94, 23.10.1997
——, Commission of the European Communities and French Republic v. Ladbroke Racing Ltd, Joined cases C-359/95 P and C-379/95 P, 11.11.1997
——, Commission of the European Communities v. French Republic, C-265/95, 09.12.1997
——, Jessica Safir v. Skattemyndigheten i Dalarnas Län, formerly Skattemyndigheten i Kopparbergs Län, C-118/96, 28.04.1998
——, Raymond Kohll v. Union des caisses de maladie, C-158/96, 28.04.1998
——, Commission of the European Communities v. Italian Republic, C-35/96, 18.06.1998
——, Commission v. France, C-225/97, 19.05.1999
——, Criminal proceedings against Maria Amélia Nunes and Evangelina de Matos ((Reference for a preliminary ruling: Tribunal de Círculo do Porto - Portugal), C-186/98, 08.07.1999
——, Commission of the European Communities v. Anic Partecipazioni SpA, C-49/92, 08.07.1999
——, Commission of the European Communities v. Federal Republic of Germany, C-184/97, 11.11.1999
——, Christelle Deliège v. Ligue francophone de judo et disciplines associées ASBL, Ligue belge de judo ASBL, Union européenne de judo (C-51/96) and François Pacquée (C-191/97), C-51/96 and C-191/97, 11.04.2000
——, Jyri Lehtonen, Castors Canada Dry Namur-Braine ASBL v. Fédération Royale Belge des Sociétés de Basket-ball ASBL (FRBSB), C-176/96, 13.04.2000
——, Roman Angonese v. Cassa di Risparmio di Bolzano SpA, C-281/98, 06.06.2000
——, Pavel Pavlov and others v. Stichting Pensioenfonds Medische Specialisten, Joined Cases C-180–184/98, 12.09.2000
——, Commission of the European Communities v. Kingdom of the Netherlands, C-144/99, 10.05.2001
——, Commission v. Italy, C-159/99, 17.05.2001
——, J.C.J. Wouters, J.W. Savelbergh, Price Waterhouse Belastingadviseurs BV v. Algemene Raad van de Nederlandse Orde van Advocaten, C-309/99, 19.02.2002
——, Criminal proceedings against Manuele Arduino (Reference for a preliminary ruling: Pretore di Pinerolo - Italy), C-35/99, 19.02.2002
——, Criminal proceedings against Manuele Arduino (Reference for a preliminary ruling: Pretore di Pinerolo - Italy), C-35/99, Opinion Advocate General Léger, 10.07.2001
——, Commission of the European Communities v. Kingdom of Sweden, C-478/99, 07.05.2002
——, Commission of the European Communities v. French Republic, C-233/00, 26.06.2003

——, Bodil Lindqvist v. Sweden, C-101/01, 06.11.2003
——, Commission of the European Communities v. French Republic, C-296/01, 20.11.2003
——, Commission of the European Communities v. Republic of Austria, C-194/01, 29.04.2004
——, Omega Spielhallen- und Automatenaufstellungs-GmbH v. Oberbürgermeisterin der Bundesstadt Bonn, C-36/02, 14.10.2004
——, Mediakabel BV v. Commissariaat voor de Media, C-89/04, 02.06.2005
——, Parliament v. Council, C-540/03, 27.06.2006
——, David Meca-Medina and Igor Majcen v. Commission of the European Communities, C-519/04, 18.07.2006
——, British Airways plc v. the Commission of the European Communities, C-95/04, 15.03.2007
——, International Transport Workers' Federation, Finnish Seamen's Union v. Viking Line ABP, OÜ Viking Line Eesti, C-438/05, 11.12.2007
——, Promusicae v. Telefónica de España SAU, C-275/06, 29.01.2008
——, Dynamic Medien v. Avides Media AG, C-244/06, 14.02.2008

B. *European Court of First Instance*

EU case-law can be retrieved from the ECJ database: http://curia.europa.eu/en/content/juris/index.htm

CFI, Stichting Certificatie Kraanverhuurbedrijf (SCK) and Federatie van Nederlandse Kraanbedrijven (FNK) v. Commission of the European Communities, T-213/95 and T-18/96, 22.10.1997
——, European Night Services Ltd (ENS), Eurostar (UK) Ltd, formerly European Passenger Services Ltd (EPS), Union internationale des chemins de fer (UIC), NV Nederlandse Spoorwegen (NS) and Société nationale des chemins de fer français (SNCF) v. Commission of the European Communities, Joined cases T-374, 375, 384 and 388/94, 15.09.1998
——, Bayer AG v. Commission of the European Communities, T-41/96, 26.10.2000
——, Institute of Professional Representatives before the European Patent Office v. Commission of the European Communities, T-144/99, 28.03.2001
——, Artegodan GmbH v. Commission, Joined Cases T-74/00, 76/00, 83/00, 84/00, 85/00, 132/00, 137/00 and 141/00, 26.11.2002
——, Atlantic Container Line AB et al. v. Commission of the European Communities, Joined Cases T-191/98 and T-212–214/98, 30.09.2003

C. *European Court of Human Rights*

CoE case-law can be retrieved from the Hudoc database: http://cmiskp.echr.coe.int/tkp197/search.asp?skin=hudoc-en

European Commission of Human Rights, Kühnen v. Germany, 12.05.1988
European Court of Human Rights, Golder v. the United Kingdom, 21.02.1975
——, Handyside v. the United Kingdom, 07.12.1976
——, König v. Germany, 28.06.1978
——, Klass and others v. Germany, 06.09.1978
——, Sunday Times v. the United Kingdom, 26.04.1979
——, Le Compte, Van Leuven and De Meyere v. Belgium, 23.06.1981
——, Silver and others v. the United Kingdom, 25.03.1983

——, Campbell and Fell v. the United Kingdom, 28.06.1984
——, Sramek v. Austria, 22.10.1984
——, Barthold v. Germany, 25.03.1985
——, X. and Y. v. the Netherlands, 26.03.1985
——, Benthem v. the Netherlands, 23.10.1985
——, Van Marle and others v. the Netherlands, 26.06.1986
——, Boyle and Rice v. the United Kingdom, 27.04.1988
——, Plattform Ärtze für das Leben v. Austria, 21.06.1988
——, Nielsen v. Denmark, 28.11.1988
——, Håkansson and Sturesson v. Sweden, 21.02.1990
——, Groppera Radio AG and others v. Switzerland, 28.03.1990
——, Autronic AG v. Switzerland, 22.05.1990
——, Philis v. Greece, 27.08.1991
——, Observer and Guardian v. the United Kingdom, 26.11.1991
——, Margareta and Roger Andersson v. Sweden, 25.02.1992
——, De Geouffre de la Pradelle v. France, 16.12.1992
——, Kraska v. Switzerland, 19.04.1993
——, Casado Coca v. Spain, 24.02.1994
——, Keegan v. Ireland, 26.05.1994
——, Pfarrmeier v. Austria, 23.10.1995
——, Goodwin v. the United Kingdom, 27.03.1996
——, Aksoy v. Turkey, 18.12.1996
——, A v. the United Kingdom, 23.09.1998
——, Pélissier and Sassi v. France, 25.03.1999
——, T. and V. v. the United Kingdom, 16.12.1999
——, Fuentes Bobo v. Spain, 29.02.2000
——, Özgür Gündem v. Turkey, 16.03.2000
——, Kudla v. Poland, 26.10.2000
——, Cyprus v. Turkey, 10.05.2001
——, VGT Verein gegen Tierfabriken v. Switzerland, 28.06.2001
——, Peck v. the United Kingdom, 28.01.2003
——, Perna v. Italy, 06.05.2003
——, Appleby and others v. the United Kingdom, 06.05.2003
——, Garaudy v. France, 24.06.2003
——, Murphy v. Ireland, 10.07.2003
——, Steur v. the Netherlands, 28.10.2003
——, Krasuski v. Poland, 14.06.2005
——, Perrin v. the United Kingdom, 18.10.2005
——, Veraart v. the Netherlands, 30.11.2006
——, Glas Nadezhda and Elenkov v. Bulgaria, 11.10.2007
——, Meltex Ltd and Mesrop Movsesyan v. Armenia, 17.06.2008
——, K.U. v. Finland, 02.12.2008

D. *US*

a. *Supreme Court*

Ashcroft v. ACLU, 535 U.S. 564 (2002)
Ashcroft v. American Civil Liberties Union, 542 U.S. 656 (2004)

Bolger v. Young Drugs Products Corp., 463 U.S. 60 (1983)
Denver Area Ed. Telecommunications Consortium, Inc. v. FCC, 518 U.S. 727 (1996)
Ginsberg v. New York, 390 U.S. 629 (1968)
Miller v. California, 413 U.S. 15 (1973)
Reno v. American Civil Liberties Union, 521 U.S. 844 (1997)
Sable Communications v. FCC, 492 U.S. 115 (1989)
United States v. Playboy Entertainment Group, Inc., 529 U.S. 803 (2000)
United States et al. v. American Library Association Inc. et al., 539 U.S. 194 (2003)

b. *Federal & District Courts*

ACLU v. Reno, 31 F. Supp. 2d 473 (E.D. Pa.1999)
ACLU v. Reno, 217 F.3d 162 (3d. Cir. 2000)
ACLU v. Ashcroft, 322 F.3d 240 (C.A.3 Pa. 2003)
American Civil Liberties Union v. Gonzales, 478 F.Supp.2d 775 (E.D. Pa. 2007)
American Civil Liberties Union v. Mukasey, 534 F.3d 181 (C.A.3 Pa. 2008)
American Library Association Inc. et al. v. United States et al., 201 F.Supp.2d 401 (E.D. Pa. 2002)
Center For Democracy & Technology v. Pappert, 337 F.Supp.2d 606 (E.D. Pa. 2004)

3. Doctrine

A. *Books*

Anderson, Craig A., Gentile, Douglas A. and Buckley, Katherine E., *Violent video game effects on children en adolescents: theory, research and public policy*, Oxford, Oxford University Press, 2007, 190 p.
Arnull, Anthony et al., *Wyatt and Dashwood's European Union law*, London, Sweet & Maxwell, 2006, 1224 p.
Ayres, Ian and Braithwaite, John, *Responsive regulation: Transcending the deregulation debate*, Oxford, Oxford University Press, 1992, 205 p.
Bainham, Andrew, *Children – the modern law*, Bristol, Family Law, 2005, 811 p.
Baldwin, Robert, Scott, Colin and Hood, Christopher (eds), *A reader on regulation*, Oxford, Oxford University Press, 1998, 522 p.
Barendt, Eric, *Freedom of speech*, Oxford, Oxford University Press, 2005, 526 p.
Barkhuysen, Tom, *Artikel 13 EVRM: effectieve nationale rechtsbescherming bij schending van mensenrechten* [*Article 13 ECHR: effective domestic legal protection against human rights violations*], Lelystad, Uitgeverij Koninklijke Vermande, 1998, 324 p. [in Dutch]
Black, Julia, *Rules and regulators*, Oxford, Clarendon Press Oxford, 1997, 285 p.
Boddewyn, Jean, *Advertising self-regulation and outside participation: a multinational comparison*, New York, Quorum Books, 1988, 384 p.
Braithwaite, John, *Restorative justice and responsive regulation*, Oxford, Oxford University Press, 2002, 314 p.
Brent, Richard, *Directives: rights and remedies in English and Community law*, London, LLP, 2001, 330 p.
Brownsword, Roger and Yeung, Karen (eds), *Regulating technologies: legal futures, regulatory frames and technological fixes*, Oxford, Hart Publishing, 2008, 396 p.

CARLSSON, Ulla (ed.), *Regulation, awareness, empowerment. Young people and harmful media content in the digital age*, Göteborg, The International Clearinghouse on Children, Youth and Media, 2006, 286 p.

CASTENDYK, Oliver, DOMMERING, Egbert J. and SCHEUER, Alexander (eds), *European media law*, Alphen a/d Rijn, Kluwer Law International, 2008, 1379 p.

COUNCIL OF EUROPE, *Freedom of expression in Europe: case-law concerning article 10 of the European Convention on Human Rights*, Strasbourg, Council of Europe Publishing, 2007, 110 p.

CRAIG, Paul and DE BÚRCA, Gráinne, *EU law: Text, cases, and materials*, Oxford University Press, Oxford, 2007, 1148 p.

CRITCHER, Cras, *Critical Readings: Moral panics and the media*, Maidenhead, Open University Press, 2006, 329 p.

DEIBERT, Ronald, PALFREY, John, ROHOZINSKI, Rafal, and ZITTRAIN, Jonathan (eds), *Access denied: the practice and policy of global Internet filtering*, Cambridge, MIT Press, 2008, 449 p.

DETRICK, Sharon, *A commentary on the United Nations Convention on the Rights of the Child*, The Hague, Martinus Nijhoff Publishers, 1999, 790 p.

DOMMERING, Egbert and ASSCHER, Lodewijk (eds), *Coding regulation: essays on the normative role of information technology*, The Hague, TMC Asser Press, 301 p.

EKKER, Anton, *Anoniem communiceren: van drukpers tot weblog* [*Communicating anonymously: from printing press to weblog*], Den Haag, Sdu Uitgevers, 2006, 286 p. [in Dutch]

EMILIOU, Nicholas, *The principle of proportionality in European law: a comparative study*, London, Kluwer Law International, 1996, 288 p.

FELDMAN, Tony, *An introduction to digital media*, London, Routledge, 1997, 173 p.

GOLDBERG, David, PROSSER, Tony and VERHULST, Stefaan (eds), *Regulating the changing media: A comparative study*, Oxford, Oxford University Press, 1998, 321 p.

GRABOSKY, Peter and BRAITHWAITE, John, *Of manners gentle: enforcement strategies of Australian business regulatory agencies*, Melbourne, Oxford University Press, 1986, 260 p.

HAMILTON, James T., *Television violence and public policy*, Ann Arbor, The University of Michigan Press, 1998, 394 p.

HARRIS, David, O'BOYLE, Michael, WARBRICK, Colin, BATES, Ed et al. (eds), *Harris, O'Boyle and Warbrick Law of the European Convention on human rights*, Oxford, Oxford University Press, 2009, 902 p.

HODGKIN, Rachel and NEWELL, Peter, *Implementation handbook for the Convention on the Rights of the Child*, New York, Unicef, 2002, 762 p.

HOFFMANN-RIEM, Wolfgang, *Regulating media: the licensing and supervision of broadcasting in six countries*, New York, The Guilford Press, 1996, 424 p.

HOLOUBEK, Michael (ed.), *Regulating content – European regulatory framework for the media and related creative sectors*, Alphen a/d Rijn, Kluwer Law International, 2007, 273 p.

JOSEPH, Sarah, SCHULTZ, Jenny and CASTAN, Melissa, *The International Covenant on Civil and Political Rights – Cases, materials and commentary*, Oxford, Oxford University Press, 2004, 985 p.

KAPTEYN, Paul and VERLOREN VAN THEMAAT, Pieter, *Introduction to the law of the European Communities – From Maastricht to Amsterdam*, London, Kluwer Law International, 1998, 1447 p.

KILKELLY, Ursula, *The right to respect for private and family life – A guide to the implementation of Article 8 of the European Convention on Human Rights (Human Rights Handbook, no. 1)*, Strasbourg, Council of Europe, 2001, 66 p.

KIRSCH, Steven J., *Children, adolescents and media violence: A critical look at the research*, Thousand Oaks CA, Sage Publications, 2006, 409 p.

Kuijer, Martin, *The blindfold of Lady Justice: Judicial independence and impartiality in light of the requirements of article 6 ECHR*, Leiden, E.M. Meijers Instituut, 2004, 497 p.
Lenaerts, Koen, Van Nuffel, Piet and Bray, Robert (ed.), *Constitutional law of the European Union*, London, Sweet & Maxwell Limited, 2005, 969 p.
Lenaerts, Koen and Van Nuffel, Piet, *Europees recht in hoofdlijnen* [*Outline of European law*], Antwerpen, Maklu, 2008, 591 p. [in Dutch]
Lessig, Lawrence, *Code and other laws of cyberspace*, New York, Basic Books, 1999, 297 p.
—, *Code version 2.0*, New York, Basic Books, 2006, retrieved from http://pdf.codev2.cc/Lessig-Codev2.pdf (on 09.06.2008)
Liebert, Robert M. and Sprafkin, Joyce, *The early window: effects of television on children and youth*, Oxford, Pergamon, 1988, 306 p.
Livingstone, Sonia, *Children and the Internet*, Cambridge, Polity, 2009, 272 p.
Livingstone, Sonia and Haddon, Leslie (eds), *Kids Online: Opportunities and risks for children*, Bristol, The Policy Press, 2009, 296 p.
Loughlin, Martin, *Public law and political theory*, Oxford, Oxford University Press, 1992, 304 p.
Macovei, Monica, *Freedom of expression – A guide to the implementation of Article 10 of the European Convention of Human Rights (Human rights handbooks, No. 2)*, Strasbourg, Council of Europe, 2004, 64 p.
Meuwese, Stan, Blaak, Mirjam and Kaandorp, Majorie (eds), *Handboek Internationaal Jeugdrecht* [*International Youth Law Handbook*], Nijmegen, Ars Aequi Libri, 2005, 693 p. [in Dutch]
Mifsud Bonnici, Jeanne, *Self-regulation in cyberspace*, Malta, 2007, 277 p.
Millwood Hargrave, Andrea and Livingstone, Sonia, *Harm and offence in media content: a review of the evidence*, Bristol, Intellect, 2006, 256 p.
—, Harm and offence in media content: a review of the evidence (abbreviated version of the book), retrieved from http://www.lse.ac.uk/collections/media@lse/pdf/Harm%20and%20Offence,%20summary.pdf (on 11.03.2008)
Mole, Nuala and Harby, Catharina, *The right to a fair trial: a guide to the implementation of Article 6 of the European Convention on Human Rights (Human rights handbooks, No. 3)*, Strasbourg, Council of Europe, 2006, 72 p.
Möller, Christian and Amouroux, Arnaud (eds), *The media freedom Internet cookbook*, Vienna, OSCE, 2004, 274 p.
Nicoll, Chris, Prins, Corien and van Dellen, Miriam (eds), *Digital anonymity and the law: tensions and dimensions*, Den Haag, TMC Asser Press, 2003, 307 p.
Nikolinakos, Nikos, *EU competition law and regulation in the converging telecommunications, media and IT Sectors*, Alphen a/d Rijn, Kluwer Law International, 2006, 698 p.
Nikoltchev, Susanne (ed.), *Audiovisual Media Services without Frontiers: Implementing the rules*, IRIS Special, Strasbourg, European Audiovisual Observatory, 2006, 76 p.
—, *Searching for audiovisual content*, IRIS Special, Strasbourg, European Audiovisual Observatory, 2008, 90 p.
Nonet, Philippe and Selznick, Philip, *Law and society in transition: toward responsive law*, New York, Harper Colophon Books, 1978, 122 p.
Nowak, Manfred, *U.N. Covenant on Civil and Political Rights – CCPR Commentary*, Kehl, N.P. Engel, 2005, 1277 p.
Oliver, Peter, *Free movement of goods in the European Community under articles 28 to 30 of the EC Treaty*, London, Sweet and Maxwell, 2003, 570 p.
Ovey, Clare and White, Robin, *Jacobs and White The European Convention on Human Rights*, Oxford, Oxford University Press, 2006, 656 p.

PRECHAL, Sacha, *Directives in EC law*, Oxford, Oxford University Press, 2005, 349 p.
PRICE, Monroe (ed.), *The V-chip debate: content filtering from television to the internet*, Mahwah, Lawrence Erlbaum Associates, 1998, 363 p.
PRICE, Monroe and VERHULST, Stefaan, *Parental control of television broadcasting*, Mahwah, Erlbaum, 2002, 314 p.
RENUCCI, Jean-François, *Introduction to the European Convention on Human Rights – The rights guaranteed and the protection mechanism*, Strasbourg, Council of Europe Publishing, 2005, 127 p.
ROTH, Peter and ROSE, Vivien (eds), *Bellamy & Child European Community law of competition*, Oxford, Oxford University Press, 2008, 1679 p.
RUXTON, Sandy, *What about us? Children's rights in the European Union? Next Steps*, Brussels, The European Children's Network, 2005, 162 p.
SEPÚLVEDA, Magdalena, *The nature of the obligations under the International Covenant on Economic, Social and Cultural Rights*, Antwerpen, Intersentia, 2003, 477 p.
SINGER, Dorothy G. and SINGER, Jerome, L., *Handbook of children and the media*, Thousand Oaks, Sage Publications, 2001, 765 p.
SNELL, Jukka, *Goods and services in EC Law – A study of the relationship between the freedoms*, Oxford, Oxford University Press, 2002, 251 p.
SPARKS, Glenn G., *Media effects research: a basic overview*, London, Thomson, 2006, 250 p.
STEINER, Josephine, WOODS, Lorna and TWIGG-FLESNER, Christian, *EU law*, Oxford, Oxford University Press, 695 p.
STRASBURGER, Victor C. and WILSON, Barbara J., *Children, adolescents & the media*, Thousand Oaks, Sage Publications, 2002, 539 p.
TAMBINI, Damien, LEONARDI, Danilo and MARSDEN, Chris, *Codifying cyberspace: communications self-regulation in the age of Internet convergence*, London, Routledge, 2008, 323 p.
TEUBNER, Gunther (ed.), *Autopoietic law: a new approach to law and society*, Berlin, Walter de Gruyter, 1988, 380 p.
TEUBNER, Gunther, *Law as an autopoietic system*, Oxford, Blackwell, 1993, 203 p.
THORNBURGH, Dick and LIN, Herbert S. (eds), *Youth, Pornography and the Internet*, Washington, D.C., National Academies Press, 2002, 450 p.
TOTH, Akos (ed.), *The Oxford Encyclopaedia of European Community law – Volume III: competition law and policy*, Oxford, Oxford University Press, 2008, 832 p.
TRIDIMAS, Takis, *The general principles of EU law*, Oxford, Oxford University Press, 2006, 591 p.
USHER, John, *General principles of EC law*, London, Longman, 1998, 167 p.
UYTTENDAELE, Caroline, *Openbare informatie – Het juridisch statuut in een convergerende mediaomgeving [Public information – The legal status in a converging media environment]*, Antwerpen, Maklu, 2002, 400 p. [in Dutch]
VALCKE, Peggy, *Digitale diversiteit – Convergentie van media-, telecommunicatie en mededingingsrecht* [*Digital diversity – Convergence of media, telecommunication ans competition law*], Brussel, Larcier, 2004, 828 p. [in Dutch]
VALKENBURG, Patti M., *Children's responses to the screen: a media psychological approach*, Mahwah NJ, Erlbaum, 2004, 164 p.
VAN BUEREN, Geraldine, *The international law on the rights of the child*, Dordrecht, Martinus Nijhoff Publishers, 1995, 435 p.
VAN CALSTER, Geert and VOS, Ellen, *Risico en voorzorg in de rechtsmaatschappij* [*Risk, precaution and the rule of law*], Antwerpen, Intersentia, 2004, 255 p. [in Dutch]
VANDE LANOTTE, Johan and HAECK, Yves, *Handboek EVRM: Deel 1 Algemene beginselen* [*Handbook ECHR: Part 1 General principles*], Antwerpen, Intersentia, 2005, 949 p. [in Dutch]

van Dijk, Pieter, van Hoof, Fried, van Rijn, Arjen and Zwaak, Leo (eds), *Theory and practice of the European Convention on Human Rights*, Antwerpen, Intersentia, 2006, 1190 p.

Verbiest, Thibault and Wéry, Etienne (eds), *Le droit de l'internet et de la société de l'information* [*Law of the Internet and the Information Society*], Brussels, Larcier, 2001, 648 p. [in French]

Verhellen, Eugeen, *Convention on the Rights of the Child: background, motivation, strategies, main themes*, Antwerpen, Garant, 2006, 193 p.

Viering, Marc, *Het toepassingsgebied van artikel 6 EVRM* [*The scope of application of article 6 ECHR*], Zwolle, W.E.J. Tjeenk Willink, 1994, 243 p. [in Dutch]

Voorhoof, Dirk, *Critical perspectives on the scope and interpretation of Article 10 of the European Convention on Human Rights (Mass media files No. 10)*, Strasbourg, Council of Europe Press, 1995, 66 p.

Weaver, C. Kay and Carter, Cynthia, *Critical Readings: Violence and the media*, Maidenhead, Open University Press, 2006, 379 p.

Whish, Richard, *Competition law*, Oxford, Oxford University Press, 2009, 1006 p.

Whiteside, Kerry H., *Precautionary politics: Principle and practice in confronting environmental risk*, Cambridge MA, The MIT Press, 2006, 182 p.

Woods, Lorna, *Free movement of goods and services within the European Community*, Aldershot, Ashgate, 2004, 307 p.

B. *Contributions in books*

Ahlert, Christian, "Technologies of control: how code controls communication", 199–136, in: Hardy, Christiane and Möller, Christian (eds), *Spreading the word on the Internet: 16 answers to 4 questions (Reflections on Freedom of the Media and the Internet Amsterdam Conference, June 2003)*, Vienna, OSCE, 2003, 224 p., retrieved from http://www.osce.org/publications/rfm/2003/06/12245_103_en.pdf (on 23.04.2007)

Akdeniz, Yaman, "Who watches the watchmen? The role of filtering software in Internet content regulation", 101–121, in: Möller, Christian and Amouroux, Arnaud (eds), *The media freedom Internet cookbook*, Vienna, OSCE, 2004, 274 p., retrieved from http://www.osce.org/publications/rfm/2004/12/12239_89_en.pdf (on 29.02.2008)

Alemanno, Alberto, "The shaping of the precautionary principle by European Courts: from scientific uncertainty to legal certainty", 11–24, in: Cuocolo, Lorenzo and Lupária, Luca (eds), *Valori costituzionali e nuove politiche del diritto: Scritti raccolti del decennale della rivisat "Cahiers Européens"*, Matelica, Halley Editrice, 2007, 232 p.

Armstrong, Kenneth A., "Mutual recognition", 225–267, in: Barnard, Catherine and Scott, Joanne, *The law of the single European market*, Oxford, Hart Publishing, 2002, 414 p.

Böttcher, Kathrin and Castendyk, Oliver, "Part III Community policies, Title III Free movement of persons, services and capital, Chapter 3 Services", 85–122, in: Castendyk, Oliver, Dommering, Egbert J. and Scheuer, Alexander (eds), *European media law*, Alphen a/d Rijn, Kluwer Law International, 2008, 1379 p.

Breyer, Stephen, "Typical justifications for regulation", 59–92, in: Baldwin, Robert, Scott, Colin and Hood, Christopher (eds), *A reader on regulation*, Oxford, Oxford University Press, 1998, 522 p.

Buckingham, David, "Children and new media", 77–89, in: Lievrouw, Leah A. and Livingstone, Sonia, *Handbook of new media – Social shaping and social consequences of ICTs*, 2006, London, Sage Publications, 475 p.

Buquicchio-De Boer, Maud, "Children and the European Convention on Human Rights",

73–89, in: MATSCHER, Franz and PETZOLD, Herbert (eds), *Protecting human rights: the European dimension (Studies in honour of Gérard J. Wiarda)*, Cologne, Carl Heymanns Verlag KG, 1988, 750 p.

BUSHMAN, Brad J. and ROWELL HUESMANN, L., "Effects of televised violence on aggression", 223–253, in: SINGER, Dorothy G. and SINGER, Jerome, L., *Handbook of children and the media*, Thousand Oaks, Sage Publications, 2001, 765 p.

CANTOR, Joanne, HARRISON, Kristen and KRCMAR, Marina, "Ratings and advisories: implications for the new ratings system for television", 179–211, in: HAMILTON, James T. (ed.), *Television violence and public policy*, Ann Arbor, The University of Michigan Press, 1998, 394 p.

CARLSSON, Ulla, 'Introduction: Media Governance – Harm and Offence in Media Content, 11–19, in: CARLSSON, Ulla (ed.), *Regulation, awareness, empowerment. Young people and harmful media content in the digital age*, Göteborg, The International Clearinghouse on Children, Youth and Media, 2006, 286 p.

——, "Violence and pornography in the media – Public views on the influence media violence and pornography exert on young people", 135–154, in: CARLSSON, Ulla (ed.), *Regulation, awareness, empowerment: Young people and harmful media content in the digital age*, Göteborg, Nordicom, 2006, 286 p.

CLAPHAM, Andrew, "The 'Drittwirkung' of the Convention", 163–206, in: MACDONALD, Ronald Saint John, MATSCHER, Franz and PETZOLD, Herbert, *The European system for the protection of human rights*, Dordrecht, Martinus Nijhoff Publishers, 1993, 940 p.

CLARK, Charles, "The answer to the machine is in the machine", 139–146, in: HUGENHOLTZ, P. Bernt (ed.), *The future of copyright in a digital environment*, 1996, The Hague, Kluwer Law International, 248 p.

COUZENS, Meda, "Autonomy rights versus parental autonomy", 419–439, in: ALEN, Andre et al. (eds), *The UN Children's rights Convention: theory meets practice* (Proceedings of the International Interdisciplinary Conference on Children's Rights, Ghent, 18–19.05.2006, Belgium), Antwerpen, Intersentia, 2007, 658 p.

CRAUFURD SMITH, Rachael, "European Community media regulation in a converging environment", 105–143, in: SHUIBHNE, Niamh Nic (ed.), *Regulating the internal market*, Cheltenham, Edward Elgar, 2006, 370 p.

CROMHEECKE, Marc and STAELENS, Valentina, "Artikel 13 – Recht op daadwerkelijke rechtshulp" ["*Article 13 – Right to an effective remedy*"], 75–126, in: VANDE LANOTTE, Johan and HAECK, Yves, *Handboek EVRM: Deel II: Artikelsgewijze commentaar (Volume II)* [*ECHR: Part II: Commentary on the articles (Volume II)*], Antwerpen – Oxford, Intersentia, 2004, 762 p. [in Dutch]

DE SMET, Bart, LATHOUWERS, Jan et al., "Artikel 6: recht op eerlijk proces" ["*Article 6: right to fair trial*"], 371–652, in: VANDE LANOTTE, Johan and HAECK, Yves, *Handboek EVRM: Deel II: Artikelsgewijze commentaar (Volume I)* [*ECHR: Part II: Commentary on the articles*], Antwerpen, Intersentia, 2004, 762 p. [in Dutch]

DOMMERING, Egbert, "Regulating technology: code is not law", 1–16, in: DOMMERING, Egbert and ASSCHER, Lodewijk (eds), *Coding regulation: essays on the normative role of information technology*, The Hague, TMC Asser Press, 301 p.

——, "Article 2 AVMSD", 847–850, in: CASTENDYK, Oliver, DOMMERING, Egbert J. and SCHEUER, Alexander (eds), *European media law*, Alphen a/d Rijn, Kluwer Law International, 2008, 1379 p.

——, "Article 2a AVMSD", 851–856, in: CASTENDYK, Oliver, DOMMERING, Egbert J. and SCHEUER, Alexander (eds), *European media law*, Alphen a/d Rijn, Kluwer Law International, 2008, 1379 p.

——, Scheuer, Alexander and Ader, Thorsten, "Article 3 AVMSD", 857–866, in: Castendyk, Oliver, Dommering, Egbert J. and Scheuer, Alexander (eds), *European media law*, Alphen a/d Rijn, Kluwer Law International, 2008, 1379 p.

Donnerstein, Ed and Smith, Stacy, "Sex in the media: theory, influences and solutions", 289–307, in: Singer, Dorothy G. and Singer, Jerome, L., *Handbook of children and the media*, Thousand Oaks, Sage Publications, 2001, 765 p.

Elspaß, Mathias and Kettner, Moira, "Rules on competition – Rules applying to undertakings", 123–149, in: Castendyk, Oliver, Dommering, Egbert J. and Scheuer, Alexander (eds), *European media law*, Alphen a/d Rijn, Kluwer Law International, 2008, 1379 p.

Frechette, Julie, "Cyber-censorship or cyber-literacy? Envisioning cyber-learning through media education", 149–171, in: Buckingham, David and Willett, Rebekah, *Digital generations: children, young people and new media*, Mahwah NJ, Lawrence Erlbaum Associates, 2006, 337 p.

Froomkin, Michael, *The Internet as a Source of Regulatory Arbitrage*, 129–163, in: Kahin, Brian and Nesson, Charles (eds.), *Borders in Cyberspace – Information policy and the global information infrastructure*, Cambridge MA, MIT Press, 1997, 374 p.

——, "Anonymity in the balance", 5–46, in: Nicoll, Chris, Prins, Corien and van Dellen, Miriam (eds), *Digital anonymity and the law: tensions and dimensions*, Den Haag, TMC Asser Press, 2003, 307 p.

Füg, Oliver Carsten, "Content ratings harmonization and the protection of minors in the European Information Society", 165–186, in: Ward, David (ed.), *The European Union and the culture industries: regulation and the public interest*, Aldershot, Ashgate, 2008, 264 p.

Goemans, Caroline and Dumortier, Jos, "Enforcement Issues – Mandatory retention of traffic data in the EU: possible impact on privacy and on-line anonymity", 161–183, in: Nicoll, Chris, Prins, Corien and van Dellen, Miriam (eds), *Digital anonymity and the law: tensions and dimensions*, Den Haag, TMC Asser Press, 2003, 307 p.

Goerens, Pierre, "Interplay between relevant European legal instruments - ECTT and TVwF Directive: competition or complementarity?", 1–11, in: European Audiovisual Observatory, *Audiovisual Media Services without Frontiers: Implementing the rules, IRIS Special*, Strasbourg, Council of Europe, 2006, 76 p.

Gormley, Laurence W., "The internal market: history and evolution", 14–28, in: Shuibhne, Niamh Nic (ed.), *Regulating the internal market*, Cheltenham, Edward Elgar, 2006, 370 p.

Greenberg, Bradley S. and Rampoldi-Hnilo, Lynn, "Child and parent responses to the age-based and content-based television ratings", 621–634, in: Singer, Dorothy G. and Singer, Jerome, L., *Handbook of children and the media*, Thousand Oaks, Sage Publications, 2001, 765 p.

Hamilton, James T., "Who will rate the ratings?", 133–156, in: Price, Monroe (ed.), *The V-chip debate: content filtering from television to the internet*, Mahwah NJ, Lawrence Erlbaum Associates, 1998, 363 p.

Harcourt, Alison, "Institutionalising soft governance in the European Information Society", 7–31, in: Ward, David (ed.), *The European Union and the culture industries: regulation and the public interest*, Aldershot, Ashgate, 2008, 264 p.

Heins, Marjorie, "Three questions about television ratings", 47–58, in: Price, Monroe (ed.), *The V-chip debate: content filtering from television to the internet*, Mahwah NJ, Lawrence Erlbaum Associates, 1998, 363 p.

Helberger, Natali, "The Media-Literate Viewer", 135–148, in: van Eijk, Nico and Hugenholtz, Bernt (eds), *Dommering-bundel: Opstellen over informatierecht aangeboden aan prof. mr. E.J. Dommering*, Amsterdam, Otto Cramwinckel Uitgever, 2008, 412 p.

HUTCHBY, Ian and MORAN-ELLIS, Jo, "Introduction: relating children, technology and culture", 1–10, in: HUTCHBY, Ian and MORAN-ELLIS, Jo (eds), *Children, technology and culture: The impacts of technologies in children's everyday lives*, Oxford, Routledge, 2001, 190 p.

JONES, Clifford, "Television without Frontiers", 299–347, in: EECKHOUT, Piet and TRIDIMAS, Takis, *Yearbook of European Law 1999–2000*, Oxford, Oxford University Press, 2000, 760 p.

KOELMAN, Kamiel, "Online intermediary liability", 7–57, in: HUGENHOLTZ, Bernt (ed.), *Copyright and electronic commerce: legal aspects of copyright management*, The Hague, Kluwer Law International, 2000, 307 p.

KOOPS, Bert-Jaap and LIPS, Miriam, "Wie reguleert het internet? Horizontalisering en rechtsmacht bij de technische regulering van het internet" ["*Who regulates the internet? Horizontalisation and jurisdiction with regard to technical regulation of the internet*"], 261–315, in: FRANKEN, Hans et al., *Zeven essays over informatietechnologie en recht* [*Seven essays on information technology and law*], Den Haag, SDU, 324 p. [in Dutch]

KÜHLING, Jürgen, "Fundamental rights", 501–547, in: VON BOGDANDY, Armin and BAST, Jürgen (eds), *Principles of European constitutional law*, Oxford, Hart Publishing, 2006, 833 p.

LAMBERS, Rik, "Code and speech. Speech control through network architecture", 91–140, in: DOMMERING, Egbert and ASSCHER, Lodewijk (eds), *Coding regulation: essays on the normative role of information technology*, The Hague, TMC Asser Press, 316 p.

LANE, Robert, "The internal market and the individual", 245–276, in: SHUIBHNE, Niamh Nic (ed.), *Regulating the internal market*, Cheltenham, Edward Elgar, 2006, 370 p.

LIERMAN, Steven, "Het voorzorgsbeginsel en gezondheidsbescherming, oude wijn in nieuwe zakken? ["*The precautionary principle and health protection: old wine in new barrels?*"], 47–68, in: VAN CALSTER, Geert and VOS, Ellen, *Risico en voorzorg in de rechtsmaatschappij* [*Risk, precaution and the rule of law*], Antwerpen, Intersentia, 2004, 255 p. [in Dutch]

LIEVENS, Eva, VALCKE, Peggy and STEVENS, David, "Vrijheid van meningsuiting", [*Freedom of expression*], in: DE CORTE, Rogier (ed.), *Praktijkboek Recht & Internet* [*Book of practice law & the Internet*], Brugge, Vanden Broele, 2005, 58 p. [in Dutch]

LIVINGSTONE, Sonia and MILLWOOD HARGRAVE, Andrea, "Harmful to children? Drawing conclusions from empirical research on media effects", 21–48, in: CARLSSON, Ulla (ed.), *Regulation, awareness, empowerment. Young people and harmful media content in the digital age*, Göteborg, The International Clearinghouse on Children, Youth and Media, 2006, 286 p.

LODDER, Arno, "Directive 2000/31/EC on certain legal aspects of information society services, in particular electronic commerce, in the Internal Market", 67–93, in: LODDER, Arno and KASPERSEN, Henrick (eds), *eDirectives: guide to European Union law on e-Commerce*, Den Haag, Kluwer Law International, 2002, 203 p.

MAJONE, Giandomenico, "The rise of the regulatory state in Europe", 192–215, in: BALDWIN, Robert, SCOTT, Colin and HOOD, Christopher (eds), *A reader on regulation*, Oxford, Oxford University Press, 1998, 522 p.

MAKKAI, Toni and BRAITHWAITE, John, "In and out of the revolving door: making sense of regulatory capture", 173–191, in: BALDWIN, Robert, SCOTT, Colin and HOOD, Christopher, *A reader on regulation*, Oxford, Oxford University Press, 1998, 522 p.

MALAMUTH, Neil M. and IMPETT, Emily A., "Research on sex in the media: what do we know about effects on children and adolescents?", 267–287, in: SINGER, Dorothy G. and SINGER, Jerome, L., *Handbook of children and the media*, Thousand Oaks, Sage Publications, 2001, 765 p.

MARSDEN, Christopher, "Co- and self-regulation in European media and Internet sectors: the results of Oxford University's study www.selfregulation.info", 76–100, in: MÖLLER,

Christian and Amouroux, Arnaud (eds), *The media freedom internet cookbook*, Vienna, OSCE Representative on Freedom of the Media, 2004, retrieved from http://www.osce.org/item/13570.html (on 30.05.2008), 274 p.

Martin, Dianne, "An alternative to government regulation and censorship: content advisory systems for interactive media", 179–194, in: Price, Monroe (ed.), *The V-chip debate: content filtering from television to the internet*, Mahwah, Lawrence Erlbaum Associates, 1998, 363 p.

McCannon, Bob, "Media literacy: What? Why? How?", 322–365, in: Strasburger, Victor C. and Wilson, Barbara J., *Children, adolescents & the media*, Thousand Oaks, Sage Publications, 2002, 539 p.

McGonagle, Tarlach, "The potential for practice of an intangible idea", 2–8, in: Nikoltchev, Susanne (ed.), *Co-regulation of the media in Europe*, IRIS Special, Strasbourg, European Audiovisual Observatory, 2003, 140 p.

McIntyre, TJ and Scott, Colin, "Internet filtering: rhetoric, legitimacy, accountability and responsibility", 109–124, in: Brownsword, Roger and Yeung, Karen (eds), *Regulating technologies: legal futures, regulatory frames and technological fixes*, Oxford, Hart Publishing, 2008, 396 p.

Montéro, Etienne, "La responsabilité des prestataires intermédiaires sur les réseaux" ["*The liability of intermediaries in networks*"], 273–295, in: Montéro, Etienne (ed.), *Le commerce électronique européen sur les rails?* [*European e-commerce on the rails?*], Cahiers du CRID, Brussel, Bruylant, 2001, 450 p. [in French]

Noorlander, Peter, "Freedom of expression and Internet regulation", 105–115, in: Hardy, Christiane and Möller, Christian (eds), *Spreading the Word on the Internet: 16 Answers to 4 Questions (Reflections on Freedom of the Media and the Internet Amsterdam Conference, June 2003)*, Vienna, OSCE, 2003, 224 p., retrieved from http://www.osce.org/publications/rfm/2003/06/12245_103_en.pdf (on 23.04.2007)

O'Leary, Síofra and Fernández-Martín, José M., "Judicially-created exceptions to the free provision of services", 163–195, in: Andenas, Mads and Roth, Wulf-Henning (eds), *Services and free movement in EU law*, Oxford, Oxford University Press, 2002, 466 p.

Paik, Haejung, "The history of children's use of electronic media", 7–27, in: Singer, Dorothy G. and Singer, Jerome, L., *Handbook of children and the media*, Thousand Oaks, Sage Publications, 2001, 765 p.

Palzer, Carmen, "Self-monitoring v. self-regulation v. co-regulation", 29–31, in: Nikoltchev, Susanne (ed.), *Co-regulation of the media in Europe*, IRIS Special, Strasbourg, European Audiovisual Observatory, 2003, 140 p.

——, "European provisions for the establishment of co-regulation frameworks", 3–13, in: Nikoltchev, Susanne (ed.), *Co-regulation of the media in Europe*, IRIS Special, Strasbourg, European Audiovisual Observatory, 2003, 140 p.

Poullet, Yves, "How to regulate Internet: new paradigms for Internet governance self-regulation: value and limits", 79–114, in: Monville, Claire (ed.), *Variations sur le droit de la société de l'information*, Cahiers du Crid, n° 20, Brussels, Bruylant, 2002, 176 p.

Price, Monroe and Verhulst, Stefaan, "In search of the self: charting the course of self-regulation on the Internet in a global environment", 57–78, in: Marsden, Christopher, *Regulating the global information society*, London, Routledge, 2000, 364 p.

Roth, Wulf-Henning, "Export of goods and services within the single market: reflections on the scope of articles 29 and 49 EC", 33–48, in: Tridimas, Takis and Nebbia, Paolisa (eds), *European Union law for the twenty-first century: rethinking the new legal order*, Oxford, Hart Publishing, 2004, 465 p.

Schulz, Wolfgang and Held, Thorsten, "Together they are strong? Co-regulatory approaches for the protection of minors in the European Union", 49–65, in: CARLSSON, Ulla (ed.), *Regulation, awareness, empowerment. Young people and harmful media content in the digital age*, Göteborg, The International Clearinghouse on Children, Youth and Media, 2006, 286 p.

SCHULZ, Wolfgang, "Regulating search engines? On the use of self- and co-regulation in the field of Internet search", 79–86, in: NIKOLTCHEV, Susanne (ed.), *Searching for audiovisual content*, IRIS Special, Strasbourg, European Audiovisual Observatory, 2008, 90 p.

SNELL, Jukka, "Private parties and the free movement of goods and services", 211–243, in: ANDENAS, Mads and ROTH, Wulf-Henning (eds), *Services and free movement in EU law*, Oxford, Oxford University Press, 2002, 466 p.

SNELL, Jukka and ANDENAS, Mads, "Exploring the outer limits: restrictions on the free movement of goods and services", 69–139, in: ANDENAS, Mads and ROTH, Wulf-Henning, *Services and free movement in EU law*, Oxford, Oxford University Press, 2002, 466 p.

SPITZER, Matthew, "A first glance at the Constitutionality of the V-chip ratings system", 335–384, in: HAMILTON, James T. (ed.), *Television violence and public policy*, Ann Arbor, The University of Michigan Press, 1998, 394 p.

TEUBNER, Gunther, NOBLES, Richard and SCHIFF, David, "The autonomy of law: an introduction to legal autopoiesis", chapter 18, in: PENNER, James, SCHIFF, David and NOBLES, Richard (eds), *Introduction to jurisprudence and legal theory*, Oxford, Oxford University Press, 2005, 1194 p., retrieved from http://www.jura.uni-frankfurt.de/ifawz1/teubner/dokumente/autonomy_of_law.pdf (on 23.06.2008)

UKROW, Jörg, "Protection of minors and public order", 699–719, in: CASTENDYK, Oliver, DOMMERING, Egbert J. and SCHEUER, Alexander (eds), *European media law*, Alphen a/d Rijn, Kluwer Law International, 2008, 1379 p.

——, "Chapter IIb Provisions applicable to on-demand audiovisual services", 919–921, in: CASTENDYK, Oliver, DOMMERING, Egbert and SCHEUER, Alexander (eds.), *European media law*, Alphen a/d Rijn, Kluwer Law International, 2008, 1379 p.

VALCKE, Peggy and DOMMERING, Egbert, "e-Commerce Directive", 1081–1107, in: CASTENDYK, Oliver, DOMMERING, Egbert J. and SCHEUER, Alexander (eds), *European media law*, Alphen a/d Rijn, Kluwer Law International, 2008, 1379 p.

VALCKE, Peggy, "In search of the audiovisual search tools in the EU regulatory frameworks", 65–76, in: NIKOLTCHEV, Susanne (ed.), *Searching for audiovisual content*, IRIS Special, Strasbourg, European Audiovisual Observatory, 2008, 90 p.

VAN DEN BOGAERT, Stefaan, "Horizontality: the Court attacks?", 123–152, in: BARNARD, Catherine and SCOTT, Joanne, *The law of the single European market*, Oxford, Hart Publishing, 2002, 414 p.

VAN DEN BULCK, Jan and VAN DEN BERGH, Bea, "Parental media guidance, communication and self-concept in pre-adolescents", 151–174, in: VAN DEN BERGH, Bea and VAN DEN BULCK, Jan (eds), *Children and media: multidisciplinary approaches*, Leuven, Garant, 2000, 235 p.

VAN HOBOKEN, Joris, "Freedom of expression implications for the governance of search", 49–62, in: NIKOLTCHEV, Susanne (ed.), *Searching for audiovisual content*, IRIS Special, Strasbourg, European Audiovisual Observatory, 2008, 90 p.

VERHULST, Stefaan G., "The regulation of digital content", 330–349, in: LIEVROUW, Leah A. and LIVINGSTONE, Sonia, *Handbook of new media – Social shaping and social consequences of ICTs*, London, Sage Publications, 2006, 475 p.

VOORHOOF, Dirk, "Media(recht) en kinder(recht)en" ["*Media(law) and children('s rights*"], Deel 1, 1.9., update 1995, 3–83, in: VERHELLEN, Eugeen (ed.), *Kinderrechtengids (KIDS): Commentaren, regelgeving, rechtspraak en nuttige informatie over de maatschappelijke en juridische positie van het kind* [*Guide to children's rights: Comments, regulation, case law and useful information about the social and legal status of the child*], Gent, Mys en Breesch, 1994 [in Dutch]

——, "Vrijheid van meningsuiting" ["*Freedom of expression*"], 837–1061, in: Vande Lanotte, Johan and Haeck, Yves, *Handboek EVRM: Deel II: Artikelsgewijze commentaar (Volume I)* [*ECHR: Part II: Commentary on the articles*], Antwerpen, Intersentia, 2004, 762 p. [in Dutch]

Weitzner, Daniel, "Yelling 'filter' on the crowded Net: the implications of user control technologies", 207–220, in: Price, Monroe (ed.), *The V-chip debate: content filtering from television to the internet*, Mahwah NJ, Lawrence Erlbaum Associates, 1998, 363 p.

C. *Articles in journals*

Amtenbrink, Fabian and van de Gronden, Johan, "Economisch recht en het Verdrag van Lissabon I: mededinging en interne markt" [*Economic law and the Treaty of Lisbon I: competition and internal market*], *SEW* 2008, No. 9, 323–329 [in Dutch]

Barber, Nicholas, "The limited modesty of subsidiarity", *European Law Journal* 2005, Vol. 11, No. 3, 308–325

Barcelo, Rosa-Juliá, "On-line intermediary liability issues: comparing EU and US legal frameworks", *E.I.P.R.* 2000, 106–119

Barcelo, Rosa-Juliá and Koelman, Kamiel, "Intermediary liability in the E-commerce Directive: so far so good, but it's not enough", *Computer Law & Security Report* 2000, No. 4, 231–239

Birnhack, Michael and Rowbottom, Jacob, "Shielding children: the European way", *Chicago-Kent Law Review* 2004, Issue 79, 101–150

Black, Julia, "Constitutionalising self-regulation", *Modern Law Review* 1996, Vol. 59, Issue 1, 24–55

Brownsword, Roger, "Code, control, and choice: why East is East and West is West", *Legal Studies* 2005, Vol. 25, No. 1, 1–21

Carlisle, George and Scerri, Jackie, "Web 2.0 and user-generated content: legal challenges in the new frontier", *Journal of Information, Law and Technology* 2007, No. 2, retrieved from http://www2.warwick.ac.uk/fac/soc/law/elj/jilt/2007_2/george_scerri (on 21.01.2008)

Carozza, Paolo, "Subsidiarity as a structural principle of international human rights law", *American Journal of International Law* 2003, Vol. 97, 38–79

Corn-Revere, Robert, "Ashcroft v. ACLU II: the beat goes on", *Cato Supreme Court Review* 2003–2004, 299–326

Coudert, Fanny and Werkers, Evi, "In the aftermath of the Promusicae case: how to strike the balance?", *International Journal of Law and Information Technology* 2008, Advanced access: retrieved from http://ijlit.oxfordjournals.org/cgi/content/full/ean015v1?maxtoshow=&HITS=10&hits=10&RESULTFORMAT=&fulltext=werkers&searchid=1&FIRSTINDEX=0&resourcetype=HWCIT (on 15.05.2009)

De Preter, Christoph, "Wie heeft nog boodschap aan de boodschap? De aansprakelijkheid van tussenpersonen onder de wet elektronische handel" ["*Liability of intermediaries under the E-commerce Act*"], *Auteurs & Media* 2003, 256–269 [in Dutch]

d'Udekem-Gevers, Marie and Poullet, Yves, "Internet content regulation: concerns from a European use empowerment perspective about Internet content regulation: an analysis of some recent statements – Part II", *Computer Law & Security Report* 2002, Vol. 18, No. 1, 11–23

EKKER, Anton, "Noot onder KU t. Finland" ["*Note under KU v. Finland*"], *Mediaforum* 2009, No. 2, 70–71 [in Dutch]

ETZIONI, Amitai, "On protecting children from speech (Symposium Do children have the same First Amendment rights as adults?)", *Chicago-Kent Law Review* 2004, Vol. 79, No. 1, 299–313

EVELAND, William. P. Jr., "A mix of attributes approach to the study of media effects and new communication technologies", *Journal of Communication* 2003, Vol. 53, No. 3, 395–410

FÜG, Oliver C., "Save the children: the protection of minors in the Information Society and the Audiovisual Media Services Directive", *Journal of Consumer Policy* 2008, Vol. 31, No. 1, 45–61

GUNNINGHAM, Neil and REES, Joseph, "Industry self-regulation: an institutional perspective", *Law & Policy* 1997, Vol. 19, No. 4, 370–380

HARCOURT, Alison and WEATHERILL, Stephen, "The Consumer, the European Union, and Media Law", *Journal of Consumer Policy* 2008, Vol. 31, No. 1, 1–4

HATZOPOULOS, Vassilis and DO, Thien Uyen, "The case law of the ECJ concerning the free provisions of services: 2000–2005", *Common Market Law Review* 2006, Vol. 43, 923–991

HAWKINS, Keith, "Rule and discretion in comparative perspective: the case of social regulation", *The Ohio State Law Journal* 1989, Vol. 50, No. 3, 663–679

HAWKINS, Keith and HUTTER, Bridget, "The response of business to social regulation in England and Wales: an enforcement perspective", *Law & Policy* 1993, Vol. 15, No. 3, 199–217

HELBERGER, Natali, "From eyeball to creator – Toying with audience empowerment in the Audiovisual Media Service Directive", *Entertainment Law Review* 2008, No. 6, 128–137

HEROLD, Anna, "Country of origin principle in the EU market for audiovisual media services: consumer's friend or foe?", *Journal of Consumer Policy* 2008, Vol. 31, No. 1, 5–24

HEUKELS, Ton, "Alternatieve implementatietechnieken en art. 189, lid 3 EEG: grondslagen en ontwikkelingen" [*Alternative implementation techniques and art. 189, para. 3 EEC: foundations and developments*], *NTB* 1993, Vol. 1, 59–74 [in Dutch]

HEYVAERT, Veerle, "Facing the consequences of the precautionary principle in European Community Law", *European Law Review* 2006, Vol. 31, Issue 2, 185–206

HUYSE, Luc and PARMENTIER, Stephan, "Decoding codes: the dialogue between consumers and suppliers through codes of conduct in the European Community", *Journal of Consumer Policy* 1990, Vol. 13, No. 3, 253–272

IDE, Nicolas, STROWEL, Alain and VERHOESTRAETE, Florence, "La Directive du 8 juin 2000 sur le commerce électronique: un cadre juridique pour l'internet" ["*The directive of 8 June 2000 on electronic commerce: a legal framework for the Internet*"], *J.T.* 2001, 133–145 [in French]

KESAN, Jay and SHAH, Rajiv, "Deconstructing code", *Yale Journal of Law & Technology* 2003, Vol. 64, 277–389

KILKELLY, Ursula, "The best of both worlds for children's rights? Interpreting the European Convention on Human Rights in the light of the UN Convention on the Rights of the Child", *Human Rights Quarterly* 2001, Vol. 23, 308–326

KLEVE, Pieter and DE MULDER, Richard, "Code is Murphy's law", *International Review of Law, Computers and Technology* 2005, Vol. 19, No. 3, 317–327

KOSTA, Eleni and DUMORTIER, Jos, "The Data Retention Directive and the principles of European data protection legislation", *Medien und Recht International* 2007, No. 3, 130–136

LATZER, Michael, JUST, Natascha, SAURWEIN, Florian and SLOMINSKI, Peter, "Regulation remixed: Institutional change through self- and co-regulation in the mediamatics sector", *Communications & Strategies* 2003, 127–157

Lessig, Lawrence, "What things regulate speech: CDA 2.0 vs. filtering", *Jurimetrics* 1998, Vol. 38, No. 4, 629–670

Lessig, Lawrence and Resnick, Paul, "Zoning speech on the Internet: a legal and technical model", *Michigan Law Review* 1999, Vol. 98, Issue 2, 395–431

Lievens, Eva, Dumortier, Jos and Ryan, Patrick S., "The co-protection of minors in new media: a European approach to co-regulation", *UC Davis Journal of Juvenile Law & Policy* 2006, Vol. 10, 97–151

Livingstone, Sonia, "Do the media harm children? Reflections on new approaches to an old problem", *Journal of Children and Media* 2007, Vol. 1, No. 1, 5–14

MacGowan, Nicholas and Quinn, Mary, "Could article 30 impose obligations on individuals?", *European Law Review* 1987, Volume 12, Issue 3, 163–178

Marsden, Christopher T., "Beyond Europe: the Internet, regulation and multistakeholder governance – Representing the consumer interest?", *Journal of Consumer Policy* 2008, Vol. 31, No. 1, 115–132

McIntyre, Thomas, "Online anonymity: some legal issues", *Commercial Law Practitioner* 2004, April, 90–106

Mifsud Bonnici, Jeanne P. and De Vey Mestdagh, Cees N.J., "Right vision, wrong expectations: the European Union and self-regulation of harmful Internet content", *Information & Communications Technology Law* 2005, Vol. 14, No. 2, 133–150

Moran, Michael, "Understanding the regulatory state", *British Journal of Political Science* 2002, Vol. 2, No. 2, 391–413

Murray, Andrew and Scott, Colin, "Controlling the new media: hybrid responses to new forms of power", *The Modern Law Review* 2002, Vol. 65, No. 4, 491–516

Newman, Abraham and Bach, David, "Self-regulatory trajectories in the shadow of public power: resolving digital dilemmas in Europe and the United States", *Governance* 2004, Vol. 17, No. 3, 387–413

Nunziato, Dawn, "Toward a constitutional regulation of minors' access to harmful internet speech", *Chicago-Kent Law Review* 2004, Issue 79, 121–174

Nunziato, Dawn C., Nunziato, Dawn C., "Technology and pornography", *Brigham Young University Law Review* 2007, Issue 6, 1535–1584

Ogus, Anthony, "Rethinking self-regulation", *Oxford Journal of Legal Studies* 1995, Vol. 15, No. 1, 97–108

Palzer, Carmen, "Co-regulation of the media in Europe: European provisions for the establishment of co-regulation frameworks", *Iris Plus* 2002, No. 6, 2–8

——, "Horizontal rating of audiovisual content in Europe – An alternative to multi-level classification?", *Iris Plus* 2003, No. 10, 2–8

Pitt-Payne, Timothy, "Privacy versus freedom of information: is there a conflict?", *European Human Rights Law Review* 2003, Special Issue, 109–119

Post, David, "What Larry doesn't get: code, law, and liberty in Cyberspace", *Stanford Law Review* 2000, Vol. 52, 1439–1459

Prosser, Tony, "Self-regulation, Co-regulation and the Audio-Visual Media Services Directive", *Journal of Consumer Policy* 2008, Vol. 31, No. 1, 99–113

Reidenberg, Joel, "Lex informatica: the formulation of information policy rules through technology", *Texas Law Review* 1998, Vol. 76, No. 3, 553–584

Reidenberg, Joel R., "States and Internet Enforcement", *University of Ottawa Law & Technology Journal* 2004, Vol. 1, No. 1–2, 213–230

——, "Technology and Internet Jurisdiction", *University of Pennsylvania Law Review* 2005, Vol. 153, 2005, 1951–1974

Ribak, Rivka, "Children & new media: some reflections on the ampersand", *Journal for Children and Media* 2007, Vol. 1, No. 1, 68–76

Rosenberg, Richard, "Controlling access to the Internet: the role of filtering", *Ethics and Information Technology* 2001, Vol. 3, No. 1, 35–54

Roth, Wulf-Henning and Oliver, Peter, "The internal market and the four freedoms", *Common Market Law Review* 2004, Volume 41, 407–441

Schauer, Frederick, "Fear, risk and the First Amendment: Unravelling the chilling effect", *Boston University Law Review* 1978, Vol. 58, Issue 5, 685–732

Schepel, Harm, "Delegation of regulatory powers to private parties under EC competition law: towards a procedural public interest test", *Common Market Law Review* 2002, 31–51

Senden, Linda, "Soft law, self-regulation and co-regulation in European law: where do they meet?", *Electronic Journal of Comparative Law* 2005, Vol. 9, No. 1, retrieved from http://www.ejcl.org/91/abs91-3.html (on 30.05.2008)

Shah, Rajiv C. and Kesan, Jay P., "Manipulating the Governance Characteristics of Code", *Info* 2003, Vol. 5, No. 4, 3–9

Sinclair, Darren, "Self-regulation versus command and control? Beyond false dichotomies", *Law & Policy* 1997, Vol. 19, No. 4, 529–559

Snyder, Francis, "The effectiveness of European Community Law: Institutions, processes, tools and techniques", *The Modern Law Review* 1993, 19–54

Sosnay, Jacob A., "Regulating minors' access to pornography via the Internet: what options do Congress have left?", *The John Marshall Journal of Computer & Information Law* 2005, Vol. 23, No. 2, 461–465

Steyger, Elies, "European Community law and the self-regulatory capacity of society", *Journal of Common Market Studies* 1993, Vol. 31, No. 2, 171–190

Svantesson, Dan Jerker B., "The characteristics making Internet communication challenge traditional models of regulation –What every international jurist should know about the Internet", *International Journal of Law and Information Technology* 2005, Vol. 13, No. 1, 39–69

Tiberi, Luca and Zamboni, Michele, "Liability of Internet service providers", *Computer and Telecommunications Law Review* 2003, 49–58

Tufte, Brigitte and Tufte, Thomas, "Parental control of broadcasting, film, audiovisual and online", *Nordicom Review* 1999, Issue 2, retrieved from http://www.nordicom.gu.se/common/publ_pdf/37_tufte&tufte.pdf (on 13.03.2008), 45–58

Valcke, Martin, Schellens, Tamara, Van Keer, Hilde and Gerarts, Marjan, "Primary school children's safe and unsafe use of the Internet at home and at school: An exploratory study", *Computers in Human Behaviour* 2007, Vol. 23, Issue 6, 2838–2850

Valcke, Peggy and Stevens, David, "Graduated regulation of 'regulatable' content and the European Audiovisual Media Services Directive: One small step for the industry and one giant leap for the legislator?", *Telematics & Informatics* 2007, Vol. 24, Issue 4, 285–302

Valcke, Peggy, Stevens, David, Lievens, Eva, Werkers, Evi, "Audiovisual Media Services in the EU: Next Generation Approach or Old Wine in New Barrels", *Communications & Strategies* 2008, No. 71, 103–118

Vandaele, Arne and Verheyde, Mieke, "Artikel 22bis van de Grondwet: een grondwettelijke bescherming in de kinderschoenen" ["*Article 22bis of the Constitution: a constitutional protection in its infancy*"], *T.J.K.* 2001, No. 1, 4–15 [in Dutch]

van Eijk, Nico, "Search engines: seek and ye shall find? The position of search engines in law", *Iris Plus* 2006, No. 2, 2–8

van Hoboken, Joris, "Legal space for innovative ordering: on the need to update selection intermediary liability in the EU", *International Journal of Communications Law & Policy* 2009, Issue 13, Winter, 49–69

VERSCHUUREN, Jonathan, "EC environmental law and self-regulation in the Member States: in search of a legislative framework", *Yearbook of European Environmental Law* 2000, Vol. 1, 103–121

VOORHOOF, Dirk, "Recente arresten van het E.H.R.M. in verband met het artikel 10 E.V.R.M. (vrijheid van meningsuiting en informatie)" ["*Recent judgments of the ECHR related to article 10 ECHR (freedom of expression and information)*"], March-May 2003, *Auteurs & Media* 2003, No. 3, 228–234 [in Dutch]

——, "Recente arresten van het E.H.R.M. in verband met het artikel 10 E.V.R.M. (vrijheid van meningsuiting en informatie)" ["*Recent judgments of the ECHR related to article 10 ECHR (freedom of expression and information)*"], September-October 2007, *Auteurs & Media* 2007, No. 6, 597–606 [in Dutch]

——, "Recente arresten van het E.H.R.M. in verband met het artikel 10 E.V.R.M. (vrijheid van meningsuiting en informatie)" ["*Recent judgments of the ECHR related to article 10 ECHR (freedom of expression and information)*"], June 2008, *Auteurs & Media* 2008, No. 4, 314–318 [in Dutch]

——, "Recente arresten van het E.H.R.M. in verband met artikel 10 E.V.R.M. (vrijheid van meningsuiting en informatie)" ["*Recent judgments of the ECHR related to article 10 ECHR (freedom of expression and information)*"], November–December 2008, *Auteurs & Media* 2009, No. 1, *in press* [in Dutch]

WEEKES, Russel B., "Cyber-zoning a mature domain: the solution to preventing inadvertent access to sexually explicit content on the Internet", *Virginia Journal of Law and Technology* 2003, Vol. 8, No. 4, retrieved from http://www.vjolt.net/vol8/issue1/v8i1_a04-Weekes.pdf (on 16.06.2008)

WERKERS, Evi and COUDERT, Fanny, "Promusicae versus Telefónica: auteursrecht en recht op privacy in de weegschaal gelegd" ["*Promusicae versus Telefónica: copyright and right to privacy put in the balance?*"], *Auteurs & Media* 2008, No. 4, 249–263 [in Dutch]

WU, Tim, "When Code isn't law", *Virginia Law Review* 2003, Vol. 89, 101–170

D. *PhD Theses*

LEMMENS, Paul, Geschillen over burgerlijke rechten en verplichtingen: het toepassingsgebied van de artikelen 6, lid 1, van het Europees Verdrag over de rechten van de mens en 14, lid 1, van het Internationaal Verdrag inzake burgerrechten en politieke rechten [*Disputes over civil rights and obligations: the scope of application of the articles 6, para. 1, of the European Convention on human rights and 14, para. 1, of the International Covenant on Civil and Political Rights*], PhD Thesis (promotor: Prof. dr. Jan De Meyer), 1987 [in Dutch]

VERDOODT, Anne-Lies, Zelfregulering in de journalistiek: de formulering en de handhaving van deontologische standaarden in en door het journalistieke beroep [*Self-regulation in journalism: the formulation and enforcement of deontological standards in and by the journalistic profession*], PhD Thesis (promotor: Prof. dr. Stephan Parmentier), 2007 [in Dutch]

4. Miscellaneous

A. *Internet and working / discussion papers*

Akdeniz, Yaman, "Stocktaking on efforts to combat racism on the Internet", Background Paper for the High Level Seminar on Racism and the Internet, Intergovernmental Working Group on the Effective Implementation of the Durban Declaration and Programme of Action, Fourth session, Geneva, 16–27.01.2006, E/CN.4/2006/WG.21/BP.1, retrieved from http://www.cyber-rights.org/reports/ya_un_paper_int_06.pdf (on 23.04.2007)

Aubry, Patrice, "The 'Television without Frontiers' Directive – Cornerstone of the European Broadcasting Policy", 2000, retrieved from http://www.obs.coe.int/online_publication/reports/TWF.pdf.en (on 09.07.2007)

Baird, Zoë and Verhulst, Stefaan, "A new model for Global Internet Governance", 2004, retrieved from http://www.markle.org/downloadable_assets/ahs_global_internet_gov.pdf (on 23.04.2007)

Baldwin, Robert, "Is regulation right?", Carr Launch paper, 2000, retrieved from http://www.lse.ac.uk/collections/CARR/pdf/IsRegulationRight.pdf (on 16.04.2008)

Berners-Lee, Tim, "New Top Level Domains .mobi and .xxx considered harmful", 2004, retrieved from http://www.w3.org/DesignIssues/TLD (on 13.06.2008)

Black, Julia, "Critical reflections on regulation", Discussion paper, January 2002, retrieved from http://www.lse.ac.uk/collections/CARR/pdf/DPs/Disspaper4.pdf (on 08.04.2008)

Center for Democracy and Technology, "Jurisdiction", retrieved from http://www.cdt.org/jurisdiction/ (on 23.04.2007)

——, "CDT calls on Senate to reject the 'Deleting Online Predators Act of 2006'", 04.08.2006, retrieved from http://www.cdt.org/speech/20060811dopa.pdf (on 27.04.2007)

——, "Child safety and free speech issues in the 110th Congress", 15.02.2007, retrieved from http://www.cdt.org/speech/20070215freespeechincongress.pdf (on 27.04.2007)

Children's Charities Coalition for Internet Safety, "Child safety online – A digital manifesto", 2004, retrieved from http://www.nch.org.uk/uploads/documents/Digital_Manifesto_web.pdf (on 23.02.2007)

Demoulin, Marie and Jacquemin, Hervé, "Bespreking van de wetten betreffende de diensten van de informatiemaatschappij" ["*Review of the acts regarding the information society services*"], retrieved from http://www.internet-observatory.be/internet_observatory/pdf/legislation/cmt/law_be_2003-03-11_cmt_nl.pdf (on 20.03.2007) [in Dutch]

du Marais, Bertrand, "Auto regulation, regulation et co-régulation des réseaux" [*Auto regulation, regulation and co-regulation of networks*], Colloque "Droit de l'Internet: approches européennes et internationales, 2001, retrieved from http://droit-internet-2001.univ-paris1.fr/pdf/vf/Marais.pdf (on 26.05.2008) [in French]

European Children's Network, "The new EU Reform Treaty – What is the impact on children's rights?", 03.12.2007, retrieved from http://www.crin.org/docs/Briefing_EURONET_EU_Reform_Treaty_Nov_07_Final.pdf (on 23.01.2008)

European Internet Coregulation Network, "Coregulation of Internet content accessed on mobile phones – Summary report and recommendations", 2005, retrieved from http://network.foruminternet.org/article.php3?id_article=24 (on 23.06.2008)

Fisher, Elizabeth, "Opening Pandora's Box: contextualising the precautionary principle in the European Union", University of Oxford Faculty of Law Legal Studies Research Paper Series, Working Paper No 2/2007, retrieved from http://papers.ssrn.com/sol3/papers.cfm?abstract_id=956952 (on 11.03.2008)

Garnham, Nicholas, "What is multimedia", 1999, retrieved from http://europa.eu.int/ISPO/legal/en/lab/lisbon/garnham.html (on 30.07.2007, no longer available)

Geist, Michael, "New Yahoo decisions raises old questions", 22.01.2006, retrieved from http://michaelgeist.ca/index.php?option=com_content&task=view&id=1083&Itemid=113 (on 23.04.2007)

Guldberg, Helene, "Challenging the precautionary principle", 01.07.2003, retrieved from http://www.spiked-online.com/Articles/00000006DE2F.htm (on 04.03.2008)

Holznagel, Bernd, "Responsibility for harmful and illegal content as well as free speech on the Internet in the United States of America and Germany", 2002, retrieved from http://www.coll.mpg.de/pdf_dat/holznag.pdf (on 12.03.2008)

Ide, Nicolas and Strowel, Alain, "Responsabilité des intermédiaires: actualités législatives et jurisprudentielles" ["*Liability of intermediaries: legislative and jurisprudential news*"], 10.10.2000, retrieved from http://www.droit-technologie.org/2_1.asp?dossier_id=32&motcle=ide+strowel&mode=motamot (on 20.03.2007) [in French]

Johnson, David, "Let's let the Net self-regulate – The case for allowing decentralized, emergent self-ordering to solve the public policy problems created by the Internet", 1998, retrieved from http://web.archive.org/web/19990210085611/www.cli.org/selford/essay.htm (on 26.05.2008)

Jordan, Andrew and O'Riordan, Timothy, "The precautionary principle: a legal and policy history", in: World Health Organisation (edited by Marco Martuzzi and Joel A. Tickner), Background document for the Fourth Ministerial Conference on Environment and Health "The precautionary principle: Public Health, the protection of children and sustainability", 07.06.2004, retrieved from http://www.euro.who.int/document/EEHC/ebakdoc09.pdf (on 11.03.2008)

Lessig, Lawrence, "The Code is the law", The Industry Standard, 09.04.199, retrieved from http://www.lessig.org/content/standard/0,1902,4165,00.html (on 09.06.2008)

Poullet, Yves, "Technologies de l'information et de la communication et 'co-régulation': une nouvelle approche?" ["*Information and communication technologies and 'co-regulation': a new approach?*"], *Droit et Nouvelles Technologies*, 27.05.2004, retrieved from http://www.droit-technologie.org/upload/dossier/doc/120-1.pdf (on 29.11.2008) [in French]

Prensky, Marc, "Digital natives, digital immigrants", 2001, retrieved from http://www.marcprensky.com/writing/Prensky%20-%20Digital%20Natives,%20Digital%20Immigrants%20-%20Part1.pdf (on 07.04.2008)

Rorive, Isabelle and Frydman, Benoît, "Regulating Internet content through intermediaries in Europe and the USA", *Droit et Nouvelles Technologies*, 19.03.2003, retrieved from http://www.droit-technologie.org/dossier-92/regulating-internet-content-through-intermediaries-in-europe-and-the-u.html (on 23.03.2007)

Ross, Patrick, "Regulation without Frontiers: Europe shows U.S. policymakers how not to embrace convergence", Progress Snapshot 1.15, September 2005, retrieved from http://www.pff.org/issues-pubs/ps/ps1.15frontiers.html (on 06.07.2006)

—, "Content Regulation without Frontiers: why the EU is indeed regulating the Internet", Progress Snapshot 1.24, December 2005, retrieved from http://www.pff.org/issues-pubs/ps/ps1.24eu.html (on 06.07.2006)

Runciman, David, "The precautionary principle – David Runciman writes about Tony Blair and the language of risk", *London Review of books*, 01.04.2008, retrieved from http://www.lrb.co.uk/v26/n07/runc01_.html (on 11.03.2008)

Schulz, Wolfgang, Held, Thorsten, Dreyer, Stephan (in cooperation with Thilo Wind), "Regulation of broadcasting and Internet services in Germany: A brief overview", Arbeitspapiere des Hans-Bredow-Instituts No. 13, March 2008, retrieved from http://www.hans-bredow-institut.de/english/publications/ap/13-2Mediaregulation.pdf (on 06.06.2008)

Scott, Colin, "Regulation in the age of governance: the rise of the post-regulatory state", National Europe Center Paper No. 100, Australian National University, 2003, retrieved from http://dspace.anu.edu.au/bitstream/1885/41716/2/scott1.pdf (on 29.11.2008)

Tambini, Damien and Forgan, Liz, "Content", Communications White Paper, retrieved from http://www.communicationswhitepaper.gov.uk/cwp_consultation/contentregulation.pdf (18.12.2003, no longer available)

Thierer, Adam, "Parents have many tools to combat objectionable media content", Progress on Point 13.9, April 2006, retrieved from http://www.pff.org/issues-pubs/pops/pop13.9contenttools.pdf (on 06.07.2006)

——, "Rep. Bean's 'SAFER NET Act': an education-based approach to online child safety", Progress on Point 14.3, February 2007, retrieved from http://www.pff.org/issues-pubs/pops/pop14.3beanbillinternetsafety.pdf (on 27.04.2007)

——, "Social networking and age verification: many hard questions; no easy solutions", Progress on Point 14.5, March 2007, retrieved from http://papers.ssrn.com/sol3/papers.cfm?abstract_id=976936 (on 16.06.2008)

——, "Parental controls and online child protection: a survey of tools and methods", July 2007, retrieved from http://www.pff.org/parentalcontrols/Parental%20Controls%20&%20Online%20Child%20Protection%20%5BVersion%202.2%5D.pdf (on 18.01.2008)

—— et al., "Cyber Safety in a Web 2.0 World: what parents and policymakers need to know", Progress on Point 14.25, December 2007, retrieved from http://www.pff.org/issues-pubs/pops/pop14.25cybersafetyweb.pdf (on 16.01.2008)

Valkenburg, Patti, "Expert opinion Schadelijke media en weerbare jeugd: een beleidsvisie 2005–2010" ["*Expert opinion Harmful media and youth: a policy vision 2005–2010*"], retrieved from http://www.ivir.nl/publicaties/vaneijk/Wijzerkijken.pdf (on 03.03.2008) [in Dutch]

Vedder, Hans, "Voluntary agreements and competition law", Working Paper Fondazione Eni Enrico Mattei, No. 79, 2000, retrieved from http://www.feem.it/NR/rdonlyres/FC5A9109-6763-4D72-B01E-A99C97874999/672/7900.pdf (on 30.10.2008)

——, "The democracy of competition – EC (Competition- law and the fine line between markets, public interests and (self-)regulation", Working Paper Annual Legal Research Network Conference, 2008, retrieved from http://papers.ssrn.com/sol3/papers.cfm?abstract_id=1282035 (on 30.10.2008)

Volokh, Eugene, "Speech and spillover", 19.07.1996, retrieved from http://www.slate.com/id/2371 (on 12.03.2008)

World Health Organisation (edited by Marco Martuzzi and Joel A. Tickner), Background document for the Fourth Ministerial Conference on Environment and Health "The precautionary principle: Public Health, the protection of children and sustainability", 07.06.2004, retrieved from http://www.euro.who.int/document/EEHC/ebakdoc09.pdf (on 11.03.2008)

B. *Research reports*

Australian Communications and media authority, Developments in Internet filtering technologies and other measures for promoting online safety – Second annual report to the Minister for Broadband, Communications and the Digital Economy, April 2009, retrieved from http://www.acma.gov.au/webwr/_assets/main/lib310554/developments_in_internet_filters_2ndreport.pdf (on 20.01.2010)

Bertelsmann Foundation, Self-regulation of Internet Content, 1999, retrieved from http://www.cdt.org/speech/BertelsmannProposal.pdf (on 12.06.2008)

Byron, Tanya, Safer children in a digital world: the report of the Byron review, 27.03.2008, retrieved from http://www.dfes.gov.uk/byronreview/ (on 04.07.2008)

Celot, Paolo (ed.), Study on assessment criteria for media literacy levels: A comprehensive view of the concept of media literacy and an understanding of how media literacy levels in Europe should be assessed, Study commissioned by the European Commission, October 2009, retrieved from http://ec.europa.eu/avpolicy/media_literacy/docs/studies/eavi_study_assess_crit_media_lit_levels_europe_finrep.pdf (on 21.01.2010)

Deloitte et al., Safer Internet: Protecting our children on the net using content filtering and parental control techniques – Test and benchmark of products and services to voluntarily filter Internet content for children between 6 and 16 years, Study commissioned by the European Union, 2008, retrieved from http://ec.europa.eu/information_society/activities/sip/docs/project_reports/sip_bench_2008_synthesis_report_en.pdf (on 22.12.2008)

Eurostat, Use of the Internet among individuals and enterprises, 2006, retrieved from http://epp.eurostat.ec.europa.eu/cache/ITY_OFFPUB/KS-NP-06–012/EN/KS-NP-06–012–EN.PDF (on 02.08.2007)

Federal Communications Commission, Report in the matter of Implementation of the Child Safe Viewing Act; Examination of parental control technologies for video or audio programming, 31.08.2009, retrieved from http://hraunfoss.fcc.gov/edocs_public/attachmatch/FCC-09–69A1.pdf (on 20.01.2010)

Grünwald, Andreas, Report on possible options for the review of the European Convention on Transfrontier Television, 24.04.2003, retrieved from http://www.coe.int/t/dghl/standardsetting/media/T-TT/T-TT(2003)002_en.pdf (on 19.05.2008)

GSMEurope, European framework for safer mobile use by younger teenagers and children: one year after – Implementation report, 06.03.2008, retrieved from http://www.gsmeurope.org/documents/gsma_implementation_report.pdf (on 28.05.2009)

——, European framework for safer mobile use by younger teenagers and children: Implementation report, 16.04.2009, retrieved from http://www.gsmeurope.org/documents/PwC_Implementation_Report.pdf (on 28.05.2009)

Hans-Bredow-Institut and EMR, Study on co-regulation measures in the media sector: Final report, Study commissioned by the European Commission, June 2006, retrieved from http://ec.europa.eu/avpolicy/docs/library/studies/coregul/final_rep_en.pdf (on 28.07.2006)

Heins, Marjorie, Cho, Christina and Feldman Ariel, Internet Filters – A public policy report, Brennan Center for Justice at NYU School of Law, 2006, retrieved from http://www.fepproject.org/policyreports/filters2.pdf (on 22.05.2006)

Helsper, Ellen, R18 material: its potential impact on people under 18: An overview of the available literature, research conducted for Ofcom, May 2005, retrieved from http://www.ofcom.org.uk/research/radio/reports/bcr/r18.pdf (on 27.02.2008)

Idate (Philippe Mathonnet and Philippe Baudouin), Final evaluation of the Safer Internet Action Plan – Final report of the expert panel, May 2006, retrieved from http://ec.europa.eu/information_society/activities/sip/docs/prog_evaluation/final_evaluation_en_siap_06112006.pdf (on 14.11.2006)

Indepen, Extension of the Television without Frontiers Directive – An impact assessment Final report for Ofcom, September 2005, retrieved from http://www.ofcom.org.uk/research/tv/twf/twfreport/twf.pdf (on 18.07.2007)

Innocenti Insight (Philip Alston and John Tobin), Laying the foundations for children's rights – An independent study of some key legal and institutional aspects of the impact of the Convention on the Rights of the Child, 2005, retrieved from http://www.unicef-icdc.org/publications/pdf/ii_layingthefoundations.pdf (on 15.05.2.2007)

Internet safety technical task force, Enhancing child safety & online technologies: final report of the Internet safety technical task force to the Multi-State working group on social networking of State Attorneys General of the United States, 31.12.2008, retrieved from http://cyber.law.harvard.edu/publications/2009/ISTTF_Final_Report (on 20.01.2010)

IPPR, A generation of youth are being raised 'online', 24.03.2008, retrieved from http://www.ippr.org.uk/pressreleases/?id=3059 (on 27.03.2008)

Kaiser Family Foundation Study, Generation M: media in the lives of 8–18 year-olds, March 2005, retrieved from http://www.kff.org/entmedia/upload/Generation-M-Media-in-the-Lives-of-8–18-Year-olds-Report.pdf (on 25.02.2008)

Keller, Daphne and Verhulst, Stefaan, Parental control in a converged communications environment: Self-regulation, technical devices and meta-information (Final report for the DVB regulatory group), October 2000, retrieved from http://ec.europa.eu/avpolicy/docs/reg/minors/dvbgroup.pdf (on 23.04.2007)

Lenhart, Amanda and Madden, Mary, Social networking websites and teens: an overview, Pew Internet and American Life Project, 2007, retrieved from www.pewinternet.org/PPF/r/198/report_display.asp (on 17.03.2008)

Lievens, Eva, Werkers, Evi, Lefever, Katrien and Volanis, Nick, Legal report: applying the current regulatory framework to Virtual Individual Networks (WP2 – Deliverable 2.1), Research report IBBT ISBO VIN project, March 2007, 72 p., not published

Livingstone, Sonia and Haddon, Leslie, *EU Kids Online: Final report*, 2009, retrieved from http://www.lse.ac.uk/collections/EUKidsOnline/Reports/EUKidsOnlineFinalReport.pdf (on 21.01.2010)

Millwood Hargrave, Andrea, Protecting children from harmful content, Report prepared for the Council of Europe's Group of Specialists on Human Rights in the Information Society, June 2009, retrieved from http://www.coe.int/t/dghl/standardsetting/media/Doc/H-Inf%282009%2913_en.pdf (on 21.01.2010)

National School Boards Association, Creating and connecting – Research and guidelines on online social – and educational – networking, July 2007, retrieved from http://www.nsba.org/SecondaryMenu/TLN/CreatingandConnecting.aspx (on 11.01.2007)

O'Connell, Rachel and Bryce, Jo, Children and young people in on-line and related off-line environments: Promoting well-being and minimising risk of harm, Study commissioned by the Council of Europe, 188 p., not published

OECD, Participative web: user-created content, DSTI/ICCP/IE(2006)7/FINAL, 12.04.2007, retrieved from http://www.oecd.org/dataoecd/57/14/38393115.pdf (on 02.08.2007)

Ofcom, Media literacy audit: Report on media literacy among children, 02.05.2006, retrieved from www.ofcom.org.uk/advice/media_literacy/medlitpub/medlitpubrss/children/ (on 14.03.2008)

OIVO, Jongeren en nieuwe technologieën [*Youth and new technologies*], May 2006, retrieved from http://www.oivo-crioc.org/teksten/pdf/1769nl.pdf (on 19.10.2006) [in Dutch]

Olsberg / SPI et al., Empirical study on the practice of the rating of films distributed in cinemas, television, DVD and videocassettes in the EU and EEA Member States: Final report, Study commissioned by the European Commission, May 2003, retrieved from http://ec.europa.eu/avpolicy/docs/library/studies/finalised/studpdf/rating_finalrep2.pdf, (on 22.12.2008)

Paul, Christian, Du Droits et des Libertés sur l'Internet – La Corégulation, Contribution Française pour une Réglementation Mondiale [*On rights and freedoms on the Internet – Co-regulation, a French contribution to universal regulation*], Rapport au Premier Ministre, May 2000, retrieved from http://lesrapports.ladocumentationfrancaise.fr/BRP/004001056/0000.pdf (on 02.06.2008)

PCMLP, Study on parental control of television broadcasting, 1999, retrieved from http://ec.europa.eu/comm/avpolicy/info_centre/library/studies/index_en.htm (on 11.06.2008)

——, Parental control in a converged communications environment: Self-regulation, technical devices and meta-information (Final report for the DVB Regulatory Group), 2000, retrieved from http://ec.europa.eu/comm/avpolicy/docs/reg/minors/dvbgroup.pdf (on 11.06.2008)

——, Self-regulation of digital media converging on the Internet: Industry codes of conduct in sectoral analysis, Study commissioned by the European Commission, 30.04.2004, retrieved from http://pcmlp.socleg.ox.ac.uk/selfregulation/iapcoda/0405–iapcode-final.pdf (on 29.05.2008)

Pew Internet and American Life Project, Teens, privacy and online social networks – How teens manage their online identities and personal information in the age of MySpace, 18.04.2007, retrieved from http://www.pewinternet.org/pdfs/PIP_Teens_Privacy_SNS_Report_Final.pdf (on 23.04.2007)

Pew Internet, Parent and teen Internet use, 24.10.2007, retrieved from http://www.pewinternet.org/PPF/r/225/report_display.asp (on 14.01.2008)

PRIME, Framework text, 13.06.2005, retrieved from https://www.prime-project.eu/prime_products/reports/fmwk/pub_del_D14.1.a_ec_wp14.1_V4_final.pdf (on 27.03.2008)

Rand Europe (Edwin Horlings, Chris Marsden, Constantijn Van Oranje and Maarten Botterman), Contribution to impact assessment of the revision of the Television without Frontiers Directive, Study commissioned by the European Commission, 11.11.2005, retrieved from http://ec.europa.eu/dgs/information_society/evaluation/data/pdf/studies/s2004_01/tvwf_rand.pdf (on 10.07.2006)

—— (Chris Marsden, Stephen Simmons and Jonathan Cave), Options for effectiveness of Internet self- and co-regulation – Inception report, Study commissioned by the European Commission, 30.04.2007, retrieved from http://ec.europa.eu/dgs/information_society/evaluation/data/pdf/studies/s2006_05/inception_final.pdf (on 08.01.2008)

—— (Chris Marsden, Stephen Simmons, Jonathan Cave, Eddy Nason, Neil Robinson), Options for and effectiveness of Internet self- and co-regulation, Phase 1 Report: Mapping existing co- and self-regulatory institutions on the Internet, Study commissioned by the European Commission, June 2007, retrieved from http://ec.europa.eu/dgs/information_society/evaluation/data/pdf/studies/s2006_05/phase1.pdf (on 02.06.2008)

—— (Chris Marsden et al.), Options for and effectiveness of Internet self- and co-regulation – Phase 2: Case study report, Study commissioned by the European Commission, 15.01.2008, retrieved from http://ec.europa.eu/dgs/information_society/evaluation/data/pdf/studies/s2006_05/phase2.pdf (on 06.06.2008)

—— (Jonathan Cave, Chris Marsden and Stephen Simmons), Options for effectiveness of Internet self- and co-regulation – Phase 3 (Final) Report, Study commissioned by the European Commission, 2008, retrieved from http://ec.europa.eu/dgs/information_society/evaluation/data/pdf/studies/s2006_05/final_report.pdf (on 30.05.2008)

Schulz, Wolfgang and Held, Thorsten, Regulated Self-Regulation as a Form of Modern Government, Study commissioned by the German Federal Commissioner for Cultural and Media Affairs, 2001, retrieved from http://www.humanrights.coe.int/Media/documents/interim-report-self-regulation.pdf (on 02.06.2008)

van der Stoel, Anne Lize, van Eijk, Nico, Hoogland, Duco, van Noorduyn, Els and Wermuth, Mir, Wijzer Kijken – Schadelijkheid, geschiktheid en kennisbevordering bij het gebruik van audiovisuele producten door jeugdigen [*Watching smarter – Harmfulness, appropriateness and advancement of knowledge*], November 2005, retrieved from http://www.ivir.nl/publicaties/vaneijk/Wijzerkijken.pdf (on 14.03.2008) [in Dutch]

Van Eijck, Nico, Asscher, Lodewijk, Helberger, Natali and Kabel, Jan, De regulering van media in internationaal perspectief [*The regulation of media in an international perspective*], Den Haag, February 2005, retrieved from http://www.ivir.nl/publicaties/overig/Media/regulering%20van%20media%20in%20internationaal%20perspect..pdf (on 01.08.2007) [in Dutch]

Walrave, Michel (ed.), Cyberkids' e-Privacy – Minderjarigen, minder rechten? (Privacy Paper Nr. 4) [*Kids' and Teens' e-Privacy at stake? An analysis of data processing and privacy statements on websites aimed at children and adolescents*], 2005, retrieved from http://www.e-privacy.be/PrivacyPaper4–Cyberkids-e-Privacy.pdf (on 14.06.2007) [in Dutch]

——, "Cyberteens@risk: Opportunities and risks of teens' ICT use analysed", TIRO (Teens and ICT- risks and opportunities) research project, February 2008, retrieved from http://www.e-privacy.be/TIRO-summary.pdf (on 29.02.2008)

Wetenschappelijke Raad voor het Regeringsbeleid, Focus op functies – Uitdagingen voor een toekomstbestendig mediabeleid [*Focus on functions – Challenges for a future proof media policy*], Amsterdam, Amsterdam University Press, 2005, retrieved from http://www.wrr.nl/dsc?c=getobject&s=obj&!sessionid=1o7p!cnhb9o!M9xXGwuyBPekM35UuYCWRZ1zyOvsfxauyo3h50uVxzYXp1K38HdW&objectid=2799&!dsname=default&isapidir=/gvisapi/ (on 27.07.2007) [in Dutch]

C. *Policy briefs & statements*

ACMA, Developments in internet filtering technologies and other measures for promoting online safety, 2007, retrieved from http://www.acma.gov.au/webwr/_assets/main/lib310554/developments_in_internet_filters_1streport.pdf (on 13.06.2008)

——, Restricted access systems declaration, 2007, retrieved from http://www.acma.gov.au/WEB/STANDARD/pc=PC_310905 (on 16.06.2008)

Ashford, Nicholas et al., Wingspread statement on the precautionary principle, January 1998, retrieved from http://www.gdrc.org/u-gov/precaution-3.html (on 04.03.2008)

Audiovisual Stakeholders, Audiovisual Media Services Draft Directive: Opinions and recommendations from stakeholders in the UK, April 2006, retrieved from http://www.audiovisualstakeholders.org/AMS_Stakeholder_Paper_FINAL_April06.pdf (on 12.07.2006, no longer available)

Australian Computer Society, Technical observations on ISP based filtering of the Internet, 2009, retrieved from https://www.acs.org.au/attachments/2009/ispfilteringoct09.pdf (on 21.02.2009)

Barlow, John Perry, Declaration of the Independence of Cyberspace, 08.02.1996, retrieved from http://homes.eff.org/~barlow/Declaration-Final.html (on 09.12.2008)

Center for Democracy and Technology, Letter submitted to the 109th Congress concerning warning labels, 02.08.2006, http://www.cdt.org/speech/20060803labeling.pdf (on 27.04.2007)

——, Policy Post 13.4: Federal Court rejects censorship, endorses user empowerment, 23.03.2007, retrieved from http://www.cdt.org/publications/policyposts/2007/4 (on 07.05.2007)

European Internet Co-regulation Network, Protecting minors from exposure to harmful content on mobile phones, July 2005, retrieved from http://www.foruminternet.org/specialistes/international/multi-fr-rapports-et-guides-en-reports-and-guides-multi/IMG/pdf/reco-mobile-20050728.pdf (on 03.03.2008)

Forum des droits sur l'Internet, Recommandation Les enfants du Net – II: Pédo-pornographie et pédophilie sur Internet [*Recommendation Children of the Net – II: Childpornography and paedophila on Internet*], 25.01.2005, retrieved from http://www.foruminternet.org/telechargement/documents/reco-enfance2–20050125.pdf (on 03.03.2008) [in French]

Global Network Initiative, Core commitments, retrieved from http://www.globalnetworkinitiative.org/index.php (on 28.05.2009)

KJM, The new German regulation for the protection of minors and digital media – The first six months, retrieved from http://ec.europa.eu/comm/avpolicy/docs/reg/minors/workshop_ring.pdf (on 26.06.2007)

Molnar, Peter et al., Budapest declaration for freedom of the Internet, 15.06.2006, retrieved from http://www.edri.org/docs/BudapestDeclaration.pdf (on 27.06.2008)

Net Consumers, Policy document: the use of rating systems, website quality assurance schemes and options for domain names, 2002, retrieved from http://www.net-consumers.org/policy/domain.htm#three (on 13.06.2008)

Ofcom, Ofcom's strategy and priorities for the promotion of media literacy – A statement, 2004, retrieved from http://www.ofcom.org.uk/consult/condocs/strategymedialit/ml_statement/strat_prior_statement.pdf (on 13.06.2008)

——, Initial assessments of when to adopt self- or co-regulation – Consultation, 27.03.2008, retrieved from http://www.ofcom.org.uk/consult/condocs/coregulation/condoc.pdf (on 04.04.2008)

——, Ofcom's response to the Byron review – Statement, 27.03.2008, retrieved from http://www.ofcom.org.uk/research/telecoms/reports/byron/byron_review.pdf (on 04.07.2008)

——, Ofcom's response to the Byron review – Annex 2: Current tools and approaches to protecting children from harmful content online, 30.11.2007, retrieved from http://www.ofcom.org.uk/research/telecoms/reports/byron/annex2.pdf (on 04.07.2008)

——, Ofcom's response to the Byron review – Annex 3: TV content regulation and child protection: policy, practice and user tools, 30.11.2007, retrieved from http://www.ofcom.org.uk/research/telecoms/reports/byron/annex3.pdf (on 04.07.2008)

——, Better policy making: Ofcom's approach to impact assessment, July 2005, retrieved from http://www.ofcom.org.uk/consult/policy_making/guidelines.pdf (on 28.12.2008)

——, Identifying appropriate regulatory solutions: principles for analysing self- and co-regulation: Statement, 10.12.2008, retrieved from http://www.ofcom.org.uk/consult/condocs/coregulation/statement/statement.pdf (on 30.12.2008)

Oftel, Communications White Paper, retrieved from http://www.communicationswhitepaper.gov.uk/pdf/ch8.pdf (on 05.05.2005, no longer available)

The organization for security and co-operation in Europe and Reporters sans Frontières, Joint declaration on guaranteeing media freedom on the Internet, 17–18.06.2005, retrieved from https://www.osce.org/documents/rfm/2005/06/15239_en.pdf (on 09.09.2008)

UN Special Rapporteur on Freedom of Opinion and Expression, the OSCE Representative on Freedom of the Media and the OAS Special Rapporteur on Freedom of Expression, Joint declaration: International mechanisms for promoting freedom of expression, 21.12.2005, retrieved from http://www.osce.org/documents/rfm/2005/12/18636_en.pdf (on 09.09.2008)

X, European framework for safer mobile use by younger teenagers and children, February 2007, retrieved from http://ec.europa.eu/information_society/activities/sip/docs/mobile_2005/europeanframework.pdf (on 28.05.2009)

X, Safer social networking principles for the EU, 10.02.2009, retrieved from http://ec.europa.eu/information_society/activities/social_networking/docs/sn_principles.pdf (on 25.05.2009)

D. *Conference proceedings*

FRYDMAN, Benoît and RORIVE, Isabelle, "Fighting Nazi and anti-Semitic material on the internet: The Yahoo! case and its global implications", Conference: "Hate and Terrorist Speech on the Internet: The Global Implications of the Yahoo! Ruling in France", Cardozo School of Law, 11.02.2002, retrieved from http://pcmlp.socleg.ox.ac.uk/YahooConference/ (on 23.04.2007)

JAKUBOWICZ, Karl, "A new notion of media?", Background text, 1st Council of Europe Conference of Ministers responsible for media and new communications services: A new notion of media?, Reykjavik, 28–29.05.2009, retrieved from http://www.ministerialconference.is/media/images/a_new_notion_of_media_web_version.pdf (on 27.05.2009)

KLEINSTEUBER, Hans, "State – Regulation – Media", OSCE Conference "Guaranteeing Media Freedom on the Internet", Amsterdam, 27–28.08.2004, retrieved from http://www.osce.org/documents/rfm/2004/08/3430_en.pdf (on 23.04.2007)

KLEIST, Thomas and PALZER, Carmen, "Co-regulation as an instrument of modern regulation", Report for working group 4 of the Expert Conference on European media policy "More trust in content – The potential of co- and self-regulation in digital media", Leipzig, 9–11.05.2007, retrieved from http://www.leipzig-eu2007.de/en/downloads/dokumente.asp (on 21.05.2008)

LATZER, Michael, "Trust in the industry – Trust in the users: self-regulation and self-help in the context of digital media content in the EU", Report for working group 3 of the Expert Conference on European media policy "More trust in content – The potential of co- and self-regulation in digital media", Leipzig, 9–11.05.2007, retrieved from http://www.leipzig-eu2007.de/en/downloads/dokumente.asp (on 21.05.2008)

VAN DEN BERGH, Roger, "Self-regulation of the medical and legal professions: remaining barriers to competition and EC-law", Paper prepared for the Conference "Pressure groups, self-regulation and enforcement mechanisms", Milan, 10–11.01.1997, retrieved from http://www.feem.it/NR/rdonlyres/DDA14FEC-D4FD-4022-9616-6105FDE83755/529/3197.pdf (30.10.2008)

VAN EIJK, Nico, "The modernisation of the European Television without Frontiers Directive: unnecessary regulation and the introduction of internet governance", paper for the ITS 19th European Regional Conference, Istanbul, 02–05.09.2007, retrieved from http://www.itseurope.org/ITS%20CONF/istanbul2007/downloads/paper/29.08.2007_Eijk.pdf (on 27.06.2008)

——, "Search engines, the new bottleneck for content access", paper for the ITS 19th European Regional Conference, Istanbul, 02–05.09.2007, retrieved from http://www.ivir.nl/publications/vaneijk/Paper_SearchEngines_ITS_2007.pdf (on 28.05.2009)

VOORHOOF, Dirk, "Internet and the right of anonymity", Proceedings of the PCMLP 2008 Belgrade Conference on Regulation of Freedom of Expression on the Internet, Belgrade, 08–09.09.2008, *in press.*

WRIGHT, Andree, "Coregulation of fixed and mobile Internet content, Safety and security in a networked world: balancing cyber-rights and responsibilities", Oxford Internet Institute, 8–10.09.2005, retrieved from http://www.oii.ox.ac.uk/research/cybersafety/extensions/pdfs/papers/andree_wright.pdf (on 06.06.2008)

E. *News articles, magazine articles & press releases*

Ars Technica (Nate Anderson), With Katrina behind it, Louisiana tackles next big problem: video games, 19.05.2006, retrieved from http://arstechnica.com/news.ars/post/20060519–6874.html (on 29.05.2006)

—— (Eric Bangeman), ESA backs Maryland video game sales restrictions, 24.05.2006, retrieved from http://arstechnica.com/news.ars/post/20060524–6907.html (on 29.05.2006)

BBC News, Net-illiterate 'failing children', 28.04.2005, retrieved from http://news.bbc.co.uk/1/hi/uk/4490879.stm (on 17.06.2008)

——, Net porn plan labelled 'obscene', 03.06.2005, retrieved from http://news.bbc.co.uk/1/hi/technology/4606125.stm (on 13.06.2008)

——, Warning over 'bullying by mobile', 07.06.2005, retrieved from http://news.bbc.co.uk/1/hi/education/4614515.stm (on 29.02.2008)

——, Violent games 'affect behaviour'; 09.01.2006, retrieved from http://news.bbc.co.uk/1/hi/health/4594376.stm (on 29.02.2008)

——, Plan for .xxx porn domain dropped, 11.05.2006, retrieved from http://news.bbc.co.uk/2/hi/technology/4760459.stm (on 13.06.2008)

——, Call to ban pro-suicide websites, 09.09.2006, retrieved from http://news.bbc.co.uk/2/hi/health/5327354.stm (on 18.09.2006)

——, Warnings over social site 'abuse', 14.09.2006, retrieved from http://news.bbc.co.uk/2/hi/technology/5344722.stm (on 18.09.2006)

——, Online time 'is good for teens', 21.11.2008, retrieved from http://news.bbc.co.uk/2/hi/technology/7740895.stm (on 21.11.2008).

CNET News (Stefanie Olsen), Parents shaky about kids' safety online, 10.08.2006, retrieved from http://www.news.com/2009–1025_3–6104028.html (on 11.01.2008)

Economist.com, Your television is ringing, 12.10.2006, retrieved from http://www.economist.com/research/articlesBySubject/displayStory.cfm?subjectid=349005&story_id=7995312 (on 16.10.2006)

EDRI, Newsletter 4.10: Draft Audiovisual Media Services Directive under criticism, 24.05.2006, retrieved from http://www.edri.org/edrigram/number4.10/audiovisual (on 29.05.2006)

Euractiv, New Commission pledges 'improved cooperation' with media industry, 19.11.2004, retrieved from http://www.euractiv.com/en/pa/new-commission-pledges-improved-operation-media-industry/article-132296 (on 23.05.2008)

Financial Times, Out of MySpace, 16.10.2007, retrieved from http://www.ft.com/cms/s/0/37d523fe-7c12–11dc-be7e-000779fd2ac.html?nclick_check=1 (on 14.01.2008, no longer available)

Gamasutra (David Jenkins), Tenessee violent game bill withdrawn, 23.05.2006, retrieved from http://www.gamasutra.com/php-bin/news_index.php?story=9416 (on 29.05.2006)

Icann, Board rejects .xxx domain application, 30.03.2007, retrieved from http://www.icann.org/en/announcements/announcement-30mar07.htm (on 22.12.2008)

Intellect, TVWF will hamper competition and harm competitiveness, says hi-tech industry, 13.12.2005, retrieved from http://www.intellectuk.org/content/view/618/108/ (on 13.07.2007)

IT Analysis (Bob McDowall), The Television without Frontiers Directive: another 'directive too far'?, 05.05.2006, retrieved from http://www.it-analysis.com/business/content.php?cid=8476 (on 12.07.2006)

Moconews.net (Dianne See Morrison), Ofcom to review code of conduct for mobile content, 21.08.2008, retrieved from http://www.moconews.net/entry/419-ofcom-to-review-code-of-conduct-for-mobile-content/ (on 23.06.2008)

NET FAMILY NEWS (Anne COLLIER), A look at MySpace software for parents, 12.01.2007, retrieved from http://www.netfamilynews.org/nl0701specialreport.html (on 13.06.2008)

OUT-LAW.COM, Michigan prosecutes spammers to protect kids, 15.08.2006, retrieved from http://www.out-law.com/page-7196 (on 29.02.2008)

——, Social networking site fined $ 1m for gathering children's data, 08.09.2006, retrieved from http://www.out-law.com/page-7279 (on 14.06.2007)

REUTERS (Andy SULLIVAN), PluggedIn: Not much to do in kids' online domain, 03.06.2005, retrieved from http://massis.lcs.mit.edu/telecom-archives/TELECOM_Digest_Online2005-1/4801.html (on 20.12.2008)

THE GUARDIAN (Alexandra SMITH), Teachers lack knowledge on internet safety, report reveals, 10.05.2006, retrieved from http://education.guardian.co.uk/schools/story/0,,1771667,00.html (on 17.06.2008)

—— (David FICKLING), Web video content could be classified, 19.06.2006, retrieved from http://technology.guardian.co.uk/news/story/0,,1801290,00.html (on 06.07.2006)

—— (Chris TRYHORN), Minister attacks EU media plans, 29.06.2006, retrieved from http://politics.guardian.co.uk/media/story/0,,1808895,00.html (on 12.07.2006)

THE NEW YORK TIMES (Brad STONE), Online age verification for children brings worries, retrieved from http://www.nytimes.com/2008/11/16/business/16ping.html?_r=1&scp=7&sq=children%20internet&st=cse (on 28.11.2008)

THE REGISTER (Mark BALLARD), EU regulation attacked as censorship, 19.05.2006, retrieved from http://www.theregister.co.uk/2006/05/19/eu_censorship/ (on 12.07.2006)

THE TIMES (Dan SABBAGH), Minister opposes EU plan to regulate Internet, 20.06.2006, retrieved from http://business.timesonline.co.uk/article/0,,13130-2001048,00.html (on 12.07.2006)

—— (Elizabeth JUDGE), Mobile firms face tough rules on internet access for children, 21.01.2008, retrieved from http://business.timesonline.co.uk/tol/business/industry_sectors/telecoms/article3221526.ece (on 23.06.2008)

THE WALL STREET JOURNAL (Emily STEEL and Julia ANGWIN), MySpace receives more pressure to limit children's access to site, 23.06.2006, retrieved from http://online.wsj.com/public/article/SB115102268445288250-YRxkt0rTsyyf1QiQf2EPBYSf7iU_20070624.html?mod=tff_main_tff_top (on 16.06.2008)

—— (Walter S. MOSSBERG), KidZui's parent plan lets children explore in safe corner of Web, 20.03.2008, retrieved from http://online.wsj.com/article/SB120597536349250547.html (on 31.03.2008)

USA TODAY (Anick JESDANUN), Age verification at social-network sites could prove difficult, 14.07.2008, retrieved from http://www.usatoday.com/tech/news/internetprivacy/2006-07-17-age-check-proves-difficult_x.htm (on 16.06.2008)

VODAFONE, Teachtoday.eu: ICT industry alliance launches TeachToday initiative, retrieved from http://www.vodafone.com/start/media_relations/news/group_press_releases/2007/ict_industry_alliance.html (17.06.2008)

WASHINGTON POST (Jonathan KRIM), Court rejects child porn internet law, 11.09.2004, retrieved from http://www.washingtonpost.com/wp-dyn/articles/A13111-2004Sep10.html (on 07.05.2007)

—— (Adam THIERER), New worlds to censor, 07.06.2005, retrieved fromhttp://www.washingtonpost.com/wp-dyn/content/article/2005/06/06/AR2005060601506_pf.html (on 04.05.2007)

WIRED NEWS (Ryan SINGEL), Internet porn: worse than crack?, 19.11.2004, retrieved from http://www.wired.com/news/technology/0,1282,65772,00.html?tw=wn_tophead_4 (on 29.02.2008)

ZDNET.BE (Pieterjan VAN LEEMPUTTEN), Veilige kinderchatbox volledig geflopt [*Safe children's chat box flopped completely*], 24.06.2008, retrieved from http://www.zdnet.be/news.cfm?id=87256 (on 16.12.2008) [in Dutch]

ZDNET UK (TOM ESPINER), Government attacks EC's 'dangerous' online media plans, 29.06.2006, retrieved from http://news.zdnet.co.uk/internet/0,39020369,39277928,00.htm (on 12.07.2006)

F. *Miscellaneous*

a. *Blog posts*

MEDIAPOST (Wendy DAVIS), Scalia: free speech trumps privacy online, 01.05.2009, retrieved from http://www.mediapost.com/publications/?fa=Articles.showArticle&art_aid=105258 (on 26.05.2009)

THE PROGRESS & FREEDOM FOUNDATION BLOG (Patrick Ross), Internet regulation without frontiers, 15.12.2005, retrieved from http://blog.pff.org/archives/2005/12/internet_regula.html#more (on 06.07.2006)

—— (Adam THIERER), Reflections on 'Beyond Censorship' Summit, 08.06.2006, retrieved from http://blog.pff.org/archives/2006/06/reflections_on_2.html#more (on 06.07.2006)

—— (Adam THIERER), Reflections on Brussels Summit on Future of free expression and child protection, 16.06.2006, retrieved from http://blog.pff.org/archives/2006/06/reflections_on_3.html#more (on 06.07.2006)

—— (Adam THIERER), Summary of latest ICRA Summit on Internet free expression and child protection, 15.09.2006, retrieved from http://blog.pff.org/archives/2006/09/summary_of_late.html#more (on 20.09.2006)

—— (Adam THIERER), A response to Sen. Lieberman's Online Child Protection Manifesto, 12.10.2006, retrieved from http://blog.pff.org/archives/2006/10/a_response_to_s.html#more (on 16.10.2006)

b. *Dictionaries*

COLLINS COBUILD, English Dictionary for Advanced Learners, Glasgow, HarperCollins Publishers, 2001, 1824 p.

MERRIAM'S-WEBSTER'S ONLINE DICTIONARY, retrieved from http://www.webster.com/dictionary/converge (on 31.07.2007)

NEWTON, Harry, *Newton's Telecom Dictionary*, San Francisco, CMP Books, 2003, 923 p.

PEARSHALL, Judy (ed.), The concise Oxford dictionary, Oxford, Oxford University Press, 1999, 1696 p.

c. *Speeches*

HINSSEN, Peter, Speech at the IBBT researchers' day, We-BBT, 19.03.2008, not published

VAN DER HAEGEN, Tony, EU view of precautionary principle in food safety, 23.10.2003, New York, retrieved from http://www.eurunion.org/news/speeches/2003/031023tvdh.htm (on 11.03.2008)

d. *Presentations*

CORONEOS, Peter, "Industry facilitated end user empowerment within a co-regulatory environment: the history and practice of online content regulation in Australia", Safety and security in a networked world: balancing cyber-rights and responsibilities, Oxford Internet Institute, 8–10.09.2005, not published

Jakubowicz, Karol, "Co-regulation as an instrument of media policy: how effective?", Presentation at the Expert Conference on European Media Policy "More trust in content – The potential of co- and self-regulation in digital media", Leipzig, 9–11.05.2007, not published

Rorive, Isabelle, "Réguler l'Internet" ["*Regulating the Internet*"], Intervention présentée au Palais de l'Europe le 31 mai 2003 dans le cadre d'une journée consacrée à La convention du Conseil de l'Europe sur l'information et la coopération juridique concernant les 'Services de la société de l'information', retrieved from http://www.coe.int/t/e/legal_affairs/legal_co%2Doperation/information_society_services/Riguler%20l%27Internet%20–%20CoE%20–%2021%20%20Mai%202003%20_version%20icrite_.pdf (on 03.04.2008) [in French]

Voorhoof, Dirk, "Co-regulation and European basic rights", Presentation at the Expert Conference on Media Policy "More trust in content – The potential of self- and co-regulation in digital media", Leipzig, 9–11.05.2007, retrieved from http://www.leipzig-eu2007.de/en/downloads/dokumente.asp (on 03.09.2008)

Westhead, Bill, "Cyberwellness and harm reduction strategies: forging a new approach", Teen works 2005: Young people and the Internet, Swansea, 15.11.2005, retrieved from http://www.wisekids.org.uk/postconference/pdfs/UCLAN.pdf (on 06.03.2008)

e. *Standards*

Etsi, Human Factors (HF); Specification and guidelines for service providers on the provision of information services to young children under twelve years of age, ETSI DTS/HF 102 745, 2008, retrieved from http://portal.etsi.org/stfs/STF_HomePages/STF323/DTS%20102745v6b.doc (on 07.04.2008)

f. *Codes and related documents*

Independent Mobile Classification Body, IMCB guide and classification framework for UK mobile operator commercial content services, 2005, retrieved from http://www.imcb.org.uk/assets/documents/ClassificationFramework.pdf (on 23.06.2008)

Australian Internet Industry Association, Internet Industry Codes of Practice – Codes for industry co-regulation in areas of mobile content (pursuant to the requirements of the Broadcasting Services Act 1992) as registered by the Australian Broadcasting Authority, May 2005, retrieved from http://www.iia.net.au/ContentCodes10_4.pdf (on 01.09.2005, no longer available)

——, Internet Industry Code of Practice – Content services code for industry co-regulation in the area of content services (pursuant to the requirements of Schedule 7 of the Broadcasting Services Act 1992 as amended), 10.07.2008, retrieved from http://www.iia.net.au/images/content_services_code_registration_version_1.0.pdf (on 24.07.2008)

O2, Orange, T-Mobile, Virgin Mobile, Vodafone, Hutchison 3G, UK Code of Practice for the self-regulation of new forms of content on mobiles, 2004, retrieved from http://www.imcb.org.uk/assets/documents/10000127Codeofpractice.pdf (on 23.06.2008)

Ofcom, UK Code of Practice for the self-regulation of new forms of content on mobiles: Review, 11.08.2008, retrieved from http://www.ofcom.org.uk/advice/media_literacy/medlitpub/ukcode/ukcode.pdf (on 18.08.2008)

Index

age verification, 82–83, 107, 189, 248–251, 316, 408–409, 509
anonymity, 54, 56–57, 65, 72, 319–323, 356, 364–365
audiovisual media services, 6, 58, 121, 180, 182, 187, 255–256, 264, 330, 333, 338–351, 353, 355, 366, 369, 451–453, 480, 505–506, 513
awareness, 87, 91, 97, 99, 105–106, 114, 117, 123, 126, 128–129, 132–134, 137, 139, 179, 186–187, 189, 202, 230, 253–254, 257–258, 264, 336, 501, 504, 522

classification (of content), 66, 68, 110, 116, 134, 201–202, 217–218, 231, 243–247, 301, 397, 441
competition, 6, 90, 156, 160, 169, 205, 264, 338, 366, 368, 378, 380, 437–438, 456–480, 497–498, 502, 506, 512, 514–516
content regulation, 5, 73, 77–78, 210, 222, 330–366, 501, 505
convergence, 2, 5, 12, 16–20, 132, 196, 499

e-Commerce, 6, 264, 331, 348, 354–366, 378, 395, 427, 440, 452–454, 505–506, 513
education, 10, 52, 86–87, 90–91, 96–97, 99, 102, 107, 114, 116–117, 133, 137–139, 179, 189, 230, 253, 255, 257–258, 270, 275, 287, 291, 295, 299, 300, 302, 341, 393, 440, 501, 504, 522
effective remedy, 6, 264, 286, 303, 323, 327–330, 377, 382, 418, 424, 426, 497, 505, 510–511, 520
empowerment, 23, 86, 130, 137–138, 201, 237, 243, 253, 258, 289–291, 393, 399, 426, 504

fair trial, 6, 264, 303, 323–327, 377, 382, 411–418, 422, 424, 496, 505, 509–510
filtering, 82–85, 91–92, 95–96, 98–99, 107–108, 116–118, 123, 126, 128–129, 189, 202, 236, 238–245, 251–252, 256, 346, 361, 364, 383, 392–401, 406, 425, 501, 503, 508–509
free movement of goods, 367, 368, 378, 427–445, 447–448, 450, 454–455, 497, 506, 511–513, 515
free movement of services, 90, 334, 354–355, 366–368, 378, 427, 443–455, 497, 506–507, 512–513
freedom of expression, 6, 24, 45, 58–61, 78–80, 83, 86, 90, 94, 98, 116, 135–136, 138, 140, 161, 197, 237, 238, 243, 251, 264, 270–273, 275–276, 281, 286–288, 292, 294, 300, 302–303, 315–317, 320–322, 328, 332–333, 343, 354, 360, 362, 370, 372, 377, 382, 383–401, 407, 411, 412, 417–418, 421–422, 424–427, 439, 451, 496–498, 500–501, 504–509, 519, 521
free speech, see freedom of expression

horizontal effect, 302, 385–388, 394, 400, 405, 407, 424–425, 427, 449, 507–509, 511, 513, 518

identification mechanism, 248–251, 274, 316, 321–322, 362, 364–366, 408, 425, 505
illegal content, 1, 4, 5, 47–52, 55, 57, 59, 60, 89, 91–95, 97–98, 104, 106–107, 129, 133–134, 138, 186, 276, 278, 299–300, 356–357, 359–362, 394
impact assessment, 133, 170, 172, 197–198, 227, 280, 299, 343, 520–521, 523
implementation (of directives), 183, 185, 350, 369, 375–378, 380, 480–496, 498, 506–507, 516–518

internal market, 6, 11, 90, 264, 333, 366–368, 378, 380, 427–455, 457, 497–498, 502, 506, 511–513

Kijkwijzer, 217–220, 244–247, 461

labelling, 91, 95–96, 99, 107, 117, 126, 139, 176, 190, 240–247, 251–252, 256, 301, 346, 383, 394, 431–433, 440–442, 512
liability, 91, 97–98, 109, 331, 356–366, 378, 392, 395, 402, 471–472, 490, 496, 506
literacy, 55, 110, 114, 117, 137–139, 189, 230, 240, 253–258, 289, 291, 501, 504, 522

media effects, 5, 30, 32–38, 46, 60, 500

precautionary principle, 5, 38–44, 60, 500
privacy, 6, 35, 72, 89, 92, 94, 98, 248, 250–251, 264, 271, 274, 286, 292, 303, 315–323, 364, 366, 377, 382, 402–412, 417, 420, 424–427, 496–498, 504–505, 508–510, 521

proportionality, 6, 42, 81, 95, 101, 140, 159, 163–164, 167, 170, 205, 215–216, 264, 299, 310, 314–315, 322, 325, 348, 366–367, 369–375, 378, 391–392, 396, 398, 400–401, 409, 425–426, 435, 441–442, 446, 448, 453, 455, 468, 471, 474, 476, 481, 488, 496–498, 500, 503, 506, 508, 512–513, 515, 516, 520, 522, 524

rating, 23–24, 91, 93, 96, 98, 107–108, 110, 123, 126, 129, 175–202, 222, 240, 243–247, 252, 256, 440, 461, 471, 501

shared responsibility, 67, 69, 519, 522
social network, 5, 12, 20–22, 24, 35, 51, 56–57, 62, 126, 132, 135, 179, 250, 258, 271, 274, 292, 524
supporting mechanisms, 5, 97, 143, 189, 230, 253–259, 263, 503–504, 522

United States, 5, 33, 43, 48, 69, 78–87, 117, 140–141, 231, 238, 244, 252, 501